# PERSIAN DREAMS

## RELATED TITLES FROM POTOMAC BOOKS

*The Wolves of Islam: Russia and the Faces of Chechen Terror*—Paul Murphy

*The Wars of Edvard Shevardnadze, Second Edition, Revised and Updated*—Melvin Goodman and Carolyn M. Ekedahl

*Kremlin Rising: Vladimir Putin's Russia and the End of Revolution, Updated Edition*—Peter Baker and Susan Glasser

# PERSIAN

**Moscow and Tehran**

# DREAMS

*Since the Fall of the Shah*

JOHN W. PARKER

POTOMAC BOOKS, INC.
WASHINGTON, D.C.

**Library of Congress Cataloging-in-Publication Data**
Parker, John W., 1945–
  Persian dreams : Moscow and Tehran since the fall of the Shah / John W. Parker.
    p. cm.
  Includes bibliographical references and index.
  ISBN 978-1-59797-236-9 (hardcover : alk. paper)
  1. Soviet Union—Foreign relations—Iran. 2. Iran--Foreign relations—Soviet Union. 3. Russia (Federation)—Foreign relations—Iran. 4. Iran—Foreign relations—Russia (Federation) I. Title.
  DK68.7.I7P36 2009
  327.47055—dc22
                          2008033716

Printed in the United States of America on acid-free paper that meets the American National Standards Institute Z39-48 Standard.

Potomac Books, Inc.
22841 Quicksilver Drive
Dulles, Virginia 20166

First Edition

10 9 8 7 6 5 4 3 2 1

For Susan

# Contents

# *Preface*

Moscow's ties with the new Islamic Republic of Iran underwent dramatic fluctuations in the quarter-century following Ayatollah Ruhollah Khomeini's triumphant return to Tehran in early 1979. After a prolonged implosion, they fitfully expanded. By summer 2006, as Iran forged ahead with its nuclear program and Iranian-backed Shia and Sunni forces flexed their muscles across the Middle East, Russian-Iranian relations again appeared to be on the threshold of an entirely new dynamic.

This book looks at Moscow's motives and approaches to dealing with Tehran, shaped not only by the rush of events in the period examined but by centuries of ingrained practices, prejudices, fears, and hopes. It weaves into the public record the recollections and analyses of Russian politicians, diplomats, and experts who dealt directly with Iran, both under the Pahlavi monarchy and after the 1979 Islamic Revolution. In both capitals, a variety of imperatives combined to override what was otherwise a mutual aversion going far back in history. Russians in fact were particularly repulsed by the fanaticism of the Khomeini-inspired theocratic regime. By 1996–97, however, the relationship had grown fairly solid—if still filled with wariness on both sides—and was even described as "strategic" by some.

Even at their low point, however, when there were no nuclear power plants or conventional weapons contracts to protect, the dominant approach in Moscow was the same as when ties were at their peak. Iran was a big neighbor, went the Russian refrain, with whom close contacts had always to be maintained lest Tehran behave badly towards Moscow's interests in the Caucasus, Central Asia, and the Middle East. This outlook in part reflected Moscow's sense of vulnerability to Iranian proselytizing inside the Soviet Union and then, after 1991, in Russia proper and in those newly independent post-Soviet nations with extensive Muslim populations. However, Moscow's concerns were probably needlessly exaggerated given the historical animosities toward Shia Iran throughout the predominantly Sunni peoples of these territories.

Shaping this Russian stance was also Moscow's historically founded wariness of spontaneous as well as inspired mob violence against Russian interests inside Iran and of the Islamic Republic's calculated use of state terrorism beyond its borders. Iranian resentment of the Russian Empire's nineteenth-century expansion into previous Iranian-controlled lands in the Caucasus and Central Asia and its imposed dominion over the Caspian Sea was still real. The bitterness provoked especially by the 1813 and 1828 treaties of Gulistan and Turkmanchai, which underscored Iran's weakness vis-à-vis Russia, still festered in Iran three decades after the Islamic Revolution.

For all the tension in the relationship, Russian politeness cum wariness toward Iran continued through all the ups and downs of the events recounted in this book. As a result, Moscow's public statements concerning Iran frequently misled observers into concluding that relations were closer than they really were. This was certainly true at their peak in 1996–97, when even those Russian leaders most intimately involved in dealing with Iran explicitly, though softly, objected to the "strategic" adjective their Iranian counterparts were prone to apply to bilateral ties. These various strands came together again in Russia's delicate handling of the Iranian nuclear issue, even after Tehran's covert activities began to come to light in late 2002.

This narrative's main text comes to a close amid all the turmoil and uncertainty of the short-lived but watershed war in Lebanon in July–August 2006. I have tried to capture and describe the atmosphere that prevailed in the conflict's aftermath on the basis of contemporary news accounts rather than reshape the analysis in the light of subsequent events. A postscript then examines the run-up to Vladimir Putin's historic October 2007 visit to Tehran—where this book's cover photo was snapped—and the first shipments of nuclear fuel to the Bushehr power plant that December. This was followed, however, by Russian disillusionment with Iran's continued resolve to pursue a nuclear enrichment program, and Russia's subsequent support in March 2008 for yet another United Nations Security Council resolution calling on Iran to suspend its enrichment activities.

The Iranian leadership appeared particularly emboldened by the outcome of the conflict in late summer 2006 in Lebanon, in which Shia Hezbollah militia forces backed by Iran stymied the objectives of the Western-supported Israeli military. In Iraq, Tehran's influence seemed to continue to wax on the strength of that country's Shia majority, newly enfranchised since the ouster of Saddam Hussein, even as Iraq teetered on the brink of full-scale sectarian war. In the Palestinian territories, the Gaza-based Hamas movement—backed by Iran even though Sunni and considered by the United States to be a terrorist organization —had outpolled the long dominant Fatah Party in January 2006 elections to the Palestinian legislative council. To some, both in Moscow and Tehran, it seemed that Iran might finally be on the verge of decisively regaining the initiative and stature it had ceded across the region in the two centuries since the bitter Gulistan and Turkmanchai treaties.

A word of caution on perspective: Although the focus of this study is the Russian-Iranian relationship, it does not intend to make the case for Tehran's primacy in Moscow's foreign policy. Iran's ties with Russia were more critical to Tehran—with important qualifications—than they were to Moscow. Indeed, even with all the bitter history between them, some in Tehran favored a "strategic partnership" between the two historic rivals. Even they, however, wanted to remain independent of Moscow and not let Russian influence simply supplant that which the United States had enjoyed during the Pahlavi era.

For Moscow, ties with Tehran were always on a lower plane than relations with the United States and other major powers. Iran was a big neighbor, yet ties with Tehran were by far not the most important relationship for Moscow. While some Russian statesmen, such as Yevgeny Primakov, favored a bigger role for Tehran in Moscow's diplomacy regionally and vis-á-vis the United States, even Primakov appeared leery of elevating Russia's relationship with Tehran to a "strategic partnership"— however defined. Even in the Middle East, Russia's dealings with some of Iran's own neighbors far outweighed those with Iran in their importance to Russia. Despite all the headlines devoted to Russian weapons sales, military technology transfers, and Bushehr nuclear power plant construction, Russia's biggest trade partner in the region was far and away Turkey and not Iran, and Russia's commerce even with Israel grew to rival that with Iran.

After a rocky start, the Islamic Republic looked to Moscow as a source of weapons and for leverage against U.S. efforts to isolate it. However, this strategy was always the subject of factional struggle. President Mohammad Khatami favored widening Tehran's international partnerships and developing a better relationship with the United States but was constrained by domestic opposition. After Khatami, President Mahmoud Ahmadinejad pursued a Look to the East policy, only to be chastised by opponents for gambling that Iran could count on Russia for help.

In Russia, amid the economic collapse of the Mikhail Gorbachev and Boris Yeltsin years, Moscow looked to Tehran for income from weapons sales and the Bushehr nuclear power plant contract. But "military-technical" contacts, contracts, and cooperation were also the subject of debate. Some in Moscow saw them as an effective way to tweak Washington and assert a distinctive Russian position. But they were opposed by those who saw a need to work with the United States on larger issues, including Russia's own security, which Putin did in the aftermath of September 11.

These tangled motives and factional infighting on both sides had implications for American policy toward Russia and Iran. It was not a simple case of Russian collusion with Iran to frustrate U.S. aims or of straightforward Russian cooperation with the United States to contain Iran, or at least its nuclear ambitions. Rather, no matter how much Russia and the United States might share security concerns over Iran's nuclear program and expanding influence in the Middle East, a common approach by Washington and Moscow was always undercut by Russia's rivalry with the United States, other interests in Iran, and the historical approach to dealing with that country.

In Russia, the Yeltsin era was reviled by many for allegedly kowtowing to Washington, yet it was during those very years that Russia signed the deal to construct

Bushehr and had the worst track record in obstructing egregious proliferation to Iran of technologies with so-called dual-use civilian and military applications. Under Putin, Yeltsin's successor, Moscow did much more to clamp down and discourage Iranian shopping trips on the Russian nuclear and missile technology and expertise market. Yet traditional Russian reluctance to give credit to Iranian capabilities until too late, failure—along with other nations, such as China—to apply maximum diplomatic pressure on Iran early on when it would have counted most, also contributed to Iran's success in developing its nuclear capacity. Iranian determination to set down the nuclear road, evident as far back as the mid-1980s, was of course primarily responsible for Iranian achievements. But by repeatedly helping to shield Iran from greater international pressure, the Putin administration contributed to increasing the odds that the Islamic Republic would eventually be able to slip out of the nonproliferation box.

To be fair, the Russian approach seemed to work until Ahmadinejad's election as president in June 2005. Up to that time, the Islamic Republic's leadership seemed willing to play for the longer game. Although not appreciated at the time, Russian leverage probably contributed to Tehran's apparent decision to disband the weaponization component of its military nuclear program in fall 2003, a decision first assessed as likely by the American National Intelligence Estimate (NIE) of late 2007. Moreover, under pressure from many countries, including Russia, Tehran had suspended nuclear enrichment in late 2003 for several years while it negotiated with European Union representatives over the future of the Iranian nuclear program. All that ended abruptly, however, when Ahmadinejad came to power. By early 2008 Tehran seemed to have skillfully used Moscow to shield its nuclear program from U.S. pressure and to have successfully maneuvered Russia into grudgingly accepting that Iran would have its own nuclear enrichment capability.

Throughout this story, the hope of fundamentally supplanting America's earlier influence in Iran under the shah no doubt flickered in Moscow and motivated Russian ambitions. However, Russia's need to work with the United States to contain the Iranian nuclear threat did not go unnoticed in the Islamic Republic, which was in any case determined to achieve independence from all foreign subordination. Moreover, Iran's historic distrust of Russia and recognition of America's greater weight, ultimately, in determining the fate of the nuclear issue and of Iran's equities in the Middle East meant that the option of dealing more closely with America remained alive in Iran, even three decades after the Islamic Revolution.

The spirited and often vicious debates in Iran over ties with the United States were themselves witness to the continuing attractiveness, even if only for tactical, utilitarian considerations, of contacts with the United States and to the widespread resentment of having to deal with Russia, Iran's historic and baggage-laden rival to the north. Still, Iran found tactical value in courting Russia. Under Ahmadinejad, hard-line conservatives could credibly argue that Russia served as a valuable buffer that mitigated the pressure and impact of U.S.-sponsored sanctions. Moreover, no matter how widespread the public and elite sentiment in Iran favoring closer relations with the United States, the ideological hatred and fear of American cultural and political inroads was always great enough, especially at the very top, to block movement in this direction.

This study actually began as an attempt to sort out and understand the complex dealings between Moscow and Tehran in 1992, when they backed opposing sides in the civil war in Tajikistan yet nourished mutual interests on other issues. It expanded from that to include those cataclysmic events that were already part of the historical record—the fall of Shah Mohammad Reza Pahlavi in early 1979 and the collapse of the Soviet Union at the end of 1991—as well as developments that were yet to occur, particularly centered on Afghanistan, Iraq, and Iran's accelerating nuclear program.

Decision-making in Moscow over these years went through three fairly distinct phases. The decade following the Soviet collapse brought with it a significant fraying of state-centered decision making under Boris Yeltsin. There frequently seemed to be multiple Russian foreign policies, often seemingly uncoordinated, pursued by a variety of state bureaucracies, business giants, and even regional administrations. In the Caspian, for example, the policies pursued by the privately controlled Lukoil company in the 1990s undermined calls from Russia's Foreign Ministry and Foreign Intelligence Service (SVR) for cooperation with Iran. Lukoil's actions contrasted sharply with those of the Ministry of Atomic Energy (MinAtom), which pursued a contract for construction of the Bushehr nuclear power plant in Iran, a goal that dovetailed with the Foreign Ministry's line of diplomacy. Lukoil and MinAtom were both motivated by profit, but their deals whipsawed Russian policy toward Iran in radically different directions—which nevertheless managed to coexist.

Only with the coming to power of Vladimir Putin did the tide shift back toward greater discipline, order, and recentralization of Russian policy, and not just toward Iran. In many ways, though, Putin simply hijacked and made his own the policies pursued earlier—without full state backing—by several of Russia's most notable post-Soviet energy titans. In the process, the Russian president quite likely amassed a personal fortune that some estimated in the tens of billions of dollars.

Many of the personalities involved on the Moscow end of the relationship were still alive and proud to share their memories and views of Russia's motivations as I began the research that eventually evolved into this book. In three trips to Moscow from December 1999 to September 2000, I was fortunate to be able to interview on-the-record a variety of officials and experts on Iran, Central Asia, and the Caucasus. For insights from a different perspective, I also managed to meet on a background basis with a number of other sources in Moscow, Baku, Ankara, Istanbul, and Washington.

In each case, I asked my informants not only to recall the past but also to speculate about the future. As luck would have it, the conversations took place as Moscow's reconsideration of its relations with Tehran was beginning to deepen after their

1996–97 high point. They were therefore of particular value to me in illuminating the reasons for this reappraisal—as well as its limits. I also combed the memoir literature by Russian personalities active during this era. Although most of these writers focused on other events and issues, their reminiscences contain nuggets relevant to this study. While I was not able to visit Iran for interviews, I have done my best to describe the view from Tehran by drawing on a variety of publicly available sources.

I am deeply grateful to the U.S. State Department's Bureau of Intelligence and Research (INR) for granting me the year to begin this study, to the U.S. Intelligence Community's Center for the Study of Intelligence for the research budget that paid for my trips during that year, and to the Woodrow Wilson International Center for Scholars for hosting me as a public policy scholar and providing great friendship and intellectual stimulation. In INR, I would like to underscore in particular the support I received for starting this study from Tom Fingar, Chris Kjom, and Jennifer Sims, and from Wayne Limberg for finishing it. At the Woodrow Wilson Center, Mike Van Dusen graciously opened the door to let me in and over subsequent years kept track of the meandering course of this manuscript to the end. Many thanks also go to the ever-helpful staff of the State Department's Ralph J. Bunche Library. Finally, this study would never have become a book without the strong encouragement of Hilary Claggett, senior editor at Potomac Books, to whom I am immensely indebted.

The narrative is naturally informed by my extracurricular research and my years following developments in the region, directly and indirectly, from my perch in INR —although of course the responsibility for the views expressed in these pages is entirely my own.

# 1

# *From the Shahs to the Ayatollah*

Centuries of tangled ties preceded the arrival of junior diplomat Nikolay Kozyrev—no relation to future Russian foreign minister Andrey Kozyrev—in Tehran in 1959. The young Kozyrev's assignment was the first of what would turn out to be four tours at the Soviet embassy in the Iranian capital. Trained as a Farsi interpreter, Kozyrev, over the next two dozen years, accompanied Soviet leaders Leonid Brezhnev, Nikolay Podgorny, and Aleksey Kosygin during their visits to Shah Mohammad Reza Pahlavi.

When Kozyrev finally left Tehran in 1983—actually, he was expelled—he felt personally and professionally deeply estranged from the Shia theocracy that replaced the Pahlavi monarchy in 1979. For much of the rest of the 1980s, Kozyrev dealt with neighboring war-torn Afghanistan. Then, after the Soviet Union's collapse, he spent six years in the 1990s as the Russian Federation's first ambassador to Ireland. Nevertheless, more than forty years after he first arrived in Tehran, the now-veteran Ambassador Kozyrev—by this time a vice rector at the Diplomatic Academy in Moscow—still recalled Iran as his first love.[1]

A century and a half before Kozyrev's diplomatic postings in Tehran, Persia lost decisively to the expanding Russian Empire in the Caucasus and became a spent power, the borders of its rule and influence already rolled back into roughly their present-day contours. Tehran formally conceded defeat and loss of its dominion over territories long part of "Greater Iran," first in the 1813 Treaty of Gulistan, which ceded control to Russia of Tbilisi and Baku and over a dozen other Caucasian provinces and khanates, and then in the 1828 Treaty of Turkmanchai, which added the khanates of Nakhichevan and Yerevan to the Russian Empire. Turkmanchai effectively divided

Persia's Azerbaijani lands, granting Russia sovereignty over all the territories to the north of the Araks River. The treaty also gave Russia exclusive right to trade, navigate, and maintain a navy on the Caspian Sea, doing away with the equal rights that Persia had enjoyed under the 1729 Treaty of Rasht.[2] Although the formal border ran to the north, Russia retained great influence in the territory around Tabriz to the south of the Araks River, now often referred to as Iranian South Azerbaijan.

Within a year of Turkmanchai, a Tehran mob killed thirty-four-year-old Ambassador Alexander Griboyedov, the treaty's principal architect—now better known as the author of the stage classic *Woe From Wit*. The emotions stirred by Turkmanchai continued to reverberate even in post-shah theocratic Iran.[3] They repeatedly resurfaced as Iran sparred with post-Soviet Russia over rights to the Caspian Sea's riches. The sense of injury was also renewed for many each time Russia voted against Iran in International Atomic Energy Agency (IAEA) and United Nations Security Council debates on Iran's nuclear program.

In Central Asia, after a weak Persian objection to Russian advances, St. Petersburg in 1869 unilaterally decreed that the border with Persia ran along the Atrak River, and Iran formally accepted this border in an agreement with Russia in 1881.[4] In fact, the Russian Empire's advance into Central Asia no longer seemed an issue for Iran. Since the 1500s Central Asia had been a backwater. Trade across the Silk Road had lost its economic importance once sea routes joining Europe and the Far East were discovered and established. Around the same time, the adoption of Shiism by the Safavid dynasty in Iran and Azerbaijan had divided Sunni Central Asia from cosectarians in the Turkish Ottoman Empire while estranging Central Asia from Iran at least on religious grounds.[5]

Iran still looked longingly eastward to where Farsi and its dialects were the dominant language—across Afghan provinces such as Herat, the great courts of Bukhara and Samarkand and lands that would later make up Tajikistan, and well into the Indian subcontinent. However, in the years leading up to World War I, Iran was so weak that Britain and Russia openly and unapologetically vied for control of its territories and riches. London and St. Petersburg formalized their division of Iranian spoils in the Anglo-Russian Agreement of August 1907. The resulting spheres of influence in the north and south of Iran, Russian and British respectively, were in effect zones of imperial occupation. During World War II, they served as templates for joint Soviet-British occupation of Iran.[6]

After the collapse of the Romanov dynasty, Iran formally claimed several territories north of the Araks River in the Caucasus and up to the Oxus River in Central Asia on the margins of the Paris Peace Conference in 1919.[7] However, while the February 26, 1921, Soviet-Persian treaty explicitly canceled the Turkmanchai Treaty and gave back to Persia equal navigation rights on the Caspian, it reaffirmed the permanence of the Russian-Iranian borders that Turkmanchai had defined nearly a century before. Moreover, the new treaty gave Soviet troops permission in advance to intervene in

Iran against hostile third powers.[8] Although Iran thus abandoned its territorial claims against the Soviet Union, they were not laid to rest in Iranian politics and over the decades occasionally resurfaced in the press.[9] As the Soviet Union collapsed seventy years later, some in Baku ascribed Iran's hesitation in recognizing Azerbaijan's post-Soviet independence to lingering reluctance to set aside these historical claims.[10]

For multiethnic Iran, the locking up of borders during Soviet times was a mixed boon. On the one hand, with the exception of the Soviet occupation of northern Iran during World War II, it quashed hopes for irredentist success among the numerous Azeris north of the Araks River and west of the Caspian Sea on the Soviet side of the long divide put in place by Turkmanchai. On the other hand, Soviet power and internal control put beyond reach, but not out of mind, Tehran's lingering territorial claims in the Caucasus. It also made difficult any Iranian efforts to influence religious brethren in Shiite though Turkic Azerbaijan, and—further away in Central Asia—ethnic brethren in Farsi-speaking though Sunni Tajikistan. After Tehran's post–World War II campaign to push Soviet forces out of separatist Azeri and Kurdish republics in northern Iran and its bloody repression of Iranian communist party, or Tudeh, officials who did not manage to escape, Soviet-Iranian relations did not warm up for over twenty years. They actually deteriorated sharply after Iran joined the pro-Western Baghdad Pact, or the Central Treaty Organization (CENTO), in 1955.[11]

Nikolay Kozyrev, who first arrived in Tehran just four years after Iran joined CENTO, four decades later recalled the development as a major failure for Soviet diplomacy. Its representatives had been negotiating a bilateral agreement in which the quid pro quo for Kremlin assurances of noninterference in Iran had been no Iranian participation in the Baghdad Pact.[12] The episode postponed the thaw in Soviet-Iranian relations until September 1962, a month before the Cuban Missile Crisis. In an exchange of notes capping several years of negotiations, the Iranian government—while remaining a member of CENTO—announced that it would not permit the basing of foreign missiles on Iranian territory. The Soviet government then declared that this signaled an end to the "existing tension in Iranian-Soviet relations."[13]

Kozyrev years later attributed a significant role in the success of the 1962 exchange of notes to Ambassador Nikolay Pegov. Pegov was skilled at dealing with people of the East, in Kozyrev's estimation, and in return the Iranians "loved him."[14] A veteran of high-level Soviet politics sent into diplomatic exile, Pegov had been a Communist Party of the Soviet Union (CPSU) Central Committee secretary and the secretary of the presidium of the USSR Supreme Soviet. After Iran, he served as ambassador to Algeria and India. In the wake of the exchange of notes, Soviet leader Nikita Khrushchev ceased to rattle rockets against Iran. In 1963 the Soviet Union made a low-interest $38.9 million loan to Iran, and Leonid Brezhnev, then-chairman of the Supreme Soviet, visited Tehran. Iran remained a firm U.S. ally, but better relations with Moscow gave the shah a freer hand to deal with mounting domestic opposition to his land and other reforms.[15]

After Brezhnev and Kosygin in October 1964 replaced Khrushchev as party and government leaders, respectively, they renewed concerted efforts to increase Soviet influence in the Middle East. This coincided with and played to the shah's own ambitious drive to assert Iranian hegemony in the Persian Gulf. The shah's campaign became even more pronounced after the British decided in January 1968 to close down all their military facilities in the Persian Gulf by December 1971. The decision culminated a series of painful choices by Britain resulting in the drawdown of its security commitments "East of Suez" and the closing of a string of military outposts that had buttressed the British Empire for a century and a half.[16]

Despite Iran's close ties to the United States, Moscow actively wooed Tehran, and the shah for his own reasons responded in kind. The shah made an official visit to Moscow in July 1965. In January 1966 the USSR loaned Iran $288.9 million for a series of industrial projects and also committed to supply Iran up to $110 million worth of military equipment in exchange for Iranian gas. In 1967 the USSR signed long-term agreements with Iran to import oil and natural gas to power industries in nearby Soviet republics. When Premier Kosygin visited Tehran in April 1968, he offered another loan of up to $300 million. In 1972 the two countries concluded a fifteen-year economic agreement. This increased the Soviet share of the Iranian import market, although that share still remained paltry compared to that of the United States and West Germany. Along with other projects, the USSR also committed to help Iran increase the capacity of the Isfahan metallurgical works to four million tons of steel per year.[17]

Shah Mohammad Reza Pahlavi adroitly used Moscow as a lever to encourage Washington to be more lavish in its armaments and technical assistance to Iran. At the same time, Moscow went along with the shah's designs for the marginal improvement that this dynamic gave the Soviet Union in the superpower competition to project and exercise influence in the Middle East and the Gulf. Soviet largesse improved Moscow's ties with Iran, but the shah remained firmly allied to the West. The Moscow connection nevertheless helped the shah advance Iran's own power objectives in the region. In the East-West zero-sum competitive spirit of the day, Soviet courting was useful to the shah in coaxing more sophisticated weapons out of Washington—lest it be outbid by Moscow—than the United States was sometimes comfortable giving him.[18]

Soviet experts on Iran looked back on the era of the shah with much fondness and outright nostalgia. Kozyrev correctly recalled decades later that the shah made four official visits to the USSR: in 1956, 1965, 1972, and 1974.[19] Vasiliy Safronchuk, a more senior diplomat who in 1979 became deeply involved in Afghan affairs, in 1999 remembered Soviet relations with the shah as excellent. According to Safronchuk, the shah's brother liked to hunt exotic game in the Pamir Mountains and in Siberia and did this so often that there was always one officer on the Iranian desk at the Foreign Ministry in Moscow whose only responsibility was to organize these visits.

There was much cooperation between Moscow and the shah, Safronchuk noted, including on gas and numerous other projects in Iran, which continued into the post-

Soviet era. In his estimation, few of the projects Russia and the Islamic Republic subsequently agreed to were new except for the Bushehr nuclear power plant.[20] Iranian expert Nina Mamedova at the Oriental Institute pointed out that Soviet specialists began the Mashhad/Tejen railroad project while the shah was still in power.[21] Middle East expert Karen Brutents, for many years with the Central Committee, observed that all the foundations for Cold War hostility between the USSR and Iran were present during that time—Pahlavi Iran was a U.S. client and hosted U.S. military bases—yet both Iran and the Soviet Union tried and succeeded in keeping an even keel.[22]

Kozyrev witnessed Soviet-Iranian cooperation in the 1960s and 1970s that ranged widely beyond the trade, industrial, agricultural, and military sectors to the educational and cultural sectors as well, including visits by ballet troupes to Iran. The Soviet Union not only had good official relations with the shah but also had close informal relations with the entire royal family. On a number of occasions in the first half of the 1970s, for example, the shah invited Ambassador Vladimir Yerofeyev and his wife to family get-togethers, and Kozyrev and his wife were at times included in these informal at-homes.

As vice rector of the Russian Foreign Ministry's Diplomatic Academy in 2000, Kozyrev made the same point stressed by Brutents: the USSR and Pahlavi Iran developed an active relationship despite the ideological barriers that divided them. In fact, Kozyrev remembered how the shah used to explain to his Soviet interlocutors that he undertook his domestic reforms precisely to neutralize communist influences that could threaten his rule. According to the shah, the more active Iran's contacts with the USSR, the less chance the Soviet Union would support subversive movements in Iran.

When Supreme Soviet Chairman Nikolay Podgorny, for example, visited Iran in the summer of 1970, he and the shah traveled to Astara on the border with Soviet Azerbaijan for the official opening of a new gas pipeline to feed the Caucasus. Riding in a convertible and with Kozyrev interpreting for them, the shah pointed to a "mullah" and told Podgorny that the cleric was applauding their joint cooperation. Though relations between the shah and the clerics were already tense, the shah asserted to Podgorny that even the Iranian clergy supported cooperation with the USSR. But the shah was mistaken, Kozyrev pointed out in 2000, because the threat to his regime came precisely from the clergy and not from the USSR.[23]

## GAMBLING ON KHOMEINI

Memories of the shah's reign still ran deep among Iranists in Moscow at the end of the twentieth century. Russian-Iranian relations, however, changed radically with Ayatollah Ruhollah Khomeini's return to Tehran in February 1979 and the subsequent establishment of the Shia-clergy dominated Islamic Republic of Iran. The shah had driven Khomeini into exile in November 1964 after the ayatollah had spearheaded the violent public campaign against the shah's reform program and denounced the Status of Forces Agreement the shah had concluded with the United States. After less than a year in Turkey, Khomeini had settled in Najaf, Iraq, the site of the most sacred Shia shrine of the Imam Ali. From his exile in Najaf, Khomeini inspired the eventual revolt against the shah's regime. This began to attain critical mass after rumors suggested that agents of SAVAK, the shah's secret police, had poisoned Khomeini's elder son Mustafa in October 1977. A year later, an uprising challenging the legitimacy of the shah's rule swept across Iran as demonstrators called for Khomeini's return. In response, the shah in October 1978 prevailed on Saddam Hussein, de facto leader of Iraq, to expel Khomeini from Najaf. From the Shia holy city, the ayatollah made his way to Paris for a few brief months before he returned triumphantly to Tehran on February 1, 1979. The shah had fled the country and in effect abandoned the Pahlavi throne two weeks before.[24]

Though Khomeini's personal and ideological bitterness was directed primarily at Baathist Iraq and the United States, it quickly became evident that he had plenty left to spew against the Soviet Union also. Even though relations between Moscow and Baghdad had deteriorated markedly by the late 1970s, the Soviet Union had continued to deal with and accord legitimacy to Saddam Hussein. Even worse, Moscow had courted the shah during all the years Khomeini had opposed his rule and had criticized the ayatollah for calling the shah's agrarian reforms un-Islamic. Soviet support for the shah did not falter until August 1978, very late in the game. However, Moscow did not side with the revolutionary wave led by Khomeini until that November, when Soviet party leader Leonid Brezhnev warned against outside interference in Iran—a gesture clearly aimed at the United States.[25]

Moscow certainly welcomed some of the Khomeini regime's early moves against the United States. These included totally abandoning CENTO, annulling the 1959 defense pact with the United States, closing U.S. intelligence bases in Iran, and opposing any American military presence in the Gulf. The moves accorded with the long-standing Soviet objectives, now suddenly and surprisingly becoming a reality, of easing the United States out of Iran and increasing Soviet influence there. Nevertheless, despite Soviet efforts to ingratiate themselves with the Islamic revolutionaries on the basis of a common anti-U.S. platform, Khomeini and his followers lost no time before declaring a policy of "neither East nor West," or "equidistance," which put both Moscow and Washington at arm's length. From Tehran's new perspective, the Soviet Union was every bit as dangerous and anti-Islamic as the United States of America.[26]

Moscow had worked hard and relatively successfully with the shah to put the Soviet-Iranian relationship on a more solid footing. Now all that the USSR had achieved in Iran over nearly two decades was threatened by the new theocratic regime's hostility toward atheistic communism. Moreover, this antipathy was soon compounded by the Soviet occupation of Afghanistan and the Soviet Union's official neutrality over the Iran-Iraq War. When Moscow's ambassador appealed for understanding of its actions in Afghanistan, Khomeini reportedly told him, "There could be no understanding between a Muslim nation and a non-Muslim government." In September 1980, in a message to pilgrims to Mecca, Khomeini drew no distinction between the United States and the USSR: "We have turned our backs on the East and the West, on the Soviet Union and America, in order to run our country ourselves. Do we therefore deserve to be attacked by the East and the West?"[27]

From the very beginning, there was debate in Moscow about the staying power of the Khomeini regime: whether it would be possible for the Soviet Union to work with it and whether the Tudeh would gain in influence as a result of its support of the revolution against the shah. As Leonid Shebarshin was preparing in 1979 for his assignment as KGB station chief in Tehran, he met with Yuri Andropov, then head of the KGB.[28] Andropov cautioned Shebarshin, "Watch out, brother, the Persians are such a people that they can make a fool of you in a flash, and you won't even have time to groan!" Andropov also warned against entertaining any illusions that the Shia clerics' power was flimsy and that their regime would be short-lived. The KGB boss suggested that Shebarshin not get his hopes up about the potential of the so-called democratic movement, presumably the Tudeh party. "It seems to me that the leftists in Iran do not have good prospects," Andropov told Shebarshin, who added that Andropov turned out to be right.[29]

Twenty years later, Oriental Institute expert Irina Zviagelskaya recalled that Russia had many unfulfilled illusions in 1979. After the Khomeini regime's first anti-U.S. moves, many in Moscow, according to Zviagelskaya, thought that Iran would have to look to its neighbor to the north for friendship. But it did not turn out to be a zero-sum game. Soviet leaders did not correctly understand the Iranian revolution. Their analysis was not expert, and the honeymoon was short-lived. The USSR turned out also to be a satan, despite the fact that—unlike what happened to the American diplomatic representation in Iran—the Soviet embassy, while attacked, was not taken over and Soviet diplomats were not held hostage, Zviagelskaya pointed out.[30]

Despite Andropov's advice to station chief Shebarshin, the Soviet embassy in Tehran apparently misjudged the flow of history outside its walls. Embassy staffer G. Avdeev wrote in his memoir, "The embassy leadership was especially irritated by the articles of *Izvestiya* newspaper political observer A. [Alexandr] Bovin, who in large part correctly detected the main tendencies of development of the revolutionary process in Iran and was not afraid to point out the definite anti-Soviet direction of the revolution itself."[31]

As early as September 1979, Bovin had written, "It is obvious to me that the fueling of religious fanaticism, anticommunist hysteria and a desire to misrepresent the policy and intentions of a friendly country will not benefit the Iranian people." As Bovin sized up the situation, "there is obviously room for doubt that a theocratic concept of the state will help Iran to become a modern and flourishing country." Bovin concluded, "All this is making the situation in the country unstable and fraught with conflicts and unexpected surprises."[32]

*Defend how? Presumably not intelligence gathering*

The Soviet ambassador to Tehran at the time was Vladimir Vinogradov. According to second secretary Vladimir Kuzichkin, about whom more later, this was the same Vinogradov who as ambassador to Cairo in July 1972 had assured Moscow that everything was normal right up to the moment Egyptian president Anwar Sadat announced the massive expulsion of Soviet advisers. Given a second chance, Vinogradov seven years later misread Khomeini and misled Moscow as badly as he had earlier misjudged Sadat and misinformed the Kremlin.[33]

Nikolay Kozyrev found it personally difficult to accept the Iranian revolution. He had already served three assignments in Tehran, beginning in 1959, during which the USSR had had good relations with what he described as an "almost European government." All this changed by the time Kozyrev began his fourth embassy tour in early fall 1979. Politically, Kozyrev could understand that the Khomeini revolution might lead to closer Soviet-Iranian relations. Personally, however, Kozyrev felt that the new Shiite regime and the cultural clampdown it instituted had suddenly thrown the country backward.

The Iranian people at first welcomed the revolution, and the USSR supported it because it was anti-monarchical and anti-imperialist, Kozyrev reflected. But against the prevailing pro-revolution sentiment in the embassy, Kozyrev felt himself in a minority. When asked, he recalled twenty years later, he would quietly caution colleagues to wait a while and see what might happen next. In fact, the U.S. embassy takeover in November 1979 was followed by a fire at the British embassy and then—within days of the Soviet invasion of Afghanistan—the first of three incursions into the Soviet embassy compound. The second assault on the embassy took only twenty minutes and resulted in the destruction of its Big Three (i.e., Joseph Stalin, Franklin Roosevelt, and Winston Churchill) Conference memorial hall, causing $500,000 damage. The Iranians never paid for the damage, Kozyrev remembered wryly, arguing that the war with Iraq made it impossible.[34]

Soon after Khomeini's return to Iran, on May 11, 1979, Tehran unilaterally annulled Articles 5 and 6 of the 1921 Soviet-Iranian treaty.[35] These prohibited any third party from using Soviet or Iranian territory for hostile acts against the other and permitted Moscow to send troops into Iran to fight any third party forces waging war against the USSR from Iranian territory.[36] In addition, Nikolay Kozyrev recalled with regret, the Khomeini regime closed down the Soviet-Iranian Cultural Cooperation Society and forced the Soviet hospital to shut down and sell off its property. A similar fate befell the Soviet insurance company operating in Iran. Even economic cooperation was sharply reduced, though not completely closed down. Kozyrev recounted that terrible controls were placed on Soviet specialists. Nevertheless, official Moscow insisted they not be withdrawn.

Two decades later, from his vice rector post at the Diplomatic Academy, Kozyrev recalled that the policy guidelines from the Soviet capital to its embassy in Tehran were that the USSR needed to be patient with Iran whatever might lay in store. Moscow wanted to have good ties with Tehran and hoped the downturn in relations would be followed by an improvement. It was, Kozyrev observed, clearly a case in which wishes were mistaken for reality. From his perspective, the Soviet invasion of Afghanistan, Moscow's reluctance to give Iran more weapons during its long drawn-out war with Iraq, the Kremlin's unwillingness to cut back on military supplies to Iraq, and the Soviet Union's atheistic ideology crystallized Tehran's anti-Soviet policy.[37]

Even future Iranian victims of the Khomeini revolution closed their eyes to the potential tragedy ahead, Nodari Simonia recalled. In the late 1970s, Simonia was an expert at the Institute of Oriental Studies and moonlighted as a Saturday lecturer for foreign party students at the Central Committee's Institute of Social Sciences in Moscow. After Khomeini came to power, Simonia argued with Iranian leftists attending his lectures that Khomeini was a reactionary and not a progressive revolutionary with whom they could work. Simonia predicted that Khomeini would destroy those who helped put him in power, just as Saddam Hussein had done to his former allies. Simonia warned the Iranians that they were in danger and needed to save themselves. But they did not heed his warnings, and they were not alone. In the Central Committee apparatus, those with a vested stake in Iran were also willing to work with Khomeini.[38]

The diplomat Bakhtiyer Khakimov, who would accompany future foreign minister Eduard Shevardnadze on critical trips to Tehran, later charted the evolution in Moscow's assessment of Iran.[39] Only after the Shia "mullahs" declared the export of the Islamic revolution as the main goal of the Islamic Republic and branded the United States, Israel, and the Soviet Union as Iran's three main enemies did views in Moscow toward Iran really change—all the more so since Iran was helping opposition Islamic organizations in Afghanistan.[40] In addition, Tehran's Ministry of Islamic Culture and Guidance began to exert a lot of influence and to target Shia Azerbaijan and Farsi-speaking Tajikistan, which Iran regarded as a related people because of their same language and culture.[41]

Fellow diplomat Safronchuk was Moscow's ambassadorial-rank foreign policy adviser to Afghan leader Hafizullah Amin from May to December 1979, when he was evacuated to Moscow shortly before Amin's overthrow and death on December 27.[42] Looking back, Safronchuk's judgment was that were it not for Afghanistan, Moscow's relations with the new regime in Tehran could have continued to be excellent on the basis of its anti-Americanism, which was reinforced by U.S. efforts to evacuate American hostages from Iran. But because of the Soviet military presence in Afghanistan, Khomeini set his sights against both East and West. The Iranians did not permit Soviet economic specialists to leave the country, in effect holding them hostage just like American embassy personnel, in Safronchuk's view. Moscow viewed the capture of the American embassy in Tehran basically as terrorism. Safronchuk argued that the USSR, while taking advantage of the Khomeini regime's anti-Americanism, never fully played the Iranian card against the Americans. Soviet ambassador to the

United States, Anatoly Dobrynin, warned against it, Safronchuk recalled, and the KGB cautioned that the Islamic revolution could next turn its attention to Afghanistan and Central Asia.[43]

>> In fact, after Ayatollah Ruhollah Khomeini toppled the shah's regime in 1979, irredentism again began to focus both Moscow and Tehran on the historically contested borderlands between them. Moscow appeared to give the go-ahead to its officials in the Azerbaijani capital of Baku to play up and project the ethnic Azeri unity issue into Iran's so-called South Azerbaijan. The gambit was probably meant as a disincentive to the Khomeini regime's initial revolutionary urge to proselytize among the Soviet Union's extensive Muslim populations in Central Asia and the Caucasus. Kremlin leaders probably calculated that the potential threat to Iran's territorial integrity would also serve to lessen Iran's opposition to the Soviet occupation of Afghanistan and
✓ perhaps also suggest to Tehran another reason to bring to an end the war with Iraq.＊

> Reacting to the Khomeini regime's antipathy, Moscow's public forbearance toward the Islamic Republic slowly though decidedly began to shift. By February 1981, in his opening report to the Twenty-sixth Congress of the CPSU, General Secretary Leonid Brezhnev conceded that the Iranian revolution was displaying "complications and contradictions." Nevertheless, he affirmed, "It is fundamentally an anti-imperialist revolution even though internal and foreign reaction is striving to change its nature."[44]

In June 1983, however, Central Committee International Department deputy head Rotislav Ulyanovskiy declared that the Iranian revolution by the end of 1981 had given birth to "Islamic despotism."[45] In August 1985 Ulyanovskiy went even further in painting the Khomeini regime not only as "despotic" but also as "reminiscent of the darkest times of the Middle Ages."[46] Vladimir Gudimenko, who joined the
> CPSU Central Committee's International Department as a young staffer in 1983, later pointed out that Ulyanovskiy had the lead on both Iran and Afghanistan in the Central Committee apparatus and supplied the ideological basis for Soviet actions in both countries.[47]

## BALANCING IRAN AND IRAQ

In January 1968 Britain had announced that it would withdraw militarily from the Persian Gulf by December 1971. In anticipation of the British withdrawal, and as part of its campaign to improve its position throughout the region, the Soviet Union was not averse to responding positively though cautiously to occasional overtures for
>> an improvement in ties by Iraq, Iran's main competitor for influence in the Gulf. Iran and Iraq were both important to Soviet ambitions, though each more so than the other in different arenas: Iraq played a larger role in Soviet diplomacy focused on the Arab-Israeli conflict; Iran in geopolitical maneuvers involving the Persian Gulf and Indian Ocean. In economic ties, the potential for further growth with Iran was always an attraction, though the volume of realized trade with Iraq—heavily concentrated in military goods—was probably greater.

Nevertheless, it would prove extremely difficult for Moscow to deal with both. Its relationship with Iraq was especially rocky during the Baath Party's brief rule in February 1963 and again when it returned to power more lastingly in July 1968. The Baathist regime's repression of the Iraqi Communist Party (ICP) made it a challenge, but so did Moscow's desire not to upset its budding relationship with Tehran. The USSR reacted to Baghdad's measures against the ICP by cutting off arms deliveries and putting economic cooperation on hold, and relations between the USSR and Iraq did not begin to improve significantly until 1970.

Meanwhile, relations between Tehran and Baghdad deteriorated as the shah intensified pressure on Iraq aimed at removing the only real obstacle to his assertion of Iran's supremacy in the Gulf. In 1969 Tehran backed a coup attempt against the Baathist regime and also unilaterally abrogated the 1937 Iraqi-Iranian agreement on navigation in the Shatt al-Arab waterway. According to its text, the Iraq-Iran border ran along the Iranian shore of the 160-mile channel into the Persian Gulf. For the Soviet Union, more important than its ties to either side was its reluctance to do anything that might cause Britain to reconsider its 1968 decision to withdraw from the Gulf by the end of 1971, so Moscow adopted a neutral stance and warned against the use of force.

In the early 1970s, the shah tried to isolate Baghdad from other Gulf Arab states and actively stoked the Kurdish rebellion in northern Iraq. Beset by low oil revenues and needing arms to deal with restless Kurds in the north, threats from Israel to the south and Iran to the east, Iraq in April 1972 signed a Treaty of Friendship and Cooperation with the Soviet Union. In part to mollify the shah's displeasure over the treaty, the Kremlin then quickly invited the shah to Moscow and signed a fifteen-year economic agreement with him. After the rise in oil revenues occasioned by the October 1973 Arab-Israeli War, however, Iraq turned away from the USSR for its investment, consumer, and military needs.

With the Algiers Agreement of March 6, 1975, Iraq finally accepted the shah's demand that the center of the Shatt al-Arab's main shipping channel (*thalweg*) rather than the Iranian shoreline mark the Iran-Iraq border. With these concessions, Iraq effectively ceded supremacy in the Gulf to Iran in order to put a stop to Iranian support to rebellious Kurds in northern Iraq. Iraq's need for Soviet military equipment eased substantially, in part because of the lower level of tensions with Iran but also because of Iraq's decision to purchase major weapons systems from France. By 1978 Baghdad had returned to repressing the ICP, and relations between Iraq and the USSR deteriorated to their low level of a decade earlier.

Despite the revolution that deposed the shah in 1979, secular Baathist-ruled Baghdad soon started to see Ayatollah Khomeini as the "turbaned shah."[48] The ayatollah appeared eager to go far beyond the shah's earlier successful challenge to Baghdad's regional writ—formalized in the Algiers Agreement of 1975—and to attack the very legitimacy of Iraq's secular—and Sunni-based—Baathist regime. The shah had met with Saddam Hussein in person to negotiate the Algiers deal. It was inconceivable that Khomeini would ever do the same. When Saddam was formally elected president of Iraq in July 1979, Khomeini was quick to denounce him as "a puppet of Satan."[49]

As had the shah before it, the Khomeini regime soon also began channeling support to rebellious Kurds, as well as radical Shia movements in Iraq. These included the Islamic Dawa Party (Hizb al-Dawa al-Islamiya, or Call of Islam Party), founded in the late 1950s. Tehran launched terrorist attacks against Iraqi officials, including Deputy Premier Tariq Aziz on April 1, 1980. That same month, Khomeini personally called on Iraqis—some 60 percent of whom were Shia, though Arab—to overthrow Saddam, whose power base was Iraq's Sunni Arab minority. Saddam's regime replied in kind, brutally repressing Dawa Party members and executing one of the movement's most authoritative Shia clerics, Mohammad Baqir al-Sadr, a colleague of Khomeini from the latter's years of exile in Najaf, and Sadr's sister.[50] Tehran was not deterred, however, and by August 1980 the confrontation between Iraq and Iran escalated to heavy border clashes.

Tehran under Khomeini both provoked and invited the attack that Iraq launched against Iran on September 22, 1980. Appealing to Iraq's Shia majority, the Khomeini theocracy from its inception had challenged the legitimacy of Saddam Hussein's secular Baathist rule. At the same time, in a frenzied hunt against internal enemies, the new Islamic Republic undermined its own defense capabilities by decimating the military officer corps inherited from the Pahlavi regime. Faced with extreme provocation by Tehran, Baghdad was presented with what looked like a good opportunity to retaliate. Saddam gambled that Iraq, though smaller and geographically more vulnerable than Iran, could take advantage of Iran's post-revolutionary chaos by striking before Tehran had a chance to sort itself out. One objective would be to cut short Khomeini's attempts to subvert Baathist legitimacy. Another goal would be to win back domination over the Shatt al-Arab access to the Persian Gulf, lost so recently to the shah in the *thalweg* compromise of the Algiers Agreement of 1975.[51]

What Saddam may have calculated would be a brief and decisive engagement, however, ended up lasting eight long and bloody years. The Khomeini regime, no matter how weakened by self-inflicted internal blows, played by new and unexpected rules, while Iraq's Shia but Arab majority remained largely loyal to Baghdad, or at least cowed by Saddam's security services. In a war that seemed like it would never end, Iraq from early on attacked Iranian civilian and military targets with chemical weapons, both sides launched bombers and missiles against the other's cities, and waves of Iranian volunteers went into battle already wrapped in death shrouds. By the end, casualties on the two sides mounted to perhaps over a million dead and wounded, and the victims were overwhelmingly Iranian—an estimated 262,000 Iranian dead compared to 105,000 on the Iraqi side—leaving Iran especially in a state of exhaustion.[52]

The Kremlin must have been just as appalled to see Khomeini bait Saddam as it was to see Saddam rise to the provocation. Soviet media occasionally depicted Iraq as the aggressor and Moscow distanced itself from the Iraqi attack, cautiously declared its neutrality, and called on both sides to negotiate a settlement. In his speech to the Soviet Communist Party Congress in February 1981, Brezhnev spelled out the line that Moscow had and would follow consistently throughout the Iran-Iraq War: The conflict was "absolutely senseless" and should "be brought to an end as soon as possible ... by political means." While it raged, it was "very advantageous to imperialism, which has constant visions of reestablishing its positions in that region."[53]

Apart from its interests in keeping the United States out of the Persian Gulf, though, Moscow wanted closer relations with both Iraq and Iran, not worsening connections with one aggravated by Soviet help provided the other. But courting Tehran was no small task given the ayatollah's own low regard for communist ideology. Moreover, the Soviet invasion of Afghanistan at the end of December 1979 frayed ties that had been uncertain from the beginning and were bound to be difficult under any circumstances. On top of Iranian invective against the Soviet occupation, economic relations began to falter as Tehran chose to strike few new agreements with the USSR. In addition, in what was ostensibly a price dispute, Iran shut off its gas pipeline to the USSR in March 1980 and declined to go forward with construction of a second pipeline.

The Soviet Union officially refrained from openly and directly supplying arms to both combatants from September 1980 to May 1982, when Iran repelled Iraqi forces and proceeded to occupy Iraqi territory. After that, the Khomeini regime repeatedly responded to Saddam's calls for a cease-fire and return to the prewar status quo with renewed calls for the ouster of the Baathist regime. In November 1982 Tehran hosted the formation of the Supreme Council of Islamic Revolution in Iraq (SCIRI), with the aim of overthrowing Saddam's regime and which two decades later—along with the Islamic Dawa Party founded inside Iraq in 1957–58—became a leading force in Iraqi political life after Saddam's toppling by Operation Iraqi Freedom.[54] Moscow in response criticized Tehran's obstinacy and began to restrict the indirect flow of its arms to Iran while increasing their direct supply to Iraq. Thereafter, the USSR sped up deliveries whenever Iranian offensives imperiled Iraq and thus became a major underwriter of Baghdad's war effort.

The Soviet Union was wary of contributing to an Iranian victory over Iraq that might inspire a triumphant Islamic Republic to increase its activities in Afghanistan and cast its eyes more ambitiously toward the Muslim regions of the Soviet Caucasus and Central Asia. What the Soviet Union wanted was a quick and inconclusive end to the Iran-Iraq War, with neither side strengthened. Instead, Iran's refusal to conclude the war in 1982 and its decision to go on the offensive compounded the challenges to Moscow's diplomacy set in motion by the Soviet Union's own invasion of Afghanistan, which many states in South Asia and the Middle East opposed. The conflict between Baghdad and Tehran increased the risk that both would turn to the United States for help. The Iran-Iraq War also diverted attention from the Arab-Israeli conflict, split the

Arab world along a new dimension between supporters of Iraq or Iran, and lessened the likelihood of Arab unity against the United States. In fact, the conflict reinforced ties between the United States and conservative Gulf states, increasingly isolated Moscow's most steadfast clients in the region, and resulted over the years in a greatly reinforced American naval presence in the Persian Gulf. Moreover, and much to Moscow's discomfort, even high-level officials in Tehran in 1985–86, including Majles Speaker Ali Akbar Hashemi Rafsanjani, were willing secretly to explore new contacts with Washington and accept some $40 million in new arms in what became known as Irangate or the Iran-Contra scandal.[55]

Early on in the Iran-Iraq War, Iranian prime minister Mohammad Ali Rajai had complained to Soviet ambassador Vinogradov of "flagrant Iraqi aggression."[56] Moscow's open provision of arms to Iraq after 1982 repeatedly rankled Tehran. Soviet pressure on Tehran to end the war without accomplishing regime change in Baghdad further aggravated relations. In 1987 Majles Speaker Rafsanjani accused the Soviet Union of colluding with the United States after Moscow sent six warships into the Persian Gulf in response to Kuwait's plea for protection of its tankers.[57] In March 1988 Rafsanjani accused Moscow of "hypocrisy and duplicity" as Iraq pounded Tehran week after week with Soviet SCUD-B missiles—the weapon of choice of both sides for attacking one another's capitals.[58]

But then the seemingly interminable Iran-Iraq War was suddenly over, as was the equally long Soviet occupation of Afghanistan. Despite its invective over the years, the Khomeini regime since 1984 had in fact begun to explore rapprochement with Moscow. By 1987 Iranian and Soviet diplomats had managed to negotiate the groundwork for the revival of economic and military relations that would unfold in 1989.

## IRAN, AZERBAIJAN, AND CENTRAL ASIA

Until the Soviet intervention in Afghanistan, the diplomat Safronchuk explained years later, the authorities in Moscow had not felt threatened by Iran in Central Asia. They therefore did not object to the many trips by Iranian embassy personnel to Tajikistan and to the heavily Farsi-speaking cities of Bukhara and Samarkand in Uzbekistan. These were not closed areas, so this travel was natural. They were just tourist trips, and the Iranian official visitors did not interfere in Soviet internal affairs.

After the Islamic Revolution, though, Moscow started looking more suspiciously at Iran's efforts to befriend the Tajiks. From 1981 to 1985, when he left Moscow for a high-ranking assignment at the UN, Safronchuk witnessed alarm in Moscow over potential Iranian export of Islamic fundamentalism to the southern Soviet republics. Moscow was on guard and stopped the visits by Iranian embassy personnel to Central Asia and to Tajikistan especially. The Ministry of Foreign Affairs could always think up a reason for denying the Iranian requests for travel to Tajik-speaking areas since the proposed trips were clearly not in Moscow's interests.[59]

According to other accounts, Moscow repeatedly turned down Tehran's petitions to open consulates in Central Asia. An appeal in 1982 for permission to establish a consulate in Dushanbe went all the way to the top before being nixed by the party Politburo.[60] As a result, the Khomeini regime turned to radio to carry its message to these newly closed off areas in Central Asia. In the Caucasus, Iranian radio also beamed north a strong signal in the Azeri language from Tabriz, the main city of Iranian so-called South Azerbaijan. For the most part, this reflected the Islamic missionary zeal of the newly empowered Khomeini regime, all the more hopeful about its prospects because of the historically Shia identification of the majority of Muslims in Azerbaijan.[61] As in Central Asia, it was doubtful that seventy years of Soviet rule had left much understanding of Sunni-Shia distinctions among Azerbaijan's Muslims, or indeed much self-identification as specifically Shia Muslims. Nevertheless, while the appeals beamed from Iran had uncertain resonance among Azerbaijan's secularized urban intellectuals, they probably had a greater impact on Azerbaijan's poor and rural populations.

With the passage of time, Iranian broadcasts may also have been motivated by hopes of neutralizing potential support for the once-again rebellious activities of ethnic Azeris in Iran's South Azerbaijan. After the collapse of the Soviet-supported autonomous regime in Tabriz—the so-called Pishevari Republic, named after its leader Sayyid Jafar Pishevari—in 1946, Tehran had reinforced its policies of Persianization and centralization.[62] As a result, the shah's regime was especially unpopular in South Azerbaijan, and the riots that began in Tabriz in February 1978 eventually crested in the nationwide movement that led to the shah's ouster and the return of Khomeini from exile.[63]

The Khomeini theocracy that replaced the Pahlavi monarchy at first relaxed restrictions on the use of the Azeri language and therefore initially enjoyed some popularity in South Azerbaijan. In addition, ethnic Azeris believed that their role in bringing back Khomeini from exile would translate into greater concern not only for their cultural grievances but also for their regional aspirations. However, their loyalties were less to Ayatollah Khomeini personally and more to Ayatollah Kazem Shariatmadari, spiritual leader of Iran's Azerbaijanis and the highest clerical authority in Iran while Khomenei had been in exile. He opposed Khomeini's elevation of the clerics to political rule, and Khomeini soon sidelined and then banished him from all power. In early December 1979, after Shariatmadari's house was attacked in Qom, demonstrators in Tabriz began another rebellion against Tehran. After the Soviet invasion of Afghanistan and Saddam Hussein's invasion of Iran, the Khomeini regime reimposed assimilationist policies on non-Persians. Still, these measures were not as harsh as those of the shah. Ethnic Azeris could still take pride in the high numbers of their co-ethnics in the upper ranks of the Khomeini regime.[64]

At the same time, though, north of the Araks River, the Turkmanchai Treaty of 1828 was increasingly seen in Soviet Azerbaijan as a glaring historical injustice for having divided the Azeri nation. In 1981 an establishment figure openly called for a national liberation front uniting Azeris in Iran and the USSR, and a historical drama discussing national unity premiered on a stage in Baku. In June 1982 the phrase "One Azerbaijan" was endorsed by many at a meeting of the Azerbaijan Writers' Union and appeared for the first time in the Soviet mass media. Support for "One Azerbaijan" appeared to surge among the Azeri creative intelligentsia, though its public expression was carefully controlled. While Moscow did not officially endorse the movement, it appeared to tolerate its expression in Baku as a pressure tactic on Tehran, which was not shy about its anti-Soviet feelings in the aftermath of the USSR's intervention in Afghanistan.[65]

The Azeri unification issue was useful to Moscow in the early 1980s to deter Tehran's impulse to proselytize in Azerbaijan and Central Asia and as a disincentive to any thought by the Khomeini regime to provide robust support to the mujahideen in Afghanistan. Azerbaijani Communist Party leader Heydar Aliyev supported rapprochement between North and South Azerbaijan while still in Baku and perhaps continued to do so in Moscow after his promotion to Soviet first deputy premier and full member of the Politburo in November 1982. On the record, Aliyev did not go beyond his 1981 endorsement of "developing broad contacts in all sectors of cultural and intellectual creativity" with South Azerbaijan.[66] Behind the curtains, however, he went much further, reportedly even telling foreign diplomats that he hoped both territories would unite in the future.[67]

Twenty years later, some in Tehran gave voice to their suspicions that Aliyev, now as president of independent Azerbaijan, was still toying with the same subversive theme. "In between the lines," charged an editorial in the *Tehran Times*, "Aliyev is trying to say that parts of Iranian Azerbaijan belong to the Azerbaijan Republic. However, historians know very well that the Azerbaijan Republic was a part of Iranian territory."[68] And after the late July 2001 armed conflict over the Alov (in Azeri), or Alborz (in Farsi), oil bloc in the southern Caspian, another Tehran commentary charged that it was enough to review Aliyev's comments about Iran in the early 1980s to "see evidence of his expansionist and hostile views toward Iran."[69]

## HITTING ROCK BOTTOM

Soviet-Iranian relations reached their low point in 1983, the year in which the Khomeini regime executed forty-five members of the Tudeh Party on charges of espionage and sedition and dissolved the Moscow-backed communist party.[70] The defection on June 2, 1982, of Soviet embassy second secretary Vladimir Kuzichkin, a KGB agent working under diplomatic cover, had set the stage for the Tudeh's demolition. Kuzichkin, who, KGB station chief Leonid Shebarshin asserted, had been working for British intelligence for a long time, fled through the Turkish border using a British passport under the name of Michael Rhode.[71] According to Western news reports several years later, British intelligence, after debriefing Kuzichkin, passed the names of Soviet agents in Iran to the American Central Intelligence Agency (CIA), which then provided them to the Khomeini regime.[72] Arrests of leaders of the People's Party of Iran (Tudeh) began in early February 1983 and soon forced the departure of Shebarshin, Kuzichkin's direct supervisor, from Iran on February 15.[73]

Years later, Nikolay Kozyrev recalled with regret that he was forced to leave Tehran after Khomeini, in May 1983, personally demanded that Soviet embassy staff be reduced and the Iranians declared eighteen staffers personae non gratae (PNG). According to Kozyrev, he was at the top of the Iranian PNG list, even though he was a "real" diplomat and his job did not include dealing with the Tudeh. In his view, his expulsion was clearly a political gesture, but since the Iranians had already closed down all the joint cooperation projects that he had negotiated, he was ready to leave anyway. Although the Iranian move against the embassy followed Kuzichkin's defection, Kozyrev concluded that it would have happened one way or another.[74]

Shebarshin rejected charges that his allegedly faulty supervision of Kuzichkin had been responsible for the destruction of the Tudeh and the Soviet agent network in Iran. In a 1991 interview, reprinted in his book, Shebarshin asserted, "The 'Tudeh' party was doomed. Kuzichkin could not add or subtract anything from its fate."[75] Kuzichkin in his memoir agreed entirely with Shebarshin on this last point: "At the time, of course, all the blame for this was laid on me in the Western press, but I feel quite sure that whether I had been there or not, the fate of the Tudeh Party would have been exactly the same."[76]

Karen Brutents recalled in retirement that Iran's new clerical regime, besides being ideologically unacceptable to the USSR, brutally tortured Tudeh's members, even ripping off their genitals. Nevertheless, Moscow still tried to repair relations with Tehran. The Soviet Union's overtures to Khomeini were meant not just to take advantage of his anti-U.S. policy but also to keep relations stable. To illustrate how far Soviet leaders went in those days not to antagonize Tehran, Brutents asserted that he personally proposed three times that Moscow publicize—even if only indirectly by leaking information to Western European newspapers—the terrible torture to which Tudeh members were being subjected, but that the Soviet leadership each time turned down his initiative.[77]

Indeed, at the pinnacle of the Soviet political pyramid high above Brutents, the Tudeh's fate apparently provoked few tears. Aleksandr Yakovlev, whom Gorbachev helped bring back from diplomatic exile as ambassador to Canada in 1983, soon became one of Gorbachev's closest political confidants and proponents of perestroika.[78] Nearly two decades later, Yakovlev recalled that the USSR was already distancing itself in 1983 from radical leftist parties and that consequently the Tudeh's demise did not upset "us" all that much. As a general proposition, according to Yakovlev, even Andropov, who was Soviet party leader at the time, understood that such parties, which the USSR had been supporting, were causing difficulties in relations with governments Moscow wished to work with. Iran's relations with the USSR were always complex, Yakovlev affirmed, but they were nevertheless better than those with the Soviet Union's other neighbors.[79]

Yakovlev's recollection of Andropov's attitude was consistent with Tehran station chief Shebarshin's assertion that Andropov as early as 1979 had assessed that "the leftists in Iran do not have good prospects."[80] Moreover, when Shebarshin not long afterward found out that his KGB section in the embassy would have to serve as postman between the Tudeh and the CPSU Central Committee's International Department, he angrily referred to the Tudeh as "that muck!"[81]

From Central Committee staffer Vladimir Gudimenko's perspective, the Tudeh's repression was yet one more consequence of the Soviet invasion of Afghanistan. Although the Khomeini regime appreciated the fact that the USSR was also anti-American and anti-imperialist, the Soviet Union had invaded Afghanistan, and Iran had to oppose this move on all fronts. Iran saw itself as encircled, Gudimenko recalled two decades later, so it made a choice. Facing an external threat, it moved to eliminate all potential internal threats. Despite Moscow's warnings to Tudeh Party leader Nureddin Kianuri, the latter labored under the "self-conceit" that the Khomeini regime would not go as far as physical extermination of his party. But the clerics were adroit at setting traps, Gudimenko noted, and these traps proved a catastrophe for the Tudeh.[82]

All in all, whatever Moscow's ambivalence toward the Tudeh's fate, the year 1983 was a terrible one in world politics from the Soviets' perspective. Moscow's reputation as a bully had been reinforced when Gen. Wojciech Jaruzelski, Poland's prime minister and Communist Party leader, imposed martial law and cracked down on Solidarity in December 1981, and the Kremlin was still trying to deal with the public relations aftereffect.[83] Party leader Andropov was absent for months at a time with a bad "cold." The September 1983 shootdown of the Korean KAL 007 passenger airliner plunged Soviet-NATO relations, already well into a deep freeze over upcoming deployments of Pershing missiles in Europe, to new depths of frigidity. And in Afghanistan, Soviet troops were getting trounced by the mujahideen backed by the United States, Pakistan, Saudi Arabia, and Iran.[84]

Even at that low point, however, Foreign Minister Andrey Gromyko extended an olive branch to Iran in a speech to the Supreme Soviet in June 1983. Nodari Simonia years later commented that Gromyko's posture during this period again proved that in reality it was not ideological interests but state interests that guided Soviet foreign policy.[85] Gromyko's words, however, were conditional and clearly barbed. While offering "normal relations of friendship," he regretted the expelling of Soviet employees from official missions in Iran, which he said did not contribute to good-neighborly contacts.

Stating that the USSR would like to see Iran continue as an independent state, the Soviet foreign minister seemed to suggest the possibility of a nonindependent alternative. Gromyko perhaps even meant to threaten Iran with what might be called the "Aliyev option" of unification of Azeris north and south of the Araks River. In retrospect, it reinforced the impression that the wily Aliyev had been acting with at least a yellow if not a green light from Moscow when he appeared to support the "One Azerbaijan" theme in Baku. Overall, however, Gromyko's speech predicated Soviet policy on "whether Iran wishes to reciprocate its actions and maintain normal relations with us or whether it has different intentions."[86]

## CLIMBING OUT OF THE HOLE

Despite Tehran's support for mujahideen elements in Afghanistan, Moscow's criticism of Tehran on this account never dominated its hopes of capitalizing on the Khomeini regime's overriding anti-Americanism.[87] A radio commentary beamed to Iran in June 1983, for example, at the nadir of relations, recalled "the Soviet Union's support for Iran's anti-shah and anti-imperialist revolution." It also asserted that at the summit of the Group of Seven (G-7) major industrialized democracies in Williamsburg, the United States and its capitalist partners had discussed plans to "poison" Soviet-Iranian relations, make Iran "retreat" to the West, and reestablish the "imperialist monopolies that ruled in your country during the shah's regime."[88]

Vladimir Gudimenko, who personally worked with Iranian leftists as a staffer in the CPSU Central Committee's International Department during the 1980s, was an insider witness to Moscow's motivation for being patient with Iran.[89] The 1979 revolution had created a new regime on Moscow's borders that was not dependent on the United States and did not host U.S. troops, he later explained. Though Moscow was aware of Islamic fundamentalism's negative potential, the Khomeini regime advertised itself as anti-U.S. and anti-imperialist. Moscow saw both the Iranian revolution and the April 1978 coup in Afghanistan as blows against American influence in the region and was determined to establish a working relationship with the Khomeini regime. The aim was not that the USSR and Iran become good allies, just reasonable neighbors. And up to the Tehran regime's suppression of the Tudeh, Moscow's gamble on being able to work with the Khomeini regime looked pretty good.

Nevertheless, Gudimenko remembered, Moscow concluded that it needed to be cold-blooded, not succumb to provocation, and continue to try to set relations right with Tehran. Iran after all remained a huge neighbor. However bad the situation inside Iran was for Soviet interests, Moscow needed to try to find a balance. The objective was to forestall a situation in which Moscow would have an open enemy on its borders working against the USSR. As a result, the Kremlin exhibited enormous forbearance, and there were no big objections to this policy of caution and patience in Central Committee offices. After Tudeh leader Kianuri's "confession" was broadcast on Iranian TV, it took great efforts to coordinate for publication in *Pravda* even a small notice about the development. The feeling was, according to Gudimenko, let's not antagonize the Iranian regime or it will repress the Tudeh even more. Critical articles became harder and harder to print and, if printed, usually cited foreign media sources.[90]

In Gudimenko's opinion, the Iranian mullahs were also ultimately interested in good relations with the USSR. Iranian propaganda among Soviet Muslim populations was not very aggressive and more or less standard fare. The clerics were convinced Islam would win on a global scale, and in Gudimenko's view they considered the USSR the only power that could help them do this. Good relations with Moscow offered economic potential and also the opportunity for military cooperation. But before the mullahs in Tehran could partake of such help, they felt they first needed to convince the USSR not to oppress Muslims and to withdraw from Afghanistan.[91]

Before long, Soviet patience seemed to begin to pay off. In June 1984 S. M. Sadr, the director general of the Iranian Foreign Ministry, paid a surprise visit to Moscow. There he met with Soviet foreign minister Andrey Gromyko and delivered a message from Iranian foreign minister Ali Akbar Velayati.[92] Tehran media reported that Gromyko stated, "Soviet leaders are prepared to have friendly relations with Iran." Sadr also met with the Soviet deputy energy minister to review economic relations, which the two sides reportedly claimed to want to expand.[93]

These initial negotiations apparently did not go beyond talk. But then the situation began to change. The Iran-Iraq War further exhausted the Iranian economy and depleted Iran's arms. In Moscow, Mikhail Gorbachev succeeded Konstantin Chernenko as Soviet party leader in March 1985. A month earlier, Majles Speaker Hashemi Rafsanjani had declared, "We are inclined to have good relations with the Soviet Union." In May 1985 Prime Minister Hossein Musavi claimed, "In our relations with the USSR, we sense a realistic approach on their part."[94] In September 1985 the Iranian Foreign Ministry's director of economic affairs met in Moscow with Soviet first deputy foreign minister Georgi Korniyenko, with whom he reportedly agreed to expand economic ties.[95]

Korniyenko's February 1986 trip to Tehran was the highest ranking official Soviet visit since the 1979 revolution, and it took place during fierce fighting between Iran and Iraq.[96] In his memoir, Korniyenko included a photograph of himself and Rafsanjani meeting in Tehran but otherwise did not deal with relations with Iran. We therefore do not know if Korniyenko gave his hosts a heads-up on Gorbachev's intention to describe the Soviet presence in Afghanistan as a "running sore" in his Twenty-seventh Party Congress speech, set to open February 25, 1986.[97] Shortly after Korniyenko's visit, however, Rafsanjani expressed "optimism" over the relationship but underscored Iran's continuing unhappiness with Moscow's support for Iraq and military intervention in Afghanistan.[98]

Nevertheless, the Iranian press reported that Korniyenko stressed expanding relations in his meetings with President Ali Khamenei, Majles Speaker Rafsanjani, Prime Minister Musavi and Foreign Minister Velayati. The two sides decided to reanimate their moribund joint economic commission: coheads were appointed with the intention that the commission should meet soon at the ministerial level. They also agreed to reestablish Aeroflot's Moscow-Tehran service.[99]

Besides economic relations, in diplomat Vasiliy Safronchuk's recollection, Korniyenko also dealt with two persistent political irritants. First, there was the continuing fallout from the Kuzichkin case and Iran's large-scale expulsion of personnel from the Soviet embassy in Tehran. Moscow expended much political capital on the issue. The other big, and related, aggravation continued to be the Tudeh's fate. The more Moscow protested the Tudeh's treatment, the more Tehran suspected Moscow of supporting Tudeh sedition. The Tudeh, after all, had been instrumental in training Afghan communists, and there were also widespread suspicions in Moscow that Kuzichkin had betrayed many in the Tudeh before his defection.[100]

Despite these unresolved issues, Korniyenko's visit to Tehran marked a definite turning of the tide. Iranian trade with the USSR began to rise in 1986.[101] By December of that year—a good year and a half before Ayatollah Khomeini died—the Iranian-Soviet Standing Commission for Economic Cooperation met in Tehran for the first time in six years. An agreement to reopen the gas pipeline from Iran to the Soviet republics in the Caucasus, which Iran had shut off in 1980 in an ostensible price dispute, was concluded that month.[102]

Soviet-Iranian rapprochement was further accelerated by developments in Iranian-American relations. After Washington had its fingers burned in the Iran-Contra affair the United States returned to a policy of trying to isolate Iran. Tehran thus began to feel like a pariah and to look for partners in its clash with the United States, Irina Zviagelskaya recalled. Even though ideological differences with the Soviet Union remained, pragmatists grew stronger in Iran in the last half of the 1980s.[103]

With negotiations over economic agreements leading the way, Soviet-Iranian contacts quickened in 1986 and 1987. Iranian foreign minister Velayati visited Moscow in February 1987, the highest ranking Iranian to visit the Soviet capital since 1979. Deputy foreign ministers exchanged visits that summer and a second visit to Tehran in August by Soviet deputy foreign minister Yuli Vorontsov resulted in agreements on projects described as "large-scale" and apparently including a new rail line and oil pipeline. With agreements on the resumption of natural gas deliveries to the USSR, construction of power plants and oil refineries in Iran, and the return of Soviet technicians to Iran, the package had all the marks of a precursor to the greatly expanded framework for future cooperation that was eventually reached in 1989.[104]

As late as early 1988, however, at least one senior Soviet official asserted to an American visitor that debate over policy toward Iran continued. One camp stressed the need for a cautious and long-term view of relations. Another camp rejected the possibility of any meaningful cooperation with the Khomeini regime.[105] In retrospect, the side arguing for persistence and engagement, however cautious, was and would continue to be dominant.

# 2

# *Gorbachev and Khomeini: Perestroika Pen Pals*

M oscow's military intervention in Afghanistan in 1979 was hastened by fears that Washington, having been kicked out of Iran by Ayatollah Ruhollah Khomeini's Islamic revolution, would move into neighboring Afghanistan to maintain its presence on the Soviet Union's southern borders. Before long, however, although well hidden from the outside world by Kremlin discipline, it became clear that the Afghan adventure was a cardinal mistake. It not only embroiled Soviet forces in a losing war but also created a huge obstacle to taking advantage of the great hostility to America exhibited by the new clerical regime in Iran. Tehran, meanwhile, began further to complicate Soviet diplomacy in the Middle East and Moscow's great power rivalry with Washington by persisting to wage war against Iraq even after Iran had blunted Baghdad's initial designs.

Only with the conclusion of the Iran-Iraq cease-fire in 1988 and the withdrawal of Soviet troops from Afghanistan in 1989 did relations between Moscow and Tehran turn around decisively and begin to regain their pre-Khomeini revolution substance. In 1989 Soviet leader Mikhail Gorbachev and his foreign minister Eduard Shevardnadze hosted Majles Speaker and soon-to-be president Ali Akbar Hashemi Rafsanjani in the Kremlin. Together, they put in place the framework that shaped relations between Russia and Iran into the twenty-first century. Moscow's withdrawal from Afghanistan and Tehran's appreciation of the pro-Soviet Najibullah regime as its best hope for resisting a Sunni Pashtun takeover of Kabul and further infringements on Afghanistan's sizeable Shia Hazara population helped make the rapprochement possible.[1]

While having categorically opposed the Soviet military intervention, Iran had limited political objectives in Afghanistan. Iran's military aid to the anti-Soviet Afghan

23

mujahideen had been much less than that of Pakistan. Nevertheless, Iran had opposed Pakistan's aspirations to achieve regional dominance in Afghanistan. Iran continued to play a limited role in Afghanistan after the Soviet pullout. This was in part because of Iran's own sectarian Shia narrow-mindedness and in part because Pakistani- and Saudi-backed Sunni groups pushed it out. But it was also in part because of Iran's improved ties with the Soviet Union and reluctance to join those trying to oust the Kabul regime installed by Moscow. At the same time, through its improved relations with Moscow, Tehran gained a foothold in Central Asia and the Caucasus, and Foreign Minister Ali Akbar Velayati visited not only Moscow but all six Muslim republic capitals in November 1991.

History took several especially ironic twists and turns over the next dozen years. Moscow and Tehran both breathed a sigh of relief when U.S.-led coalition forces drove the Taliban and al Qaeda—Moscow and Tehran's common enemy—from Kabul in late 2001. But in 1989, as after September 11, 2001, Iran's preference in Afghanistan was for a stable but loose central government in Kabul that would permit Iran wide sway along its eastern borders and in other regions of historical interest to it. Then as later, Iran's objective was to encourage the soonest possible withdrawal of all non-Iranian militaries from Afghanistan, while itself working for continued influence in that neighboring country.

## AFGHAN SCENE SETTER

The most authoritative insider's account of the reasoning and progression of the Soviet decision to intervene militarily in Afghanistan in 1979 is that of First Deputy Foreign Minister Georgi Korniyenko; other memoir writers for the most part have based their accounts on his. The most masterful outsider's reconstruction and analysis of the decision is that by Raymond Garthoff. It is based on a meticulous examination of all the primary and secondary sources that had become available by the early 1990s, including Korniyenko's recollections as well as transcripts of declassified Politburo deliberations.[2] The following sketch adds some details from memoirs published in the intervening years and from the author's interviews.

Looking back, Korniyenko wrote that the Soviet invasion was motivated by security concerns fed by the fear of "losing" Afghanistan. This fear was stimulated by concern that the United States would move to establish itself in Afghanistan after the American "loss" of Iran. Andropov had swallowed his KGB staffers' portrayal of Afghan strongman Hafizullah Amin as an American agent and their exaggerated analysis of the dangers to the USSR if Amin remained in power.[3] In addition, according to Aleksandr Yakovlev, future godfather of Mikhail Gorbachev's perestroika, Andropov had scared the Politburo with warnings that once the United States had relocated to Afghanistan and rearmed the Afghan army, the Afghans would take advantage of rising nationalism in the Soviet republics to launch provocations across the Soviet

Union's southern borders. As a result, it would be impossible for Moscow to keep Azerbaijan and the Central Asian republics in the Soviet Union.[4]

Korniyenko's account is consistent with the recollections of his longtime boss Andrey Gromyko, published by Gromyko's son Anatoly some eight years after the foreign minister's death and two years after the appearance of Korniyenko's book. Years before this, the younger Gromyko had once told an interviewer, "From what I heard from my father I drew the clear conclusion that after the downfall of the Shah of Iran there was a new danger of the US shifting its main base to Afghanistan as the spearhead for activities against our military facilities in the southern regions."[5] When the younger Gromyko's book finally came out, it contained the text of a letter the elder Gromyko had dictated for release to the first Congress of Peoples Deputies, which opened in late May 1989, should any deputies criticize him by name for his involvement in the Politburo's decision to send Soviet troops into Afghanistan.

In Andrey Gromyko's draft letter to the congress, which was not released until published posthumously by his son in 1997, he outlined the circumstances that he claimed had prompted the Politburo's decision in 1979. The American administration in Washington was allegedly striving to destabilize the Soviet Union on its southern flanks and threaten its security. From Moscow's perspective, after the United States lost its bases in Iran, Washington was determined to relocate them to Pakistan and if possible Afghanistan. Against that backdrop, Moscow saw Hafizullah Amin's murder of Afghan communist party chief Nur Mohammad Taraki as a counterrevolutionary coup that the United States and Pakistan could take advantage of to pursue their goals against the USSR. "It is possible today, ten years later, to disagree with this decision [to intervene], but there is no basis on which to cast doubt on the political underpinning of our help to Afghanistan."[6]

Some two decades later, Vasiliy Safronchuk recounted that he believed Gromyko had understood as early as March 1980 the need to look for a political exit from Afghanistan.[7] Safronchuk elsewhere suggested that Gromyko was the first Soviet leader to recognize that the Soviet invasion of Afghanistan was a "mistake of catastrophic dimensions."[8] The UN General Assembly special session on Afghanistan on January 14, 1980, underscored Moscow's diplomatic isolation. Soon after, according to Safronchuk, Gromyko began to think about "how to extricate" the Soviet Union from its "Afghan adventure using diplomacy." When Safronchuk returned from vacation at the beginning of March 1980, he joined Gromyko and others in the Foreign Ministry to work the issue.[9]

Safronchuk later agreed with most observers that the turning point did not come until 1986, when Gorbachev gave the Soviet military a year to finish the job in Afghanistan or get out. At the same time, new foreign minister Eduard Shevardnadze began to push for faster progress in Geneva at the UN-mediated "proximity" negotiations between the Kabul regime, supported by Moscow, and Islamabad, backed by Washington. The United States, gaining confidence in Gorbachev, increasingly pressured Islamabad to deal seriously with him on Afghanistan.[10]

By this time, practically no one in the Soviet leadership favored keeping Soviet troops in Afghanistan, according to Central Committee veteran Karen Brutents. Although the top level maintained great secrecy, Brutents could not detect any opposition to the Gorbachev line. The Politburo elders who had supported the invasion in the first place—KGB head Yuri Andropov, chief ideologist Mikhail Suslov, and Defense Minister Dmitri Ustinov—had all died. Gorbachev at first continued the previous policy line, giving the military a chance to show it could win but at the same time did not give the military any more troops.[11] Meanwhile, Moscow searched for Afghan political figures at home and abroad willing to form a coalition government of "national reconciliation" with a new and improved People's Democratic Party of Afghanistan (PDPA). On this last track, Moscow in May 1986 engineered the replacement of Babrak Karmal, whom Moscow had installed in December 1979 to replace the deposed Amin, by security chief Najibullah as head of the PDPA in Kabul.

As Gorbachev maneuvered to extricate the Soviet military from Afghanistan, Iran was not the most worrisome factor in terms of its activities inside that country, although Tehran of course was doing nothing to help Moscow. The Soviet occupation was a fundamental obstacle, from Tehran's point of view, to closer relations with Moscow, but that did not mean that Tehran put many resources into aiding the mujahideen fight against Soviet troops in Afghanistan. After all, from the first days of the Soviet invasion, the Khomeini regime had been preoccupied at home with securing power and dealing with internal resistance. Then, after Baghdad's attack in 1980, Tehran was almost totally focused and absorbed in fighting Iraq. In 1988 Najibullah remarked to Gorbachev that the Iranian leaders, despite all their hostility, were "being deflected from Afghanistan by the Iran-Iraq war."[12]

Aleksandr Yakovlev, who worked alongside Gorbachev throughout this period, concluded that Iran never did much in Afghanistan.[13] Although involved for centuries there, Iranian military resistance to the Soviet intervention was from the beginning overshadowed by Pakistan's efforts. Safronchuk recalled that Pakistan supported 80 percent of the mujahideen; Iran supported just 20 percent. Although Iran from the beginning was 100 percent against the Soviet occupation, the threat from Iran to Soviet troops in Afghanistan was never that great. To be sure, Tehran's Islamic Guards (i.e., the Islamic Revolutionary Guards Corps, or IRGC) helped mujahideen elements, but Iran supported only the Shiite Hazaras and even then not very actively.[14]

Karen Brutents later described part of Iran's dilemma as being that while they were fighting Soviet troops, the mujahideen were backed by the United States and Pakistan, with whom Iran was loath to coordinate let alone subordinate the fate of those forces loyal to it. Moreover, one Sunni resistance leader in particular, Gulbuddin Hekmatyar, who was closely allied to Pakistan at the time, bitterly disliked Iran, and Iran reciprocated this enmity.[15] As a result, Iranian involvement in Afghanistan by most accounts evidenced little coordination with the activities of other outside powers. It was instead focused almost exclusively on the minority (15 to 20 percent) Shia Hazaras and concentrated on those forces willing to take guidance from Tehran. Iranian support was stingy compared to what Pakistan and Saudi Arabia were giving to the commanders and political parties they backed. Tehran, it seemed, was more interested in expanding the Khomeinist presence in Afghanistan than in fighting the Soviets.[16] In a serialized memoir, Safronchuk pointed out that Iranian control of the Shia mujahideen frustrated efforts by the United States and Pakistani secret services to create a united mujahideen front.[17]

The Iranian-backed Shia resistance alliance subsequently for the most part sat on its hands and did not join in the predominantly Sunni mujahideen assault on Najibullah regime forces that followed the February 1989 completion of the Soviet troop withdrawal from Afghanistan. Soviet internal documents portrayed the campaign against Jalalabad, beginning in March 1989 and intended to set up a "transitional government" before laying siege to Kabul, as supported by Pakistan, Saudi Arabia, and the United States—with no mention of Iran.[18]

In fact, after years of encouraging the USSR to quit Afghanistan, Iran now appeared to view the Najibullah regime, which Moscow had managed to leave in place in Kabul as it began its troop withdrawals in May 1988, as Iran's best hope for blocking a Sunni Pashtun takeover of the country.[19] Longtime Afghan observer Barnett Rubin concluded, "Iranian strategy was to block a takeover by the U.S.-, Saudi-, and Pakistani-backed groups. Iran preferred Najibullah without Soviet troops to the mujahidin backed by rival states."[20] Other seasoned observers decided, "There was no doubt that some Iranian officials at least could see their way to cooperating with the Soviets to procure some sort of political settlement of the Afghanistan problem even if it involved leaving Najibullah in place."[21] Within months, Hekmatyar was publicly denouncing the Iranian leadership for Speaker Rafsanjani's contacts with Moscow and asserting that Shias in general were "not good Muslims."[22]

Summing up Tehran's posture toward Moscow and Kabul during the nine years Soviet troops were fighting in Afghanistan, Safronchuk stated that Tehran had the most clearly and sharply defined position: no negotiations with Kabul as long as Soviet troops were in Afghanistan. The Iranians did not participate in the Geneva proximity talks between Kabul and Islamabad but did ask the USSR to inform Tehran regularly of their progress. The USSR did so faithfully as Safronchuk paid yearly visits to Tehran to explain the Soviet position. When the negotiations concluded, the Iranians welcomed the withdrawal of Soviet troops, but Tehran incurred no obligations from the Geneva agreements. Iran just waited for Soviet troops to leave Afghanistan and then prepared to resume closer relations with Moscow.[23] The diplomat Nikolay Kozyrev, after leaving Tehran in 1983, was also close to the proximity negotiations. In his view, Iran's aim throughout the conflict had been to make sure that part of Afghanistan would remain in its sphere of influence, and so its support to the mujahideen had been limited, or "dosaged," as Russians like to say, to correspond to this goal.[24]

## THE ODD COUPLE

From Soviet Moscow's perspective, the major problem in relations with Iran during the 1980s was not Afghanistan but Iran's insistence on pursuing the Iran-Iraq War, which upset Moscow's basic diplomatic strategy in the Middle East. From the Khomeini regime's perspective, the fundamental problem indeed was the Soviet military occupation of Afghanistan. Only when each side abandoned the conflict of greatest concern to the other did relations between them begin to improve fundamentally. Not only that, but in a radical reversal of the long-prevailing dynamic, each side actually became useful to the other in the new environment. As Moscow withdrew from Afghanistan, Tehran did not interfere with the Soviet-installed Afghan leader Najibullah and did not join with Pakistan in supporting Sunni mujahideen warlords attacking Kabul. As Tehran settled into a cease-fire with Baghdad, Moscow abandoned its reluctance to sell Iran weapons and signed major arms deals with a Tehran anxious to reequip its depleted army.

By the end of the Iran-Iraq War, the conflict had claimed by some reckonings over one million casualties, with over a quarter million dead on the Iranian side. According to some estimates, Iran spent $74 to 91 billion to wage the war, and the direct and indirect costs of the conflict to Iran had been in the neighborhood of $627 billion.[25] Despite all of the Islamic Republic's efforts, Iraq still boasted eleven times as many main battle tanks (5,500 to 500) and seven times as many serviceable combat aircraft (513 to 70) at the war's end.[26] During the conflict's "war of the cities" last stage, as many as a quarter or more of Tehran's residents fled to avoid attacks by Iraqi missiles feared armed with chemical warheads.[27] As the war dragged on and took its toll on the Iranian economy and arsenal, Iran began to get more and more anxious to reinvigorate ties with Moscow—even in advance of a Soviet withdrawal from Afghanistan.

Moscow had all along pursued better relations with Iran and had encouraged Iran to conclude the war with Iraq. On top of Moscow's own Afghan imbroglio, Tehran's pursuit of regime change in Baghdad had complicated the playing field for Soviet diplomacy in the Middle East. With the end of the Iran-Iraq War in August 1988 and completion of the Soviet withdrawal from Afghanistan in February 1989, Moscow had reason to expect that its positioning in Middle East diplomacy would improve. At the same time, as the Soviet economy continued to decline, Moscow had an additional incentive to try to revive economic relations with Iran and even conclude new contracts for military goods.

From Tehran's point of view, purchasing arms and associated production technology from the Soviet Union—as well as from any other country willing to sell them—would be a quick way to begin to repair Iran's tattered military. The conflict had destroyed half of Iran's weapons inventory and left the other half obsolete.[28] New weapons contracts with the Soviet Union could help set the stage for Iranian indigenous programs designed better to prepare the country for future threats from regional rivals—not just Iraq—and the unwelcome presence of the United States and other nonregional powers' navies in and around the Persian Gulf.[29] Iran had already concluded new economic accords with the USSR since First Deputy Foreign Minister Georgi Korniyenko's visit to Tehran in February 1986 had broken the ice in the relationship.

The Iran-Iraq cease-fire of August 1988 and the accelerating prospects of a Soviet withdrawal from Afghanistan helped advance the revival of Soviet-Iranian ties. But the seminal breakthrough came with Ayatollah Khomeini's remarkable letter to Gorbachev in January 1989, even before the withdrawal of Soviet troops from Afghanistan was concluded the next month. As though writing to a fellow theologian, though one of a different confession, Khomeini praised Gorbachev for his reforms and in effect for burying communism, or at least confining it to the "museums of world political history." The ayatollah encouraged the Soviet leader "to seriously study and conduct research into Islam," which he said could "easily help fill up the ideological vacuum of your system." Although he declared that the Muslims of the Islamic Republic regarded themselves as "partners" in the fate of Muslims around the world, he concluded his letter by signaling Iran's readiness for a major thaw in Soviet-Iranian relations: "Our country believes in and respects good-neighborliness and reciprocal relations."[30]

As important as cessation of the Iran-Iraq War had been to Moscow, Tehran would likely have continued to hold Moscow at arm's length had the Soviet Union not pulled its forces out of Afghanistan. Khomeini's letter and the retreat home of Soviet troops underscored at least the symbolic centrality of the Afghan factor in Soviet-Iranian relations at the time. So did Soviet first deputy foreign minister Yuli Vorontsov's dual-hatted status as ambassador to Kabul and negotiator with Tehran since October 1988.[31] Other evidence followed in quick succession. Foreign Minister Eduard Shevardnadze delivered Gorbachev's reply to Khomeini's letter during a trip to Tehran in late February 1989, right after the completion of the Soviet military exit from Afghanistan. It was the highest-level Soviet visit to the Iranian capital since the Islamic Republic's foundation. Iranian foreign minister Velayati reciprocated with a trip to Moscow in March 1989 to advance Majles Speaker Rafsanjani's visit in June 1989. When Shevardnadze returned to Tehran at the end of July 1989, the positions of the two sides on an Afghan cease-fire and an "inter-Afghan dialogue" to establish a "broad-based government" reportedly were converging.[32]

In between Shevardnadze's two visits to Tehran, Rafsanjani visited the Soviet Union from June 20 to 23, 1989—even though Khomeini had died more than two weeks earlier on June 3. Although less than equivalent, Rafsanjani's was the highest level Iranian sojourn to Moscow since the shah's last appearance there in 1974. When Rafsanjani returned to Tehran, he defended dealing with the Soviet Union. Iran's own policies had not changed, Rafsanjani said in a Friday prayer lecture, but agreements were possible since Soviet policies had. Moscow's withdrawal from Afghanistan, according to Rafsanjani, had been Iran's "first demand." Other changes included diminished Soviet support for "leftist and Marxist trends" in Iran and the beginning of greater religious freedom in the USSR. "This combination prepared the grounds for a new situation for Iran with its northern neighbor," declared Rafsanjani.[33]

As Gorbachev-confidante Aleksandr Yakovlev remembered the period, the Soviet leadership for its part also clearly started to try to use Iran. Relations with the Khomeini regime were the subject of serious discussions between Yakovlev, Gorbachev, and Shevardnadze. On the one hand, they were very much aware of the possible downsides of a strong U.S. reaction to a Soviet tilt toward Tehran, and so they moved cautiously. The Soviet leaders, moreover, had plenty of their own reasons for wariness in their dealing with Tehran. Yakovlev was with Gorbachev in the Kremlin when they received the Iranian delegation, led by Khomeini's personal representative Ayatollah Javadi Amoli and Deputy Foreign Minister Mohammad Javad Larijani, there to deliver Khomeini's letter.[34] Larijani, incidentally, was none other than a brother of Ali Larijani, who gained international renown upon his appointment as Iran's lead nuclear negotiator in August 2005 after the election of President Mahmoud Ahmadinejad.[35]

Khomeini's message had come quickly and its contents were good, recounted Yakovlev. But, implicitly underscoring Moscow's distrust of Tehran by his choice of historical parallels, Yakovlev said he and his colleagues still remembered that Hitler had reassured Stalin of his good intentions right up to the moment that Nazi Germany had invaded the USSR. In not wanting to repeat Stalin's gullibility, Yakovlev and his colleagues worried about the Islamic fundamentalist threat. There was alarm that Khomeini's ideology could seriously and negatively affect Central Asia and Azerbaijan.

On the other hand, Yakovlev pointed out, the Cold War was winding down, but the rules of the game continued. Moscow thought that it could use the Khomeini regime and its anti-American and anti-Western posture to help deal with continuing pressure from Washington. The old rules of the game applied especially to the military-industrial complexes on both sides. Their overriding impulse continued to be to sell arms to anyone who would buy them. Whenever the Kremlin agreed with Washington not to sell arms to a certain country, France, Germany, and the United States would simply replace it as sellers of arms to that country. Economic ties had always played, and would always play, a big role in Moscow's relations with Tehran. Iran was a big market, and the only question Yakovlev recalled as ties took a turn for the better was how Moscow would use this market.[36]

From his vantage point inside the Central Committee's International Department, where he wrote the first draft of Gorbachev's reply to Khomeini's letter, Vladimir Gudimenko saw widespread agreement on the geopolitical imperative of dealing with Iran. It was not the subject of great debate for the bureaucratic machine as it developed information and analysis for consideration by Soviet leaders. Relations with the West were the top priority and Afghanistan the real sore spot. So it was not surprising, Gudimenko reflected, that Iran had garnered so little attention in the memoirs of the time: it was simply not a controversial issue.[37]

## AGREEMENT ON ARMS

Warming up to Rafsanjani's visit, a Moscow radio commentary forecast that Soviet-Iranian trade would exceed $1 billion in 1989, triple that in 1988.[38] After his stay in Moscow the Majles speaker traveled to Leningrad (June 22–23) and Baku (June 23). Besides Foreign Minister Velayati, Rafsanjani's official party included Mohsen Rezai, commander in chief of the IRGC, and Hassan Rowhani, chairman of the Majles's defense committee.[39] Rafsanjani, Rowhani, and Rezai all played actives roles in the development, politics, and diplomacy of Iran's nuclear program in the years ahead.

In Moscow, Rafsanjani and Gorbachev signed a joint declaration on the principles of relations and friendly cooperation between the USSR and the Islamic Republic of Iran and a long-term program for economic, commercial, scientific, and technical cooperation to the year 2000. Ministers from both sides also signed a commercial agreement and an agreement for the construction of a railway line from Mashhad in Iran across the border at Sarakhs to Tejen in Soviet Turkmenistan. They also agreed on a memorandum of mutual understanding on consular affairs. On the Persian Gulf, according to the joint communique on the visit, the two nations called for "a complete withdrawal of all the navies of foreign states, and that the security and calm of the region should be provided by the littoral states." Gorbachev, according to the communique, accepted "with thanks" Rafsanjani's invitation to visit Iran.[40]

The two leaders' initial meeting took place in the Kremlin on June 20. Gorbachev told Rafsanjani that while bilateral relations had not always gone well in the past, improving them was not a problem for Moscow. The two countries had never before had such a chance for expanding their cooperation. "We explicitly declare that our country supports your anti-imperialist revolution," said Gorbachev. In reporting the exchange, the official Iranian news agency noted that Tehran had not taken seriously Moscow's invitation two years earlier (probably during either Vorontsov's trips to Tehran or Velayati's trip to Moscow in 1987) because of Soviet support for Iraq and Moscow's military occupation of Afghanistan. But now Rafsanjani was able to tell Gorbachev, "After we got acquainted with your ideas we thought we can have good relations with you. Our assessment of the developments in the Soviet Union under your leadership is positive."[41]

The declaration of principles of relations that the two leaders signed on June 22 stated, "The emergence of the new political thinking in the Soviet Union on the one hand, and the victory of the Islamic revolution in Iran on the other hand, have created a basis for deepening ties and good-neighborly cooperation." The two sides stated that they would expand cooperation specifically "in the economic, trade, technical, and industrial sphere" as well as in "science, education, and links between universities." They pledged to "seek new forms and spheres for such cooperation, including the peaceful use of atomic energy."[42]

Gorbachev and Rafsanjani also made a side agreement on arms sales at the summit, but it was not heavily advertised. The long-term program for cooperation to the year 2000, which Gorbachev and Rafsanjani signed on June 22, outlined sixteen areas for future collaboration and inventoried past Soviet-Iranian projects according to completion dates starting in 1958 through 1988 but did not touch on military sales.[43] These were mentioned only in the declaration on principles for bilateral relations, which laconically stated, "The Soviet side agrees to cooperate with the Iranian side with regard to strengthening its defense capability."[44]

Rafsanjani held a press conference on June 22 before leaving Moscow for Leningrad. When asked about arms sales, he stressed that Iran's arms purchases abroad were based on the principles of self-sufficiency and independence. Iran was "seriously reviewing" its needs and considering expanding its production of "aircraft, missiles, artillery, and electronic equipment." All of Iran's needs in these areas could be developed at home, "but we do have certain technical needs" that Tehran hoped "to satisfy soon from various sources."[45]

After years of denouncing the USSR, the theocracy in Tehran obviously needed to explain its reversal of course toward Moscow, especially to the regime faithful back home. Much the same was true for Moscow. Press reports suggested that Moscow would supply Iran only with limited defensive weapons and not in quantities that would disrupt the regional military balance.[46] All the same, it seemed ironic that after years of frustration trying to get Tehran to stop fighting Iraq by restricting Soviet arms sales to Iran, Moscow had now turned around and agreed to sell Iran weapons. In any event, Moscow clearly found a bit touchy the criticism from abroad to its prospective new arms sales to Iran, as well as the expressions of skepticism from some influential voices at home.

Nevertheless, it would not have been difficult to make the case for going ahead with new arms contracts. The imbalance at the end of the Iran-Iraq War was staggering. Even after the upcoming buying spree, the Islamic Republic's military would still be smaller than that of the shah at the end of his reign. Despite Iraq's losses in Desert Storm in early 1991, Iraq's military even then would remain superior to Iran's.[47]

Moscow had not objected to this imbalance. The USSR in fact had contributed to it as a matter of policy during the long years of the Iran-Iraq War by restricting the flow of Soviet arms to Iran after 1982 while continuing to supply them to Iraq. The Khomeini regime had insisted on pursuing the war, which had hampered Moscow's diplomacy in the Middle East. As a result, Moscow had favored Baghdad with more weapons in an effort to make the seemingly irrational Tehran sue for peace. There was now plenty of headroom for Moscow to sell weapons to Iran without coming anywhere near to upsetting the imbalance that Iraq had obtained at the war's end.

In any event, Iran was exhausted on all fronts, not just militarily, so there was little chance of it making trouble with its new arms any time soon. Besides, Iran had at long last stopped fighting with Iraq, a step that Moscow had for years encouraged it to take. In this context, new military contracts were a payoff to Iran for ending the Iran-Iraq

War so that Soviet diplomacy could get back on track in the Middle East. Moreover, they opened the prospect of improving the Soviet Union's presence in Iran itself so as to finally realize some advantage from the American departure a decade earlier and to help keep the United States boxed out.

There was also the hope of continuing to elicit de facto Iranian neutrality toward the Najibullah regime in Afghanistan. Closer to home, given the increasingly unsteady relations between Moscow and some of the Soviet republics, especially in the Caucasus and Central Asia, the contracts may have been meant as an inducement to Iran not to muck around in the region, particularly in those republics with significant Muslim populations.[48] All of this was on top of whatever help the new arms sales would give the moribund Soviet military-industrial complex. In short, Moscow for years had been bogged down in Afghanistan; Tehran had been bogged down in Iraq. Moscow now needed to revitalize its diplomacy and salvage its economy, and Tehran needed weapons to begin to reconstitute its military standing and deterrence capability in the region.

Given what seemed the overwhelming logic of a Soviet-Iranian rapprochement that even included new military contracts, it was all the more surprising to find criticism of the development in the Soviet press. This was indicative of a persistent and jaundiced attitude among important opinion makers toward closer than necessary relations with Iran. Aleksandr Bovin, most notably, who a decade earlier had warned of the anti-Soviet potential of the Khomeini regime, now commented trenchantly on the arms sales when reviewing the Rafsanjani visit. "The advantages here are obvious. First, it means hard currency or hard currency goods. Second, it means influence in Tehran, or at least a belief that there is such influence." But in the long-term, "we are continuing to pump weapons into the most restless region of our planet; and that means we are going to promote the preservation of that restlessness and instability." This, concluded Bovin in his televised commentary, was "difficult to reconcile with the postulates of new political thinking."[49] Bovin's concerns echoed Soviet worries in the 1970s about the shah's weapons purchases from the United States[50] and would continue to be heard, as we shall see, from Russian critics of post-Soviet Russia's own weapons sales to Iran.

Nevertheless, by this time some leading Soviet economists were already declaring Gorbachev's investment policy a mistake. Moreover, the perception was hardening among the population that the economy was declining. Gorbachev had announced dramatic cuts in the Soviet army and navy the previous December at the United Nations.[51] Moscow clearly needed money and was happy to become a major arms supplier to Iran. Besides, Iraq was way behind schedule in paying for its arms purchases during the Iran-Iraq War.

Although the details would remain murky for years, Iran and the Soviet Union concluded four major weapons, spare parts, munitions, and military technical assistance contracts in the two years after Rafsanjani's visit:

- On November 25, 1989, $1.3 billion for twenty-four MiG-29 fighters, twelve Su-24MK strike aircraft, and two S-200VE Vega antiaircraft missile systems.

- On May 17, 1990, for three Kilo-class (Project 877 EKM) submarines, torpedoes, and other equipment. Although no price tag was made public, the cost of this contract and the next one below appear to have totaled around $1.6 billion.

- On April 24, 1991, for technical assistance in creating and equipping six basing facilities for the submarines.

- On November 13, 1991, $2.2 billion for licenses, technical assistance, components, and spare parts for the production in Iran of one thousand T-72S tanks and fifteen hundred BMP-2 infantry combat vehicles.[52]

Given its bitter experience in the Iran-Iraq War, the utility to Tehran of the aircraft, surface-to-air missiles, and tanks and infantry combat vehicles and associated production licenses in any new conflict with Iraq was obvious. More troubling to outside powers, of course, were the submarines. Although originally intended to counter new frigates ordered by Iraq from Italy, by the time of their delivery their mission appeared to be to deter outside powers from repeating their 1987–88 naval intervention in the Persian Gulf.[53]

All in all, the two sides reportedly agreed in principle on potentially $6 billion worth of military sales during Rafsanjani's visit, and Russia inherited these contracts after the Soviet collapse. The first Kilo was delivered in October 1992, preceded by the fall 1990 delivery of S-200s and MiG-29 fighters. The Soviet/Russian share of the Iranian arms market skyrocketed, constituting 65 percent of Iran's purchases from 1989 to 1992.[54] However, when details of the contracts surfaced a decade later, the $6 billion total was scaled back to $5.1 billion as outlined above. Moreover, the fourth contract had been significantly under-fulfilled. Because of cash flow problems, Iran by the year 2000 reportedly had assembled only 422 T-72s and 413 BMP-2s, a shortfall worth roughly some $1.5 billion.[55]

## TERRORISM AND PRAGMATISM

In January 1981 Iran finally released the fifty-two Americans held hostage since the takeover of the U.S. embassy in Tehran in November 1979. In April and October 1983, however, Iran had a hand in the bombing of the American embassy and Marine barracks in Beirut. By 1989, the United States had put Iran on the list of states that supported international terrorism (1984) and issued several iterations of sanctions on trade with Iran (1984 and 1987). In February 1989 Supreme Leader Khomeini had declared a *fatwa*, in effect a death sentence, on British citizen Salman Rushdie, author of *The Satanic Verses*. Yet despite what some leading analysts saw as the resurgence in Tehran of pragmatists, led by Rafsanjani, who was elected president in July 1989, the worst was yet to come.[56]

In the years that followed, Rafsanjani—along with Ali Khamenei, Khomeini's successor as supreme leader;[57] Minister of Intelligence and Security Ali Fallahian; and Foreign Minister Velayati—was implicated in the formal approval of state-sponsored terrorist operations by elements of the Ministry of Intelligence and Security (MOIS) and the IRGC well beyond Iran's borders. These included most notoriously the September 1992 murder of the leader of the Kurdish rebels in Iran (the Democratic Kurdish Party) and three aides in Berlin's Mykonos Café.[58] That special operation coincided with another one of pivotal importance to this narrative: the Iranian-assisted ouster from office of President Rahmon Nabiyev in Tajikistan.

As could be expected of neighbors who had clashed with each other for centuries over borderlands between them, Russia and Iran had each been responsible for numerous ugly incidents long remembered by descendants of the many victims on each side. None other than Nanuli Shevardnadze upbraided her own husband over relations with Iran when U.S. Secretary of State James Baker visited Moscow in May 1989. She told Secretary and Mrs. Baker that a chill had overcome her when she had seen a picture of her husband with Ayatollah Khomeini during Shevardnadze's visit to Tehran that February. With the seventeenth-century queen Ketevan clearly in mind, Mrs. Shevardnadze passionately recalled how the Persians had burned the dowager queen at the stake and brutally killed a half million Georgians.[59]

Nevertheless, on this occasion and in Vienna in March, while conceding that "Iran has extremists and genuine fanatics," Foreign Minister Shevardnadze argued with Baker that isolating Iran "would be the worst of all possible options." Shevardnadze said that he had "been able to ascertain that Iran has rational politicians." The bottom line for Shevardnadze was the "need for the Soviet Union and Iran, who are neighbors along a 2,500-kilometer border, to have good relations."[60]

Moscow was not alone in thinking it was possible to do business with an Iran in which pragmatists seemed to be gaining the upper hand. Moreover, even if all the instances of suspected Iranian terrorism were to be accepted and added up, they probably appeared to policymakers in Moscow insignificant compared to the atrocities inflicted by the mujahideen on Soviet forces during their unwelcome presence in Afghanistan. Indeed, from Moscow's point of view, the ascendancy of pragmatists in Tehran must have seemed to buttress Iran's shift toward policies more in line with Soviet vital interests.[61]

The strength of Tehran's pragmatists had peaked earlier in 1985–86 with what became known as the Iran-Contra deal with the United States. But leaks to the press undercut the effort, scuttled any chance of easing bitter U.S.-Iranian relations, and underscored the strength of hard-line radicals and conservatives in Tehran.[62] The August 1988 cease-fire with Iraq, however, came in the midst of another wave of pragmatism. This waned with Khomeini's fatwa against Salman Rushdie in February 1989, only to revive with Rafsanjani's election as president in July 1989.

To the extent that the pragmatists' rise made it easier for Moscow to deal with Tehran, however, it must have sparked a bit of anxiety lest those same pragmatists also let the United States get its foot back in the door to Iran. Despite the political firestorm that quickly erupted in the United States over Iran-Contra, the worrying bottom line for Moscow must have been that there had been very highly placed American and Iranian officials who had not shied away from contacts. The Iranian ambassador to Moscow later said the whole episode had been "shocking for the Soviets."[63] Moreover, despite all the harsh rhetoric exchanged between Tehran and Washington, trade between the two actually continued to grow until 1994, when its proportion of Iran's total trade actually surpassed the high point reached under the shah.[64] A year later, Minister of Atomic Energy Viktor Mikhaylov correctly noted that U.S. trade with Iran had until very recently been greater than that with Russia.[65]

## PEACE DIVIDEND

All in all, Gorbachev and Shevardnadze probably saw a post-Afghanistan win-win situation developing. They could pursue detente with the United States while taking advantage of the U.S.-Iranian estrangement to pursue a simultaneous rapprochement with Iran. Domestically, the embattled Gorbachev could use these two policy strands to appeal to both supporters of East-West detente and proponents of a more competitive anti-Western regional posture—normally not one and the same audiences. Regionally, warming ties over time could even give the USSR's presence in Iran an edge over that of the United States given what Moscow feared would be the inevitable return of America to Iran. In the meantime, closer relations with Iran would help improve the Soviet presence in the Gulf and keep some defense industry factories open.

The anticipated income from the major arms and technology contracts concluded with Iran between 1989 and 1991 was, after all, in effect a peace dividend made possible by the Soviet withdrawal from Afghanistan. In an interview with Selig Harrison, Aleksandr Yakovlev distinguished between the uniformed military and the military-industrial complex, "all those interests tied into our military production." It was the latter especially who, after Gorbachev came to power in 1985, had pressed him to go for a military solution in Afghanistan "because they were getting many benefits from the war."[66] It was easy to imagine Gorbachev using the prospect of these contracts and then their actuality to ease the opposition of Soviet military industrialists to getting out of Afghanistan. Their production lines would not have to slow down. New markets would open up as the demand for their weapons in Afghanistan eased. Besides, if the USSR did not jump into the Iranian market, some other major power unabashedly would—a belief that, as we have seen, Yakovlev maintained the Gorbachev regime regarded as a certainty.[67]

At the same time, official Moscow was probably also gambling that its arms and trade carrots would restrain Tehran's subversive impulses in Central Asia and the Caucasus. In this regard, at least some in Moscow probably felt vindicated by Rafsanjani's comments at the end of 1991 that it was no longer necessary "to speak fanatically" or "chant impractical slogans" and that what Iran required was "a prudent [*tadbir*] policy" that could be employed without accusations of "engaging in terrorism [and] without anyone being able to call us fanatics."[68] In any event, everywhere across the Soviet Union the leaders of the constituent republics had been straining at the leash for direct foreign contacts of their own, including with Iran. They desperately needed such contacts to ostentatiously demonstrate their nationalist and independent credentials in order to fend off the challenges to their legitimacy from the popular fronts that were springing up everywhere.

This, however, was a slippery slope. By July 1991 Leonid Shebarshin, expelled in 1983 from Tehran, where he had been the Soviet embassy's KGB station chief, and now head of the USSR KGB's First Main Directorate for foreign intelligence, gave a gloomy briefing on the activities of not only Iran but also Turkey on Soviet territory. Speaking to a meeting of Russian Republic security workers attended by Boris Yeltsin and other Soviet and Russian Republic political luminaries, Shebarshin asserted,

> Turkish politicians are starting to think in pan-Turkic categories and, judging by incoming information, see their sphere of influence [as extending to] the Central Asian republics and eventually Tatarstan. They are actively establishing relations with Armenia and Azerbaijan at the same time. But Iran is laying claim to influence in Azerbaijan—it is sending Islamic preachers there, propaganda literature, in a word is carrying out the material preparation for an Islamic revolution. An unheard of thing is happening—there is a clash of interests between Turkey and Iran for influence on Soviet territory.[69]

Nonetheless, as late as September 1991, a month after the August coup attempt against Gorbachev had backfired and resulted instead in the dismantlement of the Communist Party of the Soviet Union, Gorbachev sent academician Yevgeny Primakov to Tehran. Gorbachev's message to President Rafsanjani repeated his commitment to full cooperation with Iran "both through specific republics and the union as a whole."[70] Two months later, Foreign Minister Velayati visited Moscow and met with his Soviet counterpart Shevardnadze (who had resigned in December 1990 but had now been reappointed).

In addition, making full use of the Gorbachev-Rafsanjani understandings on relations not only with Moscow but also with the republics, Velayati during his November–December 1991 visit to the Soviet Union also signed an agreement with Russian Federation leader Boris Yeltsin's deputy prime minister Yegor Gaidar and visited Kazakhstan, Kyrgyzstan, Tajikistan, Turkmenistan, Uzbekistan, and Azerbaijan. Iran appeared anxious to establish ties with the Soviet Muslim republics but to do it while rendering full respect to Moscow's sovereignty over them. However, on November 9, 1991, Turkey had already recognized Azerbaijan's independence—nearly two months before the Soviet collapse and a giant psychological step ahead of Iran's own recognition of Baku.

# 3
## *Soviet Collapse: Revanche or Accommodation?*

**A** t a meeting near Brest in Belarus on December 7–8, 1991, Russian leader Boris Yeltsin and his Ukrainian and Belarusian counterparts decided to end the USSR and form the Commonwealth of Independent States (CIS). A week later, on December 12, the leaders of Central Asia requested membership in the CIS when they met in Ashgabat, Turkmenistan. Ten days later, eleven republic leaders (all but those from Georgia and the long-independent Baltic states) signed the Commonwealth Declaration in Almaty [Alma Ata], Kazakhstan. On December 25, 1991, the Soviet flag was lowered over the Kremlin for the last time and the flag of the Russian Federation was raised in its place. Soviet president Mikhail Gorbachev resigned that evening and vacated his Kremlin office, and Russian Federation president Boris Yeltsin moved in.[1]

The breakup of the USSR presented Iran with an entirely new set of dynamics to the immediate north. Iran's preferential access to Central Asia, gained after Ali Akbar Hashemi Rafsanjani's summit with Mikhail Gorbachev in mid-1989, as well as the four major arms contracts subsequently signed with the USSR, arguably inclined Iran to favor keeping the Soviet Union intact rather than seeing it disappear. Tehran had begun to look on the USSR as a major counterweight to U.S. pressure and, at long last, a more reliable source of assistance in beginning to redress the military balance with Iraq. Yet the very country on which Iran had started to count for support in overcoming its international isolation was passing into history. With so much at stake, the Soviet Union's collapse presented Tehran with major challenges and few opportunities that it regarded as compelling.

Moscow during the Soviet Union's last years probably saw closer relations with Tehran as helping to dampen the consequences of the increasing fragmentation and collapse of central authority in Central Asia and the Caucasus. Iran refused to be drawn into Azerbaijan despite the brutal Soviet suppression of the January 1990 uprising in Baku and the December 1989 crossing into Iran of thousands of Azeris from Azerbaijan's border exclave of Nakhichevan. Moreover, Iranian-backed forces for the most part did not participate in the assault on the Moscow-backed Najibullah regime in Kabul following the Soviet withdrawal. Iran's restraint in the face of what must have been the tempting turmoil in Azerbaijan and its reserved behavior in the Afghan endgame presumably went a long way in forming the foundation of what seemed Moscow's hope that Tehran would show similar self-control in Central Asia and especially Tajikistan.

It was true that the fall of communism had opened up new prospects for Tehran to proselytize on behalf of Ayatollah Ruhollah Khomeini's vision of a theocratic state in those suddenly independent territories of the former Soviet Union where Muslim citizens were in a majority. But for beleaguered Iran, all such opportunities had to be subordinated to the priority of maintaining good relations with a post-Soviet Russia that had inherited the role of Iran's partner in all the agreements just signed with the USSR. Besides, the specters of irredentism and territorial dismemberment again reared their heads. In newly independent Azerbaijan, Popular Front leader and then president Abulfez Elchibey espoused reunification of ethnic Azeris north and south of the Araks River border. A unified Azerbaijani nation could change the balance of forces in the Caspian and South Caucasus, presenting a challenge not just to a fragmented rump Iran but also to post-Soviet Russia.

Tajikistan was an entirely different matter. The number of Tajiks in Iran was minimal and Tajikistan did not border on Iran, yet the two countries' shared history, language, and culture appeared to give Iran a real purchase in the race for influence across the region after the Soviet collapse. As rival Turkey streamed into Azerbaijan and Central Asia, historical memories in Tehran of the imperial grandeur of "Greater Iran" proved tenacious. After being forced to settle for a humiliating draw in the Iran-Iraq War, frustrated Iranian leaders may have been anxious to demonstrate a dramatic success. In any event, many Iranians early on apparently looked on Tajikistan as an opportunity to make at least one of the new independent countries "Iranian" as opposed to "Turkish."

Beyond Tajikistan, once the Iranian leadership accepted the fait accompli of the Soviet collapse, it appeared to view liberated Central Asia and the Caucasus as a mixture of dangers and opportunities that required immediate attention. Iran's activism was both an attempt at preemptive damage limitation against perceived Turkish and American inroads, and a forward-leaning effort to spread its own influence by emphasizing common Islamic identities while submerging Sunni-Shia sectarianism.

Historically, Central Asia was Sunni and the majority of Azeris were Shia, but the brutalities and secular policies of the Soviet era had reduced most inhabitants of the region to theological ignorance about their specific Islamic roots. The odds were, however, that as Islam revived so would Central Asians' awareness of their ties to the Sunni world and prejudice against Shia Iran. Iran's pockets, moreover, were shallow compared to Sunni Turkey's. Iran could still offer the new countries its advantageous location to facilitate land trade and the export of the region's hydrocarbon riches to the Persian Gulf. However, beginning in spring 1993, the policy of "dual containment" of Iran and Iraq, pressed by the new administration of President Bill Clinton in Washington, would undercut Iran's potential appeal as an energy transport corridor by making it increasingly difficult to attract financing for large-scale projects.[2]

## SHATTERED FOUNDATIONS

Weak and exhausted but determined to rearm after the end of the Iran-Iraq War, the Khomeini regime had set out to improve its relations with Moscow in early 1989. All of Tehran's assumptions as to its new partner, however, began to change dramatically and rapidly toward the end of 1991 as the Soviet collapse accelerated. Tajikistan had already declared its sovereignty on August 25, 1990, and its independence on September 9, 1991. Although the Iranians hesitated to recognize Azerbaijani independence even as the Turks forged ahead, Iran opened an embassy in Dushanbe in January 1992; it was the first power to do so in that country. The United States followed in March; Russia only in April. On this and other details of establishing formal diplomatic relations in the former republics of the USSR, Moscow was distracted by the enormous sorting out of affairs that the collapse brought in its wake. It was also perhaps a victim of taking for granted its influence in what it now described as the "near abroad."

While Iran had appreciated the stability of Soviet borders and did not seem to have welcomed the Soviet collapse, it realistically and opportunistically adjusted to the new situation. With Russian influence declining, Iran moved into the Caucasus and Central Asia and tried to establish its presence. In areas such as Azerbaijan and Tajikistan, it began spending millions of dollars on religious, cultural, and political proselytizing, not excluding trying to buy the loyalty or at least neutrality of local notables by, among other things, offering cushy sinecures in joint ventures.[3] But the disappearance of the Soviet state also created dangers for Iran, in the sense that the United States and Turkey raced with it to cultivate relations with all the new states on Iran's northern borders. Instead of a friendly USSR sharing its borders, Iran now had the United States and Turkey potentially interposed between itself and a diminished—and in 1992 pro-West—Russia. When U.S. Secretary of State James Baker toured the Caucasus and Central Asia in February 1992, a primary topic in his discussions with the leaders of the newly independent countries he visited was countering Iran in the region.[4]

Looking back, foreign relations expert Nodari Simonia in Moscow concluded that Iran was confused. Leaders in Tehran were afraid as 1992 began that the new Russian Federation would not be as friendly to Iran as had been the old USSR. Ideologically and in realpolitik terms, meanwhile, it was satisfying that the communist Soviet

Union had collapsed. Iran could have some influence in Central Asia. It therefore pursued a cautious approach at the beginning, according to Simonia. As tensions later developed between Russia and the United States, Iran played up to Moscow its desire for friendship, arguing that they were neighbors compelled to cooperate with one another.[5]

Other equally astute observers painted a picture similar to that by Simonia but highlighted various aspects in darker or lighter shades. Gorbachev's former right-hand man Aleksandr Yakovlev argued that Iran could not have been in favor of the Soviet collapse. Iran had always looked at the USSR as a stable, nonthreatening neighbor and had feared it less than its other neighbors. Turkey, not Iran, had the better chances for expanding its influence in the new so-called Islamic republics, since Turkic languages were spoken everywhere except in Farsi-speaking Tajikistan. Iran understood that it would have been more secure if the republics had remained a part of the USSR, in Yakovlev's view.[6]

Years later, Party Central Committee veteran Karen Brutents reflected on Moscow's enduring approach to the issue. Russia and Iran's historically troubled relationships with Turkey predisposed both to view Ankara in a competitive vein, no matter how good ties actually were at any given time. Brutents emphasized that Turkey's competition with Iran was a constant factor in Russian-Iranian relations. This included the loyalties of the Azeri Turkic population in northern Iran. Though Russian relations with Turkey had become good a decade after the Soviet Union's collapse, Brutents opined that Russia would always tilt toward Iran on the Azeri issue.[7]

One-time Central Committee staffer Vladimir Gudimenko made the point even more strongly that Iran most likely viewed the USSR's collapse entirely negatively. From Tehran's perspective, a major source of opposition to the United States had crumbled with the Soviet Union's collapse. Under Yeltsin, new people came to power in Moscow who were entirely pro-Western. As for the Caucasus and Central Asia, Iran probably understood that it could not have a strong say there. Nevertheless, there were some very strong Iranian efforts at gaining influence in Tajikistan as Iranian hard-liners were ready to give more than just money to the opposition there. But the government line in Tehran was generally more restrained, in Gudimenko's view.[8]

From the beginning, many in Russia and Iran were probably convinced that the two countries had a common interest in limiting Turkish inroads throughout Central Asia. They would have been put on guard especially when Turkey undiplomatically jumped the gun and recognized Azerbaijani independence in early November 1991, before the Soviet collapse. Yevgeny Primakov, head of the Foreign Intelligence Service (SVR, successor to the Soviet KGB) in the first years of the Russian Federation, made clear in his memoir the jaundiced view that his organization took in those years toward Turkey and its perceived partners. "The demand for a global approach required that our foreign intelligence analyze the situation in Turkey through the prism of its membership in NATO," Primakov reminisced. "In today's conditions the SVR's priorities became exposing and countering the complicity of certain circles in Turkey with separatist forces in the northern Caucasus, the aggressive policy of Ankara with an anti-Russian bias in the Transcaucasus, Central Asia, and on Cyprus."[9]

It was not long before Russia and Iran started working together to limit the claims on the Caspian's energy resources asserted by the upstart new littoral states—so recently Moscow's subjects—and their multinational business partners. Iran and Russia were concerned that these outside partners would bring their respective governments in tow to protect their expanding business interests. Once they were established, Moscow and Tehran would not be able to reverse the process.

## ISLAMIC PENETRATION: CONTROLLABLE?

Before leaving Tehran in June 1989 for Moscow, Rafsanjani had told an interviewer that he hoped his visit would have a positive impact on the condition of the Soviet Union's 50 million Muslims.[10] In Moscow, the declaration of principles that Rafsanjani and Gorbachev signed included a provision that called for expanding knowledge and appreciation of each country's spiritual values. "The parties will facilitate visits by delegations and the establishing of contacts between religious figures of the two countries," stated the declaration.[11] This and his visit to Baku probably helped Rafsanjani counter Iranian critics of his dealings with the Satan to the north. At his press conference on June 22, Rafsanjani was asked whether he had discussed the condition of Muslims in the USSR with Gorbachev. He acknowledged that he had. The two delegations had agreed not to interfere in each other's internal affairs, but "on the whole, we perceive the Soviet leadership's domestic policy as correct."[12] In Leningrad, Rafsanjani visited the city's main mosque, which was large enough to accommodate three thousand worshipers.[13]

TASS reported that Rafsanjani in Baku said Friday prayers at the city's central mosque, called on Azerbaijani Communist Party first secretary Abdul-Rakhman Vezirov, examined Iranian and Azerbaijani classics and medieval theological texts at the Manuscript Institute, and met with Oriental scholars.[14] The official Iranian news agency IRNA reported that after Friday prayers Rafsanjani spoke to a "cheering audience of Soviet Muslims." He told them that he hoped Gorbachev's policies would make it possible for Iran to give aid to mosques and theological schools in Azerbaijan and for theologians (*ulema*) from Iran and Baku to exchange visits. According to IRNA, "traffic jammed almost all streets" during Rafsanjani's visit, and "Soviet Azerbaijanis who share cultural, religious and linguistic ties with their brethren across the borders in Iran, consoled the Iranian delegation both in Persian and the local Turkish dialect Azeri on the beloved imam's [Khomeini's] demise." Young people wept from excitement, according to IRNA, and kissed the ulema in Rafsanjani's delegation.[15]

Given the already well-established reputation of the theocratic regime in Tehran for attempting to export its political program, the self-assurance with which Moscow in 1989 gave Iran the green light for proselytizing efforts in Central Asia and the

Caucasus was remarkable. As recently as 1987, moreover, Moscow and Tehran had engaged in a well-publicized tiff over Iran's territorial claims. *Moscow News* had denounced as "absurd" *Jomhuri-e Eslami*'s call for liberating the Soviet republics of Tajikistan, Turkmenistan, and Uzbekistan and districts in Georgia, which the largest circulation Iranian newspaper had claimed was national territory.[16]

In any event, the long-term program for cooperation to the year 2000 Rafsanjani agreed to in Moscow called for developing and expanding trade between Soviet republics and Iranian provinces on the two countries' common border.[17] Strictly interpreted, this border trade would have involved only Turkmenistan, Azerbaijan, and Armenia. But the declaration of principles also endorsed the exchange of religious figures and delegations. Here the field for Iranian missionary work would have been much broader, extending to the six Soviet republics with titular Muslim populations—from Azerbaijan to Kazakhstan and Kyrgyzstan on the Chinese border—and including cities and regions in Russia and other republics with substantial Muslim concentrations, such as the Tatar ASSR.

Karen Brutents later asserted that when Gorbachev met with Rafsanjani in Moscow, the Soviet leader did not have time to think about the export of Islamic revolution by the Iranians. Events were moving too fast, and there were too many other distracting issues. The Iranians, moreover, were not interested in the USSR's collapse. The "Arabs" (that is, Iran's neighbors in the Arabic Middle East) told Brutents that the Iranians did not want the USSR to collapse and that Tehran was making this point to the Soviet Muslim republics. These southern republics, added Brutents, were of course not the instigators of the USSR's collapse.[18] From a different perspective, Central and South Asia specialist Aleksandr Umnov cautioned that in 1988 and 1989 Gorbachev was operating on pure political instinct and did not have a specialist's knowledge of the area. Umnov portrayed Gorbachev as a lost rider who had thrown down the reins in hopes his horse would find its way home out of the woods.[19]

Gudimenko had dealt firsthand with the Iranian account in the Central Committee Secretariat International Department in the 1980s. Looking back, he countered that Moscow in 1989 knew full well the potential for Islamic penetration from Iran but felt that it could control and even use it. Gorbachev's response to Ayatollah Ruhollah Khomeini's suggestion that Islam could help fill the ideological vacuum of the Soviet system had welcomed contacts with Islamic organizations. This phrasing in Gorbachev's reply to Khomeini's letter had survived from the initial draft, which Gudimenko had written as a Central Committee staffer, to the final one. It also appeared in the joint statement published on Rafsanjani's visit in June. Moscow viewed such contacts not as channels of uncontrollable Iranian subversion but as vehicles Moscow could use for developing mutual interests. The Soviet side did not give Iran carte blanche in religious contacts, stressed Gudimenko. In his view, Kremlin policy in 1989 could be best described as one of contacts with control.[20]

Besides, as the Soviet Union passed from the scene, the Islamic Republic of Iran had barely begun to recover from the economic devastation and political trauma of the eight-year-long Iran-Iraq War on its western border. Iran was still an uncomfortable host on its eastern border to several million refugees from the equally long Soviet campaign in Afghanistan. In addition, Iran was beset by the burden of hundreds of thousands of refugees from Iraq's August 1990 invasion of Kuwait and subsequent disastrous retreat in the Gulf War a half year later.

The Oriental Institute's Nina Mamedova, an expert on the Iranian economy, pointed out a decade later that in 1989 Iran was on its knees. Mamedova's colleagues traveling in Iran could not find even cooking pots for sale. No one in Moscow thought that weak Iran would or could interfere in Soviet affairs. The new economic contracts were for refurbishing and rebuilding facilities destroyed in the Iran-Iraq War. The June 1989 framework accord limited Iranian economic ties with the Soviet republics to border trade. Moscow's outlook therefore differed radically from that of Washington. Moscow did not expect any threat from Iran; its view was that there was nothing to fear, Mamedova recalled.[21]

In reminiscing on this period, Diplomatic Academy pro-rector Yevgeny Bazhanov attributed Moscow's lack of concern to its confidence that the KGB and other security organs were still in place, were strong, and could control Iranian activities in Central Asia.[22] Bakhtiyer Khakimov of the Foreign Ministry added some nuance to this assessment. Until 1985 Iranian efforts to spread its "spiritual influence" were difficult to accomplish because the Soviet KGB and other security organs were still effective and well coordinated. In 1985, however, it became possible for Iran to do much more, and by 1988 and 1989 big money had begun to flow from Iran into the region.[23]

Nevertheless, Aleksandr Yakovlev's global perspective on Iranian activities was significantly more relaxed than that of the specialized working level. Given earlier concerns, the Kremlin leadership had tasked all of the Soviet intelligence services to be on the lookout for any efforts by Iran to destabilize the situation in Central Asia and Azerbaijan. The services discovered some instances of such activities but not what appeared to be a serious, coordinated effort directed from Iran. Moreover, the individual cases seemed for the most part initiatives of separate local groups in Tajikistan, Uzbekistan, and other Soviet republics, and at that very few. In Afghanistan, the Iranian leadership's policy at the time seemed to be one of factual noninterference.[24]

## THE SUNNI-SHIA FACTOR

The Soviet collapse filled Turkey with romantic enthusiasm for spreading Turkish economic, cultural, and political influence in Turkic Azerbaijan and Central Asia. Encouraged by the United States, Turkey was fast out of the blocks in 1991–92 in launching a myriad of initiatives across the region: opening embassies, broadcasting TV, sending economic emissaries, and opening schools and offering scholarships.

For Iran, the move by its historic rival Turkey into the Caucasus and Central Asia posed a sectarian challenge in addition to a geopolitical one. Sunni Turkey and Shia Iran, with their different cultures, histories, languages, and national aspirations, had long been anathema to each other; their hostile relationship predated the Islamic Republic of Iran by centuries. Most of the former Soviet Union's 50 to 55 million Muslims were Hanafi Sunni, the sect of the Ottoman empire, and spoke Turkic languages. The main exceptions were the Azeris—Turkic-speaking but roughly 70 percent Shia—and the Tajiks, who though Farsi-speakers were predominantly Sunni.[25] Iran's past periods of expansion into the Caucasus and Central Asia had created vast reservoirs of suspicion about Iranian intentions, even while implanting deep traces of Persian culture and Farsi language. By the end of the nineteenth century the prevailing stereotype of Iranians, especially in Sunni parts of the region, tended to be negative. The American diplomat Eugene Schuyler remarked on the violent hatred of Persians as "Kaffirs and unbelievers" that he found in his 1873 travels through Central Asia.[26]

After the Soviet collapse, however, it was debatable whether Iranian hopes for influence in Central Asia were handicapped by residual Sunni prejudices. Seventy-plus years of Soviet power, seclusion, and secularization had done much to erase pre-Soviet knowledge of theological distinctions between the Sunni and the Shia sects. Azeris and Central Asians seemed to know little about their own Shia or Sunni beliefs, or of differences between the two. While these distinctions had lost little of their animosity south of the former Soviet border, north of it they had largely been repressed or erased. They did not figure prominently if at all in outsiders' impressions of the area as the Soviet Union broke up. A number of experts on the region believed that Sunni-Shia differences had largely lost their relevance and that even ten years after the Soviet collapse they operated at most on the fourth or fifth level of self-identity.[27]

Given Iranian behavior in Afghanistan, it would have been possible to speculate that Iran's influence in Central Asia and the Caucasus would initially be circumscribed less by lingering Sunni prejudices against Shia Iranians than by Iran's own likely self-limiting focus on the few Shias in the region, just as it had concentrated on the Hazaras in Afghanistan. Besides, experts pointed out that the Iranians downplayed being Shia and approached the Central Asians as fellow Muslims, not sectarian Shias.[28] In fact, the Iranians had been quite active and adept in supporting Sunni as well as Shia opposition organizations and radical secular nationalist groups throughout the Middle East.[29] But experts like Umnov in Moscow cautioned that the strengthening of Islam in the Caucasus and Central Asia could rekindle Sunni-Shia disputes and further estrange even Farsi-speaking Tajikistan from Iran.[30]

Looking back, Gudimenko did not think that the top USSR leadership gave much thought to the impact that Sunni-Shia differences might have on Iranian missionary contacts and theocratic proselytizing or was even much aware of this as an issue.[31] Indeed, some Soviet leaders appeared incredibly tone-deaf to the fine points of the world's major religions and sects.

CPSU Politburo candidate member and Central Committee secretary Vladimir Dolgikh, for example, was sent to the Armenian capital of Yerevan in February 1988 to try to dampen emotions over the disputed region of Nagorno-Karabakh in neighboring Azerbaijan. There, the Christian Armenian population had grown to outnumber the region's Muslim Azeri inhabitants, and Armenians were agitating to incorporate Nagorno-Karabakh into Armenia. Dolgikh's visit had been prompted by riots in Nagorno-Karabakh, and within days of his return to Moscow there was a bloody anti-Armenian pogrom in Sumgait, Azerbaijan. After the Soviet Union collapsed, full-scale war broke out, Armenian forces defeated those of Azerbaijan in Nagorno-Karabakh, and the local Azeri population fled the region.[32] Moreover, the conflict soon had an explosive echo as far away as Tajikistan. Amazingly, however, given the sensitivity of his mission, Dolgikh reportedly asked an audience in Yerevan why Armenians and Azeris were fighting over Nagorno-Karabakh if both were Muslims.[33]

Twelve years later, even President Putin made the mistake of telling American television interviewer Larry King, "Our Caucasus inhabitants are mostly Shiites."[34] In fact, most of the Muslim populations in Russia's Northern Caucasus territories were Sunni and not Shia. But, in the late 1980s, Soviet experts on Central Asia and the Caucasus took these differences into account and knew they were a factor that would work against any Iranian efforts to penetrate regions with significant Muslim populations. Muslim clerics in the Soviet republics, while interested in contacts with Iran, were not lovers of the Khomeini regime. For the most part Sunnis, they were little attracted by Shia Iran. In predominantly Shia but Turkic Azerbaijan, there was much Iranian radio and TV penetration but little impact on the local population. So, according to Gudimenko, Moscow viewed the situation as under control.[35]

Indeed, visitors to Baku around this time found little evidence of Islamic fundamentalism.[36] Even in nominally Shia Azerbaijan, where there should have been lasting enthusiasm for Iran if identification as Shia had played a determining role, the Azeris quickly became deeply suspicious of Iran because it sided with Armenia in the conflict over Nagorno-Karabakh and other issues. As to Farsi-speaking Tajikistan, a close observer made the case that the Tajik intelligentsia was never drawn to political Iran, neither to the Iran of the shah nor to the Iran of Ayatollah Khomeini. Rather, the initial attraction was Iran's pre-Islamic, predominantly Zoroastrian culture, which only temporarily submersed the differences between Sunni Tajikistan and Shia Iran.[37] In general, Iranian attempts to influence the Azeris and Central Asians met with mixed success at best. The countries in the region wanted good relations with Iran but not its warm embrace.[38]

## A STEP BEHIND IN AZERBAIJAN

As the Soviet Union broke up, observers could not be faulted for presuming that Iranian influence would be much greater in Azerbaijan than in Central Asia: not only because of common Shia ties but also because of Soviet-Iranian agreements that had endorsed a variety of contacts across the Araks River. Iran had long had a consulate in Baku, even during the shah's reign. Rafsanjani's 1989 summit with Gorbachev had opened up new possibilities for Iranian trade and religious work in Azerbaijan. Iranian clerics had already engaged in extensive missionary efforts in Azerbaijan even before it achieved independence.

By contrast, the Soviet regime controlled Turkish access to the Caucasus and Central Asia much more carefully, and Turkey itself was much more cautious and self-denying. Moscow had not been eager to let Turkish diplomats travel in Central Asia and Azerbaijan, and Ankara's policy was not to do anything to annoy the USSR. Although Prime Minister Süleyman Demirel had visited Uzbekistan and Azerbaijan in 1967, only in 1990 did Turkish diplomats begin extensive travel to the Turkic regions of the USSR. After President Turgut Özal's trip to Moscow in March 1991, during which he also visited Kazakhstan and Azerbaijan, movement was finally made to reopen the Turkish consulate in Baku, which had been closed for fifty years.[39] As a result, Ankara started the post-Soviet period with a self-admittedly thin understanding of the new countries opening up to its diplomats and business class.[40] Even well-educated Turks ten years later laughed when they recalled that at the time they had no idea where even Baku was and were surprised to hear Azeris and Central Asians spoke recognizably Turkic dialects.[41]

Nevertheless, under pressure from nationalists at home and in Azerbaijan, Turkey recognized Azerbaijan on November 9, 1991. It was the first country to do so—almost two months before the USSR's collapse—but later than it would have preferred. Ankara had moved slower than popular opinion would have dictated so as not to upset a big barter deal with Moscow but then jumped in with great enthusiasm.[42] Ankara's early recognition was a demonstration not only of the power of public opinion in Turkey but also that Turkey more than Iran had its finger on the pulse of events in Azerbaijan and eagerly anticipated and welcomed Azeri independence.[43]

Only by comparison to Turkey, however, was Iran late to recognize independent Azerbaijan. Iran was much faster than the United States and other Western powers to establish actual embassies in the newly independent countries and even beat Turkey to the punch in this respect in Azerbaijan. Deputy Foreign Minister Mahmoud Vaezi presided over Iran's upgrading of its consulate in Baku to embassy status on January 4, 1992, some ten days before Turkey was able to effect a similar metamorphosis of its diplomatic presence.[44] And while Iranian foreign minister Velayati toured the six so-called Muslim republics in November and December 1991, Turkish foreign minister Hikmet Çetin did not match that feat until February and March 1992, after they were all clearly independent.[45]

Iran went to great pains to be diplomatically correct in the months preceding the final collapse of the Soviet Union. At the start of Velayati's ten-day trip in November 1991, for example, he stopped in Moscow. There he met with Soviet foreign minister Shevardnadze, who encouraged Iran to open consulates in all six of the republics Velayati was about to visit.[46] In at least Bishkek (Kyrgyzstan), Ashgabat

(Turkmenistan), and Dushanbe (Tajikistan), Velayati in fact signed agreements to open Iranian consulates sometime in the future and for those Soviet republics to open representational "offices"—not consulates—in Tehran.[47]

Reflecting on his Soviet tour, Velayati laid out Iran's policy on recognition for an interviewer at home. "From the beginning," said the foreign minister, "our policy was based on two pillars. One was to respect the will of the people of those republics; the second, that we do not take advantage of the situation and become ourselves a further cause of increased tension and instability." Iran was "getting closer to the point where we can recognize some of the republics which have declared independence" and was "waiting for the legal stages of independence to take place in those countries." Iran had "no problem recognizing the republics that have passed those stages" and where people had voted, or were ready to vote, for independence. "But the legal stages should definitely be followed so that it becomes clear that that is what the people want," concluded Velayati.[48]

The popular appeal of Iran's opening an embassy in Baku in early January 1992, however, was soon undermined by Tehran's early support for Armenia in the conflict over Nagorno-Karabakh. In an attempt to mediate the dispute, Foreign Minister Velayati visited Yerevan and Baku in late February 1992. But his mission was in effect torpedoed while he was still in Baku by the February 26 Armenian attack on Khodjali and massacre of hundreds of fleeing Azeri refugees.[49] There was even some evidence of participation by Russians.[50] Tehran soon clearly tilted toward Armenia and Russian policy on the conflict over Nagorno-Karabakh. This provoked a sharp shift in attitudes toward Iran by Azeris, who were not alone in pointing out the irony of Iranian support for Christian Armenia against Shia Azerbaijan. As Azerbaijan and Turkey moved to impose a tighter blockade on commerce with Armenia, Iran became Armenia's critical trade partner through the border crossing at Meghri. In Armenia, the long and often harrowing road from Meghri to Yerevan became know as the "road of life."

The politics of the Nagorno-Karabakh conflict had an adverse impact even on the attitudes of ethnic Azeris in Iran toward Tehran. When the journalist Thomas Goltz visited the Iranian capital in April 1992, he found evidence already of a pro-Armenian tilt. The clerical regime allowed local Armenians to march in commemoration of the mass killings of some 1.5 million Armenians in the Ottoman empire beginning in 1915, which Armenians considered genocide, while it denied permission to an Azeri culture club to commemorate the Azeri victims of Armenian forces at Khodjali just that February. Such decisions started to turn some ethnic Azeris against the Khomeini regime. According to one of the members of the culture club with whom Goltz spoke: "We are second-class citizens here. We have not only been deprived of our cultural identity as Turks, but do not even enjoy the same rights as these Christians who are killing our brothers in Karabakh." Another of Goltz's contacts in Tehran told him, "I wouldn't have believed it a year ago. The mullahs are so dumb—and it is all because of Karabakh. It is going to rip this country apart."[51]

## THE "ONE AZERBAIJAN" CHALLENGE

After Gorbachev came to power in 1985 and quickened the pace of Soviet-Iranian contacts, the calls for "one Azerbaijan" that had emanated ever so carefully out of Baku under what appeared to be republic party leader Heydar Aliyev's sponsorship came to an end.[52] As Leonid Brezhnev passed from the scene earlier, Aliyev had been promoted to Moscow and risen under Yuri Andropov and Konstantin Chernenko to first deputy prime minister and full member of the Politburo. But under Gorbachev, Aliyev dropped out of sight in May 1987 and then formally retired in late October.[53] Andrey Gromyko later confirmed to his son that there had been little love lost between Gorbachev and Aliyev, whom Gromyko much admired.[54]

With nationalist fervor rising in Baku, however, December 31, 1989, was declared World Solidarity Day for Azerbaijanis.[55] Within six months of Rafsanjani's June 1989 summit with Gorbachev in Moscow, ethnic Azeris in Azerbaijan's Nakhichevan exclave, which borders on Iran, dismantled frontier barriers to gain easier access to ancestral farmlands, cemeteries, shrines, relatives, and trade on the other side in Iran.[56] Nakhichevan happened to be Aliyev's home region. A week later, even as a nationalist uprising led by the Azerbaijani Popular Front gained momentum in Baku, an editorial on January 8, 1990, in the semiofficial *Tehran Times* assured the Kremlin that Iran would "never" side with those advocating the "disintegration of the Soviet Empire."[57] Soviet troops brutally suppressed the uprising on January 20, killing at least 120 civilians. Perhaps making it easier for pragmatists in Tehran to declare a hands-off attitude to the bloodshed was the fact that President Özal in Ankara repeatedly declared, "These are internal affairs of the Soviet Union. It is impossible for us to interfere."[58] Nevertheless, zealots in Iran angrily attacked this posture. One ayatollah announced plans to send missionaries to Azerbaijan and to translate the works of Khomeini into Azeri.[59]

Thomas Goltz witnessed the vivid impact of Iranian clerical activities in Baku in spring 1991 during Ashura celebrations, the holiday commemorating the death of Imam Hussein in the Battle of Karbala, a defining moment for Shiism as a sect.[60] Goltz also reported Popular Front leader Abulfez Elchibey's comments on the consequences of the forty-five kilometer-wide passport-free border area designed to facilitate family visits, which presumably flowed out of the 1989 Rafsanjani-Gorbachev accords. According to Goltz's paraphrasing of Elchibey, "an increasing number of fundamentalist southern Azeris, connected with the Iranian regime, were appearing in 'northern' Azerbaijan, hoping to fill the philosophic void left by the demise of Marxism-Leninism with the ideology of the Islamic Republic." In Goltz's account, "While this was a real danger, Elchibey maintained that there was a flip side: Iran was inadvertently importing Azerbaijani nationalism as those same Iranian Azeris returned from their sojourns north, tainted by the vision of a unified, secular, and democratic Azerbaijan."[61]

Indeed, Tehran must have felt concern over these cross-border activities, especially in regard to so-called South Azerbaijan below the Araks River and its main city of Tabriz. During the Iran-Iraq War, the provinces of South Azerbaijan—as well as many others—had enjoyed virtual autonomy because of Tehran's preoccupation with the war effort against Iraq. Yet Moscow under Gorbachev had not fished in these troubled waters, although some in Baku certainly were not averse to doing so. Moscow early on may have been tempted to use ethnic Azeris and Kurds in Iran to encourage Tehran to do less in Afghanistan against the Soviet occupation force, but certainly under Gorbachev refrained from doing so. Brutents, in a later interview, emphatically asserted that Russia would never support Turkey or Azerbaijan in any attempt to use the South Azerbaijan issue against Tehran.[62] So, Tehran must have been grateful to Moscow on this point, adding a level of "trust" as the 1989 rapprochement developed.

Separately but cumulatively, dissatisfaction with the Islamic regime was growing everywhere in Iran, and in Iran's South Azerbaijan provinces it could always potentially mutate into demands for autonomy and even separatism.[63] The journalist Goltz happened to visit this area in April–May 1992 and ran into anticlerical comments by local Azeris in Tabriz. In Torkoman (Turkmanchai), Goltz polled a group of farmers about their identity. None answered Iranian. Asked why, one responded, "Iran is for the mullahs, and we don't want anything to do with those thieves anymore."[64]

As though underscoring its Tehran-centric mind-set, Iran first staffed its embassy in Baku exclusively with Farsi-speaking Persians, who fell flat in their attempts to cultivate the Azerbaijanis. Watching the public relations successes of the Turkish embassy, the Iranians switched quickly to Azeri speakers after they realized their mistake.[65] Soon, according to Goltz, the Iranian ambassador and most of the embassy staff were ethnic Azeris who conducted official business in Azeri and not Persian. The embassy's effectiveness improved, and Iran began bankrolling the new Islamic Party of Azerbaijan, founded in October 1992. Iranian efforts vis-á-vis Turkey were complemented by those of Russian ambassador Valter Shonia, who subtly and effectively took advantage of anti-Turkish feelings among the Russified intelligentsia in Baku.[66]

Nevertheless, observers such as Goltz concluded that Turkey had won Round One of the new "great game" for Azerbaijan and Central Asia "before the mullahs had even been able to field their team." As we have seen, however, Goltz himself recorded firsthand accounts of the Iranian clerics' activities in Azerbaijan even before diplomatic recognition by Tehran. Iran in fact was active on the ground in Azerbaijan and Central Asia well before Turkey, but within the parameters set out by the 1989 Gorbachev-Rafsanjani agreements. Those ground rules for dealing with the republics under the USSR's continuing aegis had been a great thing from the Iranian perspective, one could argue, because they gave Iran all it wanted and kept Turkey out. Iran got the green light to proselytize and do business with border and so-called Muslim republics and regions, while the Turks still faced a red light.

All the same, Azeri urban elites proved indifferent and even antagonistic to Iranian religious appeals, although the same may not have been true of Azerbaijan's poor and rural populations. Nevertheless, after 170 years of separation and almost no contacts during the Soviet period, national identity was definitely more important than religious identity for Azeris north of the Araks River, while the reverse was the case for Azeris in Iran.[67]

On balance, the Soviet collapse was not the outcome Iran seemed to have desired at this point. Iran appeared to prefer a nonindependent Azerbaijan. Tehran wanted especially to avoid the example and influence of an independent Azerbaijan on Iran's ethnic Azeris. Moreover, the disappearance of the Soviet Union finally allowed the Turks to compete with Iran for the hearts and minds of the Azeris and Central Asians, and not just for business deals with Moscow. Underscoring the attraction of Turkey, Central Asian leaders Nursultan Nazarbayev from Kazakhstan, Saparmurat Niyazov from Turkmenistan, Islom Karimov from Uzbekistan, Askar Akayev from Kyrgyzstan, and Azerbaijani prime minister Gasan Gasanov all traveled to Ankara in the Soviet Union's waning months, while only Niyazov and Azeri leader Ayaz Mutalibov trekked to Tehran.[68]

In the face of the Turkish influx into the Caucasus and Central Asia, Iranian trepidation over Turkish goals was especially the case in Azerbaijan. There the irredentist rhetoric of the Azerbaijani Popular Front and Elchibey, who became the country's first freely elected president in June 1992, put Tehran on guard.[69] Given Elchibey's closeness to politicians in Istanbul and Ankara who espoused pan-Turkish sentiments, Tehran heaved a sigh of relief when Heydar Aliyev came back to power in Baku in summer 1993. Although Aliyev had supported the "one Azerbaijan" movement in the early 1980s when he was republic party boss, a decade later he had carefully cultivated Tehran—as well as Moscow and Ankara—while leader of Azerbaijan's Nakhichevan republic.[70] Over the ensuing years, Tehran spent much money in Azerbaijan only to see Aliyev play Iran as just one more bowling pin in a skillful act that juggled the interests of all outside powers.[71]

## HISTORICAL REGRETS AND TABRIZ TREMORS

However correctly but quickly Iranian diplomacy moved after the Soviet collapse, Tehran in comparison to Ankara appeared to the Azerbaijanis to dither over the issue of recognition. To the great irritation of his listeners at a symposium in Baku on the Azeri-Persian poet Nizami, Foreign Minister Velayati argued in December 1991 that Iran wanted to wait for results of the referendum on independence scheduled for December 31.[72] What Azeris perceived as Iranian caution toward Azerbaijani independence was interpreted by some as evidence that Iran was still reluctant to give up territorial claims north of the Araks River, ceded to Russia by the 1828

Turkmanchai Treaty, and reaffirmed by the Soviet-Iranian Treaty of 1921.[73] By some accounts in Baku, Iran tried to reopen the border issue in 1991, reiterating its claims of eighty years earlier. At a press conference in Baku in December 1991, Velayati asserted, "The Azeri people know that the Iranian people have had the Azeri people in their hearts for 170 years—that is the important thing." The remarks struck some as "veiled irredentism," according to Goltz, who covered the event, since it had been 170 years earlier that Iran had withdrawn from north of the Araks River as mandated by the Turkmanchai Treaty.[74]

Ten years after the Soviet collapse, the theme that Azerbaijan rightfully belonged to Iran still resonated in the Iranian press. "Let us not forget that what is known today as the Republic of Azerbaijan was cut off from the Iranian motherland because of the incompetence of the Qajar rulers, and annexed to the Tsarist and communist regimes," intoned one article. "But the inhabitants of those parts never lost their sense of belonging to the motherland," it insisted. "This is why the people of the Republic of Azerbaijan manifested signs of a powerful desire to be reunited with the motherland as soon as—or even before—the Soviet Union collapsed. Such powerful emotions and yearnings still exist among the people of the republic, although they are gradually turning to despair."[75]

Domestic critics frequently attacked the powers-that-be in Iran for having failed to seize a wonderful opportunity to reunite North and South Azerbaijan at the end of the Soviet era. "Now, after 10 years, we remember that grand event and pity how the Iranian government was incapable at that time of thinking of a way to provide the bases for the lost Azerbaijanis to rejoin Iran in that critical situation."[76] While conceding that Azerbaijan's independence was recognized by the world, another commentary argued that Tehran's alleged "passiveness in facing the imposed situation is not the manner of wise and zealous people and the present conditions will not last forever."[77]

The theme was even applied by some Iranian lawyers to argue that the Caspian Sea should be partitioned four ways and not five, with the Azerbaijani share included in the portion that would go to Iran. Their brief asserted that because of "enormous links" the people of the Republic of Azerbaijan "would certainly wish to join Iran." Moreover, if implemented, the proposal would "put in their place" the leaders in Baku.[78] Other commentaries, with glances backward at the perceived perfidies of the Gulistan and Turkmanchai treaties of the early nineteenth century, argued that Iran should insist on 50 percent of the Caspian, since it was an issue of upholding Iran's territorial integrity.[79]

When the USSR collapsed, Iranians were convinced they could take Azerbaijan under their control, observers in Baku later recalled. But after 170 years of association with Moscow, and sixty years of rigorous border controls, Iranian culture had lost its grip on Azeris north of the Araks River under the steady gains of Russian culture, communist secularism, and Azerbaijani nationalism. Nevertheless, observers recounted, Iran had tried to gather Azerbaijan under its umbrella, spending millions of dollars in various areas. From 1994 to 1998, according to one reckoning, Iran spent $45 to 46 million in support of Khomeinist Islamist ideas in Azerbaijan. Iran sponsored Islamic clubs in different cities, bankrolled newspapers, opened bookshops in Baku, and helped establish the Islamic Party. Iran a decade later was still building mosques and religious centers in villages and using money to buy off the local clergy. Observers in Baku charged that Iran paid for students to go to Iran not just to study theology but also to turn them into spies.[80]

Many in Baku underscored that Iran was as active in 2000 as in 1992, but much more dangerous. An official inquiry concluded that the assassins of Ziya Bunyadov—deputy chairman of the ruling New Azerbaijan Party and vice president of the Academy of Sciences—had been trained in Iran for the February 1997 operation, in which they stabbed and shot Bunyadov in his apartment stairwell.[81] The Iranian MOIS had many under cover, it was said, although Azeri state security kept track of them. In 1997 450 declared Iranian diplomats resided in Baku, according to one account. According to another, in March 2000 at least forty-six cars in Baku had Iranian diplomatic plates, provoking great amazement and even greater distrust. During the 1997 trial of Islamist Party leaders convicted of spying for Iran, official testimony asserted that the party had recruited two thousand young people. Others claimed to have seen closer to four thousand training in a camp near Qom.[82]

During this period, developments inside Iran likely also contributed to rising concern for the Khomeini regime. It was commonly estimated that half of the country's 60 to 70 million people were Persian (Farsi) and a quarter Azeri. There were at least twice as many—over 15 million—ethnic Azeris throughout Iran as in Azerbaijan itself.[83] These figures may have even underestimated the ethnic Azeri population in Iran and exaggerated its Persian plurality. According to one Turkish expert observer's figures, Iran's Azeri population actually stood at 21 to 22 million, other Turkic peoples at 4.2 million, and its Farsi population far below 50 percent at only 23 to 24 million—less than the combined total of Turkic peoples. If some nearly 8 million other Indo-Iranian language groups (Kurds, Baluchis, Bakhtiaris, and Lori) were thrown in, the Farsi numbers swelled to 31 to 32 million, but this was still arguably below 50 percent of the population.[84]

Indeed, South Azerbaijan National Liberation Movement (CAMAH) activists put the ethnic Azeri population at 30 million and the total for Turkic peoples in Iran at up to 35 million.[85] Groups such as CAMAH drew inspiration from the so-called Pishevari Republic, headed after World War II by Democratic Party of Azerbaijan leader Sayyid Jafar Pishevari. To them, it was a genuine nationalist movement for cultural autonomy cynically betrayed by Stalin, who viewed it as just one more disposable tool in his dealings with Tehran.[86] In exile in Baku, Pishevari died in an auto accident, widely presumed not to have been a chance collision.[87]

The cause célèbre of CAMAH and similar groups was Professor Mahmudali Cohraqani of Tabriz University. Cohraqani had demanded the opening of Azeri-language schools and publications. He ran for a seat in the Iranian parliament in 1996 and received 100,000 votes but was not allowed to compete in the second round of voting and was later arrested. Movements such as CAMAH began under the protection of Abulfez Elchibey in 1992–93.[88]

Western soap operas and celebrity gossip shows transmitted by Turkish television may have strengthened the Turkic self-identity of Iran's ethnic Azeris. In the late 1990s, with lax enforcement of laws calling for jail sentences for those caught watching foreign television, one Turkish expert who traveled in Iran reported that 100 percent of ethnic Azeris and 80 percent of the overall population in Iran had access to Turkish television through simple antennas or satellite dishes. Ethnic Azeris understood Turkish Turkish 100 percent, and comprehension of Turkish reportedly was increasing even among Iran's Farsi population.[89]

Iran and Azerbaijan had agreed in 1992 to open consulates in Nakhichevan and Tabriz, respectively. The Iranian consulate in Nakhichevan opened in 1993, but the Azeri consulate in Tabriz did not become a reality until October 2004. Heydar Aliyev visited Tabriz while he was still living in Nakhichevan but never during official visits as president to Iran. In 1999 the student movements in Tabriz and Ardabil reportedly used Azeri slogans.[90] Tehran's reluctance to allow Azerbaijan to open a consulate in Tabriz suggested that South Azerbaijan had definitely become a sensitive issue in Tehran's eyes. One Turkish expert argued that there was a bipartisan consensus in Iran. Both moderates and radicals agreed that Iran needed to be careful about Azerbaijan. All factions in Iran were hard-liners on this issue, this observer said, and this fact produced a monolithic approach.[91]

## TWO STEPS AHEAD IN TAJIKISTAN

Across the Caspian Sea in Central Asia, off to a running start, Iran was the first country to put in place an embassy in Tajikistan. It was located on newly renamed Tehran (previously Gorky) Street and opened on January 9, 1992.[92] Aleksandr Umnov later underscored that a Farsi-speaking government in Tajikistan was important for Iran, given all the Turkic-speaking Sunni republics in the region.[93] Another source, the Iranian ambassador to Baku, when asked why Tajikistan was so important to Iran, explained that Tajikistan meant as much to Iran as Azerbaijan meant to Turkey.[94]

Many in Tehran saw in Tajikistan a country whose territory and people had formed a part of "Greater Iran" until the fifteen century, beginning under the Samanids. The Samanids were an independent dynasty that took control of most of northeastern Iran in the late ninth century as the Abbasid caliphate declined.[95] Under the Samanids and their successors, the Ghaznavids, Bukhara and Samarkand had begun to glitter as cultural centers of the Islamic world.[96] And in the rich culture of the Samanids' time—clearly predating that of Russia— Tajiks and Iranians found a common heritage as the Soviet Union collapsed. Rahmon Nabiyev, independent Tajikistan's first president, underscored Tajikistan's ancient historical and cultural ties with Iran after visiting Tehran in June 1992: "Until the 15th century we lived in a single state."[97] In 1999, under Nabiyev's successor Emomali Rahmonov, Dushanbe hosted a celebration marking the eleven hundredth anniversary of the Samanid state.

The Iranian presence in Tajikistan had grown* noticeably since Rafsanjani's visit to Moscow in 1989. The Iranian press covered the signing of agreements blessing trade and religious contacts between Tehran and the Soviet Muslim republics extensively. It continued to pay special attention to Iranian publication and distribution of Persian-language textbooks, construction of mosques and Islamic schools, opening of libraries and bookstores, exchange of cultural delegations, and the provision in June–July 1992 of Iranian television and radio programs to Tajikistan.[98] Irina Zviagelskaya of the Oriental Institute later recalled that along with the Turks, the Iranian presence became much more visible toward the end of the Soviet era in Central Asia, especially in Tajikistan. Although the Iranian influx was still not very deep, Iranian women in black, along with missionaries, businessmen, banks, and signs in Farsi's Arabic script, could be spotted in Dushanbe.[99]

The Russian Foreign Ministry's Bakhtiyer Khakimov confirmed that by 1990 not only Iran but also other states with Islamic populations had become significantly more active in the Soviet republics, which were all participating in the so-called parade of sovereignty. The vertical power structure of the KGB and other security organs was crumbling, making the ground more fertile for outsiders' activities. Many Saudis, for example, were interested in the possibilities for missionary and mercantile work in Central Asia. Saudi Arabia was home to many *basmachis* who went into exile after their revolt against Soviet power in the 1920s failed. Diplomatic relations, broken off in 1938, were resumed in September 1990.[100] The first Saudi ambassador to the USSR ** was an ethnic Uzbek, Khakimov—also an ethnic Uzbek—pointed out. In 1990 the Saudis financed the building of a big mosque in Namangan in Uzbekistan's portion of the Fergana Valley, from where many of Saudi Arabia's basmachis had originated.

Events in Afghanistan were also at work, in Khakimov's analysis. In September 1991 the United States and the USSR agreed on the "zero variant" in regard to supplying arms to forces in conflict zones, including Afghanistan. This was greatly to the advantage of the mujahideen forces, who still had access to plenty of weapons and ammunition, including from Tehran. The restraints placed on the USSR enhanced Iran's freedom to operate not only in Afghanistan, in Khakimov's view, but also north into Central Asia.[101]

# 4

# *Tajikistan: "Greater Iran" or "Near Abroad"?*

For Moscow and Tehran, the collapse of the USSR and the brutal Tajik civil war tested expected behavior on both sides. Radicals in Tehran pushed aggressively to support the so-called Islamic opposition in Tajikistan, particularly when its fortunes appeared to wax with the ouster of President Rahmon Nabiyev in Dushanbe in early September 1992. Given the painful economic dislocations in the newly independent, but diminished, Soviet successor state of Russia, the major arms contracts of 1989–91 predisposed Moscow to patience with troublesome Iranian behavior while still opposing its often vicious meddling. Still, the horrors of the Tajik conflict were such to provoke soul-searching debate in Moscow over Russia's real equities and interests in Tajikistan.

In 1992 Russian president Boris Yeltsin and his team were beset by the mind-numbing challenges of sorting out the affairs of newly independent Russia. Tajikistan was just one of their many headaches. The sudden removal of the Kremlin's heavy hand, which had set the course of Tajik politics for decades, upset the skewed distribution of power between Tajikistan's regions and left Tajik politics in turmoil. The moderate middle fractured and scattered, and the extremists became further radicalized. Moscow's initial backing for the opposition led by "democrats" and the Islamic Revival Party, evident in Gorbachev's dispatching of a team of sympathetic mediators to Dushanbe in October 1991, melted, prevaricated, and shifted.

The outbreak of civil war in Tajikistan midway through 1992 became a major challenge to Moscow and Tehran in managing their relationship. They needed to establish new ground rules for behavior in the post-Soviet environment. They had unexpectedly lost the common land border and suddenly shared a mixture of competing and common interests in the newly independent states lying between them. The challenge each presented to the other was most sharply focused in Tajikistan but was blurred by the forays into the country by Pakistani-backed radical Islamist mujahideen, who contested both Russian and Iranian interests.

In addition to the Soviet Union's collapse, the consequences of the long and catastrophic Soviet war in Afghanistan had a great impact on developments in Tajikistan. In December 1991 Tajik foreign minister Lakim Kayumov told the journalist Ahmed Rashid that Afghan mujahideen control of the long Tajik-Afghan border presented the "most difficult and complex problem" Tajikistan had ever faced. There had been mujahideen incursions into Tajikistan, and "if Islamic fundamentalism is very high in Afghanistan then it is natural it will influence Tajikistan also."[1]

According to many accounts, rival Afghan mujahideen factions actively courted the oppositionist Islamic Revival Party (IRP) in Tajikistan. The most aggressive and earliest to mount operations in Tajikistan was Gulbuddin Hekmatyar's radical Hizb-i Islami, or Islamic Party, Hekmatyar group (HIK). Since 1986–87, at the behest of the American Central Intelligence Agency (CIA) and the Pakistani Inter-Services Intelligence (ISI) directorate, Hekmatyar had been carrying out attacks across the Afghan border into Tajikistan.[2] Pakistan's role and influence as a sponsor of the anti-Soviet resistance in Afghanistan had always overshadowed that of Iran. To the extent that parties such as Hekmatyar's enjoyed Pakistan's support and were increasing their activities in independent Tajikistan, the spread of Pakistani influence from Afghanistan into Tajikistan would have been unwelcome by both Iran and post-Soviet Russia. In contrast, Turkey's presence was minimal in the Farsi-speaking country, and the United States early on made clear its noninvolvement in the Tajik civil war. In fact, Washington temporarily pulled the American embassy staff out of Dushanbe in late October 1992 as the opposing sides fought for control of the city.

Tajikistan of course was a mere footnote in the larger scheme of things. Nevertheless, the swirling of grander geopolitics in 1992 found an interesting and instructive reflection there. To Tehran, Tajikistan seemed the most natural door into Central Asia, and the Iranians knocked loud and hard on it when prospects for success seemed greatest. Some Iranian observers and radical politicians referred to Tajikistan as part of historical "Greater Iran." Radicals in Tehran saw the Soviet Union's disappearance, Tajikistan's sudden independence, and the active opposition there to President Nabiyev's old guard as presenting Iran with revolutionary opportunities. Their agitation for a more forward-leaning Iranian policy succeeded, however briefly, in August–September 1992.

For Russia, the fate of the nearly four hundred thousand ethnic Russians at risk in war-torn Tajikistan provoked an "agonizing reappraisal" of Moscow's own imperial legacy and obligations. As the conflict degenerated into civil war, Tajikistan's sizeable ethnic Russian population scrambled to leave. Besides civilians, there was also a significant military presence commanded by Russians but heavily manned at the fighting level by Tajik conscripts with conflicting loyalties. They would find it hard to stay neutral in the middle of the swirling battle. The role that Russia's Border Guard forces and especially the 201st Motorized Rifle Division (MRD) should play in the unfolding hostilities began to be hotly debated both in Russia and Tajikistan.

Tehran's reaction to the opposition's success in Tajikistan in summer 1992 challenged all of Moscow's presumed assumptions of how Iran would behave in Central Asia. Although a pro-Moscow regime retook control of Dushanbe that December, Tehran for years thereafter—along with other forces and outside powers active in Afghanistan—helped keep the Tajik opposition afloat. Nevertheless, the civil war was primarily the product of domestic Tajik dynamics, and not of Iranian—or Afghan, Pakistani, Saudi, or Uzbek—instigation, although the ambitions of all of these countries for influence in Tajikistan did feed the conflict. Moreover, though Islamic elements of the Tajik opposition reached out to Iran and to anyone else who would help them, they failed to inspire an effective and enduring mass movement in Tajikistan itself.

Russia and Iran formally adopted neutral stances while the outcome was uncertain, but then clearly displayed where their sympathies lay as first one side and then the other took the upper hand. For Russia, this meant the side that oriented itself toward Moscow, whatever this side's aversion to Yeltsin and his "democrats." Moscow's support therefore increasingly swung behind a coalition of forces from Leninobod region, long dominant in Tajik political life, and Kulob region, which backed the status quo represented by Leninobodi rule if not Leninobodi President Nabiyev personally. Iran, similarly, graduated its support from covert to overt when the IRP-led opposition ousted Nabiyev in September 1992 and briefly appeared to have triumphed.

But then the situation swiftly reversed. After the old guard Popular Front militia retook Dushanbe in late 1992, Russian and Uzbek forces openly assisted it in pushing the armed opposition into Tajikistan's hinterlands and across the border into Afghanistan. From the Russian perspective, the crisis stage in the civil war seemed to be over, and Iran—which all along had maintained close and regular contacts with Moscow—was well on its way to accepting Russian primacy in Tajikistan.

## TUMULTUOUS DUSHANBE

The politics of Tajikistan in its first year of independence were the most tumultuous in all of Central Asia. With the collapse of Soviet power, the hand of arbitration from Moscow had disappeared and the grip of Tajikistan's northern Leninobod region, which had dominated politics since the 1940s, was being challenged. The rival demonstrations that would repeatedly break out in Dushanbe were the manifestations of an increasingly bitter jockeying for a redistribution of power in newly independent Tajikistan. Even preceding the Soviet collapse, Tajik politics reflected many of the back-and-forths of political struggles in Moscow. Contending forces in the republic sought to use any advantage gained by their counterparts in the Soviet capital to advance their own fortunes in Dushanbe.

There had been large demonstrations in the Tajik capital in February 1990. They were sparked by rumors that thousands of Armenians—refugees from the conflict between Azerbaijan and Armenia over Nagorno-Karabakh recounted in the previous chapter—had been given apartments, already in critically short supply. The protests soon turned bloody when the authorities tried to disperse them with force, including gunfire. The weeklong rioting that ensued resulted in over eight hundred injured and at least two dozen officially acknowledged fatalities, though perhaps actually twice that many. In any event, the developments of February 1990 began to turn public sentiment against the regime led by Communist Party first secretary Kakhar Makhkamov and marked the beginning of a political struggle that two years later would turn into a full-blown civil war.[3]

As had been his predecessors for decades, Makhkamov was a representative of the Leninobod region in the north, often identified by its capital of Khujand.[4] Since 1946, with one exception, Leninobodis had headed Tajikistan's party and government structures. As a sop to other regions, Pamiris from the vast mountainous region of Gorno-Badakhshan, bordering on Afghanistan and China, and Garmis from districts to the east and south of Dushanbe had held the honorific post of chairman of the Supreme Soviet.[5] Now, following the example of Soviet party leader Mikhail Gorbachev—who in May 1989 became chairman of the USSR Supreme Soviet and in March 1990 USSR president—the Supreme Soviet in Dushanbe made Makhkamov its chairman in April 1990 and then elected him to the new post of president in early December 1990. Upon Makhkamov's elevation to the presidency, the Supreme Soviet promoted First Deputy Chairman Kadriddin Aslonov, a Garmi, to chairman.[6]

Eight months later, Makhkamov remained publicly silent for three days after the August 19, 1991, coup attempt against Gorbachev.[7] Soon, however, Makhkamov conceded that "Yes, in principle" he had supported the so-called Committee for the State of Emergency that had attempted to oust the Soviet leader.[8] In response to Makhkamov's failure to protest and condemn the effort to topple Gorbachev, the major opposition groups then active in Tajikistan—the IRP, the Democratic Party, the Rastokhez (Resurrection) Movement, and the Lali (Ruby) Badakhshan Society—formed a Union of Democratic Forces whose demands were backed by the republic's chief Islamic cleric (*Kazi kalon*), Akbar Turajonzoda. These forces mounted a running demonstration in support of Russian democrats and against the Makhkamov regime. The protest called for an investigation of the activities of the Tajik Communist Party during the coup attempt against Gorbachev and the suspension of the party's activities while the investigation was carried out. By August 31 the protests succeeded in ousting Makhkamov from the presidency.

The IRP was Tajikistan's largest opposition movement. While initially drawing adherents from all regions, the IRP's support base over time became identified with

Garmis living not only in the Garm region east of Dushanbe but also in Dushanbe itself and in the Kurgan-Tyube region in southern Tajikistan.[9] Significant numbers of Pamiris were also sympathetic to the IRP and, like Garmis, had been relocated under Soviet power to Kurgan-Tyube to develop the region. Many Garmi political activists now joined with Pamiri counterparts in challenging Leninobod's supremacy. Since this supremacy was associated with Communist Party rule, it was natural that the Garmis and Pamiris should gravitate to the IRP and other movements challenging the entrenched rule of the Communist Party apparatus dominated by Leninobodis.

Against these emerging forces stood the still-entrenched but reeling apparatus of Tajikistan's Communist Party. Over the years, the northern Leninobodis had used Marxism-Leninism, the Communist Party apparatus, and divide-and-balance tactics to secure their mastery over Tajikistan's other regions.[10] In what was so far a silent partner role stood the southern Kulobis, who were supportive of Leninobodis and resistant to the demands of Garmis and Pamiris. Kulobis and Leninobodis had traditionally shared a strong identification with the state: industrial Leninobod had governed Tajikistan for decades; agricultural Kulob had supplied many soldiers to the Soviet army and policemen to the republic's Ministry of the Interior.[11] In a June 1992 survey, respondents in Leninobod and Kulob expressed the strongest support for the Communist Party and almost universally rejected the idea of an Islamic state.[12] Many Kulobis had been resettled to Kurgan-Tyube and resided alongside similarly relocated Garmis and Pamiris, setting the stage for future violence.

Under pressure from the demonstration sponsored by the Union of Democratic Forces, the Supreme Soviet briefly buckled, dismissed the Leninobodi Makhkamov as president, and named Supreme Soviet chairman Kadriddin Aslonov, a Garmi, acting president on August 31, 1991.[13] It was to prove a radical shift. During what turned out to be Aslonov's brief tenure as acting head of state, the parliament declared Tajikistan independent on September 9, 1991.[14] Then, with large crowds gathering daily in downtown Dushanbe, Aslonov on September 20 resigned from the Tajik Communist Party and its Politburo; the following day approved Dushanbe mayor Maksud Ikramov's order to remove the capital's largest statue of Lenin from Lenin Square, soon renamed Ozodi (Freedom) Square; and on September 22 signed a decree suspending the activity of the republic Communist Party.[15] It had been just a month since Yeltsin on August 23 had similarly banned the Russian branch of the CPSU from operating in the Russian Federation.

The Communist Party–dominated parliament quickly retaliated and moved to reverse Aslonov's decrees. On September 23, it dismissed Aslonov as Supreme Soviet chairman and acting president; revoked his ban on the Communist Party; appointed former republic Communist Party first secretary Rahmon Nabiyev, a representative of Leninobod, new parliamentary speaker and acting president; and decreed a state of emergency throughout the republic through the end of the year.[16] Again, demonstrators quickly gathered to challenge the Supreme Soviet's reassertion of

Leninobodi supremacy, demand the reinstatement of the Garmi Aslonov as acting head of state, and call for the lifting of the state of emergency.

In the two weeks of negotiations that followed between the demonstrators and Nabiyev, film director Davlat Khudonazarov, chairman of the USSR Cinematographers Union, emerged as a leading mediator. Khudonazarov was a Pamiri, an Ismaili Shia born into a family with deep roots in Gorno-Badakhshan, but who grew up in Dushanbe and studied in Moscow. As a representative of the democratic wing of the CPSU, Khudonazarov was well-connected even in the Soviet capital. A supporter of academician Andrey Sakharov and CPSU general secretary Mikhail Gorbachev, Khudonazarov participated in the First Congress of Peoples Deputies in 1989, was a deputy to the USSR Supreme Soviet elected the same year, and became a member of the Central Committee chosen at the CPSU Twenty-eighth Congress in 1990. Khudonazarov resigned from the party after its Central Committee tried to remove Gorbachev.[17] By mid-September, Khudonazarov was already being spoken of as a candidate for president in elections that had been set earlier in the month for October 27.[18]

In negotiations with newly installed republic leader and declared presidential candidate Nabiyev, the latter accused Khudonazarov of not being neutral in pressing Nabiyev to step aside as prime minister and acting president during the election campaign. Khudonazarov responded by phoning Gorbachev's secretariat with a request that the Soviet leader send a team of impartial mediators to Tajikistan. Gorbachev assented, dispatching St. Petersburg mayor Anatoly Sobchak and academician Yevgeny Velikhov, well-known figures in the Russian democratic movement, who arrived in Dushanbe on October 3. According to Khudonazarov, those protesting the parliament's actions in Dushanbe, feeling that the Russian democrats could help them, applauded Sobchak and Velikhov the next day when they visited the square where they were gathered. The Communist Party *nomenklatura*, however, instinctively resented the fact that Sobchak and Velikhov were in Tajikistan.[19]

On October 5 Nabiyev agreed to give up his republic leadership duties temporarily. Aslonov was not reinstated, however; the Pamiri Akbarsho Iskandarov became acting chairman of the Supreme Soviet and acting president.[20] Then, on the recommendation of Sobchak and Velikhov, Iskandarov on October 6 signed a decree submitting for examination by the Supreme Soviet the question of legalizing parties of a religious nature and requesting that the presidential election be rescheduled from October 27 to November 24, which it was.[21] On October 22, after a roll-call vote, 112 of the 188 deputies present approved lifting the ban on the political activities of the IRP and other religious organizations.[22]

However, Nabiyev's temporary resignation was by and large an empty gesture since the nomenklatura did not go on vacation and kept on working for his election. Furthermore, whatever the sympathies of other Russian democrats, Boris Yeltsin— having clearly eclipsed Gorbachev in Moscow—appeared to Khudonazarov to have cast his lot with Nabiyev.[23] In any event, Nabiyev, who had been party boss in Tajikistan from 1982 to 1985, when he was swept out by Gorbachev's perestroika broom, now completed a dramatic comeback.

Seven candidates, including Nabiyev and Khudonazarov, were on the ballot on November 24, 1991. Expert sociologists predicted that Nabiyev would win the first round by around 45 percent of the vote and that Khudonazarov would come in a close second at 42 percent.[24] This would have forced a second round in which there would be no other candidates to split the anti-Nabiyev vote, thereby resulting in Khudonazarov being elected president. The official tally, however, awarded Nabiyev a lopsided 58 percent of the vote against Khudonazarov's 30 percent amid widespread charges of ballot stuffing.

Khudonazarov charged that 10 to 15 percent of the votes had been invalid.[25] Some experts estimated falsification of the results in Leninobod and Kulob regions at 30 to 35 percent.[26] Ethnic Russians throughout Tajikistan—some 7.6 percent of the country's 5.1 million population in 1989, but since then steadily dwindling—reportedly voted solidly for Nabiyev and aided and abetted the ballot tampering in his favor.[27] In addition, Khudonazarov asserted that Tashkent had directed the Uzbek diaspora—some 23 percent of Tajikistan's population at the time—to vote for Nabiyev because he was allegedly an Uzbek and that the actual results had been a much closer 41 percent for Nabiyev and 39–40 percent for Khudonazarov. In fact, Uzbekistani president Islom Karimov, who underscored to Khudonazarov that "I nursed from a Tajik mother," boasted that he had been deeply involved in making Nabiyev president.[28]

Nevertheless, it was generally accepted that Nabiyev had genuinely won a plurality of the votes if not the outright majority required by law.[29] On December 2, 1991, after claiming victory, newly elected President Nabiyev installed the hard-line procurator Safarali Kenjaev, who had managed his electoral campaign, as Supreme Soviet speaker. With this appointment, Nabiyev's already troubled victory began to go horribly awry. Rather than seeking to mend relations with the defeated opposition, Kenjaev aggressively attempted to undermine it and to roll back the advances its representatives had made in the last year. In response, radicals among the opposition did little to reach out to regime supporters and instead did much to stoke bitter and lasting resentment.

With his swings between support for Kenjaev's aggressiveness and vacillation in the face of opposition resistance, Nabiyev increasingly lost support even among his hard-core Leninobodi and Kulobi supporters and their Russian and Uzbek backers. Nabiyev was not averse to using violence but was never resolute enough to shut the opposition down. Instead, his actions resulted in both his own backers and the opposition establishing paramilitaries outside the control of the steadily weakening state. Meanwhile, operating from the middle of the political spectrum, Khudonazarov's peace-making efforts repeatedly fell victim to radicals on both sides unwilling to compromise with their opponents. Extremists soon gained control in both camps and the country began to move toward a civil war pitting Leninobodis and Kulobis against

Garmis and Pamiris, often portrayed inaccurately as a conflict between "Communists" and "demo-Islamists."

By early spring 1992 a mass demonstration challenging President Nabiyev's rule began in downtown Dushanbe on Shakhidon (Martyrs') Square, facing the Presidential Office Building, formerly the headquarters of the Central Committee apparatus of the republic Communist Party. The demonstration was provoked by a mounting series of actions by the Nabiyev administration aimed at opposition leaders. These included putting a *Rastokhez* leader on trial, starting criminal proceedings against Democratic Party leader Shodmon Yusuf, arresting Dushanbe mayor Ikramov in retribution for his sanctioning of the toppling of Lenin's statue the previous fall, and—the final straw—firing Interior Minister Mamadayoz Navjuvanov.[30] The latter, a leading Pamiri representative in Dushanbe's power structure, had antagonized Kulobis with his efforts to deprive them of their traditional influence in the country's internal security forces.[31]

The Shakhidon Square demonstration in turn provoked a counterdemonstration in support of President Nabiyev on Ozodi Square, which occupied the space in front of the complex of buildings housing the Supreme Soviet, Council of Ministers, and State Planning Committee (*Gosplan*). Although Navjuvanov was quickly reinstated and did not resign his position until September, the two demonstrations, with their numbers swelling to twenty thousand on occasion, waxed and waned for fifty-one days from late March well into May 1992.[32]

The opposition to Nabiyev was spearheaded and dominated by the Islamic Revival Party. Among the IRP's original goals—later soft-pedaled—had been an Islamic republic. The beliefs of IRP supporters spanned a wide spectrum from militant to moderate but still politicized Islam. Although the IRP generated a lot of publicity, it was not hugely popular. Polling conducted across Tajikistan in 1991 and 1992 suggested overwhelming support for secularist organizations: low (6 percent) trust in the IRP; low (5–6 percent) support for making Tajikistan an Islamic republic; and high (74–77 percent) preference for preserving Tajikistan as a secular state.[33] Khudonazarov would put support for Islamists in general at "no more than ten percent of the Tajik population."[34]

The opposition also included supporters of Kazi kalon Akbar Turajonzoda, chairman of the Muslim Spiritual Board of Tajikistan (*Kaziat*). Turajonzoda, however, maintained an ambiguous public posture throughout the crisis. Until August 1991, he had kept his distance from the IRP, even opposing its legalization in Supreme Soviet debates in which he participated as a deputy. But as demonstrations gained steam in Dushanbe against the Makhkamov regime in the wake of the coup attempt against Gorbachev, Turajonzoda joined the protestors, supported the ban on Communist Party activities, and voted for legalizing the IRP. Throughout subsequent years, Turajonzoda sought to retain freedom of maneuver while juggling alliances with elements across the political and regional spectrum.

In his public statements, the Kazi kalon repeatedly soft-pedaled the idea of an Islamic republic, suggesting that a transition lasting decades would be required before it might have a chance in Tajikistan. In the meantime, he endorsed secular democracy and later wrote that the Kaziat, "being a religious, non-political organization in accordance with its charter was not allowed to participate in political affairs."[35] In 1992, however, teachers at the new madrasah built by Turajonzoda proudly told the journalist Ahmed Rashid that the Kazi was organizing his own militia force outside Dushanbe. Rashid also learned that Turajonzoda organized the Youth of Tajikistan, sometimes called the Youth of Dushanbe, whose armed bands succeeded in forcing President Nabiyev to capitulate in early September 1992.[36]

Another major opposition figure who gained notoriety in the eyes of the Nabiyev regime and its supporters, in particular ethnic Russians, was Shodmon Yusuf, who became branded as a rabidly anti-Russian Tajik nationalist. On May 10, Yusuf told a press conference that he retained "the right to turn for aid to Afghanistan because of instances of interference by CIS forces [that is, from members of the Commonwealth of Independent States created in December 1991 as the Soviet Union collapsed] in the internal political conflict in the republic." He warned that from then on "the shadow of CIS tanks will fall on the thousands-strong Russian population of the republic."[37] Yusuf's remarks reportedly caused an immediate run on train tickets back to Russia and container reservations for shipping household goods out of Tajikistan.[38]

The Rastokhez Movement was also prone to high-profile decisions that undermined its public appeal. On May 11, the day after Yusuf's implicit threat against Russians, Mirbobo Mirrakhimov, a well-known Rastokhez activist, was appointed head of the State Committee of Television and Radio. The radical changes in programming instituted under Mirrakhimov further eroded the confidence and comfort level of Russians as well as Uzbeks in post-Soviet Tajikistan. Mirrakhimov interrupted the broadcasts of important Russian and Uzbek television channels and replaced them with programs from Iran that propagated Islam. But these new offerings, which were not pulled off the airwaves until October, irritated even wide swaths of Tajik viewers. Their reaction, according to Khudonazarov, underscored the low level of political and religious influence wielded by Iran not only in the newly independent Turkic states of Central Asia but also in Tajikistan.[39]

As rival demonstrations dragged on in downtown Dushanbe, Nabiyev increasingly turned to the southern Kulobis for support. In his courting of Kulobis, Nabiyev was helped by his opponents. In May 1992, according to Sergei Gretsky, who observed these developments firsthand, "Some leaders of the opposition indulged in the vice of localism by stirring anti-Kulob emotions that deeply offended Kulob sensibilities and made them more prone to fight the opposition to the end."[40]

Even before this, some of the anti-Nabiyev protestors on Shakhidon Square had reportedly tortured a largely illiterate but strong-willed Kulobi, Sangak Safarov, after he had called on television for reconciliation. Safarov's checkered past included twenty-three years in jail during the Soviet era on a variety of charges, including murder. Now, ironically, he became a leading defender of former republic Communist Party leader President Nabiyev and the conservative old guard and an implacable enemy of those he called "Islamic usurpers" and "democrats." Surviving his reported beating, Safarov went home to Kulob region, organized what came to be known as the Popular Front militia, and returned with some of its early detachments to Dushanbe.[41] Safarov rejected Iran's theocratic example and charged that his Islamist and "democrat" opponents were being helped by the hard-line Afghan leader Gulbuddin Hekmatyar, an ethnic Pashtun backed by Pakistan. While Sangak considered Afghanistan's Ahmed Shah Masoud "our fellow countryman—from Kulob," he did not want the support of the fabled co-ethnic Tajik warrior, preferring Russian help instead.[42]

By April 22, 1992, after taking nineteen Supreme Soviet deputies hostage, the anti-Nabiyev demonstrators in downtown Dushanbe succeeded in forcing Supreme Soviet speaker Kenjaev to resign.[43] But several days after Kenjaev's resignation, Nabiyev appointed him head of the National Security Committee (i.e., the KGB), a move that reignited the action-reaction rival demonstrations. The opposition demanded Kenjaev's ouster from the security committee, while Kulobis and Leninobodis insisted on Kenjaev's reinstatement as Supreme Soviet chairman and Turajonzoda's removal as Kazi kalon. Kenjaev in fact soon resumed his speaker duties, as the Kulobis had demanded, thus enraging the opposition.

In early May, Nabiyev distributed as many as eighteen hundred Kalashnikov semiautomatic rifles to his supporters on Ozodi Square, including Safarov's men.[44] Shooting quickly broke out, resulting in some forty (the regime's estimate) to over 110 (the opposition's claim) deaths in Dushanbe and elsewhere in the country. As the violence flared, a state farm (*sovkhoz*) director named Emomali Rahmonov distinguished himself among Safarov's followers. Rahmonov reportedly was one of the first organizers of detachments for Safarov's Popular Front and actively participated in the pro-Nabiyev demonstrations on Ozodi Square beginning in late April. Safarov and Rahmonov were from nearby Kulobi districts: Rahmonov from Dangara, whose natives would surround him once in power in Dushanbe; Safarov from the gold-mining settlement of Khovaling, which would drift into obscurity after Safarov orchestrated Rahmonov's elevation to head of state and then died unexpectedly a few months later.[45]

Meanwhile, Leninobod northerners increasingly came to see their interests, now being challenged foremost by Garmis and Pamiris, as best defended by the southern Kulobis. However, while willing to help finance and cheer on the Kulobi-based Popular Front, Leninobodis themselves were reluctant to be drawn into the fighting that ensued, apparently thinking they could ride the Kulobi tiger and then hop off and take advantage of its victories. In addition, separated from Dushanbe to the south by an imposing mountain range, Leninobod was oriented as much toward Tashkent as Dushanbe. Home to many of Tajikistan's ethnic Uzbeks, Leninobod was encouraged by Tashkent in its budding alliance with Kulob. Soon, however, it would become apparent that the Kulobis had no interest in being anybody's puppets, be it Leninobod or Tashkent. By December 1992, the Kulobi victors shoved aside their erstwhile Leninobod sponsors, and in time their Uzbek backers as well.

Nabiyev finally moved to end the escalating violence by signing a decree on May 11 approving the creation of a government of national reconciliation. Members of the opposition took eight out of twenty-four cabinet seats—a ratio the two sides would return to five years later in the June 1997 Peace Accord. (Although the anti-Nabiyev forces shared power in Dushanbe during this period in 1992, this narrative will continue to refer to them as the opposition.) Nabiyev the next day also agreed to the creation of an interim National Assembly to work alongside the Supreme Soviet until new elections set for the end of the year. Although never implemented, the eighty-member National Assembly—to be drawn equally from the Supreme Soviet and from the opposition—also bore a remarkable conceptual resemblance to the interim Commission for National Reconciliation (CNR) that would be mandated by the 1997 peace agreements that would end the civil war. On May 12 the Supreme Soviet Presidium once more relieved Kenjaev from his post as chairman of the parliament. The next day Kazi Turajonzoda encouraged the opposition to end its mass rally on Shakhidon Square.

In the next few months, however, rather than reconciling, the contending sides in the newly installed coalition government used their positions to help their respective partisans in the brutal civil war that engulfed the adjoining southern regions of Kurgan-Tyube and Kulob. Kurgan-Tyube was a focal point of much of the fighting because Garmis and Pamiris, now widely regarded as supporting the IRP, had been forcibly resettled there, together with Kulobis, beginning in the 1920s to develop the region. They all apparently retained strong identifications with their ancestral regions and the rival political movements identified with them, and fatalities quickly skyrocketed from the dozens to the tens of thousands.[46]

In neighboring Kulob, Safarov's Popular Front refused to recognize the legitimacy of the new coalition government in Dushanbe, which included the IRP. Opponents of the Popular Front in turn imposed a blockade on food shipments into Kulob region in June that tightened throughout the summer. At the end of July, a cease-fire was agreed to in negotiations held in Khorog. Safarov, however, refused to order his forces to put down their weapons and honor the agreement until the coalition government, which he continued to insist was illegal, resigned.[47] His Kulobi forces subsequently exacted savage retribution on non-Kulobi inhabitants of Kurgan-Tyube, especially anyone from Garm.

As in all civil wars, this one gave free rein to extremists on both sides and psychopaths of every type. Its combatants committed horrific atrocities against each other and against innocent bystanders. In the words of one pair of observers, "Torture in public baths, ears, noses and genitalia cut off, disembowelments and mutilations of babies—these are what the criminals fighting on both sides have introduced into the civil war."[48] To that could be added the skinning of still living victims. By early 1993 the death toll was estimated at 25,000 to 40,000, the number of displaced within Tajikistan at 500,000, the number of refugees fleeing across the border into northern Afghanistan at 75,000, and the number of houses destroyed at 150,000.[49]

The bitterness of the dislocated, orphaned, maimed, and bereaved on both sides would prove an understandable obstacle to the peace process that would take several years to gain any traction. The enmities conceived and stoked during the civil war festered and endured to the graves of many of the conflict's participants, after being further convoluted by subsequent twists and turns of fate. Kenjaev, who had managed Nabiyev's presidential campaign in 1991 before becoming the controversial speaker of the Supreme Soviet, was gunned down in Dushanbe in March 1999.[50] Otakhon Latifi, a journalist with years of experience as a Moscow correspondent and then from 1989 to 1991 a deputy premier in Tajikistan, had worked for Nabiyev's opponent, Davlat Khudonazarov, in that same campaign.[51] After years of exile, Latifi returned to Dushanbe to work on the National Reconciliation Commission, only to be murdered in September 1998.[52]

On August 24, 1992, Prosecutor General Nurullo Khuvaydulloev was forced out of his car in downtown Dushanbe and shot dead.[53] On August 31, some two to three hundred armed youths took fifty-three officials hostage. They included presidential staffers; cabinet officers, among them a first deputy prime minister and several ministers; Dushanbe's mayor; and the deputy mayor of Kulob city, the latter whom they tortured and killed.[54] The next day, September 1, a rally of some thousand Youth of Tajikistan and opposition representatives demanded President Nabiyev's resignation. One hundred or so of these charged the presidential palace when Nabiyev refused to meet with them, but he escaped to greater security in a garrison of the Russian 201st Motorized Rifle Division.[55]

On September 3, the leadership of the Supreme Soviet declared Nabiyev no longer president, but there was no vote of the parliament as a whole so the declaration was of questionable legal standing. On September 7, trapped at Dushanbe's airport, Nabiyev was finally forced—under duress by Youth of Tajikistan and opposition representatives, including Democratic Party leader Shodmon Yusuf and Kazi Turajonzoda—to sign a capitulation document, after which he fled to his hometown of Khujand.[56] The Pamiri Akbarsho Iskandarov stepped in again as acting president, asked the coalition government to stay on, and appealed for a cease-fire.[57] Then, in what may have been a bid to undercut the Kulobis by weaning away some of their Leninobod support, Iskandarov on September 21 appointed Leninobodi power broker Abdumalik Abdullojonov acting prime minister.[58]

The Kulobi-based Popular Front fought back and mounted a campaign to retake Dushanbe.[59] On November 10 acting president Iskandarov and his government were forced to resign. Then, from November 16 to December 3, 1992, a legal quorum of

197 of the Supreme Soviet's 230 deputies—elected in March 1990 and decidedly old guard—met in Khujand, capital of northern Leninobod.[60] Just three weeks earlier, Sangak Safarov had installed fellow Kulobi Emomali Rahmonov as chairman of the Kulob regional executive committee. Now Safarov orchestrated the Supreme Soviet session in Khujand, which abolished the presidency and made the forty-year-old Rahmonov parliamentary speaker and thereby the new head of state. Abdumalik Abdullojonov, from Khujand, whom Iskandarov had recently appointed acting prime minister, became fully empowered as prime minister but found himself surrounded by Kulobi ministers.[61] On December 10, Popular Front forces finally succeeded in ousting the opposition from Dushanbe, and Rahmonov and Abdullojonov returned to the capital from Khujand.[62]

In March 1993, however, kingmaker Safarov died in a mysterious shoot-out with a subordinate Popular Front commander.[63] In 1994 Safarov's acolyte Rahmonov was elected president, defeating Abdullojonov by two to one, according to the official but sharply disputed count, and sending his Leninobod would-be rival for national leadership into exile in Tashkent.

## CONFLICTED TEHRAN

Iranian behavior in 1992 suggested that there was indeed some fire behind the smoke of suspicion of Iranian involvement in Dushanbe's tumultuous politics. However, even Safarali Kenjaev, the die-hard old guard enemy of those who brought down President Nabiyev, in his memoir portrayed the opposition primarily as an eclectic bunch of Islamists and other home-grown extremists and power-hungry opportunists taking advantage of the USSR's collapse to make a grab for glory in Dushanbe. The Iranians appeared in Kenjaev's memoir as just one among several outside but largely marginal influences. It would therefore be hard to argue on the basis of even Kenjaev's account that Iran—or radical elements in Iran—instigated the Tajik revolution rather than opportunistically rendered assistance to the opposition in its own drive for power.[64]

Nevertheless, as a Turkish columnist wrote a decade after these events, Iranian policy was always a thousand-layer puff pastry with many different levels.[65] In fact, Iranian policy specifically toward Tajikistan in the wake of the Soviet collapse was complex and multifaceted, with an unknown mixture of coordination and competition between various camps. Throughout these tumultuous events, Iran had at least two lines: cautious and pragmatic versus go-for-broke and deeply committed to the Islamic opposition. Often there seemed to be no coordination at all between these two postures at various levels. This probably reflected heated debates between various institutions with separate chains of command and loyalties and willfully unilateral execution of disputed policies by those with sharply varying political outlooks.

Reflecting continuity with the cautious line of the last years of the Gorbachev era, President Rafsanjani, the Foreign Ministry, and the Iranian ambassador in Tajikistan repeatedly offered to mediate between the two sides in Tajikistan. Iran's official line was that the crisis was an internal conflict with disturbing regional consequences. It appreciated the new opportunities for Iran in Central Asia and sought to expand Iran's influence in the region with high-level visits and commerce. Apparently wary of the growing Russian and Central Asian reaction to the "Tajik syndrome," it seemed mindful of the need to balance the gains of any expansion of Iran's profile in the region against the damage it might do to Tehran's evolving relationship with Moscow and, Tehran hoped, with the Central Asian capitals, especially Tashkent.

Revolutionary Tajikistan nevertheless seemed increasingly rife with opportunities for Iran. But events elsewhere in Central Asia and in Afghanistan were threatening to move in the opposite direction. In Kabul, the predominantly Pakistani-backed mujahideen had ousted President Najibullah in April 1992. His downfall shocked Moscow and its allies in Central Asia but also had unpleasant consequences for Tehran's interests. Given the alternative of Pakistani dominance in Afghanistan, Tehran had seemed to view the Moscow-backed Najibullah regime as offering Iran the best hope for influence through the parties it sponsored, which were based predominantly on the country's Shia Hazara population. Now what could be perceived as developments favoring Pakistan not only in Afghanistan but also potentially in Tajikistan, the push by Turkey and the United States into the Caucasus and Central Asia, and the Iranian-friendly opposition's successes in Tajikistan all certainly gave ammunition to those in Tehran arguing to make one of the new post-Soviet republics "ours."

During the March–May demonstrations, the Iranian embassy in Dushanbe still gave at least the appearance of noninterference and willingness to mediate. Nevertheless, by the time journalist Ahmed Rashid visited Dushanbe in October 1992, he found a much more active posture with twenty-one official diplomats and around fifty "unofficial diplomats" staffing the Iranian mission. This compared to the mere twenty or so diplomats accredited to the six other embassies in town combined. According to a variety of Rashid's sources, the Iranians were providing "a wide range of political parties with money, food and military supplies." Foreign diplomats told Rashid that Iranian aircraft were making airdrops of weapons to the IRP. They also claimed that Iranian intelligence officials "played a major role in encouraging the opposition to topple" Nabiyev.[66]

But others were involved as well in supplying arms to the IRP and its factions. According to Rashid, KGB officials asserted that they included rival Afghan mujahideen groups loyal to the ethnic Pashtun leader Gulbuddin Hekmatyar and the ethnic Tajik commander Ahmed Shah Masoud. Moreover, behind Hekmatyar stood Pakistan's fundamentalist Jamaat-e-Islami (Islamic Society) party, which had been promoting its own vision of a radical Islamic revolution in Afghanistan since at least the mid-1970s, with at least a wink and often much more from successive Pakistani governments, before turning its attention to Tajikistan.[67] One of Iran's motives in funneling weapons and money to the IRP could well have been to prevent Pakistani influence from totally overwhelming its own not just in Afghanistan but also Tajikistan.

In any event, according to Kenjaev, the Iranian embassy funneled almost 1.5 million rubles to the Turajonzoda-controlled *Kaziat* from July to November 1992. In many places, this actually would not have been very much: from roughly $10,000 down to as little as $3,750, since the street rate of exchange declined from around 150 to the U.S. dollar in July to roughly 400 rubles in November.[68] Tajikistan was dirt-poor, however, and Kenjaev asserted that these funds made it possible for the opposition leaders to buy weapons, hire assassins from outside Tajikistan, and settle political scores.[69] In 1993 unnamed Russian intelligence sources put Iranian financial support to the Tajik opposition much higher at $3 to 4 million.[70]

However much Iran did or did not invest in poor and war-torn Tajikistan in 1992, even a little bit of money and expertise targeted effectively would have had a significant impact. Iranian complaints directed at Moscow and Tashkent conceded as much. After Russian and Uzbek forces in November 1992 began to take better control of Tajikistan's border with Afghanistan, Tehran's official news agency IRNA protested that this blocked "the only way for supply of weapons to Tajik Islamic forces" while the "communists" were free to continue stealing "ammunition, tanks, weapons, and armored personnel carriers" from CIS forces.[71]

Within the opposition in Tajikistan, there were certainly elements that appeared both to draw from and give inspiration and support to more revolutionary constituencies and government structures in Tehran. Suggestive of these possible links were the slogans of "Long Live the Islamic Republic" and "Death to America," which popped up briefly during the March–May demonstrations in Dushanbe. Even more striking were the Youth of Tajikistan, which played an important role in Nabiyev's September 1992 ouster and the defense of Dushanbe in October and December 1992 against the old guard Popular Front. More radical publications in Tehran compared the Youth of Tajikistan to the grassroots *komitehs* (committees) of Iranian revolutionary days in 1978–79. They had inspired terror among members of the shah's old regime as extralegal, armed, and undisciplined agents of Khomeini's new revolutionary authority.[72]

Going against the grain of its more restrained commentary both before and after, the semiofficial *Tehran Times* on September 9 quickly warned Russia against intervening in Tajikistan following Nabiyev's ouster from the presidency. Tehran was following events there "with particular sensitivity and interest," it said. It was "seriously concerned," it continued, "about the possibility of intervention by Russia or the other republics . . . , as any kind of insecurity and lack of stability in Tajikistan will eventually spill out." It concluded, "Russian military forces should seriously avoid any kind of intervention in the political affairs of Tajikistan."[73]

Even before Nabiyev's official resignation, and reacting to reports that Russia, Uzbekistan, Kazakhstan, and Kyrgyzstan had decided to deploy CIS forces along Tajikistan's border with Afghanistan, the *Voice of the Iranian Republic* repeatedly warned against Russian "military intervention."[74] On September 8, after Nabiyev's ouster, the

*Voice* said that his departure would enable the people of Tajikistan "to pursue the natural and irrevocable course of reforms" and that "today the Tajik people have come the closest so far to realizing their wish, which is to establish a popular government of their choice." But it betrayed some concern over the staying power of the opposition when it warned that the prerequisite for this would be preserving "unity and cohesion among the progressive political forces."[75]

This initial support from Tehran for the coup in Dushanbe suggested that Russian and others' suspicion of meddling by some Iranians was on target. Given the covert and violent strand of Iranian foreign policy activism at the time—exemplified at its worst that same September 1992 by the murder of four Kurdish opposition leaders in Berlin's Mykonos café (see chapter 2)—Tehran's participation in Nabiyev's ouster would not have been an isolated or aberrant act. The most charitable interpretation of the Iranian Foreign Ministry's tacking would have been that however much it had opposed, or not encouraged, what other institutions were doing by way of supporting the Tajik coup plotters, now that they had achieved success the Foreign Ministry could not but back the fait accompli of Nabiyev's ouster. Some analysts in Moscow, moreover, detected the ascendancy in Tehran in mid-1992 of radicals led by Spiritual Leader Ali Khamenei, who succeeded at that time in pushing President Rafsanjani and the pragmatists into the background.[76] First Deputy Foreign Minister Anatoly Adamishin portrayed it as a period in which the radicals had temporarily won out.[77]

Russia, Uzbekistan, other Central Asian countries as well as the Kulobi-based Popular Front certainly reacted as though Iran had played a hand in the roundup of Tajik government officials and the murder of Prosecutor General Khuvaydulloev in late August and then the detention and resignation under duress of Nabiyev. Even the normally more indirect President Askar Akayev of Kyrgyzstan in early November reportedly told NATO Secretary General Manfred Wörner that "the region contained forces wishing to de-stabilize the situation in Central Asia and Kazakhstan" and that he was "concerned by the politicizing of Islam from the direction of Iran."[78]

Uzbekistan's President Islom Karimov, not surprisingly, early on used a press conference to accuse Iran directly of being involved in Nabiyev's ouster.[79] By many accounts, Uzbekistan's own involvement in Tajikistan that summer had been forward-leaning and partisan. According to Democratic Party chairman Shodmon Yusuf, Karimov, with the support of unnamed Russian politicians "with a militarist disposition," had established a base in Kulob for Popular Front armed units. Helicopters and planes loaded with military cargo, according to Yusuf, made regular runs to Kulob from Tashkent and Termez.[80] None other than Safarali Kenjaev confirmed to BBC reporter Monica Whitlock, "Everything I had came from Uzbekistan."[81] Indeed, five years later Karimov publicly rebuked Tajikistan's leaders for their short memories: "Sometimes it is necessary to recall how the present leadership in Dushanbe got there, with whose help and whose vehicles were used."[82]

## DISTRACTED MOSCOW

The Russian Foreign Ministry's Bakhtiyer Khakimov, who had already been deeply involved in negotiating the exit of Soviet forces from Afghanistan, became intimately familiar with Tajikistan during many visits to the region as an expert adviser to Foreign Minister Andrey Kozyrev and First Deputy Foreign Minister Anatoly Adamishin. On one level, the contending sides were ideologically differentiated political movements and parties, and the struggle was often portrayed as a contest between Islamist and neocommunist forces. But on a second, more basic level—given the importance of regional identities and loyalties throughout Central Asia—the struggle was better understood—Khakimov and many others would argue—as one between regional interests.

Looking back, Khakimov's analysis in 1999—by then widely shared by others—was that the civil war that erupted in 1992 in Tajikistan reflected primarily regional and clan differences, and only secondarily religious differences and interethnic disputes. One-man rule had been the principle of Central Asian society, where the father's word was law. This had made the Communist Party's work easy during Soviet times but had hidden from view many stubborn realities. When the Soviet Union collapsed and communist rule broke down, it turned out that clan and regional differences were stronger in Tajikistan than any Islamist versus communist differences were. There were many slogans, but what did they really mean? People didn't really know what they were fighting for, aside from a share of power. Shodmon Yusuf, chairman of the Democratic Party, was just an ordinary Tajik nationalist and not a democrat, according to Khakimov.[83] The Islamists who entered the coalition government during summer 1992 did so as a result of interclan and interregional clashes, not on the basis of their Islamic fervor. As a result, little Islamization took place while the so-called Islamists were in power because there was no base for it. Islam in Tajikistan, after all, was not a religion but a way of life.

Two other major factors added to the turbulence, in Khakimov's view. These were the slow erosion of discipline in the Soviet Union and the long war next door in Afghanistan. Between them, they had laid the basis for anarchy and the criminalization of Tajik society. Illegal money, including profits from narcotics, had supported the fighting in Afghanistan. There, for example, Ahmed Shah Masoud, the ethnic Tajik and Panjshir Valley hero of the Afghan resistance, controlled emerald smuggling from Afghanistan's Badakhshan region bordering on Tajikistan. In Tajikistan, crime bosses were rising to power by 1992.[84] Within a decade, other observers in Moscow, including Yuri Fedorov of the USA Institute, had referred to Tajikistan as another Colombia.[85]

As to Iran, officials and experts in Moscow eight years later all recalled their concern over Tehran's role in the tumultuous politics of Tajikistan in 1992. Yevgeny Bazhanov at the Diplomatic Academy stated that in September and October 1992 it was absolutely clear to Moscow that Iran was directly supplying weapons and money to the Tajik opposition. There was great fear and unhappiness over Iranian actions.[86]

Though Bazhanov did not mention it, one story still circulating in Moscow in the year 2000 concerned the alleged scandal that had erupted at the Dushanbe airport in summer 1992. Then-foreign minister of the coalition government Khudoiberdy Kholiknazarov had returned from Tehran aboard an airplane supposedly carrying humanitarian assistance and books, but actually, so the story goes, loaded with weapons.[87]

Irina Zviagelskaya at the Oriental Institute remembered that Iran had supplied the Tajik opposition with money, literature, weapons, and military training. Was there direct Iranian involvement in Nabiyev's actual ouster in September 1992? Zviagelskaya could not say definitively but was of the opinion that Iran's support of the opposition had already in effect prepared it to do the deed.[88] Iran experts Vyacheslav Belokrenitsky and Nina Mamedova, also at the Oriental Institute, stated that it was absolutely clear that Iran had direct ties to events in Tajikistan. They knew of concerns at the working level in the Russian foreign ministry that Iran was interfering in Tajikistan on the side of anti-Russian forces. This concern was reinforced because Iran refused to state that it did not back the export of Islamic fundamentalism.[89]

Indeed, Khakimov, who was on the Iran desk in the Russian foreign ministry at that time, recalled that Iran was working actively and openly in Tajikistan. It had funded the IRP and provided money and weapons to the opposition's formations. Moscow had intelligence that Iran had supplied the substantial amount of money that had been necessary to feed and take care of the many antigovernment demonstrators who participated in the seven weeks of nonstop demonstrations in Dushanbe in March–May 1992. Whenever Moscow caught Iranian agents red-handed, Khakimov would recount, it took the evidence right to the Iranian Foreign Ministry, which of course denied any wrongdoing.

Nevertheless, although Iran had all along been clearly supporting, financing, and training the opposition, Moscow did not accuse Iran of participating directly in Nabiyev's ouster in September. By that time, noted Khakimov, it was clear to Moscow that Nabiyev had no support and that he was finished politically. This was confirmed at the November–December 1992 Supreme Soviet session in Leninobod that elevated Rahmonov to head of state. When Nabiyev appealed to the deputies to overturn as illegal the September decision to oust him, he received absolutely no support—even though Leninobod was his hometown.[90]

In the early days of 1992, Moscow was preoccupied with sorting out its own internal affairs, and largely distracted from paying much attention to developments outside the borders of the new Russian Federation. Few in Russia were interested in or knowledgeable about what was really going on in Tajikistan. Fedorov recalled that in April or May 1992 a Russian military delegation went to Dushanbe to analyze the demonstrations that were taking place. One delegation member later told a seminar (in which Fedorov participated) that he and his colleagues had been without a clue as to what was going on and what to do about it.

Moscow's understanding and assessment of the Tajik civil war underwent an evolution in 1992. In Fedorov's analysis, Foreign Minister Andrey Kozyrev and other major Yeltsin "democrats," such as State Secretary Gennady Burbulis, at first regarded events in Tajikistan as a struggle between the local opposition, seen as part of the larger post-Soviet democratic movement, and the CPSU legacy embodied in Tajikistan by President Rahmon Nabiyev. But the Tajik opposition was actually quite complex. Some of its leaders were indeed oriented toward Iran, and articles appeared in the Russian press that underscored those ties. Confusing the issue and establishing a benchmark of sorts for wackiness, other analysts in those early days argued that the West and Israel had long instigated the opposition in order to bring down the Soviet Empire. Think tank director Sergey Kurginyan, recollected Fedorov, had asserted that the opposition movement in Tajikistan had grown out of a program developed in 1976 by American and British "special services," working with the Saudis and a number of other Islamic states, to use Islam to undermine not just the Soviet Union but also Russia and even "Orthodoxy."[91]

Zviagelskaya recollected that Iran had taken advantage of the USSR's increasing weakness as it headed toward collapse and that Tehran had been excited by the spectacle of what seemed to be Islamist movements coming to the fore in Farsi-speaking Tajikistan. The truth was, however, that what was taking place in Tajikistan was a regional war and that Russia defined its course only toward the end of the conflict. In 1991 and well into 1992, Russia did not interfere in Tajikistan. The democrats in power in Moscow wanted allies in Dushanbe, Zviagelskaya emphasized, and so at first did not mind the destruction of the Communist Party apparatus in Tajikistan.[92]

But in half a year or even less, Yeltsin forces in Moscow accomplished a volte-face in their appraisal of the forces they could rely on in Tajikistan, much to their own wonderment and sense of irony. Foreign Minister Kozyrev and other democrats in Moscow swallowed hard, faced, and then accepted the dilemma. Kozyrev and fellow diplomat Khakimov years later recalled separately but still vividly how Popular Front militia leader Sangak Safarov, on a victorious roll against the opposition's armed forces in fall 1992, in their presence had told a TV interviewer, "We will resurrect Soviet power in Tajikistan, carry it to Moscow, and there shoot all the democrats." Safarov was a charismatic leader; people kissed his hand, Khakimov noted years later. Safarov loved Rahmonov and launched him on the road to power. Were these the forces Moscow should support in Tajikistan?[93]

As with Iran, but even more obvious, the events that set Moscow's reorientation in motion began in March 1992 in northern Afghanistan. There, the defection of ethnic Uzbek General Abdul Rashid Dostum and his militia from the once Soviet- and now Russian-supported regime of President Najibullah, set the stage for the Najibullah regime's collapse. On April 28, a rebel coalition ousted Najibullah, who took refuge in the UN compound in Kabul, and declared an Islamic government. Already disturbed by what was happening in Tajikistan, Central Asia's leaders were further

*How does that timing compare to developments in the Caucasus? Was Moscow continually*

traumatized by what was unfolding in adjoining Afghanistan. They no doubt identified with Najibullah and viewed the secular ex-security chief and party functionary as one of their own kind. His fall galvanized them into action, primarily to ensure that Russia pledge to preserve its military presence in Tajikistan as a security blanket for the entire region. Besides, 7.6 percent, or 388,000, of Tajikistan's population of 5.1 million were ethnic Russians, a figure that would plummet to as few as seventy to eighty thousand by 1994, and 23.5 percent were ethnic Uzbeks.[94] Both groups perceived the Islamist challenge as a threat to their own existence.

Not surprisingly, it was Uzbekistan's Karimov, announcing that "for us, the Iran model is unacceptable," who took the lead in inducing Russia to recommit to a military presence in Central Asia.[95] The Uzbek leader hosted a truncated summit of the Commonwealth of Independent States (CIS) in Tashkent on May 14, 1992. Yeltsin was the guest of honor, but five presidents did not make it, including Tajikistan's Nabiyev. He was unable to be there because of the still-continuing negotiations in Dushanbe over ending the spring's long crisis, but his country was nevertheless represented by an empowered delegation. It was at this summit, to all appearances convened at the initiative of Karimov, that the CIS Collective Security Treaty (CST) was signed.

Several months later, at the end of August 1992, just after the murder of Prosecutor General Nurullo Khuvaydulloev shocked Dushanbe, President Nabiyev proposed introducing a CIS peacekeeping force within the framework of the CST.[96] However, Nabiyev was deposed within days and the chaos of civil war in Tajikistan made the path toward CST troop commitments to the country politically torturous. The coalition government that replaced Nabiyev in September again appealed to CIS leaders for help in early October. At their summit in Bishkek on October 9, the attending CIS presidents declared themselves ready to reinforce the Russian 201st Division and send humanitarian aid, but then temporized.[97]

Left stranded in Tajikistan after the Soviet collapse, Russia's 201st MRD was a remnant of the Soviet 40th Army that had fought in Afghanistan in the 1980s. Throughout much of summer and early fall of 1992, as political tensions grew and civil war began in Tajikistan, Moscow officially assigned the 201st a basically neutral or fence-sitting role: guarding key installations, ensuring the nightly curfew, protecting itself and its equipment. While subject to widespread debate, speculation, and suspicion, the 201st's ostensible mission was ensuring the stability of the coalition government, not restoring the old guard to power. The opposition at times charged that the 201st was cooperating with old guard and Popular Front forces, but at other times the opposition called on the 201st to protect it against its enemies and preserve the coalition in which it participated in Dushanbe.

Given the lack of clear and constant guidance from Moscow, the leadership of the 201st appeared increasingly to favor the Kulobi Popular Front forces fighting the opposition. The 201st's Russian officers felt endangered by the threats to their personal safety emanating from the so-called Islamist side of the conflict.[98] By fall 1992 it was clear that despite Moscow's stated neutrality, its policy was to support the Popular Front in its battles against the opposition.[99] Right after Nabiyev's ouster, Russian Foreign Ministry spokesman Sergei Yastrzhembsky issued a warning on September 8 against outside interference in Tajikistan, which he said was in the Russian Federation's sphere of vital interests. Such interference, he stated, "cannot be justified no matter from where it comes and what it is motivated by."[100]

Despite the official bravado, the events of September and October 1992 formed a decidedly dispiriting backdrop for Moscow's deliberations over its commitment in Tajikistan. With Nabiyev out and Iran warning against Russian intervention, undeterred by Moscow's claims that Tajikistan was within Russia's sphere of interests, should Russia stay or pull out? What precisely were Russia's equities and interests in Tajikistan? Yeltsin in October was even reported by some as announcing to the Duma that he had decided to send four additional battalions to Tajikistan to form a corridor for the withdrawal of the 201st division, which would otherwise be torn to pieces.[101] The report was typical of the confusion over Moscow's policy and intentions at the time and possibly a garble of early backroom debate over various options, which would later surface at CIS summits, for reinforcing Russian forces in Tajikistan with troops from Uzbekistan, Kazakhstan, and Kyrgyzstan.

According to Yegor Gaidar, Yeltsin's acting premier, Moscow was unsure as to the real threat to the Russian population in Tajikistan. Reports from Russia's own security ministry were vague, those from its intelligence service "unreliable," and those from its embassy "utterly contradictory." So Gaidar made a quick trip to Tajikistan in October after the Bishkek summit to see for himself what was happening. In Dushanbe, Gaidar concluded that the government had "lost control of the situation" and that the 201st stood in danger of being dragged into the civil war. Given the low-tech fighting environment, the switch of even one tank or armored personnel carrier from one side to the other in a contested village could turn the tide of battle, and on occasion did just that. In fact, the very day Gaidar was in Tajikistan, a 201st soldier stole a tank and drove it over to help "his side." With the Tajik conscripts being pulled in both directions, Gaidar recommended that Moscow reinforce the 201st and the Border Guards with more Russian enlisted personnel who would not be swayed by local loyalties. Otherwise, the threat to ethnic Russians, already real, would increase as the 201st was sucked into partisan warfare.[103]

Russian determination to help stabilize Tajikistan was the order of the day, but it was repeatedly undermined by its own anxiety and uncertainty and that of its Central Asian partners. On November 4 Foreign Minister Kozyrev held an emergency meeting with four Central Asian presidents (all except Turkmenistan's Niyazov) in Almaty. On the agenda were Yeltsin's proposals to encourage a cease-fire in Tajikistan, start a dialogue between the contending groupings, and establish a national reconciliation coalition government. The participants issued a joint statement endorsing use of the

201st to protect the civilian population, guard key installations, and restore peace and order. The division should form the core of a peacekeeping force that would also include troops from other CIS states. The meeting endorsed calls by Tajikistan's acting president Akbarsho Iskandarov for the establishment of a State Council to include representatives of the major parties, movements, and regions.[103] A few days later, Iskandarov and a Yeltsin military representative signed a bilateral protocol describing the conditions under which the 201st division was to remain deployed in Tajikistan.[104]

Afterward, Kozyrev traveled to Dushanbe where he met with officers of the 201st and Russian Border Guard units and with representatives of the Russian community in Tajikistan. He told the military that their priority was to halt the bloodshed and help preserve Tajikistan's statehood while adhering to a "strictly impartial role in the country's affairs." He stressed that one of the servicemen's priority duties was to protect the Russian-speaking population. Kozyrev underscored Russia's "geopolitical interests" in Tajikistan. He argued against two extreme options: "walk away recklessly" and "intervene recklessly." "Defeatist conceptions" and a "reckless departure," he warned, would mean the "betrayal" of Russia's good neighbors. The Russian foreign minister asserted, "Russia has its geopolitical interests in Tajikistan and will be aiming not to allow extremist forces to further de-stabilize the situation in the former Soviet republic."[105]

At the end of November, Russian defense minister Pavel Grachev and his counterparts from Uzbekistan, Kazakhstan, and Kyrgyzstan met with Chief Commander of CIS Joint Forces Yevgeny Shaposhnikov in Termez on Uzbekistan's border with Afghanistan. Emomali Rahmonov, newly appointed as Tajikistan's parliamentary speaker and head of state, joined the gathering. Going into the Termez meeting, Grachev shared his unhappiness with "several political leaders" who promised contributions to a peacekeeping force but did not deliver—interpreted as an allusion to Kyrgyzstan's Akayev. The Russian defense minister's view reportedly was that simply recasting the 201st into a peacekeeping force was impermissible. Instead, it should be reorganized and incorporate a battalion from each of the countries represented at Termez.[106]

As a result, the meeting recommended a peacekeeping force consisting of one reinforced Russian battalion drawn from elements of the 201st, one battalion each from Kyrgyzstan and Kazakhstan, and two battalions from Uzbekistan. The 201st per se would not be part of the force, but would continue guarding military installations and important administrative centers in Tajikistan.[107] Nothing, however, came quickly of this recommendation, and it was nearly a year before the leaders of Russia and Central Asia finally signed a concrete agreement on a peacekeeping force for Tajikistan.[108]

## MINISTER KOZYREV'S PERSPECTIVE

In September 2000, reminiscing about events in Tajikistan in 1992 when he was Russia's foreign minister, Andrey Kozyrev emphasized that the nature of the situation was difficult to understand. He felt that even eight years later no one really knew the full story of what had happened. He had visited Tajikistan eight times in 1992, the first time when rival demonstrations were under way in Dushanbe's main squares. The so-called democratic wave was evident there as everywhere else, but it was strongly mixed in with Tajikistan's specific ethnic, regional, and religious factors. On that first visit, Kozyrev met unofficially and secretly with Kazi kalon Turajonzoda. In their long conversation, Turajonzoda portrayed himself as a religious figure who nonetheless endorsed democratic freedoms and distanced himself from Iran.

Each time Kozyrev visited Tajikistan that year, he recalled, he had met with 201st MRD and Border Guards personnel and traveled to the border with Afghanistan. After the Soviet collapse, these units at first had been subordinated to the new CIS joint command but were then placed under Russian Federation command. One of Kozyrev's priority tasks in Tajikistan was to make sure that both the 201st and Border Guards forces recognized the new Yeltsin leadership in Moscow. Moscow wanted to ensure that these forces followed its orders and were not chaotically drawn into the civil war in Tajikistan. Kozyrev therefore asked Defense Minister Grachev to fly to Tajikistan with him to deal with the situation.

Kozyrev stressed that in the fog of Soviet collapse and Tajik civil war, there were no reliable sources of information on Tajikistan. Articles by writers who did not let their complete ignorance about Tajikistan get in the way of their writing prolifically about the situation there contended with pieces ordered and paid for by rival clans to publicize their views. Kozyrev and his colleagues were aware of the views of all sides but could not guide Russian policy by them. In Dushanbe, meanwhile, Russia had no embassy to speak of and no in-country infrastructure to support its representatives. In addition, the Communist Party in Tajikistan did not welcome "democrat" emissaries from the new Yeltsin administration. Moreover, the Tajik government was in full chaos, especially after the demonstrations that spring undermined what little authority Nabiyev previously had. The warring sides did not trust each other, and no one trusted the Russians.

As a result, most of Moscow's information in 1992 came from the 201st. Since the division was the focus of a political war for its loyalties, its personnel had at their disposal information from all the forces courting it. But this information was entirely subjective, stressed Kozyrev, and the 201st was not an intelligence organization. It had many smart officers, but they were not professional analysts. Moreover, the same processes rending Russia and Tajikistan apart were at work within the 201st MRD and the Border Guards. In addition, many differences specific to the Tajik context were piled on top of the communist versus democrat split. So naturally, observed Kozyrev, there were divisions within the 201st and Border Guards units over whether to pay attention to visiting ministers, including himself, from Yeltsin's new government in Russia. And there were clearly subjective differences in the analyses of the situation in Tajikistan flowing from different elements of Russia's own military and Border Guards forces in the country.

Against this chaotic background, Kozyrev later recalled, Russian policy was guided by three principles. First, it was necessary by all means to help the newly independent government in Tajikistan stand on its own feet and secure its borders. Russia did not want a repeat of the Yugoslav disintegration scenario. For Russia, territorial integrity was fundamental, and not just for Tajikistan. Second, the Yeltsin government wanted to do whatever it could to help democratic forces in Tajikistan. But this became harder and harder to do as they splintered into rival camps, were marginalized by Tajikistan's increasingly polarized politics, and for the most part fled the country under the pressure of the civil war. Third, it was necessary to make sure that the 201st and the Border Guards remained cohesive and under Moscow's control and were not pulled apart by political passions and warring clans. Russian policy was to secure Moscow's command of these military units and to use them as the basis for helping to resurrect a stable government in independent Tajikistan.

Kozyrev stated that the Yeltsin government always placed three demands on Russian military units in Tajikistan: loyalty to Moscow, help in securing basic law and order in Tajikistan, and avoidance of direct involvement with any of the warring sides in the civil war. But Kozyrev went on to say that unspoken Russian support for the Kulobis was nevertheless present and grew over time. Moscow saw in the Kulobi-led Popular Front militia a force that could produce some order and that had the local population's support. The atrocities committed by the so-called Islamists, examples of which Kozyrev had personally seen, added to the support accorded the Popular Front.

Kozyrev recalled that he had met with Rahmonov when he was still a sovkhoz chairman in the Kulob region. He had also gotten to know Popular Front commander Sangak Safarov. Defense Minister Grachev had also visited Kulob. Kozyrev and Grachev had discussed the situation at length with the 201st leadership and the staff of Russia's new but still minuscule embassy. They all leaned toward Rahmonov and the Kulob grouping because they called for the restoration of civic order and state power. But this sympathy from the Russians was mixed with misgivings because of the Kulobis' "pink" coloration. They considered themselves communists, and Safarov even called for restoring the Soviet Union. Although Safarov said this when bullets were flying and the situation was entirely serious, remembered Kozyrev, it was nevertheless a bit comical coming from someone who had been a longtime prisoner under Soviet power.

All the same, Russia's representatives had to reconcile themselves to dealing with the Kulobis. Beneath their "red-pink" rhetoric, their core orientation was toward Moscow. The first card the Kulobis played was their desire always to be with Russia, and this naturally went over well with the command of the 201st, as did the Kulobis' emphasis on restoring order. Besides, by that time the influence of Tajik democrats had been reduced to nil. As to the Islamists, some were receiving help from Iran, others from other countries, and in general their ideology and violence did not provoke much sympathy in Tajikistan.

So, the Kulobi grouping rose to power. Kozyrev recounted that he and his Russian colleagues were not blind to the Kulobis' shortcomings and tried to turn them away from their communist ideology. They also tried to impress on the Kulobis that they would soon need to sit down with the opposition for the purpose of national reconciliation. But it was a hard task. The Kulobis' mentality was essentially Soviet, with an emphasis on force and strength and an aversion to compromise. But the same could be said about the opposition, with its proneness to violence and its corruption of Islam. In fact, the mentality of all sides was neo-Soviet, whether they were flying red flags, green flags, or any other flag. They all pushed the democratic forces completely to the side, where they split up and fled and dropped out of the political equation in Tajikistan.

As to Iranian interference in the Tajik civil war, every Central Asian leader Kozyrev met in 1992 charged that Iranian money and weapons were flowing into Tajikistan. Kozyrev stated that he never saw any hard evidence of this, but given the chorus of assertions from his Central Asian interlocutors he was persuaded it was there. At the same time, by the end of 1992 they all—even the Kulobis—agreed that Iranian interference had stopped. So Kozyrev concluded that Iran indeed had made a strong attempt to put those it favored in power in Tajikistan but then pulled back. That Iran failed in this attempt did not surprise Kozyrev, who in his account credited Tajik resistance rather than Russian claims that Tajikistan was in its sphere of interests for Iran's lack of success. Tajikistan's Islamists were first of all people with a Soviet mentality and then only Islamists. The Tajiks could never accept the Iranians. Although they were more than willing to take Iranian money, they were not willing to do so in exchange for having to read the Koran. And in any event, observed Kozyrev, the Iranians never did give the Tajiks all that much money.[109]

# 5

# *The Bait of "Strategic Partnership"*

The year 1993 saw a fundamental transition in Russian-Iranian dealings over Tajikistan and, by extension, Afghanistan. Russian emissaries paralleled efforts to encourage good behavior by Iran in Tajikistan with diplomacy focused on elevating the status of overarching Russian-Iranian relations. In Tehran in late March 1993, Foreign Minister Andrey Kozyrev claimed agreement on encouraging national reconciliation in Tajikistan. He and his aides continued to work the draft text of a new political document viewed by some as replacing the 1921 Soviet-Iranian treaty. They also dropped more broad hints about a Boris Yeltsin summit visit and the possibility of a "strategic partnership" in Central Asia and the Caucasus. These diplomatic advances were suddenly disrupted by an insurgent attack on a Russian outpost on the Tajik-Afghan border in July but then quickly resumed as Moscow persuaded Tehran to cooperate in pushing both sides in the Tajik conflict to engage in peace talks.

As the Popular Front rolled to victory in Tajikistan in late 1992, Russia had abandoned its diplomatic bashfulness. Moscow began openly to give the newly ascendant Kulobis and their emerging leader Emomali Rahmonov its full support. Iran meanwhile settled back into a policy of helping to keep combatants from the IRP and its allies alive to fight another day. Pushed out of Dushanbe and its strongholds in central and southern Tajikistan, the armed opposition retreated south and set up base camp in early 1993 in the northern Afghanistan town of Taloqan. From this low point, with apparent financial and logistical support from both Iran and Afghan mujahideen commanders, it soon began to claw its way back into Tajikistan.

Moscow and Iran struggled to keep their expanding bilateral relationship on track, even as Russian forces came under attack from—and retaliated against—the

Tajik opposition, striking from its safe havens in northern Afghanistan. Iran seemed to concede Moscow's strong position in Tajikistan for the moment. But Tehran was determined to bankroll opposition militias until their successes on the battlefield forced Dushanbe and its Russian patron into accepting the IRP's return as a player in Tajik politics. Yet as long as Iran toned down its open aggressiveness in Tajikistan, Russia and Tajikistan's Central Asian neighbors appeared willing to let Iran try to expand its commercial and cultural presence throughout the region.

In addition, policymakers in Moscow were clearly beginning to reassess the situation in Tajikistan. Their understanding of the political landscape in that country began more closely to resemble that of their experts on the region. Then–first deputy foreign minister Anatoly Adamishin, who had the lead in the MFA on Tajikistan, later recalled that the authorities in Moscow knew conclusively that Iran supported and inspired the opposition. Some of what Iran was up to in Tajikistan probably could be qualified as state-supported terrorism, Adamishin conceded, but this did not worry Russian policymakers much. They knew that there were arguments in Iran over what line to pursue in Tajikistan and that Iranian policy was influenced by domestic political debate. At first, the more aggressive side—the fundamentalist reactionaries—won out. But when the opposition was rolled back in late 1992, Iran changed its tactics because it saw that it did not have enough strength to install an Islamic government.[1]

The more radical press in Tehran bitterly condemned the Iranian government and especially the Foreign Ministry for the official policy pursued throughout 1992. It attacked it for being defensive, ineffective, and contrary to the Islamic Republic's obligations to render help.[2] It blamed official Tehran in effect for losing Tajikistan to the Tajik old guard backed by Russia and Uzbekistan. At the end of 1992, *Salam* censured what it characterized as "the depth of bestiality" of Tajikistan's "new rulers, who are protected by Russia," and called on Iran's diplomatic establishment to pay more attention to its "heavy responsibility" for developments in Tajikistan.[3] Still, such outbursts only served to underscore that the more moderate approach to dealing with that country was recovering its primacy in Tehran.

Nevertheless, Iran's policy was never either-or but rather a complex mix operating along multiple tracks. Even as official moderation again gained the upper hand, there was plenty to suggest that Iranian circles and agencies favoring a more aggressive posture continued to provide aid and comfort to Tajikistan's militant opposition, now on the run. In their Taloqan sanctuary, the armed and Islamist components of the opposition in late January 1993 founded the umbrella Movement for the Islamic Revival of Tajikistan (MIRT). IRP ruling council member Sayed Abdullo Nuri was chosen to lead the MIRT, and Tajikistan's former Kazi kalon Akbar Turajonzoda became his first deputy. Meanwhile, the secular opposition migrated largely to Moscow, where the Democratic Party, Rastokhez, and various Pamiri groups formed the Coordinating Center of Tajik Democratic Forces in the CIS.[4]

From the Russian perspective, the Tajik civil war seemed to be over except for the shouting. During his summit with Mikhail Gorbachev in June 1989, Ali Akbar Hashemi Rafsanjani had pledged noninterference in Soviet internal affairs. Even though the USSR had since collapsed, Iranian assistance to the Tajik opposition in 1992 had violated the implied understanding of the proper "code of conduct" for Iranian activities in Russia's "near abroad." Nevertheless, the chill that passed between official Moscow and Tehran did not overwhelm the overall relationship. Moscow and Tehran continued to reach out to each other even while supporting their respective clients on the civil war battlefields of Tajikistan. Career diplomat Adamishin, recalled from his ambassadorship in Rome in October 1992 to become Kozyrev's first deputy with responsibility for CIS affairs, including Tajikistan, did not visit Dushanbe for over half a year.

The bloody attack in mid-July 1993 that killed over two dozen Russian border guards on the Tajik-Afghan frontier finally riveted Adamishin's attention on Tajikistan. The massacre provoked a major crisis in Russian-Iranian relations and precipitated a major push by Moscow to get Tajik peace talks started.[5] Despite the diplomatic progress registered in the preceding months, some in both capitals called for more force as the only way to deal with the other. However, leaders in Tehran understood that they had suffered a major setback in Dushanbe the previous fall. Thus, visits by special emissary Yevgeny Primakov to Kabul and Tehran successfully advanced the idea of Tajik peace talks even as Moscow reinforced its own military presence in Tajikistan and Tehran continued to help the Tajik opposition in its pursuit of power in Dushanbe.

Besides its Tajik-specific calculations, Tehran was open to closer relations with Russia partly in reaction to renewed U.S. efforts to contain and isolate Iran. American policy, which had imposed sanctions on Iran since 1984, had just moved into the new phase of "dual containment" in spring 1993. This kept up the incentives for Tehran to cooperate with Moscow. Iran also had an interest in working with Russia to frustrate the continuing ambitions of Pakistan and Saudi Arabia in Afghanistan and Tajikistan. And Tehran wanted to dampen tensions in the region because of its sense of insecurity along its own borders, not only in so-called South Azerbaijan in the northwest but in the east adjoining Afghanistan.

Russia had its own reasons for pursuing closer cooperation with Iran. In spring 1993 the first prospects of NATO expansion had prompted anti-U.S. feelings and subsequently greater interest in some Moscow quarters in cooperation with Iran in general and in Tajikistan and Afghanistan specifically. As Russia felt itself pressed in the West, a turn toward "neo-imperialism" in Kremlin policy led to efforts to reinforce Russia's positions in the "near abroad," including Tajikistan. Moreover, since Moscow did not seem to have a problem dealing with Tehran despite the terrorism that Iran still engaged in—whether in Beirut, Berlin, or even Dushanbe—Iran was willing to cooperate. Not only did Tehran respond positively, but it also began to play on these first signs of souring relations between post-Soviet, independent Russia and Washington.

As it courted Iran to help dampen tensions in Tajikistan, Moscow benefited from Afghan mujahideen commander Ahmed Shah Masoud's desire to gain Russian help in his long-standing deadly rivalry with Pakistani-favorite Gulbuddin Hekmatyar. Hekmatyar had long been a bête noire of both Masoud and Moscow, and Masoud had resorted to tactical alliances against Hekmatyar even during the Soviet military intervention in Afghanistan. Finally, and crucially, Tajik opposition leader Nuri's ultimate desire was to regain for the Islamic Revival Party and its allies a place at the table of power in Dushanbe, not to fight the Rahmonov regime interminably.

Still, it was a hard slog, but with Moscow pressing Dushanbe and Iran leaning on the Tajik opposition, the two sides finally sat down to begin talks in April 1994—even as they continued to spar on the battlefield. The transition from civil war to a long period of peace talks, against the background of continued conflict, was complete even if imperfect.

## DRAFT POLITICAL TREATY

The Iranian side, while grousing about the reversal of its fortunes in Tajikistan, did not take long to signal that it was ready to resume the overall relationship with Moscow. When Kozyrev in early September 1992 had received Deputy Foreign Minister Mahmoud Vaezi in Moscow as the crisis in Tajikistan worsened, Vaezi reportedly had handed him a message from Foreign Minister Ali Akbar Velayati "on deepening of Tehran-Moscow relations."[6] In October, again in Moscow, the two diplomats reportedly made progress on a new political treaty, a draft of which Kozyrev and Velayati were expected to initial in Tehran in the near future in preparation for a Yeltsin-Rafsanjani summit. But Kozyrev had also registered concern over the conflict in Tajikistan and "expressed the hope that the Iranian side will take an understanding view of the situation which has arisen, since their actions with regard to the conflict will determine the future of Russian-Iranian relations."[7]

In November Russian ambassador Vladimir Gudev in Tehran told an Iranian interviewer that "we are seeking greater closeness with the Islamic Republic of Iran and soon will issue a joint Tehran-Moscow statement on measures taken in this regard" and that the statement "will pertain to overall political and economic issues."[8] After Gudev met with Deputy Foreign Minister Vaezi in Tehran on December 12, presumably after Rahmonov had relocated to Dushanbe from Khujand, the press reported that Vaezi had pronounced events in Tajikistan as "contrary to the interests of the region" but nevertheless announced "Iran's readiness to expand Tehran-Moscow relations."[9]

In his own dealings with Iranian representatives at the time, Kozyrev said that he stressed that Iran should not quarrel with Russia. Disagreements with Russia in Central Asia would have a negative impact on Iranian equities in Afghanistan, though Russia wanted to cooperate with Iran for stability in Afghanistan. When Kozyrev had traveled to the Gulf states, he had asked them to tell the Iranians that they would not get anywhere in Tajikistan. By the end of 1992, the Iranians had been convinced, and their strong interference fell off. They finally understood that there would be no easy pickings for them in Central Asia and that they would need to cooperate with Russia. Throughout it all, what was most important to Russian policy was to restrain Iran from adventurism both at home and abroad. Russia sought to orient its policy toward moderate forces in Iran and to cooperate with Iran not only on Afghanistan but also Azerbaijan, Kozyrev later pointed out.[10]

In fact, Kozyrev later described Moscow's relations with Tehran in 1992 as healthy and even quite good. Kozyrev personally advocated contacts with the Iranians and met monthly with the Iranian ambassador in Moscow. However, Kozyrev claimed, behind the scenes he categorically opposed a Yeltsin-Rafsanjani summit, which Tehran was pushing for. It was simply too early. It was true that the Iranians talked about it and that Russia was not entirely silent on the subject. (In fact, Kozyrev and his assistants were negotiating documents with their Iranian counterparts precisely for such a summit.) But it was hard for Westerners to understand, Kozyrev asserted, how deeply "Byzantine" Iranian politics were as a result of the interplay of primitive, hard-line fanatics and subtle, sophisticated pragmatists. A state visit was very important to the Iranians, so Kozyrev was convinced that Moscow had to dole out carefully any progress toward bringing about a Yeltsin summit.[11]

Diplomat Bakhtiyer Khakimov also asserted that in 1992, despite all the turmoil in Tajikistan and Iran's role in it, Russia's relations with Iran were not all that bad. Khakimov confirmed that 1992 saw preparations for a Russian-Iranian summit. Russia knew of Iranian activities in Tajikistan, warned Tehran against them, but throughout always tried to carry on a serious dialogue. Russia always dealt bluntly and candidly with Iran, asserted Khakimov. Moscow told Tehran that Tajikistan was in Russia's sphere of interests, and Iran recognized this. At the same time, Russia agreed that Iran could be active in Tajikistan. Eight years later, Iran still financed Sayed Abdullo Nuri, according to Khakimov, and Akbar Turajonzoda (whom Khakimov described as "pragmatic") had a house in Tehran where his wife and children lived.[12]

While the talk of summitry may have been a case of the Russians stringing the Iranians along, both sides were certainly publicly playing up the need for closer contacts. Kozyrev and Vaezi had made progress on a new political treaty during their meeting in Moscow in October. At the working level, Khakimov recollected, a draft was ready to go in February 1993. When Foreign Minister Kozyrev visited Tehran in late March, he and his Iranian counterpart Velayati initialed the draft treaty—or declaration, as the Iranian side preferred but did not insist on.[13] The Russian delegation regarded Article 2 of the document as a great success and of direct consequence for Tajikistan. According to it, Russia and Iran pledged "not to use force or the threat of force against each other, not to let their territories be used in launching aggressions, subversive or separatist actions against the other side, or against states friendly to it." Iran would not agree to this at first but eventually came around, Khakimov recalled years later with a touch of pride. Moscow pointed out that this would give Tehran the right to protest Russian behavior in Tajikistan, and vice versa.[14] The press described the draft as outlining the foundations of relations and the principles of good-neighborly cooperation.[15] One Russian analyst wrote that it was meant to replace the outdated Moscow-Tehran treaty of 1921.[16]

Kozyrev and Velayati also signed a protocol on regular consultations between their two ministries and a memorandum on visa-free diplomatic and official business travel. Iranian ambassador Nematollah Yazdi in Moscow later said that Yeltsin had accepted an invitation to visit Iran. The dates had not yet been agreed to, but the Iranian side hoped it would be before the year's end. Yeltsin's visit would in effect reciprocate that of Rafsanjani to Moscow in 1989.[17] In the end, however, Yeltsin never traveled to Tehran, but then Gorbachev had never returned Rafsanjani's visit either.

In Tehran in late March, Kozyrev's delegation reportedly assured the Iranians that Moscow wanted a "strategic partnership" aimed at securing stability in Central Asia and the Caucasus. But Moscow was concerned by reports that Tajik opposition detachments were training at camps in Iranian territory and that they were preparing for a major offensive against Tajik government troops. Kozyrev reportedly raised the issue even with Rafsanjani, and by the end of the visit both sides agreed on the need for a moderate leadership in Dushanbe.[18] After the talks, Kozyrev told a reporter, "We have managed to reach agreement here on not rocking this situation [in Tajikistan] and on supporting the legally elected and existing government and to motivate all sides, including the government itself, the opposition, and the Islamic opposition to embark on national reconciliation."[19]

## BORDER CARNAGE

On July 13, 1993, however, Tajik rebels reinforced by Afghan mujahideen attacked a Russian border outpost, Moskovskiy No. 12, killing twenty-two border guards and three soldiers from the 201st MRD. According to Andrey Nikolayev, commander of the Russian Federation's Border Guards, fourteen groups of Tajik opposition and Afghan mujahideen, consisting of as many as 250 fighters, participated in the assault on the outpost.[20]

Whatever the intention, the incident provoked political crises in Moscow and Tehran. Kozyrev's visit to Tehran at the end of March 1993 had broken the ice after the charges and countercharges over the events the previous fall in Tajikistan. Russian deputy foreign minister Georgiy Konatev had just been in Tehran for two days of talks pursuant to the Kozyrev-Velayati agreement on regular foreign ministry consultations. Iranian Foreign Ministry representatives had denied that Iran was arming or training the Tajik opposition, Konatev told the press, and had conveyed to him that they considered the government in Tajikistan "as legitimate."[21] Now, however, the July 13 attack threatened the desire by both sides to push past the prolonged rough patch in bilateral relations.

Ironically, the foreign ministries in both capitals took the brunt of potshots from critics. The Moskovskiy incident prompted Russian aircraft and artillery retaliatory strikes across the border into northern Afghanistan, which the Afghans complained caused extensive damage.[22] Not until two weeks after the attack, however, did the Security Council convene in Moscow on July 26 to hammer out a coherent response that gave pride of place to pushing for a political settlement.[23] By the end of the month, Russian diplomats and special envoys were working to reestablish contacts with Kabul, Tehran, and the Tajik opposition in order to get national reconciliation talks going. Moscow's two-track policy, with the two tracks arguably going in opposite directions, prompted critics to charge that Moscow in reality had no policy at all.

Without providing an alternative but pronouncing the Yeltsin administration unable to cope with the situation, Yuri Fedorov of the USA Institute wrote at the time that the "zigzags" of Moscow's "half-baked diplomacy" and its efforts to balance military and mediation tracks would not lead to success. Russia was pushing Rahmonov to compromise with his opponents, while at the same time threatening these opponents with military force. Fedorov noted that the Muscovite liberal intelligentsia had joined the Tajik opposition in calling for Russia to pull the 201st Division and the Border Guards out of Tajikistan. But a Russian departure would set the stage for a new spiral in the civil war, a spike in Russian emigration, and the need to spend "enormous sums of money" creating a new frontier line closer to home. The other Central Asian states would be sucked into the Tajikistan whirlpool in the event of a Russian withdrawal, Fedorov warned. As things stood, Central Asia was a unique "buffer zone" between Russia and the "seething Muslim world" and even China.[24]

In Tehran, radical commentary exulted that Moscow's shuttle diplomacy proved that Russia only understood force.[25] It berated the Iranian Foreign Ministry's unwillingness to press the advantage of the moment. *Salam* complained of the indifference of Iran's diplomatic apparatus and official electronic media to what it claimed were Western and U.S.-abetted Russian atrocities in Tajikistan, while Turkey was busy cultivating not only the Turkic Central Asians but also Tajikistan, once part of "Greater Iran." It demanded the Foreign Ministry make a "clear analysis of the situation and approach it accordingly" and "not forsake" the "oppressed Tajik people . . . in their difficult time of need."[26]

The attack forced Moscow's slow-moving reassessment of the Tajik situation to its conclusion. Fedorov later recalled a curious article in the military press in early 1993 that conceded that one of the weaknesses of Russian policy was that its diplomats and military representatives in Tajikistan did not understand the situation and had no real sources of information. After the USSR's collapse, according to this account, the local Tajik KGB organization controlled all the local informants, leaving Moscow blind. The Russian military did not have its own intelligence network, which was characteristic across all the former Soviet republics.[27] This allowed myths of Iranian influence to spread like wildfire, according to Fedorov. Reality was much more complex, but few at first understood it. All this, however, began to change after the massacre of the twenty-five border guards and soldiers. Something was wrong and clearly needed to be done. Moscow finally understood that what was going on in Tajikistan was fundamentally a struggle of regional clans for economic resources, including control of the narcotics traffic.[28]

In this regard, the official line when First Deputy Foreign Minister Adamishin visited the Moskovskiy No. 12 outpost not long after the carnage was that the attack had been politically motivated. However, Adamishin later remembered that he had heard during his visit that Moskovskiy was an uncorrupted post that obstructed the movement of drug traffic across the Panj River into Tajikistan. While not publicized at the time, there was speculation that the fierce attack had been meant to drive home a lesson to Moskovskiy and any other post that did not cooperate with the narco-traffickers. Of course, Moskovskiy was a vulnerable post that was open to attack from all sides by any forces that wanted to make a political statement. But the drug trafficker explanation seemed closer to reality, Adamishin concluded, although it could of course have been a combination of the two.[29] And yet a third variant that could be heard in Moscow years later was that Moskovskiy No. 12 was in fact deeply involved in narco-trafficking. According to this version, the outpost became greedy and refused to pay the local warlords cum traffickers their due after being asked to do so not just once or twice but three times.[30]

Whatever its motivation, the attack had wide ramifications in Russia itself. Public opinion was still reeling from the after-tremors of the Soviet collapse and its impact on co-ethnics in what many Russians regarded proprietarily as the "near abroad." Ethnic Russians in all of the newly independent non-Russian states were grappling with ambivalent national identities, challenged political status, and uncertain futures in the Baltics, Caucasus, and Central Asia, including even in tolerant Kazakhstan and Kyrgyzstan. Their distressing circumstances were made all the more painful by the economic collapse afflicting the entire post-Soviet space. To make matters worse, local conflicts, of which the Tajik civil war was only the most horrific, scared even Russians who had resided for generations outside of Russia—many because their ancestors had been exiled during the Stalin period—into packing their bags and migrating back to Russia, there to compete for scarce jobs and housing.[31]

All of this provoked resentment in some quarters in Russia against both the leaders of the newly independent states as well as the outside foreign powers courting them, and the Yeltsin administration began to react to the mounting political pressure. The massacre on Tajikistan's border with Afghanistan contributed to what Fedorov described as a fundamental turning point in Russian policy in July 1993. Foreign Minister Kozyrev's rhetoric began to take on a neo-imperial coloration, in Fedorov's view.[32] In January 1994 Kozyrev told a meeting of Russian ambassadors to the CIS and Baltics that these countries comprised a region of "priority vital interests for Russia." Protecting the rights of Russians abroad was a major strategic foreign policy task. It was necessary, according to the foreign minister, for Russia to maintain its "military presence in those regions which have been the sphere of Russian interests for centuries" in order to prevent hostile forces from filling the "security vacuum."[33] Russian pundits quickly began referring to the Yeltsin administration's new "Monrovsky Doctrine."[34] By December 1994 Yeltsin had launched the first war of Russia's post-Soviet era against Chechnya, which had been declared independent from the Russian Federation in 1991 by its leader Dzhokhar Dudayev.

In 1999 Fedorov speculated that some of the new hard edge was of course also influenced by Yeltsin's struggle with the Duma, which he shut down with shell fire from tanks in October 1993, and his efforts to keep the army on his side.[35] Many underscored the impact of the victory of the Communist Party of the Russian Federation (CPRF) and of Vladimir Zhirinovsky's Liberal Democratic Party of Russia (LDPR) in the December 12, 1993, elections for a new Duma.[36] Zhirinovsky had called for the restoration of the Soviet empire and denounced anti-Russian policies in Central Asia. He attributed these to "temporary presidents who have temporarily seceded" and proclaimed that "Moscow will one day become master of those lands again."[37]

Although Poland, Hungary, and the Czech Republic did not join NATO until April 1999, some also included Moscow's neuralgic reaction in fall 1993 to the first prospects of NATO expansion among the causes of the tougher rhetoric.[38] In April 1993 the leaders of these three countries broached the subject directly in Washington with President Clinton, who by January 1994 in Prague declared that the question was "no longer whether NATO will take on new members but when and how."[39] As Yevgeny Bazhanov at the Diplomatic Academy pointed out, as Russians began to feel more keenly their country's loss of status as a great power, anti-U.S. feelings rose and pro-Iranian sentiment grew.[40] In any event, Russia's nascent differences with the West coincided with Tehran's incipient greater interest in cooperation with Moscow in Tajikistan and Afghanistan, stimulated in part also by Washington's newly pronounced policy of "dual containment" of Iraq and Iran.

## PITCH TO MASOUD AND NURI

Soon after the Russian Federation Security Council met on July 26, 1993, to map out a response to the attack on the Moskovskiy border post,[41] Foreign Intelligence Service (SVR) director Yevgeny Primakov visited Tehran and Kabul—presumably to implement the council's decisions as special envoy of President Yeltsin. As he did so, Anatoly Adamishin paid calls on all five Central Asian capitals on a similar mission.

Adamishin began with a stop in Dushanbe on July 29, his first time there since becoming first deputy foreign minister in October 1992. He carried with him letters from Yeltsin to each head of state endorsing proposals that Dushanbe and the opposition participate in talks that would also include representatives from Russia, Uzbekistan, Iran, and Afghanistan.[42] The Russian president also reportedly proposed to his five counterparts that they all meet in Moscow for what would be the first such summit of Russia and the Central Asian states. Yeltsin's messages urged Kazakhstan and Kyrgyzstan to increase their contributions to the joint forces guarding the Tajik-Afghan border and the other Central Asian countries to start to share the burden.[43]

On January 22, 1993, in Minsk, a summit of the CIS leaders had declared support for the new Rahmonov leadership in Dushanbe and its call for the introduction of a collective peacekeeping force into Tajikistan. Yeltsin in Minsk said that the five states that had signed the CST in Tashkent in May 1992 would each send a battalion of five hundred troops to reinforce the Tajik-Afghan border along with Russia's Border Guards.[44] According to press reports, an Uzbek battalion had already been in Tajikistan since December.[45] Subsequently, Kyrgyzstan sent a battalion to Tajikistan in early March but then withdrew it by early April.[46] Kazakhstan's parliament in mid-April had endorsed sending a battalion to Tajikistan, but Almaty had been in no hurry to deploy the unit.[47]

Despite several CIS heads-of-government and heads-of-state summits in March and April, therefore, the January decision on sending a CST peacekeeping force to Tajikistan remained largely unimplemented.[48] Perhaps the most significant military measure taken in regards to Tajikistan had been Yeltsin and Rahmonov's bilateral signing on May 25, 1993, of what were in effect status of forces agreements governing the deployment in Tajikistan of the 201st MRD and the Russian Border Guards. The two agreements were adopted as part of a package of seven documents attached to the Friendship Treaty between Russia and Tajikistan, which Yeltsin and Rahmonov signed on the occasion.[49]

In late July, after the Moskovskiy massacre and in response to reports of preparations by the Tajik opposition and Afghan mujahideen to launch a new offensive into Tajikistan, Kyrgyzstan had again deployed a battalion to the Tajik-Afghan border.[50] Even before the Russia–Central Asia summit on August 7, Askar Akayev politely brushed off—it would be examined "most attentively"—Yeltsin's suggestion that Kyrgyzstan further increase its troop presence in Tajikistan, while Turkmenistan's Saparmurat Niyazov more bluntly told the press that he would not send any soldiers to the Tajik-Afghan border.[51] Uzbekistan's Islom Karimov, rather than underscoring the need to send more troops to participate in the joint force, now joined those urging Rahmonov to engage the opposition in talks.[52] The summit subsequently issued yet another declaration about helping defend Tajikistan's borders and sending humanitarian assistance, but there was again desultory at best follow-through from Tajikistan's Central Asian neighbors.[53]

Soon after Yeltsin's summit with the Central Asian presidents in early August, Adamishin described Russia's position as twofold. First, it was necessary to strengthen the Tajik-Afghan border and defend it against what could be a potentially "enormous" flood of "contraband, drugs, weapons, and terrorism" should Russia withdraw its forces from Tajikistan. Second, and here Adamishin said the Central Asian presidents had agreed with Yeltsin at the summit, it was necessary to push for a political solution to the conflict in Tajikistan since a military solution did not exist. Responding to an interviewer's question on Islamic extremism, Adamishin said, "I have the impression that the opposition is using the Islamic factor to a larger extent than the Islamic factor is using the opposition."[54]

Meanwhile, paralleling Adamishin's tour of Central Asian capitals, Yevgeny Primakov visited Kabul and Tehran, and the new ambassador to Islamabad, Aleksandr Alekseyev conducted talks in the Pakistani capital.[55] In Kabul, Primakov met with Afghan president Burhanuddin Rabbani and de facto defense minister Ahmed Shah Masoud, both ethnic Tajiks. The Tajik opposition, after all, had taken refuge and set up base and training camps after retreating from Tajikistan in Masoud's northern headquarters of Taloqan.[56] Primakov could not be faulted for apparently assuming that Masoud might have some influence on the Tajik opposition in exile, which he was hosting, and Primakov in fact was successful in securing a meeting with Sayed Abdullo Nuri. The mission to Kabul, Primakov told an interviewer years later, was "a diplomatic one but accomplished using foreign intelligence tactics."[57] In Tehran, Primakov conferred with President Rafsanjani and Foreign Minister Velayati, emphasizing the significance of Iran's role in the region and agreeing that the crisis on the Tajik-Afghan border should be resolved by negotiations between the Dushanbe government and the Tajik opposition.

Primakov's analysis of the situation in the region, as he laid it out in his memoir, was consistent with what others, including Adamishin, said had become the prevailing view among policymakers in Moscow at the time. The turmoil in Afghanistan was spreading to neighboring countries and "had become especially dangerous in Tajikistan, where bloody internecine battles were flaring," Primakov said. "The clashes between regional clans were intertwined with the battle between Dushanbe and the opposition, decorated in Islamic colors. It opened an anti-government front in Tajikistan itself, but for the most part based itself in Afghanistan, from where its fighters carried out daring raids, and from where flowed arms and money."[58]

Primakov met with Rabbani and Masoud on July 30. Gulbuddin Hekmatyar, described as the Pakistani ISI's favorite Pashtun at the time, had just been sworn in as prime minister on June 17 after his forces captured Masoud's defense ministry headquarters earlier in the year.[59] Hekmatyar's forces—in alliance at the time with Shia Hazara fighters—continued to attack areas of Kabul controlled by Rabbani and Masoud even during their meetings with Primakov.[60] Although Primakov would not state it quite so baldly, it appears from his account that Masoud was eager to play ball with Russia to get help in his battle with Hekmatyar, who was pressuring Masoud not only in Kabul but even around Taloqan, Masoud's regional capital.[61]

Masoud's readiness to negotiate with a representative of Moscow was not without precedent. Even though Masoud was the most legendary of the mujahideen who had battled Soviet forces during their long occupation of Afghanistan in the 1980s, he had also distinguished himself by his willingness to negotiate controversial deals with the very same Soviet commanders he was fighting. These had infuriated rival mujahideen and their Pakistan backers, and Masoud had concluded them without consulting even his political ally Rabbani.[62] Toward the end of the Soviet occupation, there had even been rumors that Moscow was considering switching its support from Najibullah to Masoud.[63]

According to U.S. ambassador Stanley Escudero, the IRP in September 1992 "enjoyed the support of the Iranians, some Saudi Wahhabis, and the fundamentalist Afghan Mujaheddin group headed by Gulbuddin Hekmatyar."[64] Similarly, the Tajik observers Gapur Khaidarov and Maksudjon Inomov in their account have pointed at support to the opposition from Iran, Saudi Arabia, and Afghanistan, in the last instance singling out Hekmatyar.[65] The Saudis along with the Pakistanis were well-known as Hekmatyar's patrons, and their rivalry with Masoud and Iran was equally well-known.[66]

Afghanistan experts Mohammad Reza Djalili and Frederic Grare have underscored that by 1993 the Tajik conflict was an extension of that in neighboring Afghanistan. Ethnic Uzbek General Abdul Rashid Dostum, Masoud, and Hekmatyar were all vying against each other for influence among the refugees from Tajikistan in northern Afghanistan.[67] Around the time Primakov visited Afghanistan, the journalist Ahmed Rashid similarly reported that Hekmatyar and Masoud were competing for influence with the Tajik opposition. Together with retired officers from ISI and members of the radical Jamaat-e-Islami (JI), the well-funded Hekmatyar was helping train some two thousand IRP fighters near Kunduz, not far from the Tajikistan border. With less support, Masoud was training perhaps only a tenth as many in nearby Taloqan.[68]

Boris Gromov, commander of the 40th Army during the Soviet intervention in Afghanistan, claimed that his command first established "solid contacts" with Masoud in 1982 and that these contacts continued until Soviet forces abandoned Afghanistan. Although other accounts place it well into 1983, it was in December 1982, according to Gromov—with what comes across as considerable professional admiration for Masoud—that representatives of the 40th Army and Masoud "personally" signed a cease-fire agreement covering Masoud's home base in the Panjshir Valley. The agreement lasted until April 1984. In return for the withdrawal of Soviet forces from the Panjshir, Masoud undertook not to allow his men to fire on Soviet columns at the southern end of the Salang Pass or to actively engage government forces, and to order his fighters to concentrate their attacks on rival mujahideen forces instead, presumably in the first instance Hekmatyar's.[69]

Over the years, Hekmatyar gained the reputation of a "total spoiler" with a particularly treacherous history.[70] It included a longtime rivalry with Masoud and Rabbani. Gromov later cited reports that Masoud and Hekmatyar had first drawn close while in exile in Pakistan in the 1970s but that a "major falling-out" between the two had forced Masoud to flee to Egypt. According to Gromov, the toll inflicted by attacks from Hekmatyar's forces on Masoud's units was one of the factors that forced Masoud to enter into the cease-fire agreement with the 40th Army.[71]

Hekmatyar had been born in Imam Sakhib near the Pyanj River border with Tajikistan. As long ago as 1986, with little urging from the American CIA and the Pakistani ISI, he had been venturing across that border to mount attacks designed to speed the Soviet withdrawal from Afghanistan. Masoud, though, had rejected participation in such tactics, which did not endear him to the ISI.[72] After the Soviet collapse, Hekmatyar had supported terrorist attacks on Russians to encourage them to quit the country.[73]

Not surprisingly, therefore, Nuri once remarked to Davlat Khudonazarov, candidate for president of Tajikistan in 1991, that his first contacts with the Afghan mujahideen were with Hekmatyar's people, at the latter's initiative, and only later with those of Masoud. It was Khudonazarov's understanding, moreover, that Masoud later on had confined his support for the Tajik opposition to humanitarian aid, thus provoking the enmity of Nuri's MIRT first deputy Turajonzoda. Consequently, Masoud over the years had problems with elements of the Tajik opposition because of their early ties with Hekmatyar. Perhaps because of the Tajik opposition's presence and their long-standing ties to Hekmatyar, Khudonazarov observed during a visit to Afghanistan that Masoud was forced to take extraordinary security precautions even in Taloqan, where the Panjshiri commander had set up headquarters not far from the Tajik border after the Soviet military withdrawal from Afghanistan in 1989. In Taloqan, Khudonazarov saw two camps for Tajiks. Iran had bankrolled one, and the other had been sponsored by Saudi Arabia.[74]

In 1993, therefore, Moscow and Masoud had strong and common interests in working together against Hekmatyar and a history of tactically cooperating with each other in the face of temporary imperatives. Primakov wrote later that during his meeting with Masoud, which was the main reason for his visit to Kabul, "I became convinced about his striving to develop multi-faceted relations with Russia especially in the area of military-technical cooperation."[75] Thus, the important chronological point was that Masoud's inclination to cooperate with Russia preceded by years the rise of the Taliban in Afghanistan in late 1994 (on which more in chapter 9) and was born of his long struggle with Hekmatyar.

Primakov apparently explained it quite directly to Masoud: the price for Russian help against his opponents in Afghanistan was Masoud's assistance in reducing Tajik opposition pressure on Dushanbe. "The three hour conversation with Ahmed Shah was maximally businesslike," wrote Primakov. "I laid out for him our view of the situation in Tajikistan and in Afghanistan." Primakov warned Masoud about the consequences of any more attacks on Russians such as that on July 13. "I told him bluntly, that we would without doubt increase our military actions if Russian and Tajik border guards were subjected to attacks. 'We have learned through bitter experience and of course are not preparing to introduce soldiers onto the territory of Afghanistan. But believe me, Ahmed Shah, we have the ability to protect our interests without a ground intervention,' I said."[76]

Then Primakov made his case for Masoud's help in setting up talks between the opposition and Dushanbe. "To establish the best conditions for a peaceful resolution [of the conflict in Tajikistan] the two sides should cease their military actions on the border, desist from infiltrating Islamic fighters into Tajikistan and begin the process of repatriating refugees, guaranteeing them security and help in settling." According to Primakov, "My interlocutor not only agreed with all this, but also showed lively interest in the organization of my meeting with Tajik-Islamic opposition leader Nuri."[77]

Primakov's meeting with Nuri took place the following day, on July 31. Primakov was the first Russian representative to meet with the leader of the MIRT. Primakov again mixed threats of retaliation with an offer of talks. "'Do you really not understand,' I said, 'that it is not in your interests to involve Russia in actions against the opposition based in Afghanistan? We will be forced to do this if they do not cease their firing on border guard bases and border guards on the border with Tajikistan. But there is a realistic alternative to this. Russia is ready to assist your negotiations with President Rahmonov.'"

Nuri responded that the opposition was not bent on overthrowing Rahmonov's government but rather participating with it in a coalition cabinet. He reportedly promised Primakov that he would do what he could to calm the border but noted that he did not control all the commanders. In fact, Primakov noted that some of Nuri's field commanders were beginning to switch their allegiance to Hekmatyar. Evidently, whatever the earlier relationship between Nuri and Hekmatyar, Nuri's inclination to deal with the regime in Dushanbe had become a source of friction between the two. "In this way," concluded Primakov, "Nuri sent us an extremely important 'signal.' The conversation with him, if I may, could be considered the starting point for the difficult, lengthy, with many digressions process of regulating relations between the Tajik leadership and the Islamic opposition." (In fact, direct negotiations between the two sides did not begin until April 1994.) With Nuri's deputy Turajonzoda, according to Primakov, "it was possible to agree on the approximate proportions of representation of the opposition and the Dushanbe leadership in the organs of power—30 percent to 70. Rahmonov supported this ratio."[78]

## TEHRAN AGREES

From Kabul, Primakov proceeded to Tehran, where he landed the evening of July 31. The next day, August 1, he met with President Rafsanjani, Foreign Minister Velayati, and Deputy Foreign Minister Vaezi. The Iranian president was especially interested in developing economic relations; the Russian side's mission was to focus on the possibilities of Iran playing a positive role in regulating the crisis in Tajikistan.[79] It would appear that Primakov played on Iranian worries over separatism, not in the South Azerbaijan provinces in Iran's northwest but on Iran's eastern borders with

by what groups?

Afghanistan. The bitter civil wars raging simultaneously in Tajikistan and Afghanistan, where Iran was clearly providing aid and comfort to some of the combatants, posed a threat to Iran's territorial integrity. Primakov later wrote that he found agreement with Velayati and Vaezi on the point that "separatist processes, whether in Afghanistan or Tajikistan, in the final analysis were fraught with a destabilizing impact on Iran itself. . . . Vaezi reacted with understanding to my words that the religious factor should not be considered the dominant one in defining the relations to opposing sides in a conflict fraught with the danger of separatism."[80]

In return, the Iranians complained to Primakov that Russia was trying to elbow Iran out of any prospective Tajik peace process. This was all the more galling to Tehran because much of the Tajik opposition leadership was by then living in Iran. Primakov in turn proposed that Moscow and Tehran coordinate their actions on Tajikistan. "I think that in Tehran they reacted with readiness to this proposal since it conformed with their striving to get out of isolation and take part in positive processes on the international arena."

Primakov allowed himself only a few indirect references in his memoir to the role of Iran in helping to fuel the Tajik civil war by its support to one of the combatants. In one passage, he noted that Tehran was ready to deal with Moscow "all the more so since by this time it had become clear that a strengthening of Iranian positions in Tajikistan was without prospects. Moreover, Iranian influence in Dushanbe and even its physical presence there had begun to wane." Primakov concluded that this visit and a subsequent one in February 1995 convinced him that Russia needed to develop not just economic but also political relations with Iran.[81]

Looking back at the assumptions underlying Primakov's diplomacy, it is important to underscore that the regional perspectives of Moscow and Tehran were fundamentally different and that Primakov played on these differences. For Moscow, Tajikistan was central and Afghanistan peripheral, though both were ultimately part of the same ball of wax. For Tehran, the reverse was true: Afghanistan and Iran's equities in its Shia Hazaras took precedence over the travails of the opposition in Tajikistan, though the latter could play a role in helping the former.

The situation was fundamentally complicated, moreover, by the ambitions of Pakistan's generals and the ISI in Afghanistan, which they wanted to dominate in their quest for strategic depth against India. Presumably, any influence Pakistan might gain in Tajikistan would be useful in this regard as well. From 1988 to 1993 Pakistan's clear instrument in Afghanistan was the ethnic Pashtun leader Hekmatyar, who was also supported both militarily and politically by Saudi Arabia. As a result, what obtained in many ways in Afghanistan was essentially a proxy war pitting Iran, later joined by Russia, against Pakistan and Saudi Arabia.[82]

Against this background, to advance Moscow's priorities in Tajikistan, Primakov in mid-1993 had to bring something to the table in order to engage Tehran, the ethnic Tajik mujahideen, and the Tajik opposition. With Tehran, it was visibility and a real role in the proffered Tajik peace process. With Masoud and Rabbani, it was support in their struggle against Hekmatyar. With Nuri and Turajonzoda, it was some tangible power in Dushanbe for them and other elements of the Tajik opposition that Tehran supported. With all concerned, however, Russian help was contingent on their severing ties, even if only tactical, to Hekmatyar and thus to his ambitions in Tajikistan.

Primakov's strategy was complicated by the Tehran-backed Shia coalition's temporary alliance with Hekmatyar during this phase of the civil war in Afghanistan. Although on its face it was counterintuitive given the long history of mutual animosity between the Hazara and Hekmatyar's forces, they were driven together for the moment by Masoud's efforts to oust both from Kabul.[83] Hekmatyar had long been the instrument of Pakistani policy in Afghanistan and by extension probably also in Tajikistan. Primakov's attempt to tilt his Afghan and Tajik interlocutors against Hekmatyar was therefore natural; it was a continuation of Moscow's resistance to Pakistan's designs against Russian interests for well over a decade.

Since the collapse of the Soviet Union and the beginning of civil war in Tajikistan, Hekmatyar and Masoud had both made inroads in Tajikistan. Moscow clearly regarded Masoud as the lesser of two evils and had experience in concluding tactical alliances with him against Hekmatyar during the earlier Soviet-period intervention. It was logical, therefore, that Russia would dangle the prospects of help against Hekmatyar to Masoud and would seek to wean the Tajik opposition away from Hekmatyar. After all, Hekmatyar had no interest in cooperating in any way with Russia in a scheme that—while giving the opposition a role in Tajik politics—would keep Rahmonov in power in Dushanbe.

When Primakov saw Nuri in Kabul, it was evident that Nuri was having the same problem with Hekmatyar that all others had had: Hekmatyar was a maximalist. He wanted those he sponsored to take over all power in Dushanbe, just as he was fighting for all power in Kabul. Hekmatyar was not interested in a power-sharing coalition. Instead, he wanted to topple Rahmonov and to terrorize ethnic Russians into leaving Tajikistan. Nuri, however, was willing to share power with Rahmonov. In the period ahead, the contested loyalties of opposition fighters in Tajikistan—tugged in opposite directions by rival mujahideen in Afghanistan—probably contributed to the fitfulness of the slowly developing peace process and its repeated setbacks, even after the Taliban's rise.

In any event, a commentary broadcast by the official *Voice of the Islamic Republic of Iran* assessed as "very positive" Primakov's efforts to enlist the help of Tehran and Kabul in a Tajik peace-making effort. It argued that if talks had already been under way, the Tajik opposition would have had no incentive to undertake an attack such as occurred on July 13.[84] By mid-September, following a phone call between Yeltsin and President Rafsanjani, the *Voice of the Islamic Republic of Iran* was exulting that the soon expected state visit by Yeltsin to Tehran would "usher in a new era in the age-old ties between the two countries" and that their cooperation could prove very effective in reducing tensions in countries such as Azerbaijan and Tajikistan.[85] Both Kozyrev and Khakimov later confirmed, as we have seen, that a Yeltsin trip to Tehran had been raised as far back as a year earlier.

## PEACEKEEPERS VERSUS OPPOSITION FIGHTERS

Russia, Kazakhstan, Kyrgyzstan, Uzbekistan, and Tajikistan finally managed to sign an agreement to establish and support a collective peacekeeping force (CPF) in Tajikistan at the September 24, 1993, CIS summit in Minsk. There had been repeated false starts since soon-to-be-deposed President Nabiyev's first proposal in late August 1992, and a reluctance—as we have seen—to come to the aid of Dushanbe militarily. Now, at last, the force was to begin functioning on October 1, 1993, with a six-month mandate. Besides the Russian 201st Division, it was to include units from Uzbekistan (two battalions) and Kazakhstan and Kyrgyzstan (one battalion apiece). The Kazakh unit especially, however, was again slow to deploy, and then only nominally at best.[86] By 1995, according to one account, the Kazakhstanis had assigned only one officer to Tajikistan, the Kyrgyz only one company, and Uzbekistan a 440-strong battalion.[87]

For all intents and purposes, the CPF consisted only of the Russian 201st Division garrisoned in Tajikistan since Soviet times. Politically, there was little public support in Russia for such a move. According to polling conducted in 1993, perhaps only a third of the Russian public favored the notion of Russian troops and border guards deployed in Tajikistan.[88] The commitment of the 201st to a CPF for Tajikistan thus came late and reluctantly, forced by the opposition's threat to the Rahmonov regime. The September 24, 1993, Minsk agreement appointed a Russian general, Boris Pyankov, as joint commander of the CPF. At the December 1993 CIS summit, Pyankov was also put in charge of all Russian forces in Tajikistan. Four months later, the April 15, 1994, CIS summit in Moscow called for sixteen thousand soldiers to man the CPF in Tajikistan.[89]

In the Tajik context, the strength of the 201st and of the total CPF was under-whelmingly low. According to various estimates, the maximum number of opposition fighters was fifteen to twenty thousand, and perhaps more realistically only seven to ten thousand. The total number of CPF (mostly the Russian 201st Division) and Tajik government soldiers, however, was in reality never sixteen thousand but rather closer to the higher end of the realistic estimate of opposition fighter strength. In mid-1994, for example, Valeriy Patrikeyev (Pyankov's successor as CPF commander) put the total CPF's strength as not much higher than 7,500, of which more than half came from the 201st Division.[90] Yet according to most expert advice on fighting insurgencies, at least a 10:1 advantage in troop strength was needed to defeat a partisan force.[91]

Numbers aside, the 201st's capabilities in real combat were also questionable. According to one expert on military matters, while the division had the guns—a critical factor in any fight—it was only a nominally effective military force. The division demonstrated weaknesses in three key areas: tactical expertise, resources, and the will to fight. The 201st's tactics were defensive and reactive. While its foes did not always have the military hardware, that was only important if they intended to take on the 201st in the open field of battle, which they did not. Instead, the 201st's opponents had the home court advantage of most guerrilla warfare scenarios: they could choose the place of battle, and they had a certain ardor for battle that many of the 201st's conscripts definitely lacked. In addition, there was another problem. A number of the 201st's ethnic Tajik conscripts found it difficult to remain neutral as they were swayed by their regional and clan loyalties into supporting one or another side in the civil conflict. Most of the Tajik conscripts were young and from the countryside. They were not in a position to exert much influence, and their Russian officers often viewed them disparagingly.[92]

> In sum, an objective analysis would have concluded that the forces supporting the Rahmonov regime in Dushanbe could not defeat the opposition fighters deployed in the Tajik countryside, who gained staying power from their sanctuary in northern Afghanistan and support from Iran. But the opposition likewise would never be able to defeat Rahmonov, as long as he had Russia standing behind him.

>> The July 1993 border outpost massacre had brought home to Moscow the renewed military vitality of the opposition it thought had been defeated, and the very real vulnerability of the Rahmonov regime to an insurgent guerrilla campaign. Given the roughly even ratio of forces facing each other in Tajikistan, Moscow had a great incentive to press Rahmonov to enter peace talks with his opposition, and the latter to explore where talks might lead. Accordingly, on a parallel track, the same CIS summit in Minsk in September 1993 that saw an agreement on establishing a CPF also issued a declaration urging the two sides in Tajikistan to find common language, according to Russian deputy foreign minister Adamishin, who followed up with another visit to Dushanbe at the end of October.

In Dushanbe, Adamishin met at length with Tajik parliamentary speaker and head of state Rahmonov, Prime Minister Abdullojonov, and Foreign Minister Rashid Alimov. Adamishin also traveled to the Tajik-Afghan border in the Gorno-Badakhshan region.[93] The two contending Tajik sides, however, continued to spar on the battlefield. Adamishin thus did not get the Tajik opposition's unambiguous agreement to negotiations with the Tajik government—under UN sponsorship with mediators and observers from Russia, Iran, and Pakistan—until he met with Iranian foreign minister Velayati and Tajik opposition representatives in Tehran on March 6, 1994.[94]

Two days after Adamishin's talks in Tehran, the radical *Salam* excoriated the Foreign Ministry for not publicizing the details of the conversations with the Russian official. With its usual reference to Spiritual Leader Khamenei, *Salam* implicitly questioned the very idea of doing business with Russia. After perpetrating "catastrophic crimes" against the "Persian-speaking Tajik people," Russia was now trying to "wrest the initiative" in the upcoming talks, "direct them toward its own long-term interests," and retain "the role of big brother." There was also implied criticism of the Foreign

Ministry for not insisting on Tehran as the venue for the first round of inter-Tajik talks—anything but the villainous Moscow.[95]

Despite the murder in Tajikistan of Deputy Prime Minister Moyonshoh Nazarshoyev and the charges and countercharges that followed,[96] the first round of negotiations managed to open in Moscow on April 5. This was the first face-to-face negotiation between Dushanbe and the opposition. Adamishin later recalled that just a month before, at his first meetings with the opposition in Tehran, it had resisted dealing with Dushanbe. Opposition negotiators had asked Adamishin why they should talk to those who took orders instead of those who gave them. He had persuaded the opposition to sit down with Tajik regime representatives in Moscow only by dangling before them the lure of ministerial posts in Dushanbe and a return to positions of influence.[97]

## THE EXPERTS REFLECT

In 1999 Adamishin recounted that when the opposition failed to hold onto power in Tajikistan, Iran started to cooperate with Russia to reconcile Dushanbe with the opposition. Iran began to calculate that it could exert more influence through the government than through its adopted clients. But why did Russia, having helped best the opposition and its Iranian (and other) supporters, invite them back into talks with the Dushanbe regime and cooperate with Iran to this end? Adamishin explained that Russia could not quit and leave Tajikistan—despite arguments by some that it should—for a variety of reasons. The Tajik border was the back door into the CIS; if Russia abandoned it, there was nothing to stop drugs, Islamist extremism, and other threats from sweeping north through Uzbekistan, Kyrgyzstan, and Kazakhstan into Russia itself. In addition, Russia also had economic interests in Tajikistan. It was potentially a very rich country. Alluding to Tajikistan's mineral resources, Adamishin underscored that all the elements in Mendeleyev's Table could be found there.

Russia realized, Adamishin explained, that the divisions in Tajikistan were along ethnic, regional, clan, and other lines, not along religious lines. Russia had to bring in the opposition and work with it to establish a political equilibrium that would bring stability to Tajikistan. As to Iran, Moscow conceded that Tehran had interests and a role to play in Central Asia. Was the decision to engage the opposition influenced by Russia's economic relations with Iran? Although he was the first to point out that Iran was one of the few countries where Russian goods could find a market, Adamishin's answer was that Russia's bilateral relationship with Iran was important in its own right. Whatever the situation in Tajikistan or elsewhere, Russia had to get along with Iran: the two countries were neighbors and if relations were allowed to deteriorate, Russia would lose any leverage and hope it might have of working with elements in Tehran to staunch the flow of Islamist extremism.[98]

By 1993 the views of experts on the region finally seemed to have gotten through to policymakers in Moscow. Central and South Asia specialist Aleksandr Umnov had long stressed that the foundation of Near and Central Asian civilization was not Islam but clan relations. Tajik-Pashtun interethnic alliances had from time immemorial been the basis for national power in Afghanistan, where there were roughly one and a half times more Tajiks than in Tajikistan.[99] The same system existed in Central Asia until the Soviets destroyed it. What Moscow accomplished in the republics during Soviet rule appeared progressive on the surface, but it destroyed local autonomy so that the center could dominate. The result was that the basis of society became separately consolidated monoethnic groups, not interethnic alliances. This presented a big danger once the Central Asian republics became independent nations, and the biggest danger of all was Tajikistan. Russia was now in essence beginning to try to put Humpty Dumpty back together again. It was not so much interested in a particular regime in Tajikistan as in the country's stability.[100]

Irina Zviagelskaya from the Oriental Institute illuminated several other facets of the story. The end of 1992 was a critical moment for Iran. It faced a choice, and even though it officially adopted a correct position, Iran continued to help the mujahideen in Tajikistan. It took until 1994 for things really to jell. In the transition period, Iran helped Russian policy aims but did not draw attention to its backstage cooperation. Opposition military pressure on Dushanbe was necessary. Without it, Dushanbe after its victory over the opposition would simply rest on its laurels. So, facing political pressure from Moscow, and opposition military action supported by Iran, Dushanbe did not have a choice. At the same time, Iran was also pushing the opposition to compromise.

In Zviagelskaya's view, Iran made a wise choice and made it within the context of Iran's search for a strategic partner in Russia. The United States was continuing to push Iran into a corner. The Iranians already saw what the United States had done to the Iraqis during the January–February 1991 Gulf War, after Iraq's invasion of Kuwait in August 1990. They regarded the Gulf War as an example of what the United States would like to do to them and concluded that the United States would never forgive their Islamist regime. As a result, the Iranians behaved themselves much better in Tajikistan than could have been expected because they felt they really needed Russia. All this, agreed Zviagelskaya, came before the rise of the Taliban in Afghanistan, which only further reinforced Iran's movement toward Moscow.

Parallel to all of this, explained Zviagelskaya, Tajik views of Iran had been changing. At first, Tajiks had looked at Iran with excited admiration. Tajiks and Iranians not only shared the same language and culture but believed Iran to be a rich country. But then, even Islamists who traveled to Iran were greatly disappointed by the reality they found. Iranians treated Tajiks snobbishly, like second-class people. To Tajiks, this treatment was insulting. Zviagelskaya had even heard from Tajiks who had visited the United States that the émigré Iranians they had met there had also treated them condescendingly. So, with the passage of time and greater exposure to each other, Tajiks unexpectedly discovered an Iran much different from their earlier assumptions.[101]

# 6

# Kilo Subs, Bushehr, and Shahab

Far from the turbulent events in Central and South Asia, but with an eye on them nevertheless, Moscow in 1989 began to develop a robust and potentially troubling arms trade partnership with Iran. With the USSR's collapse, sales from Russia to Iran soon expanded beyond state control to include illicit nuclear and missile technology transfers that increasingly worried Washington.

In the first decade after the Soviet collapse, international concern over Iran's acquisitions focused almost exclusively on their Russian origin. By 2004, however, it came to light that Pakistan had been vastly more important. In 1987, during the late stages of the Iran-Iraq War, Iran had made its first covert purchase—essentially, a rudimentary nuclear weapons starter kit—from a black-market suppliers group that included Pakistani nuclear scientist Abdul Qadeer Khan.

While diverting attention from Iran's Pakistani and other black and gray market connections, the spotlight on proliferation from Russia to Iran throughout the 1990s was nevertheless well-deserved. Soviet-era safeguards against the transfer of dual-use technology with proscribed military applications quickly frayed in the post-Soviet context of economic collapse and administrative chaos. Illicit weapons and know-how transfers from Russia to Iran became irresistible moneymakers for cash-starved factories, ministries, and research institutes.

These transfers were also expressions—often opportunistic, to be sure—of the impulse among some segments of the Russian political elite to assert an independent, anti-Western foreign policy. Nevertheless, at least a few influential Russians warned early on that in the hands of a regime such as that in Tehran, dual-use technology could be put to use in the creation of weapons of mass destruction (WMD) that could eventually threaten not just Iran's neighbors but even Russian territory.

To manage its contending American and Iranian ties, the Yeltsin government by 1993 developed essentially a two-track policy. Russia would continue doing what it regarded as legitimate and commercially defensible deals with Iran, but it would agree to discuss security issues of particular concern with Washington. This was done notably within the venue of what came to be known as the Gore-Chernomyrdin Commission, but the two sides also used several other high-level channels. The arrangement aimed to shield a growing political and economic relationship with Iran that leading lights around Yeltsin considered very much in Russian interests to pursue for a variety of reasons. It was designed to protect its domestic political flanks against accusations of catering to Washington and its foreign flanks against charges of irresponsibility toward nonproliferation obligations.

In part because of pressure from Washington, in part because of its own growing security concerns, Moscow also began in the last half of the 1990s to work out and put on the books its first export control decrees and legislation. These, however, were effective only to the extent that there was a will to enforce them and the resources to do so. Even then, a determined Iran could still find Russian institutions and individuals willing to take the risk of selling Iran forbidden know-how. Moreover, successive Russian administrations never gave nonproliferation efforts the priority they needed to shut down the troubling transfers completely.

There were ups and downs under Boris Yeltsin in dealing with Washington on nuclear and military sales to Iran. From 1992 to 1995, Moscow was not to be deterred from negotiations with Iran for a contract worth nearly $800 million for the construction of the Bushehr nuclear power station. The Russian leadership was convinced a Western power would build Bushehr if Russia did not. This predisposition was reinforced by the political backlash in Russia to Yeltsin's agreement, in July 1993, after more than a year of stonewalling, to abandon a Soviet-era contract to sell $140 million worth of missile parts, production equipment, and technology to India.[1] In its wake, Communists and other opponents of Yeltsin's "democrats" stood ready to add Bushehr to their long list of Yeltsin's perfidies should he also abandon the negotiations for the Bushehr contract. They would have painted any retreat on Bushehr as another glaring case of Yeltsin caving into Washington's demands and sacrificing Russian jobs and profits.

From 1995 to 1997, with the Bushehr deal signed, proliferation to Iran worsened even as the Yeltsin administration began to work with Washington to put in place some barriers to unauthorized exports. Intense political warfare, administrative chaos, and economic free-for-all had reigned in Russia since the Soviet collapse. Ministry of Atomic Energy (MinAtom) head Viktor Mikhaylov was able to take advantage of this environment, using the massive construction project at Bushehr as a cover under which to conduct a number of negotiations for related but dangerous technology sales to Iran. Mikhaylov reportedly did not bother to inform Yeltsin about some of the most egregious of these deals, such as for gas centrifuges that could be used to produce weapons-grade uranium.[2] The omission was all the easier given Yeltsin's heavier than usual drinking during this period and the parlous state of his health for long stretches of time.[3]

In March 1997, on the foundations of his electoral victory the previous summer and successful bypass surgery that winter, Yeltsin launched a new wave of reforms at home. They were the most significant since the privatization drive of 1992–93. Under the threat of U.S. congressional sanctions, the "young reformers" Yeltsin elevated during this period also began a sustained effort to work with the administration of President Bill Clinton to address American concerns over WMD proliferation to Iran. Their impulse was reinforced by the nuclear tests conducted by India and Pakistan in May 1998 and by ballistic missile tests conducted by Pakistan and Iran in April and July 1998, respectively. Besides simply bending to American pressure, Russian policy began to reflect a clearer appreciation of the potential implications for Russia's own security of its dual-use technology sales to Iran.

This intense phase of Russian-American cooperation on the nonproliferation front was short-lived, however. It was abruptly interrupted when the ruble collapse and currency devaluation of August 1998 forced Yeltsin to dump many of the young reformers. All the same, this period in retrospect saw a change of direction in Russian policy toward Iran that Vladimir Putin later reinforced when he succeeded Yeltsin at the end of 1999 and that Tehran clearly though mutedly came to regret.

## MONEY AND POLITICS

Post-Soviet Russia presented easy pickings for Iranian procurement agents. Defense-related Russian factories and research centers were in financial ruin and ready to work with any partner able to pay cash.[4] Given the severe economic disruptions of the 1990s, there were great incentives in Russia to turn a profit, however meager and however shortsighted for Russian security interests. Moreover, there was a widespread perception that Iran would buy the technology or know-how from someone else if Russians were not willing to deal.

Former Security Council staffer Vladimir Lebedev in an interview pointed out that the period from 1992 to 1995, immediately after the USSR's collapse, was the worst. Institutes fell into poverty, and their directors looked anywhere for saviors.[5] Moreover, as Sergo Mikoyan noted, arms sales to countries such as Iran were especially easy and undemanding for Russian factories. They required no technological or physical plant innovation, which was a good thing because there had been so little. The military-industrial complex's production lines had been in place for years. Their management and workforces were among the most resistant to adapting to post-Soviet economic conditions. Conversion to civilian production was minimal as they patiently made do and waited for better times, Mikoyan recalled.[6]

At its core, the Russian impulse to sell Iran conventional arms and to contract to build the Bushehr nuclear power plant was commercial. From Mikhail Gorbachev to

Vladimir Putin, all Kremlin administrations echoed the view of Gorbachev confidante and perestroika strategist Aleksandr Yakovlev: if Russia pulled out of the Iranian market, other powers would quickly step in and replace it. Russia's competitors would not restrain themselves.[7]

For Russia, the severe economic contraction that accelerated following the Soviet collapse magnified this basic commercial impulse. Russian arms factories were increasingly desperate to stay open and save jobs. Since NATO and other technologically advanced countries would not buy weapons from Russia, it had no alternative but to sell its arms to Iran and other similarly less demanding customers.[8] According to the analysis of foreign relations expert Nodari Simonia, during the Soviet era 80 percent of the military-industrial complex's production stayed at home, while 20 percent was exported. After the Soviet collapse, the reverse became the case: 80 percent was exported, and only 20 percent stayed at home.[9] As *The Economist* pithily put it, "Apart from raw materials, guns and vodka, Russia has few things worth exporting."[10] The bottom line was that Russia simply needed the money.

The problem was not just the giant MinAtom. There were also the occasional "bottom feeders," in the words of Carnegie Endowment nonproliferation expert Rose Gottemoeller, "small Russian industrial or research institutions that are desperate, or they wouldn't be trying to take extreme measures, such as false invoices . . . to mask their sales."[11] These sales, both legal and illicit, took place within a national security culture that had always placed much greater emphasis on intentions rather than capabilities in selling arms to neighbors who might conceivably use them to hurt Russia itself. With America having long targeted Russia with thousands of missile warheads, what were a few more far less capable weapons in the hands of Iran? It was easy to choose between a profitable contract up front and a highly improbable attack far in the future in the desperately lean years right after the Soviet collapse.

"Making a maximum profit in a minimum period of time without a proper understanding of consequences which may ensue from illegitimate commercial activity is typical of Russian exporters," wrote Lt. Gen. Gennady Yevstafyev in 1999 when Moscow's efforts to get a grip on the problem finally intensified. "This is *simply astounding*," he marveled. Even with the best of intentions, it was a tough mess to clean up. Any effort to bring it under control would need to target not just Iran but also North Korea and Pakistan. "The special services of *risk countries* are at the cutting edge of this work," explained Yevstafyev. "They have superbly developed methods of collecting that same classified technology and materials from secret (above all defense) sectors, which they then often share with each other: the Koreans advise the Pakistanis and the latter advise the Iranians."[12]

In addition, proliferators were able to cloak their pursuit of private or institutional profit under the mantle of the Russian state's geopolitical priorities, at least as argued by major establishment figures such as Yevgeny Primakov. These proliferators began their careers under Gorbachev, when little study may have been given to the ultimate security implications of some of the arms and technology transfers envisioned by the 1989 framework agreement Gorbachev signed with Rafsanjani. Proliferation became even easier under Yeltsin, especially during his first administration, as different state institutions, economic conglomerates, and regions in effect pursued their own foreign policies.[13] Even during Yeltsin's second administration, they appeared to be cheered on by key Communist and Liberal Democratic party leaders in the Duma, who in effect encouraged proliferators to deal with Iran as a way of demonstrating Russia's ability to stand up to the United States (see chapter 7).

Arms sales to Iran underscored the "independence" of Russian foreign policy in the face of American objections. In a sense, it was pure pandering to real or potential domestic political opponents. It was probably perceived as all the more necessary because the military-industrial complex was the sector of the economy hit hardest by the Soviet Union's collapse. As a result, those whose livelihoods depended most on this sector were particularly prone to despise and resent those they viewed as guilty of bringing the Soviet structure down. The military-industrial complex was home to powerful industrial leaders more than glad to work with opposition parties and leaders to subvert Yeltsin and his Western-leaning "democrats."

To make matters worse, the Russian security services that were supposed to be keeping watch over arms and technology transfers soon appeared to have turned the very trade they were supposed to be suppressing or at least controlling into their own cash cow. Federal Security Service (FSB) minders did not serve as effective deterrents to the illegal actions of corrupt proliferators from MinAtom and other entities. Both ended up having a mutual financial interest in working together to facilitate the transfer of forbidden items and technology. FSB officials often reportedly facilitated contacts between Iranian arms purchasers and Russian suppliers. They perverted their mandate to control proliferation by taking their own cut out of arms deals—an understandable temptation given their own low salaries.[14]

## EXPANSION OR REARMAMENT?

There were other incentives for arms and technology sales to Iran besides money, domestic politics, and East-West geopolitics. Once Iran by 1993–94 had clearly acknowledged Russia's primacy in Tajikistan, Russia began to see Iran as potentially helpful on new, post-Soviet regional issues. These included not only the peace process in Tajikistan, of increasing importance to the effort to contain the Taliban in Afghanistan (on which more in chapter 9) but also maintaining Russian influence in the Caucasus and limiting outside Islamic support to the independence movement in Chechnya. Bending over backward to accommodate Iranian desires for access to Russian weapons and technology must have been seen in Moscow as a necessary evil, albeit a profitable one, for keeping Iran working on the same page as Russia on critical regional issues.

In 1992 the Iranian Foreign Ministry and its embassy in Dushanbe could publicly adopt a stance of encouraging a coalition government in Tajikistan, perhaps knowing that others were busy under the table stoking what would soon turn into a full-blown civil war. But the extreme bitterness of the criticism aimed by Iranian radicals at the Foreign Ministry in Tehran suggested real differences over tactics, not just a hypocritical public relations line by the MFA. Besides protecting real and hoped for Iranian equities in Tajikistan, Azerbaijan, and Afghanistan, an important consideration for the pragmatic elements in the Iranian leadership must have been Russian help in Iranian rearmament and nuclear programs. The MFA in Tehran would have had grave concerns about an overly aggressive stance in Tajikistan upending the budding relationship with Moscow.

Moscow's policy was probably shaped by some of the same considerations. The Russian wait-and-see posture toward developments in Tajikistan was probably in part a result of its mixed feelings toward the remnants of the communist old guard and the rising strength of the Kulobis and to the battlefield standoff between Popular Front and opposition forces. While the conflict's outcome remained in doubt, Moscow's hesitation in 1992 over overtly backing the Kulobis may also have been influenced by a desire not to impede the expansion of the arms and nuclear technology supplier relationship with Iran.

Actually, even before the pot began to boil over in Tajikistan, the new post-Soviet Yeltsin regime appeared to have engaged in a quick review and reaffirmation of what had been Soviet policy toward Iran. This review appeared in great part to have been forced on Boris Yeltsin's Kremlin by George H. W. Bush's administration in Washington. Its concerns over Russian arms sales to Iran found expression in the American press and were then replayed in the Russian press. Russian skeptics and defenders alike were able to use the articles in the American press as a lead-in to their own concerns or justifications of these sales.

Their arguments were very much the same as those that Aleksandr Bovin, as already discussed, had used to question the wisdom of the Gorbachev-Rafsanjani agreements just several years earlier: Iranian politics were still subject to unpredictable swings between factions; however close it cooperated with Tehran, Moscow could not count on wielding any influence in the Iranian capital; Russia could therefore not be sure how the weapons it was supplying Iran would be used by Tehran; this was not an idle issue, since Iran shared CIS borders to the north, and the Persian Gulf and Middle East were already too well-known for their instability.

Nevertheless, even skeptics seemed to come out on the side of going ahead with the sales: the Russian economy needed the income; if Russia pulled back, other arms suppliers would simply jump in; besides, the only way to guarantee the security of the southern CIS border was a Russian policy of good-neighbor relations with Iran. So it was not surprising when the Yeltsin administration opted for continuity with the policy toward Iran developed under Gorbachev. The arguments in favor of continuity were familiar: Iranian intentions toward the CIS "space" were benign; Iran was behaving in Central Asia; and Russia needed the money.[15]

At the UN General Assembly in New York in September 1992, Foreign Minister Andrey Kozyrev reportedly vigorously defended the upcoming deliveries of Kilo-class submarines to Iran during his meeting with the American acting secretary of state Lawrence Eagleburger. Afterward, Kozyrev told the press that the deal "cannot destabilize the regional situation" and that Russia would "continue to export arms and military equipment in order to gain the necessary foreign exchange which is needed for the reconstruction of its economy."[16] When Kozyrev met with Iranian deputy foreign minister Mahmoud Vaezi in Moscow on October 14, Kozyrev's aide Galina Sidorova told the press that Russia would go ahead with arms exports to Iran. While Russia would not sell Iran weapons "capable of tipping the strategic balance of forces in the region," Russia's support for international sanctions against Libya (after its agents destroyed Pan Am flight 103 over Lockerbie, Scotland, in December 1988) and Iraq (after the 1991 Gulf War) had deprived it of significant revenues. Russia's Western partners needed to realize, stressed Sidorova, that "they will have to give room to Russian weapons makers who are in need of new export markets."[17] Delivery of the first of three contracted Kilo submarines went ahead that month.

## BUSHEHR: DELIBERATE DECOY?

After Yeltsin's October 1993 shelling of the old Supreme Soviet, his approval rating sank and by spring 1994 was down to 20 percent.[18] The new Duma elected in December 1993 was no more submissive than the old Supreme Soviet. The military-industrial complex still accounted for at least a third of GNP and a fifth of the work force. Military personnel and state enterprise workers voted heavily for Vladimir Zhirinovsky's LDPR, the election's most surprising winner.[19] Partly in response to these political challenges at home, as we have seen, Yeltsin and Kozyrev began enunciating a more flagrantly neo-imperialistic line on Russia's responsibilities for security in Tajikistan and the other Central Asian and Caucasus states.

On Iran, negotiations on a contract for a nuclear power station at Bushehr went forward despite American objections. Bushehr was a particularly useful political device to assert and make a show of standing up to the United States. The feeling in Moscow was that Russia would deal with Iran on its own terms no matter what America said and no matter how difficult it was to deal with the Iranians. With the contract on Bushehr, Yeltsin could score political points and earn significant money at the same time.

In the 1980s, however, under a veil of great secrecy, Iran had already embarked on a military nuclear program. As early as 1987, Iran had made its first purchase of nuclear enrichment components from a black-market group that included Abdul Qadeer Khan. A. Q. Khan, who would be widely regarded as the father of the Pakistani nuclear bomb when that country first tested it in 1998, in 1987 was beginning to expand from a purchaser of illicit materials for Pakistan's own nuclear program to a seller of parts and know-how to others for personal profit.[20] These first Iranian-Pakistani contacts thus occurred some five years before Iran had even initiated contract negotiations with Russia over Bushehr.

Iran's first covert dealings in 1987 with what would become the Khan network took place while the 1980–88 Iran-Iraq War was raging and were quite likely motivated by the frustrations Iran was suffering on both the battlefield and civilian fronts. The gruesome toll inflicted during that war by Iraq's chemical and other attacks on Iranian soldiers and civilians was especially horrendous and made even worse by Iran's own human-wave tactics. Psychologically, the Iraqi campaign against Iran peaked after late February 1988, when Iraq began a missile campaign against Tehran that lasted into April. Iraq launched over 150 SCUD-B missiles against Tehran, to which Iran was able to respond with only one-third as many against Baghdad. Given Iraq's chemical weapons attack on the Kurdish village of Halabja inside Iraq around the same time, Iraq's missiles aimed at Tehran were widely feared to be armed with chemical warheads. As many as a quarter or more of Tehran's population fled the capital in a panic. By that summer, after other major setbacks, Iran on July 18 accepted UN Security Council Resolution 598, which called for a cease-fire. On August 20, the cease-fire went into effect, finally bringing to an end the long war.[21]

Justifying the need for a cease-fire, Ayatollah Ruhollah Khomeini wrote a letter on July 16, 1988, that in turn cited a letter to him by Mohsen Rezai, commander in chief of the IRGC. Rezai, who within a year would accompany Majles Speaker Rafsanjani on a major visit to the Soviet Union, had written to Khomeini that Iran would need another five years to defeat the Iraqis but could do so only if Iran had 350 infantry brigades, 2,500 tanks, 600 fighter planes and helicopters, and "a considerable number of laser and nuclear weapons to confront the [Iraqi] attacks."[22]

On October 6, 1988, speaking to an IRGC audience not long after the conclusion of the Iran-Iraq War, Rafsanjani in effect seconded Rezai's comments as a guide to Iran's postwar rearmament efforts. Rafsanjani publicly urged, "[We] should fully equip ourselves both in the offensive and defensive use of chemical, bacteriological and radiological weapons."[23] Given the havoc that Iraq had caused with its repeated employment of chemical weapons during the war and its missile attacks on Tehran, Rafsanjani's call for a rearmament strategy that might give Iran the capability to deter any future such attacks had a certain military logic. Years later, it would be possible to read into Rafsanjani's 1988 statement an allusion—unappreciated at the time—to Iranian contacts already under way with the A. Q. Khan network and other nuclear black-marketers.

It also became clearer only years later that Iran and Iraq had begun a covert nuclear arms race at about the same time, perhaps unknown to each other but no doubt suspected by both. According to Mahdi Obeidi, who headed Iraq's uranium enrichment program until UN inspections shut it down in 1991, four years earlier—in

July 1987—a top deputy to Saddam Hussein had ordered a crash program to enrich uranium. Obeidi claimed that by January 1991 he had put together a prototype centrifuge system capable of producing weapons-grade fuel for a crude atomic bomb. Obeidi reportedly suspected it was for eventual use against Israel.[24] However, Charles A. Duelfer, who headed a U.S. investigation of Iraq's weapons programs after the toppling of the Hussein regime in 2003, reached a broader conclusion. According to Duelfer's report to the U.S. Congress, Hussein's nuclear, biological, and chemical weapons programs—all of which it subsequently turned out had "progressively decayed" after the Gulf War in 1991—were designed to enhance Iraq's image in the region and to deter Iran.[25]

In any event, when Rafsanjani traveled to the Soviet Union in 1989 with Rezai and others, the Majles speaker's assertion of the need for Iran to possess "chemical, bacteriological and radiological weapons" was conveniently disavowed in the agreements he signed with Gorbachev.[26] After the summit, however, the soon-to-be Iranian president and his party made a side trip to Leningrad. Rafsanjani may have wanted to visit the Baltic port city only to look over the offering of submarines available for purchase. But it was likely he also wanted to examine the city's facilities for manufacturing turbines for Iran's unfinished Bushehr nuclear power station. The Germans had started Bushehr in 1975 but abandoned the project in 1979. Tehran had been casting about for someone to complete the plant since 1984.[27] Minister for Atomic Energy Viktor Mikhaylov later dated the beginning of Moscow's role in Bushehr's rebirth to the 1989 long-term program, which contained a Section 16 on cooperation in the field of nuclear power and peaceful uses of atomic energy.[28]

By going down the nuclear path, the clerical regime in Tehran appeared intent on transforming Iran into a regional power at a less ruinous cost than the expense of a complete overhaul of its conventional arms. Iran's motives for setting out to acquire a nuclear weapons capability no doubt centered on the perceived need to deter Iraq, still vastly more powerful than Iran after the end of the Iran-Iraq War. Even after it was routed by U.S.-led coalition forces in the 1991 Gulf War, the military balance continued incontestably to favor Iraq over Iran across the full spectrum of weapons inventories.[29] Thereafter, UN inspectors largely succeeded in forcing Iraq to dismantle its nuclear, biological, and chemical WMD programs. Nevertheless, there would never be full confidence in this success, and not just in Tehran. Iranian leaders thus appear to have felt constrained to develop at least the option of a nuclear weapons capability to insure against any future resumption by Iraq of its WMD programs, including its military nuclear program.

Beyond Iraq, there was also Israel. In 1986 Mordechai Vanunu, an Israeli nuclear research center employee, had disclosed in London's *Sunday Times* the existence of an Israeli nuclear weapons program.[30] Besides Iraq and Israel, as underscored by outside analysts in the mid-1990s, Iran was surrounded by an expanding number of nuclear or threshold states, including India and Pakistan and Russia. There were also American

Navy nuclear-armed ships off Iran's shores. Analysts saw Iran as intent on acquiring the means to deter any American move against the Iranian regime or the country's vital interests.[31]

It is unknown to what extent Russia's intelligence services in the early years after the Soviet collapse were aware of Iran's clandestine dealings with Pakistani scientists active in the international nuclear black market. Russian official and unofficial sources mentioned the nuclear efforts and methods of Iran and Pakistan in the same sentence or paragraph from time to time, but more in the context of similar and parallel rather than intertwined and cooperative programs. If Russian authorities knew of Iran's covert ties to leading figures in Pakistan's nuclear sector, Moscow evidently chose to ignore or at least not publicize any evidence it had in hand.

A decade later, in late 2003 and early 2004, the IAEA pieced together how A. Q. Khan had begun in the 1980s to offer his expertise in the field of military nuclear technology to Iran, North Korea, and Libya. Reportedly using as cover a secret agreement concluded in 1986 between the Pakistani and Iranian governments for cooperation on nonmilitary nuclear programs, Khan had traveled to Iran in the late 1980s and early 1990s. In 1987, through a Dubai-based middleman, he had reportedly provided Iran with several used P-1 gas centrifuges, components, and designs and a shopping guide to black-market nuclear equipment vendors. By 1993 Iran had started a program to develop an indigenous self-sufficient capability to manufacture centrifuges for uranium enrichment on a large-scale basis. In 1994 Khan made his second sale to Iran: crate-fulls of P-1 centrifuge components and plans for a more advanced centrifuge, the P-2.[32] According to some reports, Khan continued to mentor the Iranian military nuclear program until 1996, when Iran's relations with Pakistan began to fray because of the latter's support for the Taliban takeover of Kabul. According to other accounts, Khan's cooperation with Iran continued even after that.[33]

Until 2002–2004, however, Iran managed to keep the scope of its nuclear program and the details of its nuclear cooperation with A. Q. Khan and his network largely secret. Iran's motive for contracting with Russia's MinAtom in 1995 to build Bushehr could not have been simply—if at all—to put in place an $800 million diversion of world attention from Iran's ties with Khan and other black-market suppliers. Nevertheless, the Bushehr contract and Iran's non-Bushehr contacts with Russian entities contributed to keeping Iran's dealings with Khan largely safe from view. The focus of international scrutiny and of American nonproliferation concerns in connection with Iran remained almost entirely focused on Iran's activities in Russia.

With the Iranian-Khan nuclear relationship hidden for the most part from the outside world, Foreign Minister Kozyrev in Dushanbe in early November 1992 asserted, "Russia has its geopolitical interests in Tajikistan and will be aiming not to allow extremist forces to further de-stabilize the situation in the former Soviet republic." But he also told the press that Moscow would "be struggling to find a seller's market for its military and . . . assets such as arms, uranium and space technology."[34]

At the end of March 1993, the globe-trotting minister visited Tehran. There, as we have seen, he initialed a draft treaty evidently intended to replace the outdated 1921 friendship treaty. While in Tehran, he also said that Russia was prepared to sell Iran nuclear power plants and cooperate in the nuclear field.[35] His delegation reportedly had reached an "accord" on nuclear power projects, in particular the sale to Iran of two 440-megawatt nuclear reactors, although this last deal would later be suspended.[36]

Kozyrev's announcement capped a year of intensive negotiations, during which Iran again tipped its nuclear ambitions and Moscow again largely ignored them. Deputy president Ataollah Mohajerani in October 1992 had stated, "Because the enemy [Israel] has nuclear facilities, the Muslim states too should be equipped with the same capacity."[37] As had been the case with Majles Speaker Rafsanjani's 1988 call for Iran to acquire "radiological" weapons, Mohajerani's statement was also subsequently repudiated.

In early 1992 an anonymous Russian "diplomat" disingenuously told an interviewer that there was no Russian-Iranian cooperation on nuclear technologies. "There is not even an agreement on the peaceful utilization of nuclear power between us and Iran," the "diplomat" categorically asserted.[38] Nevertheless, as MinAtom's Mikhaylov later told the story, pursuant to Section 16 of the 1989 program for long-term cooperation, Russia and Iran had been negotiating two intergovernmental agreements: the first on cooperation in the sphere of peaceful use of nuclear energy, the second on construction of an atomic power plant in Iran. They were both signed on August 25, 1992, and the Russian side designated the Ministry for Atomic Energy responsible for implementing both agreements.[39]

As he concluded his late March 1993 talks in Tehran, Kozyrev told the press, "Our friendly relations with the U.S. and Iran supplement rather than contradict each other."[40] Nevertheless, Russia's dealings with Iran quickly brought complications to its dealings with the new Clinton administration. At the April 3–4 summit in Vancouver, the first meeting between Presidents Yeltsin and Clinton, the two leaders declared a "strategic partnership." At the same time, the new U.S. team picked up the old Bush administration's policy, cautioning the Yeltsin leadership about Russia's dealings with Iran. By March 1993 the United States had declared a policy of "dual containment" aimed at both Iran and Iraq.[41]

To continue dealing with Iran while at least appearing willing to discuss American concerns, Moscow around this time settled on what amounted to a two-track policy. At Vancouver, Clinton and Yeltsin established an Intergovernmental Commission on Economic and Technological Cooperation. On March 23, just a few days before his arrival in Tehran, before winging his way back west to the Vancouver summit, the peripatetic Kozyrev had privately suggested in Washington the creation of the Gore-Chernomyrdin Commission, named after American vice president Albert Gore and Russian premier Viktor Chernomyrdin, who coheaded the commission during its first years.[42] Meeting roughly every six months, the commission quickly became an important venue for discussing American complaints about Russian proliferation of nuclear and weapons technology to Iran.

Over the years, Russia's two-track policy made neither Washington nor Tehran happy and led to pretensions by both toward Moscow. Washington from time to time could claim some credit for encouraging Moscow to police its trade with Tehran more carefully but was never fully satisfied that Russia was effectively cutting off proliferation of dangerous technologies and materials to Iran. Tehran continued to find its relationship with Moscow useful, though Iran eventually became increasingly disenchanted by Russian reluctance to sell it the most sophisticated high-end conventional weapons. In retrospect, however, it appeared that American suspicions and charges against Russia were useful to Iran in diverting attention from Iran's covert relationship on nuclear matters with Pakistan's A. Q. Khan.

In any event, at the U.S.-Russian summit in Moscow in January 1994, Kozyrev later claimed, the Russian side defended its decision to sell nuclear reactors to Iran and sought to allay U.S. objections by citing Iranian preparedness to submit its nuclear facilities to IAEA inspection.[43] Paralleling the intensification of efforts to start up peace talks on Tajikistan, Russia and Iran proceeded to negotiate a deal on installing two thousand-megawatt units (Bushehr 1 and 2) at the nuclear reactor complex at Bushehr on the Persian Gulf. After "preliminary agreements" with Tehran early in the year, Russian specialists followed up with "technical studies."[44]

In September 1994, coinciding with signature of the so-called Tehran Peace Agreement calling for a cease-fire in Tajikistan (on which more in chapter 9) experts from MinAtom's "Zarubezhatomenergstroy" arrived at Bushehr to inspect the site.[45] On the basis of this inspection, the two sides scaled back their plans from two to one unit at Bushehr.[46] The preliminary contract for $780 million, signed on January 8, 1995, called for getting one VVER-1000-megawatt unit (Bushehr 1) up and running in fifty-five months.[47] This contract became final in October 1995.[48]

## SVR SOFTENS ASSESSMENT

The two-track policy suited what Moscow calculated were its best interests—to maintain relations with both Washington and Tehran. At the same time, the policy was also two-faced in that it called for public dissembling and gilding of the lily regarding the lack of evidence pointing to an Iranian military nuclear program. Citing the failure of IAEA inspectors to find anything contravening the Nuclear Nonproliferation Treaty's (NPT) provisions at the Bushehr construction site would serve Russia conveniently for nearly a decade. Moscow evidently thought that on nuclear matters the two tracks would forever run parallel. But in 2003, IAEA inspectors found evidence of an advanced nuclear enrichment program in Iran. The two tracks began to collide, finally confronting Moscow with the need to view Iran's intentions and capabilities more realistically.

In 1995, though, as MinAtom closed in on the deal with Iran over Bushehr, there were those in Moscow eager to clear any potential bumps in the road to a contract signing ceremony. Russian SVR analyses in 1993 and 1995, made public over the signature of its then-director Yevgeny Primakov, both began with the assertion that Iran did not possess nuclear weapons. In retrospect, however, the 1993 report was fairly remarkable. After the initial denial that Iran had any nuclear weapons, it went on to state that Iran had a nuclear research program with military applications. The report even acknowledged that Iran had set up a system for circumventing Coordinating Committee for Multilateral Export Controls (COCOM) restrictions on acquiring dual-use technology abroad, and that the system was analogous to that employed by Iraq and Pakistan.

Nevertheless, the 1993 SVR report contended that, without unfettered foreign help and expenditures of $1–1.5 billion per year, it would take Iran at least ten years to create a nuclear weapon. Despite experts' worries over Iranian leadership declarations about making Iran a nuclear power and despite evidence of Iranian purchases of dual-use technology, the SVR analysis argued that there was no basis for speaking about the presence in Iran of an advanced military program in the field of nuclear weapons.[49] Thus, while the 1993 SVR report implicitly acknowledged statements such as those by Rafsanjani in 1988 and explicitly drew parallels between Iranian and Iraqi and Pakistani circumvention of COCOM restrictions, it did not suggest that Pakistani scientists and Iran were already working together in the nuclear field.

The 1995 report pulled back significantly from the 1993 assessment. By this time Moscow and Washington were engaged in an increasingly bitter debate over Russia's dealings with Iran in the nuclear field. Accordingly, the 1995 report minced words in stating, "Convincing signs of the existence in the country of a coordinated integrated military nuclear program have not been detected at this point." It asserted that construction in Iran of facilities to enrich uranium ore should not be expected before 2005. The assertions of certainty by official American representatives that Iran was putting together a military nuclear program and that Iran could have it in place by 2000 provoked "doubt," according to the 1995 SVR assessment.[50]

At his presentation of the second SVR report at a press conference on March 23, 1995, Primakov was quick to assert that Russia's provision of nuclear reactors to Iran could not help it create nuclear weapons.[51] Indeed, on the basis of SVR projections, Russians interested in doing business with Iran could have argued that the Iranians would never attain fruition in this field. The SVR assessment in 1995 asserted that without outside help, the Islamic Republic "would be unable to organize production of weapons-grade nuclear material." That flat-out statement of impossibility went beyond the 1993 report's conclusion that without such help "the appearance of nuclear weapons in the millennium is unlikely."[52]

Indeed, many Russian officials at the time, perhaps taking their cue from the SVR analysis, appeared to regard the potential threat to Russian interests of rearming Iran as either too far off to be real or altogether nonexistent given Iran's arguable inability to reach the intended goals. Sergey Tretyakov, for example, the Russian ambassador to Iran in 1995, while denying that Iran had nuclear aspirations, said that even if Iran wanted to it would take it fifty years to develop a nuclear bomb.[53]

The 1995 SVR report's projection was markedly more relaxed than the most frequent assessments in the West that Iran could accomplish the task in eight to ten years, a range extended by some at the time to seven to fifteen years. In fact, non-Russian experts agreed in pointing to significant barriers to Iranian success—as long as outside nations did not aid Iran. A survey by analyst Michael Eisenstadt concluded in the mid-1990s, for example, "Iran's generally unimpressive efforts in the field of ballistic missiles raises doubts about whether it has either the financial means or the managerial, scientific, and technical skills needed to develop nuclear weapons on its own."[54]

## ROGUE MINATOM

In the wake of the Russian-Iranian signing of the preliminary contract for Bushehr in January 1995, American frustration waxed as Clinton prepared for another summit with Yeltsin, this time in Moscow in May. The SVR assessment in March had estimated that it would be at least another decade before Iran would be able to put in place facilities to enrich uranium ore. Yet as Foreign Minister Kozyrev told the Duma in a closed-door hearing, MinAtom head Viktor Mikhaylov had concluded a secret deal with Iran to deliver a gas centrifuge, necessary to enrich uranium to weapons-grade level, without telling even Yeltsin.[55] In the lead-up to the summit, American interlocutors attempted to coax their Russian colleagues to rein in Mikhaylov. But, as Kozyrev at one point told U.S. Secretary of State Warren Christopher, Mikhaylov was "out of control."[56]

At the summit itself, Clinton led off with the Iran issue. American intelligence agencies had been tracking and assessing Pakistan's nuclear program since the 1970s, including A. Q. Khan's contributions to setting up a secret procurement network that he then began to draw upon a decade later as he expanded into a part-time purveyor of parts and plans to others, including Iran, for private gain.[57] Clinton had reportedly brought with him for Yeltsin a five-page intelligence briefing on Iran's nuclear weapons program and evidence of Pakistani, Chinese, and Russian assistance. Apparently prepared for this, Yeltsin cut the discussion short by quickly announcing that he had banned the centrifuge deal and imposed new controls on nuclear cooperation with Iran. Moreover, he agreed to Clinton's proposal that the Gore-Chernomyrdin Commission work out the details of a U.S.-Russian understanding that Russia would not transfer to Iran any nuclear technology with military applications.[58] Yeltsin's ban on the transfer of Russian centrifuges to Iran, which was enforced, and his other concessions in effect balanced the negative impact of the Bushehr contract as well as buffered it from American pressure.

After the summit, in a widely publicized article, Aleksey Yablokov, chairman of the Interdepartmental Commission for Ecological Safety of the Russian Security Council, took MinAtom's Mikhaylov to task for not coordinating the proposed sale of "military components" to Iran and for "confusing" MinAtom's own interests with Russian national interests. Quoting from the Russian-Iranian protocol of intent that Mikhaylov had signed in January with Reza Amrollahi, head of Iran's Atomic Energy Organization (IAEO), Yablokov drew attention to the joint commitment to "draw up and sign" within three months a contract for the delivery of two thousand tons of natural uranium from Russia to Iran and within six months contracts for the construction of a uranium storage facility and for the "construction of a centrifuge plant for uranium enrichment" in Iran. According to the Mikhaylov-Amrollahi protocol, MinAtom and IAEO had also agreed to cooperate in the construction of an unspecified number of "small-capacity (less than one megawatt) research reactors in Iran for training purposes."

In his article, Yablokov charged that neither Yeltsin nor Kozyrev had been consulted on these "crucial decisions in the sphere of the export of dual technologies."[59] Mikhaylov soon defended himself. Gilding the lily and ignoring the short—three and six months—deadlines called for in the January document, he described the provisions under attack as a "good carrot" and a "promise" by Russia to Iran "that if cooperation develops and nuclear power plants are built, we are prepared to examine on a broader scale all aspects related to fuel production for these power plants."[60] This last point would become an issue that would not be resolved in principle until 2002, when Iran finally agreed that all used nuclear fuel from Bushehr would be returned to Russia for reprocessing and safekeeping.[61]

Meanwhile, Russia—pursuing its now well-developed two-track policy—took other potentially useful steps on the nonproliferation front even as it began to implement the Bushehr contract with Iran. At a regular joint commission meeting on June 30, 1995, Vice President Gore and Prime Minister Chernomyrdin signed a memorandum in which Russia pledged not to ink any more arms deals with Iran and to discontinue implementing existing contracts for armaments and military hardware after the end of 1999.[62] In August 1995 Russia joined the Missile Technology Control Regime (MTCR), established in 1987 to restrain the transfer of equipment, materials, and technology contributing to the development of missiles with ranges over three hundred kilometers and payloads over five hundred kilograms.[63] In December 1995 Russia became one of twenty-eight charter members of the Wassenaar Arrangement, the successor to COCOM, aimed at curbing destabilizing transfers of conventional arms and dual-use goods and technologies.[64] In August 1996 Yeltsin signed a decree—on restricting the export of dual-use military items and technologies—intended to bring Russia in compliance with the Wassenaar agreements.[65]

## "PERSIAN THEMES"

Potentially, these measures could serve to stem the tide of proliferation of dangerous technologies and weapons to Iran, but only if they were stringently enforced. They were not, and Mikhaylov and others like him continued to pursue deals with Iran, albeit on a smaller scale. Moreover, the activities of none other than Foreign Minister Yevgeny Primakov served to undermine the intent of all these measures. In December 1996, with the Bushehr contract inked for over a year, Primakov traveled to Tehran to meet with Foreign Minister Ali Akbar Velayati, President Ali Akbar Hashemi Rafsanjani, and Majles Speaker Ali Akbar Nateq-Nuri. Primakov, in office since the beginning of the year, was an advocate of robust relations with Iran. Earlier visits to Tehran as head of the SVR—in July–August 1993 and February 1995—had persuaded him of the need for Russia to develop not just economic but also political relations with Iran.[66]

To the press, Primakov defended Russian involvement in plans to complete the Bushehr nuclear power station. During the visit, Deputy Foreign Ministers Viktor Posuvalyuk and Mohammad Javad Zarif initialed a memorandum on export control, which Primakov asserted would serve the "very noble cause" of "nonproliferation of weapons of mass destruction and corresponding technology throughout the whole world." Primakov and his counterpart issued joint statements on Tajikistan and Afghanistan. They praised each other's efforts to push for a negotiated settlement in Tajikistan—in fact, their meeting came on the same day Emomali Rahmonov and Sayed Abdullo Nuri were concluding a key round of the Tajik peace talks in Moscow. Finally, the two foreign ministers signed a memorandum of understanding on visa issues.[67]

A Moscow television commentary on Primakov's meetings in Tehran predicted that the United States would be shocked by the "Persian themes" in Russian foreign policy. Portraying Russia and Iran as "two old friends," correspondent Valeriy Skvortsov attributed the "new wave of affection" between them to the breaking off of relations with Iran by the United States after the Khomeini revolution. The establishment of a "powerful strategic alliance" with Russia was a "good New Year present" for Iran, whose leaders were seeking "supremacy" in the Near East. The memorandum of export control would help "dispel rumors about Iran manufacturing its own nuclear bomb." As did most observers at the time, Skvortsov said that there was a 100 percent probability that Speaker Nateq-Nuri would be elected president in the upcoming summer 1997 elections. Primakov's meeting with Nateq-Nuri in Tehran had ensured the "continuity" of Iran's "pro-Russia leanings," opined Skvortsov.[68] Iranian foreign minister Velayati characterized Russian-Iranian relations as the best in the "last two centuries."[69]

Nateq-Nuri was duly invited to visit Moscow. He did so beginning on April 11, 1997. It was the highest level Iranian sojourn to the Russian capital since that by Rafsanjani in 1989. By coincidence, the day before Nateq-Nuri arrived in Moscow, a court in Berlin delivered a guilty verdict in the infamous Mykonos case. In doing so, the court implicated Iran's top leadership in authorizing the September 1992 murders of four Kurdish rebel leaders in the Berlin café. In reaction to the court's action, the EU suspended its "critical dialogue" with Tehran. In stunning contrast, Moscow brushed the verdict aside. Prime Minister Chernomyrdin told Nateq-Nuri that the Mykonos case was Iran's own affair and should not stand in the way of joint investments in Iranian gas and oil fields.[70]

While in Moscow, Nateq-Nuri and Deputy Foreign Ministers Viktor Posuvalyuk and Mahmoud Vaezi signed the Intergovernmental Memorandum on Mutual Understanding on Exports Control that they had initialed in Tehran in December 1996.[70] Primakov on this occasion said it would "put an end to the conjectures that Russia maintained any relations with Iran that ran counter to international regulations."[72] However, in a major exposé of the Iranian missile program eighteen months after the signing of the memorandum, the journalist Konstantin Eggert dismissed the document as a "failed move . . . of public diplomacy, . . . an attempt to whitewash Iran," and reported that he was not able to pry a copy of it out of the MFA.[73]

## YOUNG REFORMERS SHIFT COURSE

The state of high grace between Russia and Iran, underscored by the treatment accorded Nateq-Nuri during his visit to Moscow in April 1997, was the product of the confluence of events, especially in Tajikistan and Afghanistan, and Primakov's strong encouragement, clearly reciprocated on the Iranian side. But it did not last long. To everyone's surprise, Mohammad Khatami and not Nateq-Nuri was elected president in May 1997 and soon launched a new effort to end Iran's international isolation. While Russia and Iran cooperated even more closely in arming the opposition to the Taliban in Afghanistan, Khatami's campaign to expand Tehran's external ties bore some fruit even with the United States.

At the same time, dramatic personnel changes in Moscow brought to the fore a wave of young reformers motivated to cooperate with Washington on the Iranian proliferation problem. Many would soon be removed in the wake of the ruble devaluation and economic crash of August 1998. Nevertheless, some of their successors became increasingly concerned about the long-term consequences of continued leakage of nuclear and missile technologies to Iran for Russia's own security and political interests in the Middle East. This became especially the case, as we shall see, after Iran in July 1998 first tested its Shahab-3 medium-range ballistic missile.

Yeltsin's own resounding and surprising reelection victory in June–July 1996 set the stage, but the introduction of a new push for major domestic reforms would be delayed until after Yeltsin's recovery from heart surgery that winter. Once out of the hospital, Yeltsin's recovered political standing and improved physical health allowed him to focus more consistently on the Iranian proliferation problem.

For the time being, however, Russian moves to tighten up export controls seemed to be stimulated more by the increasing threats from the U.S. Congress to impose significant sanctions, if the situation were not remedied, than by concern over the security threat to Russia posed by Iranian missile and nuclear programs. Nevertheless, already in December 1996, Defense Minister Igor Rodionov had included Iran among countries that represented an increasing military danger.[74] The Russian press immediately commented on the contradictions between Rodionov's warning and Foreign Minister Primakov's just-concluded visit to Tehran. There Primakov had declared, "Russia and Persia are neighbors and our relations are developing to mutual benefit, as well as, as we have now shown it once more, in the interests of stability in this region."[75] However, Rodionov's statement foreshadowed even stronger warnings in the Russian press about the Iranian military threat during Primakov's brief stint as prime minister in 1998–99.[76]

Almost immediately after his March 6, 1997, reformist "State of Russia" speech in the Kremlin, Yeltsin appointed Anatoly Chubays as first deputy premier to Viktor Chernomyrdin. At forty-two, Chubays had already served as Russia's "privatization tsar" under acting premier Yegor Gaidar in 1992 and then Premier Chernomyrdin until 1994; fought hyperinflation in an earlier stint as first deputy prime minister in 1994–95; and stage-managed Yeltsin's reelection battle in 1996. He was intensely hated by the antireformist, "popular-patriotic" opposition to Yeltsin and had been serving as head of the Presidential Administration, or as Yeltsin's chief of staff, since his reelection victory.[77]

A year later, in March 1998, Yeltsin appointed Sergey Kiriyenko, only thirty-five, to be Chernomyrdin's replacement as prime minister.[78] Vladimir Putin would soon serve as FSB director under Kiriyenko, and then in November 2005 as president, would put Kiriyenko in charge of RosAtom, successor to MinAtom, where Kiriyenko would preside over what appeared to be a deliberate stall by Russia on completing the Bushehr nuclear power station (see chapter 13).

Also noteworthy in March 1998 was the appointment of Andrey Kokoshin to be secretary of the Security Council. It would be an exaggeration to describe Kokoshin as the Yegor Gaidar or Anatoly Chubays of Russia's national security sector. Nevertheless, from 1992 to 1996 Kokoshin had been the first civilian to serve as a first deputy defense minister. He was then appointed secretary of Yeltsin's short-lived Defense Council, which was abolished when Kokoshin was promoted to the Security Council.[79] At fifty-two, Kokoshin was still young but all the same the oldest of those newly promoted by Yeltsin. He played an active role in elaborating and implementing new export controls designed to impede the unsanctioned flow of weapons and technology to Iran.

Within several months of his appointment as first deputy premier in March 1997, Chubays visited U.S. Deputy Secretary of State Strobe Talbott at his home in Washington. Since early that year, the Clinton administration had been confronting Russian counterparts, including Yeltsin at the Russian-American summit in Helsinki, with evidence that MinAtom and other Russian entities were supplying Iran with missile and nuclear technology. Talbott had sent a personal message to Chubays warning of the potential consequences at the upcoming summit of the Group of Seven (G-7) major industrialized democracies in Denver. Yeltsin would be attending the summit, thus marking another step toward the annual meeting's expansion to a G-8 affair including Russia. At Talbott's home, Chubays responded in person that the message had been understood. Chubays told Talbott that Yeltsin's assurances to Clinton in Helsinki—that the flow would cease—would be strictly enforced. But Chubays also confirmed that "hard-liners were exploiting resentment over NATO expansion in their advocacy of 'a strategic marriage of convenience with Iran.'"[80]

In Denver, indeed, Primakov told Secretary of State Madeleine Albright that he was sick and tired of American "pressure tactics" on Iran. He was blindsided the very next day, however, by Yeltsin's admission to Clinton that some Russian enterprises were in direct contact with Iran and were making agreements on their own about which his own watchdog commission had not provided him "with adequate information." Yeltsin proposed that both sides appoint special envoys to "get to the bottom" of the problem.[81] As a result, beginning in August 1997, Moscow worked with U.S. ambassadors Frank Wisner and then Robert Galluci to resolve some of Washington's specific concerns over the sales by a number of Russian entities of banned nuclear and missile technology to Iran.

Already on its own, and at first with no publicity, Moscow had begun what it would later claim was a clampdown on unsanctioned acquisition by Iranian agents of sensitive technology in Russia. Iranian efforts were reportedly focused on missile guidance system and liquid-fuel booster technology. As the journalists Aleksey Bausin and Erlan Zhurabayev publicized as early as May 1998, Iranian agents and their Russian contacts were resorting to false bills of sale, misleading end-user certification, chains of middlemen, phony proxy companies, and roundabout delivery routes to circumvent "tough export restrictions" in Russia and other countries. The main transgressor was the so-called Sanam Industrial Group, actually an Iranian defense industry department responsible for the country's missile program. Russian officials later asserted that everything was done quietly to prevent a negative impact on relations with Iran but that "the proper conclusions have been drawn."

According to Bausin and Zhurabayev, Russian moves against Iranian missile technology procurement efforts began in early 1997. At that time, the FSB had intervened to force the cancellation of a contract with the Kuznetsov research center in Samara for missile liquid-fuel booster components—concluded under the cover of an order for gas-distribution station equipment. In June 1997 the FSB reportedly expelled several Iranians—perhaps working for Sanam—who had attempted to obtain classified information on aviation equipment. In November, acting on what were said to be Yeltsin's personal orders, the FSB arrested Iranian Reza Teymuri at a subway station in Moscow as he met with an employee of the Mytishchi Machine Building Plant. Teymuri, who reportedly carried both a diplomatic passport and a student ID, allegedly intended to purchase design documentation for dual-use missile technology.

Also in 1997, according to Bausin and Zhurabayev, Iranian representatives attempted to sign a contract with the Central Aerodynamics Institute (TsAGI) in Zhukovskoye outside Moscow for construction of a special wind tunnel in which to test a missile model. The institute properly applied for official permission to conclude the contract, which the interagency commission on export controls then vetoed.[82]

Strong resistance to addressing the Iranian proliferation problem continued in Moscow, and it was not until early 1998 that there was any significant progress. Then, at the urging of the Clinton administration, which warned that congressional sanctions would follow if Russia failed to act, Chernomyrdin on January 22, 1998, signed a major "catchall" export control instruction, Directive No. 57, designed to close loopholes in Russian antiproliferation legislation.[83] Several months later, soon after appointing Kokoshin to the Security Council in March 1998, Yeltsin gave this body the lead in coordinating policy addressing the threat from the proliferation of dual-use technologies.[84]

On a phone call from Clinton that April, Yeltsin not only lauded Kiriyenko, his new premier, but also singled out Kokoshin for praise. Moscow and Washington soon opened a new high-level channel for work on the Iran problem—Kokoshin and Sandy Berger, Clinton's national security adviser—which, under the imminent threat of congressionally mandated sanctions, proved especially productive.[85] Kokoshin early on declared, "One of the main principles of the export of weapons should not be commercial interests, but the interests of our national security, our defense security."[86]

As the Kokoshin-Berger channel began to produce results, some Iranian press outlets began to complain, "Since last year, Russian policy has taken off on a new track; it does not appear to be shaped by the Russian Foreign Ministry."[87] The Iranian complaints suggested that Russia's more aggressive posture on nonproliferation could not be entirely dismissed as simply a public relations move. At the same time, there were Iranian hints that Tehran should abandon the NPT and the Chemical Weapons Convention (CWC). In April 1998 Seyyed Yahya Rahim-Safavi, who had replaced Mohsen Rezai as IRGC commander in chief the previous September,[88] reportedly asked, "Can we protect the Islamic Republic of Iran from the threats of America and Zionism by signing the convention banning the proliferation of chemical and nuclear weapons and international conventions?"[89] Rahim-Safavi was the head of the Iranian institution believed to be in charge of Iran's chemical, biological, and nuclear weapons programs and missile forces.

Washington meanwhile began imposing sanctions on Russian entities dealing with Iran. The State Department in mid-April had announced that it had compiled a list of Russian organizations suspected of supplying missile technology to Iran. These organizations, reportedly some twenty, would find it hard to receive any U.S. aid. They included the Central Aerodynamics State Institute (TsAGI), the Moscow Aviation Institute, and the Baltic State Technical University in St. Petersburg. One Russian newspaper reporting on the "blacklist" reached the director of TsAGI, who revealed that he had been warned about the development about two months earlier and was "taking certain steps to counter it."[90] Another paper reported that all three of these institutes had already been cut off from American funding.[91]

Years later, an "informed" source told the daily *Moskovskiy Komsomolets* that in 1998 the Presidential Administration had summoned the Iranian ambassador for a "heart to heart talk." There he was told to "stop the attempts to bribe our rectors into giving your students places to study what are for them banned subjects at our higher educational establishments." When the ambassador remonstrated, he was handed a long list of Iranians to send home.[92]

In the background, and bringing new though indirect urgency to the exchanges on Iran, India exploded several nuclear devices on May 11 and 13, 1998, and followed up with more later in the month. In response, the head of Pakistan's nuclear program, A. Q. Khan, announced that Pakistan was also ready to test, which it proceeded to do on May 28. Having just flown the Ghauri medium-range ballistic missile for the first time in April, Khan at the end of May announced that Pakistan had just tested nuclear warheads designed for the missile.[93]

In between, in what Deputy Secretary of State Talbott later described as Yeltsin's "most sober performance to date," he and Clinton participated in the first full-fledged meeting of the G-8 heads of state in Birmingham.[94] Yeltsin had arrived well prepared to defend Russia on its dealings with Iran but also ready to join Clinton in proposing inserting into the summit communiqué a call for the G-8 to strengthen controls over exports of missile and dual-use technologies.[95] After the summit, the FSB reportedly ordered MinAtom, the Russian Space Agency, and the economics, foreign trade, and science ministries not to permit export deals with several lists of foreign companies suspected of being involved in the development of WMD and delivery systems for them, singling out Iran's Sanam for special mention in FSB press releases.[96]

India and Pakistan's tit-for-tat series of nuclear tests in May 1998, following Pakistan's test of the Ghauri missile in April, reinforced Moscow's increasingly serious attitude toward Iranian efforts to acquire sensitive technologies. To the extent that Russia was by now better aware of help to Iran from elements in Pakistan, it was not surprising that some influential Russian policymakers started worrying that Iran might be able to follow Pakistan on nuclear matters much sooner than anyone had previously thought. While the nuclear genie was already out of the bottle for India and Pakistan, Russia's more critical attitude toward Iran suggested a desire at least to slow down its emergence into the nuclear club.

At the Russian Defense Ministry, a source told one Moscow daily that the Indian and Pakistani tests had created a "dangerous precedent" for Iran, South Africa, Israel, Brazil, and North Korea.[97] The SVR's spokesperson, Tatyana Samolis, likewise put Iran on the short list of "threshold countries" that could possess nuclear weapons "in the near future."[98] Even new MinAtom head Yevgeny Adamov, who had replaced

Mikhaylov in March, conceded in a remarkable radio interview, "I am sure that Iran is trying to develop nuclear weapons." Nonetheless, asserting that Russia had a greater security interest than did the United States in keeping Iran from actually getting its own nuclear arms, Adamov argued in favor of giving Iran nuclear technology "but in a way that would be least useful for weapons and most useful for the generation of energy."[99] And the official line from MinAtom spokesman Georgy Kaurov was that Iran "strictly complies with all requirements on nonproliferation of nuclear weapons."[100]

Despite signs of cross-cutting currents of opinion in Moscow, the Yeltsin administration continued to move forward in response to continuing American pressure, as well as to its newfound sense of Russia's own security priorities. As the journalist Konstantin Eggert recounted in his important chronology, Vice President Gore told the press at the end of July that Washington and Moscow had agreed to crack down on nine organizations suspected of illicit dealings with Iran. In early September, during what would be Kokoshin's last days with the Security Council, Yeltsin and Clinton at another summit in Moscow agreed to set up seven bilateral working groups to focus on dual-technology nonproliferation issues.[101]

## SHAHAB-3: WAKE-UP CALL

By 1998, on top of long-standing concern over the leakage of nuclear technology from Russia to Iran, the aggressive pursuit by Iranian agents of missile-related technology was provoking increasing worry in Washington and even Moscow. This concern spiked after Iran first tested in July 1998 what it called the Shahab-3 ballistic missile, adapted from the North Korean Nodong-1. According to Konstantin Eggert's detailed account, Iran had been interested in the Nodong-1 missile program since its inception in 1989. Not long after the first successful North Korean test flight, Iran had signed a contract for 145 of the missiles in 1993 and began taking delivery of the missiles and critical production components from North Korea around 1995. At the same time, Iran decided to diversify its sources of technology and expertise to further modify the Shahab-3 and develop follow-on longer-range versions, and for this it turned primarily to Russia.[102]

All the contacts Iran had been able to make in Russia's military-industrial sector as a result of the 1989–91 arms contracts and subsequent negotiations with MinAtom on building the Bushehr nuclear power plant gave Tehran a jumpstart in its shopping expeditions for missile technology. Iran's focus on Russia for this technology was rightly placed, since Pakistan—to whom Iran had turned in 1987 for help on nuclear technology—was as much a novice in the missile field as was Iran. A. Q. Khan also figured prominently in what was described as a barter arrangement with North Korea beginning in December 1994. Under its terms, Pakistan supplied North Korea with uranium enrichment technology and North Korea in return gave Pakistan the Nodong missile, which Pakistan renamed the Ghauri and first tested in April 1998.[103]

On July 22, 1998, Iran for the first time tested its 1,000–1,300 kilometer-range Shahab-3 surface-to-surface ballistic missile, and on September 23 displayed it for the first time in a military parade in Tehran. Although still obscured by American and other foreign accusations of Russian complicity and indifference, Iran's increasing military potential began to provoke some misgivings among thoughtful analysts and politicians in Moscow. Well before the first test in July 1998, a note of caution could be found in commentary by some national security experts. In early 1997, for example, A. Gusher (head of the Center for Strategic Development) and A. Slavokhotov (an expert at the center) had written, "Special attention is merited by the efforts of a whole list of governments (Israel, Iran, Pakistan, Saudi Arabia, India) to equip their armed forces with missile weapons of various types, as well as to create their own nuclear warheads and the means of their delivery (Israel, Pakistan, India, eventually [v perspektive] Iran)." The analysts warned, "None of these processes should fall outside the zone of view of the Russian leadership and they should all find an adequate reflection in activities to protect the security of Russia in the south."[104]

In spring 1998 FSB officer Mikhail Kirillin told the journal *Yadernyy Kontrol* that it would be "naive" to think that Russia's export control efforts were "some kind of double-dealing on our part. Let us put it frankly: Russia is considerably more interested than the United States in seeing that states with a developed long-range missile potential never, under no circumstances, appear in the immediate proximity of its— the Russian—southern borders." The Russian security services, according to Kirillin, were determined to foil Iranian attempts "to obtain access to defense information in circumvention of existing rules, above all to technologies for manufacturing so-called dual-use articles."[105]

This wariness toward Iranian intentions and concern over the implications for Russia's own security increased after the first test of the Shahab-3 and subsequent publicity about Iranian plans to move on to development of the Shahab-4 and Shahab-5, with ranges up to ten thousand kilometers.[106] Nevertheless, it was an unusually confusing period in Moscow politics. Kokoshin was out, Primakov was up, and the latter continued to make clear his lack of enthusiasm for tight restrictions on technology transfers to Iran and his support for robust relations. Washington on balance judged Russian actions in connection with Iran as "recidivism" and "severe backsliding."[107]

Movement continued on Russia's nonproliferation policy, but in different directions on different levels. The economic collapse of August made it more difficult to argue against doing business with Iran. Yeltsin quickly cast aside most of his high-profile young reformers, and elevated Primakov to the premiership in September 1998. Some of the steam seemed to go out of what little public critical questioning— originating especially from Kokoshin and the Security Council—there had been of close relations with Iran. Of that which continued, it seemed attributable in part to old momentum, in part to new worries sparked by Iran's first test firing of the Shahab-3 missile, in part to continuing intense behind-the-scenes partisan warfare. Overall, however, the Shahab-3 test meant that those advocating tighter export controls could now point to a rising security threat from Iran—and not just the threat of sanctions from Washington—as a compelling reason to impose more stringent controls on technology proliferation to Iran.

Several years later, in a memoir covering his short tenure as prime minister—it lasted only until May 1999—Primakov described his attitude toward Russia's relations with Iran. Russia would abide by all international nonproliferation regulations but was not about to let the United States impose its own "rules of the game."[108] Some of the continuing though infrequent critiques of lax dealings with Iran seemed clearly intended to undermine Primakov's well-known proclivities in this area. The month after Primakov's promotion to prime minister, to cite the most remarkable example, *Izvestiya* published Konstantin Eggert's lengthy, critical account of the Iranian missile program.

In back-to-back articles, Eggert laid out in great detail the American complaints of Russian complicity. Without any reservations, and similar to what fellow journalists Bausin and Zhurabayev had openly charged in May, Eggert described a program in which "the Iranians resort to every trick in the book: they provide false or incomplete description of the goods, name a fictitious end user, and use dummy firms and circuitous delivery routes via third countries." Eggert's two-part series was decidedly positive toward Chernomyrdin and Kokoshin and negative toward now-former FSB chief Nikolay Kovalev and Primakov. Without any attempt to defend Primakov, Eggert reported Israeli complaints to him that Primakov, after a briefing no later than January 1997 on Iranian activity in Russia, had in effect told his own experts in the Foreign Ministry, "Do not hinder them!" In Israel in October 1997, Primakov had dismissed a military intelligence briefing on the same subject as "Rubbish!"

On the national security front, Eggert concluded, "After the July 1998 [Shahab] tests, it can be said with certainty: This part of the globe will never be the same again." His impression was that "the winds blowing in Moscow's corridors of power are somewhat different" than before the Indian and Pakistani nuclear tests in May and the Iranian Shahab test that summer. In contacts with the Russian press, staffers on the Security Council—even after Kokoshin's departure—explained "quite clearly their vision of Russian-Iranian relations: It is necessary to develop political and economic relations with Tehran. But it is impermissible to supply the Iranians with technologies for mass destruction weapons and delivery vehicles for them, since this runs contrary to Russia's national interests."[109]

Nearly two years after the first Shahab test, former Security Council official Vladimir Lebedev asserted that of course Russian officials had complained directly to Iranian counterparts that the Shahab-3 posed a security threat to Russia. They are our neighbors, Lebedev explained. We understand that they are dangerous neighbors, and we understand this better than the United States does. In fact, Lebedev claimed, the last three heads of the Security Council—Andrey Kokoshin, Nikolai Bordyuzha, and Sergei Ivanov—had all warned Iran about the Shahab-3. But while the Iranians reportedly had reacted with feigned understanding, Lebedev noted that they continued to steal Russian know-how and materials, and Moscow, he claimed, continued to catch and punish them.[110]

Nodari Simonia complained similarly around the same time about the Iranian approach. Despite incantations of a desire for cooperation and friendship, in reality the Iranians were just after Russia's armaments and military technology. The Iranians had proved to be just like the Chinese, concluded Simonia: they both declared their friendship for Russia while they stole military technology and goods right out of Russia's factories.[111]

To maintain good relations, Russia continued to be generally upbeat in its public comments on Iran and pulled its punches in discussing unsanctioned weapons and technology proliferation. Nevertheless, Russia's actions would be more restrictive and nuanced than its rhetoric. Appointments such as Kokoshin's and articles such as Eggert's increasingly appeared to have marked a turning point in Russian policy. A more cautious course had been set and would by and large be maintained well into the future by Boris Yeltsin's successor Vladimir Putin.

# 7

# *The Putin Factor*

Vladimir Putin was only forty-seven years old when Boris Yeltsin appointed him acting president on New Year's Eve 1999.[1] He was still that relatively young age when elected president in his own right in March 2000. Putin differed significantly from both Yeltsin and the orientalist Yevgeny Primakov. The new president was a KGB veteran with almost five years' experience in East Germany and none in the Middle East—where Primakov had cut his professional teeth.[2] He was by all accounts very disciplined, and his judgment and follow-through—whatever else one might say of them—were not impaired by acute alcoholism, bad health, or old age.

Putin did not arrive in Moscow from St. Petersburg in 1996 with the reputation of a flaming reformer, but his early Kremlin assignments gave him a chance to find out where all the political system's dirty laundry was stashed. With time, this insider's knowledge made him uniquely qualified to have an impact on Russian nonproliferation policy and its implementation. Nevertheless, Putin held fast on Bushehr and early in his presidency abrogated the 1995 Gore-Chernomyrdin understanding on phasing out arms sales to Iran after the end of 1999, thus playing to the anti-Western galleries in Russia. But he also began to take a more judicious approach to new arms and technology contracts with Tehran and to tighten up on nonproliferation policy enforcement.

In retrospect, as we have seen, Russian-Iranian relations began to turn in 1998, just two years after Putin's transfer to the Russian capital. Ties had reached their apogee under Primakov's tutelage in 1996–97. There had then been a messy period of churning gears in 1997–98 as Yeltsin tried to advance reforms at home and reacted to disturbing events abroad. Whether intended by Yeltsin or not, some of the key individuals he promoted at that time—cohorts of Putin—had views on Iran that differed markedly from those of Primakov. Contacts were still robust, but cracks soon began to appear in Moscow's relations with Tehran.

July 1998 was a signal month in the evolution toward a more jaundiced Russian approach to Tehran. It was then that Iran first tested the Shahab-3 missile. It was then also that Washington laid down the first set of sanctions against seven Russian entities for providing missile technology to Iran. These developments, coming on the heels of the series of nuclear tests conducted by India and Pakistan in May 1998, began to provoke a serious debate in Moscow over the security implications of Russian arms and technology transfers to Iran. Coincidentally, it was also in that month, as we shall see in chapter 8, that Yeltsin broke sharply with Iran on policy toward delimiting the Caspian Sea.

Furthermore, in July 1998 Yeltsin put Vladimir Putin in charge of the FSB with what appeared to be a mandate to rein in that agency's reported collusion in the illicit transfer of dual-use technology and parts to Iran. There was indeed a noticeable shift in the enforcement of nonproliferation strictures by mid-1998. However, several of Moscow's first widely publicized enforcement actions, dating from the previous year, had the appearance of pure political contrivance, and Washington regarded them with extreme skepticism. Nevertheless, as time passed, and still leaving much room for improvement and circumvention, the actions did not appear to be totally theater of the absurd.

Putin, however, was on a fast track, and whatever his views on Iranian nonproliferation, they were subordinated to his wider political ambitions. He quickly moved on from the FSB to the Security Council to the premiership to acting president to elected president by March 2000. Putin appeared early in his presidency to be a big booster of MinAtom, Russia's main contractor on the Bushehr nuclear power station in Iran, and a promoter of renewed arms sales to Iran. Consistent with this profile, he set the stage for a summit with President Mohammad Khatami in Moscow in March 2001.

Shortly after that summit, however, Putin trimmed the sails of MinAtom's headstrong boss Yevgeny Adamov and replaced him with team player Aleksandr Rumyantsev. At the time, Adamov's firing appeared simply to be a move against a corrupt official whose dealings, only coincidentally with Iran, had gone over the line. However, and much clearer in retrospect, Adamov's corruption was just a convenient pretext for his ouster. More fundamentally, removing Adamov was Putin's first move to discipline headstrong, overly independent "capitalist ministers" inside the Russian state's own structures. Adamov's corruption was almost beside the point. After all, few Russian officials weren't corrupt to some degree.

Before long, Putin's discipline campaign extended beyond state institutions and government officials to encompass a variety of political and economic actors who had grown accustomed under Yeltsin to playing independently of Kremlin guidance or even to setting policy for the Russian state, or whom Putin may have perceived as potential rivals. Among Putin's early victims were First Deputy Prime Minister and then Railways

Minister Nikolay Aksenenko and Central Bank head Viktor Gerashchenko.[3] The string would also include media oligarchs Boris Berezovsky and Vladimir Gusinsky, Maritime Region governor Yevgeny Nazdratenko, and Gazprom CEO Rem Vyakhirev. Just two years later, with the arrest of Yukos oil company head Mikhail Khodorkovsky, Putin succeeded in intimidating and asserting vastly greater state control than had Yeltsin over freewheeling bureaucrats, regional governors, the Duma, the Federation Council, and private sector oligarchs alike. With these actions, he put in place the twin pillars of the Putin regime: the so-called vertical of power and managed democracy.[4]

His move in 2001 against Adamov had important implications on policy toward Iran, though they were obscured by the smoke and mirrors of Putin's early anticorruption posturing. With the passage of time, it would become clearer that Putin was beginning to put Moscow's relations with Tehran on a new footing, not just ousting a corrupt and overly independent head of MinAtom. In fact, he was advancing the new direction toward Iran that he personally had helped set in motion as far back as 1998, while head of the FSB.

Understandably, Washington greeted the Putin administration with the distrust born of repeated disappointments over Russia's dealings with Iran during the Yeltsin years. Nevertheless, some Moscow insiders early on argued that, if the Kremlin really wanted to crack down on illicit proliferation to Iran, then it finally had a chance to do so with Putin in charge. Indeed, before long, there was what appeared to be a debate in the Russian press over the wisdom of selling Iran advanced conventional weapons systems—despite the overturning of the Gore-Chernomyrdin understanding.

## FIRST ASSIGNMENTS AND TIES

Putin arrived in Moscow in August 1996 when he was appointed deputy to Pavel Borodin, head of the General Affairs Department—i.e., the Kremlin's business manager—and put in charge of the department's legal division and Russian overseas property. Putin was part of the wave of St. Petersburgers who transferred to the capital after Yeltsin's stunning 54 to 40 percent reelection victory over the CPRF's Gennadi Zyuganov on July 3. The future president had worked in St. Petersburg for reformist mayor Anatoly Sobchak but did not appear to have any special ties to Anatoly Chubays, the leading representative of a previous wave of St. Petersburgers who had moved to Moscow to work for Yeltsin.[5]

In March 1997 Putin was appointed deputy head of the Presidential Administration (PA) and head of its Main Monitoring Directorate. Some described this directorate as "one of the most influential departments of the Presidential Administration."[6] The position gave Putin a mandate to look into "what is happening in practically every area of government life" to ensure the implementation of President Yeltsin's decrees and instructions.[7]

Two months after taking over the directorate, Putin told reporter Yelena Tregubova on the record that Yeltsin had given him a mandate to fight corruption, especially in the Defense Ministry. He hinted that Yeltsin had fired Defense Minister Igor Rodionov—whom he replaced with Gen. Igor Sergeyev on May 23[8]—after an investigation by the Main Monitoring Directorate of state defense procurements. Off the record, Putin took aim at Governor Yevgeny Nazdratenko, who had been sponsoring rallies in his Maritime Region in the Far East calling for Yeltsin's ouster. Putin bluntly threatened to jail Nazdratenko for corruption.[9] At the end of his first year on the job, Putin told a press conference that his directorate had opened fifty criminal cases, instituted criminal proceedings against twenty people, and uncovered the "misappropriation" of some 8 trillion rubles of treasury funds.[10]

In May 1998, while holding on to the Main Monitoring Directorate, Putin was bumped up to first deputy head of the PA with responsibility for resubordinating Russia's regions to Kremlin control.[11] Of the two positions, Putin was to say later, he found the second one—where he was to start restoring the "vertical" structure of executive command—"the most interesting job." If he had not been offered it, he told his biographers, and had been stuck with only the Main Monitoring Directorate to run, he would probably have left state service and opened up a private law firm, as had many of his friends.[12]

The two hats gave Putin a great deal of authority, which he proceeded to exercise with notable self-confidence in backstage Kremlin maneuvers. They also gave him a great deal of experience in using the corruption issue as a cudgel in top-level political battles. The campaign against Nazdratenko was instructive. Putin turned the corruption investigation against the Maritime Region governor on and off without hesitation or sentimentality, adjusting it to the political exigencies of Putin's Kremlin superiors. Then, when Nazdratenko finally resigned in February 2001, now president Putin gave him the graft-rich job of head of the State Fisheries Committee and then later deputy head of the Security Council. Moreover, Putin did not stop Nazdratenko from maneuvering his protégé Sergey Darkin, who had an equally unsavory criminal reputation, into his replacement as governor. Thus, it appeared that corruption for Putin was not an evil to be fought against on all fronts but simply a useful tool to use selectively as needed in political battles.[13]

Putin's next promotion, in July 1998, was to the directorship of the FSB.[14] It was here that he began to have an impact on nonproliferation policy. In this connection, however, Primakov's memoir is fascinating. Writing of his short tenure as prime minister from September 1998 to May 1999, Primakov never linked his recollections of the Iran proliferation issue to Putin's stewardship of the FSB. Nevertheless, Primakov indirectly revealed much about what Putin was up against—including Primakov's own foot-dragging—when it came to grappling with the problem of proliferation to Iran.

Primakov only grudgingly admitted that "there wasn't smoke without fire." The Russian government could not forbid specialists to travel, he wrote disingenuously. If it had, Western "democrats" would have been the first to protest. So, it had been possible for "individual" scientists and specialists to go to Iran for "consultations," and there had been individual efforts to pass on to Iranians "classified information in the field of weaponry." But the FSB had assured him, Primakov claimed, that "not one person, directly participating on the least bit significant level in the production of weapons of mass destruction and the means for their delivery, had left the territory of Russia" in recent years.[15]

Evidence from a variety of observers did not support these assertions, imputed to the FSB by Primakov. The FSB may have placed barriers in the way of travel to Iran by some specialists but appeared to have actively facilitated the travel of others. Of course, Primakov may have been applying the narrowest of lawyerly interpretations to the population of Russian citizens "directly participating on the least bit significant level in the production of weapons of mass destruction and the means for their delivery." But that still left many Russian weapons experts and military-industrial complex managers with knowledge and wares of great interest to Tehran who were apparently free to travel to Iran and make deals.

In any event, when introducing Putin to his new subordinates in the FSB in July 1998, Premier Sergey Kiriyenko stated that Putin's work in the PA had "enabled him to get knowledge and experience in combating economic crimes."[16] One of Putin's first assignments reportedly was to ferret out corruption in the FSB itself.[17] FSB officials at the time allegedly "routinely took commissions from Iranian procurement agents in return for facilitating the travel arrangements of Russian experts."[18] From 1996 to 1998, for example, Moscow Aviation Institute missile engine expert Vadim Vorobei encountered few problems in traveling to Iran. In fact, Vorobei claimed the Russian Foreign Ministry and FSB took care of the official paperwork for his passport. This changed in 1998, however, after news in April of the U.S. State Department's "black list" of twenty Russian entities dealing with Iran. Russian security services then began to complain about Vorobei's activities to the director of his institute.[19]

While the shift predated his assumption of the leadership of the FSB, Putin seems to have been put in charge of the agency shortly thereafter because he was seen as someone more dedicated to doing the job right than his predecessor, Nikolay Kovalev. Kovalev had orchestrated the cover-up used to rebut American complaints about an attempted shipment of special steel alloys, suitable for missile fuel tanks, through Azerbaijan to Iran in April 1998. The FSB investigation reportedly concluded that the stainless steel sheets at issue in this case had widespread household uses but not military dual-use applications and therefore did not require a special export license.[20] Washington was not convinced and regarded the special steel alloy as suitable for missile fuel tanks and "little else . . . a flagrant violation of Russia's catchall decree."[21]

Toward the end of his tenure at the FSB, Kovalev tried to get out in front publicly on the nonproliferation issue, but it was apparently too late and in certain respects clearly disingenuous. While announcing unsanctioned activity at the Moscow Aviation Institute, for example, thereby confirming Vorobei's account of pressure on him around this time to ease off on his contacts with Iran, Kovalev only implicated three

*[margin handwritten notes: Why was he in Israel? Trying to save his career? ]*

Tajiks and an Iranian in the case involving steel alloys intercepted at the Azeri-Iranian border.[22] Just before being fired, Kovalev released a statement at the end of a visit to Israel. It enumerated several instances during the previous year in which the FSB had thwarted attempts to export illicit materials and know-how to foreign firms or governments, specifically mentioning Iran.[23] Kovalev perhaps chose the Israeli venue because that country's special concern about Iranian weapons programs meant that his announcement might generate more political resonance from there.

Already in January 1998, as we have seen, Prime Minister Viktor Chernomyrdin had signed Directive No. 57, a major "catchall" export control instruction. After appointing Andrey Kokoshin head of the Security Council in March, Yeltsin had given that body the lead in coordinating nonproliferation issues. By May 29, Kokoshin had established an interdepartmental working commission. By July 30, the Yeltsin administration had submitted a draft Federal Export Law to the Duma, which voted overwhelmingly for it in the first reading on December 18, 1998.[24] The bill went to second reading in May 1999 and was passed in the third reading on June 22, 1999, after which the Federation Council approved it on July 2.[25]

Although Kokoshin as secretary of the Security Council started the ball rolling in spring 1998, Putin was instrumental—according to several accounts—in driving the Federal Export Law home to adoption. Former Security Council staffer Vladimir Lebedev later argued that Putin, while FSB head from July 1998 to August 1999, was the architect of Russian nonproliferation policy.[26] Similarly, a Russian press story later attributed to Putin "the elaboration and practical imposition of export control in Russia three years ago."[27]

Underscoring his own policy lineage, Putin himself—after becoming secretary of the Security Council in March 1999 while still remaining FSB head—began his first conversation with Sandy Berger, his American counterpart in the White House's National Security Council, by conveying Kokoshin's personal greetings. It was with Kokoshin, of course, that Berger just a year earlier had felt he was finally making real progress in getting Moscow to seriously address Washington's proliferation concerns. Putin reaffirmed Russia's nonproliferation commitments to Washington for Berger and reviewed Russia's initiatives to tighten export controls.[28]

However, Putin did not stay long as Security Council secretary. Yeltsin appointed him premier in August 1999, and on December 31, 1999, designated him acting president. Just a few months later, on March 26, 2000, Putin won the elections and became president in his own right.

## FOG OF POLITICS AND POLICY

Foreign policy atmospherics in Moscow throughout this period were contradictory and acrimonious, roiled in particular by differences with Washington and European capitals over developments in the Balkans. On March 23, 1999, on the way to Washington for important economic and security talks, Prime Minister Primakov ostentatiously turned his plane around over the Atlantic and returned to Moscow. The move dramatized Moscow's objections to the imminent start of NATO air strikes against Serbia after Yugoslav president Slobodan Milosevic refused to halt the brutal campaign against ethnic Albanian separatists in the province of Kosovo. NATO launched the military action without authorization by the UN Security Council, where Russia and China had made clear they would veto any draft resolution sanctioning air strikes. Ambassador Sergei Lavrov, Russia's permanent representative to the UN, called in the Security Council for the "immediate cessation of this unacceptable aggression" but to little avail.[29] President Yeltsin then issued a statement suspending Russian participation in NATO's Partnership for Peace program and the Russian-NATO Permanent Joint Council, which Russia had joined in May 1995 and May 1997, respectively.[30]

There was subsequently lingering resentment over NATO's bombing of Serbia and continued resistance to NATO expansion. Nevertheless, relations with Europe and the United States were still Russia's highest priority and a restraining factor on the development of Russian-Iranian relations, in the view of Yevgeny Bazhanov of the Diplomatic Academy. Bazhanov asserted in December 1999 that Russia would never work together with Iran on an anti-Western or anti-U.S. platform. Nevertheless, he pointed out, there were politicians in Russia who were convinced the West wanted to dominate and diminish Russia and therefore believed that Russia should maintain an informal alliance with Iran.[31]

Certainly, not many Russians at the time seemed concerned that Iran could point its weapons north. Most experts in Russia and the West viewed Iran's military programs as focused primarily on developing assured deterrence against traditional enemies in the region, primarily Iraq. However, it did not take a Russian rocket scientist to perceive the potential threat to Russia itself of the transfer to Iran of military know-how and hardware. The Su-24s that Iran had bought from the USSR under the contract signed in November 1989 put the entire northern Caucasus region of Russia within reach of the Iranian air force, as well as the entire Caspian and half of the Black Sea. The range of the Shahab-3/Nodong 1 missiles that Iran had acquired from North Korea potentially encompassed the entire Caspian Sea littoral, most of the Black Sea, including Russian fleet facilities at Sevastopol, and extended well into Russia's Northern Caucasus zone. Sometime in the future, Iran could target all of Russia's pipeline infrastructure in and around the Caspian and in the North Caucasus across to the Black Sea, including the Caspian Pipeline Consortium (CPC) pipeline from Kazakhstan to Novorossiysk, as well as the natural gas Blue Stream pipeline under construction across the Black Sea from Russia to Turkey. And the longer range Shahab-4 and 5 would simply raise the ante.[32]

To the extent that Iran's motivations for rearming focused on deterring Iraq and improving Iran's military standing and influence in the region, miscalculations could again easily lead to war. The damage to Iraq's oil industry that would ensue would undercut Russia's own hopes of recouping massive debts owed it by the Saddam

Hussein regime. Even if Armageddon never occurred, Russia's assistance to Iran would continue to be a troublesome issue in Moscow's ties with the United States. A stronger Iran would pose a greater threat to American allies in the region and the interests, particularly in energy supplies, of the industrialized world in general.

Once operational, Iran's Shahab-3 missiles and nuclear program would constitute a special threat to Israel and not just Iraq. The sophisticated much shorter range missiles that Iran would have liked to have in its inventory would give it a choke hold on the energy-critical Strait of Hormuz at the Persian Gulf's entrance. If Iran became a greater threat to the region by upsetting prevailing power balances, the prospects went up that America's allies would invite the United States to increase its military and security presence in the area—and this was even before America's post–September 11 deployments to Afghanistan and the surrounding region.

In February 1999 Vitaly Naumkin of the Institute for Oriental Studies told Iranian interlocutors that some Russian analysts were beginning to suggest that an Iran with missiles could threaten Russia's security.[33] Some months later, a number of Russian participants at an October 7–8, 1999, conference at the Diplomatic Academy in Moscow reportedly made clear to their Iranian counterparts that they were uneasy over Iran's intentions in modernizing its armed forces. Reflecting on the conference, academy vice rector Bazhanov stated that Russia did not completely trust Iran and was uneasy about its nuclear ambitions. According to Bazhanov and his colleague Kenesh Kulmatov, Russians at the conference had made clear to Iranian participants that an Iranian nuclear bomb was an unacceptable danger to Russia. Reinforcing a point made separately by Bazhanov, Kulmatov said the Iranians had been told that any proposal for cooperation on the basis of anti-Americanism was dead on arrival.[34]

In his formal presentation at the academy conference, Kulmatov summarized the two sides of the debate in Russia. On one side were those who "instinctively distrusted the West and the U.S. in particular." Against the backdrop of NATO's bombing campaign against Serbia earlier that year, they viewed NATO's expansion to the East as a direct assault on Russian interests. In contrast, they saw in Iran a power whose interests for the most part did not contradict those of Russia and in fact often coincided with them. They assumed that an Iran armed with ballistic missiles would not threaten Russia itself. Furthermore, they believed that Iranian rocket rattling could give the United States and its allies, the Israelis in particular, just pause in the Middle East. Moreover, if Russia was drawn into Iranian military programs, it would be able to exert some control of them and thereby regain some of the influence that it had lost in the last decade in the Middle East.

The opponents of this view in essence expanded on Aleksandr Bovin's warnings a decade earlier, just after the 1989 Gorbachev-Rafsanjani summit, of the dangers of pouring more weapons into an already volatile region.[35] They warned, according to Kulmatov, that the Iranian regime would never dance to Russia's tune and that Moscow's chances of influencing Tehran's policies were slim. Moreover, "no one can predict the consequences of a total change in the balance of forces in the Near and Middle East, which would be inevitable if weapons of mass destruction and the means of delivering them get into Iranian hands." In addition, as Kulmatov laid out the case of critics of helping Iran to rearm, no one could predict the consequences for Russia's ability to retain its influence in the Caucasus and Central Asia if mass upheavals took place in the regions adjoining them.[36]

Other experts, such as Yuri Fedorov at the USA Institute, argued around the same time that Russian politicians who wanted a weighty counter to the United States should look more to India and China than to Iran. One point of view posited that Russia's geopolitical and economic interests coincided in MinAtom's sale of equipment and technology for Bushehr to Iran. Fedorov made the counterargument that relations with Iran undermined Russia's much more important ties with the West and the United States. The bottom line, in Fedorov's view, was that Russia did not really need Iran because the ultimate payback was not that great.[37]

As he prepared to assume the presidency, Putin undoubtedly heard this conflicting advice and recommendations on what policy he should steer toward Iran and the sensitive issue of arms and technology transfers. Although his track record was short, some insiders nevertheless saw grounds for maintaining that with Putin in charge there would be a chance for serious U.S.-Russian cooperation on nonproliferation.

Former Security Council staffer Lebedev argued in early April 2000, just after Putin's election as president, that Putin was a professional and that his elevation to the presidency meant continuity on this issue. Given the gravity of U.S. arms transfer charges, Lebedev predicted that Putin would involve himself personally. The United States would therefore be able to talk with the newly elected president seriously about Iran. Putin in fact appreciated the danger from Iran, said Lebedev. But Iran was Russia's neighbor, so Putin would nevertheless work with Iran on those issues the two countries had in common, such as Tajikistan.[38] Events over the next several years proved Lebedev right on all counts.

## "MR. ADAMOV" AND MINISTER ADAMOV

Well-placed Russians such as Aleksandr Bovin early on in 1989 had pointed out that arming Iran was a potential danger to Russian security interests in the Middle East (see chapter 2). But others, even leading perestroika spokesmen such as Aleksandr Yakovlev, had argued that if Russia pulled out of the Iranian arms and nuclear technology market, Western competitors would quickly step in and take Russia's place.[39] Gorbachev and Yeltsin had certainly bought this argument, and now Yeltsin's successor Vladimir Putin gave every indication of siding with this camp.

In March 1998, coinciding with Andrey Kokoshin's elevation to the Security Council and the efforts to give nonproliferation imperatives greater public profile, Yeltsin had also approved the appointment of Yevgeny Adamov to replace the controversial Viktor Mikhaylov as head of MinAtom, reportedly on the latter's recommendation.[40] The two personnel decisions were entirely contradictory in their policy implications and typified the cross-cutting and churning politics of the period.

Adamov proved no less controversial than Mikhaylov. Since 1986 Adamov had been head of a power engineering institute known by its acronym NIKIET, for Scientific Research and Design Institute for Energy Technologies. In January 1999 Washington sanctioned NIKIET for involvement in the transfer of missile and nuclear technologies to Iran.[41] According to charges that surfaced in the Russian press beginning in 1999 and culminated in early 2001, Adamov had long been involved in serious transgressions of export regulations. These included exports to Iran and did not exclude technologies, materials, and equipment for weapons of mass destruction.[42]

In an interview that Adamov gave in May 1998, just after his appointment as head of MinAtom, he in effect gave notice that he would be skirting the edge of the permissible in MinAtom's dealings with Iran, and he was proud of it. He declared, "We intend to fight aggressively for our markets wherever that does not damage our country's interest and its defense policy, even if we cannot help this causing the appropriate reaction in political circles." Remarkably, this was the same interview in which Adamov stated that he was "sure that Iran is trying to develop nuclear weapons."[43]

U.S. Deputy Secretary of State Strobe Talbott in his memoir recollected that Adamov, upon taking over MinAtom, began pressing "for cooperation with Iran in the production of nuclear-grade graphite and heavy water . . . needed to produce weapons." All of this would have violated the understanding reached at the May 1995 summit between Yeltsin and Clinton, and turned over to the Gore-Chernomyrdin Commission for elaboration, on no transfers to Iran of nuclear technology with military applications.[44]

Putin's view at first appeared to be in tune with Adamov's, in effect that whatever was good for the Ministry of Atomic Energy was also good for Russia. When Adamov met with newly appointed acting president Putin in early February 2000, the Russian press said Adamov walked out smiling.[45] It was probably more than amusement over the fact that when Putin had worked in East Germany for the KGB, he had used "Mr. Adamov" as one of his cover names. [46]

By May 2000 it was revealed that Putin had amended Yeltsin's 1992 decree "On Control Over the Export of Nuclear Materials, Equipment, and Technologies From the Russian Federation." The amendments outlined some exceptions under which Russia could export nuclear power technology to countries that had not put all their nuclear activities under IAEA control.[47] Besides the Bushehr contract signed in 1995, Russia in 1997 had already signed a $3 billion contract with China for two VVER-1000 generator units for the Tianwan nuclear power plant near the port city of Lianyungang.[48] Now in 2000, commentary in Moscow viewed newly elected President Putin's amendments to Yeltsin's 1992 decree as giving the green light to MinAtom negotiations with Iran for three more nuclear power units—to be manufactured in Putin's hometown of St. Petersburg—at a cost of about $2 billion, as well as to further MinAtom negotiations with India and Cuba.[49]

All the indications were that MinAtom remained a remarkably autonomous entity that got nearly everything it wanted. It was one of the few hopeful bright spots in Russia's sagging economy, and as such wielded considerable influence in Kremlin political circles. MinAtom's exports were said to be only a third less than the arms exports of the entire non-nuclear military-industrial complex of Soviet times.[50] In 1998, 700,000 people lived in MinAtom company towns ("closed cities"), and as many as 2.5 million people were directly dependent on the ministry.[51]

As a member of the Security Council during the last years of the Yeltsin era, MinAtom head Adamov was said to have reported directly to Yeltsin. Adamov used his Security Council seat to bypass the interagency review process mandated to coordinate trade and technological initiatives with Iran. This consisted of a commission of first deputy ministers chaired by a deputy prime minister, who unlike Adamov was not a member of the Security Council.[52]

In addition, Adamov cultivated wide political support. When the MinAtom chief went to Tehran in November 1998 for more Bushehr contract adjustment negotiations, he took along a sizable delegation from the Duma.[53] Its leading members were Anatoly Lukyanov and Vladimir Gusev from the CPRF and LDPR, respectively, vociferous advocates of closer Russian-Iranian relations.[54] In the meantime, Iran did its own stroking of these forces in Russia. According to the Carnegie Endowment's Aleksey Malashenko, the Iranian embassy in Moscow maintained a special reception room for entertaining CPRF and LDPR guests.[55]

All the indications in early 2000 were thus for continued smooth sailing for MinAtom head Adamov in his freewheeling dealings with Iran. Appearances, however, were deceiving. In late December 1999, just days short of Yeltsin's designation of Putin as acting president, Putin had authored an elaborate treatise setting out his views on how Russia should be governed. In "Russia on the Eve of the Millennium," Putin argued the notion that the state had "always played an extremely important role" in Russia and that modern Russia's society favored the restoration of "the leading and regulating role of the state to the necessary extent, taking into account traditions and the present situation in the country." Among the attributes of a strong state, Putin included the need for "more professional, better disciplined and more responsible civil servants, and stepping up the fight against corruption."[56] For his audience, Putin did not have to connect the dots: he would use the corruption issue to cow those opposed to his conception of the state.

In Putin's view, it soon became clear, the fight for state discipline began within the state itself. Before long, it appeared that Putin intended to start the process by removing none other than the freewheeling Adamov from MinAtom. Adamov was an easy target on grounds of corruption and indiscipline alone. The larger picture, however, was that his removal was part of the fitful shift in Russian policy toward cooler relations with Iran that had paralleled Putin's rise to the top of the Russian hierarchy.

Indeed, there had been inklings that Adamov's smiles could not last for long. Despite denials that NIKIET had been involved in any illegal dealings with Iran,[57] the Moscow press had published detailed support for Washington's charges. By the end of January 1999 the weekly *Itogi* reported that its sources claimed Adamov, as head of NIKIET, indeed had continued into 1998 to pursue a project in Iran for enriching uranium—despite Yeltsin's abrogation of the deal in 1995.[58] In April 1999 another publication charged that Adamov, as head of NIKIET, had repeatedly traveled to Iran from 1992 to 1998 to conduct unsanctioned negotiations, including for a project to build a "heavy-water" research reactor.[59]

With Putin having replaced Yeltsin in the Kremlin, it was decided in September 2000 to postpone and review the sale to Iran of laser technology for nuclear isotope separation, contracted by the Yefremov Institute in St. Petersburg, a subsidiary of MinAtom.[60] The move was of great significance for MinAtom's dealings with Iran and a bellwether of Moscow's changing policy toward Tehran. Indeed, by the end of the year, the prosecutor general opened a criminal investigation into charges that Adamov, while head of NIKIET, had been involved in "the illegal export of technologies, scientific and technical information and services, raw material, and materials and equipment used in the creation of weapons of mass destruction, armaments, and military equipment."[61]

Other moves were made to restrict Iranian access to dual-use technologies during Putin's first year as president. On February 11, 2000, Russia's Federal Service for Currency and Export Control ordered the Baltic State Technical University in St. Petersburg to shut down its courses for Iranian students—in Iran, no less.[62] There may have been a hope in Moscow that clamping down on such activity would make the United States at least marginally less worried about the potential of Iran using the Bushehr project as a cover for a military nuclear program. A year later, Putin on January 29, 2001, signed an edict establishing an Export Control Commission to be chaired by Deputy Premier Ilya Klebanov.[63]

Less than a year into his elected presidency, Putin began to signal publicly that he was intent on reining in some of MinAtom's freewheeling ways. At a February 22, 2001, session of the Security Council devoted to tightening export controls, Putin rebuked MinAtom for not having corrected deficiencies in this field.[64] In what began to take on the appearance of a coordinated campaign to encourage Adamov to give up his post, the Duma Commission on Combating Corruption on March 2 declassified the results of its investigation of Adamov's financial activities over the previous fifteen years. Within days, the entire report appeared online.[65]

Besides myriad allegations of financial shenanigans, the Duma report revealed that the commission had investigated charges that Adamov, while director of NIKIET, had engaged in serious transgressions of export regulations. Specifically, the report stated that it had been "established that in 1996 NIKIET concluded a contract with Iran's Atomic Energy Organization to carry out a feasibility study for the planned plant for the production of heavy water," a critical element in one method for the production of weapons-grade fissile material.[66] Mikhail Kasyanov, whom Putin had appointed prime minister after himself being sworn in as president in May 2000, soon signed a decree firing Yevgeny Fedorov, one of Adamov's deputy ministers criticized in the Duma report.[67]

By March 28, just one year and two days after his election as president, Putin replaced Adamov as head of MinAtom with Aleksandr Rumyantsev, head of the Kurchatov Institute since 1994. Putin delphically said that Adamov would explain his reasons for resigning "should it become necessary."[68] The Russian legal system, however, evidently remained notoriously subject to political intervention. In fact, the Procuracy General's office announced at the end of the year that no criminal charges would be filed against Adamov, and he returned to NIKIET as its research director.[69] He later denied ever having "sold myself" and attributed his dismissal to "state interests": "For the state I am unacceptable on account of my position in regard to India, Iran, China. I believe that that is our market. Attempts are being made to dislodge us from these positions."[70] It all seemed typical of Putin's penchant in this early period for minimizing the potential backlash by applying just enough pressure to persuade a problem official to step aside or change jobs, without casting him or her into political or financial purgatory.[71]

As a practical matter, some of Adamov's shady dealings with Iranians and others were no doubt disrupted by his abrupt departure from MinAtom but could have reasserted themselves should Rumyantsev have decided to continue pursuing them. However, Rumyantsev never gave any indication of inclinations in that direction and in any event did not appear to wield the independent clout that Adamov had had. For one thing, Rumyantsev was not a member of the Security Council, which in any event had been downgraded by the transfer of Putin-intimate Sergey Ivanov to the Defense Ministry and the appointment of Vladimir Rushaylo—not a member of Putin's inside circle—as the new Secretary of the Security Council.[72]

On the subject of the Bushehr nuclear power plant, however, which was never at issue in the lengthy Duma report on Adamov, Rumyantsev in his first public statements vigorously defended the contract with Iran. St. Petersburg, moreover, was Putin's hometown and home to major components of the Russian military-industrial complex. The Izhorskiye Zavody complex built the thousand-megawatt reactor shipped to Bushehr in November 2001 and stood ready to build more if contracts were signed.[73] Putin's modifications in May 2000 of Yeltsin's 1992 decree on nuclear export controls increased the theoretical possibility of such a sale. Other major St. Petersburg enterprises were involved in nuclear power projects for the export market. They included the Atomenergoproekt research institute, the Central Machine-Building Design Bureau, Elektrosila, and Leningrad Metal Works.[74] The city also had major shipyards that might profit from additional sales of Kilo-class submarines to Iran.

During his years as deputy mayor of St. Petersburg, Putin had worked intimately with the city's economic managers. He therefore was probably not sympathetic to arguments against selling Iran military and nuclear technology produced in St. Petersburg on the grounds that it might threaten Russia's security far off in the future. In addition, there was political pressure on Putin to keep the Moscow-Tehran connection robust and a symbol of Russia's independence and ability to resist U.S. pressure. Putin in the future repeatedly warned that he would not let Russian enterprises be pushed out of the Iranian market by Western firms that wanted to capture more market share there.

As the Putin administration in its first year considered its options, backtracking on Bushehr was not one of them. Indeed, an article in the government daily newspaper *Rossiyskaya Gazeta* portrayed the Bushehr contract as the salvation of the country's nuclear power plant construction industry, decimated after the Chernobyl disaster of 1986. Iranian payments for Bushehr were, in effect, start-up money for reviving the sector. "When Bushehr-1 is put in operation our nuclear fuel industry, specialists, and manufacturers of spare parts will acquire a new market. . . . It is the real key to the markets of the Eurasian South Arc stretching from Iran to China through India and Pakistan. . . . More than 2 billion consumers, rapidly developing economies, and the very future of the planet. Hundreds of millions of dollars spent in Bushehr are worth many billions." Moreover, the article asserted that the need to protect Bushehr would stimulate Iran to buy a variety of antiaircraft missile systems and place other military orders from Russian manufacturers.[75]

Russian officials continued to claim that U.S. objections to Bushehr were simply sour grapes over having lost the Iranian market.[76] Official Moscow seemed impervious to arguments that Tehran was using its civilian nuclear program as a cover for military research—even though this was one of the charges effectively leveled at former MinAtom head Adamov to encourage him to resign from that post. It argued that the United States supplied to the shah the one nuclear plant that was still operational in Iran. The West Germans had contracted with Iran during the shah's time to build the nuclear facility at Bushehr. If Western nations had no qualms about transferring nuclear technology to Iran, then why should Russia be prevented from engaging in similar deals? After all, Iran was still an NPT signatory, and IAEA inspectors had never found any NPT violations during their visits to Iranian nuclear facilities.

## DEBATE OVER ARMS SALES

The year 2000 was to be a year for decisions by Russia on another aspect of its relations with Iran: conventional weapons sales. The long-range program on cooperation signed by Gorbachev and Rafsanjani in 1989 was to run to the beginning of the new millennium. By fluke of history, that time frame coincided roughly with the end of Yeltsin's second presidential term. In any event, the first public hints that Moscow wanted to loosen the restrictions of the June 30, 1995, Gore-Chernomyrdin Commission memorandum, calling for an end to Russian sales to Iran by December 31, 1999, surfaced in January 1999. By way of explanation, the early leak—by Igor

Korotchenko in *Nezavisimaya Gazeta*—began with an allusion to the "marked cooling of Russian-American relations."[77]

Besides the politics of the moment, another plausible explanation was that in 1995, when Gore and Chernomyrdin worked out their understanding, Russia thought it could wind up its 1989–91 contracts with Iran by the end of 1999 and so could easily sign the memorandum. Since then, however, Iranian economic stagnation, aggravated by U.S. embargoes and Iran's spending on its missile and nuclear programs, meant that Iran had not had enough money to fulfill its conventional weapons contracts with Russia. Alternatively, Iran's progress on its missile and nuclear programs may have led it to slow down conventional weapons acquisitions. In any event, according to the grossly rounded off figures in the Russian press, only half of the $4 billion (*sic*) in commitments envisioned under the 1989–91 Russian-Iranian contracts had been fulfilled, and Moscow was loath to forgo the $2 billion from deliveries still outstanding. In addition, Iran was reportedly interested in concluding more deals worth another $2 billion.[78]

By mid-January 2000, Defense Minister Igor Sergeyev said, "Russia and Iran intend to maintain the dynamism of ties in various spheres, including the military and military-technical spheres, and will not allow third countries to interfere in this cooperation."[79] He made this comment after meeting with Hassan Rowhani, secretary of Iran's National Security Council, and after Putin chaired a session of the government commission on military-industrial questions on whose agenda reportedly were the prospects for cooperation with Iran. Sergeyev's comments were immediately interpreted as signaling Russia's possible repudiation of the 1995 memorandum.

Indeed, Security Council secretary Sergei Ivanov announced in March 2000 that the pledge to cease selling arms to Iran after the end of 1999 was being revised. Ivanov said Moscow and Washington had reached a "total mutual understanding" that Russia would not conclude any new contracts for arms to Iran but would continue to fulfill those contracts signed before the 1995 Gore-Chernomyrdin understanding.[80] According to various press reports, Russia had fulfilled only 50 percent of those contracts and needed until the end of 2010 to complete them.[81]

Deliberations on what to do about Gore-Chernomyrdin took place within the context of preparations for a Putin-Khatami summit in Moscow. Putin reportedly had invited the Iranian president to visit during the Millennium Summit at the UN in New York in September 2000.[82] By January 2001 Viktor Kalyuzhnyy, Russia's Caspian negotiator, was talking about a mid-March summit.[83] A month later, the summit was officially announced to take place on March 12–15, 2001.[84]

On November 3, 2000, Foreign Minister Igor Ivanov, who had succeeded Yevgeny Primakov after the latter had been appointed prime minister in September 1998, formally notified U.S. Secretary of State Madeleine Albright that Russia would withdraw from the 1995 agreement on December 1, 2000.[85] By that time, Security Council head Sergei Ivanov had already, in October, made a trip to Tehran, during which he conveyed a message from Putin to President Khatami. Russia, it reportedly said, is seriously "inclined towards deepening mutually advantageous Russian-Iranian cooperation in a bilateral format, at the regional and the international level." Moreover, it stressed, "We see the development of good-neighborly relations with the Islamic Republic of Iran as one of Russia's long-term foreign-policy priorities."[86] Defense Minister Sergeyev followed Ivanov's visit with one of his own in late December.[87]

As far back as 1998, Tehran had reportedly informed Moscow of its desire to purchase around $2 billion worth of new military systems.[88] Sergeyev's visit to Tehran in December 2000 was reciprocated by the visit of a high-level Iranian delegation to the Russian capital shortly before President Khatami's scheduled arrival there for his summit with Putin.[89] The priority items on the Iranian shopping list around this time and well into 2001 were said by Russian Defense Ministry sources to be an impressive array of air defense, missile, and other advanced conventional weapons systems.[90] Russian negotiators speculated that the first new arms contracts with the Iranians would be signed as early as May 2001.[91]

Estimates varied widely over what all these deals might be worth. The early 1999 slipshod estimates of a total of $4 billion—$2 billion still left over from old contracts plus another $2 billion from new contracts—had now ballooned in some circles to almost twice that figure. On both the Iranian and Russian sides, some said around $7 billion "in the near future" or "in several years." Some Russian experts, however, were much more restrained, putting potential earnings at only around $300 million a year.[92] Even skeptics in Iran called the $7 billion figure "deliberately inflated"; warned against accepting overpriced, obsolete, or secondhand weapons; and cautioned that hyping Iran's arms deals with Russia had never been to Iran's advantage since it merely aggravated American sensitivities.[93] In Moscow, the Defense Ministry conceded that besides the usual secrecy reasons, it was also avoiding divulging details of its military cooperation with "rogue" Iran because of fear of the U.S. reaction.[94]

In early December 2000, in articles keyed to Moscow's jettisoning of the Gore-Chernomyrdin accord and coinciding with Defense Minister Sergeyev's trip to Tehran, two analysts in Moscow published diametrically opposed conclusions concerning the wisdom and value of future arms sales to Iran. The point-counterpoint of these analyses probably reflected an ongoing internal debate at higher levels in Moscow over the direction of Russian-Iranian relations, in particular the arms sales dimension.

On one side of the debate was Ruslan Pukhov, director of the Center for Analysis of Strategies and Policies (Tsentr AST) in Moscow. Pukhov argued that selling more weapons to Iran would be doubly, even triply, advantageous to Russia. Russia would earn money directly from the arms sales. Iran could then use the more modern weapons systems to control the flow of oil from the Persian Gulf to the United States and Europe. The Moskit and Yakhont antiship systems, with respective ranges of 120 and 300 kilometers, could easily target the entire Strait of Hormuz and would be "an effective and fantastically inexpensive means of reducing the significance of the American fleet . . . in the Persian Gulf." Iran could use this pressure to keep oil prices on the world market high. High oil prices would benefit not only Iranian producers but also Russian oil companies. The profits from the arms sales and from higher oil prices would in turn make it easier for Russia to service its foreign debt. Russia was facing an unbudgeted $5 billion in debts to the Paris Club of creditors in 2001, which could be covered were world oil prices $5 higher per barrel, according to Pukhov's calculations.[95]

Arriving at radically different conclusions was Sergei Kandaurov, a senior analyst at the Russian Institute of Strategic Studies, who took a hard look at Iran's credit rating and potential intentions and at the opportunity costs for Russia of selling weapons to Iran. Iran's ability in the 1990s to pay for contracted conventional weapons systems—T-72S tanks and BMP-2 APCs (armed personnel carriers) in particular—had been disappointing. This was in great part because Iran had begun to accord much higher priority and funding to its missile program since signing the earlier contracts.[96] Kandaurov cautioned that counting on oil prices staying high—in the $30 per barrel range—to pay for future deliveries of Russian weapons would be "extremely risky."

Moreover, continued Kandaurov, classifying weapons such as the Yakhont cruise missile, which could threaten shipping through the Strait of Hormuz, as defensive was nonsense from the point of view of Gulf Arab regimes who feared Iran (as well as Iraq). In addition, selling weapons to cash-strapped Iran would simply stimulate the rich Arab states of the Gulf to buy more arms from the United States, France, and Great Britain. Russia should hesitate to sell Iran weapons that could threaten Russia's own southern borders, cautioned Kandaurov, and focus instead on trying to sell Iran systems for coastal and land border defense, airfield equipment, and repair facilities.[97]

Before long, other analysts reinforced Kandaurov's point about so-called defensive weapons. Even Konstantin Makiyenko, a deputy director at Pukhov's Tsentr AST, conceded that the 120-km Moskit cruise missile might "immediately provoke a political crisis" in the hands of Iran, since 60 percent of the world's oil passed through the Strait of Hormuz, which was only fifty-four kilometers wide. Makiyenko was also skeptical on two counts that Russia would sell the S-300 air defense missile to Iran. First, the system was very expensive. Second, it also could cause a serious political crisis—as had happened when Russia had tried to sell it to Cyprus and then had to back down.[98]

Against the background of discordant advice in the press, Russian sources cautioned that no new arms contracts would be signed until Khatami visited Moscow.[99] In April 2001, though, Iran's missile strikes against Iranian opposition camps in Iraq underscored the potential uses to which Tehran could put Russian-supplied systems, and Moscow quickly issued statements calling for a more restrained Iranian approach and reserved Iraqi response.[100] Indeed, not only on the security side but also on the political and financial sides, there was increasing understanding in Russia of the implications of American and European warnings about the costs to Russia of selling sophisticated conventional weapons to Iran.

At least one press commentary on Defense Minister Sergeyev's suggestion in January 2000 that Russia abandon Chernomyrdin's pledge to Gore charged that to do so would "show the whole world that Moscow is completely untrustworthy." The commentary pointed out that likely U.S. and Israeli sanctions would hurt Russia's own defense industry and arms exports. The United States could cut back further on the quota of U.S. satellites launched by Russian missiles, worth $800 million in 1999. Israel could renege on commitments to supply avionics equipment for Russian Su-30MKI multirole aircraft being outfitted for India, the A-50 AWACS (airborne warning and control system, i.e. "flying radar") aircraft being refitted for China, and the Ka-50-2 Erdogan attack helicopters that Russia hoped to sell to Turkey. "Moscow should hardly rush into any conclusions," cautioned the commentary.[101]

By March 2002 Defense Secretary Ivanov had declared that Russia and Iran had signed only one new contract for conventional weapons over the past year and a half to two years, and this one for helicopters.[102] Ivanov's assertion was a clear indication that those in Moscow arguing for caution on weapons sales to Iran had gained the upper hand.

In addition, experts such as Andrey Kokoshin, the former secretary of the Security Council who was now a deputy in the Duma, reiterated their concerns, adding that cooperating too closely with Iran would simply give grist to U.S. advocates of a national missile defense (NMD) system: "Iran's nuclear potential is an important argument for the creation of the US anti-missile system." Kokoshin drew attention to the dangers of Russian cooperation with Iran in the nuclear and missile fields and advocated working with the United States and the EU on disputes over Iranian weapons developments. "We will be the first victim in case strategic stability is disrupted," Kokoshin told an interviewer at the end of 2000. "Shahab-3—despite our very good and friendly relations with Iran—can reach the southern edge only of Russia, and not the EU or the USA. I think that neither Russia nor anybody else needs Iran as a nuclear power."[103] It was a judgment that even Vladimir Putin endorsed in the years ahead.

# 8

# Caspian Tempests

The cooling in relations between Moscow and Tehran over weapons and nuclear and dual-use technology sales was compounded by growing differences over how to delimit the Caspian Sea and regulate exploitation of its oil and gas riches. The two countries' early shared interests in the Caspian were not immutable, and they actually turned out to be fierce competitors. To some extent they cooperated—episodically and not necessarily intentionally—to frustrate outsiders' participation in exploiting Caspian energy reserves. Increasingly, however, they also tilted with each other over Caspian delimitation and control of export market share—to Turkey in particular—and even warily eyed one another's growing Caspian naval capabilities.

With the option of a condominium over Caspian resources slipping away as Russia abandoned that approach, Tehran began to insist on an equal five-way division. There were even those Iranians who suggested that anything less than 50 percent would be a national betrayal, though this extreme position was generally regarded as hopelessly unrealistic. Nevertheless, anything less than a 20 percent share of the Caspian seemed widely perceived domestically in Iran as the modern-day maritime equivalent of the despised Gulistan and Turkmanchai treaties of 1813 and 1828, by which Iranian rulers had ceded the Persian Empire's possessions in the Caucasus to the Russian Empire.

The often-asserted congruence of Russian and Iranian approaches to Caspian issues was largely a myth that began to be clearly exposed by 1998. The reality of Tehran's isolation on Caspian issues revived in Iran a deep sense of historical betrayal by Russia, now in collusion with the new post-Soviet littoral states. These included Kazakhstan and Turkmenistan but most bitterly Azerbaijan, still regarded historically by some in Iran as little more than an Iranian province that had temporarily strayed from the "Greater Iran" fold.

After Russia broke with Iran and started in July 1998 to work with Kazakhstan to delimit their joint seabed, Iran began to explore and prepare for drilling in its own self-proclaimed 20 percent sector. Iran underscored the seriousness of its position with gunboat diplomacy in July 2001, when it forcibly stopped Azeri-BP exploration of the Alborz/Alov field in what Azerbaijan claimed—and almost everyone else recognized—as Azerbaijan's national sector.

A year later, after an unproductive summit in Ashgabat, Turkmenistan, of the five presidents of the Caspian littoral states, Russia held the first major exercise of its Caspian flotilla, and the gulf between Russian and Iranian positions on delimitation became even more entrenched. With this, what seemed a prolonged but manageable stalemate settled over Caspian issues. Iran was isolated in its 20 percent demand, yet no one seemed eager to challenge Tehran's armed enforcement of its self-proclaimed exploration and drilling rights in the Caspian's southern expanses.

Russia's evolving stance on Caspian delimitation was largely defined by the then largely privatized energy giants Gazprom and Lukoil. The dynamic at play resembled MinAtom's championing of its corporate interests in the construction of the Bushehr nuclear power plant. But the implications of each were very different in their impact on Moscow's relations with Tehran. MinAtom's lobbying for Bushehr had redounded to Iran's benefit and buttressed what were described as the geopolitical imperatives of robust Russian-Iranian ties. The lobbying of Lukoil and Gazprom, in contrast, while also justified on grounds of Russian geopolitical interests, undercut rather than bolstered Iranian interest in a common approach with Russia to unresolved Caspian issues. These contradictions would not be sorted out until Putin arrived in the Kremlin and began reeling in MinAtom's independent leadership.

The early post-Soviet lobbying by Lukoil for a stake in the "deal of the century" to exploit oil off newly independent Azerbaijan's Caspian coast was the beginning of the energy-driven foreign policy that flourished a decade later under Putin. Yeltsin's successor in effect coopted Gazprom and Lukoil's policy and rewarded those oligarchs—such as Lukoil's Vagit Alekperov—who were eager to work with him and the Russian state. Those who were not, and who persisted in lobbying for projects that rivaled those favored by Putin's Kremlin, Putin destroyed: most prominently Yukos's Mikhail Khodorkovsky. Those who were willing to cash out and quietly leave the scene, Putin paid off and replaced with his own allies. Putin did this to Gazprom CEO Rem Vyakhirev, installing St. Petersburg associate Aleksey Miller in his place and turning the energy giant into a powerful vanguard of Russian foreign policy. Putin insisted that the state lead the way, and that private companies and state corporations be servants of the Kremlin, and not the other way around.

Having asserted state control of Gazprom's board of directors by June 2001, and as negotiations with Iran over Caspian delimitation stalled, Putin in January 2002 unveiled an ambitious initiative to put together a "Eurasian alliance of gas producers." The project aimed at a Gazprom monopoly on less expensive Central Asian natural gas exports in order to greatly increase Gazprom's profit margins in lucrative European markets. Together with the Blue Stream pipeline to Turkey, Putin's Gazprom-led "alliance" cemented Russia's position as the dominant supplier of natural gas to much of Europe and blocked Iran from any attempt to move in and whittle down Russia's market share.

## ALEKPEROV AND CHERNOMYRDIN

MinAtom was the proverbial six-hundred-pound gorilla in Russia's atomic energy dealings with Iran during the Yeltsin era. In the field of Caspian energy, Gazprom—together with partners such as Lukoil—was every bit MinAtom's sibling, politically perhaps even its dominant twin. Gazprom was the biggest gas company not just in Russia but around the globe. It extracted 25 percent of the natural gas in the world and controlled 30–40 percent of the world's gas reserves. It had major banks of its own and shared others with partners such as Lukoil.[1]

The interests of Gazprom and Lukoil and their intimate ties to ruling circles in Moscow had a major impact on Russian policy toward energy development in general and Caspian delimitation specifically, and consequently on policy toward Iran. The Soviet-era Oil and Gas Ministry had exploited the oil fields off the shores of Azerbaijan for decades prior to the Soviet Union's collapse and established a de facto seabed boundary with Iran for the purposes of this work. After the Soviet collapse, former ministry chiefs were reincarnated and enriched as shareholders and bosses of the ministry's post-Soviet privatized spin-off companies. With their own wallets at stake, they naturally fought fiercely to resist Iranian demands for shared access to Caspian resources in areas far beyond the de facto boundary the Soviet Union had imposed on Iran during its ministry days.

In a political system where many players regarded "conflict of interests" as an oxymoron devoutly to be sought and exploited, Viktor Chernomyrdin as Russian premier from 1992 to 1998 was widely seen as secretly in charge of Gazprom.[2] A native of the southern Urals region of Orenburg, Russia's historical gateway into Central Asia, Chernomyrdin had worked in the oil and gas sector all his life, rising during the Soviet era to become oil and gas minister from 1985 to 1989. When the ministry was reorganized and the Gazprom state consortium established in August 1989, Chernomyrdin rolled over into the position of chairman of Gazprom's board of directors. After the Soviet collapse, Chernomyrdin served as Russia's deputy premier in charge of the fuel and energy sector from May to December 1992.[3] During this period everything related to the production and distribution of natural gas was incorporated into the joint stock company Gazprom, a huge and heavily subsidized gas monopoly with some 400,000 employees.[4]

Rem Vyakhirev was Chernomyrdin's personal pick to become CEO at Gazprom and to work out the details for its privatization in early 1993. Although they steadfastly denied the reports, each allegedly held at least 1 percent of Gazprom's stock at the start. With Vyakhirev assigned control of the proxies for the Russian government's then-38 percent of Gazprom stock, he and his associates were able to dominate Gazprom's board of directors and totally obfuscate the company's statements of income and expenses flows.[5]

What was good for Gazprom was good for Prime Minister Chernomyrdin and his family. In 1994, during a crucial no-confidence vote in the Duma, Gazprom allegedly bankrolled the nearly $4 million in bribes—$15,000 per Duma deputy—that it took to ensure the vote went in favor of Prime Minister Chernomyrdin, according to one of his senior advisers.[6] Chernomyrdin's two sons, Vitaly and Andrey, were said to each own 6 percent of the stock in Stroytransgaz, Gazprom's privatized construction arm. Stroytransgaz did some $1 billion in work for Gazprom each year and by some estimates was the fourth-largest construction firm in the world.[7] Within several years, Chernomyrdin's rising fortune in Gazprom stock, by now perhaps as high as 5 percent, together with other holdings was estimated in the $4–5 billion range.[8]

Much of the Caspian story told in this chapter revolves around the activism and dynamism of Lukoil's Vagit Alekperov and his close ties to Chernomyrdin. An ethnic Azeri and native of Baku, Alekperov was born in 1950. He worked for the local Kaspromneft production association from 1974 to 1979. In 1979 he relocated to western Siberia, where he worked for the Surgutneft and Bashneft production associations before becoming general director of Kogalymneft in 1984. From 1990 to 1991, Alekperov was deputy and then first deputy minister for oil and gas. In late 1991, on the eve of the Soviet collapse, Alekperov participated in establishing the "Langepas-Uray-Kogalym-neft" concern out of three western Siberian production associations. After privatization in April 1993, this became the Lukoil Company.

In one guise or another, Alekperov was head of Lukoil from the beginning.[9] In the 1990s, although the Russian government initially owned 35 percent of Lukoil's stock, Alekperov led the way in creating a vertically integrated, market-oriented, Western-style oil company that Yeltsin set as an example for the rest of the Russian oil sector.[10] In the next decade, although president of a now largely privately held company, Alekperov distinguished himself by closely and conspicuously identifying Lukoil's interests with those of the Russian state and by endorsing and promoting Putin's statist vision. Alekperov's political agility and business acumen resulted in an extraordinarily privileged position for Lukoil under Putin.

## LUKOIL VERSUS MFA AND SVR

The Soviet Union's collapse opened up for revision the long-standing condominium in the Caspian between Moscow and Tehran as enshrined by the Soviet-Iranian treaties of 1921, 1935, and 1940.[11] These treaties, however, had focused only on navigation and fishing rights and had been entirely silent about exploitation of the Caspian's seabed resources. Over the years, various Soviet ministries had established their own practices, to which Iran did not object or at least did not dare to question publicly.

In 1935 Interior (NKVD) Minister Genrikh Yagoda by some accounts decreed a two-hundred-mile security line across the Caspian linking the Soviet land borders with Iran from Astara in the west to Gasanguly in the east. A special force was to defend this maritime line.[12] In 1949 the USSR began to extract oil off the shores of the Soviet Socialist Republic of Azerbaijan. Iran apparently did not remonstrate, but by the same token Soviet oil workers never strayed south of the Astara-Gasanguly line.[13] In 1970 the Soviet Oil and Gas Ministry established the Astara-Gasanguly line more formally for its own internal work purposes and may have even coordinated—or at least communicated—the matter confidentially with Iran.[14] When the delimitation issue heated up in the post-Soviet period, Azerbaijan rested its arguments on the basis of what it claimed was Iran's de facto recognition of the Astara-Gasanguly line during the Soviet period.[15] Iran rebutted that the Astara-Gasanguly line did not exist officially or in international law and had simply been dictated by the USSR to Iran.[16]

In dealing with the claims of the three additional sovereign states—Azerbaijan, Kazakhstan, and Turkmenistan—encircling the Caspian after 1991, Russia and Iran at first had some common interests in resolving delimitation issues. Both officially insisted that the principle of condominium should govern use and exploitation of any hydrocarbon and other riches lying beneath the Caspian's seabed. At times they argued that this was explicitly governed by the 1921 and 1940 treaties, even though it was not.[17] Occasionally they reasoned that since the condominium principle had been included in the treaties in reference to fishing and shipping, it implicitly also applied to exploitation of seabed resources. For the most part, though, the case was simply that until a new regime was negotiated and agreed to by all parties, the Soviet-era treaties should remain in force and new deals to exploit the Caspian seabed should be held in abeyance unless agreed to by all five littoral countries.[18]

In general, the impact of imposing a condominium approach to all issues after the Soviet Union's collapse would have been to give each country veto power over new projects. This would have acted as an incentive to Azerbaijan, Kazakhstan, and Turkmenistan to cut Russia and Iran into their deals in order to avoid their vetoes. This was in principle particularly valuable to Iran. If the Astara-Gasanguly line continued to restrict activities, it would limit Iran to some 11–12 percent of the Caspian seabed. This portion was thought to have few reserves. In any case, where present, the reserves would be much more difficult to extract because of the Caspian's great depth in this southern region, over a thousand meters compared to the mere six meters (twenty feet) in the Russian and Kazakhstani sectors to the north. Because of Iran's short Caspian coastline, even the more generous median line methodology, which the other countries soon began to advance, entitled Iran to the smallest national sector of all, only 13–14 percent, also bereft of major oil and gas reserves.[19] U.S. opposition, moreover—especially after passage in August 1996 of the Iran-Libya Sanctions Act (ILSA)—raised barriers to Iran's inclusion in most projects of any consequence throughout the Caspian.

Russia, in contrast, benefited not only from a longer coastline but also from the discovery of substantial energy fields in what would be its 16–19 percent sector of the Caspian under a median line delimitation regime. As a result, the condominium principle early on became of less durable interest to Russia, where powerful energy interests did not want to be left out of the high-stakes exploitation of the Caspian. Yet even in the early years after the Soviet collapse, neither Russia nor Iran was wedded to the condominium principle, and both pursued deals with other littoral states that in effect recognized separate national sectors.[20]

Years before the discovery of major hydrocarbon deposits in its North Caspian shelf, major Russian oil concerns such as Lukoil were anxious to join international consortia in developing fields lying in other Caspian states' presumed national sectors. They were opposed, however, by the Russian Foreign Ministry led by Andrey Kozyrev and the SVR under Yevgeny Primakov. Both were busily engaged with Iran in trying to get the peace process in Tajikistan started and averse to complicating MinAtom's negotiations with Iran on Bushehr. The two issues were substantial incentives for Moscow to appease Tehran when it came to the Caspian's status in the wake of the Soviet Union's disappearance.

The tug-of-war between competing lobbies in Moscow was especially noticeable in 1993–94. In November 1993 Russian fuel and energy minister Yuri Shafranik traveled to Baku and proposed that Lukoil's share in the consortium being put together to develop the Azeri, Chirag, and Guneshli fields be not just 10 percent but 20 percent. Shafranik stressed that President Yeltsin and Prime Minister Chernomyrdin had both given their blessing to his trip. While Shafranik was in town, Lukoil president Vagit Alekperov signed a pack of documents on cooperation between Lukoil and the State Oil Company of Azerbaijan (SOCAR).[21]

Nevertheless, on June 2, 1994, Russian Foreign Ministry spokesman Grigory Karasin announced that the MFA had presented a demarche to the British embassy in Moscow complaining about the Azeri project. The official note stated, according to Karasin, that since there had been no new agreement on Caspian delimitation revising the 1921 and 1940 treaties, Russia deemed invalid any agreements on developing Caspian mineral resources that had not been approved by Russia and all the other littoral countries. The note had been sent to the British embassy because British Petroleum was the lead company in the Azeri project.[22]

Azerbaijani President Heydar Aliyev soon told the press to ignore the Russian Foreign Ministry statement. He had talked by phone with Chernomyrdin and reported that the Russian premier had expressed considerable surprise over it. According to Aliyev, Chernomyrdin was not raising any questions over the Caspian's status and had no intention of doing so.[23] On July 21, 1994, nevertheless, Foreign Minister Kozyrev and SVR chief Primakov reportedly prevailed on Yeltsin to sign a secret directive that argued that Russia should preserve its sphere of influence and keep Western joint ventures out of the Caspian Sea.[24]

All the same, on September 20, 1994, Lukoil joined eight other oil companies and SOCAR in signing a project deal worth $8 billion to develop the Azeri, Chirag, and Guneshli fields in the Azerbaijani sector of the Caspian Sea. Aliyev called it the Contract of the Century. The consortium soon became better known by the acronym AIOC, for Azerbaijan International Operating Company, set up to oversee the project's day-to-day operation. A Russian Energy Ministry official—department head Stanislav Pugach—attended the signing ceremony, thereby blessing the deal and Lukoil's participation in it.[25]

The same day, however, spokesman Karasin again said Russia would not recognize the contract because the legal status of the Caspian had yet to be decided.[26] At the UN, Russia in October 1994 warned other states against unilaterally exploring the Caspian seabed.[27] Nevertheless, neither Kozyrev's MFA nor Primakov's SVR were able to keep the energy lobby in check. Aliyev telephoned Chernomyrdin and Kozyrev in mid-October 1994. Chernomyrdin affirmed that he saw no problems with the Contract of the Century. Kozyrev backpedaled and assured Aliyev that Russia was not planning to impose any sanctions on Azerbaijan.[28]

At the same time, Shafranik declared to the press that his Fuel and Energy Ministry backed the deal and that it "would have been a mistake not to take part in the project. Our position is to take an active part in international projects, especially on the territory of the CIS." Lukoil's Alekperov pointed out that "one needs much time to define the status of the Caspian Sea, but if we will be detached on-lookers, we can lose a large profit."[29] The deal went forward, as did Lukoil's 10 percent participation in the consortium, which it held on to until April 2003.[30]

So, Russia and Iran early on began to part ways on Caspian delimitation because of the interests of Lukoil and its energy lobby partners—all the way up to Prime Minister Chernomyrdin. Still, as foreign minister orchestrating the crescendo of "Persian themes" in Russian foreign policy, Primakov in late 1996 continued to fight a rearguard but ultimately losing battle on the delimitation issue. At a Caspian foreign ministers meeting in Ashgabat that November, Primakov and his counterparts from Iran and Turkmenistan declared their countries' intention to put together a joint-stock company with the right to extract mineral resources anywhere in the Caspian. But they were bitterly and uncompromisingly opposed by Kazakhstan and Azerbaijan, and the initiative—apparently designed to force the Kazakhs and Azeris into finally agreeing on the condominium approach—was stillborn.[31]

## BLUE STREAM CHALLENGE

As the successor to the Soviet Union, Russia had long had a near lock on the Turkish natural gas market. With a groundbreaking visit from Prime Minister Nikolay Tikhonov in December 1984 setting the stage, Turkey had started to import natural gas from the USSR in 1987 via a spur from the Soyuz pipeline south through Romania and Bulgaria and into western Turkey.[32] From 1987 to 1994, the Soviet Union and then Russia had been the exclusive purveyor of the product to Turkey. After the USSR's collapse, Russia did not want to lose the Turkish market, whether to Iran, Azerbaijan, or Turkmenistan bordering the natural gas-rich Caspian Sea, or to other major producers such as Algeria, from which Turkey in 1994 began to import liquefied natural gas (LNG).[33]

Iran posed the first challenge, and Russia quickly responded. In May 1995 Turkey and Iran had reached a preliminary agreement on building a pipeline for natural gas from Tabriz to Ankara. This was pushed further along during the visit of Turkish premier Necmettin Erbakan to Tehran in August 1996, just a month after his Islamic Welfare (Refah) Party had formed a ruling coalition with Tansu Ciller's True Path Party.[34] Jumping ahead, after many of the usual travails and delays of the energy business, this time aggravated by the Turkish economic crisis of 2001, the Tabriz to Ankara pipeline formally opened at its Bazargan border crossing in January 2002. Its projected maximum capacity was 10 billion cubic meters per year.[35]

One Russian Duma subcommittee chairman later characterized the Turko-Iranian project as "a direct challenge to the Russian gas policy."[36] In response to planning for the Tabriz-Ankara pipeline, Gazprom quickly began developing the concept— engineering and financing—of a Blue Stream pipeline, which it first publicized in November 1996.[37] The pipeline would send natural gas directly from Russia to Turkey under the Black Sea at a depth of over two kilometers, an unprecedented engineering challenge. However difficult to implement, such a pipeline had the attraction of avoiding the transit fees, pilfering, and security headaches of sending gas either westward through Ukraine, Moldova, Romania, and Bulgaria—as Moscow had since 1987—or "eastward" through the Caucasus using preexisting but underutilized pipelines traversing Chechnya, Georgia, and Armenia.[38]

By late August 1997, Gazprom CEO Rem Vyakhirev and Turkish energy minister Cumhur Ersumer, with Turkish prime minister Mesut Yilmaz presiding, signed an initial protocol or framework agreement for the Blue Stream project, which envisioned natural gas deliveries eventually reaching 16 billion cubic meters per year.[39] On December 15, 1997, Prime Ministers Chernomyrdin and Yilmaz signed an intergovernmental agreement for Blue Stream, while BOTAS (the Turkish pipeline company) and Gazexport signed the companion commercial agreement for the $3.2 billion project.[40]

The signing ceremony took place despite U.S. demarches to Ankara advising against the agreement.[41] Washington regarded Turkey's partnership in Blue Stream as running counter to Turkey's anticipated participation in pipelines that bypassed Russia to export Caspian oil and gas to Western markets. By 1994 the United States had settled on a policy of promoting multiple short- and long-term pipelines out of the Caspian region.[42] The policy encouraged Azerbaijan, Kazakhstan, and Turkmenistan and the multinational consortiums of which they were members to consider main export pipelines that would entirely avoid Iran and not add to Russia's monopoly on moving oil and gas out of the Caspian basin to Western markets. The "multiple pipelines" policy was in part a reaction to energy major Chevron's frustrating negotiations since 1992 with the Caspian Pipeline Consortium (CPC), originally formed by Russia, Kazakhstan, and Oman, on a pipeline designed to carry oil from Kazakhstan's giant Tengizchevroil joint venture to Russia's port of Novorossyisk on the Black Sea. Russia, controlling all the oil and gas outlets from the region at the time, had used its monopoly to pressure Kazakhstan politically and Chevron contractually over the terms for the CPC project.[43]

By 1995–96, Washington had begun specifically to endorse an ambitious proposal for side-by-side gas and oil pipelines from Azerbaijan through Georgia to Turkey. The oil pipeline eventually became known as Baku-Tbilisi-Ceyhan (BTC). It would initially deliver production from the AIOC project and extend all the way to the Mediterranean Sea. It was thought that additional oil to fill BTC could be barged across the Caspian from Kazakhstan. Not until November 18, 1999, however, was the crucial intergovernmental agreement in place. On that date, while in Istanbul for an OSCE summit, President Bill Clinton and the presidents of Azerbaijan, Turkey, and Georgia all signed a commitment to BTC.[44] Three years later, Turkey's President Ahmet Necdet Sezer traveled to Baku in September 2002 for the official kickoff of the construction phase of the $2.95 billion BTC project, and the first oil from Azerbaijan reached Ceyhan through the finished pipeline on May 28, 2006.[45]

The gas pipeline, however, was slower to take shape. It was known first as the South Caucasus Pipeline (SCP) and then as the Baku-Tbilisi-Erzurum pipeline (BTE). SCP/BTE extended from the Shah Deniz field off Baku to Erzurum in central Anatolia. Presidents Aliyev and Sezer signed the intergovernmental agreement on the project in Ankara on March 12, 2001.[46] Construction of the pipeline began in October 2004 and its completion was projected for late 2006.[47] Indeed, gas started to flow from Shah Deniz to Azerbaijan and Georgia in December 2006 and reached the Turkish system in July 2007.[48] Some envisioned additional gas for SCP/BTE piped under the Caspian from Turkmenistan via a projected Trans-Caspian Pipeline (TCP).

The aim of BTC, SCP/BTE, and their companion oil and natural gas feeder projects was to increase the market leverage of Azerbaijan and Central Asian producers vis-à-vis Russia and more widely to lessen their political vulnerability to pressure from both Russia and Iran. In proposing to deliver oil via an overland pipeline to the Turkish port of Ceyhan on the Mediterranean coast, moreover, BTC not only would provide an alternative to routes through Russia or Iran but also would avoid stressing the seventeen-mile Bosporus strait cutting through Istanbul and its population of 10 million.[49] At the same time, the BTC and SCP/BTE mainlines would ensure bountiful energy supplies for Turkey and make the country a main trans-shipment point to other world markets for the oil and gas its own economy did not need.

Blue Stream, however, undermined Iran's Tabriz-Ankara pipeline and challenged the economic viability of the American-endorsed SCP/BTE route. The Russian press thus hailed the Blue Stream project as a feather in Prime Minister Chernomyrdin's cap. On the eve of the signing ceremony, almost to the day of the fifth anniversary of his assuming office, Chernomyrdin declared, "If Turkey shakes the hand being proffered by Russia, then we will become strategic partners in the economic sphere in the 21st century."[50] At the talks, he expressed optimism about the bilateral relationship and said that Moscow viewed Turkey "as a good neighbor and a reliable partner."[51] After the ceremony, one newspaper wrote that Blue Stream would have "considerable political consequences and to a certain extent place the whole range of Russo-Turkish relations in a new context . . . [and] undoubtedly improve the overall political climate."[52]

Blue Stream was seen in some quarters as a sign of "redolent . . . pragmatism" and hailed for promoting Russia's own geopolitical goals by undermining projects such as SCP/BTE that bypassed Russia.[53] But the agreement also clearly advanced Chernomyrdin's personal and institutional economic interests. In Turkey, Blue Stream was subjected to withering criticism not only for increasing the country's energy dependence on Russia but also for the alleged corruption involved in putting the deal together.[54] Some of these allegations inevitably rubbed off on Gazprom and on Chernomyrdin personally. Chernomyrdin's sons reportedly owned 12 percent of Stroytransgaz, and it was this construction arm of Gazprom that was put in charge of building Blue Stream[55]—probably just the tip of the iceberg of Chernomyrdin's personal and family interests in Gazprom and its projects.

Construction of Blue Stream forged ahead. After starting to move natural gas under the Black Sea to Turkey on a trial basis at the end of December 2002, it shifted to regular pumping on February 20, 2003, with the flow projected to rise to sixteen billion cubic meters by 2010. Turkey's feared overdependency on Russian gas, however, almost immediately turned out to be a double-edged sword. Ankara interrupted its acceptance of Blue Stream gas from March 12 to August 1, 2003, and reopened negotiations on the terms of the contract.[56] Now the shoe was on the other foot. Some in the Russian government suggested that investing over $3 billion in a gas pipeline to be used exclusively by one consumer "may have been too radical."[57] A new agreement restructuring the price of Russian gas to Turkey was reached on November 19, 2003, however, and both sides pronounced themselves satisfied.[58]

## SHOWDOWN OVER ALBORZ/ALOV

By 1998 Russia's early policy of working with Iran to keep the West out of the Caspian had clearly failed and had begun to shift. Around the time that Yeltsin's government began taking a more dispassionate, critical approach toward security relations with Iran, the Russian president also started to revise Moscow's official state policy on Caspian delimitation. Moscow broke ranks with Tehran, abandoned the condominium approach and endorsed national sectors defined by median lines.

Azerbaijan, Kazakhstan, and Turkmenistan were all going ahead and signing up with major multinational energy consortiums to exploit fields off their coasts. Chernomyrdin and his backers clearly favored the more remunerative approach of working with Russia's own immediate neighbors to resolve exploitation rights, proceeding with exploration of potential fields, and giving the go-ahead to Russia's own energy giants to work with international consortiums, capital, and advanced technology for mutual profit. By mid-1998 Yeltsin gave his personal imprimatur to this approach.

Moscow did not want to be left behind or out of the action and so began negotiations in the first instance with Kazakhstan on an approach to delimitation which put Russia's previous much contested condominium approach—and its partner Iran—to the side.[59] To Iran's great chagrin, Yeltsin and Kazakhstani president Nursultan Nazarbayev in July 1998 signed a bilateral understanding to negotiate the division of the seabed between Russia and Kazakhstan using the modified national median line principle while sharing the water column and surface above it. It was a position that Iran promptly declared it would not recognize, but to no avail.[60]

The journalist Maksim Yusin, whose commentaries over the years often cast doubt on the wisdom of close relations with Iran, was quick to hail Yeltsin's break with Iran on Caspian delimitation. Russian diplomacy under Kozyrev and then Primakov, charged Yusin, had run "the risk of discrediting" Moscow by selling arms to the fundamentalist regime, building the Bushehr nuclear power station, and ignoring "flagrant violations of human rights" in Iran. The possible cooling of relations "with one of the most odious regimes on the planet" would be a good thing for Russia in world politics. After all, "the alliance of democratic Russia and fundamentalist Iran," wrote Yusin, had "struck many people—not only in the West but also in the East—as just too unnatural."[61]

Exploitation of already proven and yet to be discovered hydrocarbon reserves in the North Caspian was critical to the future of the Kazakhstani and Russian energy sectors. The area's riches were a powerful incentive for the two countries to reach agreement on a methodology for sorting out exploitation rights to specific energy blocks lying between them. After the July 1998 Yeltsin-Nazarbayev agreement to start sector line negotiations, Lukoil and Gazprom in November of that year signed a "strategic partnership agreement" for prospecting, producing, refining, and transporting hydrocarbon riches in the North Caspian and elsewhere in Russia.[62] In June 2001 Vagit Alekperov told an interviewer that preparing Lukoil's North Caspian holdings for development was the firm's "number one objective because we are sure that this region will give us an opportunity to remain the leader in terms of production volume in the future."[63] By May 2002 Nazarbayev and Yeltsin's successor Putin had signed a completed bilateral delimitation agreement.

The Yeltsin-Nazarbayev agreement on delimitation provoked an immediate Iranian response. Iran began to hedge its bets on the outcome, if any, of the endless rounds of delimitation talks and to stake its claim to 20 percent of the Caspian seabed through actions and not just words. On December 14, 1998, Iranian oil minister Bijan Zanganeh announced that after "more than six months of continuous work," the National Iranian Oil Company (NIOC) had that day signed an eighteen-month contract with the British-Dutch Shell and British Lasmo oil companies to explore for oil and gas in the southern Caspian. "We think this was an important step toward establishing Iran's sovereignty over its oil and gas fields in the Caspian Sea," declared Zanganeh. The project would explore ten thousand square kilometers and cost $19.8 million, just below the ILSA threshold for invoking sanctions.[64] A year later, Veba, a German oil company, joined as a partner in the exploration contract, the duration of which was now put at eighteen to twenty-four months.[65]

In March 2001, on the very eve of President Mohammad Khatami's departure for Moscow for his first summit with new Russian president Vladimir Putin, Oil Minister Zanganeh presided over another signing ceremony. The Iranian firm Sadra contracted with the Swedish company GVA to build a semisubmersible deepwater rig to drill in what the Shell-Lasmo explorations had suggested were promising oil and gas blocks. It would operate in waters as deep as a thousand meters, and drill as deep as six to seven thousand meters below the seabed. Zanganeh said Iran was operating in an area that covered 20 percent of the Caspian, which he described as Iran's "minimum entitlement." The rig would take thirty-two months to build, meaning that Iran would fully deploy the platform by 2004 if it kept to this schedule.[66]

On July 21, 2001, Iran formally protested Azerbaijan's intention to start imminently to explore the Alborz field, called Alov by Azerbaijan.[67] Tehran asserted that Alborz/Alov was situated within Iran's claimed 20 percent sector of the Caspian. When two BP-owned oil-exploration ships chartered by Azerbaijan's SOCAR nevertheless began work over Alborz/Alov on July 23, an Iranian gunboat and military aircraft forcibly chased them away.[68] The action had its intended effect. Both BP and Azerbaijan declared they would suspend work on Alov until the dispute was resolved.[69]

Alborz/Alov was located some eighty miles north of the Astara-Gasanguly line and within what would be the Azerbaijani median-line sector, neither of which Iran recognized. Since the claim to Alborz/Alov put Iran most directly in conflict with Azerbaijan, a solution might have been amenable to negotiations between Baku and Tehran. Tehran could conceivably use Alborz/Alov as a bargaining chip to win title to a national sector significantly larger than a median-line-dictated 13–14 percent but well short of its own demand for 20 percent. Spokesmen in Baku made the point that Iran should be satisfied with 13–14 percent, since this would be a decided improvement over the 11–12 percent that would belong to Iran according to the Astara-Gasanguly line, to which Iran allegedly had not objected during Soviet times.[70]

On the eve of the Alborz/Alov incident, Novruz Mammadov, head of the International Relations Department of President Aliyev's executive office, stressed that Azerbaijan had been extracting oil in the area for fifty years and would continue to do so.[71] Immediately after the incident, however, one Tehran commentary sardonically characterized Mammadov's statement as "especially interesting considering the fact that 50 years ago Azerbaijan was a remote corner of the former Soviet Union while Iran was a sovereign country."[72]

Despite the July contretemps over Alborz/Alov, Lukoil's formidable Alekperov seemed briefly to strengthen Baku's hand toward the end of the year. In June, before the incident, when asked whether the Caspian's unsettled status was a problem, Alekperov had replied that the situation was "simply keeping us a little tense. But I think the politicians will settle this problem to the benefit of all parties, especially those who are already investing in the Caspian now."[73] In December, Alekperov returned to Baku to champion a Lukoil bid for a 10–15 percent share (out of SOCAR's 40 percent share) in the Araz-Alov-Sarq project, as well as a 7.5 percent share in the Baku-Tbilisi-Ceyhan main export pipeline consortium.

The Russian government at that time was a 35 percent shareholder in Lukoil. Its approval of the Lukoil bid for a share of the Alov-inclusive project would mean that Tehran in the future would have to take into account not only Baku but also Moscow's reaction to any forcible Iranian challenge to Alov exploration. According to a source at SOCAR, Alekperov said that Lukoil "is aware of the political risk of this project and realizes that the structure is the most attractive one among the deep-water structures in Azerbaijan's sector of the Caspian." After "proper consultations" in Moscow, Alekperov hoped to have a final decision by the end of the first quarter of 2002.[74]

By April 17, 2002, however, Lukoil signaled that it did not have Moscow's backing to pursue an ownership share in the BTC pipeline project.[75] The red light from the Kremlin apparently extended to Lukoil's pursuit of a piece of the Araz-Alov-Sarq project as well. At the end of May, SOCAR first vice president (and President Heydar Aliyev's son) Ilham Aliyev said that Lukoil was willing to take part in the Alov project but that there were no ongoing talks "on its specific share."[76] With Lukoil no longer pursuing a stake in Araz-Alov-Sarq, Baku seemed to lose whatever leverage it had hoped to get from Russia in its dispute with Iran over the Alov field.

## PUTIN THREATENS 11 PERCENT

After 1998 Tehran's stance on the Caspian evolved from condominium to equal-fifths division of the seabed and water column above it. Tehran argued that it still favored a condominium, but if the others insisted on a division, then Iran would insist on a 20 percent portion of everything for each littoral country.[77]

The Iranian position was unacceptable to Azerbaijan, Kazakhstan, and even to prevaricating and unpredictable Turkmenistan—the countries with the most to gain from national sectors defined by median lines rather than the arbitrary 20 percent principle. The Iranian position implied years of haggling and uncertainty over the exploitation rights of hydrocarbon reserves located beneath and across uncertain national sector lines. Tehran's aim in threatening such legal uncertainty, besides getting Iran as big a sector as possible, seemed to be to lower the incentives for Western investment capital to pour into the region until Iran was satisfied with delimitation arrangements.

In Moscow, shortly after replacing Yeltsin, Putin at the end of May 2000 appointed Viktor Kalyuzhnyy deputy foreign minister and presidential envoy for Caspian affairs. Kalyuzhnyy fit the same mold as Chernomyrdin and Alekperov, though on a less grand scale. Kalyuzhnyy had also made his career in the energy field, starting out in the Siberian oil fields of Tomsk. In December 1998 he was appointed fuel and energy first deputy minister, and he was bumped up to minister in May 1999. As minister, Kalyuzhnyy in September 1999 engineered the appointment of Semen Vaynshtok to head Transneft, the Russian Federation's all-powerful oil pipeline monopoly.[78] Vaynshtok's takeover of Transneft was another major feather in the cap of Lukoil's Vagit Alekperov. Vaynshtok had been with Lukoil since its inception, rising to vice president from 1995 to 1999.[79]

Some had not surprisingly criticized Kalyuzhnyy, while he was fuel and energy minister, for lobbying on behalf of Lukoil and Sibneft. After his appointment as Russia's lead Caspian negotiator, Lukoil and other oil companies were said to have rejoiced over Kalyuzhnyy's new responsibilities. Putin, it was reported, wanted someone precisely like Kalyuzhnyy to put into practice what was described as the president's "new foreign policy concept." This was said to call for diplomacy to defend the interests of Russian business.[80] In reality, it would become clear with time that it was more the other way around, with big business obliged to support the priorities of the Russian state as defined by Putin and those around him. On Caspian issues, however, the priorities of both were by this time roughly the same. Long gone were the days of open conflict in Moscow over how to approach Caspian delimitation.

When Putin visited Baku in January 2001, Azerbaijan agreed to the same principle as that of the Russian-Kazakhstani understanding of July 1998: "The water is common property, but we are dividing the seabed." While unhappy with the position it found itself in, Iran agreed to a series of meetings between all the littoral states. These included a deputy foreign ministers meeting in Tehran in late February and a five presidents' summit in Turkmenistan at the end of February into early March.[81] The Tehran experts meeting in February yielded no progress, however, derailing by a year the proposed Turkmenistan summit and foreshadowing the lack of any real agreement on the delimitation issue at the March 12, 2001, summit between Putin and Khatami.[82]

With Russian-Kazakhstani and Russian-Azerbaijani understandings already reached on adjoining national sectors, Aliyev and Nazarbayev completed the triangle with a bilateral delimitation agreement of their own on the margins of the CIS summit in November 2001.[83] With that, Russia's own interests in agreed rules of the road for exploiting northern Caspian oil and gas fields were pretty much resolved. Early in 2002, Russian negotiator Kalyuzhnyy began to suggest that Iran focus on the concrete division or sharing of energy structures or blocks in the way Russia and Kazakhstan were doing. Kalyuzhnyy ruled out of hand Iran's demand for a 20 percent share and suggested the most sensible compromise would be to "leave percentage division and arrive at resource division."[84]

When Putin received Iranian foreign minister Kamal Kharrazi in Moscow on April 5, 2002, he reportedly forcefully rejected—again—Iran's demand for 20 percent of the Caspian. According to some Iranian accounts, Putin told Kharrazi that Iran would just have to settle for 11 percent, i.e., the Astara-Gasanguly line.[85]

It apparently was much the same story at the Ashgabat summit of Caspian presidents that finally convened several weeks later on April 24. Despite President Khatami's attendance and Putin's expectation in his opening speech that the summit would end with all signing a joint declaration, there was no movement in the Iranian position and no final declaration.[86] Though Putin backed Khatami's proposal to hold the next group summit in Tehran, the Russian position was that the timing would depend "on how fast the agenda for the next presidential meeting will emerge," which the Iranian side rendered more softly as "in an appropriate time."[87]

Not long after, Iranian special envoy for Caspian affairs Mehdi Safari, at a conference at Iran's Mazandaran University, reiterated Tehran's insistence on either a condominium or a minimum share of 20 percent. Alluding to the Alborz/Alov incident of July 2001, he again warned that Iran would not allow others to prospect in "its" 20 percent of the Caspian.[88] In fact, Iran's gunboat diplomacy had succeeded in backing up its claim. The demonstration of force the previous summer had evidently been enough to persuade Moscow not to risk further entangling its relations with Tehran by putting Russian equities on the line over Alov. In any event, as we have seen, within a year Lukoil's Alekperov had dropped his pursuit of a 10–15 percent stake in the Araz-Alov-Sarq project.

Meanwhile, Russia, Kazakhstan, and Azerbaijan reinforced their determination to go forward with parceling up the northern Caspian despite Iranian objections. On May 13, 2002, Putin and Nazarbayev formalized what working-level negotiators had worked out after the July 1998 Yeltsin-Nazarbayev understanding. The protocol disentangled ownership rights and established sharing arrangements in the northern Caspian using the median line principle.[89] Iran promptly rejected the agreement, again calling for consensus and warning that it considered "null and void" all "unilateral deals" concluded before the Caspian's legal regime was settled.[90] All the same, having given up trying to get Lukoil to buy into the Araz-Alov-Sarq project, and thus in effect having lost potential Russian backing for contesting the Alborz/Alov field with Iran, Azerbaijani leader Heydar Aliyev went ahead and signed an agreement on delimiting the Caspian seabed with Putin in Moscow on September 23, 2002.[91]

## FLOTILLA EXERCISE EVOKES TURKMANCHAI

Iran's positions on the Caspian factored in not only economic but also security considerations. Some ascribed the "political-security approach" to advisers of Iran's Supreme National Security Council. They noted that the 1921 and 1940 Soviet-Iranian treaties permitted ships from both sides to move freely in the Caspian and made no distinction between military and nonmilitary vessels. These advisers feared that Russia wanted to maintain a condominium approach to the Caspian's surface so that Russia's Caspian flotilla—substantially larger than Iran's—could exercise "hegemony" over the other four littoral states.[92] The advisers thus favored a complete vertical division of the Caspian, including of the surface waters, in order to interpose buffer zones belonging to Azerbaijan, Kazakhstan, and Turkmenistan between the Russian and Iranian sectors and thus to limit the movement of Russia's warships.[93] Supreme Leader Ali Khamenei appeared to support this position.[94]

Putin's announcement on April 25, 2002—the day after the unproductive Caspian summit in Ashgabat—that there would be a major exercise of Russia's flotilla later that summer reinforced this concern in Tehran.[95] According to one report, Putin chose the most forceful variant of several prepared options for his statement announcing the long-planned exercise, surprising even his navy commanders.[96] A source in the Russian navy's High Command asserted that Russian admirals had been tasked with "not just demonstrating a military presence in the region but showing the overwhelming potential of the Russian Navy in the Caspian compared with other countries' naval forces."[97] From Tehran, one commentary declared, "Putin's Russia is aware that Iran's pivotal role in the region could be an obstacle to reviving its lost might in the region and therefore he resorted to military references."[98] Iran's navy commander R. Adm. Abbas Mohtaj warned that his forces in the Caspian would defend the nation's interests in Iranian waters.[99]

The Russian exercise took place the first two weeks of August 2002. Defense Minister Sergey Ivanov called it unprecedented in either Russian or Soviet history. Russia's national security requirements in the region were changing. Noting that Afghanistan and Georgia—an allusion to Chechen rebel fighters and Arab mujahideen operating out of Georgia's Pankisi gorge—were nearby, Ivanov said the fight against terrorism was Russia's top priority. Some ten thousand servicemen were taking part in the exercise, which had deployed ninety ships and support craft, and Kazakhstani and Azerbaijani forces were also engaged.[100] Kalyuzhnyy later claimed that Russia's flotilla had been upgraded "according to scientific-technological achievements" but had not increased in numbers.[101] Demilitarization was still a realistic long-term option, according to Kalyuzhnyy, but it would take Russia time to "settle the serious problems that we are now facing in the Caucasus."[102]

Iran did not participate in the war games but did send observers. Deputy Defense Minister Adm. Mohammad Shafie Rudsari later asserted that the exercise had actually contributed to regional "security and stability" and had promoted "peace and friendship."[103] Defense Minister Ali Shamkhani, however, struck a note of caution and realism in a major interview in early September 2002. He did not consider Russia's "military maneuvers" in the Caspian a threat to Iran, he claimed, or an impediment to the continuation of "ordinary relations" between Iran and Russia. That said, Shamkhani suggested there was much that he could not predict. "Regional conditions are gradually changing and without doubt," he warned, "any sign of a regional threat to the Islamic Republic of Iran within the Caspian basin will meet with Iran's response."[104]

In Tehran, anger over Putin's announcement of the naval exercise and sudden realization of the extent of Iranian isolation on the Caspian delimitation issue led to a flurry of bitter recriminations and counterattacks in the Majles and the press. These focused not only on the negotiating record and capabilities of the Iranian Foreign Ministry but also more generally on the nature of Russian intentions and therefore the wisdom of dealing with Moscow. Extreme critics evidently charged the Iranian Foreign Ministry and Moscow were in effect no better than the Qajars and imperial Russia, who nearly two centuries before had colluded in the "shameful" Turkmanchai treaty of 1828 that had formalized Russian hegemony over the Caspian Sea and Iran's losses in the Caucasus.[105]

Some of these critics thus rejected a 20 percent portion of the Caspian as eminently unfair and demanded a 50 percent share, while others insisted on calling the Caspian the Mazandaran Sea, after Iran's northern seaside province, or *ostan*.[106] Alluding to internal debates a decade before as the Soviet Union collapsed, some regretted that Tehran had not grappled with the delimitation issue much earlier. In retrospect, they judged Iran's expectation of Russian restraint and good offices in preserving the condominium arrangement—however unfairly applied in practice during the Soviet era—a clear Iranian policy failure. Russia, they argued, though esteemed by some as Iran's "strategic friend," was in reality taking advantage of American pressure on Iran to "make its own interests last through sacrificing those of the people of Iran."[107]

More restrained critics of Tehran's dealings with Moscow joined the more extreme chorus in attacking Putin's naval exercise announcement as a threat directed against Iran. One member of the Majles's National Security and Foreign Policy Committee warned, "Russia cannot expect us to be flexible toward its demands simply because it supports us on certain issues. It would not be beneficial to Iran's national interests for us to yield to Russia's demands simply because Russia promises to support us in other areas."[108] Not a few in these two camps declared Putin an untrustworthy partner. The more bitter denounced Putin—and Azerbaijani President Heydar Aliyev—as "pupils" of the Communist Party and the KGB and found "these people" worse than their Soviet-era predecessors Aleksey Kosygin, Yuri Andropov, and "even" Mikhail Gorbachev.[109]

Defenders of putting the best face possible on the necessity of continuing to deal with Moscow, nevertheless, appeared to regain the edge for the time being in internal debates. After initial grumbling over the impending exercise, Iranian commentary began to shift as officials tried to make the best of the upcoming Russian muscle flexing. Increasingly, the line out of Tehran was that the exercise was not directed at keeping Iran down but rather at keeping the United States and NATO out of the Caspian basin.[110] Together with commentary on other issues, it was another indication that the top leadership in Tehran was determined to hang on to its Russian ties, however much Russian policy increasingly disabused Iran of its aspirations in the Caspian. Nevertheless, disagreement persisted. A commentary on Iranian state radio warned that Tehran's approval of the exercise was "like a double-edged sword" because it could open the door to "a total hegemony of one of the littoral states of the sea."[111] Others again castigated the Iranian Foreign Ministry for "our weak diplomacy in the region." The Russian exercise was a "new turning point in regional interaction" that could "indeed checkmate Iran."[112]

However critical of Iran's own Foreign Ministry and frustrated by Russia, conservatives criticized reformists in parliament for raising the Caspian issue allegedly simply to complicate relations with Russia in order to force a tilt by Iran back toward America.[113] While acknowledging the Foreign Ministry's "passivity" and lack of negotiating creativity, some more level-headed conservatives castigated those demanding 50 percent of the Caspian as totally unrealistic. They warned that Iran should search for more practical outcomes even if somewhat below 20 percent rather than risk ending up with much less.[114] They called for putting aside all illusions in dealing with Russia. "All the analysts who are waiting and hoping that our 'strategic ally' in the region will do something spectacular for us in order to make up for the Turkmanchai Treaty," they cautioned, "must know that our situation today contains even more bitter lessons."[115]

## PUTIN CAPTURES GAZPROM

On August 9, 1999, Yeltsin appointed Putin acting premier and declared that Putin was his preferred successor as president.[116] Within two weeks, Putin presided over a cabinet debate on the energy crisis then gripping Russia. There were shortages across the board: gasoline, coal, electricity, oil, and natural gas. Because of nonpayments and low payments from domestic customers, export prices that were twice as high, "barbaric" exploitation of domestic gas fields, insufficient investments and decreasing production, Gazprom had just announced its intention to reduce deliveries to the Russian and CIS market in the coming winter while continuing to honor its more lucrative contracts to markets beyond the CIS.

Putin sat "grimly silent" through three hours of debate and then lashed out at most of the participants. "The fuel and energy complex is in the hands of private owners who are standing under a golden shower," he complained bitterly. "For some reason they are convinced that they operate in the same conditions as the owners of western companies. They are mistaken." Jumping ahead, however, Putin himself in coming years would to all appearances develop an abiding liking for that same "golden shower" about which he now grumbled.

Turning to Lukoil's Alekperov, Putin asked why he did "not invest funds in Russia and build a modern oil refining system here?" More generally, Putin declared, "The state has recklessly lost its influence in the fuel and energy sector." He blamed the crisis primarily on the "diktat of monopolists" and concluded, "Solely by moderating the excessive appetites of the new owners of the fuel and energy sector we can resolve the really important problems that do pose a threat to the country's energy security: eliminate non-payments and revive the refining industry."[117]

In his "Millennium" statement at the end of 1999, Putin gave notice of his intent to restore "the leading and regulating role of the state."[118] He proceeded to do just this in the energy sector in particular. Although Putin had criticized Alekperov by name at the August 1999 cabinet session, his real target in the next few years was Rem Vyakhirev and Gazprom. As usual, insinuations of corruption featured prominently in the attacks designed to encourage Vyakhirev to retire from the field.

Putin's focus on subordinating Gazprom to the state was not an idle one and evidently had long-standing roots. According to Aleksey Venediktov, chief editor of the radio station Ekho Moskvy, Putin had set his eyes on becoming the head of Gazprom as far back as 1997.[119] Around that time, Putin had received what was described as a PhD degree from the St. Petersburg Mining Academy. Putin's thesis reportedly dealt with strategic planning and replenishment of the raw material base of St. Petersburg and the Leningrad region in a developing market economy. Although it did not focus on natural gas, it nevertheless argued, "Irrespective of who owns natural, namely mineral, resources, the state has the right to regulate their development and use."[120] In addition, Vladimir Milov, former energy deputy minister, later claimed that Putin in 1998 had asked to replace Rem Vyakhirev at Gazprom rather than be appointed FSB head.[121]

In any event, Fuel and Energy Minister Viktor Kalyuzhnyy in March 2000 used an interview in the government daily *Rossiyskaya Gazeta* to criticize the "lamentable" state of the energy complex and to deliver a withering broadside at Vyakhirev's stewardship of Gazprom. The sector had pursued a "completely ruinous tendency . . . of working chiefly for export, for the external market, satisfying the country's needs according to a principle of what was left. This finally led to the gasoline crisis of 1999." Russia needed to develop a "new ideology" for the fuel and energy sector and to adopt a "clear energy strategy." Its top priority, as set out by Putin, was to "strengthen the state's role in the fuel and energy complex." "Without this," warned Kalyuzhnyy, "we will never get out of the rut."

Under Putin's leadership, the dominance of exports had been subordinated to the priorities of Russia's domestic market, according to Kalyuzhnyy. But this had proved "highly disagreeable" to Vyakhirev in particular, who had "concluded several gas export agreements for 20–30 years into the future without any state appraisal." Vyakhirev had then compounded Gazprom's mismanagement by "messing up" its investment program. As a result, Gazprom was planning a fifty to eighty billion cubic meters cut in production between 1999 and 2001, which would punch "a sizeable hole through the country's fuel balance." Russia was being forced to make up the shortfall with imports from Turkmenistan, which charged forty-four dollars per thousand cubic meters instead of Gazprom's rate, twelve dollars. "I do not see why Russia should now depend on the political conditions in Ashgabat," groused Kalyuzhnyy.[122]

Vyakhirev's days at Gazprom were clearly numbered. By May 30, 2001, Putin protégé Aleksey Miller had replaced Vyakhirev as Gazprom's CEO. Vyakhirev remained on Gazprom's board of directors but his ouster as CEO allegedly was the beginning of the end of Gazprom's status as a "state within the state."[123] A month later, while making Vyakhirev chairman of the board, government representatives gained a majority of the seats on Gazprom's board for the first time.[124] A year later they ousted Vyakhirev from the chairmanship and replaced him with Dmitry Medvedev, deputy chief of the PA, who in 2008 would succeed Putin as Russia's president.[125] The action was a model and precursor for what the Putin regime had in store for other "strategic" sectors in coming years.

Vyakhirev's eclipse came amid long-standing and persistent reports of a government investigation that had established that at least $10 billion had "disappeared" from Gazprom's books in the previous decade. Gazprom officers and their relatives were reportedly secret owners of Itera, a Gazprom spin-off established in 1992, and were using the firm to siphon off Gazprom's assets into their own pockets. Since November 1997 Gazprom allegedly had been using Itera to privatize gas resources. Allowed virtually free access to Gazprom's pipeline network, Itera by 2001 had grown to be the second-largest gas company in Russia with some seven thousand employees in twenty-four countries.[126]

Kalyuzhnyy in his March 2000 interview had underscored that, unlike Gazprom, the oil companies had been "the first to understand that they must not be at war with the state but collaborate with it."[127] As Putin settled into office and began to bring in his own team of "statist oligarchs," Vagit Alekperov's fortunes diverged sharply from those of Vyakhirev. Indeed, by the end of 2002, Alekperov succeeded in positioning Lukoil as one of Putin's favorite privatized energy companies. The Lukoil chief did this by offering himself and Lukoil as models of what Putin seemed to be looking for in state-attuned behavior by Russia's oligarchs and the private firms and state monopolies they controlled.

Around this time, Alekperov gave a remarkable speech at Russia's General Staff Academy. The November 2002 event was billed as the first such meeting between one of Russia's premier economic leaders and the armed forces "elite." "We at Lukoil," Alekperov told the military audience, "have considered and consider ourselves to be first and foremost patriots who are working for the benefit of our great Fatherland." Alekperov's fortunes subsequently rose higher as those who flaunted their independence and even rivalry with Putin floundered and, in the case of Yukos's Mikhail Khodorkovsky, ended up in Siberian penal colonies.[128] Khodorkovsky insisted on meddling in politics. Perhaps even more egregious from Putin's point of view—as argued by Harley Balzer—Khodorkovsky's plans to sell a big chunk of Yukos to Exxon-Mobil and for changing tax legislation challenged Putin's vision of the state dominating Russia's energy and natural resources sectors.[129]

While focused on making a profit, Alekperov at the General Staff Academy asserted that Lukoil had never and would never go against Russian national interests. "Our company's long-term strategy is structured in such a manner in order to fully correspond to Russia's national interests," he stressed. "And the country's national interests outside its borders are manifested first of all through its economic expansion." Looking back at Lukoil's accomplishments since the Soviet collapse, Alekperov boasted that it had been the Russian state working with the country's oil companies that had won back Russia's position in the Caspian "rapidly and quite effectively." Together, he claimed, they had "gained strength in the Caspian economically, politically, geopolitically, culturally, and from the military point of view."[130]

## "EURASIAN GAS ALLIANCE"

Even before Alekperov congratulated himself on Lukoil's role in forging Russia's policies in the Caspian over the previous decade, Moscow had already begun to put down the foundations of a grandiose natural gas project that would multiply Russia's Caspian energy advantages in European markets for years to come. The architect of this project appeared to be none other than Putin himself. Two years earlier, Kalyuzhnyy had complained that Russia was being forced to make up for its natural gas shortfalls with imports from Turkmenistan. Now, ironically, Putin began by pitching his new project precisely to the unpredictable lifetime president of Turkmenistan.

Having asserted state control of Gazprom's board of directors by late June 2001, Putin in January 2002 unveiled an ambitious initiative to put together a "Eurasian alliance of gas producers." Receiving Turkmenistan president Saparmurat Niyazov in the Kremlin, Putin said such an alliance "would make it possible to exercise effective control over the volumes and direction of Central Asian gas exports" from Turkmenistan, Kazakhstan, and Uzbekistan as well as Russia through Gazprom's pipelines—"there are no others"—to European consumers.[131]

The project was to be a large part of the solution to the shortchanging of the Russian domestic market that had resulted from Gazprom's focus on export profits. But it went far beyond this, aiming at a monopoly on Central Asian gas in order to satisfy both domestic and export markets and to greatly increase Gazprom's profit margins in the latter. Together with the Blue Stream pipeline to Turkey, Putin's Gazprom-led "alliance" would all but deny Iran access to the European natural gas market. The two projects would also scare away financing and dampen export projections for the new and competing SCP/BTE pipeline projected to carry natural gas from Azerbaijan's Shah Deniz block to Turkey for domestic consumption and reexport to Europe.

In addition, the alliance would effectively put an end to any practical hopes Niyazov might have had for sending gas, primarily from the giant Dauletabat field on the Afghan border, east though Afghanistan to Pakistan. Should a so-called trans-Afghan pipeline (TAP) have been built, it would have deprived Russia of the volumes of Turkmen gas and profit margins it needed to cash in big on deliveries through Russia's pipelines to European markets.

Thus, a decade after the Soviet Union's collapse, Moscow and Tehran—the early partners in a condominium approach to sharing the Caspian's resources—were further apart than ever on how to share them. Some Iranian Caspian experts such as Abbas Maleki urged the authorities at long last to negotiate joint cooperation and sharing agreements covering contentious fields such as Alborz/Alov, as was Iranian practice in the Persian Gulf. Maleki seemed to suggest that Alborz was not worth the diplomatic isolation Iran now found itself in when he asserted that the field was "not all it is cracked up to be" and that there were many problems in exploiting it.[132] All the same, Iran's political leadership continued to reject Russian calls to abandon insistence on a 20 percent share and increasingly expressed contentment and even pride in not doing so. In rejecting suggestions of passivity, a Foreign Ministry spokesman underscored that "no country has been permitted to take any action or carry out drilling operations or any other action within our 20 percent perimeter. We have firmly defended the country's rights."[133]

As a result, Iran's diplomatic solitude on delimitation continued to increase. In May 2003 Russian negotiator Kalyuzhnyy and his counterparts from Azerbaijan and Kazakhstan signed a delimitation accord conforming the three states' separately negotiated bilateral seabed agreements.[134] Iranian negotiator Mehdi Safari immediately criticized the trilateral Russian-Kazakhstani-Azeri accord.[135] In Tehran, a pro-Khatami daily called the agreement a defeat for the Iranian Foreign Ministry's policy of "trust" toward Russia.[136] Although in April 2002 the five Caspian presidents had agreed in Ashgabat to meet next in Tehran, there would be no real movement on the delimitation issue for years to come despite various face-saving statements by various combinations of the parties involved.

# 9

# Taliban Threats, Tajik Accords, and U.S.-Iran Talks

Although Russia and Iran began to drift apart over Caspian and nonproliferation issues at the end of the 1990s, other developments kept them in close touch. Most prominent was the rise of the Taliban in late 1994. The Taliban challenge encouraged Moscow and Tehran to work together not just in Afghanistan but also in Tajikistan. Russian diplomacy had succeeded in persuading Iran to prevail on the Tajik opposition to begin talks with Dushanbe in spring 1994. But it was the Taliban takeover of Kabul in September 1996 that finally propelled the Tajik peace talks into their end game and the concluding agreement signed in Moscow in July 1997.

As the Taliban expanded its control over Afghan territory, Tehran and Moscow needed a stable Tajikistan through which to send arms and ammunition to the Northern Alliance's anti-Taliban forces. In a historical irony, the most prominent Northern Alliance military leader was Moscow's old foe of the 1980s, the ethnic Tajik commander Ahmed Shah Masoud from the Panjshir Valley. Masoud had frustrated Soviet ambitions in Afghanistan but had also been willing to negotiate a local cease-fire in 1983–84 and even arrangements—subsequently aborted—for the peaceful withdrawal of Soviet troops from the country in 1988–89.[1]

In 1993, before the Taliban's appearance, Russian special envoy Yevgeny Primakov had engaged Masoud, defense minister in liberated but still war-wracked Afghanistan, in Moscow's efforts to bring the Tajik opposition to the negotiating table with the regime of Emomali Rahmonov in Dushanbe. In return, Masoud had indicated interest particularly in "military-technical" help from Moscow, presumably to fight rivals such as Gulbuddin Hekmatyar.[2] Several years later, in 1996–97, Russia

169

saw in Masoud's forces the only barrier to the advance of Taliban influence into Tajikistan and thereafter to dire consequences throughout Central Asia and even across the Caspian Sea into Chechnya.

For Iran, whatever its hopes for eventually regaining and expanding influence in Tajikistan, they now became secondary to its growing and more central concern over the Taliban threat to its security interests in Afghanistan. The Taliban undermined traditional Iranian influence in Afghan border regions, a particularly sensitive issue in "Greater Iranian" Herat, and sheltered Sunni ethnic minority opponents of the Tehran regime there and in other border provinces. The Taliban also posed a constant threat to Afghanistan's minority Shia Hazaras concentrated in central Bamiyan province, supported by Iran throughout the long Soviet occupation.[3]

Iran was keen to unburden itself of some 2.5 million refugees who had sought peace and sustenance within its borders over the several decades of turmoil in Afghanistan. But the Taliban's chaotic economic policies and wide-scale repression— political, ethnic, religious, and gender—sent resurgent streams of Afghans across the border into Iran. In addition, the Taliban adopted the bad habits of many of the Afghan warlords they vanquished and soon also turned to drug trafficking to fund their theocracy. Afghanistan thus began to generate increasing and debilitating drug flows into Iran and became a greater than ever narco-threat to Russia and the countries of Central Asia.[4]

The increasing anxieties produced by the multiple Taliban challenges led to some unorthodox responses by Tehran. As would be expected, the Taliban's brief takeover of Mazar-e Sharif in northern Afghanistan in May 1997 provoked dramatically closer cooperation between Moscow and Tehran. But after the Taliban executed nearly a dozen Iranian consular officials in Mazar in August 1998, even conservatives in Tehran appeared more receptive to exploring renewed contacts with the United States— though America still remained to many Iranian hard-liners the Great Satan. Moreover, almost simultaneously with the murders in Mazar, al Qaeda terrorists truck-bombed two American embassies in East Africa. As a result, American interest in probing the possibility of contacts with Iran—already piqued by the election of reformist President Mohammad Khatami—quickened.

As targets of Taliban and al Qaeda terrorism and violence within days of each other, the United States and Iran now had some security interests in common. Subsequently, though cast into deep shadow by the glare of September 11, 2001, Tehran and Washington engaged in episodic but largely unadvertised contacts on Afghanistan that did not involve Moscow. These talks took place for several years prior to the al Qaeda attack on the Pentagon and the World Trade Center's twin towers—and even past it. To the extent that they circumvented Russian participation, the contacts probably reanimated long-standing expectations in Moscow of the inevitability of an eventual Iranian-American rapprochement.

## MOSCOW AND TEHRAN PANIC

The so-called Tehran Peace Agreement of September 1994 was the first serious accord between the two warring sides in Tajikistan. Russian SVR chief Yevgeny Primakov and First Deputy Foreign Minister Anatoly Adamishin had worked hard since the massacre of the Russian Border Guard outpost on the Panj River in July 1993 to persuade Kabul and Tehran to encourage the Tajik opposition to enter talks with Emomali Rahmonov's regime in Dushanbe. The first round of the Tajik peace talks opened in Moscow on April 15, 1994.[5] The second round concluded in the Iranian capital on September 17, 1994, with the signing of the Tehran Peace Agreement, the core of which was a cease-fire to last until November 6.[6]

At a third round of talks in Islamabad from October 20 to November 1, the warring parties prolonged the cease-fire to February 6, 1995, the first of several extensions. During this round representatives of the various opposition groups drafted a declaration on the formation of a United Tajik Opposition (UTO). They signed it on July 23, 1995, and elected MIRT leader Sayed Abdullo Nuri to head the UTO.[7] The term UTO, however, would not come into regular usage for nearly another year.

Although the two sides had agreed to hold the next round of talks in Moscow in early December 1994, the negotiations stalled.[8] The opposition denounced the presidential elections and the referendum on a new constitution held in Tajikistan on November 6, 1994, calling them illegitimate and in contradiction to the agreements reached in the first round of negotiations in Moscow. According to the official results, Head of State Rahmonov won over 58 percent of the votes in the contest against former Premier Abdumalik Abdullojonov, whom Rahmonov had forced out of office in December 1993.[9] The opposition also objected to elections for a new parliament in February–March 1995.[10] As a result, the peace talks did not resume until late May 1995, when negotiators finally met in Kabul and Almaty, under conditions that were rapidly eroding the hospitality extended to the Tajik opposition in northern Afghanistan.

A new movement, the Taliban, had sparked the new circumstances. After coming seemingly out of nowhere in October–November 1994, the Taliban was rapidly scoring unexpected successes across Afghanistan. Its appearance followed over two years of devastating fighting in the wake of the collapse of the regime led by the Soviet-installed Najibullah, who had taken refuge in the UN headquarters building in Kabul on April 16, 1992. Forces loyal to Burhanuddin Rabbani and Ahmed Shah Masoud, both ethnic Tajiks, had managed to wrest Kabul after centuries of Pashtun control. The fighting was precipitated in great measure by the ethnic Pashtun Gulbuddin Hekmatyar's quest for primacy and rivalry with Masoud and Rabbani. The latter's reluctance to cede the rotating presidency agreed to in Peshawar in April 1992 also played a part. Ethnic Uzbek strongman Abdul Rashid Dostum, whose base at Mazar-e Sharif was not far from the Uzbek border town of Termez, switched sides several times, as did the Shia Hazara forces of the Hizb-i Wahdat, originally created by Iran. Although fierce and terribly destructive, the fighting between these long-established Afghan warlords was also inconclusive.[11]

Into the power vacuum rushed the Taliban, whose name suggested its recruits came from Islamic schools in Pakistan. There was at first much speculation, later backed by solid evidence, that Pakistan, tired of the endless fighting between the various factions in Afghanistan, began to see the Taliban as a new force that might oust Masoud and Rabbani's Tajik forces from Kabul and pacify and unify the country on the basis of its substantial Pashtun plurality, which had traditionally ruled Afghanistan. A Taliban regime based in Kabul and Kandahar could more effectively support Pakistani aims such as pipelines and roads from Central Asia through Afghanistan to Pakistani ports. In any event, the Taliban soon eclipsed Hekmatyar as Pakistan's favorite vehicle for the advancement of its interests in Afghanistan.[12]

The Taliban's predominantly ethnic Pashtun composition, however, from the beginning gave it an anti-Uzbek, anti-Tajik, and anti-Hazara edge. Indeed, the Taliban's intolerance of all the mujahideen forces that had preceded it, including Hekmatyar's, served to drive those very same disparate forces together against the Taliban. One Taliban delegation reportedly urged Pakistani ISI officers to "hang all of them—*all of them.*"[13] Nevertheless, this animosity by no means ruled out shifting tactical alliances in the years ahead.

By February 1995 Taliban forces had captured twelve of Afghanistan's thirty-one provinces.[14] The Taliban's advances prompted Tehran and Moscow to draw closer to each other on regional issues. Iranian objectives in Tajikistan were clearly being overridden by more long-standing and increasingly endangered concerns in Afghanistan. The Shia Hazaras that Iran had patronized were becoming increasingly vulnerable to Sunni Taliban reprisals. The Taliban's potential for expansion beyond Afghanistan's borders worried Moscow and its Central Asian partners. As a result, Russia and Iran both pressed their respective clients in Tajikistan to come to terms on a peace agreement that would secure the country as a platform through which to channel aid to anti-Taliban forces in Afghanistan.

Consequently, President Rahmonov and MIRT chairman Nuri finally met for the first time in Kabul on May 18–19, 1995. Their get-together set the stage for the fourth round of talks beginning May 22 in Almaty, where Nuri's deputy Akbar Turajonzoda—Tajikistan's former Kazi kalon—led the opposition delegation. Turajonzoda finally conceded that the opposition would have to deal with Rahmonov, now Tajikistan's elected president, and proposed to share power with him.[15]

The opposition put on the table in Almaty a proposal for the Commission on National Reconciliation (CNR), which would wield "supreme" political-military authority during a transition period of one and a half to two years. The opposition proposed that it hold 40 percent of the seats in the CNR, the Dushanbe regime another 40 percent, and ethnic minorities the final 20 percent. The CNR would then adopt a new election law, on which basis there would be elections for a new parliament.[16]

The proportion of seats the opposition was proposing to hold in the CNR was far more generous than even the eight out of twenty-four cabinet seats it had held in the government of national reconciliation created in May 1992. Not surprisingly, Dushanbe's negotiating team turned the proposal down flat.[17] Dushanbe eventually agreed to a 50-50 split, but in an arrangement in which President Rahmonov's powers would clearly outstrip those of the CNR.

On July 19, 1995, Rahmonov again met with Nuri, this time in the Iranian presidential palace at the end of Rahmonov's first official visit to Tehran. Moscow and Tehran both seemed anxious to nudge the two sides back toward negotiations for the sake of enhancing regional opposition to the Taliban. The two leaders agreed to authorize their negotiators to the fifth round of talks—tentatively bruited for the first half of August in Ashgabat—to consider setting up a "consultative assembly of Tajik peoples."[18] There were press reports that the opposition was under "active" pressure from Tehran to soften its stance.[19] Seeing Rahmonov off at the airport, Iranian president Ali Akbar Hashemi Rafsanjani expressed "happiness" at the progress Rahmonov and Nuri had achieved. He said the only obstacle to closer Tajik-Iranian ties was the internal strife in Tajikistan, which he hoped would be "forever" resolved as a result of the agreements reached by the two Tajik leaders in Tehran.[20]

Tajikistani Foreign Ministry spokesman Zafar Saidov said Rahmonov's meeting with top Iranian leaders "in fact signifies that Tehran recognized the legitimacy of the Tajik government."[21] Tajikistan finally opened an embassy in Tehran, and the two sides signed a declaration on principles of bilateral cooperation and resumed direct flights between Tehran and Dushanbe. The opposition leadership, however, still refused to concede Rahmonov's legitimacy as head of state. Nuri insisted that he had dealt in Tehran with Rahmonov not as president of Tajikistan but as the representative of an opposition group.[22]

By August 17, 1995, thanks to shuttle diplomacy by UN special negotiator Ramiro Piriz-Ballon, Rahmonov and Nuri agreed to begin a continuous round of talks in Ashgabat on September 18. The round's objective would be a general peace agreement, with separate political, military, and refugee protocols.[23] However, subsequent disagreement over the location of the talks seemed to mask an intention by both sides to try to improve their military positions before going back to the table.[24] The fifth round finally opened in Ashgabat at the end of November but was soon interrupted when the opposition walked out on December 11.

On January 19, 1996, President Boris Yeltsin publicly pressured Rahmonov at the CIS summit in Moscow. At the press conference after the summit, Yeltsin said that Dushanbe had been asked to work harder with the opposition to set up a conciliation commission (i.e., CNR). The Russian president criticized the "passivity and permanent hope that our peacekeepers will stay on longer." He insisted, "We cannot hold Tajikistan by the hand forever, understand? . . . Our people, Russians, are dying out there." Yeltsin asserted, "We told Rahmonov today, no more extensions. You have got six months, off you go."[25]

The Ashgabat round thus resumed at the end of January 1996. The UTO started to recognize President Rahmonov's legitimacy and to back off its demand for the dissolution of parliament, while still calling for parliament to share some of its powers with the CNR.[26] Dushanbe, however, while pocketing the opposition's recognition of its legitimacy, resisted the opposition's vision of a CNR with real power, and the talks in Ashgabat broke off again on February 18.

The opposition, which in early 1996 had finally started to refer to itself as the United Tajik Opposition, began to turn the heat up on the battlefield. By May, despite pressure on their respective clients, the negotiating momentum Moscow and Tehran had generated largely dissipated. Although the negotiations resumed once more in Ashgabat on July 8, they were soon again suspended as the UTO pressed its military campaign around the strategically located town of Tavildara.[27] Despite the discomfiture of both Russia and Iran, opposition forces on September 7 seized Jirgatal and proclaimed a "Garm Islamic Republic."[28]

## KABUL FALLS

On September 27, 1996, however, the Taliban captured Kabul, ousted the Rabbani government, and forced Defense Minister Masoud to retreat to the Panjshir Valley. As they entered Kabul, the Taliban dragged deposed Soviet-era leader Najibullah out of his sanctuary in the UN compound, where he had been living since the coup against him in April 1992. Newspapers around the world carried pictures of Najibullah's mutilated body strung up for public display.

Within weeks, on October 10, the ethnic Tajiks Rabbani and Masoud, together with ethnic Uzbek General Dostum and Shia Hazara leader Karim Khalili, formed the Supreme Council for the Defense of the Motherland, better known as the Northern Alliance.[29] Hekmatyar was not part of it. Odd as it might seem, he was now in exile in Iran—always apparently amenable to hosting anyone and everyone who might someday come in handy for battling Iran's foe of the day—and many of his supporters had switched to backing the Taliban.[30] Nevertheless, Taliban representatives soon made clear to at least one American contact that, while their first priority was to defeat Masoud and the Northern Alliance, that would just be prelude to going to war with Iran.[31]

If anything, Central Asian leaders reacted with even greater anxiety than Tehran and Moscow did to the Taliban's capture of Kabul. All of their fears of 1992—when President Najibullah's ouster from power in Kabul had coincided with competing massive demonstrations in Dushanbe's major squares—returned redoubled. Besides fearing more refugees fleeing the Taliban, there was concern that the radical, hard-line Sunni theocracy being imposed on Afghanistan would soon challenge the secular power structures in Central Asia. Even more pointedly, the execution of Najibullah suggested the threat to the personal security of Central Asian presidents that a Taliban-like movement might pose.

There was another dimension to perceptions of the potential implications of the conflict in Afghanistan. Many in the region, including Russia and Iran, had become persuaded—and would remain so for years—that the United States was working with Pakistan to help put the Taliban in power.[32] One aim of this presumed cooperation between Washington and Islamabad, it was thought, was to facilitate a major project by the American oil and gas company Unocal, together with its Saudi-owned partner Delta, to build a trans-Afghan pipeline to supply natural gas, primarily from Turkmenistan's giant Dauletabat field south of Mary, through Afghanistan to energy-hungry Pakistan.[33] Indeed, one leading Afghan specialist in Washington—Zalmay Khalilzad, a future American ambassador in post-Taliban Afghanistan—went on to join a Unocal advisory board after advocating engagement with the Taliban.[34] Not surprisingly, the suspected U.S.-Pakistani angle added greatly to Russia and Iran's worries and united them in their efforts to prevent the United States from sponsoring the pipeline.[35]

In any event, amid the great horrors being perpetrated in Afghanistan, there was also great irony. In 1992 Central Asian leaders had been aghast at the fact that mujahideen leaders such as Masoud had toppled Najibullah. Now these same Central Asian leaders began to support Moscow and Tehran in their campaign to channel supplies to none other than Masoud, who had become their last hope for sustaining resistance to the Taliban. Masoud, in turn, while still among those sheltering and aiding the Tajik opposition, began to work with the Dushanbe regime to secure a supply line for military matériel to his forces fighting the Taliban.

The presidents of Kazakhstan, Kyrgyzstan, Russia (represented not by Boris Yeltsin but by Prime Minister Viktor Chernomyrdin and Yevgeny Primakov, who had replaced Andrey Kozyrev as foreign minister in January), Tajikistan, and Uzbekistan expressed "serious anxiety" over the widening violence in Afghanistan at an emergency summit in Almaty on October 4, 1996. The summit participants pledged an "adequate response" to any threat beyond Afghanistan to their common interests under Article Four of the May 15, 1992, Collective Security Treaty signed in Tashkent. Tellingly, Tajikistan's President Rahmonov announced that he had reached agreement with UTO leader Nuri to meet in Moscow in mid-October.[36]

The dramatic developments in Afghanistan continued to transform the regional context of the struggle for power in Tajikistan. Despite continued fighting, expert groups from both Tajik sides met October 15–18 in Tehran with UN special negotiator Gerd Dietrich Merrem, who had replaced Piriz-Ballon in May, to prepare a draft agreement for Rahmonov and Nuri to sign at a third meeting in Moscow a few days later. However, Dushanbe's resistance to the UTO's demands prevented closure on a draft document and delayed the Rahmonov-Nuri meeting in Moscow for two months. Backed by battlefield gains in the Garm-Karategin and Tavildara districts, the UTO was calling for parliament and Rahmonov to share real and not just "consultative" power with the CNR.[37] According to some reports, Nuri's deputy Turajonzoda was irritated by Afghan president Rabbani's alleged insistence that the UTO stop fighting and settle the Tajik civil war. Nevertheless, despite Iran's clear discomfiture over developments in Afghanistan, there were also reports, perhaps inspired by opponents—but later partially confirmed by Turajonzoda—of UTO explorations of possible relations with and support from the Taliban.[38]

Rahmonov and Nuri met next not in Moscow but in northern Afghanistan, in the settlement of Khosdeh, on December 10–11. President Rabbani hosted the meeting and Defense Minister Masoud also attended. They were the two ethnic Tajik leaders in Afghanistan to whom Primakov in 1993 had pitched cooperation with Russia to help bring the warring sides in Tajikistan to the peace table. Now in Khosdeh, the Tajik president and the UTO leader once more agreed to meet in Moscow and to ban combat operations in the Garm-Karategin and Tavildara zones during the upcoming talks.[39]

Finally, on December 23, Rahmonov and Nuri—with Russian Premier Chernomyrdin looking on—signed a protocol outlining the compromises that, when the fine print was filled in, would constitute the peace accords they would sign in Moscow in June 1997. The CNR, chaired by a representative of the Tajik opposition, would be formed and function during a transitional period of twelve to eighteen months. President Rahmonov and the CNR would exercise joint decision making in the CNR's areas of competency. Rahmonov and Nuri instructed their delegations to complete negotiations by July 1, 1997.[40]

The Moscow understandings set the stage for intensive negotiations over the next six months. Spurred by the Taliban's brief takeover of Mazar-e Sharif in May, Moscow and Tehran kept their respective clients' feet to the fire of the July 1 deadline for a finished accord. The two issues of CNR and cabinet composition were delinked, allowing for a separate compromise in each. The UTO retreated from its maximalist opening position, getting 50 percent of the CNR's seats (thirteen members from each side) but only 30 percent of the membership of the cabinet and other executive bodies. This left the opposition with the same share of seats in the cabinet that it had held in the 1992 coalition government. But, according to the agreed deal, the CNR would cease to exist after new elections, and the agreed government power-sharing quotas would also implicitly lapse with the CNR's passing.[41]

Finally, on June 27, in Yeltsin's presence in the Kremlin, Rahmonov and Nuri signed the "General Agreement to Establish Peace and National Accord in Tajikistan."[42] Russian foreign minister Primakov, Iranian foreign minister Ali Akbar Velayati, and UN Special Representative of the Secretary General Merrem witnessed the signing. Yeltsin underscored Iran's contribution to the event by holding separate meetings with Velayati as well as with Rahmonov.[43] Georgy Tikhonov, chairman of the Duma Committee for the CIS, in an interview with IRNA, thanked Iran for its "constructive cooperation," stated that Iran and Russia "would assume an essential role in helping implement the reached agreements," and declared that further coordination between Tehran and Moscow would "guarantee peace in the region."[44]

The UTO, however, never received a written commitment from the Rahmonov government on specific government posts the opposition would get as part of its 30 percent of a transition coalition government. This issue long bedeviled implementation of the peace accords. Turajonzoda claimed that the 30 percent included, besides cabinet seats and places in the executive branch from top to bottom, a first deputy premier and one of the three power ministers.[45] Not until March 10, 1998, did Rahmonov appoint Turajonzoda first deputy premier.[46] Settling on a power minister acceptable to both sides took even longer. In May 1998 the UTO nominated Mirzo Ziyoyev, its top commander during the civil war, for defense minister.[47] Facing Rahmonov's reluctance to hand over such a sensitive portfolio to a formidable recent nemesis and after haggling that lasted more than a year, the UTO finally compromised in late July 1999, and Ziyoyev wound up in the lesser post of minister for emergencies.[48]

On other issues, Turajonzoda also told a news conference in Moscow that the UTO was not demanding the withdrawal of the Russian 201st MRD or the Russian Border Guards. Tajikistan's southern borders, he said, were also CIS borders, and any CIS member country "has the right to demand good defense of the border." Somewhat contradictorily, Turajonzoda claimed that Afghanistan did not pose a threat to Central Asian countries. Confirming earlier speculation, Turajonzoda said the UTO had "excellent relations" with all groups in Afghanistan and was maintaining contact not only with the Rabbani government—which although displaced from Kabul still enjoyed overwhelming international recognition—but also the Taliban regime.[49] Years later, in the wake of September 11, retired CIA agent Robert Baer asserted—and Nuri denied—that Nuri in July 1996 had "brokered an alliance" between al Qaeda leader Osama bin Laden and Iranian MOIS officials.[50]

Rahmonov with considerable foresight worked hard to nurture Tehran's stake in a stable and prosperous Tajikistan. Even before the peace accords were signed in Moscow, Rahmonov hosted Iranian president Rafsanjani in Dushanbe in May 1997. It was the third such Tajik-Iranian summit since Tajikistan had achieved its independence.[51] Rahmonov took Rafsanjani to see the giant Sangtuda hydroelectric power station. Sangtuda's construction had begun in 1987 but had been mothballed for want of funds to complete it in the wake of the Soviet collapse and the onset of the Tajik civil war. Rahmonov touted Sangtuda and other projects to Rafsanjani as offering "enormous potential for bilateral profitable cooperation." Rafsanjani in response reportedly committed Iran to helping Tajikistan achieve energy independence through investments to help complete the Sangtuda project.[52] Given the civil war then raging in Afghanistan, however, nothing much would come of Rafsanjani's commitment to Sangtuda until 2004, after the Taliban's ouster.

## MAZAR, DAR ES SALAAM, AND NAIROBI

Turajonzoda's dismissal of the threat posed by the Taliban must have been galling to both Iran and Russia. In May 1997 the Taliban's takeover of Mazar-e Sharif, after the betrayal of local Uzbek warlord Dostum by his second in command Malik Pahlawan, had propelled Moscow and Tehran to give the final push to the Tajik peace process. The Taliban subsequently had refused to share power in Mazar, and its attempt to disarm Malik's Uzbeks and allied Shia Hazaras had sparked a popular revolt. The Uzbek and Hazara forces had then chased the Taliban out of Mazar and slaughtered many of its fighters in battles that lasted into July.[53]

Anticipating a lasting occupation of Mazar, the Pakistani ISI directorate prevailed on Islamabad formally to recognize the Taliban regime in May 1997 and persuaded Saudi Arabia and the United Arab Emirates to do so as well.[54] Although the ISI was soon disappointed by the Taliban's failure to hold the city, the scare induced by the brief takeover deeply shook Afghanistan's neighbors to the north and west. Russia closed down its consulate in Mazar in May 1997.[55] The Iranians hung on but only until disaster overtook them a year later. In the meantime, the Taliban retaliated against Iran in early June 1997 by shutting down the Iranian embassy in Kabul.

Even more ominously, after another failed attempt to recapture Mazar in late September, the Taliban charged Iran with violations of Afghan airspace. The Taliban regime suggested that it could use anti-Shia opponents of the Iranian government, which the Taliban was sheltering on Afghan territory, to make problems for Tehran. This seemed to be a reference to Sunni militants from Iran's Turkmen, Baluchi, and Afghan minorities that the Taliban regime had been secretly backing and giving sanctuary in Kandahar since 1996.[56]

The Taliban offensive against Mazar prompted Russia and Uzbekistan to reinforce the Uzbek and Tajik borders and to devise new and less vulnerable routes to supply forces of the Northern Alliance in Afghanistan. Already in June 1997, the Taliban had accused Iran of using Mazar to bring in arms for Taliban opponents. Responding to the new threats, Russia and Iran set in motion plans to make the airport outside Kulob in southern Tajikistan available to Masoud to receive arms and ammunition for onward transport to his Northern Alliance forces in the Panjshir Valley. A new landing strip outside Bamiyan in central Afghanistan also allowed Iran to begin flying in military supplies to bolster Hazara forces fending off repeated Taliban offensives there.[57] In addition, heavy weapons and ammunition began to reach Masoud's forces after a circuitous rail and truck passage from eastern Iran through Turkmenistan, Uzbekistan, Kyrgyzstan, Tajikistan, and then into northern Afghanistan.[58] The supply network underscored how relations between Russia, Iran, and some of Afghanistan's key mujahideen had been completely transformed since Moscow's occupation of Afghanistan in the 1980s.

Precisely at this point of surging Russian-Iranian cooperation, however, the Taliban threat also sparked a revival in Iranian interest in direct contact with the United States bypassing Russia. Channels of communication of any type had been largely dormant for the decade since the Iran-contra saga. This new chapter in episodic discussions with the United States peaked after September 11, 2001, when Iranian diplomats actively cooperated with American envoys at the conference in Bonn, Germany. There they worked together to nudge the various Afghan delegations toward a consensus on a post-Taliban government. Iranian-American consultations continued, though with diminished intensity, in the months before the American-led military action against Saddam Hussein in Iraq and in the period right after. They fell off after Washington's plans jelled for an American-headed Coalition Provisional Authority in Baghdad.

The surprise election in May 1997 of Iran's new President Mohammad Khatami had coincided with the beginning of the crisis in Afghanistan around Mazar. Khatami seemed intent on reversing Iran's increasing international isolation. Over the next several years, he launched diplomatic initiatives toward Arab Gulf neighbors, including Saudi Arabia, and Europe, and trial balloons for dialogue with the United States. Khatami in January 1998 invited the United States to a "dialogue between civilizations and cultures . . . centered around thinkers and intellectuals."[59] Iranian and American interests in Afghanistan began to coincide on several points in 1998–99.

Iran and the United States first discussed Afghanistan with one another in the so-called Six plus Two. In October 1997 UN Secretary General Kofi Annan established this group of concerned countries on the recommendation of his special representative to Afghanistan Lakhdar Brahimi. It was comprised of Afghanistan's neighbors Iran, Turkmenistan, Uzbekistan, Tajikistan, China, and Pakistan plus Russia and the United States. Brahimi hoped to use the forum to defuse tensions following the vicious back-and-forth fighting since May around Mazar. The Six plus Two venue became the context not just for the Taliban to negotiate fitfully and unproductively with the Northern Alliance but for Iran and Pakistan to discuss their competing equities in Afghanistan—and for Iran and the United States to compare positions on restarting some sort of peace process in the country.[60]

By August 8, 1998, tensions between Iran and the Taliban reached crisis proportions when the Taliban retook Mazar. Taliban forces inflicted vengeance on Iran's local allies by massacring five to six thousand Hazaras. They also killed eleven Iranian officials—diplomats, intelligence officers, and a journalist—after capturing them in the Iranian consulate. In September, in another blow against Iranian interests, the Taliban captured the Hazara stronghold of Bamiyan in central Afghanistan. The Iranian response was swift. By the end of the month, seventy thousand Revolutionary Guards began military exercises along the Afghan border. In October, 200,000 regular Iranian troops, Tehran's largest ever deployment in response to events in Afghanistan, began more exercises along the same border.[61]

Just one day before the Taliban murder of Iranian officials in Mazar-e Sharif, terrorist attacks on the American embassies in Kenya and Tanzania killed 257, including a dozen Americans. In retaliation, the United States on August 20 launched cruise missiles against a training camp, south of Khost in eastern Afghanistan, used by accused embassy bombing mastermind Osama bin Laden.[62] In the opinion of one U.S. official, the embassy bombings in East Africa were "a seminal moment" that changed

Washington's view of the Taliban. Officials in Washington now concluded that Taliban supreme leader Mohammad Omar was bent not just on conquering all of Afghanistan, according to this account, but on providing a safe haven for bin Laden so that al Qaeda could attack American targets around the world.[63]

The crisis over Mazar subsided after the Taliban promised to return the bodies of the Iranian officials shot there. However, relations between the Taliban and Iran and neighbors to the north, with the exception of those with Turkmenistan, failed to improve. In late August, Russian officials and the foreign and defense ministers of Kazakhstan, Kyrgyzstan, Uzbekistan, and Tajikistan met in Tashkent to consider how to deal with the Taliban advance. In October–November 1998, with the help of arms from Russia and Iran, Northern Alliance commander Masoud recaptured much of the territory the Northern Alliance had earlier lost to the Taliban along the Afghan border with Tajikistan and Uzbekistan.

In March 1999 Taliban and Northern Alliance representatives met in Ashgabat under the auspices of the UN's Six plus Two. But Mohammad Omar soon charged Masoud with duplicity and ruled out further talks. By the end of April 1999, Masoud and Hazara troops recaptured Bamiyan. Masoud earlier the same month met in Dushanbe with Russian defense minister Igor Sergeyev, who recommitted Russia to its presence in Tajikistan with talk of building a new military base there—in fact just a change in status for the 201st Division, which had already been stationed in that country for many years.[64]

Up to this point, the United States had been reluctant to supply arms to Masoud. This had been largely out of tactical considerations but also because of long-standing distrust of Masoud on a number of counts, including his dealings with Soviet forces during their occupation of Afghanistan and, more recently, his acceptance of arms from Iran.[65] By summer 1999, however, Washington privately signaled to Russia and Iran that it did not object to their providing the Afghan resistance leader with weapons. The reasoning was that it was important to keep the Northern Alliance viable in order to pressure the Taliban regime to address U.S. concerns, especially on terrorism, human rights, and narcotics.[66]

While continuing to court a still reluctant Washington and other potential donors, Masoud's most productive contacts for vital military matériel were with Russia and Iran. His aides later described at least one secret visit to Moscow, apparently in early 2001, to meet with defense officials. For the latter, Masoud was clearly the last barrier against the threat the Taliban and Osama bin Ladin posed beyond Afghanistan to Russian interests in Chechnya and Central Asia.[67]

## GENEVA INITIATIVE SUPERSEDES SIX PLUS TWO

The Six plus Two met again in Uzbekistan in July 1999 and issued a "Tashkent Declaration on Fundamental Principles for a Peaceful Settlement of the Conflict in Afghanistan," which pledged not to give any help to either the Taliban or the Northern

Alliance. Just one week after Tashkent, however, the Taliban launched a major offensive north of Kabul against the Northern Alliance.[68] After that, the Six plus Two met from time to time but languished as a forum for addressing peace in Afghanistan as the Taliban insisted on being recognized as that country's sole legitimate government. Masoud, however, refused to subordinate his Northern Alliance forces to the Taliban. Its efforts later that year to push Masoud's fighters out of the Kabul region and cut his supply lines to Tajikistan ended in failure.[69]

On February 18, 2000, Iranians went to the polls and voted for an overwhelmingly reformist parliament.[70] A month afterward, American secretary of state Madeleine Albright called on Tehran to join Washington "in writing a new chapter in our shared history." The Iranian response was mixed at best.[71] Albright, after all, had taken Iran's military to task for pursuing weapons of mass destruction and criticized its IRGC and MOIS for not getting "out of the terrorism business." Iranian security forces were subordinated to unelected Supreme Leader Ali Khamenei, not to elected President Khatami. "Until these policies change," Albright had warned, "fully normal ties" would not be possible and American sanctions would remain in place. All the same, subsequent developments suggested that both moderates and conservatives in Tehran, whether elected or unelected, found appealing the secretary's emphasis on common U.S.-Iranian concerns in Afghanistan, her endorsement of "regional discussions" on this and other sources of tension in the area, and her holding out "the possibility of a more normal and mutually productive relationship"—even if far short of normal official contacts.[72]

As events in the year 2000 unfolded, Tehran began to give what appeared to be higher priority to a new "informal" forum that referred to itself as the Geneva Initiative. Tehran warmed up to the opportunity to discuss at least Afghanistan with the United States in a more intimate setting than Six plus Two. Indeed, after the Taliban's betrayal of the July 1999 "Tashkent Declaration," the Six plus Two lost much of its appeal. The parties to the Geneva Initiative consisted of Iran, Italy, Germany, the United States, and the UN. As with the Six plus Two, the Iranians found the Geneva Initiative useful because it allowed them to meet with American representatives under a multilateral umbrella, which permitted them to claim that there had been no direct bilateral contacts. However, the Iranians evidently regarded the Geneva Initiative even more favorably precisely because—unlike the Six plus Two—it gave them the opportunity to talk with the United States about Afghanistan without having to talk with, or in the presence of, erstwhile partner Russia or bitter enemy Pakistan.[73]

Indeed, given Iran's past and continuing cooperation with Russia on Afghan issues, the Geneva Initiative was remarkable in that it did not include Russia. The Geneva Initiative "was really just a cover to allow the Iranians and the U.S. to meet," UN facilitator Lakhdar Brahimi told an interviewer years later.[74] Besides, independent contacts with Washington might have given Tehran some leverage in its dealings with Moscow. Iran was no less interested in working with Russia to supply weapons to

Masoud's forces. Iranian policy appeared predicated on the premise that Masoud could not win but could not be allowed to lose. But Iran's view of a Russian role in Afghanistan had not changed over two decades: however necessary Russian military help might be in dire straits, a commanding Russian presence in Kabul would be illegitimate. So would that of the United States, of course, but the notion of U.S. influence still apparently retained some purchase among the various Afghan political forces, among which Iran's own influence was often minimal.

The historical ironies were again almost overwhelming. The Soviet withdrawal from Afghanistan had set the stage for Moscow-Tehran rapprochement in 1989. A decade later, well before September 11, the continuing absence of peace in Afghanistan had encouraged Iran toward contacts with Washington. While still anxious for Russian help, Iran clearly was interested in a dialogue with the United States that was independent from that with Russia. At the very least, Tehran's interest in exploring contacts with Washington on the Afghan dilemma must have again put Moscow on guard, no doubt reanimating suspicions that Iranian-American rapprochement would sooner or later once again diminish Moscow's influence and importance in Tehran.

# 10

# 9/11 and Afghanistan

In August 1998 the United States launched cruise missiles against an Osama bin Laden camp in Afghanistan less than two weeks after al Qaeda terrorists had truck-bombed the American embassies in Nairobi and Dar es Salaam. The al Qaeda leader subsequently reportedly told followers he would strike against Washington in retaliation.[1] That particular account may have been apocryphal. All the same, bin Laden's anti-American resolve in fact culminated on September 11, 2001, when suicide pilots hijacked commercial airliners and flew them into the World Trade Center in New York City and the Pentagon in Washington, D.C. Two days before, by way of prelude, al Qaeda agents had assassinated legendary Northern Alliance commander Ahmed Shah Masoud, the Panjshir Valley ethnic Tajik nemesis of the predominantly Pashtun Taliban.

The international community lost no time in condemning the attacks. Invoking the UN Charter's recognition of the right of collective self-defense, the Security Council on September 12 called for "all necessary steps" to respond to the attacks and urged all states to "work together urgently to bring to justice" those responsible.[2] Within weeks of 9/11, the United States put together an international coalition to wage war against bin Laden's terrorist network and the Taliban that had sheltered him. The first CIA-led team arrived in Afghanistan on September 26. Working with opposition fighters, the team organized laser-assisted target-spotters in preparation for a dramatic air campaign. Beginning on October 7, Operation Enduring Freedom (OEF) unleashed high-tech "smart" munitions against Taliban forces in Afghanistan from bombers launched as far away as the continental United States.[3]

On November 12, after Northern Alliance forces captured Herat and local warlord Ismail Khan returned triumphantly from exile across the border in Mashhad, Iran hailed the victory.[4] On November 12–13, Northern Alliance fighters led by Gen. Bismullah Khan took over the Afghan capital.[5] Masoud's Panjshiri Tajik successors—security aide Mohammad Fahim, foreign policy aide Abdullah Abdullah and political adviser Yonus Qanooni—returned to Kabul. This time, it was Russia that found the victory particularly gratifying.[6] The Foreign Ministry welcomed Kabul's capture as an "important success."[7] A government newspaper called it a "gift for Moscow." According to the paper's correspondent, many Northern Alliance leaders viewed Russia as their "strategic partner."[8]

By December 6 the Taliban surrendered even their stronghold in Kandahar. OEF soon pushed bin Laden deep into mountain redoubts along the Afghan-Pakistani border. In Tehran, Iranian leaders grumbled about U.S. militarism but did not impede OEF. In fact, Tehran offered to help with search-and-rescue missions for downed American pilots. In Moscow, President Vladimir Putin quickly accepted the rationale for OEF access to air bases in Central Asia from which to conduct air missions over Afghanistan.

In 1979, fears that the United States might enter Afghanistan after the "loss" of Iran and the fall of Shah Mohammad Reza Pahlavi had spurred Moscow to intervene to preempt any possible American move. Now, Putin opted for cooperation with Washington in Central and South Asia, at least until the dust of OEF's defeat of the Taliban and al Qaeda had a chance to settle. At key junctures in these early days of OEF, the impulse in both Moscow and Tehran was to reach out to Washington first rather than to one another.

In the diplomatic maneuvering that paralleled OEF's military campaign, Tehran and Moscow early on dumped ethnic Tajik president Burhanuddin Rabbani, who had long before discredited himself as an effective political leader. Despite bitter internal debates, particularly in Tehran, Russia and Iran backed international efforts to help leading non-Taliban political groups cobble together arrangements for governing post-Taliban Afghanistan. This process culminated under the aegis of a UN-sponsored conference in Bonn in November–December 2001, whose participants settled on Hamid Karzai, an ethnic Pashtun, as interim leader.

As the country's near-majority ethnic group, Pashtuns had traditionally ruled in Kabul. In effect bowing to historical precedent, Russia and Iran seemed willing to accept Karzai even if he was backed by Washington—as long as their own allies retained significant influence and Karzai was not in Pakistan's pocket. Meanwhile, on top of traditional Tajik-Pashtun jockeying, Masoud's successors evidently distrusted Karzai because of his early contacts with the Taliban, and Karzai distrusted the Panjshiris because of their dealings with the Russians going back to the days of the Soviet military occupation. Over time, however, and despite their key role in ousting the Taliban, the Panjshiris lost political ground to Karzai.

After the conference in Bonn, with threats of war mounting in neighboring Iraq, Tehran was once again at great odds with Washington but increasingly comfortable with the American favorite Karzai. In contrast to the Iranian leadership, President Vladimir Putin remained close to President George W. Bush despite disagreements with the United States over Iraq. At the same time, however, Russia was increasingly frustrated with Karzai because of his seeming opposition to the influence of the Tajik Panjshiris, Russia's best contacts in Kabul. Karzai for his part behaved frostily toward Moscow but was consistently more cordial toward Tehran, with whom he shared a lingering deep antipathy toward Russia as the invader and destroyer of so much of Afghanistan in the 1980s.

With the common Taliban enemy out of power, tactical cooperation between Tehran and Moscow on Afghanistan began to fray. The Northern Alliance began to break up into its diverse components, as did its external patronage. Russia and Iran increasingly pursued their own particular paths in Afghanistan. Their agendas were not so much contradictory as simply divergent. Russia and Iran still shared the specific objectives of exterminating the Taliban, increasing border security, and decreasing drug flows. More generally, each wanted a stable and nonthreatening government in Kabul that would respect their security requirements. Achieving these goals, however, now hinged more on the policies and actions of Karzai and his rivals and on the United States and its OEF coalition allies—and less on Russia and Iran working together.

Given continuing uncertainties over Karzai's longevity and OEF's ultimate success, Moscow and Tehran both saw the need to hedge their bets. Moscow nurtured ties to those forces it had worked with in Afghanistan before 9/11, namely Masoud's ethnic Tajik Panjshiris. Iran likewise worked to maintain its influence with warlords in those regions of greatest interest to it, particularly Herat on the Iranian border.

By 2003, however, Iran's attention began to shift decidedly from Afghanistan to Iraq, where its political and security equities increasingly outweighed its stakes in Afghanistan. Russia, meanwhile, its Panjshiri Tajik card seemingly largely spent, also let its focus drift and shift to Iraq.

## PUTIN BACKS BUSH

America's reengagement in Afghanistan after a twelve-year absence and OEF's quick toppling of the Taliban in late 2001 altered the geopolitical landscape in the entire region in dramatic fashion. Since at least 1996 Moscow and Tehran had predicated their common approach on the perceived need for a stable base in Tajikistan and northern Afghanistan from which to contain the Taliban. They were united in their desire to resist any export of the Taliban's brand of Sunni extremism and, to that end, to bolster the staying power of the Northern Alliance, including its Hazara elements, inside Afghanistan. But the success of the U.S.-led OEF campaign shook the foundations of the substantial cooperation between Russia and Iran in the region and of the tentative rapprochement between Iran and America. Both dynamics had been based on shared enemies in Afghanistan.

Since the Soviet Union's collapse, and because of historical predispositions, Russia and Iran had opposed any move by the United States or its NATO allies to establish a military presence in Central Asia. But on September 11 it was Putin who placed the first phone call to President George W. Bush to express sympathy for the thousands of American and other lives lost in the terrorist actions that day in New York, Washington, and Shanksville.[9] Ten days later, Putin met with a dozen of his security chiefs in Sochi for six hours of closed-door discussions, in the middle of which he spoke with Bush on the phone.[10] The next day, still in Sochi, Putin coordinated his next moves in a series of phone calls to Tajikistan's President Emomali Rahmonov and other Central Asian leaders.[11] Only after returning to Moscow on September 24 did Putin confer with President Mohammad Khatami of Iran.[12]

Putin went on television the same day. Whatever the possible consequences for Russia's own short-term influence in Central Asia and its relations with Tehran, Putin on September 24 publicly and—for the outside world—wholly unexpectedly defended the logic of American requests to establish temporary OEF air bases in Central Asia. Putin asserted to the world that Russia herself had long been a target of international terrorism: the "events" in Chechnya had to be seen in that context. Russia would of course expand its military assistance to Northern Alliance forces and the Afghan government headed by Rabbani. But then, breaking with the conventional expectations of what Russia's policy would be, Putin announced that Moscow would share intelligence on terrorist organizations, grant overflight rights for humanitarian missions, aid international search-and-rescue efforts, and support Russia's Central Asian allies should they "offer" OEF the use of their airfields.[13]

Over the next few months, the United States signed leases for Uzbekistan's Khanabad air base at Karshi and Kyrgyzstan's Manas airport outside Bishkek. While pledging long-term security commitments, the United States underscored that the Status of Forces agreements (SOFAs) negotiated with the host countries were only temporary and only to support the fight against the Taliban and al Qaeda. At the same time, the United States made clear its desire for extended access to these or similar bases in Central Asia in the future should security imperatives require it.[14]

Before 9/11, according to U.S. Secretary of State Colin Powell, his Russian counterpart Igor Ivanov had expressed discomfort over American "meddling" in Central Asia. "I really don't like it when I see you guys doing things . . . down there. . . . That's our realm of influence," Ivanov told Powell. After 9/11, Ivanov was much more relaxed. "Now we've got bases in Uzbekistan. We've got guys running around Tajikistan," Powell recounted. "We've got guys all over the place, and all I have to do is call Igor and coordinate. He's OK."[15]

It was easy to forget that Putin's early move to accommodate the United States in Central Asia was a great gamble on the military campaign that Washington had not yet even organized. In late September 2001 no one could predict OEF's quick success in ousting the Taliban. There was nothing assured about it at the time, especially from Moscow's perspective, given the decade of abject failure by Soviet troops in Afghanistan's unforgiving topographical and tribal terrain. Many observers assumed Moscow would oppose the gathering U.S. campaign against al Qaeda and the Taliban.

Two years later, after his summit with President Bush at Camp David, Putin claimed intriguingly that "people who planned to oppose the US and did oppose the US in Afghanistan" had approached Russia as Washington began to implement its response to 9/11.[16] Putin may have been alluding to hard-line conservatives in Iran who resisted cooperation with the United States in Afghanistan that fall and well into 2002, but he offered no elaboration, then or thereafter, and we may never know for sure who these "people" were. Nevertheless, his remark served to remind his audience of the widely held assumption in September 2001 that Russia would be more a hindrance than a help to the United States in retaliating against the Taliban.

All of this underscored the radical nature of Putin's tilt toward Washington and his readiness to let lapse the earlier primacy of Moscow's coordination with Tehran in Afghanistan. There were soon other demonstrations of this change. On October 17, the eve of Putin's meeting with Bush at the Asia-Pacific Economic Community (APEC) summit in Shanghai, he announced in Moscow the closing of two Russian relics from the Cold War: its electronics facility at Lourdes in Cuba and naval base at Cam Ranh Bay in Vietnam.[17] Then, in the wee hours of October 23, on his way home from Shanghai, Putin stopped in Dushanbe for several hours of talks with Afghan leader Rabbani and Tajikistan's President Rahmonov, apparently at the latter's initiative. During the brief meeting, three weeks before the fall of Kabul, Putin and Rahmonov made it clear to Rabbani that a post-Taliban government would have to include Pashtuns and could not be an exclusively Tajik or Northern Alliance affair.[18] In Shanghai, according to Putin's account, he had a "detailed conversation" with President Bush and Secretary of State Powell, briefing them on the Russian position before he set out for Dushanbe. Nowhere was there any hint that Putin had consulted in advance with Iranian leaders on what he and Rahmonov were about to do.[19]

The decision-making sequence closely resembled that of September 22–24, when Putin had conferred beforehand with Bush and others on Russia's next steps but appeared to have informed Khatami of them only after the basic decisions had been made. In regard to distancing themselves from the discredited Rabbani, Moscow and Tehran were no doubt on the same wavelength. Nevertheless, the public optics were striking. Moscow was ostentatiously consulting with Washington. At the same time, as we shall see, Iranian representatives were huddling with American counterparts. But seemingly missing almost entirely from at least the public record of this triangular diplomacy was close coordination between Moscow and Tehran, who had worked together in recent years to buck up the Northern Alliance and keep it from being swept away by Taliban and al Qaeda forces.

Tehran's first reaction to 9/11 actually somewhat paralleled that of Moscow, although it was not in concert with Moscow. Iran convened an emergency meeting of the Geneva Initiative countries on September 21, which allowed it to consult directly with the United States, without Russia, behind the curtain of multilateral diplomacy. Tehran halted "Death to America" chants for two weeks after September 11 as some officials began to call openly for a resumption of dialogue with the United States.[20] The Bush administration reportedly sent thanks, through the Swiss embassy in Tehran, for Iran's September 11 condolences and asked Tehran to join a coalition against terrorism.[21]

Supreme Leader Ali Khamenei, however, on September 26—just after President Putin announced he would not oppose OEF use of bases in Central Asia—angrily ruled out Iranian support for U.S. attacks on Afghanistan. "Over the past 23 years, you [America] have employed everything and all your might to inflict blows on this nation [Iran] and this country. Now you expect us to help you?" By this time, regime loyalists had reverted to chanting "Death to America."[22]

However, Iran was certainly in no position to object to Moscow's acceptance of American intentions to negotiate terms for the temporary use of air bases in Central Asia. This was especially the case when the outcome of the OEF campaign was still uncertain. Moreover, despite Khamenei's outbursts, Tehran in October offered to help with search-and-rescue operations to find U.S. pilots downed in Afghanistan and to allow the United States to unload wheat at Iranian ports and truck it through northeastern Iran to Afghan refugees.[23] The same month, Iran's ambassador to the UN traveled to Washington for a dinner with a half dozen members of Congress, the first time a senior Iranian diplomat had visited the Capitol since 1979.[24] The following month, on November 12, Secretary of State Colin Powell and Foreign Minister Kamal Kharrazi shook hands at the UN at a ministerial-level meeting of the Six plus Two called to explore a post-Taliban government for Afghanistan.[25]

## KARZAI AND THE PANJSHIRIS

Tehran and Moscow both lent their weight to international efforts to forge a stable and inclusive Afghan political consensus. A UN-sponsored conference organized by Lakhdar Brahimi, the secretary general's special representative for Afghanistan, began deliberations in Bonn on November 27. Four major factions participated: the Northern Alliance, or United Front, supported by Russia and Iran; the party of Afghanistan's former king, Zahir Shah, known as the Rome Group; an exile group based in Cyprus and backed by Iran; and another group based in Peshawar and backed by Pakistan.[26]

By December 5 the Bonn Conference participants had agreed on all but two members of a thirty-seat Afghan Interim Authority (AIA) cabinet. It would be chaired by Hamid Karzai, a media-savvy English-speaking Pashtun tribal leader with three centuries of family ties to the Afghan monarchy.[27] While not an outright majority, Pashtuns had constituted a substantial plurality of Afghanistan's population on the eve of the Soviet invasion in 1979: some seven million out of more than fifteen million, or around 45 percent. The head of state had been a member of one of the most prominent groups of Pashtun tribes.[28] Karzai's father had been a deputy speaker of the Afghan parliament under Zahir Shah, who favored the traditionalist but moderate Karzai and to whom the Karzai family was related by marriage.[29] After 9/11, Hamid Karzai had been the first Pashtun tribal leader in southern Afghanistan to organize resistance to the Taliban and coordinate his efforts with U.S. officials.[30]

The Tajik-dominated Northern Alliance agreed to hand over power to the AIA in Kabul on December 22. The turnover was made easier by the fact that key posts in the thirty-member AIA cabinet (Chairman Karzai, five vice chairmen, and twenty-four other members) were to be held by Tajiks of the Northern Alliance. These included Defense Minister Mohammad Fahim, Foreign Minister Abdullah Abdullah, and Interior Minister Yonus Qanooni.[31] As such, the Tajiks, whose 3.5 million constituted between a fifth and a quarter of the country's 1979 population, were well represented.[32] Given Masoud's frustration over the years with the lack of American enthusiasm for boosting his Northern Alliance's cause, the Panjshiri Tajiks may have expected worse.[33] Even after 9/11, OEF bombing of Taliban positions closest to Northern Alliance forces had come late in the game as Washington had made clear its opposition to Tajik forces gaining political advantage by entering Kabul ahead of others. In the end, however, Tajik commanders had done just that on November 12–13.[34]

Deputy Foreign Minister Mohammad Javad Zarif headed the Iranian observer delegation to the Bonn Conference, along with delegations of monitors from Russia and the United States and a number of other interested powers. Zarif and his team contributed to the pressure on President Rabbani to make way for the new AIA headed by Karzai.[35] Zarif's intervention with Qanooni was also "decisive" in getting the Northern Alliance delegation in Bonn to accept the cabinet deal being offered it, according to James Dobbins, the U.S. envoy to the Bonn Conference.[36] Secretary of State Powell characterized Iran as helpful in the war in Afghanistan. Richard N. Haass, Secretary Powell's director for policy planning, called Iranian diplomacy in Bonn "quite constructive."[37]

Upon conclusion of the conference, Foreign Minister Kharrazi expressed pleasure and welcomed its success. From the beginning, Kharrazi elaborated, Iran had urged the Northern Alliance to participate in a broad-based government, and the United Front had been "very mature about it." Parsing the AIA's ethnic composition, Kharrazi pointed out that in addition to Karzai it comprised eleven Pashtuns, ten Tajiks, five Hazaras, and three Uzbeks. In terms of the political groups that had attended the Bonn Conference, Kharrazi's understanding at the time was that the AIA was made up of seventeen from the Northern Alliance, nine from the Rome group, and two from the Peshawar group.[38]

Kharrazi noted that Iran had shared some "common points" with the United States over Afghanistan but regretted that ties between Tehran and Washington had not improved. He conceded that "military operations may have been effective in Afghanistan" but cautioned that "Afghanistan was a special case." Iranian negotiations with the United States were "out of the question" because of what Kharrazi called the continuation of Washington's "hostile attitude."[39]

In Tehran, nevertheless, President Khatami chaired a cabinet meeting that expressed support for the results of the Bonn Conference.[40] Several weeks later, Foreign Minister Kharrazi reopened Iran's embassy in Kabul, which had been closed by the Taliban in June 1997. Iran's new ambassador would be Ebrahim Taherian, who had been head of the Foreign Ministry's department for Afghanistan and ambassador to Tajikistan and had attended the Bonn Conference as an "observer."[41] Through the good offices of UN representative Lakhdar Brahimi, Taherian over the next year evidently met from time to time at Brahimi's official residence in Kabul with American ambassador to Afghanistan Zalmay Khalilzad, who had also attended the Bonn Conference.[42]

In Moscow, Foreign Ministry spokesman Aleksandr Yakovenko pronounced the Bonn meeting "a qualitative important milestone."[43] In Dushanbe for a meeting with Afghan foreign minister Abdullah, Russian defense minister Sergei Ivanov a few days later called the Bonn Conference "a landmark event in the course of restoration of peace in the war-torn Afghanistan."[44] Most authoritatively and even more complimentary, President Putin said the outcome of the Bonn Conference had been "the optimum decision, they could have hardly made a better one."[45]

While Karzai may not have been Moscow or Tehran's first choice, neither had much trouble letting Rabbani go. Over the years, Russia and Iran had probably dealt more with Hazara commanders, such as Karim Khalili, and with Tajik commanders, especially Masoud, than with party leaders like Rabbani. Rabbani had a tortured history as president. He had angered many and contributed to the destruction of Kabul in the pre-Taliban years by not giving up his rotation as president when it should have come to an end. He had exercised bad judgment in making deals with the "spoiler" Gulbuddin Hekmatyar. Rabbani's actions had contributed to the Taliban's victory. Finally, Rabbani was from the minority Tajiks, not the Pashtuns who had historically ruled in Kabul.

The long history of friction between Masoud and Rabbani had intensified after the Taliban takeover of Kabul in 1996.[46] Five years later, a week after Masoud's successors took back Kabul, U.S. Special Representative for Afghanistan James Dobbins asked the deceased Masoud's foreign policy aide and Northern Alliance foreign minister Abdullah Abdullah what should be done about Rabbani, who had reoccupied the presidential palace. "I suggest that you tell him he has to leave," replied Abdullah.[47] At the Bonn Conference, Rabbani bitterly resisted being cast aside by a younger generation of Northern Alliance leaders and relented only under pressure.[48]

The Pashtun Karzai was from a prosperous family that had fled Kandahar to Quetta, Pakistan, after the Soviet invasion. In the 1980s, during the Soviet occupation,

Karzai had worked with the mujahideen faction of Sibghatullah Mojaddedi and had begun to cultivate contacts with a number of American diplomats. After the Soviet military departure, Karzai had lobbied American diplomats for engagement with Afghanistan's exiled king in Rome. Hard-liners in Iran presumably did not like the contacts Karzai had maintained with U.S. representatives, including with Zalmay Khalilzad, through the 1990s.[49]

Russia appeared to view Karzai with a certain degree of coolness because of his complicated relations with the Masoud camp, with which it was more comfortable. In return, Karzai probably saw Moscow through the dark lens of his treatment at the hands of Defense Minister Mohammad Fahim and his fellow Panjshiris. In early 1994, according to one account, apparently suspecting that Karzai was colluding with Pakistani intelligence agents, subordinates of Fahim, and perhaps Fahim personally, had tortured Karzai, then a deputy foreign minister in the Rabbani regime. After his release, Karzai fled Kabul for more than seven years.[50] He later attributed the wounds that were apparent after his interrogation to shrapnel from a rocket that he claimed had hit the building where he was being held. Nevertheless, he did not deny that the detention had provoked his flight from Kabul when he concluded that those around Rabbani were consumed by paranoia.[51]

Karzai spent this time in exile for the most part in Quetta, Pakistan, where his father Abdul Ahad Karzai, a former Afghan senator, was already living. When the Taliban rose to prominence, Hamid Karzai supported the movement, reportedly in part because of the challenge they posed to those who had so recently tortured him in Kabul. As the Taliban expanded its presence in Afghanistan in 1995, Karzai's support of the movement influenced those in Washington who welcomed the Taliban as a force that might finally stabilize and unite Afghanistan. In late 1996, after its takeover of Kabul, the Taliban hoped Karzai would become Afghanistan's new representative at the United Nations.[52]

By 1999, however, the Karzai family's disenchantment with the Taliban had led Abdul Ahad Karzai and his son Hamid into active opposition. This included overtures to Masoud, to Washington, to Pashtun tribal chiefs, and to prominent royalists in Pakistan and Rome, home of the exiled king. On July 15 presumed Taliban assassins retaliated and shot Karzai's father dead in Quetta. Karzai, assuming the mantle of family patriarch, redoubled his campaign against the Taliban.[53]

In 2000 Karzai joined other prominent Pashtun exiles in proposing to Masoud's representatives an alliance of forces from Afghanistan's north and south against the Taliban. In August 2001, when the Pakistani ISI directorate moved to expel Karzai from Pakistan because of his anti-Taliban activity, Karzai consulted by satellite phone with Masoud on how to join his forces in Afghanistan.[54] By September 9, however, when al Qaeda assassins finally succeeded in killing Masoud, the Northern Alliance suddenly found itself in dramatically new circumstances.

While Iran probably saw little to be gained by sticking with Rabbani, moderates and hard-liners likely argued over whether it was possible to work with the U.S. favorite Karzai. Moderates from the beginning apparently perceived they could, and hard-liners with time seemed to get more comfortable with Karzai. Moreover, when it came to influence and respect in Kabul, Tehran was able to play on the still fierce resentment of Moscow it held in common with most Afghans for the Soviet invasion and the decade of destruction that followed.

Russia's calculations no doubt differed from those of Iran. In dumping Rabbani in October–November 2001, Putin did not abandon Masoud's Panjshiri Tajiks. Rather, with Masoud now dead, Moscow's support shifted to that younger generation of Panjshiris who had served as aides to Masoud, whose alliance with Rabbani had forever been uneasy.[55] These included political adviser Yonus Qanooni,[56] foreign policy aide Abdullah, and especially security aide Fahim.[57] Russian military representatives had dealt intimately with Fahim in arranging the delivery of military supplies to Masoud's beleaguered Northern Alliance from 1997 to 2001. Putin probably calculated that Russia could wield enormous influence through Masoud's successors. Their forces held most of the guns, which were predominantly of Russian origin and manufacture, after the Taliban's ouster.

Masoud and his Panjshiri Tajiks, while spearheading the armed resistance to the Soviet occupation in the 1980s, had a long history of tactical agreements with Soviet commanders such as Boris Gromov. Masoud's aim had been to gain tactical advantage against rival mujahideen commanders, especially Gulbuddin Hekmatyar, and at the end to facilitate the departure of Soviet troops from Afghanistan. In 1993 Russian special envoy Yevgeny Primakov had sought Masoud's help in getting inter-Tajik talks going, in effect offering Masoud help against his nemesis Hekmatyar. Now, with Masoud dead, his surviving comrades in arms appeared to continue this tradition of entering tactical arrangements with Russian officials, especially in Moscow defense circles, to gain advantage against Afghan competitors, in this case Karzai. The post-Masoud Panjshiris appeared to offer Moscow, in return, the hope of political influence in Kabul through these military contacts.

Russian policymakers therefore probably figured they had time to work with what must have seemed to them the real power wielders below Karzai. Even if Moscow was skeptical that the Panjshiri Tajiks could ever rule, it may have seen in them an effective and sustainable lever for maintaining Russian influence over Karzai. It was noteworthy that when Russian Foreign Ministry Third (Asia) Department deputy director Zamir Kabulov traveled to Kabul for Karzai's swearing in as AIA chairman, Kabulov met first with Masoud aides Fahim, Abdullah, and Qanooni.[58]

## TEHRAN DEBATES CONTACTS

Although Iran had apparently been more deeply involved than Russia in facilitating the Bonn negotiations, there was much more back-biting in Tehran over their outcome than there was in Moscow. After the quick military successes of November and the installation of the Karzai-led authority in December, there was a resurgence of what appeared to be uncoordinated or contradictory Iranian policies and activities in Iran itself and in Afghanistan. The relatively unified front so recently presented by hard-liners and moderates appeared to evaporate.

Vicious factional infighting replaced what had seemed to be an emerging consensus on rapprochement, or at least quickened dialogue, with the United States. Tehran's unease over post-Taliban developments was probably provoked less by Karzai's coming to power with American support than by the increasing American and other foreign military presence in Afghanistan. Moderates presumably had backed Iran's involvement and blessing of the Bonn Conference's results in the spirit of their own earlier tentative steps toward rapprochement with Washington. Hard-liners were reportedly motivated by fear of an impending U.S. attack on Iran after the successful campaign in Afghanistan.[59]

The ambiguities and contradictions of Iranian policy often appeared to have more to do with domestic politicking than with real policy toward Afghanistan. Both sides were using the question of Iran's posture toward Karzai and the related issue of contacts with America as a cudgel against each other. According to some observers, the extreme right opposed closer ties with America not on ideological grounds but because renewed contacts would bolster the strength of the reformists.[60] In any event, hard-liners stressed the threat to Iran posed by the presence of American forces in Afghanistan and the new AIA headed by Karzai. Moderates, meanwhile, underscored the dangers to Iran of continued instability in Afghanistan. Two decades of fighting had pushed some 2.5 million Afghan refugees across the border into Iran and greatly boosted narco-trafficking into and across Iran, with debilitating consequences for Iranian society.[61]

In activities reminiscent of those in Tajikistan in 1992, Iranian military and security agencies now again appeared to be pursuing policies in Afghanistan that had not been coordinated with the more moderate positions of the Iranian Foreign Ministry, let alone Russia.[62] This was most notable in Herat close to the Iranian border. After Herat's capture by Northern Alliance forces, the Iranian media had heralded the return to the city of warlord Ismail Khan. As a young captain, Khan in March 1979 had gained fame among Afghans and notoriety among Russians when he led forces that took over Herat and killed Soviet advisers stationed there, along with their wives and children. Khan had spent recent years in exile from the Taliban in the Iranian city of Mashhad, just across the border.[63]

Now, in mid-January 2002, Iranian security elements appeared to be encouraging Khan not to submit to the authority of the new Karzai-led AIA in Kabul.[64] U.S. special envoy Zalmay Khalilzad indicated that the MOIS and the IRGC, subordinated to hard-line Supreme Leader Khamenei, had sent Iranian-trained Afghan fighters as well as money and arms to Khan's forces.[65] The U.S. envoy contrasted these objectionable activities with the more helpful posture of the Iranian Foreign Ministry, whose policies were more in line with reformist President Khatami. Khalilzad also accused officials in Khamenei's line of authority of harboring al Qaeda fighters who had fled Afghanistan to evade capture by U.S. forces.[66]

When the journalist Ahmed Rashid visited Herat in May 2002, he found Iranian diplomats conducting normal business out of the newly opened Iranian consulate. Working out of another downtown office, Rashid reported, were Iranian "military officers, spies and advisers from the hard-line [IRGC's] Sipah-e Pasdaran, or Army of God." The diplomats claimed ignorance of what this second group was up to. Rashid surmised that it was in Herat to bolster Ismail Khan in his assertion of independence from the AIA in Kabul. The Iranian nondiplomats presumably were also involved in arranging safe passage for al Qaeda fighters fleeing over the nearby border into Iran. These measures appeared meant to counter what Iranian hard-liners feared most: a secular, Western-oriented Afghanistan that would undermine the clerical regime in Iran.[67]

The IRGC certainly seemed to count for more than the Iranian Foreign Ministry in Herat. In July 2002, for example, Tehran appointed Hassan Kazemi Qomi as its new consul general there.[68] Qomi was already an old hand at operating in hot spots on behalf of the IRGC. He had earlier reportedly served in the IRGC in Lebanon. In December 2003 Qomi moved from Herat to Baghdad, where he became the charge d'affaires in the newly reopened Iranian embassy.[69]

The rash of contradictory Iranian actions reflected the long-standing divisions on policy between hard-line and moderate factions that had been subsumed in recent years to the overriding need to unite against the Taliban threat. Now, the Taliban vanquished, hard-liners in Tehran had the luxury of resuming their campaign against moderate opponents. On January 23, Supreme Leader Khamenei's chief adviser Ali Akbar Nateq-Nuri, the same cleric who had lost the presidential elections in 1997 to Khatami, charged that the Bonn Conference had been part of a plot by the United States to weaken Islam.[70]

This hard-line campaign redoubled after President Bush included Iran along with Iraq and North Korea as part of the "axis of evil" in his State of the Union address on January 29, 2002.[71] Many observers concluded that further development of U.S.-Iranian rapprochement was unsustainable. Nevertheless, there were continuing though diminishing efforts by shifting elements in Tehran to woo Washington and not let the rapprochement track lapse completely. According to U.S. special envoy Zalmay Khalilzad, U.S. and Iranian representatives had met over the winter both in Kabul and Geneva.[72]

Tehran's hardening attitude was notably out-of-step with that of Moscow. In the Caucasus, after years of claiming close links between Chechen fighters, Arab terrorists, and Afghan mujahideen, the Russian government did not object to an American proposal in February–March 2002 to send 150 to 200 military instructors to train and equip four battalions of Georgian soldiers in counterterrorism tactics.[73] Putin declared, "There is no and can be no tragedy in this. Why is this possible in Central Asia and not in Georgia? Why should certain exceptions be made for Georgia? Of course they should not."[74]

In contrast, just days after Putin's comment, Iranian defense minister Ali Shamkhani, on an official visit to the Armenian capital of Yerevan, bluntly stated that Tehran opposed the presence of third country forces in regions bordering Iran.[75] However, infighting over contacts with the United States and policy toward the Karzai interim administration continued unabated in Tehran. In late spring 2002, for example, a critique of Iranian policy published in a Foreign Ministry journal argued that Iran had missed a rare opportunity to improve its international position. After September 11, when the United States had been at its weakest, Iran could have negotiated with Washington "with a full hand." But as a result of Iran's failure to take advantage of the opportunity for cooperation with the U.S.-led antiterrorism coalition against the Taliban, "Iran did not gain any new ally, but a new enemy and rival in Central Asia."[76]

In the face of what appeared to be a wave of similar criticism of Tehran's reluctance to deal directly with Washington, Supreme Leader Khamenei on May Day again denounced contacts with the United States. "Some people can think of nothing apart from negotiation with America," he complained. "They say we should negotiate with America because this would . . . put an end to its pressures and threats, and induce it to respect our national interests," he went on. But "negotiations are not going to solve any problems."[77]

Khamenei soon upped the pressure, denouncing advocacy of talks with Washington as "both treason and foolishness."[78] Tehran's hard-line Justice Department, controlled by Khamenei, several days later decreed, "Propagating and disseminating news in support of negotiations with America will be considered an offense in accordance with the press law and in view of the Supreme Leader's ban on talks with the US."[79] The decree was apparently the first time in the history of the post-shah regime that the judiciary had declared mention of a specific issue in the press subject to criminal prosecution.[80] President Khatami endorsed Khamenei's line, declaring that "the slightest flexibility towards America" signified "disregard for the honor and interest of the Iranian people."[81]

## KARZAI PREFERS TEHRAN

Iran's endorsement of Karzai at the Bonn Conference provoked criticism from hardliners because of Washington's support for him. With time, however, even Iranian conservatives appeared to grow more comfortable with Karzai. Russia's attitude remained more complicated. Though officially correct toward Karzai, Moscow staked its influence in Kabul on close ties with Masoud's surviving and still powerful Panjshiri Tajik coterie, with whom it had worked against the Taliban. The Panjshiris, in turn, gave every sign of being locked in bitter conflict with Karzai.

Karzai from the beginning repeatedly dropped hints of his dislike for Moscow and sympathy toward Tehran—within the wider context of working closely with Washington. On this score, Karzai and Tehran had both opposed the Soviet invasion, and so both were sympathetic to each other's aversion for Russians. The Panjshiri Tajiks had also opposed the Soviet occupation, of course, but had sustained contacts with the Russian military establishment during the years of working together against the Taliban, and after the Taliban's fall they repeatedly signaled their courtship of Moscow in their intrigues against Karzai.

Not surprisingly, Karzai visited Tehran before he did Moscow, even though sparring continued in the Iranian capital over the Bonn Conference's legitimacy and its selection of Karzai as AIA chairman. In February, several Iranian publications in effect denounced him as a foreign "lackey" and argued that the Afghan population would not endure the American and UK military presence for long: "They will rise like a burning fire from under the ashes and devour all the foreigners and their domestic lackeys."[82] Others, however, while agreeing that Karzai was "the voice of the US speaking with an Afghan accent," argued that Tehran needed to use him to get its point of view across to Washington. Many experts and politicians reportedly were of the view that "the September 11th events were a suitable opportunity for resolving problems between Iran and the US."[83] In this camp apparently were those who argued that hosting Gulbuddin Hekmatyar—in exile there since 1996—was not in Iran's national interests. They urged that Tehran show him the door and in this way indicate Iran's support for the Karzai government.[84]

Karzai arrived in Tehran for his first official visit on February 24. His party included Foreign Minister Abdullah and six other ministers.[85] President Khatami endorsed the AIA and Karzai's leadership as "an Afghanistan that is moving toward progress and development." He said it was Iran's duty "to help establish a government and to help pave the way for reconstruction and progress in Afghanistan." In a subsequent meeting, Foreign Minister Kharrazi revealed that Iran had pledged $560 million over five years for Afghan reconstruction.[86] With Khatami, Karzai responded, "Iran is not only a neighboring and friendly country, it is a country that has extended great help toward the national resistance of Afghans against the Taliban and terrorism and aggressions, and has saved Afghanistan from a very dangerous situation." Commenting on American criticism of Iranian activities in Afghanistan, Karzai asserted, "We have said before that Iran is a friend and brother of Afghanistan and has saved Afghanistan from great problems."[87]

In his meeting with Karzai, Supreme Leader Khamenei expressed his "delight" over the restoration of peace in Afghanistan. Responding to Karzai's request for reconstruction help, Khamenei called for the entire Islamic world to become involved but pointedly warned the AIA not to let the West use reconstruction to "infiltrate" Afghanistan "politically and culturally." Karzai responded by thanking Iran for its "highly vital assistance" to Afghanistan during its "confrontation with the aggression of the former Soviet Union" and after that against the Taliban.[88] In his address to the Iranian Majles, Karzai returned twice to this theme of thanks to Iran for its help against the "Red Army" and other aggressors.[89] And then, in a final interview, Karzai again stressed, "No Afghan will forget . . . the Islamic Republic of Iran's assistance and cooperation during the holy war [against the Soviet Union]" and the struggle against the Taliban. And, once more, he rejected the opinion that "Iran is intervening" in Afghanistan's internal affairs.[90]

What to do with Gulbuddin Hekmatyar, whose prolonged exile in Iran had been under debate prior to Karzai's arrival, appeared to have been resolved during Karzai's visit. Tehran publicized orders to Hekmatyar to cease agitation against the AIA and close his Hizb-i Islami offices. By February 26, there were unconfirmed reports that Hekmatyar had left Iran, where he had been residing since fleeing the Taliban in 1996.[91] That, however, was by no means manifestly good news. Hekmatyar remained rabidly anti-American and anti-Karzai. He would now be personally involved on the ground in Afghanistan in the rearguard violent resistance to the AIA and the international forces engaged in trying to stabilize post-Taliban Afghanistan.[92] Arguably, the decision to encourage Hekmatyar to leave Iran probably satisfied both moderates, who wanted to improve relations with the United States, and hard-liners, who wanted to make life difficult for the United States and its allies in Afghanistan.

Next on Karzai's travel schedule was a visit to Moscow. The trip's logistics, protocol, press coverage, and atmospherics differed markedly from those of the Afghan statesman's visit to Tehran. The Moscow stop was advanced with much fanfare by Defense Minister Fahim and Interior Minister Qanooni, two of the three leaders of the Panjshiri Tajik faction in the AIA.[93] The Russian press underscored that Fahim had been responsible under Masoud for working with Russian military advisers and procuring Russian military hardware for the Northern Alliance, which had been worth $30–34 million in 2001 alone. "To this day," Fahim announced before his visit, "the manpower acquisition and command and control systems of formations and units remain Russian" as do all of Afghanistan's combat hardware.[94]

One Russian pundit observed that Karzai might turn out to be just "king for a day" and not survive in power past summer. "How everything will go there is a hazy issue and Russia is worried even now by the security of its southern borders," wrote Nikolay Ulyanov. "That is why maintaining a privileged relationship with the Northern Alliance which controls the areas of Afghanistan that border the CIS republics, evidently remains a priority for Russia's diplomats and military personnel in the region."[95]

Defense chief Fahim arrived in Moscow on February 11 and dove into talks with weapons export officials at Rosoboroneksport, the MiG aircraft company, and the Aviaeksport foreign trade association. He also met with Defense Minister Sergei Ivanov and Chief of the General Staff Anatoly Kvashnin and capped his visit with a call on President Putin.[96] At a joint news conference with Ivanov, Fahim said that

Russia had "responded positively to the request for rear-service and technical assistance for the Afghan Army."[97] Seven months later, when Sergey Ivanov visited Kabul for the first time, he revealed that the two countries' defense ministries had signed a protocol creating "a legal foundation for discussing . . . military-technical, military and personnel-training cooperation" during Fahim's February visit to Moscow.[98]

In Kabul, meanwhile, Karzai's own aides were beginning to describe his administration as "in virtual thrall to its enemies" and to claim that the demands of the Northern Alliance "prevailed without dissent" at cabinet meetings.[99] The tensions were clearly exposed by the murder on February 14 at Kabul airport of Abdul Rahman, minister for air transport and tourism. After Karzai charged a plot by senior officials in the defense, intelligence, and justice departments—all ethnic Tajiks from the Northern Alliance—Foreign Minister Abdullah publicly contradicted Karzai.[100] A senior government official several weeks later told a correspondent that "Karzai does not have any real authority. . . . Masoud followers are taking over all the important posts."[101]

Indeed, when Karzai finally visited Moscow in March, he appeared to have been all but dragged to the Russian capital by Masoud's surviving coterie of Northern Alliance Tajiks. He took with him a much larger and higher ranking delegation than the one he had traveled with earlier to Tehran. Foreign Minister Abdullah again accompanied him, as he had to Tehran. But two other ministers cum deputy chairmen of the AIA also went to Moscow, compared to none in the delegation to Tehran, as well as eight other ministers, compared to just six to Tehran.[102] In addition, Karzai's party included Afghanistan's new ambassador to Russia, Ahmed Ziya Masoud, younger brother of the deceased Ahmed Shah Masoud.[103]

When Putin received Karzai on March 12, the Russian president underscored the potential for working together against terrorism and drug trafficking, restoring Afghanistan's army, and rebuilding the country. In the war against terrorism, Putin said that Russia's support would primarily be in the "military-technical" sphere and that it would be through the central government rather than through the Northern Alliance, as had been necessary during the era of Taliban rule. Putin's formulation, of course, was technically correct. But given Fahim's control of the Defense Ministry in Kabul, it probably did little to assuage whatever concerns Karzai may have had over Russian arms going directly to his Panjshiri Tajik rivals.

In the reconstruction effort, Putin suggested to Karzai that Russia's help would best be concentrated on the more than 140 projects Moscow had built during the Soviet era. He drew particular attention to building a power station in Tajikistan to supply Afghanistan with electricity. This was an implied reference to the giant Sangtuda construction project, which had remained unfinished since the Soviet Union's collapse. However, Putin cautioned that success in cooperating on economic projects hinged on Kabul's ability to normalize political life and create a secure environment in Afghanistan.[104]

At the end of their talks, Putin and Karzai signed a joint statement pledging to build relations "on the basis of mutual trust and respect for the sovereignty, independence, territorial integrity and noninterference in each other's internal affairs."[105] Foreign Minister Abdullah reportedly reassured his Russian counterparts that Afghanistan would not end up "in the grip of US pressure."[106] Ambassador Masoud not long after the visit assured Russian interviewer Arkadiy Dubnov, "We had a good relationship with Moscow for a long time, and we are extremely eager to restore it." Defense Minister Fahim, according to the ambassador, was "quite pleased with the results."[107]

However, it soon became evident that not all had gone well. Karzai apparently had refused to assume a submissive hat-in-hand pose before Putin and other officials in Moscow. During his interview with Dubnov, Ambassador Masoud repeatedly had to smooth out the sharp edges of Karzai's alleged remarks and the purported Russian retorts to them. Karzai had reportedly rejected assertions that Western aid should foot the bill for Russian reconstruction work. The Afghan leader allegedly argued that Russia itself should pay for the restoration of the installations it had built during the Soviet era because Moscow had destroyed them during the Soviet occupation. Karzai also apparently deflected the offer by Putin to help clear Afghanistan of land mines by replying that five or six mine-clearing centers had been operating in Afghanistan already for a dozen years with European Union (EU) help. Finally, when Karzai reportedly asked whether Russia's promised military-technical assistance would be free, a high-ranking Russian official was said to have answered, "If you can stop the shipments of illicit drugs to Russia, it will be free, of course."[108]

From the public record alone it was clear that the Afghan leader did not go out of his way to embrace his Russian hosts. At the conclusion of his visit, he politely affirmed that Russia would "play an important role in Afghanistan's future." Nevertheless, he underscored that ties with Washington were the priority and relations with Iran were also important, and that Kabul would pursue both no matter what the state of relations between the United States and Iran.[109] As far as Afghans were concerned, Iran and the United States had both "assisted us greatly during our nation's sacred Jihad against the Russians, and in our war against terrorism, led by the Taliban." His trip to Iran the month before had been his best as AIA chairman, he said, and ties between Kabul and Tehran would "expand to an unprecedently high level in the future."[110] Indeed, by early 2005, Karzai would have visited Tehran four times and Moscow still only once.[111]

## DANCING WITH WARLORDS

Recognizing that developing a new Afghan army would take time, the Bonn Conference had appealed to the UN Security Council to mandate a force to "assist in the maintenance of security for Kabul and its surrounding areas. Such a force could, as appropriate, be progressively expanded to other urban centers and other areas." This would become known as the International Security Assistance Force (ISAF), which would ensure security in and around Kabul while OEF forces operated in the rest of the country. At the same time, the participants in the Bonn Conference had pledged "to withdraw all military units from Kabul and other urban centers or other areas in which the UN mandated force is deployed" and to put "all mujahidin, Afghan armed forces and armed groups . . . under the command and control of the Interim Authority."[112]

The Northern Alliance delegation to the Bonn Conference had at first categorically opposed the establishment of ISAF. "We don't feel the need for an outside force to bring security. We have our own qualified security forces and there is full security in Afghanistan," delegation head Yonus Qanooni had told a press conference.[113] The Northern Alliance had only grudgingly relented on this point. "Since we took Kabul there has been no more violence," Qanooni had argued in Bonn. "Foreign troops in Afghanistan will not resolve the problems, they will just create new ones."[114]

Russian and Iranian views on OEF and ISAF differed over time. In early May 2002 Moscow sent Mikhail Konarovsky, a diplomat with many years experience dealing with Afghanistan, to be its new resident ambassador and to reopen its Kabul embassy, shuttered in 1992 after the fall of President Najibullah.[115] Prior to setting off, Konarovsky told an interviewer that OEF and ISAF were important at the "strong-arm stage" of putting down terrorism throughout the country and ensuring security in Kabul. "At the same time," he cautioned, "it should be an important objective of theirs to prepare a very swift handover of their functions to Afghan law-enforcement bodies." The world was well acquainted, said Konarovsky, with Afghans' "allergy" to any armed foreign military presence on their territory. Therefore, he warned, "an unjustifiably long stay of either contingent could lead to an additional growth of tension in the country." Moreover, "we must also have a cautious attitude toward the possible expansion of the geographic parameters for the international forces' deployment."[116]

Despite Konarovsky's misgivings, born most recently of the Soviet Union's bitter experience in the 1980s, OEF prolonged it mission well into the first decade of the new century and ISAF fitfully expanded its mandate beyond Kabul—with little resistance from Russia. In January 2002, a 4,500-strong ISAF deployed to provide security in Kabul, as mandated by the Bonn Agreement.[117] In spring 2003, the eleven-thousand-strong predominantly American OEF forces began deploying small provincial reconstruction teams (PRTs) outside Kabul.[118] On August 11, 2003, in its first deployment outside Europe in its fifty-four-year history, NATO took over command of ISAF's multinational force.[119] Anticipating NATO's assumption of ISAF command, Russian foreign minister Igor Ivanov at a meeting with NATO foreign ministers in Moscow offered his country's intelligence and other backup support to ISAF troops in Afghanistan, but not Russian troops.[120]

That October, the UN Security Council approved NATO's request to expand ISAF's Bonn Conference mandate beyond Kabul.[121] Even before the UNSC voted, Russian defense minister Sergei Ivanov went on the record supporting the move: "We learned about these plans a long time ago . . . and we are not allergic to them."[122]The expanded mandate set the stage for NATO to begin discussing the deployment of its own PRTs outside Kabul.[123] Despite continuing clashes in Afghanistan, Putin in October 2003 asserted that the international community remained united in its approach. In this context, he called attention to the fact that Russia had signed an agreement with Germany for the transit of military cargo through Russia to Afghanistan, a first in the history of Russia's relations with NATO countries.[124]

In contrast to Moscow, Tehran from the beginning was clearly torn by the trend. It did not like U.S. and British OEF forces in Afghanistan, yet they had ousted the Taliban regime. Together with ISAF, OEF was beginning to bring enough stability for Iran to start sending its Afghan refugees home. At the same time, Iranian security and intelligence forces prudently continued to work through their own favored Afghan warlords to maintain Iran's influence in those provinces where Iranian equities were most at stake. These included western border areas most critical to Iranian security— Farah, Nimruz, and especially Herat—but also Helmand in the south and Balkh (Mazar-e Sharif) in the north. Somewhat surprisingly, the Hazara homeland in central Bamiyan did not prove receptive to such efforts. The Hizb-i Wahdat's Karim Khalili, leader of the most important and presumably Iran-bankrolled Shia Hazara component of the Northern Alliance, had declared already in early 2002, "Politically, Iran does not agree with the war of the Americans against al Qaeda and the Taliban. We are on the side of the Americans in this fight and that shows we do not agree with Iran."[125]

For Tehran and Moscow, continuing to deal with their long-standing Afghan partners was in part simply the result of the unabated momentum of earlier ties. Beyond this, however, while officially supporting Karzai in public, Russia and Iran probably saw keeping up relationships with old acquaintances as the best means to pressure Karzai to heed their views. Moscow and Tehran probably also seemed to see this as insurance in case Karzai did not last long, as may have appeared to them likely. Even if Karzai defied the odds against him, it nevertheless seemed probable that much of the country would revert to the control of warlords backed by outside powers, including the members of the OEF and ISAF coalitions and Pakistan. For all these reasons, Moscow and Tehran appeared to seek to safeguard their interests in Afghanistan by nurturing those bonds they thought they could count on and which just happened to be independent of Karzai.

At the same time, Afghan notables such as Ismail Khan in Herat and Defense Minister Fahim and fellow Panjshiri Tajiks in Kabul no doubt turned for support to their longtime outside contacts in order to garner strength with which to better press their cases on Karzai. Shortly after arriving in Moscow, Ambassador Ahmed Ziya Masoud appealed to Russia to become more involved in Afghanistan. "My late brother Ahmed Shah Masoud had very good relations with Russia," he told an interviewer. "Many states around the world are now trying to establish their spheres of influence in Afghanistan. . . . If Russia does not influence events in Afghanistan, the balance of power in the region will be upset. If this happens, both your country and mine will lose a great deal."[126] Two years later, Foreign Minister Abdullah was still sounding the same note. "We need to decide how Russian companies can be involved in Afghanistan's economic reconstruction. We believe Russia should be more actively involved in everything concerning Afghanistan," he said on the eve of a trip to Moscow.[127]

In the case of Russia, this was easier to do without appearing to contradict official support for Karzai's administration since Moscow's ethnic Tajik contacts were all high-level members of the AIA in Kabul. Russia appeared to work most assiduously with Defense Minister Fahim and other ethnic Tajiks from the Northern Alliance with whom it had cooperated closely during the pre-9/11 struggle against the Taliban. They, in turn, appeared to be coaxing Russia to involve itself more deeply in Afghan politics on their side.

The contradictions between official statements of support for Karzai and continuing collaboration with old contacts who were now rivals of Karzai were more glaring in Iranian policy. Regional warlords such as Khan in Herat were based far from Kabul and openly declared their autonomy from the capital. According to one estimate, the Iranian-backed Khan collected $100 million in customs duties in 2002 but turned only $10 million over to Kabul.[128] But the inconsistencies were no less for Russian policy even though better camouflaged by the fact that Defense Minister Fahim, for example, was officially a member of Karzai's own central cabinet.

## FOCUS SHIFTS

All the same, Karzai survived. The Bonn Conference had set out a two-year calendar for Afghanistan's post-Taliban political reanimation. The AIA was to vacate power within six months, by June 22, 2002, when an emergency *Loya Jirga* (national assembly) would choose a Transitional Authority (ATA) or government to serve for two years until elections no later than June 22, 2004. In the meantime, a constitutional Loya Jirga was to convene no later than December 22, 2003, to agree on a new constitution and the arrangements and exact date for elections.

More than fifteen hundred delegates thus duly convened in Kabul on June 11, 2002 for the emergency Loya Jirga. They elected Karzai president and head of the ATA for two years on June 13; he was sworn in on June 19.[129] After intense and prolonged debate and deal making, Karzai on June 24 finished putting together his ATA cabinet. Trying to balance faction and ethnic groups, he appointed five vice presidents: the Panjshiri Tajik Mohammad Fahim of the Northern Alliance, who insisted on retaining his defense minister portfolio; the Shia Hazara leader Karim Khalili; the governor of Nangarhar, Haji Abdul Qadir, who although a Pashtun was a member of the Northern Alliance; and lesser known Pashtun and Uzbek leaders. All were to leave their regional power bases and move to Kabul. But Abdul Rashid Dostum, the Uzbek warlord now headquartered in northern Balkh province in the city of Sheberghan, and Ismail Khan, the Tajik from Herat in the west, refused to leave their fiefdoms in exchange for vice presidential posts in Kabul.[130]

The murder of Vice President Qadir on July 6 in Kabul strained Pashtun confidence in the ATA. Qadir had been the most prominent Pashtun warlord in the Afghan cabinet, a leading member of the Northern Alliance, and as such an important bridge between Pashtuns and the Panjshiri Tajiks whom many Pashtuns now regarded as dominating the post-Taliban government in Kabul.[131] Two months after Qadir's assassination there was an even more disturbing reminder of the fragility of Karzai's balancing act. On September 5, Karzai himself narrowly escaped assassination in Kandahar, just after a huge car bomb in Kabul killed at least twenty-five people.[132]

As it watched the alarming developments next door, Tehran gave a strong boost to the emergency Loya Jirga's choice of a transitional central government. On August 13 Khatami went ahead with a visit to Kabul, the first in forty years by an Iranian head of state. There, the Iranian president repeatedly spoke of Iran's firm support for the "central government" of Afghanistan. He noted that the Kabul government, and not Herat leader Khan, would manage the five-year $560 million aid package Tehran had pledged when Karzai had visited in February. The move was sharply criticized by some in Tehran. One newspaper charged, "It is obscene to give this money to an unreliable country when our people are in such desperate straits."[133] Nevertheless, Khatami's visit was seen as a major endorsement of the Karzai administration as it contended with challenges to its authority by regional warlords.[134]

At the end of the year, on December 22, 2002, on the anniversary of the AIA's installation in Kabul after its selection by the Bonn Conference, Iranian ambassador Mohammad Taherian joined representatives from Afghanistan's five other immediate neighbors—China, Pakistan, Uzbekistan, Turkmenistan, and Tajikistan—to sign the Kabul Declaration on peace, security, and noninterference in each other's internal affairs.[135] The official Iranian news agency transmitted glowing comments from its interview with Afghan foreign ministry spokesman Omar Samad on Iran's "great effort" in making the Bonn Conference a success. Since then, according to Samad, there had been a "growing trend in Tehran-Kabul political, economic and cultural relations."[136] It was an unmistakable stamp of approval by Tehran on Karzai's leadership of the ATA and its ethnic and regional balance and marked a clear turning of the corner in Iran's relations with post-Taliban Afghanistan.

In Moscow, analysts spelled out in great detail what they saw as the fragility of the Karzai administration. The Oriental Institute's Afghan specialist Viktor Korgun—who earlier had placed much of the responsibility for the Taliban's rise on the United States—now publicly criticized Moscow's support for the Northern Alliance. It was true, conceded Korgun, that Karzai was not pro-Russian, but he was "not at all an anti-Russian politician" either. The central administration was still weak but nevertheless was "gradually strengthening, furthering the process of state building." Kabul was contending not with civil war but with the efforts of local warlords to fragment the country and secure the autonomy of their regions. In Herat, Ismail Khan had four thousand soldiers. With Iran's support, he controlled the border customs office, which gave him an income of $100–200 million annually. In the north, there was General Dostum's fiefdom. In the south and east, there were others that were similar. "There are bayonets and money everywhere, while Karzai lacks both."

"Huge money," Korgun argued, needed to come from the international community to appease "unruly and unpredictable Afghanistan." What had been pledged to date was far from enough, and what had actually been allocated was far short even of that. The United States supported Karzai, but in Korgun's opinion acted too cautiously. Meanwhile, Russia showed clear favoritism toward the Northern Alliance, and Pakistan and Iran both had their protégés. This, warned Korgun, was "a dangerous policy. It would be better if all jointly supported the Karzai provisional government." This included, but not exclusively, support for the new Afghan National Army. To date it had only fifteen hundred soldiers in Kabul, according to Korgun, facing "30,000 bayonets against them throughout the country."[137]

Nevertheless, as Zamir Kabulov of the Russian Foreign Ministry's Asia Department prepared to receive Afghan foreign minister Abdullah in Moscow in late November 2002, he implicitly defended continuing Russian ties to forces loyal to Defense Minister Mohammad Fahim—Karzai's leading rival. Kabulov stressed to the press that "most people in the [Afghan] power-wielding structures are inclined to cooperate with Russia" because "they have long been using Russian armaments and know well that they are cheaper and better suited to use in Afghanistan."[138] Kabulov as well as Deputy Foreign Minister Aleksandr Losyukov told the press that earlier hopes and even euphoria over Afghanistan were being replaced by signs that the situation in some respects was now worsening. "The potential threat of the comeback of the old forces to power in Afghanistan remains," warned Losyukov, "and correspondingly the spread of their ideology beyond the borders of the country."[139]

Still, by fall 2003 the ice of Fahim's resistance to disbanding his old Northern Alliance force was beginning to crack. At the end of October, the long-delayed push to disarm and demobilize regional militias was finally set to start.[140] On January 4, 2004, after three weeks of debate and negotiations, the Loya Jirga approved the strong presidential system favored by Karzai rather than the parliamentary system sought by Fahim. There would be no prime minister position as coveted by Fahim. Instead, there would be a popularly elected president, two vice presidents, a bicameral parliament, and provincial governors appointed by the president. The constitution called for presidential and parliamentary elections to be held in June 2004, though it was widely anticipated that the first would not be held until September and the second perhaps not until 2005.[141]

Iran and Russia both signaled their acceptance of Karzai's strengthened position and moved on. In the wake of the toppling of Saddam Hussein in April 2003, Baghdad had become far more important than Kabul to both Tehran and Moscow. Though relations between Moscow and Kabul continued to be bumpy, Putin congratulated Karzai on the adoption of the new constitution.[142] In May 2004, when Foreign Minister Abdullah visited Moscow, Foreign Ministry spokesman Aleksandr Yakovenko announced that Russia's main priority was the development of Afghanistan's "national armed forces under the control of the government of Hamid Karzai."[143] As for Tehran, months earlier, in December 2003, Iran had already transferred its consul general in Herat, the IRGC officer Hassan Kazemi Qomi, to Baghdad, where he had become the charge d'affaires in Iran's newly reopened post-Saddam embassy.[144]

# 11

# No "Strategic Partnership"

In early 2001, just a year after Putin's election as president, Russia and Iran worked their way toward a rare summit. Even as it prepared for the event, however, Moscow looked past the occasion to its developing relationship with the new American president, George W. Bush. The result was an underwhelming meeting between Putin and Iranian President Mohammad Khatami in the Kremlin. On its eve, a Russian Foreign Ministry briefer went out of his way to make sure no one was under the delusion that the Moscow-Tehran relationship was that of "strategic partners."

Weaving his way through what must have been conflicting advice on how to deal with Iran, Vladimir Putin did some skillful footwork at home and abroad during his first two years as president. He went full steam ahead on Bushehr but removed the freewheeling Yevgeny Adamov from MinAtom. He walked away from the 1995 Gore-Chernomyrdin memorandum but did not rush to conclude new arms deals with the Iranians. Putin's moves played extremely well in the Duma, which relished a show of policy toward Iran that troubled Washington. At the same time, Putin did not hesitate to agree to an early summit with President Bush and to meet frequently with him after that.

The downplaying of the Russian-Iranian relationship was in stark contrast with the sharply more upbeat atmosphere of Putin's subsequent frequent summits with Bush. In the wake of the September 11 terrorist attacks on the United States, Russian cooperation paved the way for American use of air bases in Central Asia for the campaign against the Taliban and al Qaeda in Afghanistan. In retrospect, the Moscow summit in May 2002 marked the high point in U.S.-Russian relations during the Putin-Bush era. In the same spirit, Putin's partners at the G-8 summit that June in

Kananaskis, Canada, agreed that Russia would assume the group's presidency in 2006 and host its annual summit at that time.

With Iran, Moscow finally seemed close to a deal in December 2002 on the need to return all spent fuel from Bushehr to Russia. Late in the month, after returning from Tehran, MinAtom's Rumyantsev announced to the press that the text of an agreement had been hammered out. All that was left to do was prepare the final documents. That, he said, would take "45 or 60 days," and then they could be signed. "We have got convinced," Rumyantsev declared, "that Tehran has no programs for creating military nuclear projects."[1]

Rather than laying the issue to rest, however, the nearly finalized agreement coincided with the beginning of an even more tumultuous chapter of controversy over Iran's nuclear program. This was provoked first by revelations about a vast nuclear enrichment complex under construction at Natanz and then, a year later, by the discovery that Iran had been dealing as far back as 1987 with the network of nuclear black marketers led by A. Q. Khan of Pakistan. The blockbuster revelations were followed by what seemed a deliberate slowdown by Russia on finalizing the spent fuel deal.

Not even their shared opposition to the U.S.-led military campaign against the Saddam Hussein regime in Iraq, as we shall see in chapter 12, could displace for long the growing friction between Moscow and Tehran on the nuclear issue. With another Bush-Putin summit set for Camp David outside Washington in late September 2003, and with Tehran just having begun to deploy the Shahab-3 missile, there were striking signs of concern among Russian security experts. In mid-July, for example, USA Institute head Sergey Rogov led a group of security specialists to America to discuss ideas for intensifying U.S.-Russian security cooperation against the common threats of international terrorism and WMD proliferation. In a panel discussion at the Carnegie Endowment in Washington, Rogov argued that Moscow and Washington should work together to counter and neutralize potential nuclear missile threats from Iran and North Korea. He proposed that Russia and the United States start talks on missile defense, building on the only system in the world already operational: the one around Moscow.

Rogov's proposal underscored how far Russian opinion had shifted since late 2000. Andrey Kokoshin, former secretary of the Security Council, had argued then that one reason not to cooperate too closely with Iran was that this would give grist to U.S. advocates of a national missile defense (NMD) system. Now Rogov was proposing that Russia work with the United States in creating what amounted to a joint missile defense system on Russian territory against real and potential rogue NPT breakout states, including specifically Iran.[2]

## PUTIN-KHATAMI: PERFUNCTORY SUMMIT

Andrey Nikolayev, chairman of the Duma's Defense Committee and a former commander of the Russian Federation Border Guards, was an advocate of warmer, even "strategic" partnership between Russia and Iran. In November 2000, in what seemed part of an effort to warm up the atmospherics for the upcoming Khatami visit to Moscow, Nikolayev offered to provide Tehran with a modern electronic surveillance system in the Persian Gulf and along Iran's borders with Afghanistan and Pakistan to help fight the movement of drugs, illegal migrants, and terrorists.[3] Even after a decade of rearming with Russia's help, however, Nikolayev's offer provoked many hostile responses in Tehran. "There are two countries with a 400-year-old political tradition, which have proven that they are not trustworthy and cannot be our strategic partners—one is Russia and the other is France," affirmed one professor.[4] A newspaper survey concluded that Nikolayev's proposal was aimed at gaining Russia "a foothold in Iran's eastern and southern borders and to serve her own interests. Russia is trying to fulfill its historical wish to have access to open seas, especially to the warm waters of the Persian Gulf."[5]

Nevertheless, the Russian and Iranian presidents met in Moscow on March 12–15, 2001, and summed up their discussions in a joint communiqué.[6] They also put out a joint statement on the status of the Caspian Sea,[7] which—as seen—simply papered over increasing differences over delimitation, and at long last signed the Treaty on the Basic Elements of Relations and the Principles of Cooperation.[8] As had Ali Akbar Hashemi Rafsanjani in 1989, Mohammad Khatami visited St. Petersburg, this time specifically the Izhorskiye Zavody works putting together the first reactor for Bushehr, where the director said the delivery date for the reactor unit had now slipped to early 2004. Instead of Baku, where Rafsanjani had gone twelve years earlier during the Soviet era, Khatami's third city was Kazan, the Volga River capital of the Russian Federation's Tatar Republic.[9]

Former foreign minister and prime minister Yevgeny Primakov reportedly declared on the eve of the summit that Khatami's visit was "the biggest event in the history of Tehran-Moscow relations," in the words of the Iranian IRNA press service.[10] However, despite all the hoopla and speculation, all three documents signed at the summit were remarkable for being so unremarkable. None broke new ground, and official background briefings stressed that the treaty on relations would not contain "mutual obligations of an ally or military-political nature, nor will it contain the term 'strategic partnership.'" It would simply be "a usual framework treaty, which shows that good relations are developing between Russia and Iran."[11]

In fact, although not drawn attention to in March 2001, the two sides had been working on such a document since at least September 1992. In late March 1993 Foreign Minister Andrey Kozyrev and his Iranian counterpart Ali Akbar Velayati had initialed a draft text in Tehran (see chapter 5) in anticipation of a Yeltsin-Rafsanjani summit, which never took place. Given the long gestation period, the treaty's final contents in 2001 could not be attributed to casual or sloppy drafting. On one point in particular the document was remarkably and noticeably restrained. The treaty did not commit either side to render military aid to the other in case of aggression by a third party, but merely "not give any help to the aggressor" and to assist a settlement on the basis of the UN Charter and international law.[12]

Russian commentary on the summit was quick to note that, despite Iranian wishes, Putin resisted characterizing the two countries as "strategic partners" and that there was no mention of "strategic partnership" in any of the signed documents.[13] Deputy Foreign Minister Aleksandr Losyukov, briefing the press on the eve of Khatami's arrival, stressed that "there is no question of a strategic partnership between Iran and Russia—there is no such proximity of positions."[14] One newspaper concluded that Iran for Russia was "not only a profitable partner, but also a rival."[15] Moscow's refusal to describe Russian-Iranian ties as "strategic" was all the more striking given the declaration on strategic partnership that Putin signed with Algerian president Abdelaziz Bouteflika not long after Khatami's visit.[16]

Moscow was consistent on this point. The Kremlin view under Putin reflected that of the Yeltsin era and even that during Primakov's tenure as foreign minister. In December 1996, at the height of Russian-Iranian official ardor and "Persian themes" in Russian foreign policy, Primakov personally had resisted characterizing the relationship as "strategic." Primakov was in Tehran as Tajik antagonists Sayed Abdullo Nuri and Emomali Rahmonov were in Moscow initialing a peace pact endorsed by the Iranians. When asked then to comment on the repeated mentions by his Iranian hosts of the "strategic partnership" between Russia and Iran, Primakov had demurred. "I would not use the words strategic partnership regarding anyone," he answered. "I simply want to stress that our relations are good."[17]

Primakov's unwillingness to use the term may have been tactical, on two counts. Earlier, in March 1993, when Moscow was trying to entice Tehran to support Russian efforts to start a Tajik peace process, then-foreign minister Andrey Kozyrev and his negotiators had evidently felt the need to dangle the prospect of such ties before their Iranian counterparts. By 1996 the peace process had achieved considerable traction, and Moscow no longer had to persuade Tehran to support it. In 1996, moreover, Moscow was clearly sensitive to suggestions that its ties with Iran were aimed against the United States or that they contributed to violating international nonproliferation standards. Hence, Primakov's restraint in characterizing relations with Iran as "strategic."

Certainly, Moscow had reasons other than a commitment to descriptive accuracy in shying away from calling its relations with Tehran in March 2001 "strategic." Iran's policy was not set by Khatami, warned one commentator, but by the ayatollahs. Khatami would not control the weapons Russia sold Iran; his adversaries would. In short, "the Khatami presidency is a liberal facade for the fundamentalist regime." Russia should not be surprised if a group of Islamic terrorists or separatists armed with Russian weapons sold to Iran materialized somewhere in the CIS in the next five to ten years.[18] Elsewhere, figures such as Grigory Yavlinsky, head of the liberal Yabloko Party, appeared to share the view of former foreign minister Andrey Kozyrev: Russia needed to do business with Iran, but it should also address Western concerns about the proliferation of dangerous arms technologies.[19]

Khatami's visit to Russia in 2001 was the first by an Iranian head of state since the shah's visit in 1974, although then-speaker and soon-to-be-elected president Rafsanjani had met with Gorbachev in 1989. In terms of protocol, both gestures had still not been reciprocated by a Kremlin leader's sojourn in Tehran.[20] As had Gorbachev and Yeltsin before him, Putin played hard to get, though he diplomatically accepted Khatami's invitation to visit Tehran.

By early accounts, Putin planned to travel to Tehran after the Iranian presidential elections of June 8, 2001.[21] But during Foreign Minister Kamal Kharrazi's visit to Moscow in early April 2002, there was no public mention of a bilateral summit in Tehran. Two weeks later, during Putin's bilateral with Khatami on the margins of the multilateral summit in Ashgabat devoted to Caspian issues, the Russian leader seemed to give the suggestion a polite brush off.[22] Combined with the decision by the leaders of the five littoral countries to hold their next summit in Tehran, presumably only when agreement on the Caspian delimitation issue had been reached, it suggested an indefinite postponement of a Putin trip to Tehran, since rapprochement on the thorny subject seemed further away than ever. Putin clearly seemed to be implying that he would be averse to a visit until Iran agreed to a reasonable arrangement on a Caspian regime to replace the 1921 and 1940 understandings of the Soviet era.

A year after the Putin-Khatami summit, Foreign Minister Kharrazi appeared to have come around to the Russian position that the two countries did not share a "strategic relationship." Kharrazi told a student audience at Moscow's State Institute for International Relations (MGIMO) that Russian-Iranian relations indeed could not be called "strategic" because the term "implied complete profundity of relations."[23] By that time, however, the issue of Iran's ties with Russia was caught up in Iranian domestic political maneuvering over contacts with America in the wake of September 11 as well as over open differences with Russia on Caspian delimitation.

## LOOK, BUT DON'T TOUCH

According to some press reports, Putin and Khatami had agreed to arms deals worth $7 billion during the March 2001 summit in Moscow. However, discussions in this area appeared to be continuing rather than to have been concluded, and the two sides did not sign a military-technical agreement at that time. Even before the visit, Deputy Prime Minister Ilya Klebanov, who was overseeing Russia's military-industrial complex, cautioned that discussions were focused more on implementing old contracts signed in the 1990s than on signing new deals.[24] During the visit, Russian Defense Ministry sources claimed that Defense Ministers Igor Sergeyev and Ali Shamkhani were not discussing signing any new arms purchases and that those bilateral transfers already in play included only defensive armaments.[25]

With no military-technical agreement signed during Khatami's visit to Moscow, Iranian defense minister Shamkhani was later scheduled to return in early September 2001. He was to sign the agreement with his new counterpart Sergei Ivanov, who had replaced Igor Sergeyev in late March 2001 shortly after Khatami had been in the Russian capital. The planning for Shamkhani's return to Moscow was accompanied by more realistic estimates on the Iranian side of the volume of arms sales it might potentially entail: roughly $300 million per year.[26]

Because of Israeli premier Ariel Sharon's visit to Moscow at the same time, the Iranians postponed Shamkhani's September visit at the last moment.[27] The decision came after strong criticism of the Iranian Defense Ministry by conservative quarters for even contemplating going ahead with the trip. The Israeli prime minister was a "war criminal" with a "record of war crimes in the Palestinian territories and Sabra and Shatila in Lebanon." His "brutal actions during the 11-month-old Palestinian Intifada" had "isolated him in the international arena," yet Russia had "inexplicably invited him to visit the country." The invitation to Sharon was either a "blunder" on the part of Russian officials, or intentional double-dealing toward Iran by scheduling the visit of the Israeli prime minister to coincide with that of the Iranian defense minister.[28] The invective suggested choppy waters ahead for Russian-Iranian relations.

When Shamkhani's visit finally took place at the beginning of October 2001, he and Sergei Ivanov at last signed the military-technical framework agreement.[29] But despite extensive window-shopping at major military-industrial production concerns in the Moscow region and St. Petersburg, no new contracts for advanced conventional weapons were signed during the visit.[30]

In February 2002 Ivanov asserted that Russia did not plan to cut back on its military sales to Iran, which he described as "conventional armaments and materiel . . . armored personnel carriers and anti-aircraft systems." If it did, "dozens of other states" would take its place. "Iran is our neighbor, and we have normal relations with this nation."[31] By March 2002, however, Ivanov's tune was changing. Russia and Iran, he declared, had signed only one new contract for conventional weapons over the past year and a half to two years, and this one for helicopters.[32] In September 2002 Ivanov asserted in Washington that Moscow considered only Tehran's requests for "defensive weapons." By this he meant "antitank weapons, armored personnel carriers, air-defense systems, small arms, etc., which by nature cannot destabilize the situation." Moscow, he claimed, had "so far never had any requests from Iran for the delivery of short-range missiles or anything else which could destabilize the situation in the region."[33]

A year later, Deputy Defense Minister Mikhail Dmitriyev in September 2003 estimated deliveries of Russian conventional military goods to Iran at only $25–70 million annually, "mainly repairs, upgrades and deliveries of parts."[34] By early 2004 a Russian industry weekly noted that Russian arms exporters had almost totally lost interest in the Iranian market. While exports of $300 million yearly were possible, "Russia has practically frozen the delivery of military equipment to Iran."[35] Reports on Russia's global conventional weapons sales of over $5 billion in 2003 typically highlighted India and China as Russia's biggest customers and did not even mention Iran.[36]

Tehran reacted bitterly. In an extensive interview in September 2002, none other than Defense Minister Shamkhani complained that Russia was trying to sell to Iran only weapons systems that would not provoke a reaction from America. But more fundamentally, Shamkhani emphasized, Russians did not want a stronger Islamic Republic of Iran. "On the basis of their strategic assessment, they see the presence of a powerful country within the territorial geography a danger to Russian security. That is why they refrain even from selling defensive hardware and equipment to the Islamic Republic of Iran." Asked about Bushehr, he asserted that Russia was concluding new agreements with the Bush administration that were in effect a continuation of the abrogated Gore-Chernomyrdin accords and were "aimed at controlling Iran's capabilities and maintaining technical restrictions."[37] It was an exasperated conclusion clearly not reached lightly and enunciated from the top of the military establishment in Tehran.

## BUSH-PUTIN: SHARED CONCERN

Amid all the coverage in the Russian media of the Khatami visit to Russia in March 2001, it was hard to miss the cautions over dealing with Iran and the endorsements of taking U.S. views into account. As if to underscore Moscow's concern to assuage Washington's suspicions of Russian-Iranian ties, strategic or otherwise, Security Council secretary Sergei Ivanov left for the American capital even before Khatami left Moscow. It was necessary, Ivanov said as he set off, to "make maximum efforts to have Russian-US relations be stable, pragmatic and based on consideration of mutual interests and the responsibility that our two countries bear." He hoped a Putin-Bush summit could be organized as soon as possible. Ivanov said he favored a "full-format bilateral dialogue on the entire agenda at all Russian-US levels."[38] In fact, during the subsequent visit by the other Ivanov—Foreign Minister Igor Ivanov—to Washington in mid-May 2001, it was announced that the first Bush-Putin summit would take place June 16–17 in Slovenia.[39]

At their joint press conference in Ljubljana, President Bush said that he had "brought up concerns about Iran." While he was "hesitant to put words" in Putin's mouth, he reported that the Russian president "said he's concerned as well."[40] Back in Moscow several days later, Putin openly elaborated on his unease but also underscored his determination to continue dealing with Iran. Putin described President Khatami as "a very modern person, a very strong and very worthy partner." Echoing Aleksandr Yakovlev's views about the nature of the international arms market,[41] Putin ascribed charges that Russia was rearming Iran to "political theses . . . used to squeeze Russia out of . . . the Iranian arms markets, . . . simply an instrument of unscrupulous competition." It would be a recurring theme in Putin's remarks to the press after each of his future encounters with Bush.

Nevertheless, Putin asserted that Russia was mindful of its own security interests. It had made clear to the Iranian leadership that Russia's military-technical cooperation would not include any nuclear weapon or missile technology programs. Excluding them, after all, was in Russia's "national interests." With a clear allusion to the Shahab-3 and its follow-ons, Putin suggested to his interviewers that they "check with the experts what missile weapons Iran has and what their range is, you will realize that I am not exaggerating here." On nuclear technologies, there were of course those who would try covertly to circumvent Russian state policy to make money and "we will do everything to stop this." But the United States should also take a closer look at what Iranian specialists training in American colleges and universities were really up to.[42]

A year later, the two presidents returned to these same themes in much the same tone. At their May 24, 2002, summit in Moscow, Bush told a Kremlin press conference that he was "confident that President Putin is also worried about Iran." The American president said, "We spoke very openly and honestly about the need for the non-transparent government run by radical clerics not to acquire weapons of mass destruction so as to inflict damage on us and Russia." The Russian president confirmed this and added that he agreed with President Bush's "assessment of the threats in this direction." But he then went on again to defend Russia's contract to construct the Bushehr nuclear power station.[43]

Similarly, at the G-8 summit in Kananaskis, Canada, a month later, Putin again affirmed that Russia would continue to cooperate with Iran on Bushehr.[44] The meeting participants agreed that Russia would assume the G-8 presidency in 2006 and host its annual summit that year.[45] After his bilateral with President Bush on the margins of the G-8 event in Canada, Putin declared, "Our interaction with the United States is becoming very effective not just in terms of addressing bilateral issues, but also in terms of addressing major international issues."[46]

In retrospect, the Moscow and G-8 summits in 2002 marked the high point in U.S.-Russian relations during the Putin-Bush era. It did not seem to bother Putin that Bush in late January had consigned Iran to the "axis of evil" along with Iraq and North Korea. In the wake of the September 11, 2001, terrorist attacks on New York and Washington and the subsequent American-led ouster of the Taliban regime in Afghanistan, Putin had reinforced his turn toward the West and now continued to do so. In that context, Putin's defense of Bushehr could be interpreted as a bone thrown in the direction of the clerical regime in Iran as well as Russian critics of cooperation with Washington. In fact, the Western media's amplification of the gesture made it all the more effective with these anti-Western audiences. Under the circumstances, moreover, at least some in Tehran were grateful for the favor—given what else Putin had done in spring 2002 that was not to their liking.

At the Moscow Summit in May, Bush and Putin had signed a dramatic nuclear reductions treaty—the Moscow Treaty—and issued a joint declaration on the "new strategic relationship" between Russia and America.[47] They had coordinated policies toward Afghanistan and endorsed the new NATO-Russia Council, which was approved several days later in Rome. This gave Moscow a role for the first time in the alliance's discussions of such key issues as nonproliferation, missile defense, and counterterrorism.[48] In Iran, one commentary went as far as to declare that "Russia has now turned into a NATO ally" and that the U.S.-Russia summit of May 2002 was evidence that Putin was willing to "help Bush push ahead with his plan to set a new world order."[49]

Yet some in Tehran could once again point to Putin's continued endorsement of Bushehr as evidence of Russia's "enlightened" policy and ability to resist American pressure against cooperation with Iran.[50] Indeed, as far back as Viktor Chernomyrdin's premiership in the 1990s, Moscow had given verbal assurances that MinAtom would not contract to build any more nuclear power plants in Iran beyond Bushehr.[51] Now, nevertheless, since at least the previous fall, MinAtom had been trying to interest Iran in a feasibility study for a second unit at Bushehr.[52] Moreover, a draft plan for Russian-Iranian cooperation to the year 2012, approved by Prime Minister Mikhail Kasyanov, suddenly surfaced on the Internet in late July. It included not just Bushehr-1 (under construction) and Bushehr-2 (under initial consideration) but two more units at Bushehr as well as an additional unit at Ahvaz, for a total of five plants.[53] In this regard, it was reminiscent of the various ambitious nuclear power plant proposals in play when former Foreign Minister Andrey Kozyrev had visited Tehran in March 1993. Russian planners, it seemed, could never throw a proposal away.

After strong objections from Washington, MinAtom head Aleksandr Rumyantsev assured visiting U.S. officials that "No cooperation in the nuclear sphere is in place today" other than Bushehr-1 and that the conclusion of any other further contracts would be "contingent upon many factors, including political."[54] All the same, Bushehr-2 talks continued, and in December 2002, Rumyantsev in Tehran signed a protocol calling for a joint committee to research the technical possibility of a second unit at Bushehr.[55]

It could be argued that Russia really did not need more troublesome contracts with Iran. Bushehr-1 had done its job of keeping Russia's nuclear power plant construction industry afloat as it struggled to survive and recover after the 1986 Chernobyl disaster and then the Soviet collapse. According to Yevgeny Sergeyev, director of St. Petersburg's Izhorskiye Zavody, which built the Bushehr-1 reactor, the project had given his concern a 70 percent workload and saved about three hundred enterprises in the nuclear sector from bankruptcy.[56] Since Bushehr, MinAtom had landed new contracts for building power plants in China and India—two in each—in December 1997 and November 2001, respectively.[57] By 2003 MinAtom exports would reach $3 billion.[58]

But the Russian position on a Bushehr-2 was ambiguous. There were certainly some economic incentives to MinAtom to keep open the option of another contract. Moreover, despite the downsides in the Kremlin's dealings with Washington, there were offsetting political dividends for keeping the prospect of more Bushehr start-ups alive. The high visibility project helped first Yeltsin and then Putin manage Russia's relationship with Iran, as well as handle domestic opposition to cooperative relations with Washington. Putin may have even viewed dangling the prospect of another Bushehr as a device to encourage Tehran to work with and not bolt from the IAEA, which would have forced Russia to break off its Bushehr-1 contract since it required IAEA inspections.

Indeed, the debate over Bushehr and relations with one another and with the United States continued in both Moscow and Tehran. In October 2002, for example, retired Foreign Ministry consultant Andrey Zobov rejected American "sermons" to Iran and Russia on their bilateral relations. These, he reminded his lecture audience, "came into being even before Columbus discovered America." Washington, Zobov asserted, had yet to hand over to Moscow any "reliable evidence either about Iran's nuclear missile programs or about Russian assistance" to them.[59]

Around the same time, Aleksey Arbatov, a deputy chairman of the Duma's Defense Committee and a longtime student of strategic affairs, advised another lecture audience differently: "The Americans do not believe that Iran has no plans to develop nuclear weapons, and I think we should agree with them." States such as Iran, Arbatov warned, were located very close and could eventually easily target all of Russia with their missiles and nuclear weapons. Moreover, any nuclear weapons developed in Iran could "easily get into the hands of international terrorists." Russia "verbally" supported nonproliferation, Arbatov cautioned, but did not make it a top priority. Too often, he pointed out, commercial and geopolitical interests overruled nonproliferation concerns.[60]

In Tehran, meanwhile, most of the commentary again expressed satisfaction and official gratitude that the United States had not been able to disrupt ongoing nuclear cooperation between Russia and Iran.[61] Along with that, however, there was also some suspicion of the motives behind the publicity accorded the draft long-term plan signed by Prime Minister Kasyanov. It was all a "shrewd maneuver by Moscow" designed to extract concessions from Washington, warned international law specialist Dr. Davoud Bavand. Once Moscow got what it wanted from America, it would drop its projects in Iran. Besides, Iran had no need for any more reactors, and statements that it did simply bolstered the propaganda of those suggesting that Iran was trying to acquire nuclear weapons and other weapons of mass destruction.[62]

## SHOCK OVER NATANZ AND ARAK

In August 2002 the National Council of Resistance of Iran (NCRI) pointed to the existence of two major nuclear sites some three hundred kilometers southwest and south, respectively, of Tehran at Arak and Natanz.[63] In December, a Washington think tank concluded that commercial satellite photographs suggested the Arak facility was for the production of heavy water used as a coolant in making weapons-grade plutonium and that the Natanz site was a gas centrifuge plant for enriching uranium for bombs.[64] Under pressure from these new revelations of what struck many experts as a military nuclear program, Iran began to disclose that it had embarked on an ambitious project to develop what it claimed was an indigenous, self-sufficient fuel cycle to support the equivalent of six Bushehrs.

In December Foreign Minister Kharrazi reiterated earlier claims that the plants at Natanz and Arak were designed to produce fuel for electricity-generating nuclear plants.[65] Then, on February 9, 2003, President Khatami gave an extensive public report on what he said was Iran's peaceful nuclear technology program, focusing on developing a soup-to-nuts fuel cycle. Iran was starting to mine uranium in Yazd province. An enrichment-related facility was nearing completion near Esfahan and other "huge installations" were under construction elsewhere. Russia was committed to supplying fuel for Bushehr, Khatami conceded, but Iran needed its own indigenous capability to produce enough fuel for additional nuclear power plants. These were projected to produce six thousand megawatts of electricity—six times the amount produced by Bushehr-1 alone.[66]

MinAtom Deputy Minister Valery Govorukhin immediately called into question the logic of the program outlined by Khatami. "Iran has neither the technology, the financial resources, nor the need to develop a nuclear fuel cycle," stated Govorukhin, and Russia had repeatedly told Iran that it would not offer it the relevant technologies. Khatami's statement "looks like a political one, because it is not backed up by either technological or financial resources."[67] Commentary by foreign experts and regime opponents went further and explicitly suggested that the large-scale project outlined by Khatami was in fact an elaborate but so far legal cover for a much smaller effort to produce weapons-grade fissile material.[68] Within ten days, the NCRI publicized a facility near Esfahan that might be designed to do just this.[69]

In late February 2003 Khatami's statement and the widespread questions about what Iran was really up to in the nuclear field sparked an inspection trip—originally requested for October 2002—by International Atomic Energy Agency (IAEA) director general Mohamed ElBaradei to Natanz. There he visited a gas centrifuge enrichment pilot plant as well as "a much larger enrichment facility still under construction at the same site." Over a hundred of some thousand planned centrifuges were installed at the pilot plant. Over fifty thousand centrifuges were planned for the commercial-scale facility at Natanz. ElBaradei urged Iranian authorities to agree to an additional protocol to Iran's Nuclear Safeguards Agreement with the IAEA, and they assured him that they would "actively" consider it.[70] It was the start of several years of intensive IAEA scrutiny of Iran's nuclear program. After ElBaradei's initial report in March 2003, more than a dozen IAEA Board of Governors meetings dealt with the issue of the Iranian nuclear program until it was finally reported to the UN Security Council in March and April 2006.[71]

News soon began to circulate of what ElBaradei had seen when inspecting the Natanz facility. Vladimir Frolov, deputy staff director for the Duma's International Relations Committee, declared, "Iran's uranium project cannot but arouse alarm also in Russia." Frolov reported that ElBaradei had found an experimental cascade of 160 gas centrifuges already in place and an ongoing assembly of a thousand more centrifuges. He mistakenly said the Natanz facility would eventually house five thousand centrifuges—he presumably meant to say fifty thousand—which could produce enough highly enriched uranium to arm two to three nuclear bombs each year. Although the centrifuges appeared to have been produced in Iran, Frolov reported speculation that Pakistan, China, and North Korea had provided Iran with technical assistance.

It could not be excluded, argued Frolov, that Iran was preparing for the option of breaking out of the NPT and then openly and quickly moving into the production of nuclear weapons. This made it essential that Russia work closely with the United States to encourage Iran to accept an additional protocol to its safeguards agreement with the IAEA. More intrusive inspections by the IAEA would "reduce to a minimum the risk of [Iran] switching over enriched uranium to military purposes, and also to uncover as much as is possible any secret, undeclared by Iran, nuclear-infrastructure facilities." Russia should probably rethink and scale back its cooperation with Iran in the nuclear power and other high tech sectors. "The idea that we can control Iran's nuclear ambitions through the delivery of fuel assemblies . . . and their subsequent return to Russia as spent fuel is no longer justified," concluded Frolov.[72]

## ST. PETERSBURG, EVIAN, AND VIENNA

Officials in Russia had always been less concerned than those in America over how soon Iran might really be able to develop nuclear weapons. In its 1995 report, the SVR had asserted that Iran would probably not be able to build its own enrichment facilities until at least 2005 (see chapter 6). In light of the Natanz revelations—presumably just the tip of the iceberg—Russian confidence that Iran was not capable of developing nuclear weapons any time soon was shaken.

Minister of Atomic Energy Aleksander Rumyantsev evidently could not contemplate reaching Frolov's conclusion just yet. Nevertheless, in striking contrast to the tone adopted by his MinAtom predecessors Mikhaylov and Adamov when commenting on Iran, Rumyantsev soon exclaimed, "What has recently happened has shocked the entire nuclear community." Reflecting on reports of what the IAEA had found at Natanz, Rumyantsev told a press conference that the centrifuge complex "could be a huge facility for enriching uranium that could be developed to weapons-grade status."[73] Clearly alluding to Rumyantsev's statement, Iranian Foreign Ministry spokesman Hamid Reza Asefi soon expressed his own "astonishment at these irresponsible remarks." Iran's nuclear activities were entirely transparent and peaceful.[74]

The Iranian complaints had their intended effect, but only briefly. As we shall see in chapter 12, U.S.-UK forces on March 20 had just launched Operation Iraqi Freedom despite Russian, French, and German opposition in the UN Security Council and Iranian displeasure elsewhere. Moscow and Tehran for the moment, therefore, were intent on minimizing rather than highlighting their differences on other issues wherever possible. Within days, Rumyantsev met with Iran's Ambassador Gholamreza Shafei in Moscow. Without being contradicted by Russian sources, IRNA claimed, "Rumyantsev said that Russia rests assured that the gas centrifuges set up at nuclear power plants in Natanz and Arak have nothing to do with production of nuclear arms."[75] The dictates of Russian diplomacy in the face of the conflict in Iraq, presumably, had caused Moscow to tone down its public skepticism and concern over Iran's nuclear fuel cycle program. But it was becoming increasingly hard for Moscow to exercise such restraint.

On April 9 Operation Iraqi Freedom troops reached the center of Baghdad and toppled Saddam Hussein from power—just three weeks after the campaign began. The speed of the allied operation was nearly matched by the swiftness with which Moscow returned to its increasingly critical stance toward Iran's nuclear program. On April 22 MinAtom's Rumyantsev told a press conference that the cascade of centrifuges being reported in the media as present in Iran "make it possible to enrich uranium to high weapons grade." While "an accurate picture is not known" so far, Rumyantsev conceded, "If everything that is being reported in the mass media corresponds with reality, then the situation causes concern." There needed to be IAEA "guarantees here," he concluded.[76]

Under pressure even from Moscow on the nuclear issue and apparently worried that Washington might turn its sights on Iran after having disposed so quickly of Saddam Hussein in Iraq, some in Tehran around this time—in early May 2003— discretely proposed to Washington a broad dialogue purportedly aimed at eventually normalizing relations, on which more in chapter 12.[77] Later that month, there were further reports by the NCRI of uranium enrichment facilities. Two laboratories at Ramandeh and Lashkar-Abad, in the Hashtgerd region, near Karaj, some twenty-five miles west of Tehran, were said to be intended as backups to the facilities at Natanz.[78] In July the same organization publicized what it said was yet another nuclear complex, called Kohladouz, northwest of Tehran, dispersed throughout an area controlled by the Iranian military.[79] There would be still other discoveries in the next few years of heretofore secret nuclear facilities as well as allegations of various military nuclear projects.

In Moscow, negative commentary continued, extending to Duma deputies with considerable expertise on the subject. Former Security Council secretary Andrey Kokoshin in early June 2003 commented that Iran appeared to have come right up to the "red mark" and "may indeed embark on a path of violating the nonproliferation treaty." He called for international measures to halt Iran's movement in this direction. But Sergey Reshulskiy, a leader of the Communist Party, retorted on the same radio program, "What is simply taking place is that crude pressure is being put on Russia. The President [Putin] is making concessions, losing face, and we as a free and sovereign country are losing our positions."[80]

With the IAEA Board of Governors scheduled to meet in mid-June 2003 in Vienna to discuss the nuclear developments in Iran, Putin added his own weight to the lower-level expressions of unease. Secretary of State Colin Powell, after a mid-May meeting in the Kremlin, said that Putin had shared America's "concern" over Iran's possible nuclear weapons program.[81] After his summit with President Bush in St. Petersburg, Putin told a press conference on June 1, "The positions of Russia and the USA on the issue [of the Iranian nuclear program] are much closer than they seem." As had been the case at previous summits, however, Putin added, "Russia resents nuclear programs or anything else being used as a lever in unfair competition against Russian companies on the Iranian market."[82]

At the G-8 summit in Evian, France, the next day, Putin approved the summit declaration on nonproliferation. It contained a paragraph devoted exclusively to Iran: "We will not ignore the proliferation implications of Iran's advanced nuclear program. We stress the importance of Iran's full compliance with its obligation under the NPT. We urge Iran to sign and implement an IAEA Additional Protocol without delay or conditions. We offer our strongest support to comprehensive IAEA examination of this country's nuclear program."[83]

Briefing the press after the G-8 summit, Putin said that Russia would continue to cooperate with Iran and, as usual, warned that Russia was "categorically against the dragging up of problems that could be used for unscrupulous competition, including on the Iranian market." That said, Putin went on to assert that Russia would "insist that all Iranian programs in the nuclear sphere are overseen by" the IAEA.[84] The next day, UK prime minister Tony Blair, reporting to Parliament on the G-8 summit, said, "President Putin made clear that . . . Russia would suspend its exports of nuclear fuel to Iran" until Iran complied with the G-8's call for it to sign and implement an IAEA protocol without delay or conditions.[85]

On June 6 Director ElBaradei's written report for the upcoming IAEA Board of Governors meeting, set to start June 16, stated that Iran had "failed to meet its obligations under its Safeguards Agreements with respect to the reporting of nuclear material, the subsequent processing and use of that material and the declaration of facilities where the material was stored and processed." Iran had admitted not reporting the acquisition of 1.8 tons of natural uranium in 1991. The report called on Iran to provide the IAEA with "a complete chronology of its centrifuge and laser enrichment efforts," particularly leading up to Natanz, and more information "regarding allegations about undeclared enrichment of nuclear material, including, in particular, at the Kalaye Electrical Company" outside Tehran. It addition, the report called for more enquiries concerning Iran's use and production of heavy water.[86] After the thirty-five-member board concluded its deliberations in Vienna, it issued a statement calling on Iran to "promptly and unconditionally conclude and implement an Additional Protocol to its Safeguards Agreement, in order to enhance the Agency's ability to provide credible assurances regarding the peaceful nature of Iran's nuclear activities, particularly the absence of undeclared material and activities."[87]

On June 20, as a scene-setter for his upcoming visit to London, Putin told British interviewer David Frost that Russia had "some important concerns" about the Iranian nuclear program and that "our Iranian partners are aware of those problems." His telephone conversation with President Khatami on the eve of the IAEA Board of Governors meeting was not enough to find out if Iran would fulfill its obligations. Russia would develop its nuclear relations with Iran and other countries depending on how open they were to IAEA experts. But, again, Putin warned that Russia would resist use of the nonproliferation issue "as a means of squeezing Russian companies out of the Iranian market."[88]

As the IAEA Board of Governors was meeting in Vienna, Alexander Nyago, the head of the Russian TVEL nuclear fuel producer, spoke with reporters at an economic forum in St. Petersburg. "No fuel," he stressed, "will be supplied until Iran's entire nuclear industry is put under IAEA monitoring."[89] Despite Putin's defense of Russian business interests, Russian media commentary outlined the extent of potential loses for Russia should it not go ahead with fuel supplies for Bushehr and also the magnitude of profits should its strategy succeed in dissuading Iran from developing its own nuclear fuel production complex. Several days before Nyago's statement, a television correspondent had reported that Russia expected to earn $40 million annually from uranium fuel sales for Bushehr.[90]

In late December 2002, as we have seen, MinAtom's Rumyantsev had declared that he was convinced Iran was not working on developing nuclear weapons. He had forecast that the spent fuel agreement needed just a bit more tinkering and would be ready for signing in forty-five to sixty days, i.e., by the end of February 2003 at the latest. In the wake of ElBaradei's centrifuge sightings at Natanz, however, this tight timeline gained considerable elasticity. When Asadullah Saburi, deputy head of IAEO, visited Moscow in late May, he found the spent fuel agreement still not ready and reportedly undergoing ecological vetting within the Russian bureaucracy.[91] It seemed the beginning of a deliberate slowdown on Russia's part in reaction to the revelations of what was afoot at Natanz and other nuclear facilities in Iran. In any event, the agreement would not be signed until late February 2005.

At the end of its June 16–20, 2003, meeting, the IAEA Board of Governors had called on Iran to clarify all its secret activities of the past eighteen years, rectify them, and sign an additional protocol to its Safeguards Agreement under the NPT. If implemented, this would allow unannounced inspections of Iran's nuclear sites. Rumyantsev confirmed that Russia would begin supplying fuel to Bushehr "only after Iran has put all of its nuclear facilities under the control of the International Atomic Energy Agency and provided answers to all questions the IAEA may ask."[92] After "difficult" talks in Moscow in late June and early July, IAEO director Gholamreza Aqazadeh returned to Tehran again empty handed.[93] Within days, Putin told Bush once again in a telephone call that he was concerned about Iran's nuclear program and reaffirmed that Russia would not provide it with fuel for Bushehr until Moscow was certain Iran was not developing nuclear weapons.[94]

With a Bush-Putin summit scheduled for late September 2003, opinion remained divided among Russian experts on Iran's nuclear program, though the range had shifted considerably toward assuming that Iran was much further along than previously thought on its military components. Vladimir Orlov, director of the Center for Policy Studies in Russia (PIR Center), was of the view in summer 2003 that Iran's elites were still divided over the future goals of the country's nuclear program and that they had still not made the political decision to forge ahead and actually develop nuclear weapons. This situation, in Orlov's view, meant that "Russia has much room for pursuing its foreign policy." He consequently advised that Putin not suspend cooperation on Bushehr "at least until Russia has direct proof that Iran is developing nuclear weapons of its own."[95]

Just a few months later, however, Aleksey Arbatov, a deputy chairman of the Duma's Defense Committee, again took a more jaundiced view. In a major article on nuclear deterrence, Arbatov repeatedly lumped Iran together with North Korea as nuclear "threshold" states. Together with Iraq before them, Arbatov argued that Iran and North Korea had joined the NPT "as political cover for their military programs and in order to gain easy access to information, experts, technologies and materials." Despite "serious evidence of Tehran's military nuclear activities," Arbatov argued that Russia was resisting U.S. pressure to stop construction of Bushehr because "the economic and political benefits . . . are far more appreciable than non-proliferation"— adding that the same was true of American relations with Pakistan. However, warned Arbatov, if Iran and North Korea succeeded in developing their own nuclear weapons, "a combination of numerous risk factors will make the use of nuclear weapons in foreseeable future practically inevitable."[96]

# 12

# *Operation Iraqi Freedom*

After the surprisingly rapid ouster of the Taliban from Kabul in November 2001, the lightning-quick military operation that unseated Saddam Hussein in Baghdad on April 9, 2003, once again confounded critics and skeptics alike. The similarities, however, went no further than that. Developments on the political and diplomatic fronts proceeded differently in Iraq from those in Afghanistan.

In Afghanistan, OEF had enjoyed widespread international approval. The Taliban regime had been an international pariah. It never secured accreditation for its diplomats at the United Nations, where Northern Alliance emissaries had represented Afghanistan while the Taliban actually held power in Kabul. In contrast, Saddam's representatives had always been able to avail themselves of a pulpit at the United Nations from which to state their case to the world.[1] As the United States and the UK prepared to launch Operation Iraqi Freedom (OIF), they ran into sharp resistance from other UN Security Council permanent members.

September 11 had brought Moscow and Washington together in the battle against international terrorism. Iraq, however, was repeatedly to test and strain the Russian-American relationship. Nevertheless, Moscow and Tehran drifted apart in both instances, not in opposition to one another's positions but in pursuit of different agendas, especially when it came to Iraq. Moreover, with a common enemy vanquished from power in Kabul and with Iran's bête noire Saddam Hussein deposed in Baghdad, Moscow and Tehran were soon left with less compelling reasons to coordinate with each other in the region.

Twenty years before, Iraq had been a major bone of contention between the new regime of Ayatollah Ruhollah Khomeini in Tehran and the old Soviet regime in

Moscow, which had no sympathy for Khomeini's theocracy and the ayatollah's dogged pursuit of the secular Hussein's overthrow. In the 1980s, during the painful and drawn-out Iran-Iraq War, Soviet weapons sales to the Saddam regime had contributed to a long chill in relations between Moscow and Tehran. Since 1989, however, Russian-Iranian relations had radically changed, even though Moscow continued to maintain active and profitable ties with the Saddam regime.

Particularly after 9/11, Russia and Iran shared acute concerns over the direction of U.S. policy toward Iraq, and Tehran joined Moscow in opposing the American goal of regime change in Baghdad. Neither Russia nor Iran (and especially Iran) had any pity for Saddam Hussein. However, both feared the possible downsides of what might follow Saddam's violent removal and regarded any potential gains from his ouster as uncertain at best. In the year leading up to OIF, both opposed what they perceived to be the United States pushing ahead with a military campaign to dislodge Saddam before UN weapons-of-mass-destruction (WMD) inspectors finished their job.

Although united in their opposition to the looming OIF campaign, Russia and Iran had differing stakes in opposing the shattering of the status quo in Iraq. In Tehran, the prospect of a successful U.S. effort against Saddam stoked fears within the theocratic regime that Iran itself might be President George W. Bush's next "axis of evil" target, especially given rising tensions over the fresh disclosures of Iran's covert nuclear program. Iranian leaders feared that Iraq's fragmentation might set the stage for a similar dismemberment of Iran. They also worried that the potential ensuing chaos across the region would challenge the legitimacy of their regime and its ability to govern.

For Moscow, a unilateral American move into Iraq despite Russian opposition would further undermine Russia's world power status, then principally derived from its permanent membership in the UN Security Council. It would also complicate Russia's prospects for continued profitable economic relations with whatever authority supplanted the Saddam regime. Were American intervention to go especially poorly and generate more instability in the region, it also increased the likelihood of radical forces infiltrating the Russian Federation's own territories in the North Caucasus from the Middle East and from South and Central Asia.

In addition, as we have seen in chapter 11, Russia and Iran were at increasing odds over the nuclear issue beginning in spring 2003. This clouded the incentives Moscow had to cooperate with Iran over Iraq but did not necessarily create new incentives for Russia to cooperate with the United States in Iraq. The U.S. intervention in Iraq actually sharpened the dilemma Moscow faced over its Iran policy. The revelations at Natanz added urgency to Russia's desire to contain the Iranian nuclear program. At the same time, as new revelations continued to surface even as the United States moved into Iraq, Moscow did not want to help set a precedent for an international warrant for a similar WMD-justified U.S. military attack on Iran. In the short term, at least, Russia and Iran remained united in opposing the American move into Iraq despite increasing friction over Iran's nuclear program.

After OIF toppled Saddam, Russian and Iranian core objectives in Iraq continued to differ while not contradicting each other. Russian goals remained above all economic and geopolitical, with an emphasis in the latter category on revived influence in the UN Security Council. Iranian goals were primarily political and regional, focused on increased influence in Iraq by virtue of its resurgent Shia majority. But as in Afghanistan, the two sets of national objectives—Russian and Iranian—while ultimately different nevertheless in the short term intersected and were greatly dependent on and reactive to U.S. policies.

While some accused Washington of preparing to attack Iraq for its oil, it was paradoxically Moscow and not Washington that openly and unabashedly underscored its keenness to exploit Iraq's hydrocarbon deposits. Russia's economic focus was the giant West Qurna oil field contract that Lukoil had negotiated with the Saddam Hussein regime in 1997. After Putin replaced Yeltsin, Lukoil president Vagit Alekperov continued to expand on the close ties with the Kremlin that he had forged in the 1990s when he had been so instrumental in setting Russian policy in the Caspian. But revalidating Lukoil's contract to exploit the West Qurna field was dependent on the establishment of a full-fledged government in Baghdad as well as indirectly on Iranian and American beneficence. West Qurna lay deep in the southern Iraqi Shia heartland, where Iranian Shia influence presumably was strongest. Implementing the contract could not happen until a sovereign post-Saddam government assumed office and revalidated the terms of the agreement.

Iranian political goals in turn were also affected by Washington's approach and timetable for turning sovereignty over to the Iraqis as well as by the actions of the UNSC, where Russia played a critical role but was nevertheless often outflanked by the United States. Tehran could not presume any automatic affinity from Iraq's large Shia population, which was Arab and not Persian and had by and large not defected to Iran during the prolonged Iran-Iraq War in the 1980s. However, Tehran had good grounds for anticipating that Iranian influence would grow and not diminish in post-Saddam Iraq.

## REDEFINING THE "AXIS"

After President Bush's "axis of evil" statement in January 2002 linking Iraq, Iran, and North Korea, Tehran was acutely sensitive to U.S. declarations on Iraq, regarding American policy toward Iraq as a precursor of Washington's intentions toward Iran. Tehran's worries were reinforced July 12, 2002, by President Bush's statement commemorating the anniversary of student protests in Iran in 1999.[2] Washington allusions to the need for regime change in Iraq began to weigh heavily on Iranian statements and politics. Apprehension over the potential consequences for Iran of a possible U.S. attack on Iraq was the order of the day. Hard-liners in Tehran denounced

Bush's comments as outside interference. Invoking the need for national unity, they launched a wave of newspaper closings and political repression.[3]

By mid-September 2002 Iraq had accepted in principle the return of UN weapons inspectors, whom it had expelled in 1998. On November 8 the UN Security Council unanimously adopted Resolution 1441. This gave the UN Monitoring, Verification, and Inspection Commission (UNMOVIC) and IAEA inspectors the right to search anywhere in Iraq for banned weapons. The resolution stated that failure by Iraq to comply with and fully cooperate with its implementation would constitute a further "material breach" of Iraq's obligations and would be reported to the UNSC. Upon receipt of such a report from UN inspectors, the council would convene "in order to consider the situation and the need for full compliance . . . in order to secure international peace and security." The resolution warned that Iraq would "face serious consequences as a result of continued violations of its obligations."[4] Reviewing Iraq's December 7 WMD declaration, U.S. Secretary of State Colin Powell on December 19 declared that Iraq was in "material breach" of UNSC resolutions. On January 2, 2003, U.S. Secretary of Defense Donald Rumsfeld authorized the deployment of thousands of U.S. troops to the Middle East.

Girding itself for the upcoming conflict in Iraq increasingly eclipsed Iran's earlier priorities in Afghanistan. Beyond the fear of American "regime change" intentions toward Tehran, there were other long-standing concerns. Given its long border with Iraq and bitter war during the 1980s, any instability in Iraq posed real security challenges for Iran. A major concern was that Iraq would fragment and that an independent Kurdistan in the north would appeal to Iran's Kurds to secede and join it, or at least declare autonomy within Iran—reviving memories of Soviet dictator Joseph Stalin's maneuvers at the end of World War II. Short of territorial fragmentation but related to it was the potential flow of refugees fleeing conflict in Iraq for relative security in Iran. Having just begun to relieve itself of some of the more than two million Afghan refugees who had long lived on its territory, Iran was not keen to replace them with thousands more from Iraq.

More generally and even more unpredictably, a conflict in Iraq could lead to instability throughout the entire region. Such instability could severely disrupt world oil markets and thus the Iranian state's main source of revenue. Although just four years later, with the price of oil on world markets already at over $70 per barrel, such worries were hard to appreciate, they were very real in 2002. But even more threatening, from the point of view of the theocratic regime, was that an invasion of Iraq would complete the encirclement of Iran by American forces in the region. Combined with potentially widespread disaffection inside Iran, this could threaten the regime's grip on power. Thus, however conflicted by the trade-offs, Iran in 2002 preferred the unpleasant predictability of Saddam's regime to the unpredictable volatility of whatever might come after him, all the more so since it would entail a further increase of American military might in the region.

Nevertheless, responding to the reality of U.S. preparations for the military option, veteran observers of Iranian policy toward the end of 2002 already detected a readiness by Iran not to interfere with a U.S.-led campaign against Iraq. Iran, after all, had adopted precisely such a stance toward OEF in Afghanistan in late 2001. Moreover, a decade earlier, Iran had sat on the sidelines during the 1991 U.S.-led Desert Storm war against Iraq. This time, however, Iran would be more likely to want to play a role in shaping a new regime in Baghdad.[5] Were the United States to enter Iraq—with or without explicit UNSC sanction—then the most prudent course for Iran would be to stay out of the way while preparing to capitalize on its potential assets in Iraq once the Saddam regime had been toppled.

Throughout the long buildup, to be sure, Tehran remained implacably opposed to outside military campaigns to effect regime change, in principle and specifically in Iraq. "It is not legitimate for others, regardless of how powerful they be, to intervene in other countries in order to change their regime," Foreign Minister Kamal Kharrazi declared in October 2002. Should the UN Security Council approve the use of force against Iraq, Kharrazi conceded that Iran would accept it as a fact. But he warned that Iran would nevertheless still not support the ensuing military operation.[6] In February 2003 Kharrazi put Iran's policy even succinctly: "Iran is basically against war and is not going to support either side."[7]

Already in November 2002, there were reports of "preliminary feelers" between Iranian and American officials through Arab intermediaries in a Persian Gulf nation.[8] In January 2003, on the margins of a larger gathering in Europe, U.S. and Iranian officials reportedly met directly to discuss Iranian noninterference in military operations against Iraq, assistance in search-and-rescue missions, and denial of haven to fleeing Saddam Hussein forces. The American envoys reportedly assured the Iranians that a U.S. military campaign against Iraq would not target Iran.[9]

In growing anticipation of the toppling of Saddam Hussein's hated regime, Iran's stance was best captured in what was described as its policy of "active neutrality."[10] Iran would try to gain influence in post-Saddam Iraqi politics through Iraq's Shia population, which was estimated at around 60 percent. The track record here was not good but also not hopeless. In the 1980–88 Iran-Iraq War, Iraqi Shias had remained loyal to Baghdad and not gone over to the new Islamic Republic in Tehran. Arab versus Persian ethnic and linguistic differences had proved stronger than Shia sectarian ties.[11] Nevertheless, Iran for twenty-three years had hosted the anti-Saddam opposition in exile represented by the Supreme Council of the Islamic Revolution in Iraq (SCIRI) and its Badr Brigade militia of as many as twelve thousand fighters. It had also been the refuge for leaders of the Dawa Party, the oldest Islamic movement in Iraq, since Saddam had banned the party in 1980.[12]

While not viewing the SCIRI and its Badr Brigade as Iranian puppets, there was hope in Tehran that they would at least prove a force in post-Saddam politics that would be independent from Washington.[13] As in Tajikistan during the 1992 civil war and in Afghanistan after September 11, the IRGC and the MOIS—and not the Iranian Foreign Ministry—took the lead in working with the SCIRI opposition.[14] It was therefore a good indication that Iran was preparing for all options when a representative of Ayatollah Mohammad Bakir Hakim, the Shia spiritual leader of the SCIRI, attended a meeting of the main Iraqi opposition groups in Washington in August 2002.[15]

In December 2002 the SCIRI and a number of other Iraqi opposition groups in exile met in Tehran and then also attended a U.S.-supported "unity" meeting in London, which elected a seventy-five-member Follow-Up and Coordination Committee.[16] In January 2003 members of this committee returned to Tehran to organize a follow-up to the London conference that would take place in Salah-al-Din outside Arbil in Kurdish northern Iraq.[17] At the Salah-al-Din conference, which met from February 26 to March 1, and which U.S. presidential envoy Zalmay Khalilzad attended, the opposition elected an Iraqi leadership council. Besides the SCIRI's Abdul Aziz Hakim (brother of SCIRI spiritual leader Ayatollah Hakim), it included Patriotic Union of Kurdistan leader Jalal Talabani, Kurdistan Democratic Party leader Massoud Barzani, Iraqi National Congress leader Ahmed Chalabi, Iraqi National Accord leader Ayad Allawi, and Adnan Pachachi, a pre-Baathist regime foreign minister.[18]

The final statement issued by the Salah-al-Din meeting reaffirmed that "power should be transferred to the Iraqi people and their true representatives as soon as possible."[19] At the closing news conference, the SCIRI's Hakim said the council would be responsible for leading Iraq and filling in any vacuum resulting from the overthrow of the Saddam Hussein regime. Talabani thanked U.S. envoy Khalilzad for attending the meeting and Iran for its help to the Iraqi opposition. Khalilzad reportedly stated that the United States was looking forward to working with the opposition and other Iraqis.[20] But the United States had not yet come down definitively on whether to replace Saddam Hussein with a provisional government led by Iraqis, such as those who had just met in Salah-al-Din, or whether instead to put in place an American occupation authority with Iraqis as advisers.[21]

## LUKOIL MANEUVERS

As these meetings unfolded, Moscow's security concerns were less immediate and its political objectives more geostrategic than those of Tehran. Russia did not share borders with Iraq and did not host any significant Iraqi politicians in exile. Yet a conflict in the region would affect Russia's national interests in a variety of ways, and not just because of the unpredictability of a military conflagration spreading beyond the Middle East. The Iraqi issue, after all, was under the purview of the UN Security Council, where Russia had inherited the Soviet Union's status as a permanent member with veto rights.

However much Moscow's power around the globe had ebbed since the Soviet collapse, Russia remained a big power wherever UNSC issues were engaged. Such had been the case in Iraq ever since the Gulf War in 1991. Any American and British campaign against the Saddam regime without explicit UNSC sanction would erode Russia's big power status. Moreover, depending on how strongly Russia resisted such a move in the UNSC, it would disrupt the closer Russia-U.S. relations that Presidents Vladimir Putin and George W. Bush had nourished, particularly since September 11.

Russia's emphasis on UNSC principles, however, also cloaked significant economic interests in Iraq, oil and otherwise. In the Security Council, not only Russia but also France and China, joined by nonpermanent member Germany, all objected to what they perceived as American unilateralism. They all opposed a military campaign to disarm the Saddam regime's suspected WMD programs without further inspections and explicit Security Council authorization. It was widely noted, however, that Russia, France, and China had extensive economic interests in Iraq. The three countries ranked at the top of at least forty-four from which entities and individuals had received lucrative and often illegitimately used oil vouchers during Saddam Hussein's final years in power.[22]

There were powerful financial incentives pushing Russia to keep Saddam in power, where he might eventually honor contracts and obligations toward Moscow and Russian companies. Iraq still owed Russia an estimated $8 billion in Soviet-era debt. Moreover, Russian companies had concluded a variety of contracts with Iraq that could be implemented only after the UNSC lifted its sanctions against Iraq. The most prominent was Lukoil's production-sharing agreement, signed in March 1997, to develop the giant West Qurna-2 oil deposit in southern Iraq. Lukoil president Vagit Alekperov, who had figured so prominently in setting Russian policy on Caspian exploitation and delimitation, put the "theoretical" profits to Lukoil from the West Qurna project at $6 billion.[23] Finally, many Russian companies were already profiting from contracts under the aegis of the UN Oil-for-Food (OFF) program. According to one account in late 2002, fourteen Russian companies had handled up to 40 percent of Iraqi oil exports over the previous six years, reportedly over one billion barrels valued at over $15 billion.[24] A year later the total for goods and services delivered to Iraq by Russian firms from December 1996 to March 2003 was put at $2.3 billion.[25]

The incentives were thus great for Russia to push for a peaceful resolution of the Iraqi disarmament issue and to urge Saddam Hussein to show some progress in complying with the various UNSC resolutions already on the books. While Iraqi disarmament remained an uncompleted process, Saddam had an incentive to reward Russian companies with OFF contracts in return for Moscow using its seat on the UNSC to stymie American proposals for immediate military action. Should Saddam demonstrably comply with UNSC disarmament demands, leading to the lifting of economic sanctions against Iraq, then Russian firms such as Lukoil could begin reaping profits and Russia would stand a better chance of beginning to recoup some of its Soviet-era debt.

The ouster of Saddam would threaten all these real and potential revenue streams since Moscow and Russian firms could not be sure that any post-Saddam regime would honor Saddam-era contracts.[26] Moreover, there was also the fear that Western firms entering Iraq after Saddam's fall would greatly expand Iraqi oil production, bring down world oil prices, and in doing so put a sizable dent in the Russian state budget, which was greatly dependent on taxes from Russian energy firms. The day before Saddam fell, for example, a survey in the daily *Kommersant* suggested that the occupation powers would restore Iraqi oil production to its prewar levels in about a year and that world oil prices would drop to around $20 a barrel.[27]

None of this deterred Lukoil's Alekperov, who was already looking for ways to use the Putin-Bush relationship to salvage Lukoil's positions in post-Saddam Iraq. Cooperation on energy issues was an active and expanding item on the agenda of U.S.-Russian relations in 2002. There was speculation in the Russian press that Washington had made a political decision to let Russian energy producers into the U.S. market as payback to Putin for his post-9/11 cooperation with the United States.[28] In October 2002 the Russian press widely replayed that portion of an interview with the *Financial Times* in which Alekperov had replied, "Yes, of course," when asked whether he had received a guarantee from Putin that the fate of Russian oil contracts in Iraq would be a priority in Moscow's talks with Washington.[29] A month later, President Bush affirmed in an interview with a Russian television channel that the United States understood well that Russia, and other countries, had economic interests in Iraq and that "these interests will be taken into account" in post-Saddam Iraq.[30]

It did not take Baghdad long to react. In December 2002 Iraq notified Lukoil that it was canceling the West Qurna deal. The ostensible reason was that Lukoil had not begun to fulfill the contract (even though by the contract's very terms Lukoil could not start to do so until after UNSC sanctions were lifted).[31] The real reason came out in an interview that Iraqi deputy prime minister Tariq Aziz gave about a week later. "Lukoil went to Washington to get assurances that their contract will be implemented after the removal of the Iraqi regime," complained Aziz. "This is outrageous of them because they signed a contract with us. . . . Such conduct cannot be accepted."[32] Meanwhile, a Russian government source warned Iraq through the press that cancellation of the Lukoil contract "deprives Russia of an important incentive to oppose military action against Iraq."[33] To Lukoil's protests, Iraq's ambassador in Moscow replied that Baghdad had given the West Qurna contract not to Lukoil but to Russia and that some other Russian company could take Lukoil's place.[34]

By this time, though, it was hard to draw a distinction between Russian government and Lukoil policy. According to its own press releases, Lukoil was the second largest private oil company in the world in terms of proven reserves. The company reportedly extracted 20 percent of Russia's oil.[35] Privatization had reduced Russian government ownership of Lukoil shares from 35 down to 7.6 percent. Nevertheless, Lukoil president Alekperov was wrapping the firm ever more tightly in the cloak of Russian state interests. Some even called Lukoil the Ministry of Oil, an appellation that Alekperov found appealing.[36] In November 2002, in his remarkable speech at Russia's General Staff Academy, the Lukoil chief had asserted, "We at Lukoil have considered and consider ourselves to be first and foremost patriots who are working for the benefit of our great Fatherland." In elaborating on the thesis that Russia's "national interests outside its borders are manifested first of all through its economic expansion," which Lukoil was ever ready to serve, Alekperov praised the West Qurna-2 project as "one of our best assets."[37]

Lukoil, though, was not the only Russian entity exploring post-Saddam alternatives around this time. Even the Russian Foreign Ministry was doing the same. On December 11, Vladimir Titorenko, Russia's ambassador to Iraq, met with Kurdish leaders in Sulaymaniyah in northern Iraq, an autonomous area not controlled by Baghdad.[38] Moreover, while Russian deputy foreign minister Yuri Fedotov announced that Russia would not participate in the U.S.-sponsored opposition unity meeting in London in December 2002, in November the Russian ambassador in Tehran had already met with SCIRI spiritual leader Hakim, a meeting that a Russian Foreign Ministry source confirmed.[39] Not surprisingly, it did not take long for Moscow's press to speculate that in striking out at Lukoil, "Baghdad is trying to punish Moscow for the contacts with the Iraqi opposition which have been stepped up in recent times."[40]

## RECALIBRATING AFTER SADDAM

With conflict in Iraq increasingly likely, Russia and Iran hedged their bets not only by pursuing their separate interests with Washington but also by reaffirming their ties to each other. Both hoped a war would not undo the stability that had been achieved in Afghanistan—ironically, thanks largely to the U.S.-led OEF and ISAF. Iran relished what seemed the increasing certainty of Saddam Hussein's impending ouster but had to prepare for the challenges to Iranian security and influence that would be posed by whatever regime would replace Saddam in Baghdad. More important, Iran hoped that Washington would not train its sights on Tehran after a successful campaign in Iraq. Working closely with Moscow was one way to discourage such an eventuality.

The mounting crisis served to remind both Moscow and Tehran once again that, whatever their many differences, they also shared broad common interests in the region. Continuing anxiety over Afghanistan's future and the need to prepare for the worst in Iraq sparked a new round of coordination. Iranian deputy foreign minister Mohsen Aminzade visited Moscow in mid-January 2003 for talks on Iraq, Afghanistan, and "counter-terrorism."[41] Several weeks later, Russian deputy foreign minister Yuri Fedotov was in Tehran for talks focused on Iraq. "Over the coming days and weeks we will maintain very close diplomatic contacts regarding the problems of Iraq," Fedotov told the press.[42]

Facing what seemed an inevitable U.S.-UK campaign against Iraq, Foreign Minister Igor Ivanov visited Tehran on March 11–12. The visit provided a chance to clear the air after the unproductive Caspian summit in Ashgabat in April 2002 at which President Khatami had not budged from Iran's demand for 20 percent of the Caspian despite Putin's expectation that there would be movement on the Iranian side. The sour atmospherics threatened to be revived by newly publicized evidence of an elaborate Iranian gas centrifuge uranium enrichment project underway at a facility in Natanz documented during an inspection trip by IAEA director general Mohamed ElBaradei in late February 2003. But Russia nevertheless remained opposed to helping the United States in any way on Iraq, probably now even more mindful of the precedent this might set for a similar military move into Iran in the wake of the Natanz revelations. With opposition to U.S. preparations for a military campaign in Iraq once again driving them together, both sides seemed eager to portray the Russian-Iranian relationship as moving forward. The joint statement Ivanov and Foreign Minister Kharrazi put out in Tehran once again revived the notion of a visit by Putin to Iran, which would "make a valuable contribution to strengthening Russian-Iranian relations."[43]

By early March, Russia had made clear that it would veto any UN Security Council resolution that explicitly or implicitly authorized military action in Iraq. In Paris on March 5, Ivanov joined French foreign minister Dominique de Villepin and German foreign minister Joschka Fischer in a joint statement declaring that they would not allow a resolution authorizing the use of force to be issued by the Security Council.[44] It was not an empty threat, of course, since Russia and France could both veto such a resolution. In New York on March 11, Ambassador Sergei Lavrov, Russia's permanent representative to the UN, reiterated that Russia could not accept any Security Council resolution that contained an ultimatum or provided for the automatic use of force against Iraq.[45]

On March 18, 2003, the United States, UK, and Spain withdrew their draft resolution seeking UN Security Council authorization for military action to disarm Iraq after concluding that council consensus was not possible. Nevertheless, invoking the "serious consequences" promised by UNSC Resolution 1441 of November 8, 2002, the United States and UK proceeded to launch OIF. On March 19, thirty-one teams of U.S. Special Forces entered Iraq covertly under cover of darkness. The air war began March 20 with raids near Baghdad. On March 22 ground forces began to move into Iraq. Just three weeks later, on April 9, demonstrators pulled down Saddam's statue in central Baghdad. On May 1 President Bush declared, "Major combat operations in Iraq have ended."[46]

As the first OIF strikes began to fall on Baghdad, Putin read a blistering statement. Speaking from the Kremlin, he warned Washington against replacing international law with the "law of the fist." UNSCR 1441 had not given anyone the right to use force in Iraq, he opined, but rather pointed the way to disarm Iraq by peaceful means. "The military action against Iraq is a great political mistake," the Russian president asserted, calling for it to end as soon as possible. The "central role" in resolving the Iraqi and other crises throughout the world belonged to the UN Security Council.[47]

At another Kremlin meeting four days later, however, Putin confined his remarks to a plea to Iraq to adhere to all international conventions regarding the proper treatment of prisoners of war. At the same time, Russia moved to advance its negotiations with Iran to set up a tent camp housing five thousand people just inside Iran's border with Iraq.[48] Russia's Ministry of Emergency Situations (EMERCON) announced that it was ready to help organize and supply refugee camps inside Iran's border with Iraq. Early estimates of the number of displaced Iraqis that might surge toward the Iranian border ranged from 200,000 to 800,000.[49] However, it was soon clear that some of Russia and Iran's worst fears had not come true. Iraq had not broken apart. Refugees had not streamed into Iran. And so Russia and Iran each settled down to make the best of the radically new situation in Iraq.

Putin's focus quickly shifted to restoring Moscow's relationship with Washington while at the same time upholding the primacy of the UNSC, using both venues to salvage a role for Russian companies in post-Saddam Iraq. On April 29, after a meeting with British prime minister Tony Blair, Putin stated that after the fighting ceased the role of the UN "must be not only restored but reinforced." The Security Council's role had to be clearly defined in any plan to stabilize Iraq and establish an acceptable government. "It would be unjustified," he said, "to delay the handover of power to the Iraqi people," which should happen "quite swiftly."[50]

On May 2, on the margins of a summit in Yalta with Ukrainian president Leonid Kuchma, Putin declared that Russia had to "proceed from the present-day reality and think about the future." Russia had not sided with either combatant in opposing the war. Despite all the attention that had been focused on Russia's hopes to recoup the $8 billion in Soviet-era debt owed it by Iraq, "I must tell you that . . . the Hussein regime never paid us anything." Now, "oil, money, credits" remained very important, but far more important was "what kind of peace we intend to build and what kind of international security architecture there will be."[51] Behind Putin's statesman-like formulations, the twin objectives of Russian policy were clear: secure Lukoil's West Qurna contract and preserve Russia's big power influence in the UN Security Council.

On May 14, in a meeting with U.S. Secretary of State Colin Powell, Putin declared that Russia and the United States, despite disagreements over Iraq, had "preserved the fundamental basis" of their relations.[52] A week later, Defense Minister Sergei Ivanov delivered a letter from Putin to President Bush during a visit to Washington. Briefing the press, a senior Russian official said Putin's letter called for cooperation "on all levels." According to the official, Iraq had provoked a "crisis" in Russian-American relations, but now "the most important thing is that the crisis is over."[53]

On May 22 Russia voted in favor of UN Security Council Resolution 1483. This lifted all nonweapons sanctions against Iraq and called for terminating the OFF program within six months.[54] After their summit in St. Petersburg at the beginning of June, Putin underscored to the press that Russia saw its approval of 1483 "as a serious step towards working together on the issue within the UN and together with the US."[55] Moscow clearly hoped that it had put the Iraq issue back into the UN Security Council box, and with it perhaps any U.S. thoughts of following up with a military campaign in Iran.

Meanwhile, Lukoil and other Russian economic interests in Iraq were pressing to retain their positions in the new, suddenly post-Saddam environment. According to Lukoil's West Qurna-2 contract, the company had a hundred days after the lifting of sanctions against Iraq to begin working on the project. However, several days after the UN Security Council approved Resolution 1483, Thamir Ghadhban, interim oil minister in Baghdad, reportedly again terminated—though the move was soon disavowed— Lukoil's West Qurna contract, as the Saddam regime had done in December 2002. Lukoil replied that only the International Arbitration Court in Geneva could annul a valid contract. The company was "ready to hold talks on West Qurna, when Iraq has a new officially recognized government," announced company Lukoil spokesman Dmitry Dolgov.[56]

By early June, Lukoil vice president Leonid Fedun was explaining to reporters in Moscow that Lukoil was already engaged in "consultations" on the West Qurna project with the Iraqi provisional administration. He contrasted these "consultations" with proper "negotiations," which he said could be conducted only with an "officially-elected and internationally-recognized government in Iraq."[57] All the same, several days later Fedun reported that Lukoil had reopened its office in Baghdad.[58] Lukoil was determined to begin work on West Qurna within a hundred days of the lifting of sanctions, as provided by the March 1997 contract.[59]

Meanwhile, Russian deputy foreign minister Fedotov announced that Moscow had received assurances from Washington that Russian companies could resume work in Iraq. Accordingly, representatives of Russian firms who had been participating in the UN's OFF program began to return to Baghdad in early June to negotiate renewal of their contracts.[60] The following week in Moscow, Foreign Minister Ivanov gathered representatives of fifty firms that had been active in Iraq again to reassure them that they would be able to compete on equal conditions against Western firms for OFF and other contracts.[61]

## "GRAND BARGAIN"?

Iranian policy shifted less quickly than Russia's. On April 9, as the Saddam regime was crumbling, Foreign Minister Kharrazi consulted by phone with his Russian counterpart. Both stressed, as Ivanov put it, the "pivotal role" that the UN should play in postwar Iraq in putting together an Iraqi government. Kharrazi called the American plan to put a retired general (i.e., Army lieutenant general Jay Garner) in charge of postwar Iraq "a strategic mistake."[62] Toward the end of the month, Kharrazi, during a visit to Baku, called for the early withdrawal of OIF coalition troops and the simultaneous turnover to the UN of all matters related to settling Iraq.[63]

In Rome ten days later, Kharrazi admitted that Iran was happy to see Saddam Hussein and the Taliban ousted from power in Iraq and Afghanistan but was worried by what the United States would do next. "We do not want America to maintain its presence in the region since we believe American objectives transcend eliminating the Taliban and Saddam Hussein."[64] No one was sorry to see Saddam ousted, President Khatami said a few days later, but America's military occupation of Iraq was a great mistake because it overlooked the UN and "belittled" the entire world.[65]

Tehran in its own way, however, was just as ready as Moscow to strike what amounted to its own separate deal with Washington. The fall of the minority Sunni-based regime of Saddam Hussein opened up opportunities for Iranian influence in Iraq. Behind the ever-present anti-American rhetoric, the more concrete focus of Iranian efforts since the beginning of the year—even before the launch of OIF—had become support for the principle of proportionate power for Shias. This was likely envisioned as bringing a quantum jump in influence for Iran in Baghdad and enhanced security on Iran's western border.

By May 2003 U.S. and Iranian officials had reportedly already met in Geneva three times since the beginning of the year. The third encounter had taken place on May 3, and a fourth meeting was scheduled for the week of May 19. Zalmay Khalilzad, special envoy for Iraq and Afghanistan, reportedly headed the U.S. team in the talks, which U.S. and Iranian diplomats said extended to discussions on the shape of a new Iraqi government. The venue of the talks was an evolution of the earlier Afghan-focused multilateral Geneva Initiative format. The discussions were now essentially bilateral talks on Iraq in which the Italian and German representatives did not participate. A UN official reportedly opened each session but did not always stay. Iranian UN ambassador Mohammad Javad Zarif was Tehran's lead negotiator.[66] One Iranian press report described the discussions as "direct, businesslike and serious, and without any intermediaries present."[67] The Geneva setting and the UN good offices allowed President Mohammad Khatami to portray the May 3 meeting as an almost routine continuation of two to three years of talks under UN supervision, primarily on Afghan issues.[68]

Around this time, but reported much later, a proposal for wide-ranging discussions aimed at eventually normalizing U.S.-Iranian relations was conveyed to Washington separately—not through the Geneva channel—through Swiss ambassador Tim Guldimann, who represented American interests in Tehran.[69] In his May 4 cover letter, Guldimann described the suggested agenda of WMD, sanctions, terrorism, Iraq, and the Middle East as the initiative of Sadeq Kharrazi, Iran's ambassador to France. Kharrazi was a former deputy foreign minister and nephew of Foreign Minister Kamal Kharrazi and his sister was a daughter-in-law of Supreme Leader Khamenei. In Guldimann's discussions with Kharazzi, the latter claimed to have gone over the draft of the so-called Roadmap for U.S.-Iranian negotiations in minute detail with Supreme Leader Khamenei, President Khatami, and Foreign Minister Kharrazi. The

Iranian leaders reportedly had agreed to 85–90 percent of the U.S. aims posited in the Roadmap; the rest, according to Sadeq Kharrazi, could be negotiated.[70]

There was, however, reason to be cautious about the reported proposal. According to Ambassador Guldimann, he had dealt directly only with Sadeq Kharrazi and was simply passing on to Washington what Kharrazi had claimed to him. Besides Kharrazi's own assertions as reported by Guldimann, there was no independent corroboration of Kharrazi's claims to have reviewed the Roadmap with Khamenei, Khatami, and Foreign Minister Kharrazi.[71]

The document's contents lent further grounds for raising questions about its provenance and intent. On Iraq, specifically, Iranian aims putatively included "democratic and fully representative government . . . [and] respect for Iranian national interests in Iraq." American aims in Iraq were said to be "coordination of Iranian influence for activity supporting political stabilization and the establishment of democratic institutions and a non-religious government." The proposed "first mutual step" to be taken by the two sides on Iraq was "establishment of a common group."[72] Yet the Geneva Initiative forum was precisely such a "common group," and it had already been discussing precisely these subjects for months.

Why would the authorities in Tehran have wanted to cross wires with an established negotiation that on May 3 appeared to be progressing much to Tehran's satisfaction? If Tehran were serious, why not use the Geneva channel for the new proposal? Or, at least, double-track the proposal in the Geneva talks? After all, UN ambassador Zarif was Tehran's lead negotiator in the Geneva talks. Sadeq Kharrazi had even suggested to Guldimann that Zarif might be the lead interlocutor in the proposed additional channel.[73] If Zarif were acceptable, then why not the Geneva group he already participated in? And if the Geneva channel were a problem, then why suggest as the Iranian interlocutor someone who was already part of that problem?

Finally, Sadeq Kharrazi's own history gave grounds for questioning the authoritativeness of the alleged proposal. The ambassador was apparently somewhat of a loose cannon who enjoyed protection from his family ties. Not even the posting to France could keep Kharrazi away from intrigues in Tehran. Kharazzi had actively championed talks with Washington well before the American intervention in Iraq. As a supporter of President Khatami, Kharrazi in 1998 was a committed advocate of dialogue between Tehran and Washington, although he was frustrated by what he perceived as the American lack of a positive response to Khatami's "dialogue of civilizations" initiative.[74] Four years later, in spring 2002, Tehran was wrestling with an even greater dilemma: how to respond to President Bush's "axis of evil" designation. In this highly charged context, Kharrazi lost his job as a deputy foreign minister amid swirling rumors of a "growing rift" with his uncle, Kamal Kharrazi, over the younger Kharrazi's "unlicensed contacts" in an effort to reach out to the United States.[75] Within a month, Foreign Minister Kharrazi in effect exiled his nephew Sadeq Kharrazi to Paris as Iran's ambassador.[76]

In May 2003 the Iranian leadership may indeed have been ready for far-reaching concessions after seeing what had happened to Saddam Hussein next door in Iraq. However, given Sadeq Kharrazi's apparent penchant for public controversy, he was not likely to have been Supreme Leader Khamenei's agent of choice for discreetly contacting the Americans with a genuine Iranian trial balloon or diplomatic feeler. Much more likely, it would seem, Khamenei would have preferred a private approach through the established Geneva Initiative channel. As to what Sadeq Kharrazi was up to, he may have been trying to take advantage of the heightened uncertainties in Tehran to contrive a proposal that would provoke a response from Washington that would in turn perhaps be embraced by Tehran. Indeed, there would be another demonstration of his activism along these lines after release of a letter from President Ahmadinejad to President Bush in 2006, about which more in chapters 13 and 14.

In any event, whatever and whoever lay behind the May 4, 2003, Swiss channel proposal, the next scheduled U.S.-Iranian meeting in Geneva never happened. After the bombings in the Saudi capital of Riyadh the night of May 12–13, which took thirty-four lives, including eight Americans, the United States announced suspension of the talks. Citing telephone intercepts, U.S. officials charged that Iran was harboring al Qaeda operatives involved in the preparations for the Riyadh operation.[77] At their meeting in Geneva in early May, alluding to intelligence of a possible imminent terrorist attack somewhere in the region, Khalilzad had reportedly warned his Iranian counterparts that the talks would end if the perpetrators could be traced to Iran.[78]

While generally accepting that there had been phone calls between individuals in Iran and the Riyadh bombers, critics debated their significance and argued that in any case Washington should not have used them as a pretext for not pursuing contacts with Tehran.[79] The U.S. could arguably be faulted for having missed an opening by not pursuing the Geneva channel and/or following up on the disputed May 4 proposal. The U.S. decision to break off the Geneva meetings provoked criticism in the years that followed both from those who accepted the May 4 Roadmap as a genuine proposal and others more skeptical but who nevertheless valued Geneva as a channel for testing the willingness of Tehran for compromise. After the text of the May 4 Roadmap became public, there was renewed speculation that the United States had missed an opportunity for a "grand bargain" with Tehran, which at the time had felt itself particularly vulnerable to the possibility that after Iraq a triumphant Washington might soon set its military sights next on Iran.[80]

In any event, in September 2003, while proposing that the Iraq-focused dialogue with Washington be resumed, Foreign Minister Kharrazi asserted that it had been Tehran that had decided to terminate the Geneva talks in May because the United States, he alleged, had not upheld commitments it had undertaken at the meetings earlier in the year. The one example Kharrazi gave concerned an agreement to establish a decision-making committee representing Iraqi opposition groups, which the United States then decided would have at most an advisory role.[81] This was presumably a reference to the Iraqi leadership council elected at the opposition conference in Salah-al-Din in late February 2003, which Tehran had chosen to interpret as meaning that Iraqis would quickly run liberated Iraq.[82]

The chronology of events did not contradict Kharrazi's assertion, although it may have been no more than a debating point designed to portray the United States as holding the weaker hand and therefore more in need of talks than Iran. In any event, according to the account of retired Lieutenant General Garner, the top American civilian in early post-Saddam Iraq, Garner had met with Kurdish leaders Barzani and Talabani on April 22, the general's second day in Iraq. Talabani had offered to put together an advisory group for Garner consisting of "all of us that worked with Zal [Zalmay Khalilzad]." Garner had asked Talabani to get the group to Baghdad in a week. "Look, if this works I'll make you a provisional government," Garner said he told the two Kurdish leaders. "You'll still work for me but I'll make you a provisional government."[83]

Within three weeks of Garner's meeting with Barzani and Talabani, however, L. Paul (Jerry) Bremer replaced Garner. Bremer arrived in Iraq as fully empowered presidential envoy to Iraq and head of the Coalition Provisional Authority (CPA) that would administer civilian affairs during the occupation. While Bremer was preparing for his assignment, President Bush had agreed with him to put aside Garner's plan for the "early transfer" of power to an Iraqi government by May 15. When Bremer arrived in Baghdad on May 12, he promptly postponed the meeting Garner had scheduled for him the next day with the Iraqi leadership council. Then, on May 16, well after the May 4 Roadmap proposal, Bremer informed the group of mostly exiles that the path to representative government would be "incremental" and broadly based.[84]

On Garner's return to Washington, he told Defense Secretary Rumsfeld that the dismissal of the Iraqi leadership group had been a "tragic" decision.[85] Nonetheless, Iran soon began to adjust to the new realities on the ground in Iraq. Moreover, Tehran appeared to see no sense in waiting to coordinate with Moscow, whom some Iranians saw as going its own way and pursuing its own separate interests vis-à-vis Iraq with the United States. A conservative Tehran daily would editorialize in July that "the events of Iraq, and the indecisiveness, indifference or even silence of Moscow and Beijing vis-à-vis the occupation of Iraq by America showed very clearly that even at the most sensitive junctures, these two countries are prepared to strike some kind of a deal with Washington."[86]

## IGC: NEW FACT ON THE GROUND

On July 13, the CPA appointed a twenty-five-member Iraqi Governing Council (IGC).[87] It included the half dozen who had been part of the leadership group chosen at Salah-al-Din in late February. UN Security Council Resolution 1483, approved on May 22, had called for an interim Iraqi administration, but the CPA retained the ultimate say over all decisions regarding the administration of Iraq. The IGC included thirteen Shia members, five Sunnis, five Kurds, one Turkmen, and one Christian. Of the twenty-five, three were women.

The SCIRI reportedly had hesitated to enter the IGC, questioning whether it would have enough power to make it worth joining.[88] Nevertheless, Abdul Aziz Hakim assumed a seat in the IGC. Besides the SCIRI's Hakim, the IGC included two Islamic Dawa Party representatives: spokesman Ibrahim Jafari and Basra city party leader Izzedin Salim. Like Hakim, Jafari had lived in exile in Iran since 1980.[89] UN Secretary General Kofi Annan recommended that the UN Security Council recognize the IGC as a "representative partner" with which other nations could work.[90]

In the wake of the creation of the IGC, the Kremlin continued its efforts to smooth the way for Russian interests in Iraq by conciliatory gestures toward both the Bush administration in Washington and the new authorities—both U.S.-UK and Iraqi—in Baghdad. In July, the day after the CPA appointed the IGC, Russian foreign minister Igor Ivanov declared, "We expect that this step will be followed by others, which will lead to the establishment of a legitimate Iraqi government."[91] The Russian Foreign Ministry issued a statement declaring, "Russia considers the start of the work of the Governing Council to be the first important step toward the handover of power in that country from the coalition forces to the Iraqis themselves." Russia, the statement said, was "ready for contacts with the Governing Council, and collaboration in the interests of developing traditionally friendly and cooperative relations between Russia and Iraq."[92] On August 14 Russia voted in favor of UNSC Resolution 1500. This "welcomed" the establishment of the "broadly representative" IGC "as an important step towards the formation by the people of Iraq of an internationally recognized, representative government that will exercise the sovereignty of Iraq."[93]

In Iran, although acceptance of the IGC was mixed and the reaction in some quarters at first decidedly negative, debate over its legitimacy was much more subdued than had been the case over the new Karzai administration in Afghanistan a year and a half earlier. After the IGC's appointment, an editorial in one conservative daily called it a "barely disguised act of neo-colonialism." Nevertheless, it conceded that the IGC included some "venerable figures . . . and true representatives of the Iraqi people," such as the SCIRI's Hakim and the heads of the two largest Kurdish parties, Massoud Barzani and Jalal Talabani of the Kurdistan Democratic Party (KDP) and the Patriotic Union of Kurdistan (PUK), respectively.[94] Another conservative editorial took note of the IGC's Shia majority but complained that the SCIRI's representation was "very light" and that it had been deprived of any key ministry.[95]

Debate continued even after passage of UNSCR 1500 in August. An editorial in a conservative Tehran daily called both the resolution and the IGC "instruments for lengthening the duration of the presence and domination of America in Iraq."[96] In stark contrast, an editorial in the pro-Khatami *Iran News* called the IGC the "most democratically representative government" since Iraq's creation after World War I. There was "little doubt," the editorial argued, "that the council's members—chosen extremely carefully taking into account all sensitivities—enjoy the backing of the majority of Iraqis." In both Iraq and Afghanistan, the editorial asserted, "the United States made a lot of efforts to come up with a multiethnic and broad-based government relatively representative of the entire country."[97]

In contrast to Russia's declaration of readiness to deal with the IGC, and even as reformers and conservatives in Tehran continued to debate, Iran began actually dealing with the new body. Iranian policy accommodated itself to the reality of the succession of UN Security Council resolutions recognizing the CPA as the occupation authority in Iraq and the IGC as "broadly representative" of the Iraqi people.[98] As Foreign Minister Kharrazi had in effect forecast in October 2002, the Foreign Ministry began dealing with the new facts on the ground. This was not surprising, since the immediate security threat to Iran came not from the IGC and the U.S.-UK occupation force but from Hussein loyalists who might yet overturn the IGC and even bring Saddam Hussein back to power. The former dictator, after all, would not be found and arrested until late 2003.

The clerical regime in Tehran no doubt still regarded the U.S. and UK military presence in Iraq (as well as in Afghanistan) as a long-term threat to its own hold on power in Iran. In the short run, however, this armed force was staving off the lingering twin threats of Baathist revival and Iraqi disintegration. By early August, therefore, even before passage of UN Security Council Resolution 1500, the Iranian government reportedly approved a Foreign Ministry proposal to establish three consulates in post-Saddam Iraq in the cities of Karbala, Basra, and Sulaymaniyah. According to one report, they would promote commerce with Iraq and, in the case of Karbala, serve the many Iranian pilgrims visiting the tomb of the third Shia Imam in that city.[99]

Even more telling was the visit by an Iranian Foreign Ministry delegation to Iraq at this time, the first such official exchange since Saddam's fall.[100] Iranian deputy foreign minister Gholam Ali Khoshru later asserted that Iran had been the first country to recognize the IGC and send a delegation to Iraq.[101] By late September, Foreign Minister Kharrazi called the establishment of the IGC a "step forward."[102]

## BOMBS, BUSINESS, AND BALLOTS

On August 19, 2003, a truck bomb demolished the UN headquarters in Baghdad, killing head of mission Sergio Vieira de Mello and precipitating a drastic drawdown in the UN presence in Iraq. On August 29 in Najaf, where Ayatollah Ruhollah Khomeini had spent 1965 to 1978 in exile, another huge explosion killed the SCIRI's Ayatollah Hakim, along with more than 120 bystanders, at the Imam Ali shrine, Iraq's most sacred Shiite holy place. By the time of his death, Ayatollah Hakim was considered "the most influential Iraqi cleric openly allied with the U.S.–led occupation."[103]

Moscow and Tehran both appeared to look more to Washington than to one another as they reacted to the first outbreak of large-scale violence in Iraq since the toppling of Saddam. Washington had responded to the string of horrific bombings—

starting with the attack on the Jordanian embassy on August 7—by beginning to explore with colleagues in the UN Security Council a new resolution mandating a multinational force commanded by the United States.[104] Russia's impulse was to use the incidents to shore up its UN Security Council prerogatives by maneuvering to position itself as a central decision maker in that body, in part by further mending relations with Washington. Iran's response was to support the IGC and its Shia majority, in part also by seeking to reengage with Washington.

As much as Iran opposed the U.S./UK military presence next door, it had an interest in preserving enough stability to protect its post-Saddam gains. As in Tajikistan and Afghanistan, however, Iran engaged in Iraq on several levels, with the clandestine forces of the MOIS and the IRGC not necessarily coordinating their operations with the Foreign Ministry. Rumors of covert aid to Shia forces fed suspicions of Iran's ultimate intentions. To the extent that Iranian support for radical groups prolonged the turmoil in Iraq, it complicated Russian efforts to reestablish Lukoil and other economic interests in the country. Over the next several years, Lukoil's efforts to get back into Iraq were to little avail, while Iran's political fortunes rose.

Putin signaled that he would not oppose the creation of a U.S.-led multinational force as long as it were done within the framework of a new Security Council mandate giving the UN "a serious and substantial role . . . in rebuilding Iraq and organizing economic and political life in that country."[105] Russia subsequently acted as the "principal dealmaker" in the final negotiations on the text between Washington, London, and Madrid on one side and Paris and Berlin on the other. Russia gained assurances that the U.S.-UK military occupation would end when a new Iraqi government assumed power, which the United States agreed would happen "as soon as practicable." Putin's decision on October 15 to back the amended U.S. draft made possible the unanimous (15 to 0) Security Council vote in favor of Resolution 1511 the next day.[106]

As for Iran, Foreign Minister Kharrazi, in New York for the UN General Assembly, told the *Washington Post* in late September that his country wanted a greater role for the UN but that there were "many commonalities between Iran and the United States" in Iraq. These common interests included opposition to Saddam Hussein, resolve to keep Iraq from fragmenting, and support for the establishment of a democratic government. According to Kharrazi, his government believed that restarting talks with the United States on Iraq, suspended in May, would "be very useful, as they were for Afghanistan." Tehran was "ready to work with the Americans and cooperate," but Washington had to change its approach "and bring in a new environment for cooperation."[107]

Consistent with their separate approaches, Russia objected and Iran supported the unveiling on November 15, 2003, by CPA administrator Bremer and IGC rotating president Jalal Talabani, of a timetable for the turnover of power in Iraq. The IGC would have until the end of February 2004 to draft a fundamental law. This would regulate public life until adoption of a new constitution. A Transitional National

Assembly (TNA) chosen by May 31 would elect an executive branch and appoint ministers by the end of June. On June 30, 2004, the new Iraqi executive would assume full authority, the IGC would disband, and the CPA would be dissolved. Direct elections for drafters of a new constitution would be held by March 15, 2005, and elections for a new permanent government would take place by December 31, 2005.[108]

Russian objections to the announcement were quick in coming. On November 18 Foreign Minister Ivanov told CNN that the new plan did not even begin to address the question of a UN role. What was needed was a UN-sponsored international conference such as had been convened in Bonn for Afghanistan. Iraqi, UN, and neighboring states' representatives should negotiate a plan that the UN Security Council could then consider and endorse.[109]

In contrast, Tehran almost immediately embraced the new plan's date certain of June 30, 2004, for the turnover of power from the CPA to Iraqis. Tehran also began to court IGC members more ardently. When Talabani visited Tehran just after the announcement of the timetable, President Khatami formally recognized the IGC and stated, "We believe it is capable, with the Iraqi people, of managing the affairs of the country and taking measures leading toward independence."[110]

Reflecting on Talabani's visit, a pro-Khatami daily argued that Khatami's statement had reflected the "two pillars" of Iranian policy toward developments in Iraq: support for the IGC and criticism of the U.S. presence in Iraq and Washington's policies in the region. Most of the IGC's members, it argued, were close or friendly to Iran. Insisting on holding free elections in Iraq as soon as possible to decide Iraq's future political structure should now be Iran's "main strategy."[111] The view in Tehran seemed to be that a regime in Baghdad with strong Shia representation would be disposed to warm relations with Iran, even if not necessarily inclined to follow Iran's theocratic lead.

Indicative of Iran's increased seriousness of purpose was the transfer in December 2003 of Hassan Kazemi Qomi, consul general in western Afghanistan's Herat, to Baghdad, where Qomi became the charge d'affaires in Iran's newly reopened embassy. Qomi was an IRGC officer experienced at operating in hot spots, including Lebanon.[112] The assumption by Qomi of his new job in Baghdad underscored the tipping point that Iranian policy had reached with respect to dealing with the IGC, and the shift in Iran's top priority from Afghanistan to Iraq. Indeed, the potential gains to Iranian political and security interests in post-Saddam Iraq by now far outweighed those offered by post-Taliban Afghanistan.

Seven months after the explosions in Baghdad and Najaf, another wave of violence shook Iraq. On March 31, 2004, tensions festering for nearly a year spiked in the Sunni-triangle city of Fallujah when four American security contractors were ambushed and killed and at least two of the bodies mutilated to the cheers of a crowd. Separately, in several key Shia areas, thousands of Mahdi Army militias loyal to Moqtada Sadr, a thirty-one-year-old firebrand Shia cleric, began an uprising on April 4 against OIF occupation forces in Baghdad, Najaf, Kufa, and Amara.[113] Sadr had inherited political ambitions. His uncle had been a colleague of Ayatollah Khomeini during his years of exile in Najaf and had subsequently been executed by the Saddam regime in 1980.[114] Sadr's father had been Hussein's most prominent clerical critic in the 1990s, which had made him, along with two sons, the target of assassination in 1999.[115] The Sadr and Hakim families had long feuded, and Moqtada Sadr's uprising threatened to steal the thunder from Abdul Aziz Hakim's SCIRI and to challenge the authority of Grand Ayatollah Ali Sistani.[116]

The pressure that the separate Sunni and Shia insurgencies put on the U.S.-led occupation forces again provoked different reactions in Moscow and Tehran, crystallizing the policies of each, which did not exactly mutually reinforce one another. To be sure, both appeared to want the United States to experience enough pain in Iraq to make it less likely to engage militarily elsewhere, but not so much that the United States would abandon Iraq and open the door to chaos that would make Russian and Iranian objectives difficult to achieve.[117] However, as had been the case in Tajikistan and then in Afghanistan—in part by design but perhaps even more as a result of competing political lines in Tehran—Iran continued to hedge its bets and keep all options open, including covert support for targeted political violence, which was not necessarily good for advancing Russian oil business objectives in Iraq.

Early on, American officials could find little concrete evidence that Iran was providing direct assistance to Sadr's Mahdi Army, and the SCIRI's Badr Corps, funded by Tehran, never joined Sadr's uprising. An Iranian insider with ties to President Khatami asserted that Sadr was "too radical for a majority of Iranians."[118] Within months, however, many intelligence officials reportedly concluded that money, arms, and even some fighters were flowing from Iran to insurgents in southern Iraq under Sadr's command, though the volume of this assistance was the subject of debate in Washington as well as Baghdad.[119] An Iraqi Defense Ministry official asserted, "There is no Iranian 'influence' in Basra. There is an indirect Iranian occupation of Basra." According to some city residents, Iranian intelligence agents occupied the former governor's residence, and a Western official claimed that "suitcases of cash" were "constantly ferried" across the border from Iran.[120] Indeed, Iranian defense minister Ali Shamkhani boasted in August, "We are present from Quds [Jerusalem] to Kandahar [in Afghanistan]. We are present in the Persian Gulf, Afghanistan and Iraq."[121]

Tehran could presumably be discrete in its support of deadly violence in Iraq, channeling it primarily against Baathist and other Sunni foes rather than OIF forces.[122] Nevertheless, left unchecked, meddling by Iranian elements added to potential trouble for Russian economic ambitions in Iraq and for Russian diplomatic efforts to maintain productive relations with both Iran and Iraq. In Tajikistan a dozen years earlier, Moscow had had local allies and its own deployed military with which to back up advice to Iran to temper its support to the armed opposition. In Afghanistan after the takeover by the Taliban, Moscow did not have a problem with Iranian covert activities since Russia and Iran shared the same immediate objective of preventing the Taliban's defeat of the

Northern Alliance and occupation of the entire country. Iraq, however, was in effect home-away-from-home turf for Iran, and Russia was helpless to do anything but stand by as the suspected activities of hard-line Iranian elements added to the chaos in the country. Moreover, Iranian activities could eventually provoke a backlash even among Iraqi Shias and set the stage for a reprise of the USSR's challenge two decades earlier, when Moscow had to struggle to balance relations with Baghdad and Tehran during the Iran-Iraq War.

In any event, the political timetable announced on November 15, 2003, soon began to change, a process that accelerated as violence swelled. In January 2004 Lakhdar Brahimi, instrumental in helping negotiate political arrangements for Afghanistan at the Bonn Conference in late 2001, was named the senior UN adviser for Iraq, although strictly speaking not the replacement for UN Chief of Mission Sergio Vieira de Mello, who was killed in August 2003.[123] With Brahimi's encouragement, the IGC on March 8 signed the interim constitution, or Transitional Administrative Law (TAL), negotiated in January and February under the terms of the November 15 plan.[124] The IGC also called for elections by the end of January 2005 for a 275-member TNA. The assembly would choose a Transitional Executive Authority consisting of a president, two deputy presidents, and a council of ministers. The TNA would then draft a permanent constitution and submit it to a referendum not later than October 15, 2005. If the referendum approved the permanent constitution, then there would be another round of direct elections for a new government, which would take office by December 31, 2005.[125]

Despite the tensions in Fallujah, Najaf, and elsewhere, the IGC dissolved itself on June 1. The newly designated Interim Government of Iraq (IGI) took over with Ayad Allawi, a Shia, as prime minister.[126] On June 28, two days earlier than expected, U.S. administrator Bremer dissolved the CPA and turned authority over to the IGI that had been presented to the world on June 1.[127] In mid-August, over a thousand delegates to a conference agreed to a hundred-member Interim National Assembly to act as a parliament until direct elections at the end of January 2005.[128] On September 1, this interim body convened for the first time.[129]

On November 21, Iraqi electoral officials set provincial elections and voting for the TNA for January 30, 2005.[130] Despite Sunni and some Kurdish calls for a delay of up to six months, 8.5 million Iraqis—60 percent of those eligible—cast ballots as scheduled at the end of January 2005. When the results were announced several weeks later, the Shia-dominated United Iraqi Alliance (SCIRI, Dawa, and followers of Moqtada Sadr) fell short of a majority, winning 48.2 percent of the vote, but nevertheless secured a slim margin in the TNA with 140 seats.[131]

In Tehran, government spokesman Abdollah Ramezanzadeh said Iran would cooperate with whatever government Iraqi voters chose, adding, "We hope that these elections will pave the way for ending the occupation and bring about full security in Iraq as a result."[132] Mehdi Hashemi Rafsanjani, son of Expediency Council chairman and former president Ali Akbar Hashemi Rafsanjani, bluntly declared, "We think what the Americans have done is very good for Iran."[133]

Meanwhile, Moscow had made a strategic move on the energy track at the end of September 2004. With Putin's support, the Russian government sold its 7.6 percent stake in Lukoil to the American oil major ConocoPhillips for $1.99 billion. The two companies announced several joint ventures, in particular an undertaking to revalidate Lukoil's West Qurna contract, an effort that would be accelerated after the upcoming elections in Iraq for the TNA. If successful, ConocoPhillips would acquire a 17.5 percent stake in the project. Lukoil's Alekperov asserted, "The U.S. company's joining the project will reduce the financial risks and expedite the Qurna field's commissioning."[134] Yuri Shafranik, head of Russia's Union of Oil and Gas Producers, a month later stated that Lukoil now had a good chance of working the West Qurna field.[135] This was the same Shafranik who eleven years earlier, as Russian fuel and energy minister, had helped Alekperov lobby the Russian government for permission to secure a 10 percent stake in the giant AIOC Caspian consortium for Lukoil.[136]

In February 2005, meeting with President Bush in Bratislava, Putin reminded a press conference of ConocoPhillips's purchase of Lukoil shares, adding, "I am simply sure that business and joint work between the Russian and U.S. partners will develop successfully."[137] The next day, Lukoil chief Alekperov told a press conference in Kiev that talks with Iraq over the West Qurna contract would "begin as soon as the government is formed."[138] In late June, however, announcing that he would visit Baghdad in the fall, Alekperov admitted that negotiations were difficult.[139] In fact, Lukoil's president never made it to the Iraqi capital that year and seemed to have put off his next visit indefinitely.

Unlike Russia's repeatedly frustrated efforts to revalidate Lukoil's West Qurna contract, Iran's political efforts seemed to be paying off. In Baghdad in mid-May for the first high-level call on Iraq's new government, Iranian foreign minister Kharrazi was not shy about underscoring that Iran's influence would outlast America's. Standing next to Prime Minister Jafari at a news conference and speaking English as he made the point, Kharrazi noted, "The party that will leave Iraq is the United States, because it will eventually withdraw. But the party that will live with the Iraqis is Iran, because it is a neighbor to Iraq."[140] In a joint statement at the end of Kharrazi's visit, Iraq's new leadership publicly acknowledged that Saddam Hussein's government had committed "military aggression" when it launched the Iran-Iraq War in 1980 and formally recognized that Iraq had used chemical weapons against Iran during the eight-year war that followed.[141]

That November, when Iraqi president Jalal Talabani visited Tehran, newly elected Iranian president Mahmoud Ahmadinejad waxed lyrically on the ties between the two countries. "History, religion, culture, geography and mutual interests have bound the two countries," he said. "Tehran and Baghdad have one soul in two bodies."[142]

# 13

# The Ahmadinejad Shock Wave

As the nuclear issue heated up in 2003 under pressure of headline-grabbing revelations of Iran's nearly two decades of covert activities, Moscow wanted eventually to emerge with a diplomatic solution that capped Iran's nuclear aspirations while leaving Russia's relations with Iran minimally bruised. Underpinning this approach was confidence that the revolutionary fervor of the Khomeini revolution would continue to dissipate and that the Islamic regime would steadily moderate as a younger generation reached power. The election of President Mahmoud Ahmadinejad in 2005 shook this expectation.

Moscow was determined to preserve its advantages vis-à-vis the United States in dealing with post-shah Tehran, no matter how prickly the Islamic regime installed by the Khomeini revolution twenty-five years earlier continued to behave toward Russia. Russia's goal was to remain engaged with Iran on civil terms and to minimize the inevitable rekindling of historical grievances on the Iranian side should its nuclear aspirations be frustrated with obvious Russian collusion. As a result, despite the otherwise cooling relationship, the top leadership in Tehran continued to see utility in using Moscow as a diplomatic shield against U.S. pressure.

Together with a multitude of other factors, Russian tactics contributed to permitting Iran to move ahead with its nuclear program as Tehran zigzagged to evade international sanctions and the perceived U.S. military threat. Russia wanted to remain engaged with the United States but pursue an increasingly assertive policy. Especially in the aftermath of Saddam Hussein's overthrow, this meant opposing any American push in the UN Security Council for a resolution on the Iranian nuclear issue that could conceivably be interpreted as sanctioning the use of force followed by militarily imposed regime change in Iran.

Significantly, President Vladimir Putin appointed Sergei Lavrov to replace Igor Ivanov as foreign minister in March 2004. As Russia's new top diplomat, Lavrov brought exceptional experience suited to Moscow's pursuit of revived influence at the UN. During the Soviet period, Lavrov had served in New York from 1981 to 1988. From 1988 to 1994, he had held several high-level positions at the Foreign Ministry in Moscow overseeing various facets of Russia's relations with international organizations. For the past ten years, Lavrov had been the Russian Federation's permanent representative, or ambassador, at its mission to the UN.[1] Lavrov had given voice in the UN Security Council in late March 1999 to Russia's objections to NATO launching an air campaign against Serbia without explicit Security Council authorization.[2] And again Lavrov had argued against American-led preparations to attack Iraq without unambiguous Security Council approval in spring 2003.[3]

Explicitly citing the lessons it had learned from the Iraq experience, Moscow was dead set against yielding to a reprise of Resolution 1441, which the United States and the UK had cited to justify launching OIF without returning to the UNSC for final approval. To the extent that Moscow was successful in attaining this objective as a veto-wielding permanent member of the Security Council, it meant a refurbishing of Russia's leverage and status as a major power more generally.

At times it appeared that differences over tactics would overwhelm and undermine the general consensus between Russia and the United States on the strategic goal of stopping Iran's nuclear program. Iran in fact was one issue on which Russia and the United States could still find some common ground despite increasing friction in other areas. And given America's far greater importance to Russia in world politics and economics, Moscow was not indifferent to pressure from Washington when it came to dealing with Tehran.

However, because of the publicity garnered by the clashes between Washington and Moscow over tactics, Russia's own security interests vis-à-vis Iran were often overlooked and underappreciated. Moscow had a long-standing aversion to Iran's emergence as a military nuclear power, or even one just on the threshold of nuclear status. In September 2003 Presidents Vladimir Putin and George W. Bush signaled at Camp David outside Washington that they both opposed Tehran's pur-suit of nuclear weapons and called on Iran to cooperate fully with the IAEA. In the cause of nonproliferation, Putin underscored both before and after Camp David that it was Russia and America that were "strategic partners" and by implication not Russia and Iran.

Nevertheless, Russia continued vigorously to defend its work on the Bushehr nuclear power plant project, even as it slowed down final approval of a protocol on the return of spent fuel from Iran to Russia. Putin also regularly warned other countries against using the nonproliferation and nuclear issues to wage what he described as unscrupulous economic competition against Russia for the Iranian market. Russian policymakers apparently believed they still had time before having to make a fateful choice on whether to deliver fuel to Bushehr. In any event, its projected completion date was repeatedly pushed back because of "technical difficulties."

However, Russian exasperation with Iranian behavior grew. The new administration of hard-line President Mahmoud Ahmadinejad abandoned Iran's voluntary pledge to the IAEA temporarily to suspend nuclear activities. Iran resumed conversion at Esfahan in August 2005 and enrichment at Natanz in January 2006 as it forged ahead on putting in place an indigenous nuclear fuel cycle. As a result, Russia finally supported the decision by the IAEA Board of Governors in March 2006 to move discussion of the Iranian nuclear issue to the UN Security Council, even as Russia continued to resist the imposition of sanctions and argued for another effort at finding a diplomatic solution.

In summer 2006 a leading Russian analyst argued that Russia preferred to see Iran achieve its nuclear ambitions rather than the United States succeed in preventing Iran from attaining them by military force. "When push comes to shove," wrote Dmitri Trenin, "Moscow would prefer to see Tehran pursue its nuclear program, even if it is imperfectly safeguarded, than a U.S. attack to stop it."[4] While that might ultimately prove true, Russia in fact did not want to be forced to make such a choice. Moscow thus continued to focus its efforts on encouraging Iran to resolve all its issues with the IAEA. However, Russia's success in slowing down the move toward sanctions resulted in giving Iran more time to maneuver diplomatically while its scientists improved their nuclear enrichment skills.

For many years, the Russian contention had been that Iran's ability to develop nuclear weapons was so far down the road as to be highly uncertain at best. By summer 2006, however, that assumption provided less and less comfort as a nuclear Iran appeared increasingly inevitable. Even the Duma's International Affairs Committee chairman Konstantin Kosachev worried publicly that Tehran had at last outsmarted Moscow by using Russia's diplomatic screen to advance Iranian goals that were inimical to Russia's own security interests. In any event, the premise of Russian diplomacy toward Iran appeared to shift to accommodate the perception of a changing reality. Iran's progress along the nuclear track might not be stopped. But perhaps it could still be slowed down—preferably without provoking a crisis in Russian-Iranian relations.

In Tehran, relations with Russia were the subject of renewed debate. At issue was whether Iran could count on Russia to fend off sanctions if the Iranian nuclear file were referred to the UN Security Council. In March 2006, Russia's endorsement of the file's placement on the UNSC agenda gave ammunition to those who argued the limits of Russian trustworthiness and protection. Ahmadinejad's detractors warned that Russia was at best a fair-weather friend and would end up backing the EU-3 and the United States on the nuclear issue. Opponents asserted that his Look to the East policy of trying to use Russia (and others) while shortchanging negotiations with the EU-3 and the United States had gotten Iran nothing, and in fact had led to its greater isolation.

Nevertheless, the Ahmadinejad faction continued to exploit ties to Russia to gain time for Iran's nuclear program to advance even as Tehran persisted in sorely trying Russia's diplomatic patience. Ahmadinejad and his advisers seemed to be gambling that Russia would put up with repeated disappointments from Iran on the nuclear issue in anticipation of gains and cooperation—or at least neutrality—on other issues in other areas. Ultimately, moreover, differences between Ahmadinejad and his opposition appeared primarily to be over tactics and not the goal of becoming at least a nuclear threshold state.

In any event, Tehran resisted and then attempted to bargain over the terms of a call on June 6, 2006, by the UK, France, Germany, the United States, China, and Russia—known variously as the EU-3+3 but, more frequently, as the P5+1—for Iran to suspend its fuel cycle development in return for negotiations on a new package of economic incentives. However, after Tehran in July refused to give an answer, in effect turning down the proposal, Russia joined other UN Security Council members in approving Resolution 1696. This required Iran to freeze all its nuclear enrichment–related and research-and-development activities by August 31 or face the beginning of sanctions.

Still, hard-liners in Tehran drew satisfaction from their conviction that Russia would block any Security Council resolution authorizing the use of military force under Chapter VII, Article 42, of the UN Charter. As August 31 approached, Tehran's leaders appeared confident that they could reject with relative impunity the demand that Iran suspend all nuclear activities. They seemed to regard the most likely economic sanctions as tolerable. Underlying Tehran's unwillingness to pull back was the apparent judgment that any push for serious economic measures would collapse because of lack of support from those major powers—including Russia—with vested interests in nurturing rather than sundering ties with the Islamic Republic.

## TRUTH, LIES, AND TIMING

By 2003, as we have seen in chapter 11, Iran was under great pressure from the international reaction to the mounting revelations of its covert nuclear program. The United States was charging that Iran was in material breach of the NPT and demanding that Tehran be referred to the UN Security Council for sanctions. Iran also faced calculated Russian hints of a slowdown on the sacrosanct Bushehr project and clear reluctance to expand arms sales, as bitterly noted by Defense Minister Ali Shamkhani as far back as September 2002. Though opinions varied in Moscow over how to deal with Iran, Putin gave every indication of hewing to a more demanding line.

In Tehran, factions reportedly emerged over how to respond to the IAEA's call to sign an additional protocol. One group was said to favor signing and then negotiating guarantees with the IAEA for Iran's "peaceful" nuclear program. At the opposite end were those allegedly urging not only that Iran not sign an additional protocol but also that it drop out of the NPT. In the middle, reportedly, was the

"Khatami government." It was described as positive toward the protocol, but "at the same time" wanting guarantees from the IAEA about the future of Iran's "peaceful" nuclear program. In fact, this corresponded to what Khatami had said publicly even as the IAEA Board of Governors was meeting in June.[5] In their debates, none of the factions appeared to give much prominence if any to the war in Iraq. Their talking points seemed to predate the new conflict next door and if anything were couched more traditionally in the context of Israel's possession of nuclear arms.[6]

Some Western experts believed that Tehran had "not yet made the decision to cross the nuclear threshold." Many "influential Iranians" reportedly assessed that to do so would erode rather than buttress Iran's gains in the region and increase its "strategic vulnerabilities" by providing "the pretext for further projection of US power in the region."[7] Other experts judged that Iran had already "made the decision to develop a breakout capability, which will give them the option to leave the [NPT] in the future and complete a nuclear weapon within six months or a year." According to this view, the Iranian program was "probably unstoppable through diplomatic means."[8]

Correspondents, however, often quoting the same sources, found Iranian reformers and hard-line conservatives alike unequivocally in favor of Iran developing nuclear weapons. "I hope we get our atomic weapons," stated Shirzad Bozorgnehr, reformist editor of *Iran News*. "If Israel has it, we should have it. If India and Pakistan do, we should, too."[9] Nasser Hadian, an Iranian teaching at Columbia University, expressed much the same sentiment. "These weapons would guarantee the territorial integrity and national security of Iran," Hadian told an interviewer. "We feel that we cannot possibly rely on the world to provide security for us, and this is felt by all factions."[10]

Despite mounting international demands, Iranian officials reportedly judged that the next IAEA report for the Board of Governors meeting in September 2003 would not be critical enough to increase the pressure on Iran to sign an additional protocol promptly and unconditionally, as urged by the board's meeting in June. Tehran was therefore still hoping to negotiate its own tailored conditions for additional protocol inspections—normally not negotiable with the IAEA. Foreign diplomatic observers reportedly felt that Tehran's stance was aimed at buying time and splitting the international community.[11]

However, a pro-Khatami daily cautioned against relying on help from Russia. In an editorial on the anniversary of the August 1953 coup against Prime Minister Mohammad Mosaddeq, it asserted that the Soviet Union had sided with the United States and the UK on a number of occasions despite sharp ideological differences. Today, it cautioned, "though it is Iran's most important commercial and military power [*sic*—partner?], Russia is not to be trusted and seems intent on repeating its erstwhile role in a new setting."[12]

All the same, Iran continued to court Russia, however high the mutual distrust. In Tehran, the High Council of Atomic Energy "approved" further planning for

Bushehr-2, presumably intended to encourage Moscow to continue cooperation on Bushehr-1 and to help Tehran soften anticipated criticism from the IAEA.[13] As Rumyantsev had promised during his December 2002 visit to Tehran, Russia forwarded to Tehran a "technical and feasibility study" for the construction of Bushehr-2.[14] In Moscow, Ambassador Shafei pronounced Russian-Iranian relations "quite satisfactory" after meeting with First Deputy Foreign Minister Vyacheslav Trubnikov.[15] Foreign Minister Kharrazi phoned Russian counterpart Igor Ivanov to inform him that Tehran "is prepared to broaden cooperation with the IAEA."[16]

Nevertheless, Russia gave Tehran little reason to assume that it could count on Moscow's support in evading IAEA demands. At the September 8–12 meeting of the IAEA Board of Governors, Russia joined in the unanimous call on Iran to "promptly and unconditionally" sign, ratify, and fully implement an additional protocol, freeze its uranium enrichment program, and provide a complete explanation of its nuclear program to the IAEA by October 31.[17]

As he prepared to meet President George W. Bush at Camp David outside Washington in late September, Vladimir Putin stressed to correspondents that he and Bush had "good business and personal relations" and that this was "a good factor for us to work together." Putin described the United States as Russia's "strategic partner on the problem of non-proliferation." Directly signaling Iran, President Putin endorsed the results of the September IAEA meeting, stating, "We expect that this process will be completed, and Iran will join the protocols." It was, the Russian president said, "very important for all members of the international community to influence Iran, above all IAEA members, so that Tehran agrees to sign additional protocols to the Non-proliferation agreement." Continuing to press Tehran, Putin argued, "If Iran really does not intend to create nuclear weapons, then it has no need to hide anything from the IAEA. And I see no grounds for it not to sign these additional protocols."[18]

In the joint press conference after the Camp David summit, Putin agreed with Bush that "we act not only as strategic partners, but as allies." Those in Tehran who had been repeatedly disabused in their hopes that Moscow would agree that Russian-Iranian relations were strategic must have been chagrined to see that Putin now placed Russian-American ties even higher: at the alliance level. Moreover, standing next to Bush, Putin reported, "We shall give a clear but respectful signal to Iran about the necessity to continue and expand its cooperation with IAEA." His country, said Putin, had "no desire and no plans to contribute in any way to the creation of weapons of mass destruction, either in Iran or in any other spot, region in the world."[19] According to an anonymous senior Bush administration official, Putin's remarks represented progress. "It's tilting from saying, 'You're a bunch of hypocrites who want to deprive us of our markets,' to saying, 'We'll work on this.'"[20]

Once back in Moscow, Putin again went on record with Russia's policy toward Iran. "We have our interests in Iran. Iran is our neighbor. We have a many century tradition of good-neighborly relations with this country. But regarding the problem of nonproliferation, we have full understanding with the United States." On this issue as well as on the war on terrorism, Russia and America could be "not just partners, but allies in the full sense of this word." As to Bushehr specifically, "We are not only hearing what our U.S. partners are telling us, we are listening to what they have to say, and we are finding that some of their assertions are justified." That was why, stated the Russian president, Moscow was insisting that Tehran return spent fuel to Russia. Russian specialists agreed with their American counterparts that otherwise Iran could enrich the spent fuel and use it in nuclear weapons. That was also why Russia was insisting that Tehran allow IAEA overview of Iran's nuclear programs.[21]

Pressed even by Russia, Iran on October 21, 2003, delivered what it characterized as a full declaration of its nuclear programs to the IAEA—just ten days before the deadline issued by the Board of Governors meeting in September. The same day, the foreign ministers of Britain, France, and Germany visited Tehran at the invitation of the Iranian government. The three ministers were told that the Islamic Republic had decided to cooperate fully with the IAEA and intended to sign and ratify an additional protocol as well as voluntarily suspend all uranium enrichment and reprocessing activities.[22] For the next several years, this troika—acting on behalf of the European Union and referred to as the EU-3—attempted to walk Iran back toward full compliance with its NPT Safeguards Agreement obligations by offering to negotiate a package of economic, political, and security incentives while Iran suspended its nuclear conversion and enrichment activities.

As Iran courted a favorable response to its decision from the EU-3, it also wooed Russian support. On November 10, Iranian Security Council head Hassan Rowhani traveled to Moscow. There he met with President Putin and in the Kremlin formally announced what the council had promised the EU-3 foreign ministers in Tehran the month before: the temporary and voluntary suspension of Iran's nuclear enrichment activities as well as the transmittal that day of an official letter to the IAEA formally agreeing to sign an additional protocol. Tehran subsequently signed the additional protocol on December 18, 2003, and then observed it, although the country did not ratify it for the next several years.[23] Russian experts such as Andrey Kokoshin promptly declared the "responsible decision" by the Iranian leadership a "huge achievement" for Russian diplomacy and for Putin personally.[24] Putin accepted the invitation Rowhani extended from President Khatami to visit Tehran. Yet the president once more unmistakably conditioned actually making the trip on Iranian compromise on several ticklish issues, particularly Caspian demarcation.[25]

The EU-3's public diplomacy permitted Moscow to lobby Iran behind the scenes while presenting a public face of patience and indeed even protection of Iran. Iran, however, did not make it easy for Russia to maintain confidence in Iran's intentions and to run interference for it in the international community. After Libya's decision in late 2003 to dismantle its military nuclear program, Tripoli disclosed black-market dealings and ties to Pakistan's chief nuclear scientist, A. Q. Khan. Revelations soon surfaced of

Iran's own dealings with Khan going as far back as 1987, some five years before Iran had even begun negotiations with Russia over Bushehr. If Iran had managed to keep its dealings with Khan secret so successfully for so many years, how much else had it managed to conceal about its nuclear prowess from Russia and the rest of the world, and to what end?

Matters only worsened as IAEA inspectors followed up the Libyan and other leads. They soon discovered that Iran had drawings of a more advanced centrifuge design, the P-2, which it had not declared in its October 21, 2003, submission to the agency. As the IAEA pressed its Iranian intermediaries, they asserted in late January 2004 that Iran had not imported any P-2 components and had manufactured at home all those components it possessed.[26] Upon further inquiry, however, Iran finally acknowledged on May 30, that it had actually imported some magnets, raw materials, and equipment for its P-2 centrifuges.[27] Iran subsequently proved repeatedly less than forthcoming in discussing with the IAEA the extent and origins of its nuclear enrichment technology and facilities. Iran time and time again omitted crucial information from its submissions to IAEA inspectors. It also backtracked and reversed on its pledge, albeit voluntary, to suspend all enrichment-related and reprocessing activities as a confidence-building measure.

By the time the IAEA Board of Governors met in September 2004, the list of Iran's accumulated transgressions since that spring included its announcement of plans to introduce thirty-seven tons of yellowcake at its uranium conversion facility and its continuing importation or manufacture and assembly and testing of centrifuges. As a result, the board approved a resolution that implicitly threatened to consider referring the Iranian nuclear issue to the UN Security Council at the board's next meeting scheduled for November unless Iran moved smartly to help clear up its record, suspended all conversion and enrichment activities, and ratified the additional protocol to its Safeguards Agreement.[28]

In a remarkable presentation of the quandary Iran faced after the September 2004 IAEA Board session, chief nuclear negotiator and Security Council head Rowhani that fall discretely explained to the Supreme Cultural Revolution Council (SCRC) in Tehran why the country's nuclear program found itself under such intense international scrutiny. According to the transcript of his remarks (not published until a year later) Rowhani told the session, "This is because having fuel cycle capability almost means that the country that possesses this capability is able to produce nuclear weapons, should that country have the political will to do so. . . . The country that can enrich uranium to about 3.5 percent will also have the capability to enrich it to about 90 percent." Iran had started to pursue fuel cycle technology around 1988–89 and had accelerated its efforts around 1999–2000, Rowhani recounted. Iran had tried to keep the program secret—"this never was supposed to be in the open"—but "spies exposed it."

After the "strongly worded resolution" adopted by consensus by the September 2003 IAEA Board of Governors meeting, Rowhani continued, Iran had presented to the IAEA a "complete picture" of its nuclear activities and had announced that it would sign the additional protocol. However, the report to the IAEA had omitted Iran's purchase on the black market of the more advanced P-2 centrifuge, Rowhani conceded, and the omission had "undermined the confidence-building process that we were engaged in with the Europeans." "Do you mean to say that we have lied about this?" asked an unidentified SCRC member. "No, we have not lied," responded Rowhani. "In all cases, we have told them the truth. But in some cases, we may not have disclosed information in a timely manner."

The Europeans, Russia, and China had resisted American pressure to refer the Iranian nuclear file to the UN Security Council, but the Europeans' views on Iran's possession of the nuclear fuel cycle were no better than those of the United States. "The same goes for the Russians," explained Rowhani. When Foreign Minister Lavrov visited Tehran, he had "insisted . . . that we should not have the fuel cycle." It was, Rowhani stated, "very difficult to work with the Russians." Nevertheless, Rowhani judged that Iran's position as he spoke in fall 2004 was better than it had been a year earlier. Russia and China had said they were against referring the issue to the Security Council. Had it not been for interference from the United States and England, Iran could have found an acceptable "formula" on the fuel cycle issue with Germany and France.[29]

The meeting Rowhani addressed was apparently part of the process to decide how to respond to the threat by the IAEA Board of Governors to refer the Iranian file to the UN Security Council. Finally, on November 15, 2004, Iranian representatives signed an agreement in Paris with the EU-3 to voluntarily "continue and extend" Iran's suspension of all nuclear enrichment-related and reprocessing activities as a confidence-building measure. Iran pledged to do this in time for the IAEA to be able to confirm that Iran had done so before the board met later that month. Iran warned, however, that the suspension would remain in effect only as long as "negotiations proceed on a mutually acceptable agreement on long-term arrangements."[30]

The resolution adopted by the Board of Governors on November 29, 2004, welcomed the Iranian move, underscoring that the "full and sustained implementation of this suspension, which is a voluntary, non-legally-binding, confidence building measure, to be verified by the Agency, is essential to addressing outstanding issues."[31] Only after Iran had thus committed to resuspend its conversion and enrichment activities did Russian MinAtom head Aleksandr Rumyantsev in late February 2005 finally sign with his Iranian counterpart Gholamreza Aqazadeh the spent fuel return agreement that Rumyantsev had declared in December 2002 was just forty-five to sixty days away from being finalized.[32]

## EASTERN APPROACHES

For the remainder of Khatami's presidency, Iranian diplomacy continued to hew to a posture of tactical flexibility. Meanwhile, at each IAEA Board of Governors meeting,

Russia either abstained or was part of the thirty-five-nation majority or consensus that called on Iran to cooperate fully with IAEA inspectors. Russia was content to let the United States and the EU-3 take the public lead in putting the heat on Iran as IAEA investigations went forward. However, arguing against the U.S. call for sanctions, Russia actively prevented the issue of suspected Iranian NPT violations from going to the UN Security Council. Moscow's policy appeared sustainable as long as Iran suspended its conversion and enrichment activities and was forthcoming with the IAEA in clearing up the numerous questions about its nuclear program.

Tehran's uncertainty over how long and how much it could ultimately rely on Russia to continue to stymie Security Council referral kept some pressure on Iran to cooperate, even if not fully, with the IAEA inspectors. Iran's cooperation, however, continued to be less than full and frank. From Iran's point of view, it was getting very little from the EU-3 in the way of concrete incentives in return for Iran's very real temporary suspension of its uranium conversion and enrichment activities. Increasingly obviously, Iran showed less and less willingness to compromise.

Moreover, Iran's talks with the EU-3 were desultory at best in spring-summer 2005 as the Iranian presidential campaign and two rounds of voting played themselves out. On May 25, the EU-3 promised to provide Iran its ideas for a long-term agreement in late July or early August. Not until August 5 did the EU-3 put a thirty-one-page proposal, or ideas about a proposal, on the table.[33] The EU-3 described the proposal as supporting "the development of a safe, economically viable and proliferation proof civilian nuclear program in Iran in the context of objective guarantees provided by Iran." In addition, the proposal outlined "co-operation on political and security issues as well as in economic and technological areas."[34]

By then, however, the hard-liner Mahmoud Ahmadinejad had emerged the winner in the runoff elections for president on June 24. His center-right opponent in the second round had been former president Ali Akbar Hashemi Rafsanjani, who was now chairman of the Expediency Council. Other rivals during the first round had included the hard-liner Ali Larijani and Mohsen Rezai, who dropped out of the race two days before the June 17 balloting. Rezai had been commander in chief of the IRGC during the Iraq-Iran War and had accompanied Rafsanjani on his major visit to the Soviet Union in June 1989.[35]

Ahmadinejad's election was a surprise to the world and not just to Moscow. It was the political opposite of Khatami's victory in 1997 over the hard-liner Ali Akbar Nateq-Nuri. The results now gave the upper hand to what the noted expert Shahram Chubin called the "ideological conservatives" among Iran's leadership elite, most prominently Ahmadinejad and Larijani. Such figures welcomed confrontation with the West as "an opportunity to purify the regime and society by limiting contamination from the outside and asserting the revolution's values of self-reliance and authenticity." According to Chubin, the ideologues pursued national strength so as to "impose . . . [Iran] on the region and beyond." In contrast, the election outcome disadvantaged

Iran's "pragmatic conservatives" led by Rafsanjani, Khatami, and nuclear negotiator Rowhani. As were the ideologues, the pragmatists were dedicated to making Iran a greater power in the region. But unlike the ideologues, the pragmatists favored using Iran's increased stature to reach "an accommodation with the West from a position of strength." They were open to a so-called "grand bargain" and to adjusting Iran's policies in the region "in exchange for recognition and security guarantees" from the United States.[36]

As a result, it became almost immediately more difficult for Russia to balance its relations with Washington and Tehran while safeguarding its own security interests. The immediate shift in Iran's negotiating posture with the EU-3 forced Moscow to adjust its own approach. It also cast doubt on the chances of a win-win outcome for Russia, although Moscow still went many extra miles to give Tehran a chance to agree on a face-saving solution.

Even before Ahmadinejad was sworn in as president on August 3, 2005, Iran on August 1 had notified the IAEA that it would resume uranium conversion activities at Esfahan, which it did on August 8.[37] Then, on August 15, Ahmadinejad appointed recent presidential campaign rival Ali Larijani secretary of Iran's top security decision-making body, the Supreme National Security Council, and Iran's lead nuclear negotiator, supplanting Rowhani in both positions.[38]

Larijani came from one of the Islamic revolution's most prominent families, one that had been intimately involved for decades in relations with Moscow. His brother, then-deputy foreign minister Mohammad Javad Larijani, had accompanied Ayatollah Javadi Amoli, Ayatollah Khomeini's spiritual adviser, in January 1989 to deliver the Supreme Leader's groundbreaking letter to Mikhail Gorbachev in the Kremlin. Rafsanjani, who had followed that letter up with his visit to Moscow in June 1989, had appointed Ali Larijani minister of culture and Islamic guidance after Rafsanjani's own brother had resigned from the post.[39] Larijani had then served as head of the Iranian radio and TV organization Iranian Republic of Iran Broadcasting (IRIB) for ten years. In 2004 Supreme Leader Khamenei appointed Larijani as his representative in the Supreme National Security Council.[40]

Larijani soon began signaling that Iran wanted to expand its negotiations on the nuclear issue beyond the EU-3 to other countries, including Russia, China, and members of the Non-Aligned Movement (NAM) on the IAEA Board of Governors.[41] By early September, the Iranian press was reporting that Foreign Ministry spokesman Hamid Reza Asefi was in effect describing Iran's new diplomacy as an approach that would "look toward the East." Critics immediately pointed out that a full tilt toward the East "would certainly be doomed to failure" but that a feint reminding the West of Iran's alternatives would be a shrewd move.[42] Supporters of Ahmadinejad countered that Russia's continued opposition to referral of the Iranian nuclear case to the UN Security Council was an indication that the new policy was already "relatively successful."[43]

In any event, Ahmadinejad further undermined the basis for Iran's negotiations with the EU-3 in his speech at the UN General Assembly in New York on September 17. The new Iranian president declared, "Peaceful use of nuclear energy without possession of nuclear fuel cycle is an empty proposition." Moreover, implying lack of confidence in Iran's arrangements with Russia for supplying Bushehr with fuel, and at odds with his purported Look to the East diplomacy, Ahmadinejad stated, "International precedence tells us that nuclear fuel-delivery contracts are unreliable and no legally binding international document or instrument exist to guarantee the delivery of nuclear fuel."[44]

Several days later, Larijani reiterated at a press conference in Tehran that Iran wanted to "widen the circle of talks" beyond the EU-3 and "open dialogue with Russia, China, India, the Non-aligned Countries and the Europeans." Two years of "haggling" with the EU-3 had "exhausted" Iran. If the world had in effect accepted North Korea's nuclear program, why not accept Iran's? As had Ahmadinejad, Larijani scoffed at the idea of international guarantees of fuel provision to Iran, including from Russia. All the same, he opined that Russia would not agree to any IAEA Board of Governors ultimatum to Iran to suspend its activities at Esfahan.[45]

On September 24, 2005, not surprisingly, the IAEA Board of Governors approved a resolution that "recalled" and "deplored" Iran's many "failures" to meet its obligations under its NPT Safeguards Agreement and its "policy of concealment [that] has resulted in many breaches" of these obligations. Taken together, these "failures and breaches" constituted "non-compliance" with the IAEA's statute and raised "questions that are within the competence of the Security Council."[46] The resolution passed twenty-two to one (Venezuela), with Russia and China among twelve countries abstaining but not opposing the measure.[47] In Iran, critics of Ahmadinejad and Larijani's policy quickly pointed out that Russia, China, and India had not helped Iran.[48] The "strategic policy" of "look to the East" had proved "ineffective"[49] and Larijani had "wasted three months."[50]

Facing more clearly than ever the likelihood of the Iranian issue going to the Security Council, Russia got into the negotiating act in a more public way. In early November, Moscow floated the so-called Russian plan. It proposed a face-saving arrangement that would permit Iran temporarily to participate in uranium enrichment even while the Iran-EU-3 talks continued in search of a more permanent compromise. The initiative reportedly would permit Iran to continue converting uranium at Esfahan into its gaseous form—uranium hexafluoride, or UF6—but would establish a joint venture with Iran on Russian territory for all subsequent enrichment of the UF6 into fuel.

The proposal broke new ground in conceding to Iran the right to continue to convert uranium at Esfahan but preserved the "red line" of ruling out enrichment at Natanz or anywhere else in Iran. The proposal would have also given Iran the appearance of partial ownership of a fuel cycle capability. Igor Ivanov of the Russian

Security Council reportedly put it at 35 percent when he briefed the plan in Tehran. But the initiative would not turn over to Iran any hands-on technical control of the enrichment phase.[51] To give Iran time to digest and respond to the Russian plan, the IAEA Board of Governors on November 24 refrained from issuing another resolution castigating Iran. The board opted instead for a statement by Director General Mohamed ElBaradei that expressed the "hope" that "every effort will be made so that the dialogue between Iran and all concerned parties can be resumed."[52]

Official Tehran blew cold and luke-warm over the Russian plan. Tehran's early reaction was decidedly negative: the Iranian government insisted that enrichment had to take place on Iranian territory. Gholamreza Aqazadeh, head of Iran's nuclear agency, after talks with Security Council secretary Ivanov in mid-November, maintained, "What is important for us is that we be entrusted to carry out enrichment in Iran."[53]

However, President Ahmadinejad and nuclear negotiator Ali Larijani signaled that they saw utility in not responding to Russia with a flat "No!" In mid-November, Ahmadinejad told Ivanov, "Tehran is keen on expansion of ties in all areas with Moscow and will support long-term plans which ensure the interests of both sides."[54] In early December, as negative opinion swirled in Tehran around the reported but not yet officially tabled Russian plan, Larijani described Russia as a "friend of Iran." Larijani assured a news conference that Russian officials were "clever enough" not to let the Europeans use them against Iran. Larijani predicted that Russia "has a very good maneuvering capability and will most definitely have a particular consideration for its friendship with Iran, for being a neighbor of Iran and for the level of its relations with Iran."[55]

A month later, in an extensive televised interview, Larijani repeatedly returned to the subject of Russian interests in the region and in common with Iran. "We and Russia have many interests in the region. And a small part of it can be the nuclear issue. A big part of it is other things . . . important both to us and to them," said Larijani. "The interests that Russia has in the region are much greater than the interests that the Europeans have in the region," he asserted. Therefore, "what reason can there be, in fact, for them [the Russians] to put themselves to trouble for the sake of others?" In sum, according to Larijani, "Is Russian national interest confined to the nuclear issue? It isn't. They have many other interests in the region. And in fact Iran is the key for them on some issues. Why should they squander this for the nuclear issue?"[56]

Nevertheless, the Russian plan provoked sharp debate in the Majles over Moscow's trustworthiness. "Any kind of reliance on Russia will definitely not be in the national interests of Iran," argued Majles deputy Nureddin Pir Mo'azzen from Ardebil, who denounced the "two-faced approach" of Russians coupling "policy with fraud." He instead recommended, "We should enter into negotiations with America because both the Russians and the Europeans will gain from the conflict between Iran and America."[57] Javad Jahangirzadeh of the Majles's National Security and Foreign Policy Committee intoned that the Russian plan would be "a dangerous deviation in the Islamic Republic's nuclear diplomacy" and that "there is no guarantee Russia would live up to its commitments."[58] Heshmatollah Falahatpisheh of the same Majles committee charged, "The Russians have done Iran no less injustice than the Europeans, and Russia's entry alongside the West in the negotiations with Iran can be very dangerous in creating discrimination in the right to access nuclear fuel." He warned, "The Russians, Europe and America do not on the whole differ over Iran's nuclear fuel cycle."[59]

In what may have been a Russian carrot designed to elicit Iranian buy-in to the Russian plan, Defense Minister Sergei Ivanov on December 5 confirmed news reports that Moscow at the end of November had "signed" a "contract" to deliver about thirty Tor-M1 air defense systems in the next two years. Ivanov described the Tor-M1 as "an exclusively 100 percent defensive weapon."[60] The system was the crown jewel in a package of new contracts reportedly worth more than $1 billion, including an accord to modernize Iranian air force equipment and to supply patrol craft for the Iranian navy. The Tor-M1 was described as capable of identifying up to forty-eight targets and simultaneously firing at two of them at altitudes ranging from twenty to six thousand meters.[61] Speculation was rife that Iran would use the system to protect nuclear installations such as Bushehr. But the short-range system could do so effectively only if linked to the much more sophisticated long-range S-300 system, which Iran was reportedly persistently seeking to acquire. Despite U.S. objections, confidential sources asserted that Moscow would begin deliveries as early as January 2006 upon Iranian "pre-payment of several hundred million dollars."[62]

All the same, and lost in the publicity accorded the Tor-M1 contract, there were multiple indications that sentiment ran strong in Moscow that Iran was using and fooling Russia in its nuclear diplomacy. "Iran has shamelessly exploited its Russian friends," wrote commentator Vitaliy Portnikov. Iran's nuclear advances meant that Russia's regional influence was weakening and Russia ran the danger of ending up "on the periphery of world politics."[63] "The Iranian ayatollahs's policy toward Russia is already extremely ambivalent," said Mikhail Rostovskiy. "There are grounds to believe that the cunning Persians are simply using us."[64]

Even the government daily *Rossiyskaya Gazeta* carried a piece by Yevgeniy Shestakov that complained, "Russia has found itself dragged into" Iran's skillful "Byzantine game" of using "bribery and generous promises of profitable oil contracts" to gain time to develop its nuclear weapons while Moscow "selflessly protected Iran against international sanctions."[65] The state-owned Rossiya TV channel gave time to Konstantin Kosachev, chairman of the Duma's International Affairs Committee, who agreed, "Iran is really using Russia" and "is an extremely difficult partner." Russia had to continue "persuading Iran to show good will." But Russia was "running a risk" that Iran was "fooling its closest partners and the UN" and could become a nuclear state, which was "obviously not in anyone's interests, including Russian interests."[66]

In late December 2005, even as Majles deputies continued to denounce the Russian plan as a "dirty trick" and a "devious and distorted suggestion," Javad Vaeedi, deputy head of the Supreme National Security Council, said in Tehran that Iran would "seriously and enthusiastically" study Moscow's proposal.[67] One newspaper commentary in Tehran praised talking with Moscow while moving ahead on gradually ending the suspension of Iran's nuclear activities. Russia would ultimately side with the West, according to this commentary, but in the meantime, "By dragging the talks to another round, Tehran has once again succeeded in making use of diplomatic negotiations in her favor."[68]

## END OF SUSPENSION

In fact, Russian and Iranian representatives met on January 8, 2006, even as detractors continued to argue in Tehran that the Russian plan was just an American initiative written in Russian; that Russian delays on Bushehr were "unconvincing"; that Russian behavior brought to mind "bitter memories of the infamous Turkmanchai and Gulistan treaties" of 1813 and 1828 which had deprived Iran of extensive territories in the Caucasus and critical navigation rights in the Caspian; and that Russia had never used its veto in the UN Security Council to support Iran.[69] Russian negotiators explained their proposal and "insistently advised" Iran not to abandon its enrichment moratorium.[70]

Nevertheless, Iran that same day ordered IAEA inspectors to remove their seals from the nuclear facility at Natanz and on January 10 resumed enrichment activities there, thus ending the two-year suspension.[71] Russian Foreign Minister Sergei Lavrov reported to President Putin his "concern" over Iran's "defiance of the moratorium agreed upon between Iran and European nations, as well as in defiance of the International Atomic Energy Agency." Putin's "instructions" to Lavrov did not waver: "to contribute to a solution to the Iranian nuclear problem in a way that will help avoid violating the nuclear nonproliferation regime" through diplomatic channels and safeguarding Russian economic interests.[72] In Tehran, critics of the Ahmadinejad administration's diplomacy charged, "Countries that were the core of Iran's strategy of 'Look at the East' have joined Iran's opposing group. It seems that Iran's nuclear diplomacy has been incapable of keeping its allies."[73]

On February 4, 2006, a special meeting of the IAEA Board of Governors expressed its "serious concern" about the continuing lack of clarity surrounding Iran's nuclear program. It underscored in particular "possible activities which could have a military nuclear dimension" and the "lack of confidence" in Iran's intentions in developing a "fissile material production capability." The Board of Governors adopted a resolution requesting that Director General ElBaradei "report" to the UN Security Council all the actions required of Iran by the IAEA as well as all IAEA reports and resolutions relating to the Iranian issue, including those of the next regular Board of Governors meeting in March.[74]

Russia and China joined the twenty-seven members of the board that voted in favor of the resolution—Syria, Cuba, and Venezuela voted against; five countries abstained—after getting agreement that any action against Iran would be postponed at least until March. President Ahmadinejad immediately criticized the board for caving in to "political pressure of a few countries and without any legal justification." He declared that Iran's voluntary implementation of the additional protocol would have to be suspended.[75]

The Russian vote in favor of the resolution castigating Iran was met with "utter disbelief" in Tehran.[76] For the moment totally abandoning any pretense of confidence in Russia, Ahmadinejad's ridicule of the Russian plan for enrichment outside Iran went into high gear as tensions flared. "They say that they will produce the fuel somewhere else and then they will hand it over to us. . . . Do you expect us to be stupid enough to believe you?"[77] Majles deputy Jahangirzadeh denounced the Russian plan as "more disgraceful than the Turkmanchai and Gulistan treaties."[78]

The two treaties were effective buzzwords in Tehran debates on both the Caspian and nuclear issues. Gulistan and Turkmanchai still stirred bitter memories. Mentioning them was a quick and effective way to rekindle the sense of injury inflicted by Russia nearly two hundred years earlier. As the Ahmadinejad administration dealt with Russia, it had to be careful not to inadvertently set off the emotional charge still conveyed by the two treaties. At the same time, policymakers in Moscow also had to tread with caution given the still vivid historical memories associated with Gulistan and Turkmanchai in Tehran.

More objectively, Russia's vote in favor of the IAEA Board of Governors' resolution served as the hook for Iranian critiques of Ahmadinejad's tactics on the nuclear issue. "The Islamic Republic of Iran is not a primary or even a secondary priority in Russia's foreign policy and this country views Iran as a temporary need and regulates its ties on the basis of short term interests," wrote the academic Kabak Khabiri. "Russia and the Islamic Republic of Iran have never been strategic partners and the Russians have never been prepared to accept the use of this term in ties with this country, in spite of the inclination demonstrated by Iranian officials to use this term."[79]

In Moscow, an unidentified expert said to be close to the negotiations criticized Ahmadinejad and others for "playing and speculating on our pseudo-dependence on cooperation with them." The expert counseled continued patience but warned that Iranian nuclear weapons deployed near Russian borders were "the last thing we need" and did not rule out an American missile strike against Iran if tensions continued.[80] Russian General Staff chief Gen. Yuri Baluyevsky pointedly advised Iran that given the tense conditions "reason should prevail, above all from the Iranian side."[81]

On March 8, the IAEA Board of Governors did not adopt a resolution but instead approved a neutral summing-up by the board's chairman of the various positions expressed by several groups of "some members" at the meeting.[82] In concluding remarks, Director General ElBaradei underscored the need for more transparency from Iran and the lack of confidence in the nonmilitary nature of Iran's nuclear program. But he also stressed the need for "cool headed approaches . . . to lower the rhetoric." He described the UN Security Council's upcoming discussions of the Iranian nuclear file as "simply a new phase of diplomacy" to assist the parties in returning to the negotiating table.[83] That same day, ElBaradei transmitted his report on Iran's nuclear program to the UN Security Council.[84]

Despite ElBaradei's call for a cooling of rhetoric in the IAEA, Russian comments directed at Iran became sharper—and more frustrated with Iran's behavior—than ever. On March 13, announcing that Russian and Iranian negotiators would meet again soon, Foreign Minister Lavrov chastised Tehran's performance. "We are very disappointed at how Iran has been conducting itself during these talks, absolutely not helping those who would like to ensure that peaceful ways of settling the situation in connection with the Iranian nuclear program are found," he said. On the Russian proposal, Lavrov complained, "Conflicting signals are coming from Iran—first they refuse to do it and then they don't."[85]

Some press commentary was much less forgiving. The Iranian nuclear issue was a Russian diplomatic failure equal to the "Orange Revolution" in Ukraine, wrote Marat Khayrullin and Olga Pavlikova, alluding to the victory of the pro-western Viktor Yushchenko in presidential elections in that country in December 2004. "Iran was using Russia for its own ends right from the start. . . . The most important thing for the ayatollahs now is not to resolve the problem but to create the semblance of resolving it."[86] Russian specialists on Iran reportedly took perverse pride in their clients: "They are Persians, and you cannot outsmart them." Russian scientists reportedly estimated that Iran would come close to creating a nuclear weapon in five to six years.[87]

In any event, the UN Security Council finally formally discussed the Iranian nuclear file on March 29. After what were reported as difficult negotiations, its fifteen members adopted a nonbinding statement that expressed "serious concern" over Iran's nuclear program three times but avoided any threat of sanctions or military actions. At the insistence of Russia and China, the statement also gave Iran thirty days rather than two weeks to comply with the UNSC's call for it to resuspend its uranium enrichment program, at which time it requested that IAEA Director General ElBaradei report back on Iranian compliance.[88]

The following day the foreign ministers of the P5+1 met in Berlin. They again called on Iran to suspend its enrichment activities, but Russia and China again opposed moving toward sanctions. Foreign Minister Lavrov told the press, "Russia doesn't believe that sanctions could achieve the purposes of settlement of various issues." In Vienna, Ali Asghan Soltanieh, Iran's representative to the IAEA, declared, "This enrichment matter is not reversible."[89]

## DEBATES IN TEHRAN

Iran in fact continued thumbing its nose at the IAEA and the UNSC. On April 11, 2006, Ahmadinejad announced that Iran had "joined the nuclear countries of the world" by succeeding in enriching uranium at Natanz to 3.5 percent. Iranian spokesmen underscored that this was adequate for powering a plant such as Bushehr but not for manufacturing a nuclear weapons charge.[90] Several days later, Ahmadinejad dismissed all those who objected to Iran attaining the full nuclear cycle: "We say, be angry and die of this anger." At the same time, he acknowledged debate on the issue within Iran. "There are some coward elements who are trying to create difference among people," he stated. "They get together, talk and create propaganda and psychological war. But we laugh at them. They call us and say that crisis is on the way, but we believe that the enemy has a crisis."[91] On April 23 Iranian Foreign Ministry spokesman Hamid Reza Asefi declared that Iran's nuclear enrichment and research and development activities were "irreversible."[92]

Within the ruling elite in Iran, three currents were reported to be contending over nuclear policy. President Ahmadinejad was the leader of the radicals in the first current. They were said to be ready to risk confrontation with the international community and pay the price to defend Iran's right to enrich uranium on its own territory. Chief nuclear negotiator Ali Larijani was among the "realistic hard-liners" who comprised the second current. They were willing to settle for enrichment on a limited scale but still on Iranian territory, and did not want to risk diplomatic isolation.

The third current was said to include reformist supporters of former President Khatami and "neoconservative" supporters of Rafsanjani. They opposed Ahmadinejad's policy of confrontation. They were willing to live with a temporary enrichment freeze in order to return to developing a full nuclear fuel cycle on Iranian territory once international tensions dissipated. Many in this camp reportedly endorsed talks with the United States on the nuclear issue and argued that Russia and China were not dependable allies. Supreme Leader Khamenei, concerned over the prospects and costs of international isolation and the reported challenge to his authority by President Ahmadinejad, was said to be leaning toward the Khatami-Rafsanjani line.[93]

Indeed, the signs of factional fighting that kept popping up in the Iranian press pointed to differences over diplomatic tactics rather than the ultimate strategic goal of making Iran a nuclear power, or at least moving closer to that status. Leaders such as Rafsanjani had supported Iran's nuclear program from the beginning. But that did not mean that they did not have ideas of their own on how best to minimize the negative international reaction and keep the effort going forward. Rafsanjani, after all, on October 6, 1988, not long after the conclusion of the Iran-Iraq War and when Iran's secret contacts were already under way with the A. Q. Khan nuclear black-market network, had publicly urged, "[We] should fully equip ourselves both in the offensive and defensive use of chemical, bacteriological and radiological weapons."[94] More recently, Rafsanjani had touched on Iran's nuclear aims, albeit with artful indirection and ambiguity, in a Friday sermon on December 14, 2001: "If one day, the Islamic world is also equipped with weapons like those that Israel possesses now, then the imperialists' strategy will reach a standstill because the use of even one nuclear bomb inside Israel will destroy everything. However, it will only harm the Islamic world."[95] Rafsanjani seemed to be touting nuclear weapons as Iran's ultimate deterrence against attack, though not recommending such arms as a first-strike option.

Besides Rafsanjani, the "cowards" Ahmadinejad derided seemed to include Mohsen Rezai. In 1988, as we have seen in chapter 6, Rafsanjani and Rezai had both cited Iran's need for nuclear and other weapons to deal with Iraq. As such, they had both been present at the creation of Iran's nuclear program, something Ahmadinejad could not claim. In June 1989 Rezai had accompanied Rafsanjani when he visited the Soviet Union to meet with Mikhail Gorbachev. The visit had amounted to a giant shopping trip kicking off Iran's post-Iraq war rearmament effort. Now, in early May 2006, Rafsanjani and Rezai both openly counseled the need for moderation, negotiations, and diplomacy, in effect criticizing Ahmadinejad's line. Rafsanjani recommended refraining from "any provocative statements." Rezai called for a switch from "simplistic" to "serious negotiations and diplomacy." "In our struggling situation," he advised, "negotiation is a kind of revolutionary diplomacy."[96]

While vigorously opposing any UNSC movement toward sanctions or military action, Russia may have been playing on these signs of differences in Tehran in an effort to apply leverage behind the scenes. By April, no Tor-M1 systems had been delivered despite the reports in December that their transfer to Iran would happen early in 2006. A Russian television report described what had been signed in November as a "protocol of intent" and said, "It is still too soon to speak of a deal."[97] Later that month, a source close to Rosoboronexport, the Russian government's arms export agency, asserted that deliveries would not begin until the fall "because the personnel for them have not yet been trained."[98] General Baluyevsky, while asserting that the Tor-M1 contract would be executed, stated, "I don't think that [the equipment] will be delivered to Iran either tomorrow, or the day after tomorrow." Baluyevsky told the press that Russia would not support either side should conflict break out with Iran.[99] In fact, as we have seen, the Russia-Iran Treaty signed in Moscow during the March 2001 Putin-Khatami summit did not commit either side to render military aid to the other if attacked but merely "not [to] give any help to the aggressor." By mid-June, Iranian defense minister Mostafa Mohammad Najjar, when asked about the Tor-M1 deal, said merely, "The purchase of such items is being looked into."[100]

There were also indications that the projected completion date for the Bushehr nuclear power plant was again slipping, much to the irritation of Iranian officials. In November 2005 Putin had replaced Aleksandr Rumyantsev as head of MinAtom, now renamed the Federal Atomic Energy Agency, or RosAtom, with Sergey Kiriyenko. Putin had explained that he wanted an experienced manager to carry out a major reorganization of RosAtom.[101] Putin and Kiriyenko had known each other for close to a decade, at least, and it had been then-briefly Prime Minister Kiriyenko who had informed Putin of his appointment by President Boris Yeltsin as director of the FSB in July 1998.[102] Kiriyenko and Putin had been part of the wave of younger officials promoted under Yeltsin around that time as Russia's policy toward Iran had begun to toughen on the nonproliferation front.

Now, in 2006, there were no indications that Kiriyenko's replacement of Rumyantsev at RosAtom meant a change toward Iran on the nuclear issue. Mohammad Sa'idi, the deputy head for international affairs of IAEO, hoped in May that Bushehr would be ready "within the next few months." Sa'idi asserted, "There are no obstacles in the way, and Russia should deliver the fuel for Bushehr . . . as soon as possible."[103] A few days later, however, an unnamed senior RosAtom official declared that it was "utterly clear to the professionals that it is not possible to complete the construction of the station in a few months." According to the official, the Iranian assertions that it was otherwise were "causing bewilderment and distress in RosAtom." The realistic completion date for Bushehr, he emphasized, was 2007.[104] In late June, Iranian deputy foreign minister Mehdi Safari complained about the six-year delay in Bushehr's projected completion date. Work had gone fast while Yevgeny Adamov had been in charge, he said, but there had been "no progress whatsoever" under Rumyantsev. Now Kiriyenko had promised to speed up the work, Safari said, leaving unspoken whether he actually expected this to be the case.[105]

On another front, Iranian observers could not have missed the statement in late May by former Russian defense minister Igor Sergeyev that "Russia is more interested in an Iran without nuclear weapons than the US, because the missiles Tehran has today are capable of reaching Russian territory."[106] The remark was reminiscent of the assessment ten years earlier by then-defense minister Igor Rodionov that Iran was in the group of countries representing an increasing military threat to Russia.[107]

At the end of April, IAEA Director General ElBaradei, as mandated by the UN Security Council at the end of March, submitted an update on Iranian compliance to both the UNSC and the IAEA Board of Governors (although the board had not met at that time). The lengthy eight-page report charted in detail Iran's shortcomings in resolving old and new questions regarding its nuclear program. It concluded that the gaps in knowledge and understanding of Iran's nuclear program after three years of inspections remained a "matter of concern." Cooperation and transparency beyond adherence to the Safeguards Agreement and the additional protocol, the latter of which Iran had ceased to implement in February 2006, were necessary to clear up the record on Iran's twenty years of secret nuclear activities. The report confirmed President Ahmadinejad's claim that Iran had enriched UF6 at Natanz to the 3.5 or 3.6 percent level. It also reported continuing conversion and production of UF6 and expanding enrichment. UF6 was being fed into the 164-centrifuge cascade completed in March and two additional cascades of the same size were being assembled.[108]

As Tehran faced expanding pressure from the international community, the lines of contending Iranian views seemed to be drawn sharper than ever in the press. Although it was unclear what the relative strength of the opposing sides was behind each argument, Tehran's policy seemed best and most accurately described in the conservative daily *Keyhan*. "First, maintain national consensus," wrote Mehdi Mohammadi. "Second, Iran negotiates about the future, not about what it already has; and, third, Iran strengthens its position at the negotiating table by moving in the direction of increasing its technical capabilities rapidly."[109] Around this main line, however, swirled controversy. At heart, the debate was over the wisdom of relying on Moscow to shield Iran from sanctions *versus* displaying more flexibility and even striking a deal with the EU-3 and perhaps even Washington. The arguments on each side were marshaled with greatest clarity in two articles appearing within a day of each other in *Keyhan* and the reformist *Aftab-e Yazd*.

In *Keyhan*, the same Mehdi Mohammadi put forward the "Russia as effective shield" argument. He asserted that Russia and China together "are thinking about a strategic unity between themselves and Iran, which will neutralize the danger of the West's complete domination forever. In fact, the signs of this strategy can be seen in their invitation to Iran to attend the summit of the Shanghai members."[110] This was a reference to the fifth anniversary summit of the Shanghai Cooperation Organization (SCO) scheduled for June 15 in Shanghai. Indeed, although Iran was only an observer and not a full member, it had just been announced that President Ahmadinejad would attend the SCO summit and meet there with Putin.[111]

In stark contrast, an unsigned editorial in *Aftab-e Yazd* the next day criticized "the pursuit of what was called the 'Look East' policy [that] showed the determination of Ahmadinejad and his followers to make fundamental changes in Iran's foreign relations." It cautioned that the "nuclear dossier however is particularly sensitive and complex and any negligence in that regard can have irreparable consequences and even fatal dangers." It claimed, "Developments in Iran's nuclear dossier in recent months have not directly yielded anything for Iran, and have even harmed Iran with the suspension of many large-scale economic activities." And it warned that a continued flat-out rejection of the EU-3 proposal would simply push "other countries, including Russia and China," toward supporting American efforts to increase pressures on Iran.[112]

A signed article the same day in *Aftab-e Yazd* was even more polemical. It asserted that Russia actually wanted to encourage Iran's continued resistance to the Europeans' proposals. This would allow the Russian "bears" to gain a "superior geoeconomic position" in the region. Repeating a centuries-old myth about a nonexistent document, the author argued that this would allow the Russian "bears" to pursue Peter the Great's "will and testament . . . [according to which] if they gain access to the warm waters of the Persian Gulf they will rule the world."[113]

## LETTER AND SANCTIONS

In this contentious environment, President Ahmadinejad on May 8 released a highly unusual, surprise letter to President Bush.[114] Although the message was an extensive laundry list of Iranian grievances against America, some Iranian officials rushed to portray it as an invitation to direct talks between Tehran and Washington. Among the first out of the block with this line was none other than Sadeq Kharrazi, the driving force behind the May 4, 2003, Roadmap proposal allegedly approved by Supreme Leader Khamenei and others. Dismissed as ambassador to France the previous fall by the then-new Ahmadinejad administration, Kharrazi in April 2006 had told an interviewer, "I supported the idea of Iran-US talks from the very beginning and suffered for it."[115] Now, just two weeks later, Kharrazi told a U.S. wire service that Ahmadinejad's letter "could have been a turning point in relations."[116] According to others, if America recognized Iran's role in the region and foreswore "regime change," Iran allegedly could help America out in Iraq, Afghanistan, Lebanon, and Syria.[117]

All in all, however, it seemed a stretch to conclude—as did some Western correspondents in Tehran—that Ahmadinejad's confrontational letter was in reality a cover for "a desire to mend relations."[118] In actual fact, the text and tone of the letter—as we shall see in chapter 14—was fully consistent with the views of hard-line conservative clerics who wanted no truck with the West and whose backing was important to Ahmadinejad's political longevity. At the same time, it was probably also a ploy to fend off those Iranian elites critical of Ahmadinejad's unbending line toward the West on the nuclear issue. Some of these very same critics appeared to have tried to guild the lily in hopes of provoking a positive response from Washington to the letter that would put pressure on Ahmadinejad to engage with Europe and the West.

In the meantime, American policy toward Iran was evolving. After her session with P5+1 counterparts in Berlin on March 30, Secretary of State Condoleezza Rice, who had replaced Colin Powell in January 2005, began to formulate a new approach. On May 30 American and European officials said that Washington had agreed to rule out the immediate threat of military force—that is, not to invoke Chapter VII's Article 42—in the UN Security Council resolution then under negotiation. In an effort to get Russia on board, the United States would agree instead to cite only Article 41, which excluded the use of force.[119] The following day Secretary Rice announced that the United States now offered to join the EU-3 in direct talks with Iran provided Iran suspended its nuclear enrichment and reprocessing activities.[120]

After further negotiations by the P5+1 foreign ministers in Vienna on June 1, EU foreign policy chief Javier Solana presented the new package they endorsed to Ali Larijani in Tehran on June 6.[121] As described in the press, it required Iran to "suspend all enrichment-related and reprocessing activities" during negotiations on the new proposal. The formal paper did not discuss possible penalties if Iran refused to comply, but Solana reportedly told Larijani that there would be "serious consequences" for Iran in the UN Security Council. The incentives reportedly included greater access to world markets and capital, support for Iran's entry into the World Trade Organization, promotion of greater trade and investment, and consideration by the United States of lifting sanctions on the sale of commercial aircraft, farm equipment, and telecommunications technology.[122] As Tehran mulled over the offer, diplomatic sources suggested Solana's presentation left the definitions of "suspension" and "enrichment-related and reprocessing" vague. Negotiations were therefore likely to focus on where to draw the line on conversion and enrichment activities at Esfahan and Natanz and how long suspension would need to last.[123]

The very day Solana presented the new package to Larijani, however, Iran restarted pouring UF6 into its functioning 164-centrifuge cascade at Natanz.[124] After that, Iran stalled on its response, despite repeated prodding by the P5+1 for an answer within weeks, certainly before the G-8 summit scheduled for July 15–16 in St. Petersburg. At the SCO summit in Shanghai in mid-June, Putin said after meeting with Ahmadinejad that Iran "in the very near future . . . will formulate its position on a timetable for these talks."[125] Ahmadinejad, however, while describing the new proposal as "a step forward," said only that Iran would respond "in due time."[126] A week later, on June 21, Ahmadinejad said Iran would not have a formal response ready for more than a month, apparently not until mid-August.[127]

Tehran's delaying tactics were no doubt deliberate but perhaps also attributable to continuing debate in Tehran. In mid-June, for example, an editorial scathingly reviewed Iran's foreign policy during the first year since Ahmadinejad's election as president. His "pro-Eastern approach" of drawing closer to Russia, China, and India and giving priority to regional states and the Islamic world had "not resulted in the creation of any opportunities" and threatened "a loss of opportunity for the greater interests of the country" and "a heavy price." On the nuclear issue, it had pushed Europe "to join the ranks of those calling for the exerting of pressure on Iran."[128] Several days later, an early post-shah foreign minister wrote a commentary in a reformist daily urging direct nuclear talks with the United States: "History shows that holding direct talks is the surest and healthiest option for two nations to solve their differences."[129]

Around this time, indeed, Supreme Leader Khamenei appointed the moderate and now ex-foreign minister Kamal Kharrazi to head a new foreign policy committee for five years. The June 25 decree establishing the Strategic Council for Foreign Relations was interpreted as possibly signaling the Supreme Leader's dissatisfaction with President Ahmadinejad's brashness. It was perhaps aimed at establishing a counterbalance that might serve as a back channel for contacts with the United States. In fact, Khamenei let it be known that if Iran's right to pursue nuclear power were recognized, then "we are willing to negotiate over controls, inspections and international guarantees." However, the Supreme Leader also stated bluntly, "Negotiation with the United States has no benefits for us."[130]

In Moscow, surprisingly, it appeared that the cup of Putin's patience had still not runneth over. "The Iranian administration said that they will be ready for dialogue in August," Putin said while taking questions on July 6. "To our mind, they could have done that earlier. However, we must take into account the opinion of the other party—Iran. We should not anticipate events or escalate tensions. Let us give the professionals a chance to work."[131]

Whether or not Tehran thought that it had at least a yellow light from Moscow to keep trying the patience of the P5+1, when Larijani met with Solana and representatives of the EU-3 and Russia on July 11, the Iranian negotiator continued to stall on a response to the new incentives offer. Rather than eliciting flexibility, Putin's comments seemed to confirm Tehran in its conviction that Russia would continue to soften the international reaction.

In the short run, however, the opposite happened. The EU-3 and Russian foreign ministers, joined by their Chinese and American counterparts—in other words, the full P5+1—met in Paris on July 12 and agreed to resume negotiations in the UNSC on a resolution demanding that Iran suspend its nuclear enrichment activities or face economic sanctions. Provoked by Tehran's stonewalling on July 11, the meeting in Paris suddenly cleared the deck of differences among the major powers over referral of the Iranian nuclear file to the UNSC on the eve of the G-8 summit that same weekend in St. Petersburg.[132] Foreign Minister Lavrov underscored the common disappointment over the lack of a positive response from Larijani in the meeting with Solana on July 11. At the same time, Lavrov emphasized that the P5+1 agreement reached in Paris "absolutely excluded" using force against Iran should it refuse to suspend its nuclear enrichment program.[133]

After further fine-tuning, the Security Council passed Resolution 1696 on July 31 by a vote of fourteen to one. Citing Article 40 of Chapter VII of the UN Charter and noting "outstanding issues and concerns on Iran's nuclear program, including topics which could have a military nuclear dimension," it called for "full and sustained" suspension by Iran of "all enrichment-related and reprocessing activities, including research and development," by August 31. Otherwise, Iran would face "appropriate measures" under Article 41 of Chapter VII, to be specified by "further decisions" of the UNSC, to encourage it to comply with the requirements of UNSCR 1696. In his statement, Russian Permanent Representative Vitaly Churkin underscored that "It was crucial to note that . . . any additional measures that could be required to implement the resolution ruled out the use of military force." Churkin's allusion was to Article 41's restriction to "measures not involving the use of armed force." The use of military force against Iran could be sanctioned only under Article 42 of the charter's Chapter VII, which Resolution 1696 did not invoke or explicitly foreshadow.[134]

In Tehran, the debate on tactics continued throughout July and into August even as the leadership appeared to have set its course on refusing to heed the Security Council's demands. In the reformist press, one could read that "ill-considered and half-baked action by our politicians" had pushed Iran into isolation as even "friendly" countries such as Russia had allied themselves with Europe and the United States on the issue of Iran's nuclear program.[135] Commentary in the hard-line *Keyhan*, however, reflected the prevailing views at the top: there were no incentives that could justify suspending Iran's uranium enrichment program; the vote in favor of UNSCR 1696 served Russia and China's interests vis-à-vis the United States but did not harm or impose "any real cost" on Iran; any future substantial economic sanctions would be unenforceable; moreover, Washington would find itself entirely isolated should it try to "confront" Iran and "replace the diplomatic process with undiplomatic measures."[136]

From the hard-liners' perspective, it appeared, Tehran had successfully used Moscow to stave off any military threat from the United States, and economic or diplomatic sanctions would not be sufficiently serious to cause the Iranian leadership to suspend its nuclear program.

# 14

## *Beyond Turkmanchai?*

On July 12, 2006, Russia had at last agreed with the P5+1 to help draft a UN Security Council resolution demanding that Iran suspend its nuclear enrichment activities or face sanctions. That same day, war broke out in the Middle East after Iranian-supported Lebanese Hezbollah forces crossed the border into Israel, killed eight Israeli soldiers and kidnapped another two. Israel responded by air and land against Hezbollah targets across Lebanon in a war that ground on for thirty-four days.

The same weekend the Lebanese war broke out, Russian president Vladimir Putin hosted the G-8 summit in St. Petersburg, an event meant to showcase and publicize post-Soviet Russia's final coming of age on the world stage. But front-page stories of the Lebanon conflict buried coverage of Putin's long anticipated star turn deep inside newspapers around the world.

The outcome of the Lebanese conflict was widely seen as heralding a new chapter in the expansion of Iranian influence across the Middle East and well beyond. In Iraq, where Russia remained stymied in its efforts to revalidate Lukoil's contract to develop the giant West Qurna oil field, Iranian meddling waxed as sectarian violence engulfed that country and challenged the ability of U.S.-led forces to slow the slide toward civil war. In the West Bank and Gaza Strip, Iranian-supported Hamas had won parliamentary elections in January, which put an end to Fatah's long domination of the Palestinian Authority. In Afghanistan, President Hamid Karzai reciprocated Tehran's nurturing of warm ties even as Kabul's relations with Moscow remained soured and the Taliban began to threaten a comeback.

In the Caucasus and Central Asia, Iran had less to show for its efforts but was raising its still very low standing by a policy of dampening tensions and improving relations. This included studiously staying out of the Chechen conflict in Russia's own north Caucasus. Moscow, meanwhile, profited considerably from the flight toward safety by entrenched leaders and elites after the various "color" revolutions of 2003–2005. In addition, Gazprom by late 2005 had begun to reap great profits selling cheap Central Asian gas on the premium European markets as Putin realized his vision of a "Eurasian gas alliance."

After Russia at the end of July 2006 joined other UN Security Council members in threatening Iran with sanctions over its nuclear activities, there were those in Iran who bitterly recalled the still reviled early nineteenth-century treaties of Gulistan and Turkmanchai imposed on a humbled Iran by the victorious Russian Empire. At the same time, in what amounted to a historical mirror image, there were those in Moscow who feared that Iran's advances that summer, showcased by Hezbollah successes in Lebanon and Iran's refusal to suspend its nuclear enrichment program, could mark the reversal of the tide of history. Iran in coming decades just might manage, according to this view, to take back at Russia's expense much of what Iran had lost and still coveted through those same two treaties almost two hundred years earlier.

## LEBANON: ADVANTAGE IRAN

As the war eclipsed public attention to the Iranian nuclear issue, civilian casualties in Lebanon mobilized not just Shia but Sunni sentiment against Israel and the United States in the Middle East and beyond. Together with Hamas' electoral victory and subsequent power-sharing agreement with Fatah in the Palestinian territories, the performance of the Lebanese Hezbollah was seen in many quarters as underscoring Iran's growing influence and self-confidence not just in post-Hussein Shia-dominant Iraq but throughout the region.[1]

The events and trends of July and August 2006 contributed to flux and uncertainty in the Middle East and in Russian-Iranian relations. There was much speculation that Iran had ordered the Hezbollah to attack Israel in order to divert attention from the nuclear issue and to remind all of Iran's power and leverage in the region. Whether such speculation was on the mark or not, the Lebanese Hezbollah succeeded in using its Iranian-supplied arsenal and training to prevent Israel from attaining all its military goals. This was enough for Iranian Supreme Leader Ayatollah Ali Khamenei on August 17 to congratulate Hezbollah chief Hassan Nasrallah on his "victory for Islam" over Israeli forces in Lebanon and for thwarting the "illusory plan for the Middle East" of the United States and Israel. The day before, President Mahmoud Ahmadinejad had called for the United States and United Kingdom to be expelled from the UN Security Council and face a war crimes tribunal.[2]

Emboldened by Hezbollah's performance, Tehran's claims fed the aura of expanding Iranian influence across the Middle East, particularly in those regions and countries with concentrations of Shias. Some observers portrayed the conflict as a proxy war between Iran and the United States. Others argued that it was the first move in an American plan to attack Iran: the war would wipe out Hezbollah's arsenal and deprive Iran of an effective way to retaliate against the United States by attacking Israel; the war would also be an opportunity to test the best methods for the United States to destroy Iran's tunnels and underground nuclear facilities.[3] In the war's aftermath, however, many observers concluded that even if the United States were to contemplate acting militarily against Iran without UNSC authorization, the chances of success were diminished—perhaps to the point that the United States would abandon plans for a military solution.

In Moscow, veteran pundit Sergei Karaganov declared, "Iran turned out the unquestionable winner. The war in Lebanon distracted attention from its nuclear program, whereas its ally and client Hezbollah won a political victory." According to Karaganov, "It became more obvious that Tehran has the political will and craft to play and win convoluted political stratagems. It is entering the new round of bargains over the prospects of its nuclear potential with better cards." As for Iraq, "It has become obvious that the United States has lost Iraq and that the situation in that country is sliding toward civil war, which is going to suck in contiguous countries."[4]

## IRAQ: SECTARIAN VIOLENCE

The prospects for greater Iranian influence in Iraq were indeed high but nevertheless mixed. A referendum had approved a permanent constitution on October 15, 2005. There had been a second round of post-Saddam elections for a permanent parliament on December 15. The official election results were announced on January 20, 2006.[5] The 275-member parliament opened on March 16, with the Shia United Iraqi Alliance coalition controlling 130 seats, but with Sunni Arabs, Kurds, and secular parties controlling 133 seats.[6] After tortuous negotiations, Nuri al-Maliki eclipsed interim premier Ibrahim Jafari, both of the Dawa Party, and emerged as prime minister of Iraq's first post-Saddam permanent government on April 22.[7] The same day, Hassan Kazemi Qomi, who in December 2003 had transferred from consul general in Herat to charge d'affaires of Iran's reopened embassy in Baghdad, was promoted to ambassador. The next day new Iranian foreign minister Manouchehr Mottaki congratulated Iraq on the establishment of a permanent government.[8]

In late November 2005, as Iraq headed into uncharted waters with the impending elections to a permanent parliament, U.S. Secretary of State Condoleezza Rice confirmed that Ambassador Zalmay Khalilzad in Baghdad had been authorized to talk directly with Iranian diplomats about developments in Iraq. However, Rice ruled out broader talks because they would "run the risk of granting legitimacy to a government that does not deserve" it.[9] In Tehran more than three months later, amid reports of widespread unhappiness over President Ahmadinejad's mismanagement of the economy and foreign policy,[10] Ali Larijani, chief nuclear negotiator and head of the Supreme National Security Council, announced acceptance on March 16 of talks with the United States about Iraq.[11] Just two days later, however, the hard-line *Kayhan* daily warned in an editorial that dialogue with the United States would be a "destructive trap."[12] By April 24 Ahmadinejad declared "no need" for talks with the United States because there was now a "permanent government of Iraq."[13]

In truth, however, the Iraqi parliament did not approve Prime Minister Maliki's new cabinet until May 20, 2006. Even then, the critical defense, interior, and national security posts were left unfilled because of continuing disagreements among Shia, Sunni, and Kurdish leaders. Nevertheless, the United Iraqi Alliance occupied seventeen of the thirty-six posts that were filled, and Shias assumed the leading if not uncontested role in the country's first permanent post-Saddam government.[14]

As Iraqi politicians bickered over cabinet seats, security in Iraq deteriorated. The bombing of the Askariya Shia Shrine in Samarra on February 22, 2006, sparked a tsunami of horrific sectarian violence that killed over ten thousand by August.[15] In July, according to the Iraqi Health Ministry, there were 3,438 civilian deaths across the country, nearly twice that in January. In Baghdad, the city morgue received 1,855 bodies in July, 18 percent more than in June.[16] Of these, 90 percent were judged to be the result of executions.[17] What some were already declaring a full-blown civil war challenged the ability of the new authorities to govern the country. Even Gen. John P. Abizaid, commander of American forces in the Middle East, told a Senate committee, "I believe that the sectarian violence is probably as bad as I've seen it, in Baghdad in particular, and that if not stopped, it is possible that Iraq could move towards civil war."[18]

An American air strike killed Abu Musab al-Zarqawi, leader of the radical Sunni Arab al Qaeda in Iraq, on June 7, 2006.[19] According to Gen. George Casey, commander of the multinational force in Iraq, Zarqawi's death hurt but did not finish off his movement. Moreover, armed groups of criminals were adding to the "complexity of the security environment." The Sunni insurgency may not have been growing, but it was concentrating its attacks on Baghdad.

Meanwhile, on the Shia side, Iranian activities had become a major element in Iraq's security. According to General Casey, "we are confident that the Iranians, through their covert special operations forces, are providing weapons, IED [improvised explosive device] technology and training to Shi'a extremist groups in Iraq, the training being conducted in Iran and in some cases probably in Lebanon through their surrogates." Iran was using these surrogates operating on its behalf "to conduct terrorist operations in Iraq, both against us and against the Iraqi people." Iran was "supporting . . . not all of the groups, but a wide variety of groups across southern Iraq," stated General Casey.[20]

To the extent that Iran had stoked the fire to encourage America and the multinational OIF to withdraw their forces from Iraq, it may also have helped create a conflagration that it could not rein back in. The revived specter of the country's fragmentation rekindled the threat of streams of refugees, which Iran had feared in

2003 but which had never developed. The prospects for a new recarving of borders in the Middle East seemed greater than ever since the toppling of the Saddam Hussein regime three years earlier, and with it the secession of Iraqi Kurdistan that Iran so strongly opposed.[21] As much as Iran welcomed the pressure that these developments put on the U.S.-led coalition to leave Iraq, it was hard to see how Tehran would be able to exert effective leverage in the chaos that would likely follow and against the opposition of Arab Sunni regimes in the region.

Meanwhile, Russia's hopes for reestablishing its economic presence in Iraq were left dangling. Moscow's calculations in regard to revalidating and moving ahead with Lukoil's West Qurna contract appeared to rest in great part on expectations of considerable Iranian influence not just in post-Hussein Baghdad but especially in Iraq's southern Shia heartlands, where the West Qurna field lay. Indeed, the economic motive behind Russia's persistence in trying to smooth the waters of the Iranian nuclear case was arguably more Lukoil's anticipated potential profits from West Qurna than finishing out MinAtom's Bushehr contract. But even after joining forces with the American oil major ConocoPhillips in September 2004, Lukoil had been forced to cool its heels as it waited for the situation to resolve itself.[22] The company's contract to exploit the giant West Qurna oil field in North Rumaila, west of Basra, had still not been revalidated, even though there was now a permanent government in Baghdad.

In summer 2006 the prospects and timing for the revalidation of the West Qurna contract still seemed as uncertain as ever. Even if it happened forthwith, the mounting violence in Iraq would make it nearly impossible for Lukoil to go forward with the work it had so long coveted. To some extent, Lukoil in summer 2006 may have viewed the unexpected tripling of oil prices on the world market since the ouster of Saddam Hussein as helping make up for a portion of the income it had anticipated from West Qurna. All the same, there had been nearly three hundred attacks by insurgents on pipelines and other oil installations in Iraq since 2003.[23] Even more ominously, five Russian embassy employees in Baghdad were abducted and killed in June 2006 by a group reportedly linked to al Qaeda.[24] As a result, Lukoil had to content itself with an announcement in August 2006 that it had "fully fulfilled its obligation regarding the technical portion of the humanitarian aid program for the Iraqi Oil Ministry." This meant training of Iraqis at Russian and Azerbaijani oil and gas institutes and the provision of thirty pieces of equipment worth $5 million to the Iraqi Oil Ministry, according to the memorandum Lukoil president Vagit Alekperov had signed in March 2004 with then Iraqi oil minister Ibrahim Bahr al-Ulum.[25] Actually getting to work on West Qurna still seemed more a glimmer in Alekperov's eye than a sure thing.

## AFGHANISTAN: TALIBAN REDUX

In Afghanistan, Hamid Karzai won a five-year term as the country's first popularly elected head of state with 55.4 percent of the vote in presidential elections finally held on October 9, 2004. His main rival, Yonus Qanooni, who had taken over political leadership of the Panjshiri Tajiks after the assassination of legendary commander Ahmed Shah Masoud on September 9, 2001, came in a distant second with 16.3 percent, but well ahead of sixteen other candidates.[26] According to a survey by U.S. elections observers, Karzai got not only 86 percent of his coethnic Pashtun vote but also 40 percent of the Tajik, 21 percent of the Hazara, and 16 percent of the Uzbek vote.[27] However, Karzai reportedly got only 1 percent of the vote in the Panjshir Valley, the stronghold of Masoud and his successors: Qanooni, Defense Minister Mohammad Fahim, and Foreign Minister Dr. Abdullah Abdullah.[28]

Karzai was sworn in as president on December 7, 2004.[29] Later that month, when he formed his new cabinet, he dropped Fahim from the Defense Ministry, replacing him with Gen. Rahim Wardak, an ethnic Pashtun who had been serving as senior deputy defense minister since October 2003. Unhappy Tajiks complained that Karzai was "Pashtunizing" the government.[30] Qanooni set about establishing the New Afghanistan Party to contest the elections for a bicameral national assembly, eventually held on September 18 and November 12, 2005.[31]

When the new parliament opened, its lower house elected Qanooni chairman by a vote of 122 to 117, with nine abstentions, against a Pashtun ally of President Karzai.[32] However, the parliament in April 2006 also approved Karzai's appointment of Rangeen Dadfar Spanta as new foreign minister, replacing Dr. Abdullah.[33] With Abdullah's departure from the cabinet, Karzai had finally succeeded in sidelining the last of the troika of Panjshiri Tajiks, who since the Bonn Conference in late 2001 had appeared to spearhead Karzai's opposition. To the extent that they had been favorably disposed to overtures from Moscow as an avenue to bolstering their influence in Afghan domestic politics, Moscow's leverage in Kabul, always low, shrank even further.

Moscow and Tehran both supported Karzai's election but neither seemed to abandon longtime contacts not in Karzai's camp. In Russia, Putin underscored the need to take into account the interests of all political forces and ethnic groups. He even baldly suggested that "for objective reasons" and because of "difficult conditions" this had not happened in October 2004.[34] Defense Minister Sergei Ivanov, echoing Afghan Tajik complaints, claimed concerns "about the attempts to Pashtunize Afghanistan."[35] In Iran, however, the Foreign Ministry spokesman called the presidential elections a "positive move" for Afghanistan's political stability and economic development. Then–foreign minister Kamal Kharrazi represented Iran at Karzai's inauguration ceremony. But state radio broadcasts from the northeastern city of Mashhad denounced the elections as meant to legitimize "an occupation and the appointment of the occupiers' favorite government."[36]

Russian spokesmen continued to fret over the dangers of terrorism and drugs emanating from Afghanistan. They suggested they were in no hurry to see OEF forces leave that country until threats to the security of Russia and its neighbors were definitely eliminated. Defense Minister Ivanov called the situation "unclear and unstable" and "quite contradictory." The Taliban still controlled large areas of Afghanistan and the threat of international terrorism still emanated from the country.[37] Russian ambassador Zamir Kabulov, despite his public complaints, conceded that the U.S. military presence in Afghanistan was not against Russian interests "for the time being."[38]

As for Tehran, Karzai's firing of Iranian-favorite Ismail Khan as governor of Herat province in September 2004 had been followed by the U.S. occupation of the Soviet-era air base at Shindand, less than twenty miles from the Iranian border. Despite concern over the American move into Shindand, Iranian officials claimed they did not object to Khan's appointment as minister of power in Kabul because they supported Karzai's efforts to subdue provincial warlords who undermined the central government's authority.[39] In any event, Khan's departure from Herat did not slow down Iran's growing influence in the region, which it had long regarded as an important buffer zone.[40]

Khan's eclipse also did not impede Tehran's cordial ties with Karzai. In May 2006 Karzai visited Tehran for the fifth time as president. In his meeting with President Ahmadinejad, Karzai expressed gratitude for the support extended to Afghanistan by Iran over the past thirty years.[41] The Afghan president and his retinue of nine ministers signed a total of seven agreements and memoranda of understanding with their Iranian counterparts.[42]

In contrast, Karzai's relations with Moscow continued to be strained despite occasional efforts to patch them up. In June 2006 Karzai and Putin met in Almaty, Kazakhstan. It was their only bilateral meeting since then–newly installed Afghan president Karzai had visited Moscow in March 2002. Putin expressed "good feelings" for the Afghan people and stated that Russia would continue, "within its possibilities," to help Afghanistan rebuild. Karzai responded that "Your Afghan friends are pinning serious hopes on you playing a great role in rebuilding Afghanistan's economy and making investments in this economy."[43] The two leaders appeared to be trying—though not very successfully—to put behind them another ugly dispute over debts and reparations. The summer before, Russia had demanded $10.5 billion from Afghanistan to repay past state debts. Afghanistan had countered that Russia actually owed Afghanistan $70 billion in war reparations for damages inflicted by the Soviet occupation.[44]

As Karzai engaged in summitry with his Iranian and Russian counterparts, his political position at home began to slip as increasing violence took its toll.[45] In Kabul, a fatal accident involving a U.S. military truck at the end of May 2006 sparked the worst unrest in the capital since the fall of the Taliban.[46] By July, as NATO prepared to take over command of international forces in Afghanistan's southern provinces by the end of the month, a resurgent Taliban was inflicting the highest casualty rates on government and Western forces—the latter now up to some forty thousand—since 2001–2.[47] Observers reported that the escalating insurgency and widespread corruption were provoking a loss of faith and confidence in Karzai among domestic and foreign supporters.[48]

In early 2006 Iran's new foreign minister Mottaki had called for a timetable for the withdrawal of foreign forces from Afghanistan.[49] The available evidence suggested that Iran at that time had little to do with the newly concerted campaign of al Qaeda and Taliban attacks on OEF and ISAF soldiers that accelerated in the months that followed Mottaki's call.[50] All the same, Iran probably viewed some anti-Western violence in Afghanistan's heavily Pashtun southern provinces—such as Kandahar and Helmand across the border from sanctuaries in Pakistan—as useful. Along with mounting unrest in Iraq, it presumably discouraged American thoughts of a military campaign against Iran, then the subject of rampant speculation in the press.[51] To some extent, Iran had the luxury of having its cake and eating it too since Herat and other key buffer provinces along the Iranian-Afghani border remained comparatively more peaceful and stable. Indeed, the last thing Iran wanted was the return of the Taliban to power across Afghanistan, and especially along Iran's eastern borders.

For Russia, aside from the perverse pleasure some might derive from seeing U.S. and NATO objectives frustrated in Afghanistan, there was no real advantage in a resurgent Taliban anywhere in that country. Chaos in Afghanistan would revive the security worries of Russia and its Central Asian neighbors and frustrate hopes for economic gain opened up by a prosperous Afghan market and secure transit for energy and other products to India and Pakistan. By summer 2006, besides a spiraling insurgency, it appeared Afghanistan's opium harvest would reach record levels, up 50 percent from the year before, and that the projected 6,100 metric tons would amount to 92 percent of the global supply.[52] Foreign Minister Sergei Lavrov declared that Afghanistan was "on the brink of becoming a narco-state."[53]

## CAUCASUS AND CENTRAL ASIA: ADVANTAGE RUSSIA

Despite early fears in the West and early expectations in Iran, efforts by the Islamic Republic to gain influence in the Caucasus and Central Asia after the collapse of the Soviet Union had not enjoyed particular success. Since its failed attempt in Tajikistan, Iran appeared to have given up on any effort to spark an Islamic revolution in Central Asia and Azerbaijan. Tehran in effect had ceded primacy to Russia and turned to pursuing a long-term strategy of trying to improve its presence and influence in the region through economic diplomacy rather than Islamic revolution.

Looking back, Majles member Dr. Elaheh Koulaei declared in 2004, "Iran's opportunities in Central Asian republics are unfortunately gone with the wind." In the months after the collapse of the Soviet Union, Iran had focused on the region through ideological prisms, ignoring its more important interests in Central Asia. Russia had effectively used the threat of rising fundamentalism, which it ascribed to the Islamic Republic of Iran, to secure its military presence in Central Asia. In fact, argued Dr. Koulaei, "the Sunni majority in Central Asian republics never had any interest in establishment of a system using the Islamic Republic of Iran as a model." Iran had never posed much of a threat to Russia in the region and never had "such potential influence" there either.[54]

That said, there were those in Iran who still nourished long-term hopes of gaining a greater presence across the swath of lands in the former Soviet republics that had historically been regarded as in "Greater Iran's" sphere of influence. Iranian diplomats would need to keep active in the area to defend the Foreign Ministry against charges of having "lost" these territories after the breakup of the Soviet Union had once again reopened the historical bidding for them. Iran's security services, subordinate to much harder-line elements in the Islamic theocracy, would presumably also keep working to develop nondiplomatic options for exerting pressure throughout the region on behalf of their superiors in Tehran.

Although Russia was satisfied with Iran's "good" behavior in the region since helping forge a peace agreement in Tajikistan, there was plenty of lingering mistrust of long-term Iranian objectives and presumed ongoing quiet work to advance its goals. Nevertheless, Iranian influence in the former Soviet lands did not seem likely to rise dramatically in the near future. Years before the wave of sectarian violence in Iraq focused the world's attention on the issue, Central and South Asia specialist Umnov had speculated that resurgent Islam in Tajikistan and Central Asia could revive ancestral, pre-Soviet Sunni-Shia differences and prejudices and actually lessen Iran's cultural and political purchase in the region.[55] Although Iran might reap rewards in Central Asia by playing on shared pre-Islamic Zoroastrian roots and Persian culture, overbearing clerics and widely perceived Iranian arrogance were likely repeatedly to undermine moves in this direction.[56]

Iran had clearly failed to fulfill its early expectations, misjudged the preferences of the peoples of the Caucasus and Central Asia, and mismanaged its own policies. Nevertheless, it could not be excluded that judicious Iranian diplomacy and sensitive cultural outreach programs, emphasizing not just Islamic but also pre-Islamic historical, cultural, and linguistic ties, could noticeably strengthen Iranian influence at least in Tajikistan. President Mohammad Khatami struck precisely these themes in a swing through Central Asia—particularly during his stop in Tajikistan—after the Caspian summit in Ashgabat in April and May 2002.[57]

Only time would tell how sustained this more subtle Iranian approach would prove. It may have been just a temporary defensive response to public criticism back home in the wake of setbacks on the Caspian delimitation and post-Taliban Afghanistan issues. Nevertheless, Khatami's successor Ahmadinejad, despite his confrontational posture toward the West, appeared in his first year in power to be comfortable with a continuation of the soft-touch Khatami line in Central Asia and the Caucasus, perhaps as part of Ahmadinejad's so-called Look to the East diplomatic orientation. Russia even accommodated Iranian policy in this respect by voting it observer status in the Shanghai Cooperation Organization (SCO), dominated by Russia and China, at the organization's summit in Astana in July 2005, and permitting Ahmadinejad to attend in that capacity at its summit the following summer in Shanghai.[58] But across Central Asia, after the dust of the Soviet collapse and the Tajik civil war had settled, Russian primacy vis-à-vis Iran was clear already in the Yeltsin years and remained so throughout the Putin era.

Nevertheless, Putin's decision not to oppose the use of military bases in Central Asia by the OEF Coalition after 9/11 had provoked criticism at home and from Iran for ceding too much to Washington in Moscow's so-called backyard. Rather than struggling to evict OEF forces from Central Asian air bases, however, Putin in June 2002 used the continuing threat from international terrorism to justify the redeployment of Russian warplanes and the CIS Collective Security Treaty's Rapid Reaction Force to Kant Air Base in Kyrgyzstan.[59] Putin and Kyrgyz president Askar Akayev presided over the air base's ceremonial opening in October 2003.[60] However, the Kant force's modest numbers suggested that the real aim of the deployment, at least initially, was to offset the public relations impact of the OEF presence at nearby Manas International Airport outside Bishkek.[61]

As time passed, Putin's support for OEF bases in Central Asia became less than rock-ribbed. On May 23, 2005, President Hamid Karzai signed a "strategic partnership" declaration with President Bush in the White House.[62] Although it made no mention of a permanent American military presence in Afghanistan, there was much speculation to that effect in the press. [63] Concern over U.S. intentions in Afghanistan as well as Central Asia may have prompted Putin to support the call on July 5, 2005, by the SCO summit meeting in Astana, Kazakhstan, for OEF coalition members to "set final deadlines for the temporary use" of bases in Central Asia and their deployments of military forces in the region.[64] But Putin's desire to take advantage and curry favor with Uzbekistani president Islom Karimov, at odds with the United States and many other countries over his brutal suppression of demonstrators in Andijon on May 13, 2005, was in all likelihood the more important factor in the development of the SCO call.[65]

By now, in contrast to right after 9/11, Putin's policies in Central Asia and the Caucasus had the full backing of traditionalist forces at home, including the defense and security (*siloviki*) lobbies. Moreover, the Rose Revolution in Georgia (November 2003), the Orange Revolution in Ukraine (December 2004), and the Tulip Revolution in Kyrgyzstan (March 2005), combined with assertions about American use of nongovernmental organizations (NGOs) to topple local regimes, had driven leaders across Central Asia, particularly Uzbekistan's Karimov, closer to Russia in search of stability and political survival.

On July 29, 2005, within hours of the departure of 439 Andijon refugees from Kyrgyzstan to Romania, Tashkent gave the United States 180 days to abandon the Karshi-Khanabad Air Base in southern Uzbekistan.[66] The decision brought to an end the agreement on use of the base signed on October 8, 2001—in the glow of Putin's statement on September 24, 2001, which had removed any Russian objections to such "temporary" OEF deployments in Central Asia.[67] But in Bishkek, President Kurmanbek Bakiyev, Akayev's successor, ignored the SCO call for the departure of foreign troops from the region. Instead, Kyrgyzstan negotiated a new deal for continued use of Manas airport by American and OEF forces for support of operations in Afghanistan.[68]

Meanwhile, Putin had largely succeeded in stitching together the "Eurasian alliance of gas producers" that he had suggested in early 2002. By late 2005 all the pieces were in place for what some analysts described as a Russian-controlled OPEC-like cartel that kept Iranian gas out of Europe and assured Russia's position as the dominant supplier of natural gas to European markets.[69] Together with the windfall profits from sharply higher world oil prices, the development increasingly led observers to call Russia an energy superpower.

In April 2003 Gazprom had concluded a twenty-five-year agreement with Turkmenistan for virtually all of its natural gas production. The price was set at $44 per thousand cubic meters for the first three years, then subject to renegotiation.[70] In addition, Uzbekistan and Kazakhstan not only produced natural gas for export but also were crucial for the transit of the much larger volumes of Turkmen gas to Russia and onward to Western markets. In September 2005 Gazprom had contracted for nearly all the capacity of the pipelines in Uzbekistan. Gazprom also had a deal to buy nearly all of Uzbekistan's gas for $60 per thousand cubic meters. In November 2005 Gazprom had struck a similar deal with KazMunaiGaz for Kazakhstan's transit capacity and gas export output at $50 per thousand cubic meters.[71] In 2006 Turkmenistan, Uzbekistan, and Kazakhstan all bargained for higher rates from Gazprom, but still far below the $230–240 per thousand cubic meters that Gazprom was fetching from Europe at the other end of its pipelines for the same gas.[72]

In June 2005 the Russian government paid $7.11 billion for over 2.5 billion shares of Gazprom stock, or 10.74 percent, giving the Russian state a controlling stake of over 50 percent of Gazprom shares.[73] By 2006 Gazprom supplied 25 percent of Italy and France's gas imports; 44 percent of Germany's; and all of the gas bought by Finland, Slovakia, and other countries in Eastern Europe.[74] Thanks largely to Gazprom's favorable contracts with Central Asian producers, its monopoly on gas export pipelines from the region, and myriads of acquisitions, Gazprom's evaluation had risen to more than $240 billion. It was the fifth-largest corporation in the world.[75]

Putin personally had reportedly become immensely wealthy thanks to his control of the state and of firms such as Gazprom. One analyst estimated that the Russian president's net worth would reach at least $15 billion by the time he left office in 2008.[76] If true, that would far surpass the $4–5 billion that former prime minister Viktor Chernomyrdin was estimated by some to have amassed during the 1990s.[77] The allegations suggested that Putin had developed a strong liking of his own for that "golden shower" that Putin had accused an earlier generation of energy moguls of enjoying to excess shortly after he became acting prime minister in August 1999.[78]

In any event, Gazprom more than ever was widely seen as a tool of the Russian state. In June 2005, board chairman Aleksey Miller announced that Gazprom would begin charging CIS and Baltic countries in 2006 according to what he called "purely market mechanisms."[79] Russia subsequently used Gazprom's natural gas dominance in January 2006 to put the squeeze on Georgia and Ukraine. From Georgia, Gazprom demanded an increase from the old price of $63 per thousand cubic meters to a new price that it set at $110. From Ukraine, it demanded a nearly fivefold increase from $50 per thousand cubic meters to $230, eventually settling for a short-term deal at $95 per thousand cubic meters. In both cases, state-controlled Gazprom's sudden demands in the middle of a harsh winter—backed up by interruptions in gas supplies—were widely seen as political retribution against the Rose and Orange revolutions that had brought to power pro-Western presidents Mikhail Saakashvili in Georgia and Viktor Yushchenko in Ukraine.[80]

## OPEN DOOR IN TAJIKISTAN

In Tajikistan, after all the bloodshed of the civil war and the torturous negotiations leading to the 1997 peace accords, President Emomali Rahmonov effectively coopted or suppressed warlords from both sides and brought a modicum of peace and stability to the country. While giving them a seat at the table of power in Dushanbe, Rahmonov also marginalized Iranian-supported forces in the ensuing political struggle.[81]

Rahmonov took advantage of internal rifts in the Islamic Revival Party (IRP). Two years after the peace accords, the United Tajik Opposition's (UTO) Akbar Turajonzoda, who had eventually joined the IRP, was elected a deputy chairman of the IRP when Sayed Abdullo Nuri replaced Mohammadsharif Himmatzoda as chairman. But then Turajonzoda almost immediately broke with the IRP, endorsing Rahmonov and his People's Democratic Party (PDP) in the November 1999 presidential and the February 2000 parliamentary elections. Turajonzoda even accused the IRP of using "the holy laws of Islam" for its own selfish political ends, thus in effect defending Islam from the very same Iranian-supported Islamists to whom he had hitched his political wagon for the previous eight years of turmoil in Tajikistan.[82] The IRP's leadership summarily expelled Turajonzoda from the party.[83] By summer 2006 IRP leader Sayed Abdullo Nuri was dead, leaving the future of the party in doubt.[84]

On the external front, Rahmonov made use of 9/11 to gain room for maneuver with partners other than Russia and Iran. As early as December 2002, the Tajik president declared at the White House that his country was ready "to be a reliable and stable partner of the United States for a long-term perspective."[85] Nevertheless, Rahmonov maintained correct relations with Tehran, and Dushanbe's ties with Moscow were as always preeminent.

After the fall of the Taliban, Rahmonov played on the desire in both Tehran and Moscow to leverage energy investments in Tajikistan to improve their influence not only in Tajikistan but throughout Central and South Asia. In March 2002 Putin highlighted to the visiting Afghan leader Karzai the idea of Russia building a power station in Tajikistan to supply Afghanistan with electricity.[86] With the Afghan economy beginning to rebound, the press reported potential markets for profitable electricity sales to that country as well as to Iran, Kazakhstan, Pakistan, and even China. There were also plans to expand the use of Central Asian energy grids through Uzbekistan and Kazakhstan to export Tajik and Kyrgyz energy to Omsk and other Siberian regions in Russia.[87]

In the meantime, the Iranian company Sabir International began in December 2003 to cut an all-season traffic tunnel through the critical Anzob pass linking northern and southern Tajikistan.[88] The $31 million initiative was part of an ambitious Iranian plan for a road from China to the Persian Gulf.[89] Underscoring Iran's continuing efforts in Tajikistan ahead of other Central Asian states, President Ahmadinejad visited the country and together with President Rahmonov presided at the official opening of the Anzob tunnel on July 26, 2006.[90]

Rahmonov's campaign to sell Tajikistan as an energy producer and exporter went into high gear when he met with Putin in Sochi in July 2004,[91] then received Iranian president Mohammad Khatami in Dushanbe in September,[92] and Putin the next month.[93] The end result was agreement by all three countries in January 2005 that Russia, with an investment of $250 million, would be the majority stockholder in the Sangtuda-1 hydroelectric power station project. Iran, with a commitment of $180–200 million, would take the lead on a lesser but still substantial power plant, referred to as Sangtuda-2.[94]

Putin and Rahmonov in October 2004 also agreed on the final details of converting the status of the 201st Motorized Rifle Division's deployment in Tajikistan to that of a Russian military base[95] and confirmed the final stages of the withdrawal of Russian Border Guard forces from Tajikistan. Ongoing since 1998, that withdrawal would be completed in July 2005, bringing to an end Russia's 110-year presence on the Tajik-Afghan border.[96]

## AZERBAIJAN AND TERRITORIAL INTEGRITY

As in Central Asia, many described Russia and Iran as strategic enemies but tactical allies in the Caucasus. Russia and Iran were of a common mind in wanting to minimize any long-term Western military influence in the Caspian basin. But Russia understood that Iran in the long run wanted to supplant Russia in the Caucasus, taking advantage of those areas where the populations were Muslim, and Tehran understood that Moscow would resist this.[97]

In Azerbaijan, Tehran's overwhelming concern had been its unease over the aspirations of ethnic Azeris in Iran's South Azerbaijan, whose desire for cultural and even political autonomy had waxed and waned over the years. Tehran's supreme interest was to contain this pressure, especially given demographic trends that may already have produced an Iranian population with a predominantly Azeri Turkic majority (see chapter 3). There was great irony in the fact that the one post-Soviet state with the greatest number of at least nominal Shias was the one Iran worried the most about because of the potential for ethnic-based irredentism. However exaggerated and unreciprocated some Azerbaijani claims, Tehran did not want to take any chances with the disaffection that certainly existed in northwestern Iran as well as in other provinces.[98]

Azerbaijan's longtime Soviet and then post-Soviet leader Heydar Aliyev was well-versed in playing the Azeri unity theme, with experience going back at least to the early 1980s. But his administration clearly recognized the territorial integrity of Iran, even as it argued that the cultural rights of ethnic Azeris in Iran must be protected. As such, the issue served to remind Tehran of Baku's usefulness in keeping the ethnic Azeri movement under control and was a disincentive to excessive Iranian meddling in Azerbaijani affairs. But it was a doubled-edged sword, for whenever Aliyev wanted to improve relations with Iran, as he periodically did, Tehran could insist that he clamp down on the activities of groups active south of the Araks River in Iran and make their sanctuary north of the river in Azerbaijan less comfortable.[99]

With both sides apparently intent on dampening tensions, President Heydar Aliyev chose not to visit Tabriz, the main city in Iranian South Azerbaijan, nor raise the long contentious issue of an Azerbaijani consulate there when he finally visited Tehran in May 2002 after repeated postponements.[100] Under the terms of the Friendship and Cooperation Accord that Presidents Aliyev and Khatami approved during the visit, according to skimpy media accounts, Iran recognized Azerbaijan's territorial integrity and both countries pledged not to allow their territories to be used for hostile moves against the other.[101] It was highly unlikely that either side put much stock in the accord's obligations as a restraining factor either on its own or the opposite side's behavior. Nevertheless, the agreement was evidence of the great sensitivity of the ethnic Azeri cross-border issue to Iran: whether the tug of Azeri irredentism toward Baku or the pull of "Greater Iranian" loyalties back to Tehran would win out in South Azerbaijan.

In October 2003 Ilham Aliyev succeeded his father as elected president; Heydar Aliyev died soon after in January 2004. In August 2004 President Khatami visited Baku, the first Iranian leader to do so in over a decade since President Rafsanjani had been there in October 1993.[102] As a house-warming gift to the new leader in Baku, Khatami confirmed Iran's support for Azerbaijan's territorial integrity, adding that Nagorno-Karabakh belonged to Azerbaijan. He also agreed that Azerbaijan's consulate in Tabriz could at long last open, which it did in October 2004.[103] Ilham reciprocated by visiting Iran in January 2005. Unlike his father, he was able to include in his itinerary not just Tehran but also Tabriz.[104] Several months later, Iranian defense minister Ali Shamkhani and his Azeri counterpart Safar Abiyev signed a memorandum of understanding on defense cooperation that Shamkhani described as a nonaggression pact. According to him, the agreement's fifth clause "prohibits establishment of any base by a third state on either country for attack on the other."[105]

Presidents Heydar and Ilham Aliyev, however, consistently gave pride of place to Russia over ties with Iran. Putin's visit to Baku in January 2001, and Heydar Aliyev's return state visit to Moscow in January 2002, had "raised Russian-Azerbaijani relations to the highest level in the last 10 years," Heydar Aliyev was quick to tell the press.[106] Although none of the documents they signed contained the phrase, Aliyev described Azerbaijan as Russia's "strategic partner." Novruz Mammadov, Aliyev's aide for international relations, told the press, "Russia understands that Azerbaijan can be Russia's most reliable partner and support on an equitable basis as a young and independent state in the South Caucasus."[107] When son Ilham came to power and paid his first official visit to Moscow in February 2004, he confirmed to Putin in the Kremlin, "Russia remains a strategic partner for Azerbaijan; we are loyal to this partnership, and will pursue this course continuously."[108]

Such expressions of closeness to Russia, however, were a requisite for both Aliyevs to pursue relations with the United States. Ilham continued this policy when he visited Washington in April 2006. But ever the balancer, he brushed off suggestions that Azerbaijan might cooperate with the United States in military moves against Iran and its nuclear program. After all, Azerbaijan and Iran had an important bilateral agreement that "clearly says that the territories of our countries cannot be used for any danger towards each other."[109] This was presumably a reference to the Friendship Treaty signed in 2002 by his father and Khatami and reinforced by the May 2005 memorandum of understanding between the defense ministers of both countries.[110]

A month after Ilham Aliyev visited Washington, he hosted Iranian president Ahmadinejad in Baku, where representatives from Turkey, Pakistan, Kazakhstan, Kyrgyzstan, Tajikistan, Turkmenistan, and Uzbekistan as well as Azerbaijan and Iran met for a summit of the Economic Cooperation Organization (ECO).[111] While relations with the new Ahmadinejad government were superficially cordial, the dispute over the Alov/Alborz energy bloc in the Caspian remained at least publicly unresolved since an Iranian gunboat and military aircraft had stopped Azeri exploration of the area in July 2001.

In 2002, as first vice president of SOCAR, Ilham Aliyev had declared, "There can be no concessions to Iran over the Araz-Alov-Sarq oil field."[112] Despite the bravura, he later confirmed that "SOCAR does not want to exert pressure on BP in the development of the Araz, Alov and Sarq structures" but promised to return to the issue after Iran and Azerbaijan resolved their dispute over Alov.[113] This had not yet happened by summer 2006. Meanwhile, construction for Iran of the deep-water rig to exploit blocs such as Alov/Alborz was running at least two years behind the 2004 scheduled completion date.[114] Whenever the rig was finally ready to go, its potential deployment over the Alov/Alborz field could severely challenge the so-called nonaggression pact between Iran and Azerbaijan.

## THE CHECHEN EXCEPTION

In the Northern Caucasus, Iran studiously if painfully steered clear of the Chechen conflict within Russia's own borders. As early as 1993, well before the Taliban made its appearance in Afghanistan, Iranian officials had been quite frank with their Russian interlocutors in speaking of their concerns over the repercussions of conflict in Tajikistan and Afghanistan on Iran's own internal stability. They had reportedly assured Foreign Minister Andrey Kozyrev in Tehran that they had no official contacts with separatist forces in the Russian Federation regions of Chechnya and Tatarstan and did not intend to establish them.[115]

Majles deputy Dr. Elaheh Koulaei contrasted Iranian policy toward Tajikistan and Chechnya. "We did not repeat in Chechnya what we did at the beginning of the civil war in Tajikistan because we had learnt a lesson from the Tajik war," Koulaei told a university seminar. In Tajikistan, Iran had been motivated by ideology and the impulse to expand Islamic influence, but it had entered the civil war without "a clear grasp of the nature of that war and the disputes among Tajikistan's political forces." Iran's subsequent lack of support for Chechnya's Muslims against Russia demonstrated, asserted Dr. Koulaei, that Iran had learned "to understand and differentiate between our interests and the values which we defend." Different circumstances demanded different means to defend Iran's values.[116]

However, Moscow had few illusions about the potential for Tehran-sponsored terrorism. Experts such as Yevgeny Bazhanov of the Diplomatic Academy and officials such as Semyon Gregoryev of the Foreign Ministry echoed each other in their refrain that Russia appreciated Iranian policy not because Iran was behaving well but because Russia feared Iran could behave much worse and interfere in Central Asia and the Caucasus.[117] There had been those in Iran who did not shy away from criticizing Russian policy and actions specifically in Chechnya, including branding President Putin the "butcher of Chechnya."[118]

Nevertheless, given Iran's own internal fragilities and sensitivities to developments just over Iran's borders—especially the ever-touchy ethnic Azeri issue and common interests with Russia in opposing the Taliban—it was no wonder that official Tehran never supported the Chechen drive for independence. Moreover, as much as they might have been tempted to criticize Moscow over Chechnya, and occasionally in fact did so, Iranian officials may have been dissuaded lest Russian opponents of close relations use any incautious statements to call into question Iran's trustworthiness as a partner. In 2002, for example, after the traumatic incident at the Dubrovka theater in Moscow, in which 129 hostages died after Russian security forces pumped a disabling gas into the auditorium, the journalist Maksim Yusin took Iranian statements of sympathy toward Chechnya—in a newspaper Yusin asserted was controlled by Supreme Leader Ali Khamenei—as a sign of "betrayal" and contrasted them to Washington's reaction of "restraint, sympathy, and compassion" toward Moscow.[119]

In late 1999 the Diplomatic Academy's Bazhanov noted that Iran was behaving better than could be believed in Chechnya. It was not providing any weapons to the Chechen "bandits," or any other overt or covert support. While Iran decried civilian deaths in Chechnya, observed Bazhanov, it recognized Chechnya as an internal Russian matter.[120] In commenting on events in Chechnya, Iran deplored military solutions and condemned terrorist acts while consistently underscoring its respect for the territorial integrity of the Russian Federation.[121] Iran's hands-off stance was reminiscent of its refusal to contribute to the disintegration of the Soviet Union during the nationalist uprising in Baku in January 1990.[122] During President Khatami's three-year (1997–2000) chairmanship of the Organization of the Islamic Conference, Iran was especially helpful to Moscow in tempering criticism over Chechnya from the Islamic world.[123] In this regard, Chechen rebel commander Shamil Basayev once remarked on the lack of Iranian involvement in supporting the Chechen cause, suggesting that Iran was afraid of Russia and of course needed Russian cooperation in building a "nuclear bomb."[124]

## PSYCHOLOGICAL WATERSHED

Nearly a dozen years after Basayev's remark, and against the backdrop of all the uncertainties in Lebanon, Iraq, and Afghanistan, Russia joined other members of the UN Security Council on July 31, 2006, in approving Resolution 1696. Reacting to its call on Iran to suspend all nuclear enrichment–related and research and development activities by August 31 or face economic sanctions, Iran's top nuclear negotiator, Ali Larijani, and the Iranian Foreign Ministry called the resolution illegal. The Russian Foreign Ministry quickly reminded Tehran that, according to Article 25 of the UN Charter, "the Members of the United Nations agree to accept and implement the decisions of the Security Council in accordance with the Charter."[125]

Moscow's pique was understandable. Russia had successfully used its veto power in the Security Council to resist a rush to sanctions against Iran. Moscow was therefore clearly not amused by Tehran's thumbing its nose at the Security Council's authority, one of Russia's principal claims to status and respect as a major power. To the extent, however, that Russia—supported most prominently by China—continued to block Chapter VII, Article 42 military measures to arrest Iran's nuclear program and effectively to slow down and soften adoption of economic sanctions against Iran, it encouraged Iranian leaders' growing sense of impunity.

Russia may have taken satisfaction in its ability to use its leverage within the Security Council to shape the council's decisions on Iran. But Russia's own caution in enforcing the council's judgment against Iran undercut the very authoritativeness of the body that Russia had been so eager to bolster since the U.S./UK-led toppling of the Saddam Hussein regime in April 2003. Indeed, Tehran quickly shifted back to playing on Russia's—as well as the EU-3 and China's—tactical differences with Washington. Nevertheless, some commentators and Majles parliamentarians continued to pick at the still itchy scabs of the early nineteenth-century Gulistan and Turkmanchai treaties in denouncing Russia's votes against Iran in the UN Security Council. There were few if any left in Tehran or Moscow to argue that ties between Iran and Russia qualified as a "strategic partnership."

The shift in the role played by the Iranian nuclear issue in Russian-American relations underscored the changed atmospherics. In the 1990s Russia's dealings with Iran in this area had been the biggest irritant in relations with Washington. By 2006 it was one of the few remaining areas in which some cooperation was still possible as disputes grew over other issues in the run-up to the G-8 summit set to be hosted by President Putin in St. Petersburg in July.

That winter, Russia had provoked an uproar in the West when Gazprom had subjected Ukraine and Georgia to sudden gas cutoffs and price hikes. By March 2006 a task force of the American Council on Foreign Relations had criticized Russia for rolling back democratic reform at home; using energy exports as a political weapon against neighboring states; trying to curtail OEF access to air bases in Central Asia; and inviting to Moscow the leaders of Palestinian Hamas, which the United States regarded as a terrorist organization; but had applauded Russia for its support in containing Iran's nuclear program.[126] Two months later, endorsing the litany of criticisms voiced by Vice President Richard Cheney in Vilnius, Secretary of State Condoleezza Rice nevertheless had underscored that on Iran, "The Russians don't want the Iranians to have a nuclear weapon. Of that I'm quite certain."[127]

As the year 2006 unfolded, it appeared increasingly likely that it would become a psychological watershed in the history of Russian-Iranian relations. Iran's success as a sponsor of Hezbollah in Lebanon and Hamas in the Palestinian territories and its ability to outfox Russian diplomacy on the nuclear issue threatened to alter at least the perception of the correlation of forces in the region. Iran's refusal to halt its nuclear program and its successes in playing to the anti-Western street in the Middle East—on the strength of its anti-Israeli, anti-American, Islam-versus-the-West propaganda—already translated into an Iran less constrained and more self-confident as a regional power. Iran's increased profile challenged not just Western but also Russian influence. No matter what the short-term outcome of the nuclear issue, Russia could no longer be confident that it could maintain the edge that it had enjoyed for nearly two centuries in dealing with Iran since the signing of the Turkmanchai Treaty in 1828.

At the very least, Iran was threatening to become a gray nuclear power. By March 2006 experts at the Moscow-based Council for Foreign and Defense Policy concluded that "Iran is keen on getting nuclear weapons" and, in the opinion of most of the contributors to the study, would be able to do so within five years.[128] Two months later, in the mass-circulation *Moskovskiy Komsomolets*, the journalist Mikhail Rostovskiy wrote, "The American and Russian plans for restraining Iran both have rather mediocre chances of succeeding." Rostovskiy concluded, "The most terrifying thing is that the Tehran ayatollahs have every chance of getting through."[129]

The international community, led by the United States and the EU-3, had engaged in intensive negotiations among themselves and Tehran to constrain Iran's nuclear program. Rather than working toward a compromise, Tehran after the election of President Ahmadinejad had pocketed Russian insistence on patience and forbearance while continuing to plow full steam ahead. Despite considerable inducements, Tehran had repeatedly rejected calls to suspend its conversion and enrichment activities and insisted on Iran's right to develop a full nuclear fuel cycle capability on its own territory under its own control. Compared to the new Ahmadinejad "bosses" in Tehran, observed Rostovskiy, Iraq's Saddam Hussein and Serbia's Slobodan Milosevic seemed in retrospect "almost like masters of compromise."[130]

Russia's earlier certainty that Iran would never be able to develop a mature nuclear program without outside assistance was overtaken by Iran's success in maintaining a covert program that was not discovered until 2002. Russia's belief that it would be able to impose a compromise on Iran by patient perseverance was upset by the Ahmadinejad administration's success in using Russian diplomacy to buy time to push Iran's program seemingly beyond the point of no return. Even if Ahmadinejad were pushed aside by more flexible Iranian conservatives, the Iranian nuclear program had already acquired a more advanced base from which a future administration could launch another push forward. Moscow would have to deal with the consequences for decades to come.

"World diplomacy has made a big mistake in underestimating" President Ahmadinejad, warned Yevgeny Satanovsky, head of the Near East Institute in Moscow.[131] The Iranian leader "is a man of a Hitlerite type." He was "testing the region's strength" and would have nuclear weapons in "two or three years' time."[132] According to Satanovsky, "The Shiite crescent, from Lebanon and Syria to the south of Iraq, Saudi Arabia's eastern province, and the minor monarchies of the Persian Gulf, are a priority zone of interest." Iran's "nuclear programs and, in the very near future, nuclear weapons are a guarantee of its inviolability." Alluding to sentiment in Iran for rolling back the results of the Gulistan and Turkmanchai treaties, Satanovsky speculated that after settling matters with its Persian Gulf rivals, Iran would turn its sights to its former "northern territories" in the Caucasus and Central Asia. By 2050, Satanovsky predicted, Russia's population would shrink to 100 million while Iran's would grow by 20 million, and Iran would "be fully organized in terms of oil, gas, and nuclear technologies."[133]

Russia and others had successfully moderated pressure in the UN Security Council for harsher sanctions against Iran. All the same, there were increasingly unambiguous expressions of concern in the Moscow press that Russian diplomacy—while tactically adept toward Washington—might prove strategically inept toward Tehran. Iran in the end could well slip away and emerge from the grasp of the international community and its nonproliferation regime on the threshold—at least—of becoming the world's newest nuclear power.

Russia's insistence on a peaceful solution to the Iranian nuclear issue had given Iran time to draw closer to the very goal that Moscow had no interest in Iran attaining. As a result, Russian policy—while consistent—seemed tied in knots. "Russia cannot decide what to do," observed Aleksandr Khromchikhin of Moscow's Institute of Political and Military Analysis. "It does not want to quarrel with the West, with Europe in particular, but it does not want to quarrel with Iran either. . . . In the meantime, while everyone is playing for time Iran continues to develop nuclear weapons."[134]

Over the years, statements by Russian experts and officials had strongly suggested that Russia never expected that Iran would manage to accomplish what it had in developing its nuclear program. Moscow no doubt also never expected an Ahmadinejad-type of leader to come to power after years of banking on the gradual moderation of the revolutionary Islamic regime in Tehran. The combination meant that no matter how successful Russia might be in reasserting the prerogatives of its UN Security Council status vis-à-vis the United States, Iran in the end might succeed in radically changing the correlation of forces between itself and Russia in the Middle East, the Caucasus, Central Asia, and South Asia by becoming a nuclear power. Even if still years away from possibly attaining this status, its early threshold achievements were already earning Iran increased attention throughout the region.

"Russia is not going to be friends with Iran to its own detriment," intoned Mikhail Margelov, head of the International Affairs Committee of the Federation Council. "Only an idiot would dream of having a neighbor with a nuclear bomb in his pocket on a troubled southern border."[135] But Moscow vigorously claimed to fear that any move to forcibly prevent Iran from going nuclear would have unforeseen consequences that would challenge Russian security interests by creating "zones of instability at Russia's borders."[136]

If it came to pass, the consequences of a nuclear Iran would dwarf the dangers posed by a conventionally rearmed Iran. Even a near-nuclear Iran could eventually begin to challenge the legacy of the Persian Empire's defeats at the hands of the Russian Empire. As Aleksandr Bovin had warned as far back as Rafsanjani's 1989 visit to Moscow, even a conventionally powerful Iran could wreak havoc in the Persian Gulf with unpredictable consequences for the Middle East and far beyond. But Iran's Shahab-3 missiles would present a much more direct challenge to Russian security should they ever be armed with nuclear weapons. Their very existence would mean a more influential Iran not just in the Middle East but across the Caucasus and Central Asia. Moreover, according to Rostovskiy, should other countries follow in Iran's proliferation wake, the value of Russia's own nuclear weapons, "one of our main trump cards," would decline "drastically."[137]

## POLITICS, NOT ECONOMICS

Despite the looming challenge, there was great consistency and continuity in the Russian view on how to deal with Iran over the decades covered in this narrative.

Patience, albeit frequently tested, was the byword. This was the case whether economic ties were anemic or a bit more substantial. In contrast to the aggressive bluster that Moscow did not hesitate to deploy against a number of other capitals, large and small, Russian diplomats persistently clothed Moscow's opposition to Iranian nuclear ambitions with expressions of extreme politeness. This was not just to protect Russia's financial interest in the Bushehr nuclear power plant, for example. Rather, and much more broadly, it exemplified the basic Russian attitude on how best to deal with Iran and had less to do with economics than with politics, history, and perceptions of lessons learned over the centuries.

Even at the lowest point in relations during the period covered by this study, Moscow in the 1980s kept assiduously in touch with Tehran to inform it of diplomatic developments relating to the Soviet Union's military presence in Afghanistan. Moscow likewise proved adept during the Tajik civil war in the 1990s at simultaneously opposing Iranian revolutionary aspirations in that country while conducting negotiations on what would eventually turn out to be the contract to build the Bushehr nuclear power plant. A decade later, a determination to manage the relationship by staying in close touch even while disagreeing over the increasingly troublesome nuclear issue remained the keystone of Moscow's approach to Tehran.

Moscow's ginger approach seemed predicated on a number of factors. In part, it was the victor's condescension in centuries of skirmishing over borderlands between the two former empires. In other ways, however, it was motivated by wariness of Iran's lingering influence and calculations of how best to discourage its potential bad behavior. Russians still feared the trouble that Iran might be able to stir up especially in Shia Azerbaijan, Persian Tajikistan, and separatist Chechnya. In the Middle East and South Asia, Russian ambitions had to contend with the unchanging reality of Iran's shadow across both regions.

By the time Putin became president, it was easy to demonstrate that Russia was disenchanted by its economic ties to Iran. Despite press hype, they were never robust. In 1998 oil had been selling at only $14 a barrel, Russia had defaulted on more than $40 billion of Soviet-era Paris Club debt, and the Yeltsin administration had precipitated a financial crisis at home when it devalued Russia's own currency. Yet, even with financial chaos still gripping Russia in 1999, Moscow's disappointment over Iran's preference for barter deals and unwillingness or inability to boost non-arms cash-for-goods imports was palpable. Analysts such as Yuri Fedorov dismissively contended that doing business with Iran did not stimulate any serious economic transformations in Russia and so was not worth pursuing.[138]

Even on the widely publicized issue of conventional arms sales, others pointed out that the $200–300 million a year in weapons sales to Iran represented only around 10 percent (actually, even less) of Russia's global arms exports.[139] In fact, China and India, not Iran, were Russia's most lucrative arms customers. By 1999 they were already responsible for more than half of Russia's $4.8 billion in yearly weapons sales, a proportion that rose to more than 80 percent of the $5.12 billion of Russian arms sold in 2004.[140]

In February 2002, Putin had modestly declared "between $20 and $25 to the barrel" to be the optimum price level for oil.[141] By July 2006 the price of oil had hit $78 a barrel. In August Moscow wiped out its Soviet-era debt with a $23.7 billion transfer to the Paris Club of creditors. However important the Bushehr deal and arms sales had been to the cash-strapped Yeltsin government in the 1990s, they were by now of vastly less importance to the oil and gas revenue-flush Putin government.[142]

In Moscow, sober analysts pointed out that Iran in 2006 did not hold great economic interest for Russia as a whole, although it certainly did in a few specific sectors. Though having bested Iran in the battle for Caspian energy resources, Russian energy majors were not shy about courting Iran for stakes elsewhere. Maintaining good relations with Iran was important to Russia's hopes for eventual Lukoil profits from the West Qurna project in Iraq, as well as Lukoil and Gazprom ambitions to become partners in joint ventures with Iranian oil and gas companies working rich land and offshore deposits in Iran itself.[143]

Nevertheless, Russia's worldwide exports the previous year had reached around $250 billion, of which trade with Iran had been less than $1 billion, according to some (actually, somewhere between $1 and 2 billion). Still, Iran represented "very serious political factors" for Russia—in the Caucasus, Central Asia, Afghanistan, and the Caspian basin—and because of these "Russia cannot afford to quarrel with Iran."[144] In Tehran, there were also those who recognized that the approach of both China and Russia to the nuclear issue with Iran "has less to do with commerce and more with politics and influence."[145]

When it came to economics, Russian foreign policy under Putin, with its emphasis on using and advancing economic interests, certainly found Turkey more interesting than Iran, even though Turkey was a historical rival of both going back centuries to the epoch of round-robin wars between the Ottoman, Persian, and Russian empires. The Friendship Treaty that President Boris Yeltsin and Prime Minister Süleyman Demirel had signed on May 25, 1992, had become the basis for a significant expansion of relations between Russia and Turkey.[146] These ties in many significant respects had come to rival and even surpass those between Moscow and Tehran. Putin's unprecedented presidential trip to Ankara in December 2004 underscored the increasing importance of Russian-Turkish relations relative to Russian-Iranian ties.[147] When Putin then returned to Turkey's Black Sea port of Samsun in November 2005 for the official opening of the Blue Stream gas pipeline, trade was approaching the $15 billion level and nearly two million Russians had visited Turkey that year.[148]

The contrast was glaring with Russian-Iranian trade—which had spiked at around $2 billion in 2005 but then plummeted[149]—and the lack of any Putin trip to Iran despite the occasional diplomatic promise of one.[150] There had been numerous teases since Rafsanjani's 1989 visit to Moscow, but neither Gorbachev nor Yeltsin had ever made it to Tehran for a summit. In fact, the only supreme Kremlin leader ever to have done so had been Joseph Stalin. However, Stalin had been there in November–December 1943 for the wartime conference with Franklin Roosevelt and Winston Churchill, not to meet with any Iranian counterpart.[151]

Russia's ties even with Israel rivaled those with Iran and certainly far outweighed them in terms of cultural affinity. A large Russian-speaking population had immigrated to Israel in recent decades. Since 1985 Moscow had pursued rapprochement with Israel—the primary target of Iranian-sponsored state terrorism—even as it began to cultivate relations with the Islamic Republic. Moscow had insisted on its right to reestablish and maintain relations with all of Iran's neighbors, including Israel and Iraq, whatever the level of Tehran's hostility toward them. According to Gorbachev's perestroika comrade in arms Aleksandr Yakovlev, when Tehran complained to Moscow about its reestablishment of relations with Israel, Moscow explained that it would have relations with all counties that wished to have relations with it.[152] Retired CPSU Central Committee official Karen Brutents contended that Russia would avoid being forced to make a choice between Iran and Israel.[153]

In April 2005 Putin became the first Kremlin leader, Soviet or Russian, ever to visit Israel. For years, many Russians had underscored the impact of more than 800,000 immigrants from Russia or the former Soviet Union on relations between Tel Aviv and Moscow. Yuri Fedorov of the USA Institute noted in 1999 that Israel offered Russia many more advantages than did Iran: from expertise in airborne warning and control systems (AWACs) to counterterrorism.[154] Russia's trade with Israel had surpassed $500 million in 1995 and then after the conclusion of a free trade agreement reached up to $1 billion, a figure Putin underscored during Prime Minister Ariel Sharon's visits to Moscow in September 2001 and a year later.[155]

On October 26, 2005, after President Ahmadinejad said that Israel "must be wiped off the map," Foreign Minister Sergei Lavrov called the statement "unacceptable."[156] When Ahmadinejad returned to the subject on December 14 and called the Holocaust a "myth," the Russian MFA issued a formal rebuttal.[157] Yet much to Israel's dismay and Iran's pleasure, Putin in late January 2006 refused to call Hamas a terrorist organization after its success in Palestinian parliamentary elections. Putin then proceeded to invite a Hamas delegation for talks in Moscow in early March, even though Hamas continued to refuse to recognize Israel's right to exist.[158]

## WATCHING THE POT

Years before the nuclear issue attained its critical profile, Kenesh Kulmatov of the Diplomatic Academy maintained that popular opinion in Russia did not expect anything good to come from the Russian-Iranian relationship.[159] Yet however prone to fraying and competition from other partners and even historical enemies, the level of political relations that Russia and Iran achieved by 2006 was remarkable given the unpopularity of each among the other's public and their relatively modest trade relations.

As distasteful as it was to deal with a theocratic regime so near its borders, Moscow over the quarter century surveyed on these pages had been determined to establish a modus vivendi and to do so much on its own terms. To Moscow, the Islamic Republic was a prickly neighbor that could not be avoided and that had to be dealt with, but that still offered some advantage and profit—though not to be exaggerated. As Brutents portrayed Russian policy in the 1980s and 1990s, Moscow's steadfast approach toward the Islamic Republic was to keep the pot from boiling over, prevent relations from snapping, and maintain a measure of good neighborly relations.[160]

Among a generation of Russian officials with vast experience in the region, the Foreign Ministry's Bakhtiyer Khakimov represented a similar consensus in 1999—as Putin edged closer to the presidency—in arguing that it was easier to find common ground with Iran when direct contact was maintained. Iran would always be one of the biggest countries in the region, no matter how serious its economic troubles. Iranians could not be chased into a corner, warned Khakimov, who had personally participated in the budding rapprochement with Iran both before and after the Soviet collapse.

In Khakimov's view, the bottom line was that Moscow got and was still getting good results from this approach. Yes, there were problems with the current regime, Khakimov said while the moderate reformer Khatami was still president, but you could not change it overnight. The situation required an evolutionary, not revolutionary, approach. Rafsanjani earlier, just like Khatami after him, had tried to go faster but ran into obstacles. The outside world needed slowly to encourage the Iranians to change and come out of their self-isolation, recommended Khakimov.[161]

In 2006 surveying the waters roiled by Khatami's successor Ahmadinejad, Russian officials were likely to judge Khakimov's advice all the more necessary given the new Iranian president's radical hard-line politics. For those with long memories, KGB head Yuri Andropov's advice to Tehran station chief Leonid Shebarshin in 1979 probably seemed as adept as ever: "Watch out, brother, the Persians are such a people that they can make a fool of you in a flash, and you won't even have time to groan!"[162]

Tehran's handling of Moscow on the nuclear issue threatened to prove Andropov's warning prescient and to have arguably caught his KGB-trained successor Vladimir Putin short. Yet Russian officials repeatedly acted with great self-restraint toward Iran, whatever the short-term costs. They were ever guided, it seemed, by the view that "any jerky movements can derail the fragile chance to reach a compromise."[163] But it was an accurate reading of this historical hesitation in Moscow that allowed hard-liners in Tehran to push forward with their nuclear program. As the Soviet Union collapsed in 1991, the Iranian leadership had arguably worried that it was losing a valuable counterweight to pressure from the United States. A decade and a half later, however, post-Soviet Russia was still serving that purpose on the nuclear issue so critical to Iran.

In Tehran, there was a tendency in leading quarters to see in the relationship with Russia a guarantee against the threat of international isolation posed by being included in President Bush's "axis of evil," although this was subject to heated debate and distrust of Russian motives. The ultimate preference of significant segments in both Russia and Iran was for better ties with the United States rather than with one another, all of which contributed to the bumpy ride of Russian-Iranian relations. "The prevailing mood among the Russian elite is to identify itself with the West and to be guarded and sometimes hostile toward Islamic countries and Iran," conceded even those in Moscow who argued for closer relations with Iran at the beginning of the Putin years.[164]

Russian diplomat Semyon Gregoryev observed that twenty years after the Islamic revolution, Iran was still very much oriented toward the West economically, technologically, and even psychologically and that it would take work for Russia to strengthen its economic potential there.[165] However, while repulsed by the religious fanaticism of Iran's clerical regime, Moscow was more than willing to profit from the reluctance of Iran's hard-line clerics to enter into regular contacts with Washington, let alone reestablish diplomatic relations.

In the view of the Carnegie Endowment's Aleksey Malashenko, the Russian MFA in the last half of the 1990s actually feared rather than welcomed the rise of Iranian moderates. The MFA foresaw problems when Khatami was first elected in 1997, according to Malashenko, and Russian diplomats on balance had preferred to deal with the harder-line ayatollahs because they were anti-Western.[166] Indeed, the Kremlin had rolled out the red carpet for hard-line Speaker Ali Akbar Nateq-Nuri in April 1997. The MFA under Primakov clearly saw him as the sure winner in the upcoming elections—as did the rest of the world. But eight years later, all were again surprised by Mahmoud Ahmadinejad's election and his subsequent sharp swing of the pendulum away from Mohammad Khatami's policies.

Moscow all along found itself in a Catch-22 situation, or at least fearful of its potential traps. There were those who argued that Russia could deal with the pragmatists in Tehran and indeed should try to help them strengthen their power. Yet these same Iranian pragmatists were most prone to renewing ties with Washington, and the radicals would most bitterly oppose moves in this direction. When Bazhanov visited Iran in early 2000, he was struck by the broad public's love for everything American, and its dislike or at least disinterest in things Russian. But the clerics still hated the United States, perceived Bazhanov, so the Iranian MFA had to tread a fine line in responding to any U.S. overtures.

There was therefore always a modicum of fatalistic unease throughout the 1990s—long predating September 11—over the near-term stability of Russia's relationship with the Islamic Republic, the constancy of Tehran as a partner, and the unpredictability of Iran's ultimate intentions. Carnegie Endowment expert Malashenko argued in late 1999 that while Russian-Iranian ties for the moment were not bad, for Russia cooperation was a strategy, for Iran just a tactic.[167] Russian foreign policy experts who visited Tehran in April 2000 likewise reported that their Iranian colleagues wanted continued contacts with Moscow but needed Washington more, and so were undecided on what kind of a relationship they ultimately wanted with Russia. They did not regard ties to Russia as a priority but judged them nevertheless as helpful to getting Iran back into the club of modern nations. These Iranians had no special affinity to Russia, and their Russia policy was increasingly becoming just one direction of policy among others.[168]

The veteran diplomat Nikolay Kozyrev, whose experiences with Iran dated back to several embassy tours in Tehran during the shah's era, argued toward the end of his career that Iran had always viewed Russia and the United States as competitors and had tried and would continue to try to play on this competition.[169] Oriental Institute expert Irina Zviagelskaya cautioned midway during the Khatami period that the Iranians were rational and would eventually want to maintain a balance in their relations with the United States and with Russia. In fact, Iran's not having another major outside power to balance against Russia was an anomaly. Historically, Iran had usually maintained leverage by having two counterbalancing powers—even the shah cultivated Moscow as well as Washington. Many in Moscow were probably right to fear that the prevailing abnormal situation would be short-lived, that the United States would inevitably be back in Iran, and that Iran would in fact pursue a policy that yielded this result and therefore limited or at least balanced Russian influence.[170]

Six years later, however, the limited contacts between Iran and the United States over Afghanistan in late 2001 and Iraq in early 2003 seemed a dim memory and had not led to wider consultations on other issues, much less to the return to diplomatic relations. In Tehran, government officials touted President Ahmadinejad's letter to President Bush in May 2006 as an invitation to renewed contacts (see chapter 13). In the West, some analysts saw Ayatollah Khomeini's letter to Soviet leader Mikhail Gorbachev in January 1989, which had set the stage for President Rafsanjani's visit to Moscow that summer and the improved Russian-Iranian relations that followed, as a precedent. However, while there were some parallels between the two letters, there were also crucial differences and good reasons to be skeptical.

Khomeini's letter twenty-five years earlier had opened with well wishes to Gorbachev and the Soviet nation and praised Gorbachev's "courage and boldness." It had urged Gorbachev not to fall into the "prison of the West and the Great Satan." It had made but the briefest of mentions of the Soviet invasion of Afghanistan, which it euphemistically referred to as the "issue of Afghanistan." And it had closed with the affirmation that Iran "believes in and respects good-neighborliness and reciprocal relations." This had been widely interpreted as sanctioning the revitalization of relations and putting behind the decade-long Soviet invasion of Afghanistan and Moscow's refusal to fully back Iran in the Iran-Iraq War.[171]

In contrast, Ahmadinejad's letter to President Bush in May 2006 totally lacked any praise. Instead, it was an extensive laundry list of Iranian grievances against America, from the 1953 coup to the "attacks" on Afghanistan and Iraq to the campaign against

Iran's nuclear program. Unlike Khomeini's passing anodyne reference to Afghanistan in his letter to Gorbachev, Ahmadinejad's letter to Bush made no attempt to let bygones be bygones. It once more justified Iran's neuralgic takeover of the American embassy in Tehran in 1979 and even suggested the official collusion of American security and intelligence services in the September 11 attacks. Ahmadinejad's only "invitation" was for Bush to return to the teachings of the prophets, not to enter into a dialogue between Iran and the United States. Rather than cooperation, Ahmadinejad challenged Bush in effect to submit to the court of opinion of the Muslim and nonaligned street.[172] Indeed, a conservative daily described the president's letter as an "ultimatum" to world leaders and praised Ahmadinejad for demonstrating "the intelligent bravery and the glory and power of Islamic Iran once again."[173]

The challenge to the theocratic regime that contacts with America would bring made it highly unlikely that Tehran's ruling hard-line clerics would encourage contacts once any immediate danger was past—such as right after 9/11 and then right before and after the invasion of Iraq—or expand them to include items not on Iran's own agenda. The theocracy would pursue contacts with the United States only if it could assure itself that they would not impact on its domestic grip on power. Hoseyn Shariat Madari, editor in chief of the *Keyhan* newspaper, bluntly told a Russian television interviewer, "I think that our confrontation [with America] will continue exactly as it is now, the way it has been for more than twenty-seven years. I don't think that a day will come when we will not oppose each other. It may be that sometime both sides will agree not to touch each other. But anyway, I know one thing: we cannot find a common language." This was the same Shariat Madari who reportedly met weekly with Spiritual Leader Khamenei over tea to discuss current events.[174]

As the Diplomatic Academy's Bazhanov had argued in early 2000, Tehran would always have plenty of reasons to keep working with Moscow even after any possible rapprochement with the United States.[175] Ahmadinejad's surprise election in June 2005, however, was a mixed blessing for Russian interests. A year later, it was still too early to tell whether it signaled the durable rejuvenation of the Islamic revolution or its troubled last gasp, a victim to its own incompetence and unpopularity. For the time being, the rise of a new generation of Iranian hard-liners again not only put off the return of America to Iran but also meant continued prickly relations with Russia.

In the 1960s and 1970s Soviet diplomats such as the trained Iranist expert Nikolay Kozyrev had felt at home with the shah's "almost European government." After its passing, they had been decidedly estranged by the Islamic theocracy that had toppled it.[176] In summer 2006 the ideologues seemed to be strengthening their grip on power in Tehran and the pragmatists appeared in retreat. A younger generation of Russian diplomats, it seemed, would have to bide its time before having a chance to deal with anything akin to that "almost European" regime that the now elder statesman Ambassador Nikolay Kozyrev so fondly recalled.

# Postscript:
# The Road to Tehran

From summer 2006 into spring 2008, Moscow and Tehran continued their uneasy push-pull-but-don't-let-go dance. Russia awkwardly tried to lead Iran toward better behavior on the nuclear issue, presumably calculating that its kid-glove treatment would strengthen Russian long-term influence in Iran against other historical suitors, particularly the United States. Iran went through the ostentatious motions of partnering with Russia but effectively used Russia's lead and ambitions to frustrate those powers, especially the United States, that were pressing Iran to comply with UN Security Council demands to suspend Iran's nuclear enrichment activities.

Cash-rich and more than fully recovered from the economic collapse of 1998,[1] Russian policy grew still more assertive toward the West. At the same time, Moscow continued—in its own fashion, according to its own lights, always claiming to rule out military measures—to contribute to the international effort to restrain Iran's nuclear program. President Vladimir Putin in Munich in February 2007 sparked headlines when he bitterly charged that the United States had "overstepped its national borders in every way." Yet in the same speech, he also stressed that Russia was engaged with America in developing stricter nonproliferation measures. All but unnoticed, Putin reiterated that Russia still had "concerns about the character and quality of Iran's nuclear programs."[2]

Indeed, after prolonged bargaining, Russia in December 2006 had already joined other UN Security Council members in unanimously approving Resolution 1737, which for the first time called for sanctions against Iran for failing to suspend its nuclear enrichment activities.[3] Iranian president Mahmoud Ahmadinejad lost no time in dismissing the resolution: "Nuclear technology is our right, and no one can take it

301

away from us." Chief nuclear negotiator Ali Larijani vowed that Iran would immediately "begin activities at Natanz . . . and we will drive with full speed."[4]

A month later, Supreme Leader Ali Khamenei, in a transparent effort to sidetrack any follow-on resolution, reportedly conveyed to Putin—through visiting Security Council secretary Igor Ivanov—a proposal for a strategic alliance, including Russian-Iranian cooperation in the Middle East and Central Asia.[5] Detractors at home, however, again criticized Tehran's Look to the East policy for foolishly counting on Russia to block Security Council pressure. Moscow's behavior was "unseemly," charged one reformist daily, and optimism in regard to Russian policy was "unscientific."[6] Sadeq Kharrazi, who had authored the widely publicized Roadmap proposal of May 2003 for U.S.-Iran talks, told the press that counting on Moscow's support had been a mistake from the beginning of the nuclear debate.[7] In fact, Putin reportedly politely brushed aside the strategic relationship offer, as he had done before and as had even Yevgeny Primakov as foreign minister ten years earlier when he had steered bilateral ties through their warmest times.[8]

Nevertheless, Tehran still resisted changing course. Supporters of the hard line pointed out that Resolution 1737's sanctions would have been more severe had it not been for opposition from Russia and the Europeans. They argued that Russia disagreed with American efforts to isolate Iran and asserted that Russia and Iran were consulting together on how to "neutralize American conspiracies . . . through joint security and strategic cooperation."[9] However, they were soon disabused of their confidence in Moscow by Russian approval in March 2007 of Resolution 1747, which broadened Resolution 1737's sanctions. Ahmadinejad immediately called the new resolution's demands "not legal" and cut back even further on Iran's cooperation with the IAEA.[10]

Meanwhile, Iranian politics grew more vicious. In February 2007 Supreme Leader Khamenei renewed the call for national unity in the face of what he labeled the West's psychological warfare.[11] At the end of April, Hossein Mousavian, a former ambassador to Germany and nuclear negotiator, was arrested. The move sent a chill through pragmatist and moderate circles in Tehran. In January Mousavian had called for heeding the UN Security Council and returning to the negotiating table.[12] Then, on May 8, Iranian authorities imprisoned Haleh Esfandiari, director of the Woodrow Wilson International Center for Scholars' Middle East Program, after months of house arrest and weeks of questioning. On May 29 they formally charged Esfandiari and two other dual American-Iranian citizens with espionage.[13] They and Mousavian were just the most publicized of thousands of cases of intimidation and repression. Across the country, Iranians reportedly were increasingly unhappy with the 20 percent inflation rate and 25 percent rise in the price of gasoline brought on by Ahmadinejad's economic and foreign policies.[14]

In January 2007 Deputy Prime Minister and Defense Minister Sergei Ivanov announced that Russia had completed delivery to Iran of the Tor-M1 systems, whose contract he had publicized in December 2005 (see chapter 13).[15] However, while helping to upgrade Iran's air defenses, the deliveries could not provide much comfort to the guardians of Iran's nuclear facilities. As analyst Pavel Felgenhauer pointed out, the relatively short-range Tor-M1s could not defend hardened nuclear sites against blockbuster munitions released from high-flying stealth bombers.[16] To do that, the long-range S-300 was necessary. Beyond the profits from the Tor-M1 deal, fulfillment of the contract seemed more of a political gesture given the system's limited defensive capability. Indeed, a month later, Putin in Munich asserted, "We did this so that Iran did not feel it had been driven into a corner." The Russian president hoped that "the Iranian party will understand and hear our signals."[17]

Moscow, however, was not averse to mixing sticks with carrots. In February 2007 IAEA inspectors reported that Iran had finished installing two 164-centrifuge cascades at Natanz (of the eighteen cascades, or 2,952 centrifuges, planned for the facility).[18] Around the same time, Russia again slowed down work on the Bushehr nuclear power plant.[19] Although publicly disavowed, Russian National Security Council secretary Igor Ivanov the following month reportedly delivered an ultimatum to Tehran: Russia would not deliver fuel for Bushehr unless Iran suspended uranium enrichment.[20] By May, however, Iran had eight cascades up and running at Natanz, and another five either under construction or undergoing tests.[21]

Subsequently, after charging Tehran with falling behind on its payments, Moscow cited technical disruptions in explaining a further delay in the target date for completion of Bushehr. When the original contract had been signed in October 1995, Bushehr had been projected to be finished by spring 2000. By summer 2007 Bushehr's completion date had slipped to fall 2008 at the earliest.[22] The move provoked bitterness in Tehran. An editorial in a reformist daily intoned, "The people may rightfully ask now of the supporters of the Look East policy to openly admit to the abusive conduct and unreliable nature of the Russians."[23] Mohammad Nabi Rudaki, vice chairman of the Majles National Security and Foreign Policy Committee, charged Russia with "repeatedly" stabbing Iran "in the back."[24]

Putin sprung yet another surprise on Tehran on June 7, 2007. For months, Russia had been complaining about American plans to install radars in the Czech Republic and missile interceptors in Poland to defend against missiles from Iran. As recently as June 1, the Russian president had threatened to target the new facilities if the United States went ahead with its missile defense plan.[25] But just a few days later, Putin made an unexpected proposal to President George W. Bush on the margins of the G-8 summit in Heiligendamm, Germany: that Russia and America share real-time data from the Qabala radar installation Russia leased from Azerbaijan.[26] Putin expanded on the offer when he met again with the American president at the Bush family compound at Kennebunkport in early July.[27]

In its delivery, the proposal bore a similarity to Putin's surprise acquiescence in September 2001 to American use of airfields in Central Asia and to his jawboning the next month of Afghan leader Burhanuddin Rabbani to contemplate sharing power in a post-Taliban Kabul (see chapter 10). There was no sign that the Russian president had consulted in advance with Tehran on the Qabala radar offer, even while Putin claimed to have done precisely that with Azerbaijan president Ilham Aliyev. The reformist press in Tehran quickly pounced on the absence of consultation. There were charges that Putin's initiative again proved that Russia "will proceed easily to the brink of officially declaring hostility against countries with which it has friendly relations."[28] When the Iranian Foreign Ministry response finally came on June 17, it was lame. "It looks like Russia doesn't intend to create instability and bring detriment to security in the region where it [Qabala] is located," stated a spokesman, who then tried to shift attention to the Caspian foreign ministers meeting coming up on June 20 in Tehran.[29]

At that ministerial, Foreign Minister Lavrov unexpectedly suggested that it might finally be time for a Caspian summit in Tehran even though the five littoral countries had not reached final agreement on delimitation and other thorny issues.[30] After years of stalling on another five-party summit in the wake of the inconclusive first such meeting in Ashgabat in April 2002, Lavrov's initiative may have been calculated to ease the shock in Tehran over Putin's Qabala initiative. It may have also been intended as an incentive for Iran to cooperate with the IAEA in order to forestall yet another round of debate in the UN Security Council in September and October 2007 and another resolution with yet more stringent sanctions.

Despite the concession on holding a Caspian summit, Moscow did little else to warm relations. When Ahmadinejad attended the SCO summit in Bishkek, Kyrgyzstan, in August 2007, Russia did not make an effort to upgrade Iran's status from observer to full member.[31] Not only that, but there was evidently no Putin-Ahmadinejad bilateral meeting on the margins of the Bishkek multilateral session, and the apparent snub by Russia again became grist for Ahmadinejad's critics at home.[32] Nevertheless, Ahmadinejad a week later in Baku was able to announce a Caspian summit in Tehran for October 16, 2007, and there were consultations in Moscow at the end of August on preparations for the meeting.[33]

Moscow's stalling on Bushehr while holding out the prospect of a Putin visit to Tehran probably contributed to Iran's reanimation of engagement with the IAEA. By the end of August 2007, after a series of meetings beginning with IAEA Director General Mohamed ElBaradei's visit to Tehran on July 11, Iran had negotiated a so-called work plan that would put Iran's intentions to the test over the next few months.[34] As a consequence, a vote in the UN Security Council on a third sanctions resolution was deferred. This was even though the IAEA had reported that Iran now had twelve cascades—nearly two thousand centrifuges—in full operation, with four more cascades—an additional 656 centrifuges—on the way.[35]

In his speech on September 25 to the UN General Assembly, President Ahmadinejad asserted that Iran's nuclear file was no longer the proper business of the Security Council.[36] Still, by late September, Lavrov and Rice and their P5+1 counterparts reached agreement on a two-track approach: await the results of talks between Iran and IAEA Director General ElBaradei and EU foreign policy chief Javier Solana; at the same time, continue to negotiate the text of another resolution that would be considered in November should the results of the ElBaradei and Solana talks with Iran prove unproductive.[37]

In the meantime, after years of polite brush-offs, Putin on October 16 became the first supreme Kremlin leader to visit Tehran since Joseph Stalin attended the wartime summit with Franklin Roosevelt and Winston Churchill in 1943. On that earlier occasion, the Big Three had not even officially informed the Iranian government about their arrival until gossip had first spread the word.[38] Now Putin crammed the Caspian summit, a joint press conference, a solo session with the Iranian press, a bilateral meeting with President Mahmoud Ahmadinejad, and then another meeting with Supreme Leader Ali Khamenei all into one very long day. Putin did not seem to want to spend even one night in Tehran.

The joint statement issued after Putin's meeting with Ahmadinejad touted the "working visit" to Iran as the first ever "in the whole history of relations between the two countries" by a Russian head of state.[39] Khamenei, however, lamented to Putin that "unfortunately, you have been in Tehran not very long."[40] Neither party was reported to have called the other a "strategic partner," although Putin as usual described Russia and Iran as "neighbors and friendly countries" and Ahmadinejad characterized them as "two natural allies."[41]

Aside from the presence of Putin in Tehran, neither the Caspian nor the bilateral summit documents broke any significant ground. The agreement for regular meetings of foreign ministers and presidents by the five Caspian leaders served to underscore that much work remained to resolve seabed delimitation and other sticky issues. The nonaggression language in the Caspian declaration—"the Parties stress that under no circumstances will they allow their territories to be used by other states to commit aggression and other military actions against any of the Parties"—simply paraphrased the 1921 Soviet-Iranian Treaty (minus its language giving Soviet troops the green light in advance to intervene in Iran against any hostile third power) and the more recent 2001 Russia-Iran Treaty and the 2002 Azerbaijani-Iranian Accord (see chapters 1 and 14).[42]

Similarly, the call in the Russia-Iran bilateral statement for agreement on a long-term plan for the development of "trade and economic, industrial and scientific and technical cooperation and an agreement on facilitating and protecting capital investment" merely resurrected the negotiations apparently dropped after 2003, when an earlier draft had been initialed at the deputy minister level by both sides (see chapter 11).[43] Gorbachev and Rafsanjani had actually signed such a document in 1989 to run until 2000 (see chapter 2). Although Ahmadinejad touted possible deals to construct a Bushehr-2 and 3, they were not mentioned in the statement.[44] The statement, moreover, did not spell out when Russia would deliver fuel for Bushehr, and Putin in his meeting with Iranian journalists would not be pinned down: "I only made promises to my mother, when I was a little boy."[45]

Still, Putin's visit was immensely valuable to Ahmadinejad and Khamenei, given the domestic criticism of their policy of gambling that Russia would shield Iran from serious sanctions by the UN Security Council. However, Putin's meetings may have been a diplomatic cover for delivering a more serious message on the nuclear issue in private in Tehran. Indeed, within days there were press reports that Putin had "offered a special proposal."[46] The source of those reports, however, was Ali Larijani, who a few days later was replaced as Iran's lead nuclear negotiator by Saeed Jalili. The latter was reportedly a close friend and confidant of Ahmadinejad, and the switch sparked much speculation about a hardening in Iranian nuclear tactics.[47]

In early October, however, even before visiting Tehran, Putin had dropped strong hints that he would remain in power as prime minister after relinquishing the presidency.[48] By December 17, Putin declared he was "ready" to become prime minister if First Deputy Prime Minister Dmitry Medvedev were elected president on March 2, 2008.[49] The forty-two-year old Medvedev had first worked with Putin in St. Petersburg for city mayor Anatoly Sobchak in the early 1990s.[50] In June 2002 President Putin had installed then-deputy chief of the Presidential Administration Medvedev as Gazprom board chairman (see chapter 8). The state takeover of Gazprom had been the model for what the Putin regime had in store for other "strategic" sectors. More than five years later, the prospective Medvedev-Putin tandem augured not only continuity in Russian policy but also safekeeping of Putin's personal wealth, now estimated by some at over $40 billion.[51]

Since Putin was clearly not a lame duck, Tehran would have to give serious consideration to whatever it was that he had suggested while in the Iranian capital. If the Islamic Republic's leadership chose simply to pocket Putin's visit yet yield nothing on the nuclear issue, the slight could be expected to further complicate future relations between Moscow and Tehran.

A month after the Tehran summit, however, the IAEA reported that Iran had finished installing all eighteen cascades at Natanz and that the facility's nearly three thousand centrifuges were up and running. The agency noted that its knowledge of Iran's nuclear program was "diminishing" and that it was "not in a position to provide credible assurances about the absence of undeclared nuclear material and activities in Iran without full implementation of the Additional Protocol."[52] In Moscow, the Foreign Ministry spokesman underscored that the UN Security Council's demands remained in effect and again called on Iran to suspend all its enrichment work and implement the additional protocol.[53]

On December 3, to wide surprise, an unclassified version of the key judgments of a National Intelligence Estimate (NIE) released in Washington stated with "high confidence" that Iran had "halted its nuclear weapons program" four years earlier, in fall 2003. A footnote explained that the halt applied only to "Iran's nuclear weapon design and weaponization work" and to its "covert" uranium conversion and enrichment efforts. The NIE estimated that with the declared centrifuges operating at Natanz, "Iran probably would be technically capable of producing enough HEU [highly enriched uranium] for a weapon sometime during the 2010–2015 time frame" and that "Iran has the scientific, technical and industrial capacity eventually to produce nuclear weapons if it decides to do so."[54] Although not remarked in the NIE's key judgments, Iran also had a delivery vehicle—the Shahab-3 ballistic missile—already developed should it choose to go forward with weaponization.

Release of the NIE's conclusions immediately took the steam out of efforts to move toward another sanctions resolution in the UN Security Council.[55] The next day, when Putin met in Moscow with Saeed Jalili, the Russian president noted, "Our cooperation is becoming more active almost in every area." Nevertheless, Putin did not second Jalili's assertion that Russian-Iranian relations were "at the stage of strategic partnership." Instead, Putin again urged Iran to comply with the IAEA's inspection requirements and with the demands of the UN Security Council, including its call on Iran to freeze its uranium enrichment activities.[56]

Commenting on the U.S. NIE, Foreign Minister Lavrov was quick to crow that Russia had no data of its own that Iran had been engaged in a military nuclear program even before 2003.[57] Still, Putin and Lavrov had good memories. Though before their watch, Russia's own SVR had publicly concluded as far back as 1993 (see chapter 6) that Iran had a nuclear research program with military applications. More recently, none other than then–Russian MinAtom head Aleksandr Rumyantsev had declared in 2003 (see chapter 11) that the single experimental cascade discovered that year at Natanz made it "possible" for Iran "to enrich uranium to high weapons grade."[58] Even Iranian nuclear negotiator Hassan Rowhani had conceded in 2005 (see chapter 13) that "having fuel cycle capability almost means that the country that possesses this capability is able to produce nuclear weapons, should that country have the political will to do so." Lavrov's insistence that Iran "should not have the fuel cycle" did not appear to have surprised Rowhani at the time.[59]

What was true of Iranian capabilities as far back as 2003, when Tehran had only one experimental cascade in operation, was no less true four years later, when eighteen full cascades were up and running at Natanz. In retrospect, Russia could take some—albeit unvoiced—credit for having contributed to the pressure that apparently caused Iran to halt its weaponization program in 2003 and, for a time, suspend its enrichment effort. After the discoveries at Natanz, Russia had stalled the negotiations on the protocol for handling spent fuel from Bushehr for over two years until Iran had committed to resuspend its conversion and enrichment activities (see chapter 13). Since then, in what was widely interpreted as continued pressure on Iran, Russia had repeatedly pushed back the date on which it expected Bushehr to be operational, and thus the time frame in which Russia would actually begin to ship fuel for Bushehr (see chapter 13 and above).

Nevertheless, without any apparent positive response by Iran to whatever Putin had proposed while in Tehran in October, Moscow on December 16 at last began to ship fuel to Bushehr. This was a clear reversal of long-standing policy. In March 2007, as we have seen, Security Council secretary Igor Ivanov reportedly had told Tehran that Russia would not deliver fuel for Bushehr unless Iran suspended its uranium enrichment activities. As recently as October, Putin had refused to be pinned down in Tehran on when fuel deliveries would begin. As long ago as June 2003, Putin reportedly had pledged to his counterparts at the G-8 summit in Evian that Russia would not deliver fuel to Bushehr until Tehran unconditionally signed and implemented an IAEA additional protocol. That same month, MinAtom head Rumyantsev had asserted that Russia would supply fuel to Bushehr "only after Iran has put all of its nuclear facilities under the control of the International Atomic Energy Agency and provided answers to all questions the IAEA may ask" (see chapter 11).

Now the argument was turned around. The Russian Foreign Ministry asserted that the fuel shipments should make it possible for Iran to comply with IAEA and UN Security Council demands, especially for suspension of Iran's uranium enrichment activities, since the Russian fuel supplies made it unnecessary for Iran to produce its own.[60] All the same, Iran countered that it would not suspend since it needed additional fuel for another power plant, at Darkhovin north of Bushehr, which it said it was building on its own.[61] Iranian energy minister Parviz Fatah asserted that Bushehr would start operating at half capacity as early as March 21, 2008.[62] Sergei Shmatko, head of Russia's Atomstroyexport, rebutted that the start-up of Bushehr "cannot be guaranteed before the end of 2008."[63]

As 2007 drew to a close, a pro-government conservative newspaper in Iran asserted, "The start of the new nuclear interaction between Tehran and Moscow coincides with the recognition of Iran as a powerful nuclear power by the world."[64] The oppositionist press, however, warned that Russian policy toward Iran continued to be "ambiguous, equivocal and contradictory." Moscow's latest postponement of a start-up date for Bushehr, it argued, was just "the most recent promise broken by the Russians," who "should not be trusted anymore."[65] Indeed, in Russia the press carried speculation that Moscow was still using the Bushehr launch date as a "strong diplomatic lever" on Iran to comply with IAEA and UN Security Council demands.[66]

Moscow had probably made the decision to ship fuel to Bushehr before release of the American NIE but nevertheless benefitted from the publicity over the document. The U.S. intelligence services' conclusion that Iran had likely disbanded its weaponization program in 2003 allowed Moscow to argue that there was more time for diplomacy, even while Russia was retreating from its own criteria for moving ahead with fuel shipments to Bushehr. The go-ahead on fuel was also consistent with Russia's line from the beginning, that Bushehr was independent from other Iranian nuclear issues, even though Russia in practice had linked Bushehr to them as a way of getting Tehran's attention. Moreover, although the financial importance of Bushehr was no longer as great given high oil prices, Russia was still looking for more nuclear power plant customers and wanted to behave as a reliable contractor.

All the same, Moscow at the end of 2007 was faced with an Iran that had a large-scale nuclear fuel cycle in development, something Moscow had opposed for years. ✓ Putin and his advisers in all likelihood finally calculated that outside pressure no longer stood a fair chance of reversing that Iranian accomplishment, and they were not willing to sacrifice Russian interests in Iran to do so. Moscow appeared resigned to living with the reality of an Iranian enrichment capability, while continuing to maneuver with those levers it still had at its disposal to encourage Iran not to expand its enrichment potential any further and not to reconstitute its suspended nuclear weaponization program. Besides, in going ahead with fuel for Bushehr, Moscow could continue to flaunt an increasingly assertive and distinctive policy vis-à-vis Washington, while at ✓ the same time working with Washington to constrain Iran's future development as a nuclear power.

Indeed, in late December 2007, Defense Minister Mostafa Mohammad Najjar announced that Iran had finalized a contract with Russia for future delivery of the S-300 air defense missile system. This was a considerably more advanced and longer-range system than the Tor-M1 and had been on Iranian shopping lists as far back as 1998 (see chapter 7).[67] Should Russia indeed go ahead and sell it to Iran, Tehran would finally have a three-tiered, echeloned air defense capable of protecting sites such as Bushehr and Natanz from an extensive array of air attacks. Despite Russian denials of Najjar's assertion, there were several detailed accounts in the Russian media of negotiations over the system going back several years. What appeared to be deliberate stringing out of actual deliveries was seen by some as another Russian effort to encourage Iran to come to acceptable terms on its nuclear enrichment program with the international community.[68]

In January 2008 Foreign Minister Lavrov joined his P5+1 counterparts in Berlin. There they all finally agreed on the draft of the third sanctions resolution, which they had been negotiating since summer 2007. They would next submit it to the other members of the Security Council for their amendments.[69] Lavrov reacted pointedly several weeks later to Iran's February 4 announcement that it had tested what it called a space launch vehicle, which experts evaluated as an advanced version of the Shahab-3 ballistic missile.[70] "Russia does not approve of constant demonstration of [Iran's] intention to develop the missile sector and to enrich uranium," complained the foreign minister.[71]

On March 3 in Vienna, IAEA Director General Mohamed ElBaradei reported that new evidence on Iran's past efforts to develop nuclear weapons was of "serious concern." Later the same day in New York, the UN Security Council finally approved Resolution 1803, in gestation since the previous summer. This authorized a further expansion of international sanctions against Iranian nuclear program–related activities.[72] A P5+1 ministerial statement made public after the vote promised to freshen up the package of incentives offered to Iran in June 2006 (see chapter 13) and urged Tehran to return to negotiations.[73] Deputy Foreign Minister Sergey Kislyak, Russia's chief negotiator, called UNSCR 1803 "another signal to Tehran about the need to cooperate with the IAEA and the UN Security Council."[74]

President Ahmadinejad, however, again brushed off the resolution as of "no importance or prestige."[75] He had just returned from Baghdad—the first visit to Iraq by an Iranian leader since the 1979 Islamic Revolution—and was feeling his oats.[76] In May the Iranian leadership would have more reason to take satisfaction from developments in the region after the Iranian-supported Shia-based Hezbollah deployed armed militias in the middle of Beirut and won veto power in future Lebanese governments.[77] In addition, international sanctions were pinching Iran less sharply than they otherwise might have. The price of oil had surged past $100 per barrel on world markets in February.[78] In May it would spike at one point to over $135 a barrel.[79]

Putin and Bush met together for the last time as presidents in Sochi on April 6. As had become routine, their joint declaration again included a call for Iran to comply with the requirements of the UNSC, now spelled out by Resolutions 1737, 1747, and 1803.[80] Already by this time, however, at least one major Russian newspaper had editorially concluded that Moscow had failed in "tying" Russia's "strategically important southern neighbor to itself." Instead, argued *Nezavisimaya Gazeta,* it turned out the other way around: Russia had wound up "tied to the geopolitical strategy of its Islamic neighbor state." Moreover, Iran did not intend to sacrifice its "own interests for the sake of 'friendship with the great Russian people.'"[81]

On May 7 Dmitry Medvedev assumed the presidency. The next day a still very powerful and arguably still dominant Putin became premier.[82] On May 13 Iran presented its own proposal for negotiations to the P5+1. While appealing for wide-ranging talks, it rejected abiding by the three UNSC resolutions and made no pledge to suspend uranium enrichment.[83]

With centuries of dealing with Iran, Moscow continued to play for the long-term, sensitive to the reality that it would always have Iran as a near neighbor. In the short run, Iran played for more time in which to develop its nuclear enrichment capabilities and missile delivery know-how and saw Russia's policy of slowing and watering down American and European pressure as useful. Russia remained opposed to Iranian efforts to develop nuclear weapons and the missiles with which to deliver them. Nevertheless, Russia continued to judge them as further away than did the United States, and so apparently calculated that it still had time to brake Iranian efforts if not reverse them. Left up in the air was how far the Iranian programs would advance by the time they were stopped, if they were stopped.

In the meantime, the Islamic Republic might be a prickly regional actor with no particular fondness for Russia. The Iranian public and oppositionist elites might still prefer to deal more closely with the West and the United States in particular. But the clerical leadership entrenched at the top still kept alive the anti-American animus of the Khomeini Revolution three decades earlier. That opened up continuing opportunities for Moscow as it dealt with a Tehran to all appearances determined to steer clear of any broad rapprochement with Washington but also for Iran to push forward a nuclear program that could eventually pose a security threat to Russia itself.

# *Notes*

## CHAPTER 1: FROM THE SHAHS TO THE AYATOLLAH

1. Nikolay Ivanovich Kozyrev, interview by author, Moscow, September 18, 2000. After leaving Tehran, Kozyrev served from 1984 to late 1986 as minister-counselor in the Soviet embassy in Kabul and simultaneously as foreign policy adviser to the Afghan Ministry of Foreign Affairs (MFA). Kozyrev succeeded Vasiliy Stepanovich Safronchuk in this double-hatted capacity after the 1982–1983 interregnum of Stanislav Gavrilov, who died in July 1983 after a heart attack. From November 1986 to December 1991, Kozyrev worked out of the Foreign Ministry in Moscow as ambassador-at-large for Afghanistan, observer at the UN proximity talks on Afghanistan, and secretary to the Politburo Commission for Afghanistan, which was headed by Foreign Minister Shevardnadze. From 1992 to 1998, Kozyrev was the Russian Federation's first ambassador to Ireland.

2. Barbara Janusz, *The Caspian Sea: Legal Status and Regime Problems*, Russia and Eurasia Program, Briefing Paper, REP BP 05/02 (London: Chatham House, August 2005), 2.

3. Laurence Kelly, *Diplomacy and Murder in Tehran: Alexander Griboyedov and Imperial Russia's Mission to the Shah of Persia* (London: I. B. Tauris, 2002), passim; Firuz Kazemzadeh, "Iranian Relations With Russia and the Soviet Union, to 1921," in *The Cambridge History of Iran*, ed. Peter Avery, Gavin Hambly, and Charles Melville (Cambridge: Cambridge University Press, 1991), 7: 338–339; and Tadeusz Swietochowski, *Russia and Azerbaijan: A Borderland in Transition* (New York: Columbia University Press, 1995), 5–7.

4. Kazemzadeh, "Iranian Relations," 341; and George Lenczowski, *Russia and the West in Iran, 1918–1948: A Study in Big-Power Rivalry* (Ithaca: Cornell University Press, 1949), 3.

5. James Critchlow, "Caravans and Conquests," *The Wilson Quarterly* 16, no. 3 (Summer 1992): 29–30.

6. Kazemzadeh, "Iranian Relations," 343–344; Lenczowski, *Russia and the West*, 5, 42–43, 168–172, and 194–199; Sandra Mackey, *The Iranians: Persia, Islam, and the Soul of a Nation* (New York: Plume Books, 1998), 160–165; and Amin Saikal, "Iranian Foreign Policy, 1921–1979," in *The Cambridge History of Iran*, 7: 434.

7. Lenczowski, *Russia and the West*, 49–50; and Swietochowski, *Russia and Azerbaijan*, 229.

8. Kazemzadeh, "Iranian Relations," 340–347; Lenczowski, *Russia and the West*, 50–51 and 317–318; and Janusz, *Caspian Sea*, 2.

9. In 1951, for example, Darius Foruhar founded the ultranationalist Pan-Iranist Party of Iran (Hizb-i Pan-Iranist-i Iran), which called for the reabsorption of the Caucasus, Afghanistan, and Bahrain into Iran. Foruhar and his wife, well-known dissidents

decades later, were brutally murdered in November 1998, the first in a string of such assassinations around this time. On Foruhar and his pan-Iranist party, see Michael Rubin, *Into the Shadows: Radical Vigilantes in Khatami's Iran* (Washington, DC: Washington Institute for Near East Policy, 2001), 90. In 1987 *Moscow News* rebutted the claim made in the newspaper *Jomhuri-e Eslami* that Tajikistan, Turkmenistan (Turkmenia), Uzbekistan, and some Georgian districts ought to be liberated from the USSR (Moscow World Service, May 20, 1987, in Foreign Broadcast Information Service, *Daily Report for the Soviet Union* (Springfield, VA: National Technical Information Service, May 20, 1987), H 2 [FBIS-SOV-87-097, May 20, 1987, H 2]).

10. Background interviews by author, Baku, April 2000.

11. Saikal, "Iranian Foreign Policy," 446–447.

12. Nikolay Kozyrev, interview.

13. Quoted in Rouhollah K. Ramazani, *Iran's Foreign Policy, 1941–1973* (Charlottesville: University Press of Virginia, 1975), 316. See also Shahram Chubin and Sepehr Zabih, *The Foreign Relations of Iran: A Developing State in a Zone of Great-Power Conflict* (Berkeley: University of California Press, 1974), 50–69.

14. Nikolay Kozyrev, interview.

15. Robert O. Freedman, *Soviet Policy Toward the Middle East Since 1970*, 3rd ed. (New York: Praeger, 1982), 19–21.

16. Efraim Karsh, "From Ideological Zeal to Geopolitical Realism: The Islamic Republic and the Gulf," in *The Iran-Iraq War: Impact and Implications*, ed. Efraim Karsh (New York: St. Martin's Press, 1989), 26–27; and Jeffrey Pickering, *Britain's Withdrawal From East of Suez: The Politics of Retrenchment* (New York: St. Martin's Press, 1998), 174 and 185.

17. Freedman, *Soviet Policy*, 27, 35, and 113.

18. Ibid., 28 and 119.

19. Nikolay Kozyrev, interview. See also Galia Golan, *Soviet Policies in the Middle East: From World War Two to Gorbachev* (Cambridge: Cambridge University Press, 1990), 178 and 181; Freedman, *Soviet Policy*, 27; and Firuz Kazemzadeh, "Soviet-Iranian Relations: A Quarter-Century of Freeze and Thaw," in *The Soviet Union and the Middle East: The Post-World War II Era*, ed. Ivo J. Lederer and Wayne S. Vucinich (Stanford: Hoover Institution Press, 1974), 72 and 76.

20. Vasiliy Stepanovich Safronchuk, interview by author, Moscow, December 8, 1999. Safronchuk was deputy head, Second European Department, USSR MFA, until April 1979. From May to December 1979, he served as foreign policy adviser with the rank of ambassador to Afghanistan prime minister and then head of state Hafizullah Amin. From March 1980 to 1982, Safronchuk was adviser with rank of ambassador to Foreign Minister Shah Mohammad Dost and Soviet observer to Afghan proximity talks in Geneva. From July 25, 1982, to 1985, Safronchuk was head of the Middle East (Afghanistan, Iran, Turkey) Department in the Soviet Foreign Ministry. From 1985 to 1986, he was deputy USSR UN Permanent Representative. From 1985 to 1992, Safronchuk served as undersecretary general for political and Security Council affairs at the United Nations in New York City. He passed away in March 2004.

21. Nina Mikhaylovna Mamedova, interview by author, Moscow, December 6, 1999. Mamedova was head of sector for Iran, Institute of Oriental Studies.

22. Karen Nersesovich Brutents, interview by author, Moscow, December 9, 1999. Now retired, Brutents served for many years as one of Boris Ponomarev's deputies in the CPSU Central Committee's International Department. For an extensive analysis of the 1970s and 1980s writings of Brutents and a number of other Soviet specialists cited or interviewed years later in the present work—including Rotislav Ulyanovskiy,

Nodari Simonia, Alexander Yakovlev, Yevgeniy Primakov, and Anatoly Gromyko—see Rajan Menon, *Soviet Power and the Third World* (New Haven: Yale University Press, 1986), 19–88.

23. Nikolay Kozyrev, interview.
24. Shaul Bakhash, *The Reign of the Ayatollahs: Iran and the Islamic Revolution* (New York: Basic Books, 1984), 9–18 and 35–51; and Mackey, *Iranians*, 248–249 and 273–285.
25. Golan, *Soviet Policies*, 185–186.
26. Ibid., 186–189.
27. Quoted in Odd Arne Westad, *The Global Cold War: Third World Interventions and the Making of Our Times* (New York: Cambridge University Press, 2005), 330; and Jussi Hanhimäki and Odd Arne Westad, *The Cold War: A History in Documents and Eyewitness Accounts* (New York: Oxford University Press, 2003), 564. For another excellent analysis of Moscow's intertwined approaches to Tehran and Kabul in the decade leading up to the Soviet military intervention in Afghanistan, see Malcolm Yapp, "Colossus or Humbug? The Soviet Union and its Southern Neighbours," in *The Soviet Union and the Third World*, ed. E. J. Feuchtwanger and Peter Nailor (New York: St. Martin's Press, 1981), 137–163.
28. Shebarshin is not precise on when he arrived in Tehran. Vladimir Kuzichkin, however, puts it in May 1979. Kuzichkin also recounts Shebarshin's introduction of himself to the KGB staff at the embassy, in which he told the staff about his meeting with Andropov. See Vladimir Kuzichkin, *Inside the KGB: My Life in Soviet Espionage* (New York: Pantheon Books, 1990), 280–281.
29. Leonid Vladimirovich Shebarshin, *Ruka Moskvy: Zapiski nachal'nika sovetskoi razvedki* [The hand of Moscow: Notes of the chief of soviet espionage] (Moscow: Tsentr-100, 1992), 175. Shebarshin ended his KGB career as head of its First Main Directorate (for foreign intelligence) from February 6, 1989, to September 23, 1991. After the Soviet Union's collapse, this directorate was transformed into what became the Foreign Intelligence Service (SVR) of the Russian Federation (see "Russia: Foreign Intelligence Service [SVR] Press Service Director on Differences Between SVR and Former KGB's First Main Directorate," *Voyenno-Promyshlennyy Kuryer*, August 4, 2004 [FBIS: Open Source Center, https://www.opensource.gov; or World News Connection, http://wnc.dialog.com]).
30. Irina D. Zviagelskaya, interview by author, Moscow, December 7, 1999. Zviagelskaya worked in the Central Asia Department at the Institute of Oriental Studies and was vice president of the International Center for Strategic and Political Studies.
31. G. Avdeev, "Dom na Vesal-e Shirazi" [The Building on Vesal-e Shirazi], *Aziya i Afrika segodnya*, no. 2 (2000): 55.
32. Alexandr Bovin, "With Koran and Saber!!!" *Nedelya*, no. 36, signed to press September 4, 1979 [FBIS-SOV-79-176, September 10, 1979, H 1].
33. Kuzichkin, *KGB*, 88–89, 132, 225, and 270–272.
34. Nikolay Kozyrev, interview. The Soviet embassy was attacked on January 1, 1980; on December 27, 1980, the first anniversary of the Soviet invasion of Afghanistan; and in early March 1988, when Tehran was hit by Soviet SCUD missiles during the "war of the cities" phase of the Iran-Iraq War. See Shebarshin, *Ruka*, 128–130.
35. This was actually the second time; the first had been on February 3, 1959. Each time, Moscow refused to recognize Tehran's action. See T. B. Millar with Robin Ward, eds. "Treaty of Friendship Between Persia and the Russian Federal Soviet Republic," in *Current International Treaties* (New York: New York University Press, 1984), editors' footnote, 408. See also Golan, *Soviet Policies*, 177 and 189.
36. Lenczowski, *Russia and the West*, 50–51 and 317–318.

37. Nikolay Kozyrev, interview.

38. Nodari A. Simonia, interview by author, Moscow, April 4, 2000. Simonia served as deputy director of the Institute of World Economy and International Relations (IMEMO).

39. Bakhtiyer Marufovich Khakimov, interview by author, Moscow, December 6, 1999. Khakimov at the time was director of the First CIS Department (general CIS problems) in the Russian Foreign Ministry. Earlier, he had worked on the Iran Desk of the Foreign Ministry, from at least 1989 to 1996; then he was Russian Federation ambassador to Namibia. Khakimov accompanied Foreign Ministers Eduard Shevardnadze and Andrey Kozyrev and First Deputy Foreign Minister Anatoly Adamishin on many of their trips to Iran and Tajikistan.

40. In August 1980 Iranian foreign minister Sadeq Qotbzadeh wrote a public letter to Soviet foreign minister Andrey Gromyko charging, "You have proved in practice that you are no less satanic than the US." Gromyko in turn had charged, also publicly, that Qotbzadeh's effort to "disgrace" the Soviet Union by placing it "on the same level as the United States" amounted to "irresponsible behavior" and "completely baseless claims." (See Dilip Hiro, *Iran Under the Ayatollahs* (London: Routledge & K. Paul, 1985), 285–286; and "Gromyko Replies to 'Baseless Claims' in Qotbzadeh Letter," Moscow in Persian to Iran [FBIS-SOV-80-170, August 29, 1980, H 1-2].) Much had changed since March 1979, when rebels in Herat province (led by Ismail Khan, who would govern Herat after the ouster of the Taliban in late 2001) had mounted a brief but bloody uprising against the Peoples' Democratic Party of Afghanistan (PDPA) regime of Nur Mohammad Taraki and Hafizullah Amin in Kabul. The PDPA had cried Iranian interference, and Safronchuk, who had still not arrived in Kabul at the time, later wrote that the rebellion's foreign support came mostly from Iran. (See Vasiliy Safronchuk, "Afghanistan in the Taraki Period," *International Affairs*, January 1991, 84; and Raymond L. Garthoff, *Détente and Confrontation: American-Soviet Relations From Nixon to Reagan*, rev. ed. (Washington, DC: Brookings Institution, 1994), 995–996, for a more nuanced assessment.) Moscow, nevertheless, was still hoping at that time to be able to work with the new regime in Tehran, and Soviet ambassador to Kabul Aleksandr Puzanov "warned Taraki not to provoke an open Afghan-Iranian conflict while the Soviet Union took 'new initiatives' with the Ayatollah Khomeini." (See Odd Arne Westad, "Prelude to Invasion: The Soviet Union and the Afghan Communists, 1978–1979," *The International History Review* 16, no. 1 (February 1994): 57.)

41. Khakimov, interview.

42. In his interview with this author, Safronchuk said that Soviet commandos had hoped that Amin would be captured alive. In his written memoir, Safronchuk wrote that Amin was killed by enemies within the PDPA in their armed assault on the Kasre Darul Palace. They also had hoped to capture Amin alive and had gotten Amin's doctor and cook to slip him a large dose of soporific. Amin had grown suspicious, however, had his stomach pumped, grabbed a Kalashnikov, and was killed resisting the assault on his quarters. See Vasiliy Safronchuk, "Afghanistan in the Amin Period," *International Affairs*, February 1991, 95–96.

43. Safronchuk, interview.

44. Leonid Brezhnev, "Accountability Report of the CPSU Central Committee to the 26th CPSU Congress and the Immediate Tasks of the CPSU in the Field of Domestic and Foreign Policy," Moscow Domestic Service, February 23, 1981 [FBIS-SOV-81-036, February 24, 1981, Supplement, 10].

45. R. Ulyanovskiy, "Moral Principles in Politics, and Policy in the Sphere of Morals: Iran—What Next?" *Literaturnaya Gazeta*, June 22, 1983 [FBIS-SOV-83-127, June 30, 1983, H 5].

46. Rotislav Ulyanovskiy, "The Fate of the Iranian Revolution," *Kommunist*, no. 8 (May 1985), 107 and 110.

47. Vladimir Ivanovich Gudimenko, interview by author, Moscow, March 31, 2000. From 1983 to August 18, 1991, Gudimenko had worked as a staffer, then a senior staffer ("referent") in the sector for Iran, Afghanistan, and Turkey of the CPSU Central Committee's International Department. He had handled Gorbachev's correspondence with Khomeini in 1989. On Ulyanovskiy, see also Safronchuk, "Taraki," 88–89; Georgiy Markovich Korniyenko, *Kholodnaya Voyna* [Cold War] (Moscow: Mezhdunarodnyye Otnosheniya, 1995), 190; Karen Nersesovich Brutents, *Tridtsat' let na Staroy Ploshchadi* [Thirty years on Old Square] (Moscow: Mezhdunarodnyye Otnosheniya, 1998), 451; and Kuzichkin, *KGB*, 288.

48. Shahram Chubin and Charles Tripp, *Iran and Iraq at War* (Boulder: Westview Press, 1988), 26.

49. Mackey, *Iranians*, 317.

50. Rodger Shanahan, "The Islamic Da'wa Party: Past Development and Future Prospects," *Middle East Review of International Affairs* 8, no. 2 (June 2004): 17–18. None other than Sadr's nephew Moqtada Sadr attained prominence in post-Saddam Iraq. In 1999 Moqtada Sadr's father also lost his life to the Hussein regime.

51. On the origins and events leading up to the war's outbreak and on the war aims of Iran and Iraq, this account draws on Bakhash, *Reign*, 125–129; Chubin and Tripp, *Iran and Iraq*, 13–67; Golan, *Soviet Policies*, 157–196; Stephen R. Grummon, *The Iran-Iraq War: Islam Embattled* (New York: Praeger, 1982), 1–21; Dilip Hiro, *The Longest War: The Iran-Iraq Military Conflict* (New York: Routledge, 1991), 7–39; Karsh, "From Ideological Zeal to Geopolitical Realism," 26–30; and Oles M. Smolansky, *The USSR and Iraq: The Soviet Quest for Influence*, with Bettie Smolansky (Durham: Duke University Press, 1991), 188–229.

52. Hiro, *Longest War*, 250–251.

53. Brezhnev, "Accountability Report." [FBIS-SOV-81-036, February 24, 1981, Supplement, 11 and 15–16]. On the December 1980 proposal, see Garthoff, *Détente and Confrontation*, 1108–1109. On Soviet diplomatic initiatives toward the Persian Gulf during the war's early phase, see also Grummon, *Iran-Iraq*, 57 and 63–71.

54. Hiro, *Longest War*, 97, 179, and 197–198; and Shanahan, "Da'wa Party," 16–25.

55. This account of the initial and middle periods of the Iran-Iraq War draws on Amazia Baram, "Iraq: Between East and West," in *Iran-Iraq War: Impact and Implications*, 78–97; Chubin and Tripp, *Iran and Iraq*, 188–240; Freedman, *Moscow*, 71–204; Hiro, *Longest War*, 215–222; Robert S. Litwak, "The Soviet Union and the Iran-Iraq War," in *Iran-Iraq War: Impact and Implications*, 200–214; and Smolansky, *USSR and Iraq*, 230–248.

56. As quoted in Freedman, *Moscow*, 215. Rajai, appointed prime minister in August 1980, by June 1981 succeeded in ousting Abolhassan Banisadr, elected in January 1980 as Iran's first president. Before Rajai could be elected president in his own right, however, he was killed by a bomb on August 30, 1981. Ali Khamenei was then elected president in October 1981. See Bakhash, *Reign*, 90–91, 106, 114, 125–165, 219, and 224.

57. The United States by September 1987 had sent a convoy of some forty warships into the Persian Gulf to protect twelve reflagged Kuwaiti tankers. The USSR to some extent mollified Iran by calling for the withdrawal of all American and allied warships from the Gulf but stopped short of the Iranian insistence that all foreign navies should leave the Gulf. Moscow also suggested a multilateral naval presence authorized by the UN Security Council, which presumably would have included Soviet ships. See Chubin and Tripp, *Iran and Iraq*, 226–228, 233, and 237.

58. Tehran Television, March 24, 1988, as quoted in W. Raymond Duncan and Carolyn McGiffert Ekedahl, *Moscow and the Third World Under Gorbachev* (Boulder: Westview Press, 1990), 130.

59. Safronchuk, interview.

60. Richard Herrmann, "The Role of Iran in Soviet Perceptions and Policy," in *Neither East nor West: Iran, the Soviet Union, and the United States*, ed. Nikki R. Keddie and Mark J. Gasiorowski (New Haven: Yale University Press, 1990), 81; and Fred Halliday, "The Iranian Revolution and Great-Power Politics," in *Neither East nor West*, 254.

61. Swietochowski, *Russia and Azerbaijan*, 186.

62. Ibid., 170.

63. Ibid., 185. Tabriz in fact was the cradle of four revolutions in Iran in the twentieth century. These revolts were not, however, for independence, but rather for provincial autonomy in the context of grievances against violations of the constitution by the shah reigning in Tehran at the time: the 1908 uprising led by Sattar Khan; the 1920 Mohammad Khiabani rebellion; the 1945–46 Autonomous Government of Azerbaijan led by Sayyid Jafar Pishevari; and the riots of February 1978, which culminated in the overthrow of the shah in January 1979. On all of these, see Swietochowski, *Russia and Azerbaijan*, passim.

64. Ibid., 187–191. On Shariatmadari, see also Bakhash, *Reign*, 89–90 and 223; and Mackey, *Iranians*, 307–308. On the complexities of Azeri ethnic identification and the issue's impact on the downfall of the Pahlavi monarchy and politics during the first decades of the Islamic republic, see Brenda Shaffer, "The Formation of Azerbaijani Collective Identity in Iran," *Nationalities Papers* 28, no. 3 (September 2000): 449–477; and Brenda Shaffer, *Borders and Brethren: Iran and the Challenge of Azerbaijani Identity* (Cambridge: MIT Press, 2002), 109–115. For a review of the history of ethnic (not just Azeri) and related sectarian tensions and the Iranian state's (both Pahlavi monarchy and Islamic theocracy) policies to impose unity, see A. William Samii, "The Nation and Its Minorities: Ethnicity, Unity State Policy in Iran," *Comparative Studies of South Asia, Africa and the Middle East* 20, nos. 1–2 (2000): 128–142.

65. David B. Nissman, *The Soviet Union and Iranian Azerbaijan: The Use of Nationalism for Political Penetration* (Boulder: Westview Press, 1987), 73–75; and Swietochowski, *Russia and Azerbaijan*, 192.

66. Heydar Aliyev, Speech to the VIIth Congress of Writers of Azerbaijan, quoted in Nissman, *Soviet Union*, 70–71. On Aliyev and this period in Azerbaijan, see also Shaffer, *Borders*, 103–109.

67. Swietochowski, *Russia and Azerbaijan*, 191, citing *The Times* [London], November 29, 1982.

68. *Tehran Times*, June 21, 2001 [FBIS].

69. *Norooz*, July 28, 2001 [FBIS].

70. Golan, *Soviet Policies*, 189–190.

71. For Kuzichkin's own account of his defection, see Kuzichkin, *KGB*, 372–384. For an account that alleges "unforgivable errors" by Shebarshin in his handling of Kuzichkin, see interview by Nataliya Gevorkyan, "KGB Staffer Discusses Intelligence Directorate, Its Leadership," *Moscow News*, no. 41, October 13, 1991, 16 [JPRS Report, JPRS-UPA-91-047, December 10, 1991, 39–41]. For an account that limits itself to charges of "bungling" by Shebarshin, see "Excerpts From Kalugin Memoirs," *Moskovskiye Novosti*, no. 2, January 10, 1993 [JPRS Report, FBIS-USR-93-038, March 26, 1993, 1–6].

72. Cited by Maziar Behrooz, "Trends in the Foreign Policy of the Islamic Republic," in *Neither East nor West*, 22; and Chubin and Tripp, *Iran*, 210–211.

73. Shebarshin, *Ruka*, 166–168.

74. Nikolay Kozyrev, interview.
75. Shebarshin, *Ruka*, 348. According to the journalist Iona Andronov, in 1990 Nikolay Kozyrev at the MFA and Shebarshin at the KGB worked together informally to carry out KGB chief Vladimir Kryuchkov's instructions to frustrate Yeltsin's efforts to obtain the release of Russian POWs from the Afghan mujahideen. See Iona Ionovich Andronov, *Moya voyna* [My war] (Moscow: Delovoy mir 2000, 1999), 136–147.
76. Kuzichkin, *KGB*, 358.
77. Brutents, interview.
78. For Yakovlev's own take on his relationship with Gorbachev, see Aleksandr Yakovlev, *Omut pamyati: Ot Stolypina do Putina* [Whirlpool of memory: From Stolypin to Putin] (Moscow: Vagrius, 2001), 2: 5–85.
79. Aleksandr Nikolayevich Yakovlev, interview by author, Moscow, April 4, 2000. Yakovlev was then serving as president of the International Democracy Foundation. From 1986 to 1990, Yakovlev was CPSU Central Committee secretary, and from 1990 to 1991, he was a member of the USSR Presidential Council. In January 1987 he was elected a candidate member of the CPSU Central Committee Politburo, and in June 1987 he rose to full member of the Politburo. Yakovlev passed away on October 18, 2005.
80. Shebarshin, *Ruka*, 175.
81. Ibid., 285 and 288.
82. Gudimenko, interview. For another take on Kianuri's self-delusions and deliberate exaggeration of Tudeh's importance in reporting to Moscow, see Kuzichkin, *KGB*, 264 and 289–295. In the eyes of the Khomeini regime, of course, it did not help Kianuri and the Tudeh that the Soviets had earlier pressured them into defending the Soviet invasion of Afghanistan. On this point, see Richard W. Cottam, "U.S. and Soviet Responses to Islamic Political Militancy," in *Neither East nor West*, 279. Moreover, according to Safronchuk, the Tudeh had played a role in training Afghan communists (Safronchuk, interview). Twenty years later, the Iranian press invoked a tie to Kianuri as yet one more reason not to accept Britain's nominee, David Reddaway, for its new ambassador to Tehran. Besides being "originally a Jewish person and . . . affiliated with MI6," Reddaway's wife, an Iranian, was said to be a niece of Kianuri's wife. See *Keyhan*, January 6, 2002 [FBIS].
83. Interestingly, Kuzichkin underscores that it was the imposition of martial law in Poland that was the key event that pushed him and his friends into opposition, however silent and covert, against the Soviet regime. See Kuzichkin, *KGB*, 371. It was, of course, the Polish crisis and not the Afghanistan invasion that prompted Moscow to resume radio jamming, which had ceased in 1973, of foreign news broadcasts on August 20, 1980. For more on this point, see John W. Parker, *Kremlin in Transition*, vol. 1, *From Brezhnev to Chernenko, 1978 to 1985* (Boston: Unwin Hyman, 1991), 50–51.
84. For a review and analysis of this period, see Parker, *Kremlin*, 1: 213–332.
85. Simonia, interview.
86. TASS, June 16, 1983 [FBIS-SOV-83-118, June 17, 1983, R 16].
87. Golan, *Soviet Policies*, 194.
88. Vera Lebedeva commentary, Moscow in Persian to Iran, June 21, 1983 [FBIS-SOV-83-121, June 22, H 1].
89. Kuzichkin would explain that the International Department ran all contacts with communist parties everywhere, which was consistent with Gudimenko's assertion that he dealt firsthand with Iranian leftists. However, the International Department maintained its contacts at times indirectly through KGB and GRU officers, who were sworn not to reveal the details of their assignments even to their home organizations.

In this capacity Kuzichkin got stuck, despite his misgivings, as a KGB liaison between Tudeh Party leaders in Tehran and the CPSU International Department in Moscow. See Kuzichkin, *KGB*, 284–287.

90. See, for example, "On the Persecutions of Members of the People's Party of Iran (Tudeh)," *Pravda*, June 23, 1983 [FBIS-SOV-83-125, June 28, 1983, H 3-4], which cites Reuters on the torture of Kianuri. *Pravda* earlier had run its own bitter editorials on the arrests of Kianuri and other Tudeh members ("Against Iran's National Interests," *Pravda*, February 20, 1983 [FBIS-SOV-83-036, February 22, 1983, H 6-7]) and their televised confessions ("Concerning the Anti-Soviet Campaign in Iran," TASS, May 6, 1983 [FBIS-SOV-83-089, May 6, 1983, H 1-2]). For a review and analysis of these articles and other Soviet media play, see Freedman, *Moscow*, 160–161, 192–193, 252, and 287; and Smolansky, *USSR and Iraq*, 238–240, 244–246, and 252.

91. Gudimenko, interview.

92. KUNA (Kuwait), June 4, 1984 [FBIS-SOV-84-109, June 5, 1984, H 1]; and TASS, June 6, 1984 [FBIS-SOV-84-111, June 7, 1984, H 1].

93. Tehran Domestic Service, June 7, 1984 [FBIS-SOV-84-112, June 8, 1984, H 1].

94. Quoted by Chubin and Tripp, *Iran*, 224.

95. Smolansky, *USSR and Iraq*, 246.

96. Alvin Z. Rubinstein, "Moscow and Tehran: The Wary Accommodation," in *Regional Power Rivalries in the New Eurasia: Russia, Turkey, and Iran*, ed. Alvin Z. Rubinstein and Oles M. Smolansky (Armonk, NY: M. E. Sharpe, 1995), 28.

97. For the photograph, see Korniyenko, *Kholodnaya voyna*, 285.

98. Smolansky, *USSR and Iraq*, 253.

99. IRNA and Tehran Domestic Service, February 3 and 4, 1986 [FBIS-SOV-86-023, February 4, 1986, D 1–2].

100. Safronchuk, interview.

101. Soviet-Iranian trade fell by half to its lowest point after the televised Tudeh confessions in 1983. See Behrooz, "Trends," 21.

102. Rubinstein, "Moscow and Tehran," 28.

103. Zviagelskaya, interview.

104. For the visits in 1986–87 that followed that of Korniyenko to Tehran, see Golan, *Soviet Policies*, 191 and 286; Rubinstein, "Moscow and Tehran," 28; and Smolansky, *USSR and Iraq*, 53–255, 260, and 268–272.

105. See Gary Sick, "Slouching Toward Settlement: The Internationalization of the Iran-Iraq War, 1987–1988," in *Neither East nor West*, 228.

## CHAPTER 2: GORBACHEV AND KHOMEINI—PERESTROIKA PEN PALS

1. Ahmed Rashid, *Taliban: Militant Islam, Oil and Fundamentalism in Central Asia* (New Haven: Yale University Press, 2000), 199; and Barnett R. Rubin, *The Search for Peace in Afghanistan: From Buffer State to Failed State* (New Haven: Yale University Press, 1995), 116.

2. Garthoff, *Détente and Confrontation*, 985–1046.

3. Korniyenko, *Kholodnaya voyna*, 190–197. Elsewhere, according to Korniyenko, Central Committee Secretariat International Department head Boris Ponomarev and Rotislav Ulyanovskiy, his deputy for Iran and Afghanistan, had begun arguing that Afghanistan was a "nearly socialist" country. This convinced the Brezhnev regime's chief ideologist and gray eminence Mikhail Suslov to support the invasion in order to prevent not just the loss of a friendly neighboring country but also the rollback of socialism's borders. See also Anatoliy Sergeyevich Chernyayev, *Shest' let s Gorbachevym* [Six years with Gorbachev] (Moscow: Progress-Kul'tura, 1993), 38, and *Moya zhizn i moye vremya* [My

life and times] (Moscow: Mezhdunarodnye Otnosheniya, 1995), 401; Diego Cordovez and Selig S. Harrison, *Out of Afghanistan: The Inside Story of Soviet Withdrawal* (New York: Oxford University Press, 1995), 44–49; and John W. Parker, *Kremlin in Transition*, vol. 2, *Gorbachev, 1985 to 1989* (Boston: Unwin Hyman, 1991), 3–58.

4. Yakovlev, *Omut pamyati*, 1: 530.
5. Alexei Vassiliev, *Russian Policy in the Middle East: From Messianism to Pragmatism* (Reading: Ithaca Press, 1993), 259.
6. Gromyko added that Taraki's murder had shocked Brezhnev, who as a result felt that Amin was capable of conspiring with the United States. See Anatoly Andreyevich Gromyko, *Andrey Gromyko: V labirintakh Kremlya* [Andrey Gromyko: In the labyrinths of the Kremlin] (Moscow: Avtor, 1997), 186–188. In Kabul, according to Vasiliy Safronchuk, who was there until late 1979 as foreign policy adviser to Amin and saw him every day, everyone in the Soviet embassy was against the invasion, as was the Foreign Ministry (everyone but Foreign Minister Gromyko, apparently) back in Moscow. Safronchuk did not believe Amin was an American spy. Rather than advocating counterrevolution, Amin had insisted to Safronchuk that Afghanistan was not just oriented toward socialism but also bypassing the stage of developed capitalism on its way to socialism. Safronchuk and Amin had debated how to interpret the then-famed article by Soviet Central Committee International Department deputy head Rotislav Ulyanovskiy, "On Socialism-Oriented Countries," in *Kommunist*, no. 11 (July 1979), 114–123. See Safronchuk, "Amin," 94.
7. Safronchuk, interview.
8. V. Safronchuk, "Afganistan pri Babrake Karmale i Nadzhibulle" [Afghanistan under Babrak Karmal and Najibullah], *Aziya i Afrika segodnya*, no. 6 (1996): 14. Possibly confirming Safronchuk's conclusion, Anatoly Gromyko wrote that Afghanistan was one subject that his father hardly ever discussed with him. The younger Gromyko believed that his father's involvement in the decision to intervene was possibly the single instance in his long career at the top when he ignored his own "golden rules" about the need to rely on diplomacy and not strength. See Gromyko, *Gromyko*, 186.
9. Safronchuk, "Afganistan," no. 6 (1996): 11 and 13–14. Gorbachev aide Anatoly Chernyayev later recalled the early regrets of Central Committee Secretariat International Department head Boris Ponomarev and the early efforts by academician Georgi Arbatov to lobby KGB head Yuri Andropov on the need to withdraw Soviet troops from Afghanistan. See Chernyayev, *Moya zhizn*, 403–406; and, more generally, Christian Friedrich Ostermann, "New Evidence on the War in Afghanistan: Introduction," *Bulletin*, no. 14/15, Woodrow Wilson International Center for Scholars, Cold War International History Project, Washington, DC (Winter 2003–Spring 2004): 140.
10. Safronchuk, interview.
11. Brutents, interview. Brutents's assertion that Gorbachev met little opposition on Afghanistan is supported by notes of Politburo discussions on November 12, 1986, and January 21–22, 1987 (Cold War International History Project, *Bulletin*, no. 14–15: 143–145).
12. "Record of a Conversation of M. S. Gorbachev With President of Afghanistan, General Secretary of the CC PDPA Najibullah, 13 June 1988, " Cold War International History Project, *Bulletin*, no. 14–15: 184.
13. Yakovlev, interview. Yakovlev was skeptical of the view that Iran pulled punches in Afghanistan over concern that the USSR would respond by increasing its support to Baghdad in the Iran-Iraq War. But Yakovlev was certain that the USSR would indeed have pulled out all the stops against Iran if Tehran had mounted a big campaign against Moscow in Afghanistan. On speculation and assertions of a linkage between

Soviet support to Iraq and Iranian support to the mujahideen in Afghanistan, see Chubin and Tripp, *Iran and Iraq*, 231 and 239.

14. Safronchuk, interview. In a secret report to the CPSU Central Committee in October 1980, Soviet Defense Minister Ustinov counted forty-two training camps in Pakistan versus thirteen in Iran, which had sent into Afghanistan fifty thousand and three thousand trained mujahideen, respectively (*Bulletin*, no. 8–9, Woodrow Wilson International Center for Scholars, Cold War International History Project, Washington, DC (Winter 1996–1997): 176).

15. Brutents, interview.

16. Edward Girardet, *Afghanistan: The Soviet War* (New York: St. Martin's Press, 1985), 200–201.

17. Safronchuk, "Afganistan," no. 1 (1997): 38–39.

18. "On additional measures to influence the Afghan situation," note from L. Zaikov, E. Shevardnadze, D. Yazov, and V. Kruychkov to the CC, CPSU, May 12, 1989, Cold War International History Project, *Bulletin*, no. 8–9: 184.

19. Rashid, *Taliban*, 199.

20. Rubin, *Search for Peace*, 116.

21. Amin Saikal and William Maley, *Regime Change in Afghanistan: Foreign Intervention and the Politics of Legitimacy* (Boulder: Westview, 1991), 130.

22. Ibid., 128.

23. Safronchuk, interview.

24. Nikolay Kozyrev, interview. The recollections of Safronchuk and Kozyrev are consistent with those of Diego Cordovez, who as UN undersecretary general for special political affairs from 1981 to 1988 negotiated the Soviet withdrawal from Afghanistan. Iran played only a distant and marginal role in the negotiations and only at the very end did the Tehran-supported parties come into play. See Cordovez and Harrison, *Out of Afghanistan*, 320, 371, 374, and 384. On Cordovez's dealings with Safronchuk, see especially 99–100 and 133; and with Kozyrev, 178 and 183–84.

25. Hiro, *Longest War*, 250–251.

26. Shahram Chubin, *Iran's National Security Policy* (Washington, DC: Carnegie Endowment, 1994), 36. See also Hiro, *Longest War*, Appendix II and Appendix III, 297 and 299, for similar though somewhat less disproportionate ratios.

27. Michael Eisenstadt, *Iranian Military Power: Capabilities and Intentions* (Washington, DC: Washington Institute for Near East Policy, 1996), 28; and Chaim Herzog, "A Military-Strategic Overview," in *The Iran-Iraq War: Impact and Implications*, 263, with the lower estimate of 1.5 million of Tehran's 8 million residents, or 18.75 percent.

28. Chubin, *Iran's National Security Policy*, 21, 29, and 36.

29. Ibid., 17–19, 40, and 44–45.

30. Tehran Domestic Service, January 8, 1989 [FBIS-NES-89-005, January 9, 1989, 57–59]. See also Mohiaddin Mesbahi, "Gorbachev's 'New Thinking' and Islamic Iran: From Containment to Reconciliation," in *Reconstruction and Regional Diplomacy in the Persian Gulf*, ed. Hooshang Amirahmadi and Nader Entessar (London: Routledge, 1992), 269–270.

31. Parker, *Kremlin*, 2: 261–275. On Vorontsov's tenure in Kabul from 1988 to 1989, see also Rubin, *Search for Peace*, 102 and 154–155.

32. TASS, August 1, 1989 [FBIS-SOV-89-147, August 2, 1989, 23–24].

33. Tehran Domestic Services in Persian, June 30, 1989 [FBIS-NES, July 13, 1989, 63-67], as quoted by Mesbahi in "Gorbachev's 'New Thinking,'" 267–268.

34. *Pravda*, January 5, 1989 [FBIS-SOV-89-003, January 5, 1989, 18–19].

35. Mohammad Quchani, "The Larijani Brothers," *Asr-e Azadegan*, April 22, 2000 [FBIS].

36. Yakovlev, interview.
37. Gudimenko, interview.
38. Moscow in Persian to Iran, June 20, 1989 [FBIS-SOV-89-119 of June 22, 1989, 29].
39. *Pravda*, June 21, 1989 [FBIS-SOV-89-118, June 21, 1989, 18–19].
40. *Pravda*, June 24, 1989 [FBIS-SOV-89-121, June 26, 1989, 19–20].
41. *Pravda*, June 21, 1989, and IRNA, June 20, 1989 [FBIS-SOV-89-118, June 21, 1989, 18–20].
42. For the text of the declaration of principles of relations, see TASS, June 22, 1989 [FBIS-SOV-89-119, June 22, 1989, 23–24.]
43. "Dolgosrochnaya Programma torgovo-ekonomicheskogo i nauchno-tekhnicheskogo sotrudnichestva mezhdy Soyuzom Sovetskikh Sotsialisticheschikh Respublik i Islamskoy Respublikoy Iran, na period do 2000 goda." Text in author's archives.
44. For the text of the declaration of principles of relations, see TASS, June 22, 1989 [FBIS-SOV-89-119, June 22, 1989, 23–24].
45. *Izvestiya*, June 23, 1989 [FBIS-SOV-89-121, June 26, 1989, 20–21].
46. Duncan and Ekedahl, *Moscow and the Third World*, 131. All the same, Baghdad immediately criticized Moscow's "opportunistic behavior" and failure to consult with Iraq as called for by the 1972 Soviet-Iraqi Friendship Treaty (*Al Iraq*, July 2 and 3, 1989, as cited by Duncan and Ekedahl, 133).
47. Chubin, *Iran's National Security Policy*, 35–38.
48. Ibid., 8.
49. Moscow Television Service, "International Panorama," July 2, 1989 [FBIS-SOV-89-127, July 5, 1989, 16].
50. Golan, *Soviet Policies*, 182.
51. Parker, *Kremlin*, 2: 26 and 277–278.
52. Igor Korotchenko, "In Spite of U.S. Pressure," *Nezavisimoye Voyennoye Obozreniye*, September 21, 2000 [FBIS]. Korotchenko gives $5.1 billion as the total value for all four contracts, and it is from this figure that the $1.6 billion for the submarines and basing contracts is derived.
53. Chubin, *Iran's National Security Policy*, 40 and 44–45.
54. Ibid., 33.
55. Korotchenko, "In Spite of U.S. Pressure."
56. White House, Office of the Press Secretary, "Fact Sheet: Iran-Libya Sanctions Act of 1996," Washington, DC, August 6, 1996, http://www.usembassy-israel.org.il/publish/press/security/archive/august/ds1_8-7.htm ; and Eisenstadt, *Iranian Military Power*, 67
57. Ali Khamenei, elected president in October 1981 and reelected in August 1985, was quickly chosen as the new supreme leader on June 5, 1989. Presidential elections were then advanced from August to July 30, when Rafsanjani was duly elected by a lopsided majority. See Anoushiravan Ehteshami, *After Khomeini: The Iranian Second Republic* (London: Routledge, 1995), 33–35.
58. For details on this and other acts of Iranian state-sponsored terrorism in the 1990s, including the findings of a German court in April 1997 on the Mykonos case, see William Drozdiak, "German Court: Tehran Ordered Exile Killings; Verdict Blaming Top Iranians Ruptures Ties," *Washington Post*, April 11, 1997; Michael Eisenstadt, "Dilemmas for the U.S. and Iran," Washington Institute for Near East Policy, *PolicyWatch*, no. 414 (October 8, 1999), http://www.washingtoninstitute.com/. See also U.S. Department of State, "Iran Report on Human Rights Practices for 1996," Washington, DC, January 30, 1997, http://www.state.gov/www/global/human_rights/1996_hrp_report/iran.html; and Eisenstadt, *Iranian Military Power*, 65–75.

59. Shah Abbas the Great's scorched-earth campaigns in eastern Georgia against Kartli and Kakheti in the early seventeenth century resulted in the deaths, imprisonment, and deportation of several hundred thousands and the martyrdom of Dowager Queen Ketevan in 1624 in Shiraz. See Ronald Grigor Suny, *The Making of the Georgian Nation* (Bloomington: Indiana University Press, 1988), 50–51; *Bol'shaya Sovetskaya Entsiklopediya*, vol. 13, 2nd ed. (Moscow: Bol'shaya Sovetskaya Entsiklopediya, 1952), 43–44; and David Marshall Lang, *Lives and Legends of the Georgian Saints*, 2nd rev. ed. (Crestwood, New York: St. Vladimir's Seminary Press, 1976), 169–172.

60. James A. Baker III, *The Politics of Diplomacy: Revolution, War and Peace 1989–1992*, with Thomas M. Defrank (New York: G. P. Putnam's Sons, 1995), 66 and 78.

61. The analysis here draws heavily from David Menashri, *Revolution at a Crossroads: Iran's Domestic Politics and Regional Ambitions*, Policy Paper, no. 43 (Washington, DC: Washington Institute for Near East Policy, 1997), 21–23, 27–29, and 70–71.

62. Tehran released U.S. hostage David Jacobsen two hours before Election Day in the United States on November 2, 1986. The next day the Beirut newspaper *Ash Shiraa* broke the story of National Security Adviser McFarlane's visit to Tehran.

63. Sick, "Slouching," 227. See also Freedman, *Moscow*, 248.

64. Menashri, *Revolution*, 75.

65. Viktor Nikitovich Mikhaylov, interview by I. N. Arutyunyan, "Nuclear Cooperation With Iran: The View From Ordynka," *Priroda*, no. 8 (August 1995): 3–11 [FBIS]. Iran's combined imports-exports with the United States dropped from $3,054,000,000 in 1994 to $1,238,000,000 in 1995 to $86,000,000 in 1996, compared to the rise in Iran's trade with Russia from $342,000,000 in 1994 to $430,000,000 in 1995 to $693,000,000 in 1996 (International Monetary Fund, *Direction of Trade Statistics Yearbook: 2000* (Washington, DC: IMF, 2000), 261).

66. Cordovez and Harrison, *Out of Afghanistan*, 187 and 246.

67. Yakovlev, interview.

68. Cited in Menashri, *Revolution*, 27, from Radio Tehran, December 20, in *DR*, December 23, 1991.

69. Shebarshin, *Ruka*, 266.

70. Rubinstein, "Moscow and Tehran," 31.

## CHAPTER 3: SOVIET COLLAPSE—REVANCHE OR ACCOMMODATION?

1. Jack F. Matlock Jr., *Autopsy on an Empire: The American Ambassador's Account of the Collapse of the Soviet Union* (New York: Random House, 1995), 3–5 and 634–647.

2. Martin Indyk, "The Clinton Administration's Approach to the Middle East," Washington Institute for Near East Policy, Soref Symposium, 1993, http://www.washingtoninstitute.org/print.php?template=C07&CID=61; and Rosemarie Forsythe, *The Politics of Oil in the Caucasus and Central Asia*, IISS, Adelphi Paper 300 (Oxford: Oxford University Press, 1996), 24–25, 46–47, 53–54, and 56–57.

3. Baku, background inteviews.

4. Baker, *Politics of Diplomacy*, 625–633.

5. Simonia, interview.

6. Yakovlev, interview.

7. Brutents, interview.

8. Gudimenko, interview.

9. Yevgeny Maksimovich Primakov, *Gody v bol'shoi politike* [Years in big politics], (Moscow: Kollektsiya "Sovershenno Sekretno," 1999), 137.

10. IRNA, June 20, 1989 [FBIS-SOV-89-118, June 21, 1989, 19].

11. For the text of the declaration of principles of relations, see TASS, June 22, 1989 [FBIS-SOV-89-119, June 22, 1989, 23–24].

12. *Izvestiya*, June 23, 1989 [FBIS-SOV-89-121, June 26, 1989, 21].
13. TASS, June 23, 1989 [FBIS-SOV-89-120, June 23, 1989, 17].
14. TASS, June 23, 1989 [FBIS-SOV-89-121, June 26, 1989, 22].
15. IRNA, June 23, 1989 [FBIS-SOV-89-121, June 26, 1989, 22].
16. Moscow World Service, May 20, 1987 [FBIS-SOV-87-097, May 20, 1987, H 2]. See also former ambassador to Tehran Vladimir Vinogradov's May 27, 1987, radio broadcast riposte [FBIS-SOV-87-110, June 9, 1987, E 7].
17. "Dolgosrochnaya Programma torgovo-ekonomicheskogo i nauchno-tekhnicheskogo sotrudnichestva mezhdy Soyuzom Sovetskikh Sotsialisticheschikh Respublik i Islamskoy Respublikoy Iran, na period do 2000 goda," Section 13, page 8. Text in author's archives.
18. Brutents, interview.
19. Aleksandr Yurevich Umnov, interview by author, Moscow, December 1, 1999. Umnov was a senior research fellow at the Institute of World Economy and International Relations (IMEMO) and a chief expert at the Institute of Israeli and Middle Eastern Studies.
20. Gudimenko, interview.
21. Mamedova, interview.
22. Yevgeny Petrovich Bazhanov, interview by author, Moscow, December 2, 1999. Bazhanov was vice rector of the Diplomatic Academy of the Foreign Ministry of the Russian Federation.
23. Khakimov, interview.
24. Yakovlev, interview.
25. With the exception of the Ismaili Shiite population in the mountainous eastern region of Gorno-Badakhshan.
26. Eugene Schuyler, *Turkistan: Notes of a Journey in Russian Turkistan, Kokand, Bukhara and Kuldja*, ed. Geoffrey Wheeler and abrid. K. E. West (New York: Praeger, 1966), 237–238, 284. Schuyler was the U.S. consul general in St. Petersburg when he made his seven-month journey through Central Asia in 1873.
27. Background interviews by author in Moscow, Baku, Ankara, and Istanbul, 1999–2000.
28. Ankara and Baku, background interviews.
29. Eisenstadt, *Iranian Military Power*, 72.
30. Umnov, interview.
31. Gudimenko, interview.
32. For a balanced account of the early years of this conflict, see Matlock, *Autopsy*, 165–168 and 715–716.
33. Aleksey Malashenko, conversation with author at Carnegie Endowment, Washington, DC, March 1, 2004. On Dolgikh's visit, see Hamburg DPA, February 26, 1988 [FBIS-SOV-88-038, February 26, 1988, 42]; and Yerevan Domestic Service, February 28, 1988 [FBIS-SOV-88-039, February 29, 1989, 68–69].
34. *Izvestiya*, September 12, 2000 [FBIS]; and *Nezavisimaya Gazeta*, September 12, 2000 [FBIS].
35. Gudimenko, interview.
36. See Marat Akchurin, *Red Odyssey: A Journey Through the Soviet Republics* (New York: HarperCollins, 1992), 388.
37. Moscow, background interview. Ironically, there were some parallels with the shah's efforts, culminating in the celebration at Persepolis in 1971 of the 2,500th anniversary of the Iranian nation under Cyrus, to appeal to a national identity older than Shia Islam. The shah's campaign made much use of Ferdowsi's *Shahnameh*. See Mackey, *Iranians*, 234–235.

38. Ankara, background interview. For an interesting analysis of regional influences in Central Asia, including the Iranian-Turkish rivalry, by a high-level Kyrgyz diplomat and future foreign minister, see Alikbek Djekshenkulov, *Novye nezavisimye gosudarstva Tsentral'noi Azii v mirovom soobshchestve* [The new independent governments of Central Asia in the world community] (Moscow: Nauchnaya Kniga, 2000), 184–195.

39. George S. Harris, "The Russian Federation and Turkey," in *Regional Power Rivalries*, 16. Iran and Iraq both had consulates in Baku prior to the USSR's collapse. The only Turkish consulate at the time of the collapse was in Batumi (Georgia), although there had also been one in Odessa (Ukraine) before World War II. After the collapse, Turkey in 1996 opened a consulate in Kazan, capital of the Russian Federation's Tatar Republic, and in January 2005 in the Black Sea port of Novorossyisk (Ankara and Baku, background interviews; and "First General Consul of Turkey in Kazan Will Represent His Country in Novorossiysk," Information Agency of Tatarstan, January 30, 2005, http://eng.tatar-inform.ru/news/society/?ID=359).

40. Ankara, background interviews.

41. Background interviews by author, Washington, DC, 1999–2000.

42. Thomas Goltz, *Azerbaijan Diary: A Rogue Reporter's Adventures in an Oil-Rich, War-Torn, Post-Soviet Republic* (Armonk, NY: M. E. Sharpe, 1998), 106–107.

43. Ankara, background interviews.

44. Interfax, January 5, 1992 [FBIS-SOV-92-003, January 6, 1992, 67]; and *Postfactum*, January 5, 1992 [FBIS-SOV-92-007, January 10, 1992, 53]. Turkey and Azerbaijan signed a treaty in Baku on the restoration of diplomatic relations on January 14, 1992 (*Postfactum*, January 15, 1992 [FBIS-SOV-91-014, January 22, 1992, 91]). Turkey then apparently succeeded in accrediting an ambassador to Azerbaijan before Iran did (*Milliyet*, January 15, 1992 [FBIS-SOV-91-014, January 22, 1992, 92]).

45. Duygu Bazoğlu Sezer, "Turkish-Russian Relations: From Adversity to 'Virtual Rapprochement,'" in *Turkey's New World: Changing Dynamics in Turkish Foreign Policy*, ed. Alan Makovsky and Sabri Sayari (Washington, DC: Washington Institute for Near East Policy, 2000), 95 and 99.

46. Voice of the Islamic Republic of Iran, November 26, 1991 [FBIS-NES-91-228, November 26, 1991, 57].

47. Tehran IRIB Television, November 29, 1991 [FBIS-SOV-91-233, December 4, 1991, 81]; Tehran IRIB Television, December 1, 1991 [FBIS-SOV-91-233, December 4, 1991, 85]; and Radio Dushanbe, December 2, 1991 [FBIS-SOV-91-233, December 4, 1991, 83–84]. In the case of Dushanbe, Velayati spoke of this exchange occurring in the next three months (Radio Dushanbe, December 2, 1991 [FBIS-SOV-91-233, December 4, 1991, 84]). Oles M. Smolansky, "Turkish and Iranian Policies in Central Asia," in *Central Asia: Its Strategic Importance and Future Prospects*, ed. Hafeez Malik (New York: St. Martin's Press, 1994), 283–310, presents much valuable information on the early relations between Iran and the newly independent former Soviet republics. See also Edmund Herzig, *Iran and the Former Soviet South* (London: Royal Institute of International Affairs, 1995), passim.

48. Tehran IRIB Television, December 19, 1991 [FBIS-NES-91-245, December 20, 1991, 40–41].

49. Goltz, *Azerbaijan Diary*, 117–123.

50. For assertions and some evidence of Russian involvement in this and other actions in Nagorno-Karabakh, see ibid., 124 and 263–264.

51. Ibid., 162–163.

52. Swietochowski, *Russia and Azerbaijan*, 193.

53. Parker, *Kremlin*, 2: 202 and 223–234.

54. Gromyko, *Gromyko*, 86–87 and 154–155.
55. Shaffer, *Borders*, 197–198.
56. Audrey L. Altstadt, *The Azerbaijani Turks: Power and Identity Under Russian Rule* (Stanford: Hoover Press, 1992), 211.
57. "Iran Will Not Take Advantage of Domestic Soviet Problems," *Tehran Times*, January 8, 1990 [FBIS-NES-90-009, January 12, 1990, 35].
58. Swietochowski, *Russia and Azerbaijan*, 208. On Black January 1990, see Altstadt, *Azerbaijani Turks*, 210–219.
59. Swietochowski, *Russia and Azerbaijan*, 208–209.
60. Goltz, *Azerbaijan Diary*, 21–25. On the historical background of Ashura, see Mackey, *Iranians*, 54–56.
61. Goltz, *Azerbaijan Diary*, 62–63.
62. Brutents, interview.
63. For examinations of the impact of Russia, Iran, and Turkey on Azeri identity, see Altstadt, *Azerbaijani Turks*, passim; Goltz, *Azerbaijan Diary*, 18–20 and passim; Shireen T. Hunter, "Greater Azerbaijan: Myth or Reality?" in *Le Caucase Post Sovietique: La Transition Dons le Conflict*, ed. Mohammad-Reza Djalili (Brussels: Bruylant, 1995), 115–142; Shaffer, "Formation," 449–477; and Swietochowski, *Russia and Azerbaijan*, passim.
64. Goltz, *Azerbaijan Diary*, 171 and 175.
65. Ankara, background interviews.
66. Goltz, *Azerbaijan Diary*, 165 and 283–284.
67. Swietochowski, *Russia and Azerbaijan*, 223.
68. Multiple press reports, August to December 1991 [FBIS].
69. On Elchibey and unification, see Shaffer, *Borders*, 197–200.
70. Swietochowski, *Russia and Azerbaijan*, 219–225; Elizabeth Fuller, "Azerbaijan at the Crossroads," in *Challenges for the Former Soviet South*, ed. Roy Allison (Washington, DC: Brookings Institution Press for the Royal Institute of International Affairs, 1996), 134–135; and Goltz, *Azerbaijan Diary*, 287.
71. On Aliyev's ability to play the Turks, Russians, Americans, and Iranians at the same time, see Goltz, *Azerbaijan Diary*, 371–372.
72. Goltz, *Azerbaijan Diary*, 107–109.
73. Kazemzadeh, "Iranian Relations," 340–347; Lenczowski, *Russia*, 49–51 and 317–318; and Swietochowski, *Russia and Azerbaijan*, 229.
74. Goltz, *Azerbaijan Diary*, 108.
75. *Jomhuri-ye Eslami*, October 12, 2000 [FBIS]. See also "North Azarbayjan Liberation Movement: Goals and Solutions," *Misaq* (Tabriz), December 31, 2001 [FBIS].
76. *Azarbayjan* (Tabriz), January 8, 2002 [FBIS].
77. *Azarbayjan*, October 30, 2001 [FBIS].
78. *Abrar*, November 22, 2000 [FBIS].
79. *Aftab-e Yazd*, April 13, 2002 [FBIS].
80. Baku, background interviews.
81. *Yeni Musavat*, October 6, 2000 [FBIS]. Those convicted in the murder reportedly were associated with the Islamic terrorist organization Vilayat-e Hezbollah al-Faqih and had targeted Bunyadov because of his alleged attacks on Islam. For details from the two trials of those charged, see Turan, February 21, 2001 [FBIS]; *Obshchaya Gazeta*, No. 10, March 8–14, 2001 [FBIS]; and *Zerkalo*, December 13, 2003 [FBIS].
82. Baku, background interviews.
83. According to the CIA, 24 percent, or 15,643,140, of Iran's population of 65,179,752 in July 1999 was Azeri, compared to 90 percent, or 7,117,402, of Azerbaijan's total

population of 7,908,224. See U.S. Central Intelligence Agency, *The World Factbook 1999* (Washington, DC: Central Intelligence Agency, 1999), 33 and 231.

84. Ankara, background interviews. Two years later, an Iranian publication reportedly put the number of Azeris at around 20 million—close to the Turkish estimate just cited—out of a total population for Iran of 61.9 million (*Baku Turan*, August 29, 2002 [FBIS]). For a listing of major ethnic groups and estimated numbers several decades earlier, see John W. Limbert, *Iran: At War With History* (Boulder: Westview Press, 1987), 21, Table 2.1.

85. Baku, background interviews. Two years later, CAMAH leader Dr. Mahmudali Cohraqani put the number of ethnic Azeris in Iran at 32 million (*Baku Space TV*, April 25, 2002 [FBIS]).

86. Baku, background interviews. CAMAH assertions are buttressed by Soviet archives. See Natalia I. Yegorova, "The 'Iran Crisis' of 1945–1946: A View From the Russian Archives," Woodrow Wilson International Center for Scholars, Cold War International History Project, Working Paper, no. 15, May 1996, 10, 21, and 23–24.

87. Baku, background interviews; and, for example, Vassiliev, *Russian Policy*, 163.

88. Cohraqani is also rendered Chekhragani, Johragani, or Chehregani. In 1997, reportedly at the initiative of Elchibey, the Azerbaijani Popular Front gave the Mamed Emin Rasulzade award, named after the founder of the first Azerbaijani Democratic Republic of 1918–20, to Dr. Cohraqani (*Turan* (Baku), May 22, 1997 [FBIS]). Cohraqani arrived in Baku on March 15, 2002, for what appeared to be a lengthy visit.

89. Ankara, background interviews.

90. Baku, background interviews.

91. Ankara, background interviews.

92. Dushanbe Radio, January 9, 1992 [FBIS-SOV-92-007, January 10, 1992, 47].

93. Umnov, interview.

94. Washington, DC, background interviews.

95. The Shiite Buyid dynasty ruled western Iran at this time, and the Ziyarid dynasty—also Shiite—the Caspian coastal region of Mazanderan [Limbert, *Iran*, 65–66; for a map of Iran's traditional provinces, see Limbert, *Iran*, 5, Map 1.2]. Even before Kievan Rus redirected trade down the Dnieper and across the Black Sea to Byzantium's Constantinople, Rus scattered across the Upper Volga reaches and the Baltics had engaged in voluminous though indirect exchange of furs for the silver *dirhams* (coins) of the Samanid dynasty (Simon Franklin and Jonathan Shepard, *The Emergence of Rus: 750–1200* (London: Longman, 1996), 63–65, 125–130, and 156).

96. During this period Ferdowsi wrote the epic poem *Shanameh* (*Book of Kings*), "the great hymn of Iranian nationalism," that depicted the greatness and uniqueness of a thousand years of pre-Islamic Iranian identity that was forced to come to terms with the Arab conquest and attendant Muslim beliefs (Mackey, *Iranians*, 64). At this time, Kiev was not much more than a log house town and Moscow was not even on the map.

97. *Narodnaya Gazeta*, July 18, 1992, 1–2, as cited by Mohiaddin Mesbahi, "Tajikistan, Iran, and the International Politics of the 'Islamic factor,'" *Central Asian Survey* 16, no. 2 (1997): 144.

98. David Menashri, "Iran and Central Asia: Radical Regime, Pragmatic Politics," in *Central Asia Meets the Middle East*, ed. David Menashri (London: Frank Cass, 1998), 87.

99. Zviagelskaya, interview.

100. TASS, September 18, 1990 [FBIS-SOV-90-182, September 19, 1990, 4]. For an overview of prior Saudi-Soviet relations, which included diplomatic ties from 1926

to 1938, see Mark N. Katz, *Russia & Arabia: Soviet Foreign Policy Toward the Arabian Peninsula* (Baltimore: Johns Hopkins University Press, 1986), 131–139.

101. Khakimov, interview.

## CHAPTER 4: TAJIKISTAN—"GREATER IRAN" OR "NEAR ABROAD"?

1. Ahmed Rashid, *The Resurgence of Central Asia: Islam or Nationalism?* (Atlantic Highlands, NJ: Zed Books, 1994), 172.

2. Rubin, *Search for Peace*, 65 and 81.

3. Muriel Atkin, "Thwarted Democratization in Tajikistan," in *Conflict, Cleavage, and Change in Central Asia and the Caucasus*, ed. Karen Dawisha and Bruce Parrott (Cambridge: Cambridge University Press, 1997), 284–285; and Davlat Khudonazarov, interview by Yevgeniy Tsymbal, "Ya daval slovo, chto budu delat' vsyo, chto smogu. I ya starayus' eto slovo derzhat" [I gave my word that I will do everything that I can. And I am trying to keep my word], *Vestnik Instituta Kennana v Rossii* (Moscow), no. 2 (2002): 71–72.

4. The region was renamed Soghd in August 2000 (*Hakikat-i Leninobod*, August 5, 2000 [FBIS]).

5. Davlat Khudonazar (Khudonazarov), "The Conflict in Tajikistan: Questions of Regionalism," in *Central Asia: Conflict, Resolution, and Change*, ed. Roald Z. Sagdeev and Susan Eisenhower (Chevy Chase, MD: CPSS Press, 1995), 254–255.

6. TASS, April 12, 1990 [FBIS-SOV-90-072, April 13, 1990, 105]; and "Vremya" newscast, Moscow Television Service, December 3, 1990 [FBIS-SOV-90-234, December 5, 1990, 86–87].

7. *Komsomolskaya Pravda*, August 27, 1991 [FBIS-SOV-91-167, August 28, 1991, 118]. On the coup attempt, see Matlock, *Autopsy*, 578–604.

8. Interview by Otakhon Latifi in the weekly *Soyuz*, as cited in "Events of the Week," Radio Dushanbe Network, September 1, 1991 [JPRS Report, FBIS-USR-91-028, September 6, 1991, 76–77].

9. Among the other elements of the opposition, the Democratic Party drew support from younger reform-minded intelligentsia in Dushanbe and other urban centers across Tajikistan. In its early years, it appealed beyond Tajiks, both secular and pious, to Uzbeks and even some Russians, and did not exclude Communist Party members though few were likely to be full-time functionaries. Rastokhez considered itself a nationalist-democratic movement whose aim was the revival of Tajik culture and sovereignty. It attracted moderate oppositionists and even some government workers. The Lali Badakhshan Society represented the interests of Pamiris in the sparsely populated but extensive region of Gorno-Badakhshan. See Atkin, "Thwarted," 285–287; Sergei Gretsky, "Civil War in Tajikistan: Causes, Developments, and Prospects for Peace," in *Central Asia*, 221; and Aleksandr Verkhovskiy, *Srednaya Azia i Kazakhstan: Politicheskiy spektr* [Central Asia and Kazakhstan: Political spectrum], 2nd ed. (Moscow: Informatsionno-ekspertnaya gruppa "Panorama," October 1992), 77–93.

10. Gretsky, "Civil War," 221.

11. Saodat Kuziyevna Olimova and Muzaffar Abduvakkosovich Olimov, *Tadzhikistan na poroge peremen* [Tajikistan on the threshold of change] (Moscow: Tsentr strategicheskikh i politicheskikh issledovaniy; Nauchno-analiticheskiy tsentr "Shark," 1999), 45.

12. In the same poll, the notion of an Islamic state still enjoyed some support in regions such as Kurgan-Tyube (18.6 percent) and Dushanbe (14.7 percent). Support for the IRP was 18.4 percent in Dushanbe and 17.5 percent in Kurgan-Tyube region. The Democratic Party enjoyed its highest support in Dushanbe at 25.7 percent. Support for the Communist Party was weakest in Dushanbe, where it garnered only three percent (Grigorii G. Kosach, "Tajikistan: Political Parties in an Inchoate National

Space," in *Muslim Eurasia: Conflicting Legacies*, ed. Yaacov Ro'i [London: Frank Cass, 1995], 135–136).

13. The charge against Makhkamov was led by Safarali Kenjaev, who would play a key role in future president Nabiyev's ill-starred administration. Makhkamov suffered a whole-scale loss of confidence in the Supreme Soviet, where 124 out of 172 deputies present voted to dismiss him (All-Union Radio Mayak, August 31, 1991 [FBIS-SOV-91-170, September 3, 1991, 114–115).

14. The Supreme Soviet had asserted the republic's sovereignty on August 25, 1990.

15. All-Union Radio First Program Radio-1 Network, September 20, 1991 [FBIS-SOV-91-185, September 24, 1991, 90]; TASS, September 23, 1991; and Interfax, September 23, 1991.

16. Interfax, September 23, 1991.

17. Ivan Podshivalov, "Surprise Choice," *Moscow News*, no. 26, July 8–15, 1990 [JPRS Report, JPRS-UPA-90-046, July 31, 1990, 70]; and Khudonazarov, "Ya daval slovo," 67–71.

18. *Komsomolskaya Pravda*, September 12, 1991 [FBIS-SOV-91-179, September 16, 1991, 102–103]; and *Trud*, September 18, 1991 [FBIS-SOV-91-186, September 25, 1991, 84].

19. Davlat Khudonazarov, interview by author, Moscow, September 20, 2000. This was one of several interviews with Khudonazarov in Moscow in 1999–2000 and in Washington, D.C., in 2005.

20. *Krasnaya Zvezda*, October 5, 1991 [FBIS-SOV-91-196, October 9, 1991, 73]; and AFP, October 8, 1991 [FBIS-SOV-91-196, October 9, 1991, 74].

21. "Decision of the Supreme Soviet Presidium of the Republic of Tajikistan on Numerous Measures to Democratize Public Life in the Republic of Tajikistan," Dushanbe Radio, October 6, 1991 [FBIS-SOV-91-195, October 8, 1991, 84–85]; and *Izvestiya*, October 8, 1991 [FBIS-SOV-91-198, October 11, 1991, 72].

22. Interfax, October 22, 1991 [FBIS-SOV-91-205, October 23, 1991, 72].

23. Khudonazarov speculated that Yeltsin perhaps preferred Nabiyev because he regarded him as a docile and malleable drunk, as President Islom Karimov in neighboring Uzbekistan probably also did. In addition, the Russian mediators may have gone back to Moscow with the impression that it would be a mistake to support the moderate secularist opposition in Tajikistan because the Muslim clergy would ultimately control it (Khudonazarov, interviews, December 2, 1999, and September 20, 2000).

24. Igor Rotar, "The Next Presidential Elections in Tajikistan Will Be Called Early," *Nezavisimaya Gazeta*, December 4, 1991 [JPRS Report, FBIS-USR-92-006, January 21, 1992, 67–68].

25. Radio Dushanbe, November 26, 1991 [FBIS-SOV-91-229, November 27, 1991, 72].

26. Oleg Panfilov, "Republic Marks Independence Day; All Russia Was for Me, Assures Emomali Rakhmonov (Rahmonov)," *Nezavisimaya Gazeta*, September 9, 1993 [JPRS Report, FBIS-USR-93-129, October 6, 1993, 98–100].

27. Atkin, "Thwarted," 298.

28. Khudonazarov, interviews, December 2, 1999, and April 2, 2005. Although Karimov, born in Samarkand in 1938, took the Uzbek nationality of his father, his mother was an ethnic Tajik (for a biography of Karimov, see V. Pribylovskiy and I. Suchkova, *Rukovoditeli Gosudarstv na Territorii Byvshego SSSR* [Leaders of governments on the territory of the former USSR] (Moscow: Panorama, 1999), 157–159). According to Khudonazarov, his own assertions in 1991 as to voting fraud and actual balloting were based on the calculations of the Russian elections expert Aleksandr Sobyanin.

29. U.S. Department of State, "Tajikistan," *Country Reports on Human Rights Practices for 1992* (Washington, DC: U.S. Government Printing Office, 1993), 929.

30. Khudonazar, "Conflict," 258 and 263n14. Ikramov was imprisoned in Khujand and not released until October (U.S. Department of State, "Tajikistan," 925).

31. Irina Zviagelskaya, *The Tajik Conflict* (Moscow: Russian Center for Strategic Research and International Studies, 1997), 6. Navjuvanov had been appointed minister in 1989 (*Tojikstoni Soveti*, April 11, 1989 [FBIS-SOV-89-079, April 26, 1989, 68]), replacing K. Pulatov, presumably an ethnic Uzbek from the Leninobod region. On March 25, 1992, Kenjaev publicly accused Navjuvanov of official corruption, which provoked a demonstration outside Nabiyev's residence the next day by Pamiris who called for a public apology by Kenjaev (Oleg Panfilov, "Tajikistan," *Nezavisimaya Gazeta*, March 27, 1992 [JPRS Report, FBIS-USR-92-046, April 24, 1992, 80–81]).

32. On Navjuvanov's resignation, see ITAR-TASS, September 1, 1992 [FBIS-SOV-92-171, September 2, 1992, 1–2]). On the number of protestors, see U.S. Department of State, "Tajikistan," 927.

33. While this polling was conducted in regions that included Kurgan-Tyube, it was not done in the Pamiri region of Gorno-Badakhshan and may not have extended to Garm and other nearby important components of IRP support. See Kosach, "Tajikistan," 133–136.

34. Gregory Freidin, "The Horror in Tajikistan," *Central Asia Monitor*, no. 5 (1992): 9.

35. Akbar Turajonzoda, "Religion: The Pillar of Society," in *Central Asia*, 269.

36. Rashid, *Resurgence*, 177 and 180.

37. ITAR-TASS, May 11, 1992. For more on Yusuf's inflammatory rhetoric, see Atkin, "Thwarted," 298 and 310n77.

38. S. Yegorov and S. Dzeglov, "Novosti" newscast, Teleradiokompaniya Ostankino, May 18, 1992.

39. Khudonazarov, interview, December 2, 1999; Verkhovskiy, *Politicheskiy spektr*, 92; and U.S. Department of State, "Tajikistan," 927.

40. Gretsky, "Civil War," 222.

41. Rakhmon Aziz and Timur Kadyr, "Sangak Safarov: A Tajik Chapayev," *Megapolis-Express* (Moscow), February 24, 1993 [JPRS Report, FBIS-USR-93-045, April 10, 1993, 131–134].

42. Vadym Belykh and Nikolay Burbyga, "Hostages of Terror," *Izvestiya*, September 9, 1992 [FBIS-SOV-92-177, September 11, 1992, 43–44]. For a photograph of Safarov, see Gregory Gleason, *The Central Asian States: Discovering Independence* (Boulder: Westview, 1997), 104. As for Safarov's reference to Masoud as a fellow Kulobi, the Tajik commander set up headquarters after the Soviet military withdrawal in Taloqan, not far across the border in northern Afghanistan.

43. The Supreme Soviet did not formally accept his resignation until August 11, when it elected the Pamiri Akbarsho Iskandarov to the post (*Moscow News*, No. 44, November 1–8, 1992 [JPRS Report, FBIS-USR-92-153, November 30, 1992, 107–109]).

44. Igor Rotar, with brief interviews of Tajik political figures Davlat Khudonazarov and Langari Langariyev, "The War Without Victors—The Tajik Democrats Gave the Uzbek President a Gift," *Nezavisimaya Gazeta*, September 30, 1992 [JPRS Report, FBIS-URS-92-131, October 16, 1992, 99–102].

45. Oleg Panfilov, "Unofficial Biography of the Appointed President: Emomali Rakhmonov Will Hardly Bring About a Drastic Change in the Country's Fortunes," *Nezavisimaya Gazeta*, November 19, 1994 [JPRS Report, FBIS-USR-94-132, 99–101].

46. Rotar, "War Without Victors."

47. *Nezavisimaya Gazeta*, July 28, 1992 [JPRS Report, FBIS-USR-92-103, August 14, 1992, 80–81].

48. Aziz and Kadyr, "Sangak Safarov."

49. Nassim Jawad and Shahrbanou Tadjbakhsh, *Tajikistan: A Forgotten Civil War*

(Manchester, UK: Manchester Free Press, 1995), 20; and Stanley T. Escudero, "Rat-a-tat-tat in Tajikistan; U.S. Embassy People Have to Get Out," *State*, no. 365 (April 1993): 18.

50. ITAR-TASS, March 30, 1999 [FBIS].

51. Although Latifi described himself as Khudonazarov's campaign manager, Khudonazarov pointed out that Turajonzoda arranged to send Latifi to Tehran for two weeks in October 1991 in order to weaken Khudonazarov's campaign against Nabiyev (Khudonazarov, interview, December 2, 1999).

52. ITAR-TASS, September 22, 1998 [FBIS].

53. ITAR-TASS, August 24, 1992 [FBIS-SOV-92-164, August 24, 1992, 48–49].

54. Andrey Pershin, Andrey Petrovskiy, and Vladimir Shislin, Interfax, September 1, 1992; and U.S. Department of State, "Tajikistan," 924.

55. AFP, September 1, 1992 [FBIS-SOV-92-170, 46–47]; and Oleg Panfilov, "Another President Overthrown in Tajikistan; Russian Troops Asked Not to Concern Themselves," *Nezavisimaya Gazeta*, September 2, 1992 [JPRS Report, FBIS-USR-92-120, 70–71].

56. Radio Dushanbe, September 8, 1992 [FBIS-SOV-92-174, September 8, 1992, 48–49]; and "President Nabiyev Reportedly Forced to Resign," AFP, September 7, 1992. For Nabiyev's account, see Igor Rotar's interview with him in "Ousted President Hopes for Revenge," *Nezavisimaya Gazeta*, October 1, 1992 [FBIS-SOV-92-192, October 2, 1992, 35–36].

57. Iskandarov had served as acting speaker and acting president a year earlier while Nabiyev ran for president and, on August 11, 1992, had been elected full-fledged Supreme Soviet chairman (*Moscow News*, No. 44, November 1–8, 1992, [JPRS Report, FBIS-USR-92-153, November 30, 1992, 107–109]).

58. ITAR-TASS, September 21, 1992 [FBIS-SOV-92-183, September 21, 1992, 53].

59. In late October, as fighting spread across the city, Ambassador Stanley T. Escudero and his staff evacuated the American embassy when forces led by Kenjaev entered the capital in an unsuccessful coup (Escudero, "Rat-a-tat-tat," 13–18). U.S. personnel returned to Dushanbe in spring 1993.

60. On attendance at the Supreme Soviet session, see U.S. Department of State, "Tajikistan," 929.

61. Oleg Panfilov, "Sangak Safarov: 'We Will Cleanse Tajikistan and Russia of the Democratic Scum!' The 16th Session of the Supreme Soviet of Tajikistan Summed Up More Than Six Months of Civil War in the Republic," *Nezavisimaya Gazeta*, December 5, 1992 [JPRS Report, FBIS-USR-92-163, 121–122]; and Panfilov, "Unofficial Biography of the Appointed President," 99–101.

62. Sometime in December, Safarov reportedly ordered the killing of Kadriddin Aslonov, the Garmi who as acting president a year earlier had presided over the banning of the Communist Party, the toppling of Lenin's statue in downtown Dushanbe, and Tajikistan's declaration of independence. More recently Aslonov had briefly been the opposition's last-ditch appointee as governor in embattled Kurgan-Tyube. Upon his arrest, Aslonov was charged with maintaining contacts with Afghanistan's Gulbuddin Hekmatyar and planning to eliminate the Kulobi leadership (Panfilov, "Republic Marks Independence Day"). Aslonov served in Kurgan-Tyube from October 8, 1992 (Radio Dushanbe, October 8, 1992 [FBIS-SOV-92-197, October 9, 1992, 34]) to around October 25, 1992, when he was arrested (Interfax, November 9, 1992 [FBIS-SOV-92-218, November 10, 1992, 65]).

63. The Rahmonov regime blamed the opposition for the deaths of Safarov and Fayzali Saidov on March 30, 1993, while others attributed it to a power struggle between the two men (Igor Lenskiy, "Tajikistan: Assassination Attempt or Quarrel," *Pravda*, April 1, 1993 [FBIS-SOV-93-062, April 2, 1993, 62]).

64. Safarali Kenjaev, *Perevorot v Tadzhikistane* [Upheaval in Tajikistan], vol. 1 (Dushanbe: Dushanbinskiy Poligrafkombinat, 1996), passim. This is apparently the only volume of Kenjaev's series of three volumes of memoirs in Tajik that has been translated into Russian. For the original, see Safarali Kenjaev, *Tabadduloti Tojikiston* [Upheaval in Tajikistan], 3 vols. (Dushanbe: Fondi Kenjaev, 1993–95).

65. Enis Berberoglu, "Tehran Is Between Two Mosques but Doesn't Pray," *Hurriyet*, October 3, 2001 [FBIS].

66. Rashid, *Resurgence*, 180–181.

67. Ibid., 177, 180, 183 and 215–216; Rubin, *Search for Peace*, 26–27 and 35–37; and Steve Coll, *Ghost Wars: The Secret History of the CIA, Afghanistan, and Bin Laden, From the Soviet Invasion to September 10, 2001* (New York: Penguin Books, 2005), 27, 86, 114, 181, and 284.

68. On the exchange rate, see V. Koen and E. Meyermans, "Exchange Rate Determinants in Russia: 1992–93," *Tijdschrift voor Economie en Management* 40, no. 3–4, 1995, 253, graph, http://www.econ.kuleuven.be/tem/jaargangen/1991-2000/1995/TEM1995-3&4/TEM1995-3&4_247-268p.pdf.

69. Kenjaev, *Perevorot*, 258–259.

70. Mohiaddin Mesbahi, "Iran and Tajikistan," in *Regional Power Rivalries*, 141n64 (reference to *New Times*, but no issue number given). Some have also claimed that Saudi secret services gave Kazi kalon Turajonzoda $50 million, which he then used to buy weapons for forces loyal to him. See Gapur Khaidarov and Maksudjon Inomov, *Tajikistan: Tragedy and Anguish of the Nation* (St. Petersburg: LINKO, 1993), 78.

71. IRNA, November 10, 1992 [FBIS-NES-92-220, November 13, 1992, 53].

72. Mesbahi, "Iran and Tajikistan," 120–121; and Mesbahi, "Tajikistan, Iran, and 'Islamic Factor,'" 143. For an overview of the activities of the local revolutionary *komitehs* in Iran, see Bakhash, *Reign*, 56–59.

73. *Tehran Times*, September 9, 1992 [FBIS-NES-92-185, September 23, 1992, 44].

74. Voice of the Islamic Republic, September 5, 1992 [FBIS-NES-92-175, September 9, 1992, 49].

75. Voice of the Islamic Republic, September 8, 1992 [FBIS-NES-92-176, September 10, 1992, 37].

76. Vyacheslav Ushakov, "What Is Impeding Cooperation?" *Pravda*, July 24, 1993 [FBIS-USR-93-107, August 18, 1993, 65–67].

77. Anatoly Adamishin, interview by author, Washington, DC, November 17–18, 1999. Adamishin was Russian Federation first deputy foreign minister from October 1992 to October 1994 with responsibility for Tajikistan and had served as ambassador to Italy and the UK.

78. Interfax, November 5, 1992 [FBIS-SOV, 92–216, November 6, 1992, 58–59].

79. *Nezavisimaya Gazeta*, September 17, 1992 [FBIS-SOV-92-181, September 17, 1992, 52].

80. Shodmon Yusupov (Yusuf), "A Letter to *Nezavisimaya Gazeta*," dated August 1993, *Nezavisimaya Gazeta*, August 25, 1993 [JPRS Report, FBIS-USR-93-122, JPRS, September 22, 1993, 78–82].

81. Monica Whitlock, *Land Beyond the River: The Untold Story of Central Asia* (New York: St. Martin's Press, 2002), 170.

82. Interfax, October 30, 1997 [FBIS]. While the Popular Front forces accepted Uzbekistan's help in their struggle against the Tajik opposition, it was out of dire necessity and not affinity. After ousting the opposition from Dushanbe, Tajikistan's leaders under Emomali Rahmonov cast their lot with Moscow, which rankled Tashkent. In coming years, Uzbekistan provided sanctuary to a renegade Tajik

Popular Front commander, Col. Mahmud Khudoyberdiyev, who—after revolting in August 1997—mounted incursions from Uzbekistan into Tajikistan in October 1997 and November 1998. Karimov's retort cited above came after Dushanbe complained about Khudoyberdiyev's first incursion. After the second incursion, Rahmonov openly accused Tashkent, including President Karimov and Rahmonov's 1994 presidential election rival Abdumalek Abdullojonov, of supporting Khudoyberdiyev's forces (Russian Public Television, November 12, 1998 [FBIS]).

83. In September 1994 Yusuf broke with the opposition and began to support Rahmonov. See Sergei Gretsky, "Russia and Tajikistan," in *Regional Power Rivalries*, 249.

84. Khakimov, interview.

85. Yuri Fedorov, interview by author, Moscow, December 6, 1999. Fedorov was head of section, USA and Canada Institute, and professor, Moscow State Institute of International Relations (MGIMO). In fact, Colombia was also well known for emerald smuggling long before it became even better known for narco-trafficking.

86. Bazhanov, interview.

87. Moscow, background interview.

88. Zviagelskaya, interview.

89. Mamedova, interview; and Vyacheslav Yakovlevich Belokrenitsky, interview by author, Moscow, December 6, 1999. Belokrenitsky was head of the Near and Middle East Department of the Institute of Oriental Studies. Article 3, Point 16 of the Constitution of the Islamic Republic of Iran (http://www.iranchamber.com/government/laws/constitution_ch01.php) calls for "framing the foreign policy of the country on the basis of Islamic criteria, fraternal commitment to all Muslims, and unsparing support to the freedom fighters of the world." I am grateful to William A. (Bill) Samii for calling this to my attention.

90. Khakimov, interview.

91. Fedorov, interview. For a sample of Kurginyan's thinking, including his analysis of what happened in Tajikistan, possible future parallels in Russia (e.g., Moscow and St. Petersburg as the Russian Khujand, Nizhniy Novgorod or the Urals as Garm, and the Kursk, Lipetsk, etc. "red belt" as Kulob), and criticism of Kozyrev, see Kurginyan's interview in *Pravda*, August 10, 1993 [JPRS Report, FBIS-USR-93-117, September 8, 1993, 83–86]; and his analysis, apparently submitted to the Supreme Soviet, reprinted in *Sovetskaya Rossiya*, July 29, 1993 [JPRS Report, FBIS-USR-93-117, September 8, 1993, 66–80].

92. Zviagelskaya, interview.

93. Khakimov, interview; and Andrey Kozyrev, interview by author, Moscow, September 13, 2000. Kozyrev was Russian foreign minister from October 1990 to January 1996.

94. Figures are from the 1989 USSR Census, according to which 62.3 percent of Tajikistan's population was ethnic Tajik. See Gosudarstvennyi komitet SSSR po statistike [USSR State Committee for Statistics], *Natsionalnyi sostav naseleniya SSSR: Po dannym vsesoyuznoy perepisi naseleniya 1989 g.* [National composition of the population of the USSR: Data from the 1989 all-union population census] (Moscow: "Finansy i Statistika," 1991), 17.

95. Moscow Teleradiokompaniya Ostankino Television First Program, May 14, 1992 [FBIS-SOV-92-095, May 15, 1992, 7–8].

96. ITAR-TASS, August 28, 1992 [FBIS-SOV-92-168, August 28, 1992, 45].

97. Interfax, October 9, 1992 [FBIS-SOV-92-198, October 13, 1992, 2].

98. For some examples, see Gretsky, "Russia and Tajikistan," 238–239.

99. Escudero, "Rat-a-tat-tat," 14–15.

100. ITAR-TASS, September 8, 1992 [FBIS-SOV-92-175, September 9, 1992, 11].

101. Interfax, October 6, 1992 [FBIS-SOV-92-195, October 7, 1992, 29].

102. Yegor Timurovich Gaidar, *Days of Defeat and Victory* (Seattle: University of Washington Press, 1999), 176–178.

103. ITAR-TASS, November 5, 1992 [FBIS-SOV-92-215, November 5, 1992, 3].

104. Interfax, November 6, 1992 [FBIS-SOV-92-217, November 9, 1992, 45].

105. Interfax, November 6, 1992 [FBIS-SOV-92-217, November 9, 1992, 44].

106. Interfax, November 30, 1992 [FBIS-SOV-92-231, December 1, 1992, 4].

107. *Krasnaya Zvezda*, December 3, 1992 [FBIS-SOV-92-234, December 4, 1992, 4].

108. For an overview of CIS decision making on sending a peacekeeping force to Tajikistan, see A. I. Nikitin and others, *Mirotvorcheskiye Operatsii v SNG* [Peacemaking operations in the CIS] (Moscow: Moskovskii Obshchestvennii Nauchnii Fond, 1998), 36–48 and 96–97.

109. Andrey Kozyrev, interview.

## CHAPTER 5: THE BAIT OF "STRATEGIC PARTNERSHIP"

1. Adamishin, interview.

2. Mesbahi, "Tajikistan, Iran, and 'Islamic Factor,'" 150. As noted previously, Article 3, Point 16 of the Constitution of the Islamic Republic of Iran calls for "framing the foreign policy of the country on the basis of Islamic criteria, fraternal commitment to all Muslims, and unsparing support to the freedom fighters of the world."

3. "The People of Tajikistan: Multiplied Oppression," *Salam*, December 31, 1992 [FBIS-NES-93-020, February 2, 1993, 70–71].

4. Gretsky, "Civil War," 236–237.

5. Adamishin, interview, and *Rossiyskiye Vesti*, December 23, 1993 [FBIS-SOV-93-246, December 27, 1993, 33–36].

6. IRNA, September 5, 1992 [FBIS-NES-92-175, September 9, 1992, 48].

7. Russian Television Network, October 14, 1992 [FBIS-SOV-92-200, October 15, 1992, 8].

8. *Abrar*, November 9, 1992 [FBIS-NES-92-222, November 17, 1992, 52].

9. IRNA, December 12, 1992 [FBIS-NES-92-240, December 14, 1992, 38]. The Russians were not alone in continuing high-level contacts with the Iranians during this period, as Kazakhstan's Nursultan Nazarbayev (October 31–November 3) and Uzbekistan's Islom Karimov (November 24–25) both stopped in Tehran that fall.

10. Andrey Kozyrev, interview. Unfortunately, time did not permit exploring the Azerbaijan angle in our interview.

11. Ibid.

12. Khakimov, interview.

13. Kozyrev and Velayati news conference, ITAR-TASS, March 29, 1993 [FBIS-SOV-93-059, March 30, 1993, 11–12].

14. Khakimov, interview; and Interfax, March 31, 1993 [FBIS-SOV-93-060, March 31, 1993, 9].

15. ITAR-TASS, March 29, 1993 [FBIS-SOV-93-059, March 30, 1993, 10–11].

16. Vyacheslav Ushakov, "What Is Impeding Cooperation?" *Pravda*, July 24, 1993 [FBIS-USR-93-107, August 18, 1993, 65–67].

17. *Izvestiya*, July 24, 1993 [FBIS-SOV-93-142, July 27, 1993, 10].

18. Maksim Yusin, "Moscow Offers Tehran 'Strategic Partnership,'" *Izvestiya*, April 1, 1993 [FBIS-SOV-93-061, April 1, 1993, 8].

19. "Novosti" newscast, Moscow Ostankino Television First Channel Network, March 31, 1993 [FBIS-SOV-93-061, April 1, 1993, 6].

20. Andrey Ivanovich Nikolayev, *Na perelome: Zapiski russkogo generala* [At the turning point: Notes of a Russian general] (Moscow: Sovremennyi pisatel, 1999), 150.

21. Radio Moscow, July 18, 1993 [FBIS-SOV-93-137, July 20, 1993, 14].

22. In his memoir, Gorbachev's aide Anatoly Chernyayev takes Shevardnadze to task for proposing cross-border strikes in 1989 (Chernyayev, *Shest' let*, 269–273). In May–June 2000, Russian officials again threatened such strikes, this time in response to alleged Taliban support for Muslim rebels fighting in Chechnya (see Pamela Constable, "Russia, U.S. Converge on Warnings to Taliban; Ex-Rivals Fear Afghan Support for Terrorists," *Washington Post*, June 4, 2000).

23. Yuri Fedorov, "Russia Has Neither the Forces to Get Out Nor the Forces to Remain: An Analysis," *Obshchaya Gazeta*, No. 5, August 20–26, 1993 [FBIS-USR-93-121, September 20, 1993, 13–14].

24. Ibid.

25. See, for example, "The Russians on the Path of No Return," *Salam*, July 19, 1993 [FBIS-NES-93-147, August 3, 1993, 45].

26. Kamal Hoseyni, "The Domain of Iranian Culture and Civilization in Danger of a Foreign Onslaught," *Salam*, August 4, 1993 [FBIS-NES-93-161, August 23, 1993, 69–70].

27. As cited earlier, this is consistent with what former acting premier Yegor Gaidar reported in his memoir and what Andrey Kozyrev related to the present author was the case in Tajikistan in 1992 while he was dealing with the trouble spot as foreign minister.

28. Fedorov, interview.

29. Adamishin, interview.

30. Moscow, background interview.

31. For country-by-country surveys of developments in this period, see Matlock, *Autopsy*, 678–740. See also Karen Dawisha and Bruce Parrott, eds., *Russia and the New States of Eurasia: The Politics of Upheaval* (Cambridge: Cambridge University Press, 1994), passim; *Democratic Changes and Authoritarian Reactions in Russia, Ukraine, Belarus and Moldova* (Cambridge: Cambridge University Press, 1997), passim; and *Conflict, Cleavage, and Change in Central Asia and the Caucasus* (Cambridge: Cambridge University Press, 1997), passim.

32. Fedorov, interview. Kozyrev in December 1992 had already shocked counterparts at the CSCE ministerial summit in Stockholm when he stated, but then retracted as a "rhetorical technique," that "the former Soviet Union . . . is post-imperial territory where Russia will have to defend its interests by using all available means, including military and economic ones." (ITAR-TASS, December 14, 1992 [FBIS-SOV-92-241, December 15, 1992, 7–8]).

33. ITAR-TASS, January 18, 1994 [FBIS-SOV-94-011, January 18, 1994, 1–2].

34. Alexei G. Arbatov, "Russian National Interests," in *Damage Limitation or Crisis? Russia and the Outside World*, ed. Robert D. Blackwill and Sergei A. Karaganov, CSIA Studies in International Security, no. 5 (Washington, DC: Brassey's, Inc., 1994), 59–60, citing V. Portnikov, "Andrei Kozyrev Defines Priorities," *Nezavisimaya Gazeta*, January 20, 1994. On Yeltsin and Kozyrev's hardening rhetoric during this period, see also Nikitin and others, *Mirotvorcheskiye Operatsiy*, 77–78.

35. Fedorov, interview.

36. The LDPR won 22.9 percent of the popular vote, while the CPRF and its Agrarian allies garnered 20.4 percent. See Michael Urban and Vladimir Gel'man, "The Development of Political Parties in Russia," in *Democratic Changes*, 203, table 5.3.

37. Catherine Poujol, "Chronology of the Russian Involvement in the Tajik Conflict, 1992–1993," in *Tajikistan: The Trials of Independence*, ed. Mohammad Reza Djalili, Frederic Grare, and Shirin Akiner (Richmond, Surrey: Curzon Press, 1998), 117.

38. Jonathan Valdez, "The Near Abroad, the West, and National Identity in Russian Foreign Policy," in *The Making of Foreign Policy in Russia and the New States of Eurasia*, ed. Adeed Dawisha and Karen Dawisha (Armonk: M. E. Sharpe, 1995), 98.

39. Strobe Talbott, *Russia Hand: A Memoir of Presidential Diplomacy* (New York: Random House, 2002), 93 and 111.

40. Bazhanov, interview.

41. Fedorov, "Russia Has Neither."

42. ITAR-TASS, July 29, 1993 [FBIS-SOV-93-145, July 30, 1993, 50].

43. *Izvestiya*, August 5, 1993 [FBIS-SOV-93-149, August 5, 1993, 5–6].

44. See Yeltsin's comments at the post-summit news conference, Moscow Teleradio-kompaniya Ostankino Television First Program Network, January 22, 1993 [FBIS-SOV-93-014, January 25, 1993, 8].

45. Interfax, March 10, 1993 [FBIS-SOV-93-045, March 10, 1993, 16–17].

46. ITAR-TASS, March 3, 1993 [FBIS-SOV-93-041, March 4, 1993, 58]; and interview with Air Marshal Yevgeny Shaposhnikov, commander of CIS Joint Armed Forces, Moscow Ostankino First Channel Network, April 23, 1993 [FBIS-SOV-93-078, April 26, 1993, 1–4].

47. Interfax, April 13, 1993 [FBIS-SOV-93-070, April 14, 1993, 73]; and *Nezavisimaya Gazeta*, April 29, 1993 [FBIS-SOV-93-082, April 30, 1993, 13–14].

48. CIS prime ministers met in Moscow on March 12 and in Minsk on April 28. CIS heads of state met at Zaslavl near Minsk on April 16 and in Moscow on May 14, 1993.

49. *Krasnaya Zvezda*, May 27, 1993 [FBIS-SOV-93-102, May 28, 1993, 11–12]; and Ministerstvo inostrannykh del Rossiyskoy Federatsii [Ministry of foreign affairs of the Russian Federation], *Vneshnayaya Politika Rossii: Sbornik dokumentov: 1993: Kniga 1: Yanvar' – Mai* [Foreign policy of Russia: Collected documents: 1993: Book 1: January–May] (Moscow: Mezhdunarodnyye otnosheniya, 2000), 472–482, 482–486, and 487–498.

50. Moscow Radio Rossii Network, July 30, 1993 [FBIS-SOV-93-146, August 2, 1993, 73].

51. *Izvestiya*, August 5, 1993 [FBIS-SOV-93-149, August 5, 1993, 5–6].

52. *Nezavisimaya Gazeta*, August 6, 1993 [FBIS-SOV-93-151, August 9, 1993, 1–2].

53. Nikitin and others, *Mirotvorcheskiye Operatsii*, 43.

54. *Moskovskiye Novosti*, no. 33, August 15, 1993 [FBIS-SOV-93-155, August 13, 1993, 1–2].

55. *Rossiyskiye Vesti*, August 6, 1993 [FBIS-SOV-93-152, August 10, 1993, 5].

56. On Masoud's control of Taloqan, see V. G. Korgun, *Afganistan: politika i politiki* [Afghanistan: Politics and politicians] (Moscow: Institute of Oriental Studies of the Russian Academy of Sciences, 1999), 119 and 123. Though by 1995 Turajonzoda was living in Tehran, see his remarks on Taloqan and the first congress of the MIRT held in Taloqan at the end of January 1993 in his interview by David Nalle with Sergei Gretsky, "Interview with Qadi Akbar Turajonzoda," *Central Asia Monitor*, no. 2 (1995): 9–11.

57. Moscow Center TV, February 1, 2001 [FBIS].

58. Primakov, *Gody*, 179.

59. Rashid, *Taliban*, 129.

60. As Primakov notes, Hekmatyar occupied the area of Kabul where the old, completely destroyed Soviet embassy building was. Primakov, *Gody*, 180.

61. For details on Masoud's longtime rivalry with Hekmatyar, see Barnett R. Rubin, *The Fragmentation of Afghanistan: State Formation and Collapse in the International System*, 2nd ed. (New Haven: Yale University Press, 2002), 158, 250–251, and 277; and Coll, *Ghost Wars*, 121, 181–184, 202, 211–214, 236–237, and 262–263.

62. Rubin, *Fragmentation*, 220.

63. "Soviets to Embrace Afghan Foe?" *Christian Science Monitor*, October 19, 1988, as cited by Cordovez and Harrison, *Out of Afghanistan*, 380.

64. Escudero, "Rat-a-tat-tat," 14. The article includes a photograph showing the view of the Kaziat compound from the American mission.

65. Khaidarov and Inomov, *Tajikistan*, 17, 26, 43, 74, and 77.

66. See, for example, Coll's treatment of Masoud and Hekmatyar in *Ghost Wars*, passim.

67. Mohammad Reza Djalili and Frederic Grare, "Regional Ambitions and Interests in Tajikistan: The Role of Afghanistan, Pakistan and Iran," in *Tajikistan*, 121.

68. Ahmed Rashid, "Playing With Fire," *Herald*, June 15, 2003 [JPRS-NEA-93-107, October 27, 1993, 13–14].

69. Boris V. Gromov, *Ogranichennyi Kontingent* [Limited contingent] (Moscow: Progress-Kultura, 1994), 189–192. On the cease-fire, see also Girardet, *Afghanistan*, 85–87; Rubin, *Fragmentation*, 220; and Coll, *Ghost Wars*, 118–119.

70. William Maley, *The Afghanistan Wars* (Houndmills, Basingstoke, Hampshire: Palgrave Macmillan, 2002), 198–199.

71. Gromov, *Ogranichennyi Kontingent*, 189–192.

72. Rubin, *Search*, 65 and 81. Steve Coll briefly refers to assertions that Masoud, as early as spring 1985, mounted some of the first cross-border incursions into the Soviet Union (*Ghost Wars*, 106) but otherwise does not dwell on Masoud in this context and does not discuss at all any similar operations by Hekmatyar. On balance, Rubin's account is more persuasive and accords with other assertions pointing to early activities by Hekmatyar rather than Masoud in Soviet Tajikistan.

73. Djalili and Grare, "Regional Ambitions," 121.

74. Khudonazarov, interview, September 11, 2000. For firsthand accounts vividly depicting life in Afghanistan's Kunduz and Takhar provinces just across the border from Tajikistan during the decades of strife inflicted by the Soviet invasion, mujahideen infighting, and then the Taliban regime, see Alex Klaits and Gulchin Gulmamadova-Klaits, *Love and War in Afghanistan* (New York: Seven Stories Press, 2005), passim.

75. Primakov, *Gody*, 180.

76. Ibid., 181–182.

77. Ibid., 182.

78. Ibid., 182–183.

79. Ibid., 184.

80. Ibid., 185; and again in Yevgeny Maksimovich Primakov, *Minnoye pole politiki* [The minefield of politics] (Moscow: Molodaya Gvardiya, 2007), 147. When Kozyrev had been in Tehran in March, some Iranian officials had also expressed fear of "unpredictable" developments flowing from the conflict in Tajikistan. One confided to a Russian correspondent, "If the Afghan Tajiks (Rabbani and Masoud) join forces with the opposition in Tajikistan, this will lead to breaking up Afghanistan and jeopardize stability in Iran, where many Tajiks live." See Interfax, March 31, 1993 [FBIS-SOV-93-060, March 31, 1993, 9].

81. Primakov, *Gody*, 185. Primakov in his memoir did not comment further on his February 1995 trip to Tehran. It may have been to consult over the Taliban's ongoing assault on Kabul. It may also have been to preview for Tehran what an upcoming SVR report would have to say on Iranian nuclear programs (see chapter 6).

82. Rubin, *Search*, 121 and 128–129.

83. Ibid., 129–130.

84. Voice of the Islamic Republic of Iran, August 2, 1993 [FBIS-NES-93-147, August 3, 1993, 43].

85. Voice of the Islamic Republic of Iran, September 16, 1993 [FBIS-NES-93-179, September 17, 1993, 52–53].
86. *Rossiyskiye Vesti*, January 11, 1994 [FBIS-SOV-94-008, January 12, 1994, 1–2]; and *Nezavisimaya Gazeta*, July 23, 1994 [FBIS-SOV-94-142, July 25, 1994, 63–64].
87. Nikitin and others, *Mirotvorcheskiye Operatsii*, 98. *Krasnaya Zvezda* of July 1, 2000 [FBIS] put the number of soldiers in Tajikistan in 1994 at 322 from Uzbekistan and 108 from Kyrgyzstan.
88. U.S. Department of State, Office of Research, "Russians See No End to Chechen Conflict, Feel Vulnerable to Terrorism," Opinion Analysis, M-145-01, Washington, DC, July 9, 2001.
89. Nikitin and others, *Mirotvorcheskiye Operatsii*, 44–46.
90. *Krasnaya Zvezda*, July 20, 1994 [FBIS-SOV-94-140, July 21, 1994, 2].
91. Nikitin and others, *Mirotvorcheskiye Operatsii*, 97–98; and *Krasnaya Zvezda*, July 1, 2000 [FBIS]. The actual strength of both the 201st and the Border Guards was subject to conjecture over the years, but in any event both were heavily local ethnic Tajik. Around 1994 the 201st was manned by only some 6,000 soldiers (Nikitin and others, *Mirotvorcheskiye Operatsii*, 46; and *Krasnaya Zvezda*, July 1, 2000 [FBIS]). Six years later, in 2000, according to observers in Moscow, the 201st's manpower stood at around 8,500, though a year later the Russian press put the number closer to 7,000, all contract soldiers (background interview, Moscow, March 2000; and *Moskovskiy Komsomolets*, June 14, 2001 [FBIS]). Russian Border Guards personnel ranged from 10,000 to 12,000. The 201st and Border Guards were led almost exclusively by Russian officers. However, the conscripts and contract soldiers of the Russian Border Guards were predominantly local ethnic Tajiks, and Tajiks made up from a quarter to a third of the 201st Division's contract soldiers (*Kraznaya Zvezda*, March 7, 2001 [FBIS]; *Moskovskiy Komsomolets*, June 14, 2001 [FBIS]; *Agentsvo Voyennykh Novostey*, January 23, 2002 [FBIS]; and *Agentstvo Voyennykh Novostey*, October 11, 2002 [FBIS]).
92. Background interviews, Washington, DC, 1999–2000; and Nikitin and others, *Mirotvorcheskiye Operatsii*, 98.
93. ITAR-TASS, October 30, 1993 [FBIS-SOV-93-209, November 1, 1993, 57–58]; and Moscow Ostankino Television First Channel and Orbita Networks, November 3, 1993 [FBIS-SOV-93-213, November 5, 1993, 71–72].
94. Voice of the Islamic Republic of Iran, March 6, 1994 [FBIS-NES-94-045, March 8, 1994, 65–66].
95. *Salam*, March 8, 1994 [FBIS-NES-94-050, March 15, 1994, 41].
96. ITAR-TASS, March 11, 1994 [FBIS-SOV-94-048, March 11, 1994, 46–47]; and Radio Rossi Network, March 12, 1994 [FBIS-SOV-94-049, March 14, 1994, 54–55].
97. Adamishin, interview.
98. Ibid.
99. According to estimates for July 1999, Tajiks constituted 64.9 percent of Tajikistan's population of 6,102,854 in July 1999, and 25 percent of Afghanistan's 25,824,882. See U.S. Central Intelligence Agency, *The World Factbook 1999* (Washington, DC: Central Intelligence Agency, 1999), 1 and 471.
100. Umnov, interview.
101. Zviagelskaya, interview.

## CHAPTER 6: KILO SUBS, BUSHEHR, AND SHAHAB

1. The trade Moscow worked out with Washington gave a green light to U.S.-Russian space cooperation and opened the door to lucrative commercial space launch contracts for Glavkosmos, Russia's Main Administration for the Development and Use of Space

Technology for the National Economy and Scientific Research. It would be formally subordinated to the Russian Space Agency at the beginning of 1998 (*Rossiyskaya Gazeta*, May 20, 1998 [FBIS]). Nevertheless, the agreement to give up the deal with India provoked a storm of criticism of Yeltsin and resentment of Washington in the Russian military-industrial complex and Duma opposition (see Talbott, *Russia Hand*, 81–83, 158–159, and 441nn5–6).

2. *Kommersant-Daily*, May 18, 1995 [FBIS]; and Talbott, *Russia Hand*, 158–159.

3. For tracking Yeltsin's health and drinking, the index entries in Talbott, *Russia Hand*, and Leon Aron, *Yeltsin: A Revolutionary Life* (New York: St. Martin's Press, 2000), are particularly useful.

4. Konstantin Eggert, "'Meteor' for the Ayatollahs: Iran Needs Ballistic Missiles in Order to Become a World Power," *Izvestiya*, October 21, 1998 [FBIS].

5. Vladimir V. Lebedev, interview by author, Moscow, April 4, 2000. Lebedev at the time was deputy head, National Security Studies Center, Moscow State University; deputy director of the International Relations Department of the Moscow city government; head of the International Department of the Otechestvo movement; and coordinator for "Otechestvo i Vsya Rossiya" (OVR) in the Duma. Earlier, Lebedev had served as assistant to Security Council Chairmen Andrey Kokoshin and Nikolay Bordyuzha. For a firsthand account by Vadim Vorobei, the head of the faculty of engine production at the Moscow Aviation Institute, see Michael Dobbs, "The Missile Trail: A Story of Iran's Quest for Power," *Washington Post*, January 13, 2002.

6. Sergo Anastasevich Mikoyan, interview by author, Moscow, December 3, 1999. Mikoyan, former director of the Latin America Institute in Moscow, was at this time chief researcher, Center of Peace Studies, Institute of World Economy and International Relations (IMEMO) and the compiler and editor of several volumes of posthumous memoirs by his legendary father, Anastas Mikoyan.

7. Yakovlev, interview.

8. The view of Dmitri Babich, foreign editor of the *Moscow News*, as reported in the *Washington Post*, August 16, 2002.

9. Simonia, interview. See also Nodari Simonia, "Domestic Developments in Russia," in *Russia and Asia: The Emerging Security Agenda*, ed. Gennady Chufrin (Oxford: Oxford University Press, 1999), 64.

10. "Surplus to Requirements," *The Economist*, July 8, 2000, 79.

11. As quoted by Scott Peterson in "Russian Nuclear Know-How Pours Into Iran," *Christian Science Monitor*, June 21, 2002.

12. *Yadernyy Kontrol*, no. 3 (May–June 1999): 8–13 [FBIS].

13. On this theme, see Eugene B. Rumer, *Dangerous Drift: Russia's Middle East Policy* (Washington, DC: Washington Institute for Near East Policy, 2000), passim.

14. Dobbs, "Missile Trail." For more detail, see chapter 7.

15. See especially *Izvestiya*, February 6, 1992 [FBIS-SOV-92-026, February 7, 1992, 33–35], in which Vladimir Skosyrev juxtaposed the concerns of critics with the defense by an anonymous "diplomat"; and Vadim Makarevsky, "To Sell or Not to Sell?" *New Times*, no. 16 (April 1992): 30–32.

16. Radio Moscow, September 25, 1992 [FBIS-SOV-92-188, September 28, 1992, 9].

17. Interfax, October 14, 1992 [FBIS-SOV-92-200, October 15, 1992, 7].

18. Aron, *Yeltsin*, 571.

19. Ibid., 559–561.

20. Douglas Frantz and Catherine Collins, *The Nuclear Jihadist: The True Story of the Man Who Sold the World's Most Dangerous Secrets . . . and How We Could Have Stopped Him* (New York: Twelve, 2007), 156–161. See also John Lancaster and Kamran Khan, "Pakistan

Fires Top Nuclear Scientist," *Washington Post*, February 1, 2004; and Douglas Frantz, "From Patriot to Proliferator," *Los Angeles Times*, September 23, 2005.

21. This summary of the last months of the Iran-Iraq War and their heavy toll draws from Eisenstadt, *Iranian Military Power*, 28; Shahram Chubin, "Iran and the War: From Stalemate to Ceasefire," in *The Iran-Iraq War*, 21–22; Thomas McNaugher, "Walking Tightropes in the Gulf," in *The Iran-Iraq War*, 187–191; Herzog, "A Military-Strategic Overview," 263–264; Mackey, *Iranians*, 316–333; Hiro, *Longest War*, 200–201 and 249–251; and Smolansky, *USSR and Iraq*, 259 and 265–268.

22. Cited by Nazila Fathi, "An Old Letter Casts Doubts on Iran's Goal for Uranium," *New York Times*, October 5, 2006; and Bill Samii, "Battles Begin as Assembly Experts Await Vetting," *RFE/RL Iran Report*, October 17, 2006, http://archive.rferl.org/reports/Archive.aspx?report=571&year=2008. In 1987 Rezai had included "rocket, chemical, bacteriological and nuclear industries" among Iran's research and production industrial groups (quoted by Chubin, *Iran's National Security Policy*, 26). Rezai's 1988 list of requirements would resurface in 2006 in an entirely different political context.

23. Cited in Chubin, *Iran's National Security Policy*, 26 and 52; and "NTI: Iran Nuclear Chronology 1988," http://www.nti.org/e_research/profiles/Iran/1825_1858.html.

24. Bob Drogin, "Iraq's 'Nuclear Mastermind' Tells Tale of Ambition, Deceit," *Los Angeles Times*, October 3, 2004.

25. Dana Priest and Walter Pincus, "U.S. 'Almost All Wrong' on Weapons," *Washington Post*, October 7, 2004.

26. The declaration Rafsanjani and Gorbachev signed in Moscow in June 1989 stated that Iran and the USSR would cooperate in working for the prohibition and elimination of nuclear, chemical, and other types of weapons of mass destruction. For the text of the declaration of principles of relations, see TASS, June 22, 1989 [FBIS-SOV-89-119, June 22, 1989, 23–24]. After his own allusion in 1988 to the need for nuclear weapons, Rezai likewise perished the thought in subsequent declarations. In 1995, for example, he told an interviewer, "We do not want to move toward strategic weapons; and the Western propaganda that Iran is trying to acquire nuclear weapons is an outright lie" (*Resalat*, September 24, 1995 [FBIS-NES-95-193, October 5, 1995, 1–4]).

27. Eisenstadt, *Iranian Military Power*, 14. For an overview of Iran's nuclear ambitions and programs under the shah, and of the contradictory American, British, French, and German reactions to them, see Frantz and Collins, *Nuclear Jihadist*, 55–60.

28. Mikhaylov, "Ordynka."

29. Chubin, *Iran's National Security Policy*, 35–38.

30. For a review of the 1986–87 revelations about Israel's nuclear weapons program—which presumably had an impact on Tehran's assessment of its military requirements—by Israeli nuclear research center employee Mordechai Vanunu, see the *Washington Post*, November 25, 1999. See also the reportage occasioned by Vanunu's release from prison (*Washington Post*, April 21 and 22, 2004).

31. Chubin, *Iran's National Security Policy*, 55–56; and Eisenstadt, *Iranian Military Power*, 10–11.

32. Joby Warrick, "Nuclear Program in Iran Tied to Pakistan," *Washington Post*, December 21, 2003; and John Lancaster and Kamran Khan, "Pakistan Fires Top Nuclear Scientist," *Washington Post*, February 1, 2004. See also David Rohde and David E. Sanger, "Key Pakistani Is Said to Admit Atom Transfers," *New York Times*, February 2, 2004; Frantz, "From Patriot to Proliferator;" Frantz and Collins, *Nuclear Jihadist*, 160–161, 198–199, and 211–213; and David Armstrong and Joseph Trento, *America and the Islamic Bomb: The Deadly Compromise* (Hanover, NH: Steerforth Press, 2007), 158–161 and 167–169.

33. Douglas Frantz, Paul Watson, and Mubashir Zaidi, "Pakistan Caught in a Web of Evidence," *Los Angeles Times*, February 3, 2004.

34. Interfax, November 6, 1992 [FBIS-SOV-92-217, November 9, 1992, 44].

35. Andrey Kamorin, "Moscow to Sell Nuclear Reactors to Tehran," *Izvestiya*, March 31, 1993 [FBIS-SOV-93-061, April 1, 1993, 7–8]; and "Russia, Iran Sign Agreements," *RFE/RL Newsline*, March 30, 1993.

36. *Izvestiya*, March 31, 1993 [FBIS-SOV-93-061, April 1, 1993, 7–8].

37. Cited in Eisenstadt, *Iranian Military Power*, 11.

38. *Izvestiya*, February 6, 1992 [FBIS-SOV-92-026, February 7, 1992, 34].

39. Mikhaylov, "Ordynka." By November 1992, the two sides had signed a protocol covering both spheres. See London *Al-Hayah*, November 25, 1992 [FBIS-SOV-92-229, November 27, 1992, 17]. One of these agreements culminated with the signing in October 1995 of a final contract by which Russia would install a thousand-megawatt reactor at the Bushehr nuclear power plant (Mikhaylov, "Ordynka").

40. Kozyrev and Velayati news conference, ITAR-TASS, March 29, 1993 [FBIS-SOV-93-059, March 30, 1993, 11–12].

41. Indyk, "Clinton Administration's Approach." For one chronology of Washington's pressure on Moscow re Iran, see *Russkiy Telegraf*, March 11, 1998 [FBIS].

42. Talbott, *Russia Hand*, 64–65 and 424.

43. Interview with Andrey Kozyrev in *Al-Wasat*, June 12–18, 1994 [FBIS].

44. *Jomhuri-Ye Eslami*, April 13, 1994 [FBIS-NES-94-079, April 25, 1994, 82]; and IRNA, June 16, 1994 [FBIS-NES-94-123, June 27, 1994, 72–73].

45. Boris Konovalov, *Izvestiya*, June 22, 1995 [FBIS].

46. As early as Kozyrev's March 1993 stop in Tehran, the two sides had also concluded a contract on construction of two additional units (Bushehr 3 and 4) to be fitted out with VVER 440 megawatt light-water reactors. This contract, however, was subsequently suspended at Iran's initiative. See Veronika Romanenkova, interview with Georgiy Kaurov, Head, Public Relations Department, Russian Ministry for Atomic Energy, "No Secret Nuclear Deals," ITAR-TASS, September 15, 1995 [FBIS].

47. See text in Eisenstadt, *Iranian Military Power*, 106–107.

48. The final contract had to be renegotiated in September 1998, when Russia committed to finishing Bushehr within fifty-two months, that is, by February 2003, some four years behind the original schedule (IRNA, January 30, 2001 [FBIS]; and Viktor Vishniakov, "Russian-Iranian Relations and Regional Stability," *International Affairs* 45, no. 1 (1999): 151–152). Even that target date proved too ambitious and had to be repeatedly put back.

49. Sluzhba vneshnei razvedki Rossii, otkrytyi doklad SVR za 1993g, "Novyi vyzov posle 'kholodnoi voiny': rasprostraneniy oruzhiya massovogo unichtozheniya: Iran," http://svr.gov.ru/material/2-1.html and http://svr.gov.ru/material/2-13-9.html.

50. Sluzhba vneshnei razvedki Rossii, otkrytyi doklad SVR za 1995g, "Dogovor o nerasprostranenii yadernogo oruzhiya: Problemy prodleniya: Iran," http://svr.gov.ru/material/4-0.html and http://svr.gov.ru/material/4-iran.html.

51. *Rossiyskaya Gazeta*, March 25, 1995 [FBIS-SOV-95-058, March 27, 1995, 4–5].

52. During his February 1995 trip to Tehran (see chapter 5), Primakov may have previewed what the SVR's report on the operation of the NPT—in connection with the upcoming conference in New York on extending the NPT's operation—would have to say on Iran.

53. *The Independent*, May 30, 1995.

54. Eisenstadt, *Iranian Military Power*, 9n1, 10n3, and 32.

55. *Kommersant-Daily*, May 18, 1995 [FBIS].

56. Talbott, *Russia Hand*, 158.
57. Armstrong and Trento, *America and the Islamic Bomb*, 161–162, 169, and 219–220; and Frantz and Collins, *Nuclear Jihadist,* 36–48, 201–203, 208–210, 213, 216, and 219–221.
58. Talbott, *Russia Hand*, 161 and 445n7; Bill Clinton, *My Life* (New York: Knopf, 2004), 655; Jim Hoagland, "Briefing Yeltsin on Iran," *Washington Post*, May 17, 1995; and Frantz and Collins, *Nuclear Jihadist*, 214–215.
59. "Atomic Energy Ministry Confused Its Own Interests With National Interests in Signing the Protocol With Iran," *Izvestiya*, June 2, 1995 [FBIS]. See also the televised debate in which Yablokov accused MinAtom Deputy Minister Yevgeniy Reshetnikov of "having the intention to violate national security in the interests of the ministry," while Reshetnikov defended the protocol as simply instructing "the appropriate bodies to look at the possibility of selling Iran a diffusion plant" (Russian Public Television, June 4, 1995 [FBIS]).
60. Mikhaylov, "Ordynka."
61. *New York Times*, August 22, 2002.
62. *Nezavisimaya Gazeta*, January 27, 1999 [FBIS]; and Talbott, *Russia Hand*, 255 and 451n1.
63. For Russian Government Decree No. 737, signed by Premier Chernomyrdin on July 24, 1995, and instructing the Foreign Ministry to forward the appropriate MTCR membership documents, see *Rossiyskaya Gazeta*, August 18, 1995 [FBIS].
64. AFP, December 19, 1995 [FBIS].
65. Presidential Edict No. 1268, "On Control Over the Export of Dual-Purpose Goods and Technologies From the Russian Federation," signed August 26, 1996. See *Rossiyskaya Gazeta*, September 3, 1996 [FBIS].
66. Primakov, *Gody*, 185.
67. Interfax, December 23, 1996 [FBIS]; and ITAR-TASS, December 23, 1996 [FBIS].
68. Valeriy Skvortsov, report on the results of Foreign Minister Yevgeny Primakov's visit to Iran, from the "Vesti" newscast, Russian Television Network, December 23, 1996 [FBIS].
69. ITAR-TASS, December 23, 1996 [FBIS].
70. IRNA, April 15, 1997 [FBIS].
71. Interfax, April 11, 1997 [FBIS].
72. As reported much later in ITAR-TASS, June 25, 2000 [FBIS].
73. Eggert, "'Meteor' for the Ayatollahs," October 21, 1998.
74. The others were the United States, NATO, Turkey on its own, Iran, Pakistan, Japan, and China. See *Kommersant-Daily*, December 26, 1996 [FBIS].
75. Russian Television Network, December 23, 1996 [FBIS].
76. See especially Eggert, "'Meteor' for the Ayatollahs," October 21 and 22, 1998.
77. Aron, *Yeltsin*, 649 and 658–659.
78. Ibid., 679.
79. *Kommersant-Daily,* March 4, 1998 [FBIS].
80. Talbott, *Russia Hand*, 255.
81. Ibid., 255–257.
82. Aleksey Bausin and Erlan Zhurabayev, "The Iranian Connection: A Partner With Whom One Has to Be on One's Guard," *Obshchaya Gazeta*, May 7–13, 1998 [FBIS]. See also ITAR-TASS, April 13, 1998 [FBIS].
83. Talbott, *Russia Hand*, 258–260; and David Hoffman, "Russia Was Lab for Theories on Foreign Policy," *Washington Post*, June 4, 2000.
84. Eggert, "'Meteor' for the Ayatollahs," October 22, 1998.

85. Talbott, *Russia Hand*, 267–273.
86. Ekho Moskvy, March 4, 1998 [FBIS].
87. *Iran News*, April 30, 1998 [FBIS].
88. IRIB Television First Program Network, September 10, 1997 [FBIS].
89. *Jame'eh*, April 29, 1998 [FBIS].
90. *Obshchaya Gazeta*, no. 16, April 23–29, 1998 [FBIS]. The first shoe dropped in July 1998, when Washington imposed sanctions on seven of these entities. The other shoe followed on January 12, 1999, when Washington added the Scientific Research and Design Institute for Energy Technologies (NIKIET), the Mendeleyev Institute of Chemical Technology (RKhTU), and the Moscow Aviation Institute (MAI) to this list for their involvement in the transfer of missile and nuclear technologies to Iran. See *Segodnya*, January 14, 1999 [FBIS], for the full list of the entities involved in the July 1998 action and for some of the initial reaction to the January 1999 announcement of sanctions.
91. *Izvestiya*, April 22, 1998 [FBIS].
92. Mikhail Rostovskiy, "Ahmadinejad Isn't Mean When It Comes to the Troubles He Could Bring to Russia and the World," *Moskovskiy Komsomolets*, May 23, 2006 [FBIS].
93. *Novyye Izvestiya*, May 13, 1998 [FBIS]; and *Kommersant-Daily*, May 30, 1998 [FBIS]. India had first tested a nuclear device in 1974; the 1998 series was Pakistan's first.
94. Talbott, *Russia Hand*, 269.
95. ITAR-TASS and Interfax, May 17, 1998 [FBIS]. For an extensive defense of Russian nuclear ties with Iran around this time by Yeltsin's press secretary Sergey Yastrzhembskiy, see ITAR-TASS, May 21, 1998 [FBIS].
96. *Izvestiya*, May 22, 1998 [FBIS]; and Interfax, May 28, 1998 [FBIS].
97. *Kommersant-Daily*, May 30, 1998 [FBIS].
98. Interfax, June 1, 1998 [FBIS].
99. Interview by Aleksey Venediktov, Ekho Moskvy, May 11, 1998 [FBIS].
100. Interfax, June 3, 1998 [FBIS].
101. Eggert, "'Meteor' for the Ayatollahs," October 22, 1998.
102. Eggert, "'Meteor' for the Ayatollahs," October 21, 1998.
103. John Lancaster and Kamran Khan, "Musharraf Named in Nuclear Probe," *Washington Post*, February 3, 2004.
104. A. Gusher and A. Slavokhotov, "Strategiya natsional'noi bezopasnosti Rossii na yuge" [Russia's strategy of national security in the south], *Aziya i Afrika segodnya*, no. 1 (1997): 35.
105. See Mikhail Kirillin, interview by *Yadernyy Kontrol*, "Mikhail Kirillin: Several U.S. Firms Engaged in Developing Missile Equipment Have Links With Iranians," *Yadernyy Kontrol* 38, no. 2 (March–April 1998): 37–43 [FBIS], for Kirillin's full interview. See also the extensive treatment of this issue in the report by Ivan Safranchuk of the PIR-Center, "Scientific Notes No. 8: The Nuclear and Missile Programs of Iran and Russian Security—The Framework of Russian-Iranian Collaboration," *Nauchnyye Zapiski* 8 (May 5, 1999): 1–36 [FBIS].
106. See, for example, the commentary by Vladimir Dunayev in *Izvestiya*, September 28, 2000 [FBIS]; and the series by Konstantin Eggert, "'Meteor' for the Ayatollahs," October 21 and 22, 1998. Western military experts regarded the first Shahab-3 test as unsuccessful. At the time of a second test, apparently more successful, in summer 2000, Iran said the Shahab-3 had a range of 800 miles and speed of 4,320 miles per hour with a one-ton warhead (*Washington Post*, July 16, 2000). During a third test in September 2000, the missile exploded shortly after liftoff (*Washington Times*, September 22, 2000). Subsequently, the success of the second test was ascribed by

U.S. and Israeli experts to Iran's replacement of an indigenously produced engine with one of a dozen North Korean engines delivered in November 1999 (Dobbs, "Missile Trail"). In May 2002, Iran confirmed reports of a successful fourth test flight of the Shahab-3 (Associated Press, *Washington Post*, May 27, 2002). A year later, after further tests and a final successful test in June 2003, the missile was slated to go into production and to be turned over to the Iranian armed forces for deployment (*New York Times*, July 8, 2003).

107. Talbott, *Russia Hand*, 294.
108. Yevgeniy Maksimovich Primakov, *Vosem' mesyatsev plyus* . . . [Eight months plus . . . ] (Moscow: "Mysl,'" 2001), 142–143.
109. Eggert, "'Meteor' for the Ayatollahs," October 21 and 22, 1998.
110. Lebedev, interview.
111. Simonia, interview.

## CHAPTER 7: THE PUTIN FACTOR

1. Putin was born October 7, 1952.
2. Nataliya Gevorkyan, Natalya Timakova, and Andrei Kolesnikov, *First Person: An Astonishingly Frank Self-Portrait by Russia's President Vladimir Putin* (New York: Public Affairs, 2000), 67.
3. Andrey Grigoryev, "Chubays Is to Blame for Everything," *Kompaniya*, April 8, 2002 [FBIS]; and Valeriy Vorontsov, *V koridorakh bezvlastiya (Premyeri Yeltsina)* [In the corridors of impotence (Yeltsin's premiers)] (Moscow: Akademicheskiy Proyekt, 2006), 851–852, 868, 900, and 902.
4. For good accounts, see Andrew Jack, *Inside Putin's Russia* (Oxford: Oxford University Press, 2004), 174–215, 229–237, and 313–320; Lilia Shevtsova, *Putin's Russia*, rev. ed. (Washington, DC: Carnegie Endowment for International Peace, 2005), 90–133 and 275–289; and Peter Baker and Susan Glasser, *Kremlin Rising: Vladimir Putin's Russia and the End of Revolution* (New York: Scribner, 2005), 83–87 and 272–292. On all of these, and especially on Putin's accompanying suppression of the mass media, see the classic by Yelena Tregubova, *Bayki kremlevskogo diggera* [Tales of a Kremlin digger] (Moscow: Ad Marginem, 2003), passim.
5. For Putin's account, see Gevorkyan and others, *First Person*, 125–128 and 192–193.
6. NTV, July 26, 1998 [FBIS].
7. NTV, February 13, 1998 [FBIS]; ITAR-TASS, May 25, 1998 [FBIS]; Interfax, June 4, 1998 [FBIS]; and NTV, July 26, 1998 [FBIS].
8. ITAR-TASS, May 23, 1997 [FBIS].
9. Tregubova, *Bayki*, 142–145.
10. Mikhail Shchipanov, "Vladimir Putin Has Taken Up the Challenge," *Rossiyskaya Gazeta*, January 11, 2000 [FBIS].
11. Yelena Tregubova, "Personnel Revolution Reaches Kremlin: President Puts His Own House in Order," *Russkiy Telegraf*, May 26, 1998 [FBIS].
12. Gevorkyan and others, *First Person*, 129.
13. Tregubova, *Bayki*, 146–148; Aleksey Chernyshev and Ilya Bulavinov, "Governor Nazdratenko's Fate Is Decided," *Kommersant*, February 6, 2001 [FBIS]; and Inna Lukyanova, "Contemporary History—Darkin From the Sea," *Profil*, July 16, 2001 [FBIS].
14. Putin found out directly from then Prime Minister Sergey Kiriyenko that Yeltsin had just signed the decree making him FSB director (Gevorkyan and others, *First Person*, 130).
15. Primakov, *Vosem' mesyatsev*, 142–143; and again in Primakov, *Minnoye pole politiki*, 288.

16. ITAR-TASS, July 27, 1998 [FBIS].

17. Interfax, November 20, 1998 [FBIS].

18. This was the finding of the prominent journalist Yevgenia Albats, as reported by Dobbs in "Missile Trail."

19. Dobbs, "Missile Trail." By Vorobei's own account, he continued to work with Iran by setting up a private business outside his institute until well into 2000. In 2004, when the United States accused Vorobei of violating weapons and technologies export controls, the Russian press reported that he had traveled to Iran some ten times between 1996 and 2000 to deliver lectures in his specialty (*Nezavisimaya Gazeta*, April 4, 2004 [FBIS]).

20. RIA, June 27, 1998 [FBIS].

21. Talbott, *Russia Hand*, 265–266. A Russian expert later made the point that dual-use materials and technology could be found everywhere, often unexpectedly, but that trade with countries such as Iran could not be closed down just because of this. By way of example, his recollection was that the specialty steel turned out to be stainless steel for urinals—certainly a household use, although not found in most homes—but he conceded it was indeed true that it could also be used in missiles (Moscow, background interview).

22. ITAR-TASS, July 13, 1998 [FBIS].

23. *Ma'ariv* (Tel Aviv), July 20, 1998 [FBIS].

24. Nikolay Uspenskiy, "Export Control Is a Key Element of National Security," *Yadernyy Kontrol*, no. 3 (May–June 1999): 5–8 [FBIS].

25. It covered all types of foreign trade, including military products. For the draft text, see *Yadernyy Kontrol*, no. 3 (May–June 1999): 39–50 [FBIS]. For the final text, see *Rossiyskaya Gazeta*, July 29, 1999 [FBIS]. On its endorsement by the Security Council while it had been headed by Kokoshin, see Eggert, "'Meteor' for the Ayatollahs," October 22, 1998.

At the same time, Yeltsin signed a decree in January 1999 amending and expanding his August 1996 Wassenaar-related decree on controlling the export of dual-use goods and technologies. For the text of the decree signed on January 4, 1999, and titled "Introduction of Changes and Additions to the List of Dual-Purpose Goods and Technologies Whose Export Is Controlled, Approved by a Decree of the President of the Russian Federation of 26 August 1996 No. 1268: On Control of Dual-Purpose Goods and Technologies From the Russian Federation," see *Rossiyskaya Gazeta*, January 14, 1999 [FBIS]. Pursuant to this decree, Putin signed lists of controlled goods on August 11, 2001.

26. Lebedev, interview.

27. *Nezavisimaya Gazeta*, February 23, 2001 [FBIS].

28. Talbott, *Russia Hand*, 355.

29. The United States argued that the Security Council had authorized the use of military force the previous October when it had invoked Chapter VII of the UN Charter in calling for a cease-fire in Kosovo. See Barton Gellman, "U.S., Allies Launch Air Attack on Yugoslav Military Targets: Two MiGs Reported Shot Down," *Washington Post*, March 25, 1999. On Primakov's aerial U-turn and the diplomatic moves leading up to the start of the NATO campaign, see *Washington Post*, March 22 and 24, 1999.

30. David Hoffman, "Moscow Recalls NATO Delegate to Protest Raids: Yeltsin 'Deeply Angered' by Assault," *Washington Post*, March 25, 1999. See also the account of these critical events in Talbott, *Russia Hand*, 164–165, 245–246, and 298–306.

31. Bazhanov, interview.

32. See the maps in Eisenstadt, *Iranian Military Power*, 29; and in Dobbs, "Missile Trail."

33. V. V. Naumkin, "Rossiya i Iran v Tsentralnoy Azii i Zakavkaz'ye v Regional'nom i Global'nom Kontekste" [Russia and Iran in Central Asia and the Caucasus in regional and global context], in *Doklady Rossiyskikh Uchastnikov 5-oy Konferentsii "Kruglogo Stola" po Rossiysko-Iranskim Otnosheniyam* [Reports by Russian participants in the fifth "round table" conference on Russian-Iranian relations], ed. V. V. Naumkin (Moscow: Tsentr Strategicheskikh i Politicheskiykh Issledovaniy, 1999), 30.

34. Bazhanov, interview; and Kenesh Nurmatovich Kulmatov, interview by author, Moscow, December 2, 1999. Kulmatov, a former ambassador to Sri Lanka, Maldives, Nepal, and Tanzania, was serving as deputy to Vice Rector Bazhanov at the Diplomatic Academy. On the conference, see Ye. P. Bazhanov and V. Ye. Dontsov, eds., *Rossiysko-iranskoye sotrudnichestvo (vzglyad iz Rossii): Materialy mezhdunarodnoy konferentsii* [Russian-Iranian cooperation (the view from Russia): Materials from international conference] (Moscow: Diplomaticheskaya Akademiya MID Rossii, 2000).

35. Moscow Television Service, "International Panorama," July 2, 1989 [FBIS-SOV-89-127, July 5, 1989, 16]. For Bovin's response to Israeli concerns about Iran, which he used during the years he served as Moscow's ambassador to Israel from December 1991 to May 1997, see Aleksandr Yevgenevich Bovin, *5 let sredi evreev i midovtsev* [Five years among the Jews and MFA-ers] (Moscow: Zakharov, 2000), 63–64. In addition to his official talking points, Bovin liked to say that he was indeed worried about Russian scientists reportedly working in Iran, Iraq, Libya, and Brazil but that he was even more concerned by what the thirty-seven Russian nuclear scientists who he claimed were working at Israel's own nuclear reactor facilities might be doing.

36. K. N. Kulmatov, "Vospriyatiye Irana razlichnymi sloyami obshchestva v Rossii" [Impressions of Iran by different strata of society in Russia], in *Rossiysko-iranskoye sotrudnichestvo*, 78–79.

37. Fedorov, interview.

38. Lebedev, interview.

39. Yakovlev, interview.

40. ITAR-TASS, March 25, 1998 [FBIS].

41. *Segodnya*, January 14, 1999 [FBIS].

42. *Itogi*, January 26, 1999 [FBIS]; *Novaya Gazeta Ponedelnik*, April 26, 1999 [FBIS]; "Materials From the State Duma Commission for Struggle Against Corruption. (Delivered by the Commission to State Duma Deputies 1–2 March)," Compromat.ru, March 7, 2001 [FBIS]; and *Segodnya*, March 3, 2001 [FBIS].

43. Interview of Yevgeny Adamov by Aleksey Venediktov, Radiostantsiya Ekho Moskvy, May 11, 1998 [FBIS].

44. Talbott, *Russia Hand*, 161 and 265.

45. *Kommersant*, February 3, 2000 [FBIS].

46. Michael Wines, "Putin Was Once Decorated as a Spy; Few Agree on His Deeds," *New York Times*, January 10, 2000. .

47. ITAR-TASS, May 7, 2000 [FBIS].

48. Xinhua, December 29, 1997 [FBIS]. First Deputy Premier Boris Nemtsov, who traveled to Beijing with MinAtom head Viktor Mikhaylov to sign what was billed as the largest ever Russian-Chinese contract, extolled it for providing jobs to sixty thousand Russian workers in a hundred enterprises (RIA, December 30, 1997 [FBIS]). MinAtom Deputy Minister Yevgeny Reshetnikov two years later claimed the project would provide jobs for 220,000 Russian workers in seven hundred firms (ITAR-TASS, October 21, 1999 [FBIS]).

49. *Kommersant*, May 11, 2000. Subsequently, in a contract worth $1.5–2 billion, MinAtom on November 6, 2001, agreed to supply two VVER-1000 units for India's Kudankulam

nuclear power station (Interfax, November 6, 2001 [FBIS]; and online report at Nuclear. ru, December 20, 2001 [FBIS]). New MinAtom chief Aleksandr Rumyantsev said that the contract was legal because it was grandfathered by the Soviet-Indian agreement of November 20, 1988, but that new contracts were ruled out because India had not placed all its nuclear activities under IAEA guarantees (Interfax, November 6, 2001 [FBIS], and *Gazeta*, July 3, 2003 [FBIS]).

50. *Nezavisimaya Gazeta*, March 20, 2001 [FBIS].

51. Rumer, *Dangerous Drift*, 39n16. By 2005, and perhaps using different accounting categories, Rumyantsev put the number of workers in the nuclear industry at 330,000 in some one hundred enterprises scattered across the Russian Federation (*Elektrostal Atompressa*, no. 40 (672), October 31, 2005 [FBIS]).

52. Rumer, *Dangerous Drift*, 19–20 and 28n11. On Adamov's membership in the Security Council, see Yeltsin's reshuffle of November 1998 in ITAR-TASS, November 20, 1998 [FBIS].

53. Vishniakov, "Russian-Iranian Relations," 151–152. According to Vishniakov, during the November 21–24, 1998, delegation visit to Iran, "a protocol was signed on the turn-key project involving the construction of the first generator of a VVER-1000 (water-cooled) reactor to be completed by the Russian side in May 2003. Iran also turned to Russia with an offer, in addition to the 1995 contract on building the nuclear plant, to study the possibility of building right there in Bushehr three more generators at an approximate cost of $3 billion. During the course of the visit, the Iranian leaders stressed on more than one occasion the absence in Iran of the desire to create a nuclear weapon."

54. ITAR-TASS, November 21, 1998 [FBIS]; Gusev at that time was chairman of the Duma's Committee for Industry, Construction, Transport, and Energy. The CPRF may even have had a direct financial interest in MinAtom and its RosEnergoAtom subsidiary. The economic journalist and detective thriller novelist Yuliya Latynina, while carefully qualifying her work as sheer "creative invention," later suggested that so-called leftist-patriotic forces in the Duma actually milked the atomic industry sector and laundered campaign and other expenses through it. See Yuliya Latynina, *Okhota na izyubrya* [Stag hunting] (Moscow: Olma-Press and Neva, 1999), 145–149.

55. Aleksey Malashenko, interview by author, Moscow, November 30, 1999.

56. V. V. Putin, "Russia on the Eve of the Millennium," Moscow Russian Government, December 28, 1999 [FBIS].

57. ITAR-TASS, January 13, 1999 [FBIS]; and *Segodnya*, January 14, 1999 [FBIS].

58. *Itogi*, January 26, 1999 [FBIS].

59. *Novaya Gazeta Ponedelnik*, April 26, 1999 [FBIS].

60. *Washington Post*, June 15, 2001; *Vremya Novostey*, September 21, 2000 [FBIS]; and *Nezavisimaya Gazeta*, September 22, 2000 [FBIS].

61. "Materials From the State Duma Commission."

62. For university rector Yuri Savelyev's justification of this activity, see *New York Times*, May 10, 2000.

63. *Rossiyskaya Gazeta*, February 3, 2001 [FBIS].

64. *Kommersant*, February 23, 2001 [FBIS].

65. *Segodnya*, March 3, 2001 [FBIS].

66. For a discussion of the diversion, plutonium production, and uranium enrichment routes to obtaining fissile material for nuclear weapons, see Eisenstadt, *Iranian Military Power*, 16–22.

67. Interfax, March 14, 2001 [FBIS].

68. RTR, March 28, 2001 [FBIS]. The change at MinAtom was announced at the same time as a half dozen major "power ministries" changes, including Sergey Ivanov's

appointment as defense minister and former Interior Minister Vladimir Rushaylo to replace Ivanov as head of the Security Council.

69. The announcement was made on December 19, 2001, according to Konstantin Smirnov, "The Prime Minister in a State of War," *Kommersant-Vlast*, May 28, 2002 [FBIS].

70. Adamov interview in *Izvestiya*, March 29, 2002 [FBIS]. See also his elaborate defense a year later in "Ye. Adamov: 'Civil Service Was a Forced Step for Me to Preserve the Sector,'" Nuclear.ru, April 8, 2003 [FBIS].

71. Jack, *Inside Putin's Russia*, 318–319. In May 2005, however, Adamov was arrested in Switzerland at the request of U.S. authorities. At the end of the year he was extradited to Moscow, where he was charged with large-scale fraud and abuse of office (ITAR-TASS, January 30, 2006 [FBIS]; ITAR-TASS, April 28, 2006 [FBIS]; and Interfax, April 28, 2006 [FBIS]).

72. The changes were announced on March 28, 2001 (see RIA, Ekho Moskvy, and others, March 28, 2001 [FBIS]). For a short history of the Russian Federation Security Council and its membership as of June 2001, see Aleksey Fomin, "Union of Sword and Plowshare," Moscow Stringer News Agency, June 7, 2001 [FBIS]. For a subsequent Putin edict on membership of the Security Council, likewise bereft of MinAtom representation, see *Krasnaya Zvezda*, April 27, 2004 [FBIS].

73. ITAR-TASS, November 16, 2001 [FBIS].

74. *Vedomosti*, October 11, 2000 [FBIS]; and Interfax, July 18, 2003 [FBIS].

75. Vladimir Kucherenko, *Rossiyskaya Gazeta*, May 25, 2001 [FBIS].

76. Mariya Ignatova, *Izvestiya*, January 18, 2000 [FBIS].

77. Igor Korotchenko, *Nezavisimaya Gazeta*, January 27, 1999 [FBIS].

78. *Nezavisimaya Gazeta*, January 27, 1999 [FBIS]. For the more accurate arithmetic on the 1989–91 contracts, see chapter 2.

79. *Kommersant*, January 15, 2000 [FBIS].

80. *Kommersant*, March 15, 2000 [FBIS]; and *Washington Post*, March 16, 2000.

81. *Nezavisimaya Gazeta*, January 27, 1999, October 19, 2000, and November 24, 2000 [FBIS]. According to other reports, Russia already had started deliveries under a new contract of five military-transport helicopters to the Iranian navy. Moscow was also reportedly deliberating over resuming sales to Iran of tactical missiles, antiaircraft systems, naval weapons, and modern aircraft (*Kommersant* and *Nezavisimaya Gazeta*, January 15, 2000 [FBIS]; see also *Segodnya*, January 26, 1999 [FBIS] and *Nezavisimaya Gazeta*, January 27, 1999 [FBIS]). For examination of the issue in the U.S. press after it was raised in the course of the U.S. presidential campaign, see *New York Times*, October 13, 2000; and *Washington Post*, October 14, 2000.

82. Interfax, November 25, 2000 [FBIS].

83. IRNA, January 15, 2001 [FBIS]; and *Izvestiya*, January 17, 2001 [FBIS].

84. IRNA, February 15, 2001 [FBIS].

85. Jim Hoagland, "From Russia With Chutzpah," *Washington Post*, November 22, 2000; and John M. Broder, "Russia Ending Deal on Arms Negotiated by Gore," *New York Times*, November 23, 2000.

86. Interfax, October 16, 2000 [FBIS]; and IRNA, October 17, 2000 [FBIS].

87. *Nezavisimaya Gazeta*, December 30, 2000 [FBIS].

88. This was said to include eight S-300PMU1 antiaircraft missile system battalions, a thousand Igla portable antiaircraft missile systems, twenty-five Mi-17-1V military transport helicopters, eight Su-25 attack planes, plus S-300VM antiaircraft missile systems, Gamma-DYe and Kasta-2Ye2 radar stations, and other equipment (Igor Korotchenko, "In Spite of U.S. Pressure," *Nezavisimoye Voyennoye Obozreniye*, September 21, 2001 [FBIS]).

89. It was led by division general Golalali Rashid, first deputy chief of staff of the Iranian army (Agentstvo Voyennykh Novostey, March 7, 2001 [FBIS]).
90. An expansion of the 1998 wish list, the array included the long-range S-300PMU-1 and S-300PMU-2 Favorit systems for protecting Bushehr and other strategic sites, the medium-range (forty-two kilometers) Buk-M1 system, and the short-range (twelve kilometers) Tor-M1 system. The list also included antiship cruise missiles (among them the Yakhont, with a 300-kilometer range, and the Moskit-Ye, with a 120-kilometer range), MI-17 helicopters (a variant of the MI-8 Hip), Su-25 Frogfoot attack planes, and Su-27 fighters. The Iranians reportedly were also interested in patrol boats for their navy and in modernizing their air force's inventory of thirty-five MiG-29 Fulcrum and twenty-four Su-24 Fencer planes. Their long shopping list also included up to 450 modern T-90S tanks, BMP-3 and BTR-90 armored vehicles, KA-50 helicopters, the Smerch and Uragan multiple rocket launcher artillery systems, the Igla multiple rocket launcher air defense system, and more diesel submarines. See Agentstvo Voyennykh Novostey, March 1, 2, 5, and 7, 2001 [FBIS]; *Kommersant*, March 15, 2001 [FBIS]; *Nezavisimaya Gazeta*, March 16, 2001 [FBIS]; *Izvestiya*, August 25, 2001 [FBIS]; Igor Korotchenko, "In Spite of U.S. Pressure," *Nezavisimoye Voyennoye Obozreniye*, September 21, 2001 [FBIS]; and *Moskovskiy Komsomolets*, October 2, 2001 [FBIS]. On the capabilities of the Buk-M1, see Agentstvo Voyennykh Novostey, October 10, 2001 [FBIS]. For those of the Tor-M1, see Russian Public Television (ORT), October 14, 2001 [FBIS].
91. Agentstvo Voyennykh Novostey, March 5, 2001 [FBIS].
92. Agentstvo Voyennykh Novostey, March 1, 2001 [FBIS]; and Interfax, March 2, 2001 [FBIS].
93. *Jame'eh-ye Madani*, March 17, 2001 [FBIS].
94. *Nezavisimaya Gazeta*, March 16, 2001 [FBIS].
95. Oleg Leonov, "Expert Politics—Double Strike: Arms Exports to Iran Will Help Moscow Deal With Paris Club," *Ekspert*, December 4, 2000 [FBIS].
96. Ironically, although Kandaurov did not make the point, to the extent that Russian firms and institutes were assisting the Iranian missile program covertly and illegally, they were also in effect contributing to a situation in which the Iranians were strapped for cash and not in shape to follow through on the substantial and above the board conventional weapons contracts they signed in 1989–91. For a list of Russian entities suspected of having assisted the Iranian missile program, see Michael Eisenstadt, "Russian Arms and Technology Transfers to Iran: Policy Challenges for the United States," *Arms Control Today*, March 2001, http://www.armscontrol.org/act/2001_03/eisenstadt.asp.
97. Sergey Kandaurov, "VTS Between Russia and Iran: Possibilities and Prospects," *Eksport Vooruszheniy*, November–December 2000, 5–10 [FBIS].
98. Interfax, March 10, 2001 [FBIS].
99. Agentstvo Voyennykh Novostey, December 20, 2000 [FBIS].
100. Interfax, April 20, 2001 [FBIS].
101. Ilya Bulavinov, *Kommersant*, January 15, 2000 [FBIS].
102. Agentstvo Voyennykh Novostey, March 11, 2002 [FBIS]. For details on the helicopter sale, see chapter 11, n32.
103. Ekho Moskvy Radio, December 18, 2000 [FBIS].

## CHAPTER 8: CASPIAN TEMPESTS

1. *Sovetskaya Rossiya*, April 16, 1998 [FBIS].
2. *Moskovskiy Komsomolets*, May 22, 2001 [FBIS]; Steven Erlanger, *New York Times*, July 3,

1995; and Peter Fuhrman, "Robber Baron," *Forbes*, September 11, 1995, 208–220.

3. For Chernomyrdin's biography, see ITAR-TASS, August 23, 1998 [FBIS]; and Anvar Amirov, *Kto yest' kto v mire nefti i gaza Rossii 2000: Kratkiy biograficheskiy spravochnik* [Who is who in the world of oil and gas in Russia in 2000: Short biographic directory], 3rd ed. (Moscow: Panorama, May 2000), 186–191. After leaving the premiership in 1998, Chernomyrdin dabbled in politics while nurturing his business interests until Putin appointed him ambassador to Ukraine in May 2001 (NTV, May 10, 2001 [FBIS]).

4. Anders Aslund, *How Russia Became a Market Economy* (Washington, DC: Brookings Institution, 1995), 159, 274, and 311.

5. Fuhrman, "Robber Baron," 208–220; Jack, *Inside Putin's Russia*, 206; and Amirov, *Kto yest' kto*, 39–41.

6. Fuhrman, "Robber Baron," 208–220.

7. *Moskovskiy Komsomolets*, September 3, 1999 [FBIS]; Florian Khassel [Hassel] and Leonid Bershidskiy, "About Daughters and Subsidiaries," *Vedemosti*, May 21, 2001 [FBIS]; and Douglas Frantz, *New York Times*, June 8, 2001. Rem Vyakhirev reportedly also owned 7.14 percent of Stroytransgaz stock, and his daughter was one of its biggest shareholders. Vyakhirev's son Yuri and daughter Tatyana Dedikova reportedly were able to obtain shares at firesale prices in this and other companies doing business with Gazprom.

8. *Sovetskaya Rossiya*, April 16, 1998 [FBIS]; and Florian Hassel, "All Stays in the Family," *Frankfurter Rundschau* (Internet version), May 21, 2001 [FBIS].

9. For Alekperov's biography, see Amirov, *Kto yest' kto*, 9–11; and RussiaToday.Info, "Russia's Who's Who," http://russiatoday.ru/en/top100/most_fam/13557.html.

10. David E. Hoffman, *The Oligarchs: Wealth and Power in the New Russia* (New York: Public Affairs, 2002), 299.

11. Janusz, "Caspian Sea," 2. For the text of the February 26, 1921, Treaty of Friendship, see Leonard Shapiro, ed., *Soviet Treaty Series* (Washington, DC: Georgetown University Press, 1950), 1: 92–94. For the March 25, 1940, Treaty of Trade and Navigation and four of the five supplemental notes exchanged on the same day, see Jane Degras, ed., *Soviet Documents on Foreign Policy* (London: Oxford University Press, 1953), 3: 424–435.

12. For Azerbaijani presidential staffer Rustam Mammadov's account, see *Zaman* (Baku), January 20, 2001 [FBIS]. Gasanguly is also rendered Gasan-Kuli, Esenguly, or Hosseinqoli.

13. SOCAR vice president Khoshbakht Yusifzade in ANS (Baku), November 18, 1997 [FBIS].

14. On this point, see IRNA, August 12, 2001 [FBIS].

15. See, for example, the official statement of Ministry of Foreign Affairs in Baku in *Khalg Gazeti*, December 11, 1998 [FBIS].

16. See the illuminating news conference debate between presidential staffer Rustam Mammadov and Ahad Qaza'i, the Iranian ambassador in Baku, in *Ekho* (Baku), July 25, 2001 [FBIS].

17. Iran's Caspian envoy Mehdi Safari conceded the point when he told an interviewer that the 1921 and 1940 agreements had been "silent on the area under the seabed" but nevertheless went on to defend joint ownership as the "best option" (*Iran*, October 6, 2002 [FBIS]).

18. For the arguments used by the five littoral states either invoking or rejecting the relevance of the 1982 UN Convention on the Law of the Sea, see Geoffrey Kemp, "U.S.-Iranian Relations: Competition or Cooperation in the Caspian Sea Basin," in *Energy and Conflict in Central Asia and the Caucasus*, ed. Robert Ebel and Rajan Menon (Lanham, MD: Rowman & Littlefield, 2000), 148–149.

19. *Izvestiya*, January 17, 2001 [FBIS]; and *Krasnaya Zvezda*, October 5, 2000 [FBIS]. Russian deputy foreign minister Boris Pastukhov in 1998 gave the following sectoral percentages, which would accrue to each of the littoral states based on their coastlines: Kazakhstan—29 percent; Turkmenistan—22 percent; Azerbaijan—19 percent; Russia—16 percent; and Iran—14 percent (*Zerkalo* [Baku], August 1, 1998 [FBIS].) The chairman of the International Institute for Caspian Studies in Tehran around the same time gave the following percentages of surface area accruing to each state based on the use of the median line: Kazakhstan—28.4 percent; Azerbaijan—21 percent; Russia—19 percent; Turkmenistan—18 percent; and Iran—13.6 percent (Abbas Maleki, "The Legal Status of the Caspian Sea: Discussions of Different Iranian Views," International Institute for Caspian Studies, Tehran, January 2001, www.cpf. az/caspsea/109-the-legal-status-of-the-caspian-sea.html ).

20. Forsythe, *Politics of Oil*, 15–17, 23–26, and 29–31.

21. Turan, November 19, 1993, and November 20, 1993 [FBIS-SOV-93-223, November 22, 1993, 70–71].

22. *Kommersant-Daily*, June 4, 1994 [FBIS-SOV-94-109, June 7, 1994, 16–17]. See also *Izvestiya*, June 7, 1994 [FBIS-SOV-94-109, June 7, 1994, 17].

23. *Rossiyskaya Gazeta*, June 11, 1994 [FBIS-SOV-94-114, June 14, 1994, 11].

24. Forsythe, *Politics of Oil*, 15–16 and 29–30.

25. Turan, September 20, 1994 [FBIS-SOV-94-183, September 21, 1994, 81–82].

26. Turan, September 21, 1994 [FBIS-SOV-94-184, September 22, 1994, 67–68].

27. Forsythe, *Politics of Oil*, 16, 30, and 39–41.

28. ITAR-TASS, October 14, 1994 [FBIS-SOV-94-199, 8].

29. Turan, October 14, 1994 [FBIS-SOV-94-200, October 17, 1994, 68].

30. Interfax, April 28, 2003 [FBIS]. There were probably contending views on the Iranian side as well. According to some accounts, Iran had lobbied strongly to participate in the AIOC consortium to develop the Azeri-Chiraq-Guneshli fields, but the consortium's American companies—holding a 43.8 percent share in the AIOC—vetoed the Iranian bid. See Forsythe, *Politics of Oil*, 24 and 40–41.

31. See the report in *Nezavisimaya Gazeta*, November 13, 1996 [FBIS]; and the extracts from the stenographic record of the foreign ministers' statements in *Rossiyskaya Gazeta*, December 7, 1996 [FBIS].

32. Harris, "Russian Federation and Turkey," 10.

33. Algerian LNG imports captured 28.5 percent of the Turkish market by 1996, but Russia still held more than 70 percent of it (International Energy Agency, *Energy Policies of IEA Countries: Turkey 1997 Review* (Paris: OECD/IEA, 1997), 64–67). Russia controlled 69.7 percent of the Turkish natural gas market in 2000 (International Energy Agency, *Energy Policies of IEA Countries: Turkey 2001 Review* (Paris: OECD/ IEA, 2001), 76).

34. *Milliyet* (Istanbul), December 27, 1995 [FBIS]; and IRNA, August 12, 1996 [FBIS].

35. IRNA, January 22, 2002 [FBIS].

36. Vishniakov, "Russian-Iranian Relations," 148.

37. *Finansovyye Izvestiya*, November 4, 1997 [FBIS].

38. ITAR-TASS, November 4, 1997 [FBIS]; *Rabochaya Tribuna*, December 5, 1997 [FBIS]; *Flag Rodiny* (Sevastopol), December 3, 1997 [FBIS]; and *Rossiyskaya Gazeta*, December 19, 1997 [FBIS].

39. TRT Television Network, August 29, 1997 [FBIS]; *Kommersant*, September 9, 1997 [FBIS]; and *Finansovyye Izvestiya*, November 4, 1997 [FBIS].

40. *Hurriyet*, December 15 and 16, 1997 [FBIS].

41. *Hurriyet*, December 15, 1997 [FBIS].

42. Forsythe, *Politics of Oil*, 19.

43. Ibid., 49–52; and Richard D. Kauzlarich, "Time for Change? U.S. Policy in the Transcaucasus" (New York: Century Foundation, 2001), 22–26. See also Rustam Narzikulov, "Caspian Pipeline on Brink of Financial Collapse: 'Chevron' Trying to Renew Negotiations With Russia on Company's Participation in CPC," *Segodnya*, September 5, 1995 [FBIS].

44. *Kommersant*, November 19, 1999 [FBIS].

45. Anatolia, September 18, 2002 [FBIS]; and Istanbul NTV, May 29, 2006 [FBIS].

46. Interfax, Presidential Bulletin, March 13, 2001 [FBIS]. Nevertheless, it was not until February 2003 that all the partners in the Azerbaijan Gas Supply Company consortium agreed to sanction implementation of Stage 1 of the $3.2 billion project, with Norway's Statoil designated the consortium's lead operator (Interfax, February 21, 2003 [FBIS]; *Aftenposten* (Oslo), February 27, 2003 [FBIS]; and *Nezavisimaya Gazeta*, February 28, 2003 [FBIS]).

47. Turan, October 18, 2004 [FBIS]; and ITAR-TASS, July 21, 2006 [FBIS].

48. BP Press Release, "2007 First Half Results Media Briefing by the BP Azerbaijan Leadership Team," August 15, 2007, http://www.bp.com/genericarticle.do?categoryI d=9006615&contentId=7037409.

49. On the tanker threat to the Bosporus, see *New York Times*, January 28, 2001.

50. *Izvestiya*, December 16, 1997 [FBIS].

51. Interfax, December 15, 1997 [FBIS].

52. *Segodnya*, December 17, 1997 [FBIS].

53. *Respublika Armenia*, December 24, 1997 [FBIS].

54. See, for example, Cengiz Candar, *Yeni Safak* (Istanbul), May 23, 2001 [FBIS]. For an analysis of Turkey's contractual commitments for natural gas, see Bulent Aliriza and Seda Ciftci, "Turkey's Caspian Energy Quandary," Center for Strategic and International Studies, Caspian Energy Project, Caspian Energy Update, Washington, DC, August 13, 2002.

55. Douglas Frantz, "Russia's New Reach: Gas Pipeline to Turkey," *New York Times*, June 8, 2001.

56. Anatolia, April 25, 2003 [FBIS]; Interfax, August 22, 2003 [FBIS]; and *Gazeta*, July 3, 2003 [FBIS].

57. *Izvestiya*, July 15, 2003 [FBIS].

58. Interfax, November 20, 2003 [FBIS]; and *Milliyet*, December 6, 2003 [FBIS].

59. *Kommersant-Daily*, July 7, 1998 [FBIS].

60. *Izvestiya*, July 9, 1998 [FBIS].

61. Maksim Yusin, "'Honeymoon' Over: First Conflict Between Moscow and Tehran," *Izvestiya*, July 9, 1998 [FBIS].

62. ITAR-TASS, November 24, 1998 [FBIS].

63. See *Izvestiya*, June 28, 2001 [FBIS].

64. Tehran IRIB Television First Program, December 15, 1998 [FBIS]; and IRNA, December 14, 1998 [FBIS].

65. IRNA, November 28, 1999 [FBIS].

66. Vision of the Islamic Republic of Iran, March 9, 2001 [FBIS]; Voice of the Islamic Republic of Iran, March 10, 2001 [FBIS]; and *Iran*, March 13, 2001 [FBIS].

67. Vision of the Islamic Republic of Iran, July 21, 2001 [FBIS].

68. The two ships were the Geofizik-3 and the Alif Haciyev. For the Azerbaijani Foreign Ministry's protest, see *Azerbaijan*, July 24, 2001 [FBIS]; for BP's account, see ANS-ChM Television, July 24, 2001 [FBIS]; for Iranian accounts, see *Tehran Times*, July 24

and 25, 2001 [FBIS]. For more background on the incident, see *The Economist*, August 4, 2001, 41, which includes a useful map.

69. IRNA, August 1, 2001 [FBIS].
70. Presidential staffer Rustam Mammadov in *Ekho* (Baku), July 25, 2001 [FBIS].
71. Turan, July 23, 2001 [FBIS].
72. *Tehran Times*, July 25, 2001 [FBIS].
73. *Izvestiya*, June 28, 2001 [FBIS].
74. Turan, December 24, 2001 [FBIS].
75. Lukoil vice president Jevan Cheloyants told an energy conference in London, "Our company intends to participate in the project only as a user, but will not finance and take part in the construction of the pipeline" (Media-Press News Agency [Baku], April 18, 2002 [FBIS]). By the end of the year, as part of what Alekperov described as a "company restructuring program," Lukoil had also decided to sell its 10 percent share in AIOC—which it had bought in September 1994 after Alekperov's vigorous lobbying in Moscow—to Japan's INPEX Corporation (ITAR-TASS, November 16, 2002 [FBIS]; and Interfax, December 20, 2002 [FBIS]). Once SOCAR gave its consent, the sale was completed in April 2003 (Interfax, April 28, 2003 [FBIS]).
76. Sarq News Agency [Baku], May 30, 2002 [FBIS].
77. See, for example, the various commentaries on the evolution of Iran's position and options in *Hayat-e Now*, September 10, 2001 [FBIS].
78. Amirov, *Kto yest' kto*, 223–224. After more than three years, Putin replaced Kalyuzhnyy with Igor Yusufov as presidential representative for international energy cooperation (Interfax, August 27, 2004 [FBIS]). On the Oil Transporting Joint Stock Company Transneft, see "About Transneft," http://www.transneft.ru/About/Default.asp?LANG=EN.
79. Amirov, *Kto yest' kto*, 31–32.
80. *Kommersant*, June 1, 2000 [FBIS].
81. *Izvestiya*, January 17, 2001 [FBIS].
82. The lack of agreement was papered over by a "joint statement" on the subject ("On the Legal Status of the Caspian Sea," Ministry of Foreign Affairs of the Russian Federation, (Internet text), March 21, 2001 [FBIS]).
83. Sarq News Agency (Baku), March 13, 2002 [FBIS].
84. Interfax, February 26, 2002 [FBIS].
85. *Siyasat-e Ruz*, April 25, 2002, as quoted by Hoseyn Bastani in "The Hidden Half of Iran's Caspian Share," *Bonyan*, May 2, 2002 [FBIS]; and also by Esma'il Amini in "Our Comprehensive Diplomacy," *Hayat-e Now*, April 27, 2002 [FBIS].
86. "Speech of Russian Federation President V. V. Putin at Meeting of Heads of Caspian States" on April 23 in Ashgabat, Moscow Russian Federation President (Internet text), April 24, 2002 [FBIS]; and ITAR-TASS, April 24, 2002 [FBIS]. In addition, there was a harsh exchange between Presidents Aliyev and Niyazov. For a summary of the positions of the five presidents at the summit, see the report by Mariya Arzumanova, *Strana.ru*, April 24, 2002 [FBIS].
87. "Putin Holds Several Bilateral Meetings in Ashgabat," Interfax Presidential Bulletin, April 24, 2002 [FBIS]; and IRNA, April 24, 2002 [FBIS].
88. IRNA, May 30, 2002 [FBIS].
89. Interfax, May 13, 2002 [FBIS].
90. IRNA, May 15, 2002 [FBIS].
91. ITAR-TASS and ORT Television, September 23, 2002 [FBIS].
92. In 2002 V. Adm. Vladimir Masorin, commander of the Caspian flotilla, put the number of Russia's combatant and auxiliary naval units in the Caspian at three hundred, an

increase of 150 percent over recent years. Masorin put the number of Iran's ships and craft at eighty-eight, which could be supplemented by nearly fifty other craft, including two midget submarines, moved from the Gulf (*Argumenty I Fakty*, May 21, 2002 [FBIS]). In 1998 Russian navy ships in the Caspian were said to number almost sixty, in addition to some thirty Border Guard vessels based in Nikolokomarovka (lower Volga), Makhachkala and Kaspiysk (*Russkiy Telegraf*, April 29, 1998 [FBIS]).

93. See Maleki, "Legal Status."

94. IRNA, May 3, 2001 [FBIS].

95. For the announcement, see Russian Public Television (ORT 1), April 25, 2002 [FBIS]; and Interfax, April 25, 2002 [FBIS].

96. Yuriy Golotyuk, "The President Has Summed Up the Summit," *Vremya Novostey*, April 26, 2002 [FBIS].

97. Aleksandr Plotnikov, "Caspian Monsters Spread Their Wings," *Grani.ru*, June 7, 2002 [FBIS].

98. *Iran Daily*, May 1, 2002 [FBIS].

99. IRNA, May 15, 2002 [FBIS].

100. Interfax, August 8, 2002 [FBIS]. See also *Krasnaya Zvezda*, August 2, 2002 [FBIS].

101. ITAR-TASS, May 14, 2003 [FBIS].

102. Agentstvo Voyennykh Novostey, May 12, 2003 [FBIS].

103. IRNA, August 28, 2002 [FBIS].

104. Defense Minister Adm. Ali Shamkhani, interview by Mohammad Safari, in *Resalat*, September 2, 2002 [FBIS]. For an overview of the five Caspian littoral countries' navies at the beginning of 2004, see *Nezavisimoye Voyennoye Obozreniye*, January 16, 2004 [FBIS].

105. For allusions to this line of criticism, see *Aftab-e Yazd*, April 13, 2002, and May 21, 2002 [FBIS] and *Nowruz*, May 22, 2002 [FBIS]; and especially *Aftab-e Yazd*, April 13, 2002 [FBIS]; and *Mardom Salari*, June 2, 2002 [FBIS].

106. *Bonyan*, April 6, 2002 [FBIS]; Iranian Students News Agency (Tehran), April 20, 2002 [FBIS]; and Kazakh Commercial TV (Almaty), April 11, 2002 [FBIS].

107. Ardeshir Amiri, "Khatami should reconsider," *Entekhab*, April 15, 2002 [FBIS]. On these themes and the criticized fecklessness of Iranian regional policy in the decade after the Soviet collapse, see also *Aftab-e Yazd*, April 22, 2002 [FBIS]; *Bonyan*, May 4, 2002 [FBIS]; and *Mardom Salari*, June 2, 2002 [FBIS].

108. *Siyasat-e Ruz*, April 30, 2002 [FBIS].

109. *Azad*, April 28, 2002 [FBIS].

110. See the comments by Dr. Seyfolreza Shahabi in *Hayat-e Now*, July 8, 2002 [FBIS]; and by former Foreign Minister Ali-Akbar Velayati in *Tehran Times*, August 6, 2002 [FBIS].

111. Quoted by Bill Samii, "Tehran Objects to Russia's Caspian Maneuvers," *RFE/RL Iran Report*, August 5, 2002, http://archive.rferl.org/reports/Archive.aspx?report=571&year=2008

112. *Seda-ye Edalat*, August 4, 2002 [FBIS].

113. *Keyhan*, April 29, 2002 [FBIS].

114. *Asia* as reported by IRNA, April 6, 2002 [FBIS]; *Seda-ye Edalat*, April 27, 2002 [FBIS]; and *Siyasat-e Ruz*, April 27, 2002 [FBIS].

115. *Bonyan*, May 2, 2002 [FBIS].

116. ITAR-TASS, August 9, 1999 [FBIS].

117. Vladimir Kucherenko, "Winter 2000: Oil Producers Celebrate, but Will the Country Weep? Economy Urgent," *Rossiyskaya Gazeta*, August 24, 1999 [FBIS]. On the August

20 cabinet session, see also *Nezavisimaya Gazeta*, August 21, 1999 [FBIS]; and *Moskovskiy Komsomolets*, August 24, 1999 [FBIS].

118. V. V. Putin, "Russia on the Eve of the Millennium," Moscow Russian Government website, December 28, 1999 [FBIS].

119. Interview with "Echo Moskvy": "Putin schätzt diese Loyalität," *Spiegel Online*, December 13, 2005, http://www.spiegel.de/politik/ausland/0,1518,390146,00.html. I am grateful to my INR colleague Robert Otto for drawing my attention to this interview.

120. RenTV, February 2, 2006 [FBIS]. On Putin's ideas concerning the energy sector, see also the two useful articles by Harley Balzer: "The Putin Thesis and Russian Energy Policy," *Post-Soviet Affairs* 21, no. 3 (July–September 2005): 210–225; and "Vladimir Putin's Academic Writings and Russian Natural Resource Policy," *Problems of Post-Communism* 53, no. 1 (January–February 2006): 48–54. The latter contains Professor Balzer's translation of Putin's 1999 article on "Mineral Natural Resources in the Strategy for Development of the Russian Economy," originally published in the St. Petersburg State Mining Institute's *Zapiski Gornogo Instituta* 144 (1999): 3–9.

121. Vladimir Milov, "Gazoviy Prezident," *Novaya Gazeta*, no. 97 (December 26, 2005), http://www.NovayaGazeta.Ru/data/2005/97/17.html. Milov cites "evidence from various sources." I am again indebted to Robert Otto for drawing my attention to this article.

122. Interview by Vladimir Kucherenko, "Viktor Kalyuzhnyy: 'The Fuel and Energy Complex Should Banish All Thoughts of Its Being an Exception,'" *Rossiyskaya Gazeta*, March 25, 2000 [FBIS].

123. Jack, *Inside Putin's Russia*, 206; *Rossiyskaya Gazeta*, May 31, 2001 [FBIS]; and *Moskovskiy Komsomolets*, June 1, 2001 [FBIS].

124. Interfax Daily Financial Report, June 29, 2001 [FBIS].

125. Interfax, June 28, 2002 [FBIS].

126. *Moskovskiy Komsomolets*, September 3, 1999 [FBIS]; Florian Hassel, "All Stays in the Family," *Frankfurter Rundschau* (Internet version), May 21, 2001 [FBIS]; *Moskovskiy Komsomolets*, June 6, 2001 [FBIS]; and *Rossiyskaya Gazeta*, August 1, 2001 [FBIS].

127. Kucherenko, "Kalyuzhnyy."

128. On the ambitions and fate of Mikhail Khodorkovsky, head of the private Yukos oil company, whose $35 billion market value at one time was more than half of the Russian Federation's budget, see Jack, *Inside Putin's Russia*, 206–215; and Shevtsova, *Putin's Russia*, 275–285.

129. Balzer, "The Putin Thesis," 210–211 and 216.

130. *Krasnaya Zvezda*, December 6, 2002 [FBIS].

131. "Speech by Russian Federation President V. V. Putin During Enlarged Russian-Turkmenistani Meeting," Russian Federation President (Internet text), January 22, 2002 [FBIS]. See also Caspian envoy Viktor Kalyuzhnyy's commentary on the project in *Kommersant*, February 19, 2002 [FBIS].

132. *Iran News*, January 19, 2003 [FBIS].

133. Interview by Hamid Reza Asefi, *Aftab-e Yazd*, January 29, 2003 [FBIS].

134. Khabar Television, May 14, 2003 [FBIS].

135. IRNA, May 14, 2003 [FBIS].

136. *Mardom Salari*, May 20, 2003 [FBIS].

## CHAPTER 9: TALIBAN THREATS, TAJIK ACCORDS, AND U.S.-IRAN TALKS

1. Gromov, *Ogranichennyi kontingent*, 191–192 and 326–328.

2. Primakov, *Gody*, 180.

3. For a map of the concentration of Sunni Muslim and other minority religions in Iran, see Limpert, *Iran*, 31, map 2.2.
4. A. William Samii, "Drug Abuse: Iran's 'Thorniest Problem,'" *Brown Journal of World Affairs* 9, no. 2 (Winter–Spring 2003): 283–299.
5. Interfax, June 6, 1994 [FBIS-SOV-94-109, June 7, 1994, 61–62]; and Interfax, June 23, 1994 [FBIS-SOV-94-122, June 24, 1994, 14].
6. The Dushanbe government also agreed to amnesty for forty detainees whom the opposition regarded as political prisoners in exchange for which the opposition pledged to hand over fifty-four captured government soldiers. Although the opposition also demanded that the government postpone presidential elections and a referendum on a new constitution, government negotiators would have none of it (Interfax, September 21, 1994 [FBIS-SOV-94-184, September 22, 1994, 63–64]).
7. Gretsky, "Civil War," 237.
8. Adamishin had already left Moscow for London as the new Russian ambassador there, and Deputy Foreign Minister Albert Chernyshev took over the Tajikistan portfolio.
9. Dushanbe Radio Tajikistan Network, November 12, 1994 [FBIS-SOV-94-219, November 14, 1994, 42–43]. Since then, Abdullojonov had been serving as Tajikistan's ambassador in Moscow; he now went into exile in Tashkent.
10. ITAR-TASS, March 13, 1995 [FBIS-SOV-95-048, March 13, 1995, 72].
11. Rubin, *Fragmentation*, 265–274; and Rashid, *Taliban*, 11.
12. Coll, *Ghost Wars*, 282–294; and Rashid, *Taliban*, 21–30.
13. Coll, *Ghost Wars*, 293.
14. Rashid, *Taliban*, 29–31.
15. Turajonzoda in Interfax, May 25, 1995 [FBIS].
16. See Turajonzoda interview in Almaty, *Panorama*, May 27, 1995 [FBIS]; and Gretsky, "Civil War," 244.
17. In early 1997 Zafar Saidov, Rahmonov's press spokesman, asserted that only 5–6 percent of the population supported the opposition (*Rossiyskaya Gazeta*, January 6, 1997 [FBIS]). While not suggesting opposition support was that low, a veteran Tajikistan observer and U.S. diplomat not long after personally regarded as "doubtful" that the opposition commanded 30 percent of national support. See Daria Fane, "Tajikistan: Conflict and Conflict Resolution" (paper presented at annual meeting of the Association for Studies of Nationalities, Columbia University, New York, April 1999), 8.
18. Foreign Minister Ali Akbar Velayati's letter to UNSYG Butrus-Ghali, IRNA, August 5, 1995 [FBIS].
19. ITAR-TASS, July 19, 1995 [FBIS].
20. IRNA, July 19, 1995 [FBIS].
21. Interfax, July 19, 1995 [FBIS]. Iran reportedly in effect conceded the point as far back as July 1993, when Deputy Foreign Minister Georgiy Konatev visited Tehran (Radio Moscow, July 18, 1993 [FBIS-SOV-93-137, July 20, 1993, 14]).
22. *Jomhuri-Ye Eslami*, July 24, 1995 [FBIS].
23. ITAR-TASS, August 18, 1995 [FBIS]; and "Protocol on the fundamental principles of establishing peace and national accord in Tajikistan," signed August 17, 1995, in Kamoludin Abdullaev and Catherine Barnes, eds, "Politics of Compromise: The Tajikistan Peace Process," special issue, *Accord*, no. 10 (2001): 67.
24. Dushanbe continued to favor Ashgabat, but the opposition suggested a variety of other venues, including Vienna. See *Pravda*, August 2, 1995 [FBIS]; and Interfax, October 31, 1995 [FBIS].
25. Yeltsin press conference after the CIS summit, Russian Television Network, January 19, 1996 [FBIS].

26. ITAR-TASS, March 12, 1996 [FBIS].

27. The UTO forces in the Tavildara sector were led by Mirzo Ziyoyev, whom the UTO two years later unsuccessfully nominated for defense minister in a coalition government, and his close associate Juma Namangani, of future Islamic Movement of Uzbekistan (IMU) notoriety (Dushanbe *Vecherniye Vesti*, September 5, 1996 [FBIS]).

28. *Komsomolskaya Pravda*, September 10, 1996 [FBIS].

29. Rashid, *Taliban*, 48–53.

30. Coll, *Ghost Wars*, 345–346. Given Hekmatyar's long history of enmity toward Iran, Tehran's motives for giving him safe haven were puzzling. One can only speculate that perhaps some officials in the MOIS or IRGC calculated that he might still prove of some use, but whether they had something definite in mind is hard to say.

31. Ibid., 340.

32. According to the Russian scholar Viktor Korgun, for example, Senate foreign affairs South Asia subcommittee chairman Hank Brown in August 1996 met with Taliban leader Mullah Mohammad Omar in Kandahar (after meeting with Rabbani, Masoud, and Dostum). The American ambassadors to New Delhi and Islamabad did the same. The Americans talked with Omar about opening a road through Afghanistan from Turgundi (Torgundi) on the Turkmenistan border to Spin-Buldak on the Pakistani border to link Central Asia and Pakistan. Pakistani minister of internal affairs Nasirullah Babar accompanied the Americans. Korgun concluded that it was already clear who the Taliban's main sponsors were—Saudi money, Pakistani weapons, and American political support—and that it was a repetition of the mujahideen war against the pro-Soviet Najibullah government (Korgun, *Afganistan*, 123). For a more dispassionate look at American policy around this time, characterized as dominated by "indifference," see Coll, *Ghost Wars*, 14–15, 298–300, and 334–335. For another perspective, see Rashid, *Taliban*, 45–46 and 166.

33. Rashid, *Taliban*, 160–168, 173–174, and 178–179. In April 1998 American UN ambassador Bill Richardson and assistant secretary of state Karl Inderfurth met in Kabul with Mullah Omar's deputy, Mohammad Rabbani. An American reporter who sat in on the meeting later wrote that Richardson, besides expressing concern about the Taliban sheltering Osama bin Laden, also raised "the possibility of running an oil [*sic*] pipeline across parts of Taliban territory." See Jeffrey Goldberg, "A Reporter at Large: The Unknown," *New Yorker*, February 10, 2003, 41.

34. Coll, *Ghost Wars*, 339.

35. In August 1998, after the al Qaeda bombings of the American embassies in Kenya and Tanzania were followed by U.S. cruise missile strikes on Afghanistan, Unocal indefinitely suspended its pursuit of a trans-Afghan pipeline project (*Russkiy Telegraf*, August 25, 1998 [FBIS]).

36. *Kazakhstanskaya Pravda*, October 8, 1996 [FBIS]; and Radio Tajikistan, October 5, 1996 [FBIS].

37. Voice of Free Tajikistan, October 16 and 31, 1996 [FBIS]; and interview with government negotiator Ibrohim Usmonov and opposition negotiator Haji Akbar Turajonzoda in Voice of the Islamic Republic of Iran, October 18, 1996 [FBIS].

38. ITAR-TASS, October 7, 1996 [FBIS]; and Interfax, June 28, 1997 [FBIS].

39. Interfax, December 10, 1996 [FBIS]; Radio Tajikistan, December 12, 1996 [FBIS]; "Protocol on settlement of the military and political situation in the areas of confrontation," signed December 11, 1996, in Abdullaev and Barnes, "Politics of Compromise," 68; and "Joint statement by the President of the Republic of Tajikistan, E. Sh. Rakhmonov, and the leader of the United Tajik Opposition, S. A. Nuri," signed December 11, 1996, http://www.c-r.org/our-work/accord/tajikistan/key-texts4.php.

40. Interfax, December 23, 1996 [FBIS]; Radio Tajikistan, December 24, 1996 [FBIS]; and "Agreement between the President of the Republic of Tajikistan, E. Sh. Rakhmonov, and the leader of the United Tajik Opposition, S. A. Nuri, on the result of the meeting held in Moscow on 23 December 1996," and "Protocol on the main functions and powers of the Commission on National Reconciliation," signed December 23, 1996, in Abdullaev and Barnes, "Politics of Compromise," 69 and 69–70, respectively.

41. For the texts of the numerous agreements hammered out during these months of intensive negotiations, see Abdullaev and Barnes, "Politics of Compromise," 66–80; and http://www.c-r.org/our-work/accord/tajikistan/key-texts.php.

42. Russian Public Television, June 27, 1997 [FBIS]; and Khovar, June 28, 1997 [FBIS]. The "General Agreement" catalogued the various protocols that had been agreed to along the way and the dates they had been agreed to. The protocols were then attached as appendices to the "General Agreement" ("General Agreement on the Establishment of Peace and National Accord in Tajikistan," "Protocol on mutual understanding between the President of Tajikistan, E. Sh. Rakhmonov, and the leader of the United Tajik Opposition, S. A. Nuri," and "Moscow declaration," all signed June 27, 1997, in Abdullaev and Barnes, "Politics of Compromise," 78, 78–79, and 79, respectively).

43. ITAR-TASS (various), June 27, 1997 [FBIS].

44. IRNA, June 27, 1997 [FBIS].

45. Interfax, June 28, 1997 [FBIS].

46. Radio Tajikistan, March 10, 1998 [FBIS]. For Turajonzoda's news conference on the occasion, see Voice of the Islamic Republic of Iran (Mashhad), March 10, 1998 [FBIS].

47. *Vecherniy Dushanbe*, May 15, 1998 [FBIS].

48. *Nezavisimaya Gazeta*, July 30, 1999 [FBIS]. On this and other problems in implementation of the peace accords, see Irina Zviagelskaya, "The Tajikistan Conflict," in *SIPRI Yearbook 1999: Armaments, Disarmament and International Security* (New York: Oxford University Press, 1999), 63–75; Fane, "Tajikistan"; R. Grant Smith, "Tajikistan: The Rocky Road to Peace," *Central Asian Survey* 18, no. 2 (1999): 243–251; R. Grant Smith, "Tajikistan: Implementing the Peace Accords" (paper presented at the UN University for Peace Conference, Dushanbe, Tajikistan, June 2002); and Rashid G. Abdullo, "Implementation of the 1997 General Agreement," in Abdullaev and Barnes, "Politics of Compromise," 48–53.

49. Interfax, June 28, 1997 [FBIS].

50. Robert Baer, *See No Evil: The True Story of a Ground Soldier in the CIA's War on Terrorism* (New York: Crown, 2002), 166. Baer, who left Tajikistan in 1995, does not give a source for this assertion. For Nuri's less than absolute denial of the thrust of Baer's claim, see *Asia-Plus* (Dushanbe), January 18, 2002 [FBIS]. According to Nuri, he had seen Taliban leader Mullah Mohammad Omar when his, Nuri's, plane had been forced down in Shindand on its way from Mashhad to Kunduz in 1996, but he had never met Osama bin Laden.

51. Rahmonov's predecessor Nabiyev had been in Tehran in June 1992, and Rahmonov had made a trip of his own in July 1995.

52. Dushanbe Radio Tajikistan (various), May 10, 1997 [FBIS].

53. Rashid, *Taliban*, 57–59.

54. Coll, *Ghost Wars*, 349. No other countries ever recognized the Taliban regime.

55. It did not reopen until October 2002 (Interfax, October 14, 2002 [FBIS]).

56. Rashid, *Taliban*, 202–204.

57. Ibid., 60–61, 69–70, 72, and 203–204.

58. Robin Bhatty and David Hoffman, "Afghanistan: Crisis of Impunity: The Role of Pakistan, Russia, and Iran in Fueling the Civil War," *Human Rights Watch* 13, no. 3(C) (July 2001): 36–39, 44–45, and 50–53.

59. CNN interview, IRNA, January 8, 1998 [FBIS]. For the U.S. response, see Secretary of State Madeleine K. Albright, remarks at Asia Society dinner, New York City, June 17, 1998, http://hongkong.usconsulate.gov/ushk_state_1998061701.html.

60. Brahimi pulled back temporarily from active involvement in the Afghan peace process in October 1999, when Francesc Vendrell took over as the Secretary General's personal representative on Afghanistan. For final reports on Brahimi's activities, see UN Secretary General, "The Situation in Afghanistan and Its Implications for International Peace and Security: Report of the Secretary General," S/1999/994, September 21, 1999, http://www.un.org/Docs/sc/reports/1999/sgrep99.htm; and UN Press Briefing, "Briefing by Special Envoy to Afghanistan," October 20, 1999, http://www.globalsecurity.org/military///library/news/1999/10/19991020-brahimi-doc.htm. Brahimi then rejoined the process after September 11, 2001, and coordinated the Bonn conference that agreed on a post-Taliban interim administration for Afghanistan.

61. Rashid, *Taliban*, 72–77 and 205.

62. Coll, *Ghost Wars*, 409–411.

63. See the account of U.S. contacts with the Taliban by David Ottaway and Joe Stephens, "Diplomats Met With Taliban on Bin Laden; Some Contend U.S. Missed Its Chance," *Washington Post*, October 29, 2001.

64. Rashid, *Taliban*, 75–78; and *Jang* (Rawalpindi), October 4, 1998 [FBIS]).

65. Coll, *Ghost Wars*, 184, 211, 431, and 463.

66. Ibid., 464–465.

67. Ibid., 518–519 and 559.

68. UN Secretary General, "The Situation in Afghanistan."

69. Rashid, *Taliban*, 76–78.

70. After run-off elections on May 5, an estimated 222 out of 290 seats in the Majles were held by reformers.

71. For two analyses, see *Eqtesad-e Asia*, April 1, 2000 [FBIS]; and *Iran-e Farda*, April 12, 2000 [FBIS].

72. Secretary of State Madeleine K. Albright, "Remarks Before the American-Iranian Council," Washington, DC, March 17, 2000, http://secretary.state.gov//www/statements/2000/000317.html.

73. The Geneva Initiative group met at least four times in the course of 2000 and 2001 in Geneva: in December 2000; in April 2001; on September 9, 2001; and then, at the initiative of Iran, on September 21, 2001—just ten days after the momentous al Qaeda attacks on the World Trade Center and the Pentagon (AFP, September 21, 2001 [FBIS]; and *New York Times*, September 26, 2001).

74. Maggie Farley, "U.S. and Iran Have Been Talking, Quietly," *Los Angeles Times*, March 9, 2007.

## CHAPTER 10: 9/11 AND AFGHANISTAN

1. Dana Milbank and Walter Pincus, "Declassified Memo Said Al Qaeda Was in U.S.," *Washington Post*, April 11, 2004.

2. UN Security Council, Resolution 1368, September 12, 2001, S/RES/1368 (2001), http://www.un.org/Docs/sc/unsc_resolutions.html.

3. For a fascinating account of the air campaign, see Mark Bowden, "The Kabul-ki Dance," *Atlantic Monthly* 290, no. 4 (November 2002): 65–87. For an insider's view by

the leader of the CIA team that arrived first on the ground in Afghanistan, see Gary C. Schroen, *First In: An Insider's Account of How the CIA Spearheaded the War on Terror in Afghanistan* (New York: Ballantine Books, 2005), passim. See also Dana Priest, "'Team 555' Shaped a New Way of War," *Washington Post*, April 3, 2002; and Bob Woodward, "Doubts and Debate Before Victory Over Taliban," *Washington Post*, November 18, 2002, excerpted from Bob Woodward, *Bush at War* (New York: Simon & Schuster, 2002), passim.

4. IRNA, November 12, 2001 [FBIS]; Voice of the Islamic Republic of Iran, November 12, 2001 [FBIS]; and Vision of the Islamic Republic of Iran, November 13, 2001 [FBIS].

5. Gary Berntsen and Ralph Pezzullo, *Jawbreaker: The Attack on Bin Laden and Al Qaeda: A Personal Account by the CIA's Key Field Commander* (New York: Three Rivers Press, 2005), 168–183; and Woodward, *Bush at War*, 304–313.

6. AFP, November 13, 2001 [FBIS].

7. ITAR-TASS, November 13, 2001 [FBIS].

8. Vladislav Kulikov, *Rossiyskaya Gazeta*, November 14, 2001 [FBIS].

9. For the chronology of U.S.-Russian contacts in the immediate aftermath of September 11 and of decision making on the Russian side, see Alan Sipress, "U.S., Russia Recast Their Relationship; Anti-Terror Agenda Appears to be Framework for Future," *Washington Post*, October 4, 2001.

10. The session and the phone call took place on September 22, 2001. For one of the fullest accounts of the deliberations in Sochi, see Nikolay Gulkovskiy, "Vladimir Putin Mobilizes the Security People," *Kommersant*, September 24, 2001 [FBIS]. On the Bush-Putin phone call, see Woodward, *Bush at War*, 118–119.

11. Asia-Plus, September 24, 2001 [FBIS].

12. ITAR-TASS, September 24, 2001 [FBIS].

13. Russian Public Television, ORT 1, September 24, 2001 [FBIS]. Putin's televised statement was all the more surprising given Defense Minister Sergei Ivanov's immediately negative response on September 14 at a news conference in Yerevan: "There are absolutely no grounds, even hypothetical, for suppositions on a possibility of any NATO military operations in the Central Asian states, forming the CIS" (ITAR-TASS, September 14, 2001 [FBIS]).

14. Vernon Loeb, "Footprints in Steppes of Central Asia," *Washington Post*, February 9, 2002.

15. Robin Wright, "Ties That Terrorism Transformed," *Los Angeles Times*, March 13, 2002.

16. Moscow Russia TV RTR, September 27, 2003 [FBIS].

17. "Speech by Russian Federation President V. V. Putin at Russian Federation Ministry of Defense Conference," Russian Federation President (Internet text), October 18, 2001 [FBIS].

18. The Russian president's understanding of the situation seemed well in tune with that of specialists such as Aleksandr Umnov, as touched on in chapter 5. Umnov in late 1999 had stressed to this author the importance of interethnic alliances for stability in both Tajikistan and Afghanistan. Commenting on Moscow's Soviet-era responsibility for the subsequent ethnic fragility in both countries, Umnov had warned of the dangers deriving from the separately consolidated monoethnic groups that Soviet rule and long years of military intervention had brought about (Umnov, interview).

19. *Kommersant*, October 23, 2001 [FBIS]; and Moscow Russian Federation President (Internet text), October 22, 2001 [FBIS].

20. *New York Times*, December 10, 2001.

21. *Washington Post*, September 25, 2001.
22. Voice of the Islamic Republic of Iran, September 26, 2001 [FBIS]. Outside in the streets, however, in response to televised appeals by Zia Atabay, an Iranian exile broadcasting via satellite from a Los Angeles studio, thousands of youth carried candles to show solidarity with the United States. See Michael Lewis, "The Satellite Subversives," *New York Times Magazine*, February 24, 2002, 33.
23. *Washington Post*, October 29, 2001.
24. *USA Today*, October 25, 2001.
25. *Washington Post*, November 13, 2001.
26. *Washington Post*, November 27, 2001.
27. *Washington Post*, December 5 and December 6, 2001.
28. Rubin, *Fragmentation*, 26.
29. Jon Lee Anderson, "The Man in the Palace," *New Yorker*, June 6, 2005, 65–66.
30. Schroen, *First In*, 268 and 273–274.
31. AFP, December 5, 2001 [FBIS].
32. Rubin, *Fragmentation*, 26.
33. Coll, *Ghost Wars*, 363–364, 560–564, and 571–572.
34. Berntsen and Pezzullo, *Jawbreaker*, 168–177 and 183; Schroen, *First In*, 193, 326–328, and 342–351.
35. *Washington Post*, January 19 and February 4, 2002.
36. Maggie Farley, "U.S. and Iran Have Been Talking, Quietly," *Los Angeles Times*, March 9, 2007. See also Woodward, *Bush at War*, 314–315; and Robin Wright, "Diplomatic Exit," *Washington Post*, April 15, 2007.
37. Eric Schmitt, "A Nation Challenged: Regional Politics: Iran Exerts Sway in Afghan Region, Worrying the U.S.," *New York Times*, January 10, 2002.
38. According to a different tally, the breakdown was eighteen from the Northern Alliance, eleven from the Rome Group, and one from the Peshawar Group. The Iran-backed Cyprus Group backed the results of the Bonn Conference but chose not to participate in the AIA (Al-Manar Television, December 6, 2001 [FBIS]).
39. IRNA, December 7, 2001 [FBIS]; and Vision of the Islamic Republic of Iran, December 7, 2001 [FBIS].
40. IRNA, December 5, 2001 [FBIS].
41. Dushanbe Asia-Plus, December 5, 2001 [FBIS]; Voice of the Islamic Republic of Iran, December 21, 2001 [FBIS]; and Vision of the Islamic Republic of Iran Network 1, May 11, 2002 [FBIS].
42. Farley, "U.S. and Iran."
43. Ekho Moskvy, December 5, 2001 [FBIS].
44. ITAR-TASS, December 7, 2001 [FBIS].
45. ITAR-TASS, December 9, 2001 [FBIS].
46. Coll, *Ghost Wars*, 124 and 344; and Schroen, *First In*, 258.
47. Berntsen and Pezzullo, *Jawbreaker*, 224.
48. *New York Times*, December 4, 2001; *Washington Post*, December 13, 2001; Deutschlandfunk, December 1, 2001 [FBIS]; and AFP, December 5, 2001 [FBIS]. CIA operative Gary Schroen, who had met with Masoud over the years and had led the team that arrived in the Panjshir Valley on September 26 to coordinate OEF with the anti-Taliban resistance after 9/11, was persuaded that Masoud intended to politicize his Northern Alliance military organization in the event he managed to defeat the Taliban and to use it to isolate Rabbani. While working with Fahim, Schroen witnessed what appeared to be clear signs of rivalry between Fahim and Rabbani. However, Schroen also saw indications that while Fahim was recognized as the military commander of Panjshiri

forces, Masoud's successors—certainly future AIA foreign minister Abdullah—had markedly less confidence in Fahim's political talents (Schroen, *First In*, 91, 96–101, 244, and 257–259).

49. Coll, *Ghost Wars*, 206, 285–286, and 551.

50. Ibid., 286–287.

51. Anderson, "Man in the Palace," 68.

52. Coll, *Ghost Wars*, 285–287, 299, and 335.

53. Ibid., 461–462.

54. Ibid., 519, 571–573.

55. Ibid., 124 and 344; and Schroen, *First In*, 258.

56. Qanooni served as defense minister and then interior minister in the Rabbani government and led the Northern Alliance delegation to the UN-sponsored peace talks with the Taliban in Ashgabat, Turkmenistan, in March 1999.

57. Coll, *Ghost Wars*, 123 (Abdullah) and 286–287 (Fahim). Abdullah early on used only that one name, but with time became known more frequently as Abdullah Abdullah.

58. Interfax, December 18, 2001 [FBIS]; and RIA-Novosti, December 19, 2001 [FBIS].

59. Camelia Entekhabi-Fard, "Afghan Leader's Visit to Iran Hands Political Victory to Reformists in Tehran," *Eurasia Insight*, February 27, 2002, http://www.eurasianet.org.

60. Amy Waldman, "In Louder Voices, Iranians Talk of Dialogue With U.S.," *New York Times*, December 10, 2001.

61. *New York Times*, February 25, 2002.

62. Adding to Western concerns, Iranian elements working with the Lebanese Hezbollah were suspected of having attempted to smuggle fifty tons of weapons aboard the ship *Karine A*—captured by Israeli commandos in a January 3 raid in the Red Sea— to elements within the Palestinian Authority for use against Israel (*Washington Post*, February 4, 2002; see also the in-depth reporting by Douglas Frantz and James Risen, "A Secret Iran-Arafat Connection Is Seen Fueling the Mideast Fire," *New York Times*, March 24, 2002).

63. Vision of the Islamic Republic of Iran, November 13, 2001 [FBIS]; and Coll, *Ghost Wars*, 40.

64. For a firsthand account of an audience with Ismail Khan in January 2002, the reach of Khan's authority eastward from Herat into Ghowr province, and then its eclipse by that of Karim Khalili in Bamiyan province, the heart of the Hazarajat, see Rory Stewart, *The Places in Between* (Orlando, FL: Harcourt, 2004), passim. Stewart walked from Herat to Kabul in thirty-six days in January–February 2002.

65. For the particulars of Iranian activities in Herat, spelled out by sources other than Khalilzad, see Anthony Shadid and John Donnelly, "Fighting Terror/The Struggle for Influence; Iranian Arms Goods Flood Afghan Region," *Boston Globe*, January 25, 2002.

66. *Washington Post*, January 19, 2002.

67. Ahmed Rashid, "Afghan Warlord Finds Chaos Is Just the Ticket," *Wall Street Journal*, May 17, 2002, and Ahmed Rashid, "Warlord, Profiteer, Ideologue, Chief," *Far Eastern Economic Review*, May 23, 2002.

68. Herat Television, July 8, 2002 [FBIS].

69. Bill Samii, "Is an Iranian Hand Stirring the Iraqi Pot?" *RFE/RL Iran Report*, April 12, 2004, http://archive.rferl.org/reports/Archive.aspx?report=571&year=2008.

70. Patrick Clawson, "Iran as Part of the Axis of Evil (Part II): U.S. Policy Concerns," Washington Institute for Near East Policy, *PolicyWatch*, no. 601, February 5, 2002, http://www.washingtoninstitute.org/templateC05.php?CID=1479.

71. *New York Times*, January 30, 2002.

72. The meeting in Geneva had been in January, according to Khalilzad. See Camelia Entekhabi-Fard's interview with him, "US National Security Expert Says Internal Rivalries Influence Iranian Foreign Policy," *EurasiaNet Q & A*, March 15, 2002, http://www.eurasianet.org/departments/qanda/articles/eav031502.shtml. On the debates in Tehran over contacts with the United States, see Nazila Fathi, "A Nation Challenged: Tehran; Iran's Leader Backs Effort for Talks With U.S.," *New York Times*, March 18, 2002; Bill Samii, "Iran-U.S. Dialogue Controversial for Both Sides," *RFE/RL Iran Report* 5, March 18, 2002, http://archive.rferl.org/reports/Archive.aspx?report=571&year=2008; and Ray Takeyh, "Iran: Scared Straight?" Washington Institute for Near East Policy, *PolicyWatch* no. 622, May 3, 2002, http://www.washingtoninstitute.org/templateC05.php?CID=1500. In April there was even criticism of the fundamentalists' support for "violent conflict" by Palestinians against Israel. See "The Palestinians and the Supporters of Republicanism in Iran," *Bonyan*, April 4, 2002 [FBIS].

73. *Washington Post*, February 27, March 2, and April 28, 2002; and *New York Times*, April 30, 2002.

74. For the transcript of Putin's remarks at the CIS summit in Almaty on March 1, see the official website of the Russian Federation President, March 4, 2002, http://www.president.kremlin.ru [FBIS].

75. Arminfo (Yerevan), March 4, 2002 [FBIS].

76. Nabi Sonboli, "Iran and the Post-9/11 Security Environment of Central Asia," *Central Asia and the Caucasus Review*, no. 37 (Spring 2002): 103–122 [FBIS].

77. Voice of the Islamic Republic of Iran, Radio 1, May 1, 2002 [FBIS].

78. Voice of the Islamic Republic of Iran, Radio 1, May 22, 2002 [FBIS].

79. IRNA, May 26 and May 27, 2002 [FBIS].

80. Associated Press, "Iran Bans the Mention of Possible U.S. Talks," *Washington Post*, May 26, 2002.

81. Vision of the Islamic Republic of Iran, Network 1, May 29, 2002 [FBIS].

82. *Resalat*, February 2, 2002 [FBIS]; and *Jomhuri-ye Eslami*, February 24, 2002 [FBIS]. The quote is from the latter. This explicit argument was similar to that put forth more implicitly by Russian observers.

83. *Azad*, February 25, 2002 [FBIS].

84. *Azad*, February 13, 2002 [FBIS]. For an interview with Hekmatyar in a government guesthouse in a Tehran suburb around this time, see *Al-Sharq al-Awsat*, February 11, 2002 [FBIS].

85. IRNA, February 24, 2002 [FBIS].

86. IRNA, February 25, 2002 [FBIS].

87. Voice of the Islamic Republic of Iran, February 24, 2002 [FBIS].

88. Vision of the Islamic Republic of Iran, February 25, 2002 [FBIS]. For interesting analysis on Iranian factional fighting over Afghan policy in connection with Karzai's visit, see Entekhabi-Fard, "Afghan Leader's Visit"; and Camelia Entekhabi-Fard and Idi Verani, "Afghan Reconstruction Effort Poses Major Test for Iranian Policy Makers," *Eurasia Insight*, February 27, 2002, http://www.eurasianet.org.

89. Bakhtar News Agency, February 25, 2002 [FBIS].

90. *Iran*, February 28, 2002 [FBIS].

91. Reuters, February 26, 2002; and Bill Samii, "Hekmatyar's Unclear Objectives," *RFE/RL Iran Report*, March 18, 2002, http://archive.rferl.org/reports/Archive.aspx?report=571&year=2008.

92. In May, the American CIA reportedly fired missiles at a meeting of Hekmatyar and his aides outside Kabul (*Washington Post*, May 10, 2002). In a handwritten letter at the end of May and in a tape-recorded message in September, Hekmatyar attacked the United

States, its allies, and the Karzai administration (Associated Press in the *Dallas Morning News*, May 31, 2002; and *The Times* (London), September 6, 2002).

93. Qanooni was in Moscow from February 28 until March 2, during which time he met Foreign Minister Igor Ivanov, Interior Minister Boris Gryzlov, and other Russian officials (Bakhtar News Agency, March 2, 2002 [FBIS]).

94. *Nezavisimaya Gazeta*, February 12, 2002 [FBIS].

95. Nikolay Ulyanov, "Moscow Looks One Step Ahead in Its Relations With Kabul," *Strana.ru*, February 4, 2002 [FBIS].

96. *Nezavisimaya Gazeta*, February 12, 2002 [FBIS]; and RIA-Novosti, February 12, 2002 [FBIS].

97. *Krasnaya Zvezda*, February 13, 2002 [FBIS].

98. ITAR-TASS, September 6, 2002 [FBIS]. See also *Kommersant*, September 7, 2002 [FBIS]. Two years later, a source at the Russian Defense Ministry said that Russia in the protocol had pledged to give the Afghan military $110 million in aid. This consisted of two hundred trucks, jeeps, and land rovers and spare parts for artillery systems and armor but no weapons or ammunition (ITAR-TASS, October 7, 2004 [FBIS]). A week later, Defense Minister Ivanov put the level of "annual free material-technical aid" to the Afghan army at around $100 million, again insisting that none of it consisted of munitions or combat matériel (ITAR-TASS, October 14, 2004 [FBIS]).

Ivanov clearly misspoke in describing this as the value of "annual" aid. As Ambassador Zamir Kabulov stated a year later, "Russia has donated approximately $100 million to Afghanistan since the fall of the Taliban regime." Kabulov said this included "hundreds of military trucks, jeeps, radios, wireless and communications units and heavy artillery spare parts to the newly-established national army of Afghanistan. We have also repaired six military helicopters of the Afghan National Army." Kabulov said he was "puzzled" by the failure of Afghan authorities to make any mention of the Russian aid to the ANA (*Kabul Weekly*, August 10, 2005 [FBIS]).

99. *Washington Post*, February 24, 2002.

100. Michael Hirsh, "Tensions at the Top," *Newsweek* [Web Exclusive], February 19, 2002; and Pamela Constable, "Afghan Government Backs Off Conspiracy Charge in Airport Killing," *Washington Post*, February 24, 2002. An official investigation eventually concluded Rahman had been the victim of an angry mob of hajj pilgrims stranded at the airport and that there had been no plot (Peter Baker, "Afghans Say Killing of Official Was No Plot," *Washington Post*, April 25, 2002).

101. Mehrdad Balali, "Dead Hero Masood Continues to Rule in Afghanistan," Reuters, March 5, 2002.

102. IRNA, February 24, 2002 [FBIS]; and Bakhtar News Agency, March 11, 2002 [FBIS].

103. Asia-Plus, March 11, 2002 [FBIS].

104. "Russian Federation President V. V. Putin's Speech and Meet the Press Session at the Close of Talks With Head of Afghanistan's Interim Administration H. Karzai," Russian Federation President (Internet text), March 13, 2002 [FBIS].

105. *Krasnaya Zvezda*, March 14, 2002 [FBIS].

106. *Kommersant*, March 13, 2002 [FBIS].

107. Arkadiy Dubnov, "Russia Is a Great State," *Vremya Novostey*, March 20, 2002 [FBIS].

108. Ibid.

109. ITAR-TASS and Interfax, March 13, 2002 [FBIS].

110. IRNA, March 13, 2002 [FBIS].

111. Three of Karzai's trips to Tehran were official visits (February 26–28, 2002; June 18–20, 2003; and January 26–27, 2005) and one a stopover on the way to Turkey at

Tehran's Mehrabad Airport during which he conferred with several Iranian officials and also Pakistani President Pervez Musharraf (October 13, 2002).

112. "Agreement on Provisional Arrangements in Afghanistan Pending the Re-establishment of Permanent Government Institutions with Annexes I—III," German Foreign Ministry (Internet text), December 5, 2001 [FBIS].

113. AFP, November 28, 2001 [FBIS]. For his reversal, see Berlin ddp, November 29, 2001 [FBIS].

114. AFP, December 1, 2001 [FBIS].

115. *Izvestiya*, March 6, 2002 [FBIS]; and Interfax, April 25, 2002 [FBIS].

116. Arkadiy Dubnov, "Afghanistan Is Not the Place for Geopolitical Games," *Vremya Novostey*, April 29, 2002 [FBIS].

117. *Christian Science Monitor*, January 3, 2002.

118. Laurel Miller and Robert Perito, "Establishing the Rule of Law in Afghanistan," U.S. Institute of Peace, Special Report 117, March 2004, http://www.usip.org/pubs/specialreports/sr117.html.

119. *New York Times*, August 12, 2003.

120. *Moscow Times*, June 5, 2003.

121. *Washington Post*, October 14, 2003.

122. ITAR-TASS, October 7, 2003 [FBIS].

123. *Washington Post*, November 16, 2003; *New York Times*, February 23, 2004; and *London Financial Times*, March 11, 2004. As of September 2005, twenty-two PRTs were in Afghanistan: thirteen led by the United States and nine by ISAF (Robert M. Perito, "The U.S. Experience With Provincial Reconstruction Teams in Afghanistan," U.S. Institute of Peace, Special Report 152, October 2005, http://www.usip.org/pubs/specialreports/sr152.html.

124. Interfax, October 19, 2003 [FBIS].

125. For a roundup of Iranian military and security activities in these provinces, see Bill Samii, "Afghans Struggle With Iranian Interference," *RFE/RL Iran Report*, February 11, 2002, http://archive.rferl.org/reports/Archive.aspx?report=571&year=2008. Khalili quote is from AFP as cited by Samii.

126. Aleksandr Khokhlov, "Ahmad Zia Mas'ud: Everybody Is Devoting Time to Our Youth Except the Russians," *Izvestiya*, May 15, 2002 [FBIS].

127. Interfax, May 5, 2004 [FBIS].

128. According to a report from a Council on Foreign Relations–Asia Society panel, Kabul collected only $80 million of such revenues nationwide from provincial governments in 2002. See *Inside the Pentagon*, July 3, 2003.

129. *New York Times*, June 20, 2002.

130. *New York Times*, June 20 and 28, 2002.

131. Ahmed Rashid, *Wall Street Journal*, July 8, 2002.

132. There was speculation that Gulbuddin Hekmatyar was behind the attacks (*New York Times* and *Washington Post*, September 6, 2002).

133. From *Entekhab* as quoted by Ardeshir Moaveni, "Iran Probes for Diplomatic Openings to Avoid Strategic Encirclement," *Eurasia Insight*, August 20, 2002, http://www.eurasianet.org. The aid package was sometimes put at $550 million.

134. *New York Times*, August 14, 2002.

135. IRNA, December 22, 2002 [FBIS].

136. IRNA (Kabul dateline), December 22, 2002 [FBIS].

137. Interview with Viktor Korgun by Anatoliy Shapovalov, "The Year of Karzai: One Will Have to Pay Much and Long to Pacify and Rebuild Afghanistan," *Rossiyskaya Gazeta*, December 18, 2002 [FBIS]. The Western press put the number of irregular militia as

high as 100,000, of which less than two-thirds may have been actual fighters (*Wall Street Journal*, March 14, 2005). Actually, the "30,000 bayonets" cited by Korgun were probably closer to the mark. Right after September 11, 2001, the CIA put Northern Alliance forces at between ten and thirty thousand in a briefing for Vice President Richard Cheney and Secretary of State Condoleezza Rice (Woodward, *Bush at War*, 156). Of these, probably a third was loyal to Defense Minister Fahim. CIA operative Gary Schroen estimated there were still some twelve thousand fighters under General Fahim's command in mid-2004 (Schroen, *First In*, 357).

138. ITAR-TASS, November 22, 2002 [FBIS]. See also Ahmed Rashid, "Jockeying for Influence, Neighbors Undermine Afghan Pact," *Eurasia Insight*, January 15, 2003, http://www.eurasianet.org/.

139. Interfax, November 25, 2002 [FBIS].

140. *Washington Post*, October 6, 2003.

141. *New York Times*, December 21, 2003, and January 5, 2004; *Washington Post*, January 5, 2004; and *Christian Science Monitor*, January 6, 2004.

142. Interfax, January 9, 2004 [FBIS].

143. ITAR-TASS, May 6, 2004 [FBIS].

144. Bill Samii, "Is an Iranian Hand Stirring the Iraqi Pot?"

## CHAPTER 11: NO "STRATEGIC PARTNERSHIP"

1. ITAR-TASS, December 27, 2002 [FBIS].

2. Author's notes on the panel discussion, supplemented by Carnegie Endowment for International Peace, "U.S.-Russian Security Cooperation in the Run-Up to the Next Bush-Putin Summit Meeting," July 17, 2003, http://www.ceip.org/files/events/events.asp?EventID=632. Col. Gen. (ret.) Viktor Yesin (Esin) of the Academy for Security, Defense, Law and Order Studies, who had earlier worked on the staff of the Security Council, and Maj. Gen. (ret.) Pavel Zolotarev of the Foundation for Military Reform accompanied Rogov. In his remarks, Yesin expressed skepticism that Iran could produce a nuclear weapon anytime soon but nevertheless argued that it was important to guard against it. No one in Russia, Yesin asserted, wanted Iran to become a nuclear power. Zolotarev added that Russia and the United States could deploy a joint warning system on Russian territory, which could cover all the regions of concern. Such a system would make it senseless for any country to want to develop nuclear weapons.

3. Interfax, November 30, 2000 [FBIS]; ITAR-TASS, November 24, 2000 [FBIS]; and *Krasnaya Zvezda*, January 5, 2001 [FBIS].

4. *Entekhab*, December 5, 2000 [FBIS].

5. *Jam-e Hafteh*, December 9, 2000 [FBIS]. See also *Entekhab*, December 2, 2000 [FBIS]. The proposal was still being considered but apparently going nowhere when Iranian Defense Minister Shamkhani visited Moscow in October 2001 (see ITAR-TASS, October 2, 2001 [FBIS]; and Agentstvo Voyennykh Novostey, October 3, 2001 [FBIS]).

6. ITAR-TASS, March 15, 2001 [FBIS].

7. Signed March 12, 2001. Available at Moscow Ministry of Foreign Affairs of the Russian Federation website, March 21, 2001 [FBIS].

8. ITAR-TASS, March 12, 2001 (not full text) [FBIS].

9. Interfax, March 13, 2001 [FBIS]; and *New York Times*, March 16, 2001. Ali Akbar Nateq-Nuri had also visited Kazan in April 1997.

10. IRNA, March 11, 2001 [FBIS].

11. *Presidential Bulletin*, vol. no. 46 (2291), Interfax, March 11, 2001 [FBIS].

12. ITAR-TASS, March 12, 2001 [FBIS]. On another point, the 2001 treaty stopped short of language agreed to eight years earlier. In the final version Putin and Khatami signed, each side undertook "not to use force or threat of force in mutual relations and not to use its territory for committing aggressions, subversive and separatist actions against the other side." This significantly abbreviated the formulation initialed in March 1993 by Kozyrev and Velayati, which had extended this pledge to include "or against states friendly" to each (Interfax, March 31, 1993 [FBIS-SOV-93-060, March 31, 1993, 9]).

This earlier formulation was a point that the diplomat Bakhtiyer Khakimov, as noted in chapter 5, later recalled with what appeared to be some pride of authorship. It would have given Iran, he had argued, a contractual base on which to lodge complaints about Russian actions in Tajikistan, for example. Now that phrase had disappeared, presumably reflecting Russia's lack of interest in propitiating Iran any further given that the Tajik civil war had ended some four years earlier (Khakimov, interview).
13. *Izvestiya*, March 13, 2001 [FBIS].
14. Interfax, March 11, 2001 [FBIS].
15. *Nezavisimaya Gazeta*, March 13, 2001 [FBIS].
16. *Izvestiya*, April 6, 2001 [FBIS].
17. Report by Aleksandr Shkirando, Russian Public Television, First Channel Network, December 23, 1996 [FBIS].
18. Maksim Yusin, "Dangerous Deal," *Izvestiya*, March 14, 2001 [FBIS].
19. Patrick Tyler, "Russians Question Wisdom of Their Coziness With Iran," *New York Times*, March 16, 2001.
20. *Izvestiya*, January 17, 2001 [FBIS]. Kozyrev in June 1994 had described relations with Iran as "good" and, returning to a subject raised as far back as 1992, said he hoped for a Yeltsin visit to Tehran that year (*Al-Wasat*, June 12-18, 1994 [FBIS]). A year later, in May 1995, President Rafsanjani also spoke of an upcoming Yeltsin visit to Tehran. But Rafsanjani said the date still had not been fixed and did not suggest it could be that year—perhaps an indication that it was becoming a remote possibility (IRNA, May 30, 1995 [FBIS]; and ITAR-TASS, May 31, 1995 [FBIS]). That fall, when Yeltsin's protocol chief Vladimir Shevchenko was asked whether a visit was being prepared, he responded, "This question has not even been considered here yet" (*Komsomolskaya Pravda*, September 22, 1995 [FBIS]). In fact, this may have been the last mention in the press of a Russian-Iranian summit involving a Yeltsin visit to Tehran.
21. Interfax, March 15 and September 11, 2001 [FBIS].
22. "Putin Holds Several Bilateral Meetings in Ashgabat," Interfax Presidential Bulletin, April 24, 2002 [FBIS]; and IRNA, April 24, 2002 [FBIS].
23. ITAR-TASS, April 4, 2002 [FBIS]. For a contrary analysis, published several months after Khatami's trip to Moscow, see Brenda Shaffer, *Partners in Need: The Strategic Relationship of Russia and Iran*, Policy Paper, no. 57 (Washington, DC: Washington Institute for Near East Policy, 2001).
24. ITAR-TASS, February 28, 2001 [FBIS].
25. IRNA, March 13, 2001 [FBIS].
26. Interfax, September 11, 2001 [FBIS].
27. IRNA, September 3, 2001 [FBIS]; and Interfax, September 11, 2001 [FBIS]. The same thing would happen two years later in November 2003 with a scheduled visit to Moscow by Hassan Rowhani, head of Iran's Supreme National Security.
28. *Tehran Times*, September 2, 2001 [FBIS].
29. Interfax, October 2, 2001 [FBIS].
30. *Vedemosti*, October 2, 2001 [FBIS]; *Rossiyskaya Gazeta*, October 3, 2001 [FBIS]; Agentstvo Voyennykh Novostey, October 3, 2001 [FBIS]; and ITAR-TASS, October 3, 2001 [FBIS].

31. Agentstvo Voyennykh Novostey, February 4, 2002 [FBIS].
32. Agentstvo Voyennykh Novostey, March 11, 2002 [FBIS]. Several months after Shamkhani's October 2001 visit, one press report asserted that Iran had placed a $150 million order for thirty Mi-17 military transport helicopters. The report described it as the first contract within the framework of the new military-technical agreement (*Vremya MN*, December 7, 2001 [FBIS]). Another report referred to a contract signed in April 2001 for twenty-one helicopters that would be completed with the delivery of the last two helicopters to Iran in January 2002; this report also referred to a second contract, for thirty Mi-171Sh combat helicopters equipped with the Shturm antitank system, to be delivered to Iran in 2002–3 (ITAR-TASS, December 24, 2001 [FBIS]). Press stories in October 2002 specified that twenty-one Mi-171 helicopters delivered to Iran in 2001–2 were being used to fight narcotics traffic in Iran and that Iran had signed a new contract in 2001 for thirty more Mi-171 helicopters to be delivered in 2002–3 (ITAR-TASS and IRNA, October 25, 2002 [FBIS]). In addition, the U.S. State Department disclosed in September 2003 that it had sanctioned the Tula Instrument Design Bureau (KPB) for selling to Iran lethal military equipment, reportedly an undisclosed number of laser-guided artillery shells (*Washington Times*, September 16, 2003; and *Los Angeles Times*, September 17, 2003).
33. ITAR-TASS, September 18, 2002 [FBIS]. A contract worth $100 million for 550 BMP-3 infantry fighting vehicles from the Kurgan Machine-Building Plant was said after Khatami's visit to be ready for signing (*Kommersant*, March 15, 2001 [FBIS]). But in late August and early October 2001, the BMP-3 contract was still being described only as "prepared for signing" (*Izvestiya*, August 25, 2001 [FBIS]; and *Moskovskiy Komsomolets*, October 2, 2001 [FBIS]). Although one publication a year and a half later described the BMP-3 contract as "being implemented successfully," the overall level of hype on this and other accounts in the article invited caution in accepting the claim literally (*Vremya Novostey*, May 29, 2003 [FBIS]).
34. Interfax, September 19, 2003 [FBIS].
35. *Promyshlennyy Yezhenedelnik*, February 24, 2004 [FBIS].
36. See, for example, ITAR-TASS, February 13, 2004 [FBIS]; and Moscow Channel One TV, April 22, 2004 [FBIS].
37. *Resalat*, September 2, 2002 [FBIS].
38. Interfax, March 13, 2001 [FBIS].
39. *Washington Post*, May 19, 2001.
40. *New York Times*, June 17, 2001.
41. Yakovlev, interview.
42. *Strana.ru*, June 19, 2001 [FBIS].
43. For the transcript, see Moscow ORT Television, May 24, 2002 [FBIS].
44. ITAR-TASS, June 27, 2002 [FBIS]; and Voice of the Islamic Republic of Iran, June 28, 2002 [FBIS].
45. "Kananaskis Summit Document: The Kananaskis Summit Chair's Summary," Kananaskis G-8 Summit official website, June 27, 2002 [FBIS].
46. NTV Mir, June 27, 2002 [FBIS].
47. Interfax and ITAR-TASS, May 24, 2002 [FBIS].
48. *New York Times*, May 29, 2002.
49. *Iran Daily* ("Media Monitor" from *Khorasan*), May 23, 2002 [FBIS].
50. See, for example, Foreign Minister Kharrazi's comments as reported by IRNA, May 26, 2002 [FBIS]; the unattributed editorial, "Why Moscow Won't Shelve Third World Allies for Washington," *Iran News* (Internet version), May 26, 2002 [FBIS]; and the coverage of Kananaskis by Voice of the Islamic Republic of Iran, June 28, 2002 [FBIS].

51. See MinAtom First Deputy Minister Lev Ryabev reiteration of these assurances in ITAR-TASS, January 13, 1999 [FBIS].
52. ITAR-TASS, September 4, 2001, and April 4, 2002 [FBIS]; and Interfax, September 17, 2002 [FBIS].
53. Prime Minister Kasyanov signed Decree No. 556, "On the Long-Term Program for Development of Trade and Economic, Industrial, and Scientific-Technical Cooperation Between the Russian Federation and Islamic Republic of Iran for the Period up to 2012," on July 24, 2002 (pravitelstvo.ru, July 26, 2002 [FBIS]). Although five units were listed in the document, many commentaries rendered it inaccurately as Bushehr-1 plus six more. A year later, in July 2003, Russia and Iran signed a draft memorandum of understanding (MOU) on the same subject, with annexes to the MOU scheduled to be signed in September 2003 (IRNA, July 18, 2003 [FBIS]). After that, the paper trail on the fate of the "Long-Term Program" goes cold—until a similar notion was resurrected in the bilateral statement issued after Putin's visit to Tehran in October 2007 (see Postscript).
54. *Washington Post*, August 3, 2002.
55. Voice of the Islamic Republic of Iran, Radio 1, December 26, 2002 [FBIS]; and Interfax, February 11, 2003 [FBIS].
56. *Izvestiya*, December 27, 2002 [FBIS].
57. Interview with MinAtom's Aleksandr Rumyantsev, Ekho Moskvy, October 21, 2002 [FBIS].
58. Interfax, February 3, 2004 [FBIS].
59. Andrey Zobov, "The Non-Proliferation of Weapons of Mass Destruction as a Topic Issue of the Third Millennium: Regional and Global Aspects," lecture delivered October 11, 2002, Moscow Center for Arms Control, Energy, and Environmental Studies (Internet text), November 6, 2002 [FBIS].
60. Aleksey Arbatov, lecture delivered at the Moscow Institute of Physics and Technology on October 4, 2002, Moscow Center for Arms Control, Energy, and Environmental Studies (Internet text), [FBIS].
61. Bill Samii, "Tehran Pleased With U.S. Failure to Hinder its Nuke Pursuits," *RFE/RL Iran Report*, August 5, 2002, http://archive.rferl.org/reports/Archive.aspx?report=57 1&year=2008.
62. Dr. Davoud Bavand, "Saddam's Poisonous Olive Branch," *Iran*, August 19, 2002 [FBIS].
63. *Iran Mojahedin* (Internet text), August 14, 2002 [FBIS].
64. *USA Today*, December 13, 2002; and *Washington Post*, December 14, 2002.
65. IRNA, December 16, 2002 [FBIS].
66. Vision of the Islamic Republic of Iran, Network 1, February 9, 2003 [FBIS].
67. *Nuclear.ru*, February 10, 2003 [FBIS]; and ITAR-TASS, February 11, 2003 [FBIS].
68. *New York Times*, February 10, 2003; and *Washington Post*, December 19, 2002, and February 11, 2003.
69. *Washington Post*, February 20, 2003.
70. IAEA, Board of Governors, Director General Mohamed ElBaradei, "Introductory Statement to the Board of Governors," March 17, 2003, http://www.iaea.org/NewsCenter/Statements/2003/ebsp2003n008.shtml#iran; and IAEA, Board of Governors, Report by the Director General, "Implementation of the NPT Safeguards Agreement in the Islamic Republic of Iran," June 6, 2003, GOV/2003/40, http://www.iaea.org/NewsCenter/Focus/IaeaIran/index.shtml.
71. Following Director General ElBaradei's report in March 2003 on his delegation's safeguards discussions with Iranian officials, the IAEA Board of Governors took

up the issue at its meetings in June, September, and November 2003; March, June, September, and November 2004; March, June, August, September, and November 2005; and February, March, and April 2006. Relevant documents for each meeting are available at http://www.iaea.org/NewsCenter/Focus/IaeaIran/index.shtml.

72. Vladimir Frolov, "Iran's Nuclear Surprise," *Vremya MN*, March 12, 2003 [FBIS].

73. Interfax, March 24, 2003 [FBIS].

74. Iranian Students News Agency, March 27, 2003 [FBIS].

75. IRNA, March 29, 2003 [FBIS].

76. ITAR-TASS, April 22, 2003 [FBIS].

77. Guy Dinmore, "Washington Hardliners Wary of Engaging With Iran," *Financial Times*, March 16, 2004; and Glenn Kessler, "In 2003, U.S. Spurned Iran's Offer of Dialogue; Some Officials Lament Lost Opportunity," *Washington Post*, June 18, 2006.

78. *New York Times*, May 27, 2003; and *Washington Post*, June 23, 2003. For an analysis and overview of all these revelations, see Douglas Frantz, "Iran Closes in on Ability to Build a Nuclear Bomb," *Los Angeles Times*, August 4, 2003. For a primer on the alternative methods of weaponizing uranium, see Valerie Lincy and Gary Milhollin, "Iran's Nuclear Program: For Electricity or a Bomb?" *New York Times*, August 3, 2003.

79. *International Herald Tribune*, July 9, 2003.

80. Ekho Moskvy, June 3, 2003 [FBIS].

81. Ekho Moskvy, May 15, 2003 [FBIS].

82. Joint News Conference, Russia TV RTR, June 1, 2003 [FBIS].

83. G-8 Summit Declaration, "Non-Proliferation of Weapons of Mass Destruction," Paris G-8 Evian Summit (Internet text), June 2, 2003 [FBIS].

84. Russia TV RTR, June 3, 2003 [FBIS].

85. "UK Prime Minister Blair Briefs Parliament on G-8 Summit," London 10 Downing Street (Internet text), June 4, 2003 [FBIS].

86. IAEA, "Implementation of the NPT Safeguards."

87. IAEA.org, News Center, "Statement by the Board," Media Advisory 2003/72, June 19, 2003, http://www.iaea.org/NewsCenter/Focus/IaeaIran/index.shtml.

88. BBC1 Television, interview recorded on June 20, 2003, broadcast June 22, 2003, [FBIS].

89. Interfax, June 18, 2003 [FBIS].

90. Moscow RenTV, June 16, 2003 [FBIS].

91. *Kommersant*, May 27, 2003 [FBIS].

92. ITAR-TASS, June 20, 2003 [FBIS].

93. *Kommersant*, July 3, 2003 [FBIS].

94. According to a "senior U.S. official," AP story datelined Washington, in *Moscow Times*, July 7, 2003.

95. Vladimir Orlov, "Patient in Coma?" *Russia in Global Affairs* 1, no. 3 (July–September 2003): 115–119, http://www.ceip.org/files/projects/npp/resources/moscow2003/orlovreport.pdf.

96. Aleksey Arbatov, "Nuclear Deterrence and Proliferation Yesterday, Today, and Tomorrow . . ." *Strategicheskaya Stabilnost*, December 6, 2003 [FBIS].

## CHAPTER 12: OPERATION IRAQI FREEDOM

1. Although the Iraqi ambassador and his deputy left New York shortly after the start of OIF, lower-ranking members of the Saddam-era-appointed delegation stayed on well into the summer of 2003 (*Washington Times*, July 3, 2003).

2. President Bush called on the "unelected . . . rulers" of Iran to listen to the Iranian

people, the "vast majority" of which had voted for "political and economic reform" in recent elections. He promised that as the Iranian people moved toward "a future defined by greater freedom, greater tolerance, they will have no better friend than the United States of America." See White House, Office of the Press Secretary, "Statement of the President," July 12, 2002, http://www.whitehouse.gov/news/releases/2002/07/20020712-9.html.

3. Bill Samii, "Khamenei and Khatami See Eye-to-Eye on Bush," *RFE/RL Iran Report*, July 23, 2002, http://archive.rferl.org/reports/Archive.aspx?report=571&year=2008; and *Washington Post*, August 3, 2002.

4. UN Security Council, Resolution 1441, S/RES/1441 (2002), November 8, 2002, http://www.un.org/Docs/sc/index.html.

5. Elaine Sciolino, "To Iran, Iraq May Be the Greater Satan," *New York Times*, November 3, 2002.

6. *London Times*, October 25, 2002.

7. *Washington Post*, February 8, 2003.

8. Barbara Slavin, "Iranians May Aid U.S. War on Iraq," *USA Today*, November 15, 2002.

9. Peter Slevin, "U.S. Met With Iranians on War," *Washington Post*, February 8, 2003.

10. Karl Vick, "Iran-Backed Militia Seen Moving Into Iraqi Kurdish Zone," *Washington Post*, March 7, 2003.

11. Steve Fairbanks, "Iran's Interest in Shia Iraq," *RFE/RL Iran Report*, March 20, 2003, http://archive.rferl.org/reports/Archive.aspx?report=571&year=2008.

12. *London Times*, October 25, 2002; Keyhan, July 21, 2003 [FBIS]; and Shanahan, "The Islamic Da'wa Party," 16-25.

13. Vick, "Iran-Backed Militia."

14. Bill Samii, "Tehran Organizing Iraqi Opposition," *RFE/RL Iran Report*, February 3, 2003, http://archive.rferl.org/reports/Archive.aspx?report=571&year=2008.

15. Sciolino, "To Iran."

16. *New York Times*, December 13, 2002; and *Entekhab*, January 7, 2003 [FBIS].

17. Samii, "Tehran Organizing Iraqi Opposition"; and *Al-Jazirah Television*, January 15, 2003 [FBIS].

18. Al-Sulaymaniyah KurdSat, February 28, 2003 [FBIS].

19. "Final Statement Issued at the End of the Coordination and Follow-up Committee Meeting," *Arbil Brayati*, March 2, 2003 [FBIS].

20. Salah-al-Din Kurdistan Satellite TV, March 1, 2003 [FBIS].

21. Jon Lee Anderson, "American Viceroy," *New Yorker*, December 19, 2005, 64.

22. According to the report written by Charles A. Duelfer, the chief U.S. weapons inspector (*Washington Post*, October 7, 2004).

23. On this and other evaluations of the size and potential profits from West Qurna, there were wildly different estimates in the press. Alekperov, however, put West Qurna reserves at over 7 billion barrels of oil and stated that the overall cash flow involved in the project was $20 billion. See his interview in *Itogi*, December 24, 2002 [FBIS]. The consortium to develop the West Qurna-2 field included Lukoil (68.5 percent), Zarubezhneft (3.25 percent), Mashinimport (3.25 percent), and the Iraqi Oil and Gas Ministry (25 percent.)

24. Yevgeniy Kalyukov, "Iraq Separates Lukoil From Oil," *Gazeta.ru*, December 16, 2002 [FBIS].

25. According to Russian deputy foreign minister Yuri Fedotov in Interfax, November 20, 2003 [FBIS].

26. For an overview of the choices Moscow faced around this time, see Mark N. Katz,

"Losing Balance: Russian Foreign Policy Toward Iraq and Iran," *Current History* 102, no. 666 (October 2003): 341–345.

27. Yuriy Kogtev and Roman Simonenko, "Pipe Calls Oilmen to China: Russia Forced to Correct Export Plans," *Kommersant*, April 8, 2003 [FBIS].
28. *Nezavisimaya Gazeta*, October 1, 2002 [FBIS].
29. See, for example, *Izvestiya*, October 15, 2002 [FBIS].
30. NTV Mir, November 21, 2002 [FBIS].
31. Interfax and Ekho Moskvy Radio, December 12, 2002 [FBIS].
32. Interview with Canada's *National Post* as reported by Reuters, December 18, 2002. There were also occasional assertions in the press of Lukoil contacts with Iraqi opposition groups (*Izvestiya*, June 11, 2003 [FBIS]).
33. Olga Pashkova, "Iraq Versus Lukoil," *Politkom.ru*, December 16, 2002, [FBIS].
34. Kalyukov, "Iraq Separates Lukoil."
35. Interfax, January 9, 2004 [FBIS].
36. See the interview with Alekperov in *Profil*, no. 33 (September 8, 2003): 34–37 [FBIS]. In late 2003 Alekperov reportedly controlled 10.38 percent of Lukoil stock (*Kompaniya*, November 3, 2003 [FBIS]).
37. *Krasnaya Zvezda*, December 6, 2002 [FBIS].
38. *Kurdistani Nuwe* (Sulaymaniyah), December 11, 2002 [FBIS].
39. Interfax, November 18, 2002 [FBIS]; *Al-Hayah* (London), December 7, 2002 [FBIS]; *New York Times*, December 13, 2002; and *Entekhab*, January 7, 2003 [FBIS].
40. *Itogi*, December 24, 2002 [FBIS].
41. Interfax, January 15, 2003 [FBIS].
42. RIA-Novosti, February 3, 2003 [FBIS].
43. ITAR-TASS, March 11, 2003 [FBIS].
44. LCI Television (Paris), March 5, 2003 [FBIS].
45. ITAR-TASS, March 11, 2003 [FBIS].
46. On the campaign and some of the key political and military planning that went into it, see Peter J. Boyer, "The New War Machine," *New Yorker*, June 30, 2003, 55–71.
47. RTR TV, March 20, 2003 [FBIS].
48. *Kommersant*, March 25, 2003 [FBIS].
49. Interfax, March 19, 2003 [FBIS]; and Bill Samii, "Iran to Fend Off Refugee Influx," *RFE/RL Iran Report*, March 20, 2003, http://archive.rferl.org/reports/Archive.aspx?report=571&year=2008.
50. Russian Federation President official website, www.kremlin.ru, April 29, 2003 [FBIS].
51. Ibid., May 2, 2003 [FBIS]
52. ITAR-TASS, May 14, 2003 [FBIS].
53. *New York Times*, May 23, 2003.
54. UN Security Council, Resolution 1483, S/RES/1483 (2003), May 22, 2003, http://www.un.org/Docs/sc/index.html.
55. Joint News Conference, RTR TV, June 1, 2003 [FBIS]. UNSCR 1483 was approved unanimously on May 22, 2003, by a 14-0 vote (Syria did not vote).
56. ITAR-TASS, May 26, 2003 [FBIS]; and *Izvestiya*, June 11, 2003 [FBIS].
57. Interfax, June 2, 2003 [FBIS].
58. Interfax, June 6, 2003 [FBIS].
59. *Izvestiya*, June 11, 2003 [FBIS].
60. *Vremya MN*, June 7, 2003 [FBIS].
61. *Politkom.ru*, June 16, 2003 [FBIS].
62. Voice of the Islamic Republic of Iran, April 9, 2003 [FBIS].
63. ITAR-TASS, April 29, 2003 [FBIS].

64. IRNA, May 9, 2003 [FBIS].

65. Vision of the Islamic Republic of Iran, May 14, 2003 [FBIS].

66. Barbara Slavin, "Iran, U.S. Holding Talks in Geneva," *USA Today*, May 12, 2003; and Barbara Slavin, *Bitter Friends, Bosom Enemies: Iran, the U.S., and the Twisted Path to Confrontation* (New York: St. Martin's Press, 2007), 201–202.

67. *Iran News*, May 13, 2003 [FBIS].

68. Vision of the Islamic Republic of Iran, May 14, 2003 [FBIS].

69. *London Financial Times*, March 17, 2004; Glenn Kessler, *Washington Post*, June 18, 2006; and Glenn Kessler, "2003 Memo Says Iranian Leaders Backed Talks," *Washington Post*, February 14, 2007.

70. Trita Parsi, *Treacherous Alliance: The Secret Dealings of Israel, Iran, and the United States* (New Haven: Yale University Press, 2007), Appendix A: Iran's May 2003 Negotiation Proposal to the United States, 341–342; and Appendix C: Letter From Ambassador Guldimann to the U.S. State Department, 345–346.

71. Parsi, *Treacherous Alliance*, Appendix C. Parsi was head of the National Iranian American Council and an advocate of U.S.-Iranian talks. In writing that the "proposal" was "authoritative," had the "approval" of the Supreme Leader, and was "authentic" (244 and 248), Parsi—as did some others—ascribed greater authoritativeness to the Roadmap than did Ambassador Guldimann in his cover letter.

   In addition, Kharrazi told Guldimann that he had told Khamenei that the Roadmap was an Iranian initiative. Contradicting this, Parsi published another document, which he presented as the initial proposal that had allegedly come from a high official in Washington and had then been edited by Kharrazi and his contacts in Tehran (Parsi, *Treacherous Alliance*, Appendix B, 343–344). However, no one in Washington ever took credit for authorship of the alleged initial American draft. In a town remarkable for its "leaks," such modesty was unusual.

72. Ibid., Appendix A.

73. Ibid., Appendix C. According to Parsi's recounting of these events, but without clear attribution, Ambassador Zarif had also reviewed the proposal (243). But in Ambassador Guldimann's cover letter, he did not report that Sadeq Kharrazi had claimed this to him (Appendix C).

74. See, for example, the interview with Kharrazi in "American's Iran Policy Is Confused," *Iran Daily*, May 30, 1998 [FBIS].

75. "Sadeq Kharrazi: Removal or Resignation?" *Entekhab*, April 22, 2002 [FBIS]; and Ali Nurizadeh, "Khamenei Intervenes in the Issue of Dialogue With Washington and Restricts Authority to Conduct Contacts to Khatami's Government," *Al-Sharq al-Awsat*, April 24, 2002 [FBIS]. See also "A Report on Meetings and Talks on Iran-American Relations," *Iran*, April 22, 2002 [FBIS]; and "Sadeq Kharrazi Was Sacked: What Is Going on Behind the Scenes?" *Mardom Salari*, April 24, 2002 [FBIS].

76. "Sadeq Kharrazi Appointed as Iran's Ambassador to France," *Azad*, May 18, 2002 [FBIS].

77. Robin Wright, "U.S. Ends Talks With Iran Over Al Qaeda Links," *Los Angeles Times*, May 21, 2003; and Robin Wright, "Iran Points Out Its Al Qaeda Arrests," May 22, 2003.

78. Karl Vick, "Iran Agrees to Talk With U.S. About Iraq; White House Says Agenda Is Limited, but Tehran Signals Hopes for More," *Washington Post*, March 17, 2006.

79. Parsi, *Treacherous Alliance*, 252–253; and Slavin, *Bitter Friends*, 203–204.

80. See, for example, Parsi, *Treacherous Alliance*, 243; Slavin, *Bitter Friends*, 204–206; and the transcript of the discussion by Barbara Slavin and Suzanne Maloney in "U.S.-Iran Relations," Council on Foreign Relations, October 31, 2007, http://www.cfr.

org/publication/14723/. Writing before accounts of the Roadmap proposal surfaced, however, Kenneth Pollack had cautioned that while "The Grand Bargain has a great deal to recommend it . . . the problem is . . . it doesn't work in practice." See Kenneth M. Pollack, *The Persian Puzzle: The Conflict Between Iran and America* (New York: Random House, 2004), 395 and 395–400.

81. Glenn Kessler, "Iran Signals Readiness to Cooperate; Change in U.S. Approach Necessary, Official Says," *Washington Post*, September 25, 2003.

82. Voice of the Islamic Republic of Iran, Radio 1, April 20, 2003 [FBIS].

83. Bob Woodward, *State of Denial* (New York: Simon & Schuster, 2006), 174–175. Garner represented the Pentagon's Office of Reconstruction and Humanitarian Assistance (ORHA).

84. L. Paul Bremer, *My Year in Iraq: The Struggle to Build a Future of Hope*, with Malcolm McConnell (New York: Simon & Schuster, 2006), 5–12 and 43–49.

85. Woodward, *State of Denial*, 219.

86. *Jomhuri-ye Eslami*, July 9, 2003 [FBIS].

87. For an inside account of how the IGC was put together, see Bremer, *My Year in Iraq*, 78–100.

88. *Los Angeles Times*, June 22, 2003.

89. *Washington Post*, July 14, 2003; "Iraqi Governing Council Members," BBC News, July 14, 2003, http://news.bbc.co.uk/2/hi/middle_east/3062897.stm; and *Keyhan*, July 21, 2003 [FBIS].

90. *Washington Post*, July 21, 2003; and *Christian Science Monitor*, July 22, 2003.

91. Interfax, July 14, 2003 [FBIS].

92. Ibid.

93. UN Security Council, Resolution 1500, S/RES/1500 (2003), August 14, 2003, http://www.un.org/Docs/sc/index.html.

94. *Keyhan International*, July 15, 2003 [FBIS]. For the affiliations of all twenty-five IGC members, see "Iraqi Governing Council Members"; and *Keyhan*, July 21, 2003 [FBIS].

95. *Resalat*, August 4, 2003 [FBIS].

96. *Jomhuri-ye Eslami*, August 17, 2003 [FBIS].

97. *Iran News*, August 20, 2003 [FBIS].

98. UNSCR 1483 of May 22, 2003; and UNSCR 1500 of August 14, 2003.

99. *Farhang-e Ashti*, August 10, 2003 [FBIS].

100. *E'temad*, August 6, 2003 [FBIS].

101. *Kommersant*, October 27, 2003 [FBIS].

102. IRNA, September 25, 2003 [FBIS].

103. *Washington Post*, August 30, 2003.

104. Richard L. Armitage, Deputy Secretary of State, "Roundtable With Domestic Syndicates," August 26, 2003 [released on August 28, 2003], http://www.state.gov/s/d/former/armitage/remarks/23581.htm. As later catalogued by the Security Council, there was also the assassination of IGC member Akila Hashimi on September 25, the murder of a Spanish diplomat on October 9, and the bombing of the Turkish embassy on October 14 (UN Security Council, Resolution 1511, S/RES/1511 (2003), October 16, 2003, http://www.un.org/Docs/sc/index.html).

105. Interfax, August 30, 2003 [FBIS]. Putin was speaking at a news conference in Sardinia.

106. S/RES/1511 (2003), October 16, 2003. On the culminating exchanges between U.S. and Russian representatives, see also Colum Lynch, "U.S. Gets Backing for More U.N. Aid in Iraq," *Washington Post*, October 16, 2003.

107. *Washington Post*, September 25, 2003.

108. "The November 15 Agreement: Timeline to a Sovereign, Democratic and Secure Iraq," http://www.iraqcoalition.org/government/AgreementNov15.pdf. See also *Washington Post*, November 16, 2003; and *Washington Post*, December 16, 2003, which contains a useful chart of the various processes involved in the agreed transition to Iraqi sovereignty.

109. CNN interview with Igor Ivanov, November 18, 2003, as posted on the Russian Foreign Ministry website, November 20, 2003 [FBIS].

110. *Iran News*, November 20, 2003 [FBIS].

111. *Iran,* November 25, 2003 [FBIS].

112. Bill Samii, "Is an Iranian Hand Stirring the Iraqi Pot?"

113. *Washington Post*, April 5 and 11, 2004.

114. Chubin and Tripp, *Iran and Iraq at War*, 25–27; Karsh, "From Ideological Zeal," 29–30.

115. Anthony Shadid, "Call of History Draws Iraqi Cleric to the Political Fore," *Washington Post*, February 1, 2004; Nicholas Blanford, "Iran, Iraq, and Two Shiite Visions," *Christian Science Monitor*, February 20, 2004; and Shanahan, "The Islamic Da'wa Party," 16–25.

116. *Washington Post*, April 11, 2004; and *New York Times*, April 21, 2004.

117. According to an Iranian Foreign Ministry source, "It would be a tragedy for the United States . . . to withdraw its troops from Iraq too soon" (*Iran*, April 18, 2004 [FBIS]).

118. "Is Iran Provoking the Unrest?" *Time*, April 19, 2004. See also Samii, "Is an Iranian Hand Stirring the Iraqi Pot?" Samii concluded, "There is no publicly available substantive evidence of an Iranian role, but . . . actors in the Iranian foreign policy field have the motivation and the means to interfere in Iraqi affairs."

119. *Los Angeles Times*, August 12, 2004; and *New York Times*, September 20, 2004.

120. George Packer, "Letter From Basra: Testing Ground," *New Yorker*, February 28, 2005, 39.

121. *USA Today*, September 14, 2004.

122. Sunni insurgents were made up overwhelmingly of Baathist diehards and lesser numbers of fresh Arab recruits, including suicide bombers from Abu Musab Zarqawi's foreign-dominated al Qaeda in Iraq and other terrorist forces, many of whose activities were not desirable from Tehran's point of view. In Fallujah, for example, American troops found a letter dated April 4 from an apparently non-Iraqi Sunni combatant urging a friend to join him in the "beautiful" fight against Shia "nonbelievers" and Americans. "This is like Iran, there are many Shiites and we need to fight them" (*Washington Post*, April 12, 2004). One study a year later estimated around thirty thousand insurgents, of which only 4–10 percent consisted of non-Iraqi foreign elements. See Anthony Cordesman and Nawaf Obaid, "Saudi Militants in Iraq: Assessment and Kingdom's Response," Center for Strategic and International Studies, Washington, DC, September 19, 2005, http://www.csis.org/ press/wf_2005_0919.pdf.

123. *Washington Post*, January 12, 2004.

124. Interfax, March 8, 2004 [FBIS]; and IRNA, March 8, 2004 [FBIS].

125. *Washington Post*, March 9, 2004.

126. *Washington Post*, June 2, 2004. On June 8, after intense bargaining and many revisions, the UNSC finally approved by 15-0 a new resolution on Iraq. UNSCR 1546 "endorsed" the new political timetable rolled out by the IGC on March 8. It also accommodated a watered-down version of Russia's demand since the previous November for an international conference (*Washington Post*, June 8 and 9, 2004; and UN Security Council, Resolution 1546, S/RES/1546 (2004), June 8, 2004, http://www.un.org/Docs/sc/index.html). Brahimi's initiatives in April had been crucial in all these developments (*Washington Post*, April 15, 16, and 17, 2004; and *New York Times*, April 28, 2004).

127. *Washington Post*, June 29, 2004.
128. *New York Times*, August 19, 2004.
129. *Washington Post*, September 2, 2004.
130. *New York Times*, November 22, 2004.
131. *Washington Post*, November 28 and December 7, 2004; *New York Times*, January 31, 2005; and *Washington Post*, February 14 and 15, 2005.
132. Bill Samii, "Tehran Anticipates End of Iraqi Occupation," *RFE/RL Iran Report*, February 7, 2005, http://archive.rferl.org/reports/Archive.aspx?report=571&year=2008.
133. *USA Today*, January 31, 2005. According to later press reports, Iran had pumped considerable money and effort into supporting United Iraqi Alliance candidates friendly to Iran in the January 2005 elections (David Ignatius, "Bush's Lost Iraqi Election," *Washington Post*, August 30, 2007).
134. The sale upped the proportion of Lukoil's privately owned shares to 100 percent. Several months after the initial purchase, the American company increased its stake in Lukoil to 10 percent (*Washington Post*, September 30, 2004; Interfax, September 29, 2004 [FBIS]; and Interfax, December 23, 2004 [FBIS]).
135. ITAR-TASS, October 27, 2004 [FBIS].
136. Turan, November 19 and 20, 1993 [FBIS-SOV-93-223, November 22, 1993, 70–71].
137. Russia TV RTR, February 24, 2005 [FBIS].
138. ITAR-TASS, February 25, 2005 [FBIS].
139. ITAR-TASS, June 28, 2005 [FBIS].
140. *New York Times*, May 18, 2005.
141. *New York Times*, May 20, 2005. Iran had proposed these and Sulaymaniyah in August 2003 (*Farhang-e Ashti*, August 10, 2003 [FBIS]).
142. Associated Press, *USA Today*, November 22, 2005.

## CHAPTER 13: THE AHMADINEJAD SHOCK WAVE

1. Interfax, March 9, 2004 [FBIS]. Igor Ivanov became secretary of the Security Council upon leaving the Foreign Ministry.
2. Barton Gellman, "U.S., Allies Launch Air Attack on Yugoslav Military Targets; Two MiGs Reported Shot Down," *Washington Post*, March 25, 1999.
3. ITAR-TASS, March 11, 2003 [FBIS]; and David E. Sanger, "Threats and Responses: Diplomacy; U.S. May Abandon UN Vote on Iraq, Powell Testifies," with Warren Hoge, *New York Times*, March 14, 2003.
4. Dmitri Trenin, "Russia Leaves the West," *Foreign Affairs* 85, no. 4 (July–August 2006): 94.
5. IRNA, June 18, 2003 [FBIS].
6. "Iran's Negotiations Aimed at Signing the Additional Protocol," *Yas-e Now*, August 14, 2003 [FBIS]; and Kamyar Rowshan-Dezh, "Nuclear Ambiguity," *Yas-e Now*, August 14, 2003 [FBIS]. For a report on debate among Majles deputies, see "Shall We Accept or Reject the Additional Protocol?" *Aftab-e Yazd*, August 6, 2003 [FBIS].
7. Ray Takeyh, "Iran's Nuclear Skeptics," *Washington Post*, April 25, 2003.
8. Gary Samore, quoted in Douglas Frantz, "Iran Closes In on Ability to Build a Nuclear Bomb," *Los Angeles Times*, August 4, 2003.
9. Karl Vick, "Iranians Assert Right to Nuclear Weapons," *Washington Post*, March 11, 2003.
10. Frantz, "Iran Closes In."
11. *London Financial Times*, August 20, 2003.
12. Hamid Kushki, "Lest History Repeat Itself," *Mardom Salari*, August 18, 2003 [FBIS].

13. IRNA, August 14, 2003 [FBIS].

14. *Nuclear.ru*, August 20, 2003 [FBIS].

15. IRNA, August 11, 2003 [FBIS].

16. Interfax, August 18, 2003 [FBIS].

17. IAEA, Board of Governors, "Implementation of the NPT Safeguards Agreement in the Islamic Republic of Iran: Resolution Adopted by the Board on 12 September 2003," GOV/2003/69, http://www.iaea.org/NewsCenter/Focus/IaeaIran/index.shtml.

18. Excerpts from transcript of Russian President Vladimir Putin's interview with U.S. journalists near Moscow on 20 September, Moscow Ministry of Foreign Affairs (Internet text), September 24, 2003 [FBIS].

19. White House, Office of the Press Secretary, "President Bush Meets With Russian President Putin at Camp David: Remarks by the President and Russian President Putin in Press Availability Camp David," September 27, 2003, http://www.whitehouse.gov/news/releases/2003/09/20030927-2.html.

20. Dana Milbank, "Putin Agrees in Spirit but Little Else," *Washington Post*, September 28, 2003.

21. Steven Lee Myers, "Putin Says U.S. Faces Big Risks in Effort in Iraq," *New York Times*, October 6, 2003; and "Interview With President Putin," *New York Times*, October 5, 2003, http://www.nytimes.com/2003/10/05/international/06PTEXT-CND.html?ex=1216526400&en=6ba8d161cd2c462f&ei=5070.

22. IAEA, Board of Governors, "Implementation of the NPT Safeguards Agreement in the Islamic Republic of Iran," Report by the Director General, February 24, 2004, GOV/2004/11, http://www.iaea.org/NewsCenter/Focus/IaeaIran/index.shtml; and IAEA.org, News Center, In Focus: IAEA and Iran, "Statement by the Iranian Government and Visiting EU Foreign Ministers," October 21, 2003, http://www.iaea.org/NewsCenter/Focus/IaeaIran/statement_iran21102003.shtml.

23. IAEA.org, News Center, Top Stories, Staff Report, "Iran Signs Additional Protocol on Nuclear Safeguards," December 18, 2003, http://www.iaea.org/NewsCenter/News/ 2003/iranap20031218.html.

24. Agentstvo Voyennykh Novostey, November 11, 2003 [FBIS].

25. Vision of the Islamic Republic of Iran, November 10, 2003 [FBIS]; and Interfax, November 10, 2003 [FBIS].

26. IAEA, GOV/2004/11.

27. IAEA, Board of Governors, "Implementation of the NPT Safeguards Agreement in the Islamic Republic of Iran," Report by the Director General, June 1, 2004, GOV/2004/34, http://www.iaea.org/NewsCenter/Focus/IaeaIran/index.shtml.

28. IAEA, Board of Governors, "Implementation of the NPT Safeguards Agreement in the Islamic Republic of Iran: Resolution Adopted by the Board on September 18, 2004," GOV/2004/79, http://www.iaea.org/NewsCenter/Focus/IaeaIran/index.shtml.

29. Text of speech by Supreme National Security Council Secretary Hassan Rowhani to the Supreme Cultural Revolution Council, "Beyond the Challenges Facing Iran and the IAEA Concerning the Nuclear Dossier," *Rahbord*, September 30, 2005 [FBIS].

30. IAEA.org, "Communication Dated 26 November 2004 Received From the Permanent Representatives of France, Germany, the Islamic Republic of Iran and the United Kingdom Concerning the Agreement Signed in Paris on 15 November 2004," Information Circular, INFCIRC/637, November 26, 2004, http://www.iaea.org/Publications/Documents/Infcircs/2004/infcirc637.pdf.

31. IAEA, Board of Governors, "Implementation of the NPT Safeguards Agreement in the Islamic Republic of Iran: Resolution adopted by the Board on November 29, 2004," GOV/2004/90, http://www.iaea.org/NewsCenter/Focus/IaeaIran/index.shtml.

32. RIA-Novosti, February 27, 2005 [FBIS].

33. The number of pages in the proposal comes from *New York Times*, June 15, 2006.

34. IAEA.org, "Statement by the United Kingdom on behalf of the European Union at the IAEA Board of Governors, August 9, 2005," News Center, In Focus: IAEA and Iran, Timeline Archive, http://www.iaea.org/NewsCenter/Focus/IaeaIran/bog092005_statement-eu.pdf.

35. Bill Samii, "As Winners Head for Runoff, Losers Complain of Fraud," and "Excess of Presidential Candidates Worried Hard-Liners," *RFE/RL Iran Report*, June 20, 2005; and Samii, "A New Paradigm and New Math," *RFE/RL Iran Report*, June 27, 2005, http://archive.rferl.org/reports/Archive.aspx?report=571&year=2008.

36. Shahram Chubin, *Iran's Nuclear Ambitions* (Washington, DC: Carnegie Endowment for International Peace, 2006), 32, 34, and 36.

37. The IAEA Board of Governors on August 11 urged Iran to reestablish full suspension and requested an update on the Iranian nuclear file for Director General ElBaradei for the next scheduled board meeting in late September (IAEA, Board of Governors, "Implementation of the NPT Safeguards Agreement in the Islamic Republic of Iran: Resolution Adopted on August 11, 2005," GOV/2005/64, http://www.iaea.org/NewsCenter/Focus/IaeaIran index.shtml).

38. IRNA, August 15, 2005 [FBIS]; and *Sharq*, August 16, 2005 [FBIS].

39. Mohammad Quchani, "The Larijani Brothers," *Asr-e Azadegan*, April 22, 2000 [FBIS].

40. "Leading Iranian Presidential Candidate Profiles," BBC Monitoring, May 18, 2005 [FBIS].

41. Voice of the Islamic Republic of Iran Radio 1, August 25, 2005 [FBIS].

42. Shahab Kashefi, "The Ugliness and Beauty of Looking Toward the East," *Mardom-Salari*, September 10, 2005 [FBIS].

43. *Siyasat-e-Ruz*, September 15, 2005 [FBIS].

44. Full text of President Mahmoud Ahmadinejad before the Sixtieth Session of the UN General Assembly, IRNA, September 17, 2005 [FBIS].

45. News conference by Ali Larijani, Islamic Republic of Iran News Network Television, September 20, 2005 [FBIS].

46. IAEA, Board of Governors, "Implementation of the NPT Safeguards Agreement in the Islamic Republic of Iran: Resolution Adopted on September 24, 2005," GOV/2005/77, http:// www.iaea.org/NewsCenter/Focus/IaeaIran/index.shtml.

47. *New York Times*, September 25, 2005.

48. Mohammad Quchani, "Ways of Friend Finding," *Sharq*, September 26, 2005 [FBIS]; and Arash Yavari, "New Experiences in Iran's Diplomacy," *Mardom Salari*, September 28, 2005 [FBIS].

49. Nabi'ollah Ebrahimi, "Play With Red Card," *Sharq*, October 2, 2005 [FBIS].

50. BBC Monitoring: Press Quotes From Iranian Newspapers, *Mardom-Salari*, November 13, 2005 [FBIS].

51. *New York Times*, November 10, 2005; *Financial Times*, November 10, 2005 [FBIS]; and *Washington Post*, November 17, 2005.

52. IAEA, Board of Governors, "Introductory Statement to the Board of Governors: Implementation of the NPT Safeguards Agreement in the Islamic Republic of Iran,"

Statements of the Director General, November 24, 2005, http://www.iaea.org/ NewsCenter/Focus/IaeaIran/index.shtml; and Alissa J. Rubin, "The West Signals Patient Approach on Iran," *Los Angeles Times*, November 23, 2005.

53. Associated Press, *Los Angeles Times*, November 13, 2005.
54. IRNA, November 12, 2005 [FBIS].
55. Islamic Republic of Iran News Network Television, December 5, 2005 [FBIS].
56. Vision of the Islamic Republic of Iran, Network 2, January 2, 2006 [FBIS].
57. *Mardom-Salari*, November 23, 2005 [FBIS].
58. Mehr News Agency, November 26, 2005 [FBIS].
59. *Aftab-e Yazd*, December 3, 2005 [FBIS].
60. Rossiya TV, December 5, 2005 [FBIS].
61. Agentstvo Voyennykh Novostey, December 2, 2005 [FBIS].
62. Aleksandr Babakin and Vladimir Ivanov, "Bombshell for Greater Middle East? Delivery of Surface-to-Air Missile Systems to Iran Threatens to Have Explosive Consequences," *Nezavisimoye Voyennoye Obozreniye*, December 9, 2005 [FBIS]; Aleksandr Kostin, "Iran Is Ready to Arm Itself With Russian Pechora-2A SAM's," *Grani.ru*, December 15, 2005 [FBIS]; *Argumenty i Fakty*, No. 51, December 20, 2005 [FBIS]; and ITAR-TASS, December 23, 2005 [FBIS]. The Tor-M1 had been on the shopping list of the high-level Iranian delegation in Moscow shortly before President Khatami's visit in March 2001 (see chapter 7).
63. *Politkom.ru*, December 6, 2005 [FBIS].
64. *Moskovskiy Komsomolets*, December 14, 2005 [FBIS].
65. *Rossiyskaya Gazeta*, December 15, 2005 [FBIS].
66. Rossiya TV, December 21, 2005 [FBIS].
67. *New York Times*, December 29, 2005; and Bill Samii, "Iran: Distrustful of Russia, Legislators Want Nuclear Diplomacy," RFE/RL, January 25, 2005, http://www.rferl.org/featuresarticle/2006/01/a03fc925-3a74-4f42-a7c0-a24eeaa89ef3.html.
68. *E'temad*, January 10, 2006 [FBIS].
69. *Iran Daily*, January 10, 2006 [FBIS].
70. Statement by the Russian Ministry of Foreign Affairs, "Regarding the Announcement by Tehran of Its Decision to Resume Scientific Research Into Uranium Enrichment," January 10, 2006 [FBIS].
71. *Washington Post*, January 11, 2006.
72. Agentstvo Voyennykh Novostey, January 10, 2006 [FBIS].
73. BBC Monitoring, Press Quotes from Iranian Newspapers, *E'temaad-e-Melli*, February 2, 2006 [FBIS].
74. IAEA, Board of Governors, "Implementation of the NPT Safeguards Agreement in the Islamic Republic of Iran: Resolution Adopted on February 4, 2006," GOV/2006/14, http://www.iaea.org/NewsCenter/Focus/IaeaIran/index.shtml.
75. *Washington Post*, February 5, 2006.
76. *Siyasat-e Ruz*, March 4, 2006 [FBIS].
77. *Washington Post*, February 15, 2006.
78. Quoted in Vahid Sepehri, "Consensus That Russia and the West Are Not Iran's Friends," *RFE/RL Iran Report*, March 8, 2006, http://archive.rferl.org/reports/Archive.aspx?report=571&year=2008.
79. *E'temade-e Melli*, February 21, 2006 [FBIS].
80. Interfax, February 7, 2006 [FBIS].
81. Agentstvo Voyennykh Novostey, February 16, 2006 [FBIS].
82. IAEA, Board of Governors, "Chairman's Conclusion on Sub-item 5(b): Report by the Director General on the Implementation of the NPT: Safeguards Agreement in

the Islamic Republic of Iran," IAEA Staff Report, March 8, 2006, http://acdn.france. free.fr/spip/article.php3?id_article= 168&lang=en.

83. IAEA.org, "Transcript of Director General's Remarks at Conclusion of IAEA Board Meeting," News Center, March 8, 2006, http://www.iaea.org/NewsCenter/ Transcripts/2006/transcr08032006.html.

84. IAEA.org, "Report on Iran's Nuclear Program Sent to UN Security Council," Staff Report, March 8, 2006, http://www.iaea.org/NewsCenter/ News/2006/bog080306. html.

85. Interfax, March 13, 2006 [FBIS].

86. *Gazeta*, March 13, 2006 [FBIS].

87. *Politkom.ru*, April 5, 2006 [FBIS].

88. Colum Lynch, "Security Council Pressures Tehran," *Washington Post*, March 30, 2006; and UN Security Council, Statement by the President of the Security Council, S/PRST.2006/15, March 29, 2006, http://www.un.org/Docs/sc/unsc_pres_ statements06.htm.

89. Glenn Kessler, "Iran Warned, but Russia, China Dissent on Action," *Washington Post*, March 31, 2006.

90. *New York Times*, April 12, 2006.

91. *New York Times*, April 14, 2006.

92. Mehr News Agency, April 23, 2006 [FBIS].

93. Abd-al-Karim Abu-al-Nahar, "The Secrets of the Nuclear and Political Struggle in Iran; Arabs Are Worried That Supporters of 'Radicals' May Win," *Al-Nahar* (Beirut), March 17, 2006 [FBIS].

94. Cited in Chubin, *Iran's National Security Policy*, 52; and Nuclear Threat Initiative, "Iran Profile: Nuclear Chronology: 1988," http://www.nti.org/e_research/profiles/ Iran/1825_1858.html.

95. Quoted in Bill Samii, "Shamkhani: No Nukes," *RFE/RL Iran Report*, February 11, 2002, http://archive.rferl.org/reports/Archive.aspx?report=571&year=2008.

96. Quoted in Mehdi Khalaji, "Iran: International Pressure and Internal Conflict," The Washington Institute for Near East Policy, *PolicyWatch*, no. 1106, May 24, 2006, http:// www. washingtoninstitute.com/.

97. RenTV, April 2, 2006 [FBIS].

98. *Vedemosti*, April 18, 2006 [FBIS].

99. Interfax, April 19, 2006 [FBIS].

100. Iranian Labor News Agency, June 16, 2006 [FBIS].

101. ITAR-TASS, November 15, 2005 [FBIS]; and Rossiya TV, November 22, 2005 [FBIS].

102. Gevorkyan and others, *First Person*, 130.

103. IRNA, May 11, 2006 [FBIS].

104. ITAR-TASS, May 15, 2006 [FBIS].

105. Mehdi Safari, Interview by Nadezhda Kevorkova, *Gazeta*, June 27, 2006 [FBIS].

106. Interfax, May 24, 2006 [FBIS].

107. *Kommersant-Daily*, December 26, 1996 [FBIS].

108. IAEA, Board of Governors, "Implementation of the NPT Safeguards Agreement in the Islamic Republic of Iran: Report by the Director General, April 28, 2006," GOV/2006/27, http://www.iaea.org/NewsCenter/Focus/IaeaIran/index.shtml.

109. Mehdi Mohammadi, "What Is Happening in New York?" *Keyhan*, May 11, 2006 [FBIS].

110. Mehdi Mohammadi, "Europe's Authority Has Waned," *Keyhan*, May 21, 2006 [FBIS].

111. *Nezavisimaya Gazeta*, May 17, 2006 [FBIS].
112. Editorial, "We Are Not at a Juncture," *Aftab-e Yazd*, May 22, 2006 [FBIS].
113. Behrad Farahmand, "A Piece of Advice for the Bears," *Aftab-e Yazd*, May 22, 2006 [FBIS]. For an overview of scholarship on the myth of Peter's "testament," which never existed except in forgeries, see Muriel Atkin, "Myths of Soviet-Iranian Relations," in Nikki R. Keddie and Mark J. Gasiorowski, editors, *Neither East nor West: Iran, the Soviet Union, and the United States* (New Haven: Yale University Press, 1990), 110–111.
114. Text in *Le Monde*, May 9, 2006 [FBIS].
115. "Sadeq Kharrazi: I Believe in Negotiations With America, and Have Suffered for It," *Aftab-e Yazd*, April 27, 2006 [FBIS].
116. Ali Akbar Dareini, "Iranians Fault Rice's Dismissal of Letter," May 10, 2006, *washingtonpost.com*, http://www.washingtonpost.com/wp-dyn/content/article/2006/05/09/AR2006050900197_... On the dismissal of Kharrazi and a number of other ambassadors, see Nilufar Mansurian, "Called-In Ambassadors," *Sharq*, October 31, 2005 [FBIS].
117. Trudy Rubin, "Talk of Tehran: U.S.-Iran Talks," *Philadelphia Inquirer*, May 28, 2006.
118. Michael Slackman, "Iran Chief Eclipses Clerics as He Consolidates Power," *New York Times*, May 28, 2006.
119. *New York Times*, May 31, 2006.
120. *Washington Post*, June 1, 2006, and June 4, 2006.
121. *Washington Post*, June 2, 2006, and June 7, 2006.
122. *New York Times*, June 15, 2006; and *Washington Post*, July 14, 2006. See also *Washington Post*, June 7, 2006, and *New York Times*, June 8, 2006.
123. Elaine Sciolino and William J. Broad, "At the Heart of the United Front on Iran, Vagueness on Crucial Terms," *New York Times*, June 18, 2006.
124. *New York Times*, June 9, 2006.
125. ITAR-TASS, June 15, 2006 [FBIS].
126. *Washington Post*, June 17, 2006.
127. *New York Times*, June 22, 2006.
128. *E'temad-e Melli*, June 17, 2006 [FBIS].
129. Dr. Ebrahim Yazdi, "Iran, United States, Nuclear Issue," *Sharq*, June 20, 2006 [FBIS].
130. *New York Times*, June 28, 2006; and Bill Samii, "New Foreign Policy Council Could Affect Iran-U.S. Relations," *RFE/RL Iran Report*, July 7, 2006, http://archive.rferl.org/reports/Archive.aspx?report=571&year=2008.
131. Agentstvo Voyennykh Novostey, July 6, 2006 [FBIS].
132. *New York Times*, July 12 and 13, 2006.
133. "Transcript of Remarks and Replies to Media Questions by Russian Minister of Foreign Affairs Sergey Lavrov Following Six Foreign Ministers' Meeting on Iran, Paris, July 12, 2006," Moscow Ministry of Foreign Affairs WWW-Text, July 13, 2006 [FBIS].
134. UN Security Council, Resolution 1696, S/RES/1696 (2006), July 31, 2006, http://www.un.org/Docs/sc/index.html. UN Security Council, Press Release, SC/8792, July 31, 2006, http://www.un.org/News/Press/docs/2006/sc8792.doc.htm, also contains the text of UNSCR 1696 as well as summaries of national statements. See also *Washington Post*, August 1, 2006; and text of the "Charter of the United Nations" at http://www.un.org/aboutun/charter/contents.htm.
135. *E'temad-e Melli*, July 13, 2006 [FBIS].
136. *Keyhan International*, July 12, 2006 [FBIS]; and *Keyhan*, July 31, 2006 [FBIS].

## CHAPTER 14: BEYOND TURKMANCHAI?

1. See, for example, Robert Lowe and Claire Spencer, eds., "Iran, Its Neighbours and the Regional Crises," Royal Institute of International Affairs, Chatham House, Middle East Programme Report, August 23, 2006, http://www.chathamhouse.org.uk.

2. Bill Samii, "Hailing Hizballah 'Victory,' Iranian Officials Condemn U.S., Israel, and UN," *RFE/RL Iran Report*, August 22, 2006, http://archive.rferl.org/reports/Archive. aspx?report=571&year=2008.

3. For reporting on this view, see Seymour M. Hersh, "Watching Lebanon," *New Yorker*, August 21, 2006, 28–33.

4. Sergei Karaganov, "Tasks for the Year; What Should Russia Do in Changing World?" *Rossiyskaya Gazeta*, August 29, 2006 [FBIS].

5. *Washington Post*, January 21, 2006.

6. *Washington Post*, March 3 and 17, 2006.

7. *Washington Post*, April 23, 2006.

8. Bill Samii, "Tehran Hails Political Developments in Baghdad," *RFE/RL Iran Report*, May 3, 2006; and Samii, "Is an Iranian Hand Stirring the Iraqi Pot?" *RFE/RL Iran Report*, April 12, 2004, http://archive.rferl.org/reports/Archive.aspx?report=571&year=2008.

9. Barbara Slavin, "Rice Defends Tactics That She Says Thwart Major Terror Attacks," *USA Today*, November 29, 2005.

10. John Daniszewski and Alissa J. Rubin, "Iran May Finally Be Ready to Talk," *Los Angeles Times*, March 14, 2006; and John R. Bradey, "Tehran Elite Turning on Extremist Presidency," *Washington Times*, March 14, 2006.

11. Vick, "Iran Agrees to Talk With U.S. About Iraq."

12. Karl Vick, "Iranians See Talks With U.S. as Historic," *Washington Post*, March 20, 2006.

13. *International Herald Tribune*, April 25, 2006.

14. *New York Times*, May 21, 2006.

15. *Washington Post*, February 23 and 28 and August 25, 2006.

16. *New York Times*, August 16, 2006.

17. Michael R. Gordon, "Iraqi Casualties Have Risen 51%, U.S. Study Finds," *New York Times*, September 2, 2006, reporting on the most recent U.S. Defense Department quarterly report on "Measuring Security and Stability in Iraq."

18. *New York Times*, August 4, 2006.

19. *Washington Post*, June 9, 2006.

20. U.S. Department of Defense, News Briefing with Secretary Donald Rumsfeld and Gen. George Casey, News Transcript, June 22, 2006, http://www.defenselink.mil/transcripts/ 2006/tr20060622-13318.html.

21. See, for example, Daniel L. Byman and Kenneth M. Pollack, "Iraq Runneth Over. What Next?" *Washington Post*, August 20, 2006.

22. By the end of 2005, ConocoPhillips had increased its stake in Lukoil to 16.1 percent of company shares and over the course of 2006 planned to push this to 20 percent (Interfax, January 9, 2006 [FBIS]).

23. Andrea R. Mihailescu, "Moscow Eyes Lost Oil Contract in Iraq," *Washington Times*, April 5, 2006.

24. ITAR-TASS, June 27, 2006 [FBIS].

25. Interfax, August 9, 2006 [FBIS].

26. Afghanistan Television, November 3, 2004 [FBIS].

27. *Washington Times*, October 14, 2004.

28. Anderson, "Man in the Palace," 70.

29. *New York Times*, December 8, 2004.
30. Anderson, "Man in the Palace," 70.
31. *New York Times*, December 26, 2004, September 19, 2005, November 13, 2005, and December 4, 2005.
32. *New York Times*, December 22, 2005.
33. *New York Times*, April 20 and 21, 2006.
34. ITAR-TASS, October 18, 2004 [FBIS]; Interfax, November 3, 2004 [FBIS]; and "Speech at a Conference in the Jawaharlal Nehru Memorial Foundation," December 3, 2004, President of Russia Official Web Portal, http://www.kremlin.ru/eng/text/speeches/2004/ 12/03/123.
35. ITAR-TASS, December 1, 2004 [FBIS]. The comment drew sharp complaints from Kabul that Ivanov was interfering in Afghanistan's internal affairs and reminders of the damage Moscow's intervention had done to Afghanistan in the 1980s. For the Afghan Foreign Ministry press release, see Radio Afghanistan, December 4, 2004 [FBIS]. For less restrained retorts, see *Anis*, December 4, 2004 [FBIS]; Afghanistan Television, December 5, 2004 [FBIS]; and *Erada*, December 12, 2004 [FBIS].
36. Bill Samii, "Tehran Talks Out of Both Sides of Mouth on Afghan Elections," *RFE/RL Newsline*, October 18, 2004, http://archive.rferl.org/reports/Archive.aspx?report=571&year=2008; and *Washington Post*, December 8, 2004.
37. RIA-Novosti, July 28, 2005 [FBIS]; and ITAR-TASS, July 28, 2005 [FBIS].
38. *Kabul Weekly*, August 10, 2005 [FBIS].
39. Amin Tarzi, "Is Herat a Prelude to the End of Afghan Warlordism?" *Eurasia Insight*, September 26, 2004, http://www.eurasianet.org; David S. Cloud, "Afghan Warlords Slowly Come in From the Cold," *Wall Street Journal*, March 14, 2005; and Ahmed Rashid, "Afghan Neighbors Show Signs of Aiding in Nation's Stability," *Wall Street Journal*, October 18, 2004. Presumably driven in part by the same concern at that time, the Iranian government in December 2004 froze the bank accounts of Hizb-i Eslamin leader Gulbuddin Hekmatyar (Bill Samii, "Tehran Freezes Hekmatyar's Assets," *RFE/RL Iran Report*, December 27, 2004, http://archive.rferl.org/reports/Archive.aspx?report=571&year=2008).
40. Mohsen Milani, "Iran's Policy Towards Afghanistan," *The Middle East Journal* 60, no. 2 (Spring 2006), 252–254.
41. IRNA, May 27, 2006 [FBIS].
42. IRNA, May 28, 2006 [FBIS].
43. RTR Planeta TV, June 17, 2006 [FBIS].
44. *Eslah*, August 23, 2005 [FBIS]; Agentsvo Voyennyk Novostey, November 10, 2005 [FBIS]; and ITAR-TASS, January 27, 2006 [FBIS].
45. Pamela Constable, "Afghanistan Rocked as 105 Die in Violence," *Washington Post*, May 19, 2006.
46. *Washington Post*, May 30, 2006.
47. Carlotta Gall, "U.S. Hands Southern Afghan Command to NATO," *New York Times*, August 1, 2006; and Pamela Constable, "Suicide Bomber Kills 21 Civilians In Afghanistan," *Washington Post*, August 4, 2006. For an overview of developments in Kandahar, where President Hamid Karzai grew up but also where the Taliban first developed, see *Washington Post*, August 19, 2006. On the timetable for the expansion of ISAF operations and contraction of OEF responsibilities, see *New York Times*, December 11, 2005.
48. Pamela Constable, "Afghan Leader Losing Support," *Washington Post*, June 26, 2006; and Carlotta Gall, "Nation Faltering, Afghans' Leader Draws Criticism," *New York Times*, August 23, 2006.
49. IRNA, January 31, 2006 [FBIS].
50. David Montero, "Iran, US Share Afghan Goals," *Christian Science Monitor*, May 4, 2006; Pamela Constable, "Dozens Are Killed in Afghan Fighting," *Washington Post*, May 23,

2006; and Eric Schmitt, "Springtime for Killing in Afghanistan," *New York Times*, May 28, 2006.

51. See especially Seymour M. Hersh, "The Iran Plans: Would President Bush Go to War to Stop Tehran From Getting the Bomb?" *New Yorker*, April 17, 2006, 30–37.

52. *New York Times*, September 3, 2006.

53. Interfax, June 28, 2006 [FBIS].

54. IRNA, May 5, 2004 [FBIS].

55. Umnov, interview.

56. Some Turkish experts were the first to agree that neither Turks nor Islamic Republic Iranians had made themselves popular in Central Asia, although the Iranians with their religious rhetoric, abstinence from alcohol, and shunning of shaking hands with women had done themselves the most damage (Ankara, background interviews).

57. For a sampler of remarks in Dushanbe and Khojand, see IRNA, May 1 and 2, 2002 [FBIS].

58. ITAR-TASS, July 5, 2005 [FBIS]; and ITAR-TASS, June 15, 2006 [FBIS]. In addition to SCO full members Russia, China, Kazakhstan, Kyrgyzstan, Tajikistan, and Uzbekistan, the Astana summit granted "observer" status to India, Pakistan, and Iran. Mongolia had been accorded similar status a year earlier. For a review of the SCO's origins and history, see Jefferson E. Turner, "What Is Driving India's and Pakistan's Interest in Joining the Shanghai Cooperation Organization?" *Strategic Insights* 4, no. 8 (August 2005), http://www.ccc.nps.navy.mil/si/2005/Aug/turnerAug05.asp. For the SCO's limitations, see the views of Richard Weitz of the Hudson Institute and Daniel Kimmage of RFE/RL in "The Limits of the Shanghai Cooperation Organization," RFE/RL Press Releases, August 7, 2006, http://www.rferl.org/content/PressRelease/1105890.html. .

59. Kyrgyz Radio One, June 28, 2002 [FBIS]; Agentstvo Voyennykh Novostey, December 4, 2002 [FBIS]; and *New York Times*, December 4, 2002.

60. ITAR-TASS, October 23, 2003 [FBIS].

61. *Izvestiya*, December 11, 2002 [FBIS]; Agentstvo Voyennykh Novostey, March 13, 2003 [FBIS]; and *Nezavisimaya Gazeta*, September 23, 2003 [FBIS]. The force at Kant initially consisted of some seven hundred personnel supporting five SU-27 interceptors and five SU-25 ground-attack warplanes, four transport aircraft, and several MI-8 helicopters. It was supplemented by six Russian SU-25s attached to the 201st division in Dushanbe ("Oborona I Bezopasnost Kolonka Analitika," *WPS* (Moscow), January 24, 2003 [FBIS]).

62. *Los Angeles Times*, May 24, 2005; and *Washington Post*, May 25, 2005.

63. *Washington Post*, April 14, 2005.

64. ITAR-TASS, July 5, 2005 [FBIS].

65. For a review and analysis, see International Crisis Group, "Uzbekistan: The Andijon Uprising," Update Briefing, Asia Briefing, no. 38, Bishkek/Brussels, May 25, 2005, http://merln.ndu.edu/archive/icg/uzbekistanandijonuprising.pdf. A year earlier, after terrorist attacks in Tashkent in March 2004, Karimov and Putin on June 16 had signed a "Strategic Partnership Treaty" (for text, see *Narodnoye Slovo*, June 22, 2004 [FBIS]). They followed this up with a "Treaty on Allied Relations" signed on November 14, 2005 (for text, see *Kremlin.ru*, November 14, 2005 [FBIS]).

66. *Washington Post*, July 30, 2005; and *New York Times*, July 31, 2005.

67. Uzbek Radio 1, October 8, 2001 [FBIS]; ITAR-TASS, October 7, 2001 [FBIS]; and *Washington Post*, October 14, 2001.

68. Robin Wright, "Kyrgyzstan Agrees to Continuing U.S. Military Presence at Key Air Base," *Washington Post*, October 12, 2005; and Thom Shanker, "U.S. Reaches Deal With

Kyrgyzstan for Continued Use of Air Base," *New York Times*, July 15, 2006.

69. Stephen Blank, "Russia Realizes Its Cartel," and Mamuka Tsereteli, "The Blue Stream Pipeline and Geopolitics of Natural Gas in Eurasia," both in *Central Asia-Caucasus Analyst*, Central Asia-Caucasus Institute, Johns Hopkins University, November 30, 2005, http://www.cacianalyst.org/issues/20051130Analyst.pdf.

70. "Agreement Between the Russian Federation and Turkmenistan on Cooperation in the Gas Sector," Russian Federation President (Internet text), April 10, 2003 [FBIS]; and *Neytralnyy Turkmenistan*, April 16, 2003 [FBIS].

71. Jakub Siekierzynski, "Gazprom Monopolizes Gas Supplies From Central Asia to Europe," *EastWeek Analytical Newsletter for Eastern Europe, Russia, Caucasus, and Central Asia*, Warsaw Eastern Studies Center, November 24, 2005 [FBIS]; Roman Kupchinsky, "East: Ukraine, Russia Spar Over Turkmen Gas," RFE/RL, April 18, 2005, http://www.rferl.org/content/Article/1058531.html; and Daniel Kimmage, "Eurasia: Central Asian Gas Powers Regional Aspirations," RFE/RL, January 25, 2006, http://www.rferl.org/content/article/1065068.html.

72. Daniel Kimmage, "Turkmenistan: The Achilles' Heel of European Energy Security," RFE/RL, June 30, 2006, http://www.rferl.org/content/article/1069597.html.

73. FBIS Report, "FYI—Deal Finalized for Russian Government to Acquire Control of Gazprom," citing Gazprom press release as quoted by Interfax, June 16, 2005 [FBIS].

74. According to the U.S. Energy Information Administration, as cited by Glenn Kessler in "Rice Warns Against Russian Gas Monopoly," *Washington Post*, April 26, 2006.

75. Andrew E. Kramer, "Gazprom Becomes the Bear of Russia," *New York Times*, December 27, 2005; and Andrew E. Kramer and Steven Lee Myers, "Workers' Paradise Is Rebranded as Kremlin Inc.," *New York Times*, April 24, 2006.

76. Stanislav Belkovskiy, "The Riddle of Vladimir Putin," *Lenta.ru*, March 6, 2006 [FBIS].

77. *Sovetskaya Rossiya*, April 16, 1998 [FBIS]; and Florian Hassel, "All Stays in the Family," *Frankfurter Rundschau* (Internet text), May 21, 2001 [FBIS].

78. Vladimir Kucherenko, "Winter 2000: Oil Producers Celebrate, But Will the Country Weep? Economy Urgent," *Rossiyskaya Gazeta*, August 24, 1999 [FBIS].

79. Radio Rossii, June 24, 2005 [FBIS].

80. Gennadiy Sysoyev, "Cubic Meters as a Weapon," *Kommersant*, December 30, 2005 [FBIS]; Peter Finn, "Russia Cuts Off Gas to Ukraine in Controversy Over Pricing," *Washington Post*, January 2, 2006; and "Gazprom Official Outlines Main Points of Russia-Ukraine Gas Deal," Channel One TV, January 4, 2006 [FBIS].

81. Amid numerous charges of election rigging, Rahmonov officially won almost 97 percent of the vote with a 98 percent turnout for presidential elections on November 6, 1999. A mere 2 percent plus of the votes went to his Islamic Revival Party (IRP) rival Davlat Usmon (Interfax, November 7, 1999 [FBIS]; and *Kommersant*, November 9, 1999 [FBIS]). In the parliamentary elections held on February 27, 2000, Rahmonov's ruling People's Democratic Party (PDP) officially won 70 percent of the votes; the Communist Party some 12–15 percent; and the IRP came in third with no more than 12 percent of the votes cast (*Izvestiya*, March 1, 2000 [FBIS]; and *Kommersant*, March 1, 2000 [FBIS]).

82. Radio Tajikistan, First Channel Network, October 16, 1999 [FBIS]; and *Kommersant*, March 1, 2000 [FBIS].

83. Voice of the Islamic Republic of Iran (Mashhad), October 18, 1999 [FBIS].

84. Avesta, August 9, 2006 [FBIS].

85. ITAR-TASS, December 12, 2002 [FBIS].

86. "Russian Federation President V. V. Putin's Speech and Meet-the-Press Session at the Close of Talks With Head of Afghanistan's Interim Administration H. Karzai," Russian Federation President (Internet text), March 13, 2002 [FBIS].

87. *Avesta*, June 9, 2004 [FBIS]; Tajik Television First Channel, August 2, 2004 [FBIS]; Interfax, September 12, 2004 [FBIS]; *Kommersant*, September 14, 2004 [FBIS]; and *Kommersant*, October 18, 2004 [FBIS].

88. Rahmonov got the ball rolling on the Anzob project during his visit to Tehran in June 2003 (Dushanbe Asia-Plus, June 17, 2003, and January 8, 2004 [FBIS]).

89. Kambiz Arman, "Investing in Tunnel, Iran Nurtures Ambitions in Tajikistan," *Eurasian Insight*, August 1, 2003, http://www.eurasianet.org.

90. Tajik Television First Channel, July 26, 2006 [FBIS].

91. RIA-Novosti, June 4, 2004 [FBIS]; and *Vedomosti*, June 7, 2004 [FBIS].

92. ITAR-TASS and Interfax, September 12, 2004 [FBIS]; IRNA, September 12, 2004 [FBIS]; and *Kommersant*, September 14, 2004 [FBIS].

93. Russia TV RTR, October 16, 2004 [FBIS]; Tajik Television First Channel, October 17, 2004 [FBIS]; *Kommersant*, October 18, 2004 [FBIS]; *Kuryer Tajikistana*, October 21, 2004 [FBIS]; and Khovar News Agency, October 28, 2004 [FBIS].

94. ITAR-TASS, January 10, 2005 [FBIS]; Tajik Television First Channel, January 12, 2005 [FBIS]; and IRNA, January 13, 2005 [FBIS]. The "bidding" had started in 2001 with Iran proposing to invest some $12.5 million in Sangtuda-1 (Asia-Plus, June 4, 2001 [FBIS]). With Russia, an interlinked package of agreements signed during Putin's visit in October 2004 wiped out Tajikistan's $300 million plus external state debt to Russia, turned over to Russia the Okno space tracking station at Norak, and committed—though there would be little follow-up—the Russian Aluminum company to invest $1.5 billion in Tajikistan over ten years (ITAR-TASS, June 3, 2005 [FBIS]).

95. President Boris Yeltsin and Rahmonov had witnessed their defense ministers sign the bilateral agreement on April 16, 1999, in Moscow, but at Tajik insistence the details of the status of forces understanding were later renegotiated to move the headquarters of the 201st out of downtown Dushanbe to a southern suburb (see NTV, April 16, 1999 [FBIS]; and Interfax, August 14, 2002 [FBIS]). The CIS peace-keeping mandate for the operations of the 201st in Tajikistan had expired at the end of 1997 (see "Where Our Peacekeepers Are Located," *Krasnaya Zvezda*, November 28, 1998 [FBIS]).

96. ITAR-TASS, May 27, 2005 [FBIS]; and Avesta, July 13, 2005 [FBIS].

97. Much in this section draws from the author's background interviews in Baku. Many of these themes also appear independently in the article by Douglas Frantz, "Islamic Fervor From Iran Puts Azerbaijan on Alert for Unrest," *New York Times*, February 4, 2001.

98. In Qazvin, for example, regular army units refused to quash riots that broke out in August 1994 (Eisenstadt, *Iranian Military Power*, 41).

99. See, for example, *Mahd-e Azadi* (Tabriz), March 4, 2000 [FBIS].

100. See especially Aliyev's press conference in Baku on return from Tehran (Baku Azerbaijani TV 1, May 20, 2002 [FBIS]). For Iranian argumentation and conditions for improving relations with Azerbaijan, see Akbar Mirza Hosseini, "Relations between Iran and the Republic of Azerbaijan: Walking in a Fuddled Atmosphere," *Bonyan*, April 4, 2002 [FBIS]; and Ramin Hashemi, "A New Horizon in Baku-Tehran Ties," *Iran*, August 1, 2002 [FBIS].

101. Baku Space TV, May 18, 2002 [FBIS]; Baku ANS Television, May 20, 2002 [FBIS]; and Aliyev's own description of it shown by Azerbaijani TV 1, August 6, 2002 [FBIS].

102. *Izvestiya*, October 29, 1993 [FBIS-SOV-93-210, November 2, 1993, 20].

103. Azerbaijani TV 1, August 6, 2004 [FBIS]; *Shargh*, August 7, 2004 [FBIS]; and IRNA, October 20, 2004 [FBIS].

104. IRNA, January 26, 2005 [FBIS].

105. IRNA, May 16, 2005 [FBIS].

106. Azerbaijani TV 1, January 27, 2002 [FBIS].

107. Baku ANS Television, January 29, 2002 [FBIS].

108. ITAR-TASS, February 6, 2004 [FBIS].

109. Robert McMahon, "Azerbaijani President Stresses Military Cooperation With U.S. in Afghanistan, Iraq—but Not Iran," News Briefing, Council on Foreign Relations, April 26, 2006, http://www.cfr.org/publication/10545/azerbaijani_president_stresses_military_cooperation_with_us_in_afghanistan_iraqbut_not_iran.html.

110. In addition, President Ilham Aliyev in August 2004 reportedly signed a new law on national security banning the deployment of foreign bases and troops in Azerbaijan. However, a member of the parliamentary commission for defense and security issues stated, "If the situation changes, it will not take long to introduce amendments to the law." See Interfax, August 6, 2004 [FBIS].

111. IRNA, May 5, 2006 [FBIS].

112. *Bilik Dunyasi* (Baku), May 31, 2002 [FBIS].

113. MPA (Baku), November 18, 2002 [FBIS].

114. In 2005 completion of the rig had been pushed back to at least May 2006 ("Strategic Drilling in Caspian Sea to Begin Next Year," MehrNews.com, July 11, 2005, http://www.mehrnews.com/en/NewsPrint.aspx?NewsID=205307).

115. See Interfax, March 31, 1993 [FBIS-SOV-93-060, March 31, 1993, 9].

116. Iranian Students News Agency, August 19, 2002 [FBIS].

117. Bazhanov, interview; and Semyon Vyacheslavovich Gregoryev, interview by author, Moscow, December 7, 1999. Gregoryev at the time was acting chief on the Iran Desk in the Third Department (for Asia) of the Russian Foreign Ministry. He had spent seven years, beginning in 1990, working in Moscow's embassy in Tehran.

118. *Jomhuri-ye Eslami*, January 17, 2000 [FBIS].

119. *Izvestiya*, November 1, 2002 [FBIS]. In 1999, Yusin had called Iranian demands for an end to Russian military operations in Chechnya a "stab in the back" that should have dispelled the "illusions" of the "geopolitical plans diligently laid by Russian diplomats over the past five years" (*Izvestiya*, October 7, 1999 [FBIS]).

120. Bazhanov, interview.

121. On this point, see A. William Samii, "Tehran's Take on the Moscow Hostage Crisis," *RFE/RL Iran Report*, November 4, 2002, http://archive.rferl.org/reports/Archive.aspx?report=571&year=2008.

122. *Tehran Times*, January 8, 1990 [FBIS-NES-90-009, January 12, 1990, 35].

123. When he received Russia's then-Foreign Minister Igor Ivanov in late 1999, for example, Khatami defended Russia's territorial integrity and noninterference in Russia's internal affairs (IRIB Television First Program Network, November 28, 1999 [FBIS]).

124. *Lidove Noviny* (Prague), July 18, 1995 [FBIS]. Basayev was killed early on July 10, 2006, according to FSB chief Nikolay Patrushev (Interfax, July 10, 2006 [FBIS]).

125. Interfax, August 3, 2006 [FBIS]; and *New York Times*, August 7, 2006.

126. Council on Foreign Relations, *Russia's Wrong Direction: What the United States Can and Should Do*, Task Force Report, no. 57, John Edwards and Jack Kemp, chairs, and Stephen Sestanovich, director, March 2006, http://www.cfr.org/content/publications/attachments/Russia_TaskForce.pdf.

127. "Strong Rebuke for the Kremlin from Cheney," *New York Times*, May 5, 2006; and Condoleezza Rice, "Interview With the Associated Press Editorial Board," New York City, May 8, 2006, http://www.state.gov/secretary/rm/2006/65975.htm.

128. Interfax, March 3, 2006 [FBIS].
129. Mikhail Rostovskiy, "Ahmadinezhad Isn't Mean When It Comes to the Troubles He Could Bring to Russia and the World," *Moskovskiy Komsomolets*, May 23, 2006 [FBIS].
130. Ibid.
131. *Nezavisimaya Gazeta*, August 15, 2006 [FBIS].
132. *Izvestiya*, August 10, 2006 [FBIS].
133. *Izvestiya*, August 14, 2006 [FBIS].
134. "Russia's Position on Iran's Nuclear Issue 'Schizophrenic,' Pundits Tell Radio," Mayak Radio, May 29, 2006 [FBIS].
135. Mikhail Margelov, "We Were the United States' 'Nice Guy'" for a Long Time," *Komsomolskaya Pravda*, May 18, 2006 [FBIS].
136. Anatoliy Tsyganok, "Nuclear Ping-Pong. Russia Will Not Support America in Use of Force Against Iran," *Voyenno-Promyshlennyy Kuryer*, May 24, 2006 [FBIS].
137. Rostovskiy, "Ahmadinezhad Isn't Mean."
138. Fedorov, interview.
139. *Kommersant*, January 15, 2000 [FBIS].
140. *New York Times*, August 21, 2000; and Agentstvo Voyennykh Novostey, February 8, 2005 [FBIS].
141. "Russian President V. V. Putin Interview With *Wall Street Journal*," Russian Federation President (Internet text), February 11, 2002 [FBIS].
142. *Washington Post*, August 22 and September 10, 2006.
143. On Lukoil, see ITAR-TASS, April 18, 2005 [FBIS]. On Gazprom, see RIA-Novosti, June 26, 2006 [FBIS].
144. Aleksandr Pekayev, deputy chairman of "Scientists for Global Security," interviewed by Vladimir Averin, "Panorama" program, Mayak Radio, April 12, 2006 [FBIS].
145. S. Sadeqi, *Iran Daily*, May 23, 2006 [FBIS].
146. See Sezer, "Turkish-Russian Relations," 95 and 99.
147. *Kommersant*, December 7, 2004 [FBIS]. It had been scheduled for early September 2004 but was postponed in the wake of the Beslan hostage tragedy.
148. Anatolia, October 20, 2005 [FBIS]; Interfax, November 16, 2005 [FBIS]; and ITAR-TASS, November 17, 2005 [FBIS].
149. "Russia-Iran Trade Shrinks by Half in the First Quarter of 2006," Interfax, August 25, 2006 [FBIS]. The volume of Russian-Iranian trade in 2003 had been $1.39 billion and slightly more in 2004 (IRNA, December 18, 2004 [FBIS]. Ironically, at $4.4 billion in 2005, Turkish-Iranian trade was much greater than Russian-Iranian trade ("Iran-Turkey Trade Increases 37% and Reaches $1.1b in 3 Months," *The Journal of Turkish Weekly*, May 1, 2006, http://www.turkishweekly.net/news.php?id =30837.
150. In spring 2005, after meeting with Russian Foreign Minister Sergei Lavrov, Hussein Mousavian, secretary of the Iranian Supreme National Security Council's Foreign Policy Committee, hoped that Putin would visit Tehran "in the near future" (ITAR-TASS, April 19, 2005 [FBIS]). This was one of the last mentions of a possible Putin visit to Tehran, until revived in late summer 2007 (see Postscript).
151. George Lenczowski, *Russia and the West in Iran, 1918–1948* (Ithaca: Cornell University Press, 1949), 176. Brezhnev, Kosygin, and Podgorny, who visited either as heads of state or premiers in the 1960s and 1970s, were obviously subordinate to the top party leader at the time.
152. Yakovlev, interview. According to long-time Kremlin aide Anatoly Chernyayev's memoir, as early as 1972, after Sadat kicked Soviet advisers out of Egypt, Brezhnev ordered Andropov and Gromyko to resume efforts to establish contacts with Israel. In November 1973, Brezhnev again told Gromyko he wanted to reestablish diplomatic

relations with Israel, which Moscow had broken off in 1967. See Chernyayev, *Moya zhizn*, 291 and 301.

153. Brutents, interview.
154. Fedorov, interview. Fedorov was referring to the A-50 AWACS aircraft being refitted with Israeli assistance by Russia for China.
155. Interfax, September 4, 2001 [FBIS]; and Russian Federation President, www.president. kremlin.ru, September 30, 2002 [FBIS].
156. *New York Times*, October 27, 2005; and Interfax, October 27, 2005 [FBIS].
157. *Washington Post*, December 15, 2005; and ITAR-TASS, December 15, 2005 [FBIS].
158. *Jerusalem Post*, February 3, 2006 [FBIS]; RIA-Novosti, February 9, 2006 [FBIS]; and ITAR-TASS, March 5, 2006 [FBIS].
159. Kulmatov, interview.
160. Brutents, interview.
161. Khakimov, interview.
162. Shebarshin, *Ruka Moskvy*, 175.
163. Pekayev, "Panorama" program.
164. Vishniakov, "Russian-Iranian Relations and Regional Stability," 143.
165. Gregoryev, interview.
166. Malashenko, interview.
167. Ibid.
168. Moscow, background interviews.
169. Nikolay Kozyrev, interview.
170. Zviagelskaya, interview.
171. Text dated January 1, 1989, Tehran Domestic Service, January 8, 1989 [FBIS-NES-89-05, January 9, 1989, 57-59].
172. Text in *Le Monde*, May 9, 2006 [FBIS].
173. *Resalat*, May 9, 2006 [FBIS].
174. Russian Center TV, July 28, 2006 [FBIS].
175. Bazhanov, interview, Moscow, March 30, 2000.
176. Nikolay Kozyrev, interview.

## POSTSCRIPT: THE ROAD TO TEHRAN

1. See, for example, Steven Pearlstein, "Oil, Oligarchs and Opulence," *Washington Post*, July 6, 2007.
2. "Russian President Addresses Munich Forum [on February 10], Answers Questions on Iran," Moscow Ministry of Foreign Affairs (Internet text), February 12, 2007 [FBIS].
3. UN Security Council, Resolution 1737, S/RES/1737 (2006), December 23, 2006, http://www.un.org/Docs/sc/index.html.
4. *New York Times*, December 25, 2006.
5. "Iran Consults With Russia on Security," *Kommersant.com*, February 9, 2007 [FBIS].
6. *E'temad-e Melli*, February 24, 2007 [FBIS].
7. "Sadeq Kharrazi: The Present Circumstances Can Be Managed," *E'temad*, February 6, 2007 [FBIS].
8. "Iran Consults With Russia."
9. Mehdi Mohammadi, "When the West Comes to Its Senses," *Keyhan*, February 25, 2007 [FBIS].
10. Thom Shanker and William J. Broad, "Iran to Limit Cooperation With Nuclear Inspectors," *New York Times*, March 26, 2007; and UN Security Council, Resolution 1747, S/RES/1747(2007), March 24, 2007, http://www.un.org/Docs/sc/index.html.

As foreshadowed by United Nations Security Council Resolution 1696 of July 31, 2006, Resolutions 1737 and 1747 both invoked Article 41 of Chapter VII of the UN Charter.

11. IRNA, February 22 and March 22, 2007 [FBIS]. See also the commentary ("Iranian Paper Says Enemy Behind Accusations Against Eminent Politicians") on Khamenei's February 22 remarks in *Jomhuri-ye Eslami*, February 28, 2007 [FBIS].

12. Golnaz Esfandiari, "Iran: Former Nuclear Negotiator Arrested on Security Charges," RFE/RL, May 3, 2007, http://www.rferl.org/content/article/1076263.html.

13. *Washington Post*, May 9, 22, and 30, 2007.

14. Robin Wright, "Iran Curtails Freedom in Throwback to 1979," *Washington Post*, June 16, 2007.

15. Interfax, January 16, 2007 [FBIS].

16. Pavel Felgenhauer, "Iran Takes Delivery of Russian Tor-M1 Missiles," Jamestown Foundation, *Eurasia Daily Monitor* 4, no. 12 (January 17, 2007), http://www.jamestown.org/ print_friendly.php?volume_id=420&issue_id=3975&article_id...

17. "Russian President Addresses Munich Forum [on February 10], Answers Questions on Iran," Moscow Ministry of Foreign Affairs (Internet text), February 12, 2007 [FBIS].

18. IAEA, Board of Governors, "Implementation of the NPT Safeguards Agreement and Relevant Provisions of Security Council Resolution 1737 (2006) in the Islamic Republic of Iran," Report by the Director General, February 22, 2007, GOV/2007/8, http://www.iaea. org/NewsCenter/Focus/IaeaIran/index.shtml.

19. Andrew E. Kramer, "Russia Will Slow Work on Iran's Nuclear Plant," *New York Times*, February 20, 2007.

20. Elaine Sciolino, "Russia Gives Iran Ultimatum on Enrichment," *New York Times*, March 20, 2007.

21. IAEA, Board of Governors, "Implementation of the NPT Safeguards Agreement and Relevant Provisions of Security Council Resolutions in the Islamic Republic of Iran," Report by the Director General, May 23, 2007, GOV/2007/22, http://www.iaea.org/NewsCenter/ Focus/IaeaIran/index.shtml.

22. Ivan Groshkov, "Tehran Wants to Take Moscow to Court: That Is Iran's Reaction to Moscow's Readiness to Postpone the Delivery of Fuel Assemblies for the Bushehr Nuclear Power Station," *Nezavisimaya Gazeta*, August 13, 2007 [FBIS].

23. "Vulgarity in Opportunism!" *Aftab-e Yazd*, June 10, 2007 [FBIS].

24. "National Security Committee Members React to Russia's Breach of Promise," *Aftab-e Yazd*, July 7, 2007 [FBIS].

25. ITAR-TASS, June 3, 2007 [FBIS]; and Sheryl Gay Stolberg and David E. Sanger, "Bush to Seek a Bit of Unity With Putin," *New York Times*, June 5, 2007.

26. Sheryl Gay Stolberg, "Putin Presents Bush With Plan on Missile Shield," *New York Times*, June 8, 2007; Michael A. Fletcher, "Putin Offers to Join Missile Shield Effort," *Washington Post*, June 8, 2007; "Putin News Conference: Missile Defence, Democracy, Kosovo," Vesti TV, June 8, 2007 [FBIS]; and "Putin and Bush in Defense of Europe," *Kommersant.com*, June 8, 2007 [FBIS]. As far back as July 2003, USA Institute head Sergey Rogov had suggested that Russia and the United States cooperate on missile defense (see chapter 11).

27. ITAR-TASS, July 3, 2007 [FBIS].

28. Ja'far Golabi, "Russia's Strange Proposal," *E'temad*, June 10, 2007 [FBIS].

29. ITAR-TASS, June 17, 2007 [FBIS].

30. "Summary of Opening Remarks by Sergey Lavrov at Caspian States Foreign Ministers

Conference, Tehran, June 20, 2007," Moscow Ministry of Foreign Affairs (Internet text), June 20, 2007 [FBIS].

31. See Aleksandr Losyukov's comments in "Shanghai Organization Members Agree to Retain Moratorium on Expansion," ITAR-TASS, August 13, 2007 [FBIS].

32. "Daily Sees Missed Opportunity for Iran in Recent Asian States Meeting," *Aftab-e Yazd* (Internet text), August 19, 2007 [FBIS].

33. Vision of the Islamic Republic of Iran, August 22, 2007 [FBIS]; and ITAR-TASS, August 31, 2007 [FBIS].

34. IAEA.org, "Communication Dated 27 August 2007 From the Permanent Mission of the Islamic Republic of Iran to the Agency Concerning the Text of the 'Understandings of the Islamic Republic of Iran and the IAEA on the Modalities of Resolution of the Outstanding Issues,'" with attached text of the "Understandings," August 27, 2007, INFCIRC/711, http://www.iaea.org/Publications/Documents/Infcircs/2007/infcirc711.pdf.

35. IAEA, Board of Governors, "Implementation of the NPT Safeguards Agreement in the Islamic Republic of Iran," Report by the Director General, August 30, 2007, GOV/2007/48, http://www.iaea.org/NewsCenter/Focus/IaeaIran/index.shtml.

36. Warren Hoge, "Iran President Vows to Ignore U.N. Measures," *New York Times*, Septebmer 26, 2007.

37. Neil King Jr., "Iran Action Stalls at U.N.," *Wall Street Journal*, September 29, 2007; Sergei Kislyak's comments in "Six FMs Meeting on Iran Not Easy, but Substantial—RF Diplomat," ITAR-TASS, September 29, 2007 [FBIS]; and Condoleezza Rice's statements in "FM Livni's 17.10.07 Press Conference With US Secretary of State Rice," Jerusalem Government Press office (e-mail text), October 18, 2007 [FBIS].

38. Lenczowski, *Russia and the West*, 176.

39. "Russian and Iranian Presidents' Joint Statement," ITAR-TASS, October 16, 2007 [FBIS]. This was technically correct. As noted in chapter 1, heads of state Brezhnev and Podgorny, who visited Iran in 1963 and 1970, respectively, were at the time chairmen of the USSR—not Russian—Supreme Soviet, and Kosygin, who visited in 1968, was Soviet—not Russian—premier.

40. "Putin Meets With Ayatollah Khamenei," Interfax, October 16, 2007 [FBIS].

41. "Putin Discusses Bushehr Project, NATO Expansion, ABM With Iranian Media," Moscow Vesti TV, October 16, 2007 [FBIS]; and "Russia-Iran Relations Should Be Maximally Developed—Ahmadinejad," ITAR-TASS, October 16, 2007 [FBIS].

42. "The Declaration of the Republic of Azerbaijan, the Islamic Republic of Iran, the Republic of Kazakhstan, the Russian Federation and Turkmenistan," Fars News Agency, October 16, 2007 [FBIS]. On the earlier documents, see chapters 1, 8, 11, and 14.

43. "Russian and Iranian Presidents' Joint Statement," ITAR-TASS, October 16, 2007 [FBIS].

44. "Iran Supreme Leader Urges to Expand Cooperation With Russia," ITAR-TASS, October 17, 2007 [FBIS].

45. "Putin Discusses Bushehr Project."

46. Nazilla Fathi, "Putin Is Said to Offer Idea on Standoff Over Iran," *New York Times*, October 18, 2007.

47. Robin Wright, "Iran's Nuclear Negotiator Resigns," *Washington Post*, October 21, 2007; Nazila Fathi and Michael Slackman, "Iran's Nuclear Envoy Quits: Talks in Doubt," *New York Times*, October 21, 2007; Sasan Aqa'i, "Why Larijani Left," *E'temad-e Melli*, October 24, 2007 [FBIS]; and Medi Khalaji, "Larijani's Resignation: Implications for Iranian Nuclear Policy and Internal Politics," Washington Institute for Near East

Policy, *PolicyWatch*, no. 1296, October 25, 2007, http://www.washingtoninstitute. org/.

48. Peter Finn, "Putin Suggests He'd Be Premier," *Washington Post*, October 2, 2007.
49. Interfax, December 17, 2007 [FBIS].
50. Peter Finn, "Putin Anoints Successor to Russian Presidency," *Washington Post*, December 11, 2007.
51. Stanislav Belkovskiy, interview by Manfred Quiring, "One Should Not Overestimate Putin's Active Role," *Die Welt*, November 12, 2007 [FBIS]; and Oleg Salmanov, "Money—Equidistant," *The New Times*, November 14, 2007 [FBIS]. This was more than twice Belkovskiy's previous estimate, as we have seen in chapter 14 (Stanislav Belkovskiy, "The Riddle of Vladimir Putin," *Lenta.ru*, March 6, 2006 [FBIS]).
52. IAEA, Board of Governors, "Implementation of the NPT Safeguards Agreement and Relevant Provisions of Security Council Resolutions 1737 (2006) and 1747 (2007) in the Islamic Republic of Iran," Report by the Director General, November 15, 2007, GOV/2007/58, http://www.iaea.org/NewsCenter/Focus/IaeaIran/index.shtml.
53. "MFA Spokesman Mikhail Kamynin's Response to a Media Query on IAEA Director General's Report on Iranian Nuclear Program," Moscow Ministry of Foreign Affairs (Internet version), November 19, 2007 [FBIS].
54. National Intelligence Council, "Iran: Nuclear Intentions and Capabilities," National Intelligence Estimate, November 2007, http://www.odni.gov/press_releases/ 20071203_release.pdf.
55. Elaine Sciolino, "Europeans See Murkier Case for Sanctions," *New York Times*, December 4, 2007.
56. Interfax, December 4 and 5 (various), 2007 [FBIS].
57. ITAR-TASS, December 5, 2007 [FBIS].
58. ITAR-TASS, April 22, 2003 [FBIS].
59. Text of speech by Supreme National Security Council Secretary Hassan Rowhani to the Supreme Cultural Revolution Council, "Beyond the Challenges Facing Iran and the IAEA Concerning the Nuclear Dossier," *Rahbord*, September 30, 2005 [FBIS].
60. ITAR-TASS, December 17, 2007 [FBIS].
61. Helene Cooper, "Iran Receives Nuclear Fuel in Blow to U.S.," *New York Times*, December 18, 2007.
62. Ilya Kononov, "Iran Needs 20 Nuclear Power Stations; Launch of Bushehr Nuclear Power Station Remains Subject of Speculation," *Nezavisimaya Gazeta*, December 25, 2007 [FBIS].
63. Interfax, December 20, 2007 [FBIS].
64. Hanif Ghaffari, "Failure of the Neoconservatives' Tradition," *Resalat*, December 18, 2007 [FBIS].
65. Iraj Jamshidi, "The Russians' New Game," *E'temad*, December 22, 2007 [FBIS].
66. Kononov, "Iran Needs 20 Nuclear Power Stations."
67. C. J. Chivers, "Iran: Russia Denies Planning Missile System," *New York Times*, December 29, 2007.
68. Konstantin Lantratov and Alexandra Gritskova,"Iran Shields Its Nuclear Activities by Russian Missiles," *Kommersant.com*, December 26, 2007 [FBIS]; Yakovina Ivan and Ilya Kramnik, "Superiority Complex; Russia Prepared to Give Iran the Chance Not to Be Intimidated by United States," *Lenta.Ru*, December 27, 2007 [FBIS]; and "Russian Deputy Minister Stresses Importance of Cooperation With Iran," ITAR-TASS, December 27, 2007 [FBIS].
69. Robin Wright, "Six Powers Back U.N. Draft on Iran," *Washington Post*, January 23, 2008.

70. Michael Evans, "Spy Photos Reveal 'Secret Launch Site' for Iran's Long-Range Missiles," *London Times,* April 11, 2008.
71. "Russian Foreign Minister Warns Iran Over Nuclear Plans," ITAR-TASS, February 13, 2008 [FBIS].
72. Warren Hoge and Elaine Sciolino, "Security Council Adds Sanctions Against Iran," *New York Times,* March 4, 2008; and UN Security Council, Resolution 1803, S/RES/1803(2008), March 3, 2008, http://www.un.org/Docs/sc/index.html.
73. Disarmament Documentation, "UNSCR on Nonproliferation, Statements by Permanent Members of the Security Council, 3 March 2008," Acronym Institute for Disarmament Diplomacy, http://www.acronym.org.uk/docs/0803/doc08.htm.
74. "SC Resolution on Iran Does Not Call for Large-scale Sanctions," ITAR-TASS, March 4, 2008 [FBIS].
75. "Tehran Rejects UN Resolution," ITAR-TASS, March 5, 2008 [FBIS].
76. Sudarsan Raghavan and Amit R. Paley, "Iranian Leader, in Baghdad, Hails 'New Chapter' in Ties With Iraq," *Washington Post,* March 3, 2008; and Solomon Moore and Mudhafer Al-Husaini, "Iran President, in Baghdad, Calls for U.S. to Leave," *New York Times,* March 4, 2008.
77. Anthony Shadid and Alia Ibrahim, "Lebanon Accord Offers a Respite," *Washington Post*, May 22, 2008.
78. Steven Mufson, "Oil Closes Over $100 for 1st Time," *Washington Post,* February 20, 2008.
79. "Stocks Find a Foothold as Oil Takes a Breather From Its Run," *Washington Post,* May 23, 2008.
80. White House, Office of the Press Secretary, "U.S.-Russia Strategic Framework Declaration," April 6, 2008, http://www.whitehouse.gov/news/releases/2008/04/print/20080406-4.html.
81. "Nuclear Ties: How Russia Should React to Iran's Activity in Nuclear Sphere," *Nezavisimaya Gazeta,* March 18, 2008 [FBIS].
82. Peter Finn, "For Russia, a Second Center of Power," *Washington Post,* May 8, 2008.
83. Robin Wright, "Tehran Urges New Round of Talks," *Washington Post,* May 21, 2008.

# Selected Bibliography

Abdullaev, Kamoludin, and Catherine Barnes, eds. "Politics of Compromise: The Tajikistan Peace Process." Special issue, *Accord*, no. 10 (2001).

Akchurin, Marat. *Red Odyssey: A Journey Through the Soviet Republics.* New York: HarperCollins, 1992.

Aliriza, Bulent, and Seda Ciftci. "Turkey's Caspian Energy Quandary." Center for Strategic and International Studies, Caspian Energy Project, Caspian Energy Update. Washington, DC, August 13, 2002.

Altstadt, Audrey L. *The Azerbaijani Turks: Power and Identity Under Russian Rule.* Stanford: Hoover Institution Press, 1992.

Amirov, Anvar. *Kto yest' kto v mire nefti i gaza Rossii 2000: Kratkiy biograficheskiy spravochnik* [Who is who in the world of oil and gas in Russia in 2000: Short biographic directory]. 3rd ed. Moscow: Panorama, May 2000.

Anderson, Jon Lee. "American Viceroy." *New Yorker*, December 19, 2005, 54–65.

———. "The Man in the Palace." *New Yorker*, June 6, 2005, 60–73.

Andronov, Iona Ionovich. *Moya voyna* [My war]. Moscow: Delovoy mir 2000, 1999.

Arbatov, Alexei G. "Russian National Interests." In *Damage Limitation or Crisis? Russia and the Outside World*, edited by Robert D. Blackwill and Sergei A. Karaganov, 55–76. CSIA Studies in International Security, no. 5. Washington, DC: Brassey's, Inc, 1994.

Arman, Kambiz. "Investing in Tunnel, Iran Nurtures Ambitions in Tajikistan." *Eurasian Insight*, August 1, 2003. http://www.eurasianet.org.

Armstrong, David, and Joseph Trento. *America and the Islamic Bomb: The Deadly Compromise.* Hanover, NH: Steerforth Press, 2007.

Aron, Leon. *Yeltsin: A Revolutionary Life.* New York: St. Martin's Press, 2000.

Aslund, Anders. *How Russia Became a Market Economy.* Washington, DC: Brookings Institution, 1995.

Atkin, Muriel. "Myths of Soviet-Iranian Relations." In *Neither East nor West: Iran, the Soviet Union, and the United States*, edited by Nikki R. Keddie and Mark J. Gasiorowski, 100–114. New Haven: Yale University Press, 1990.

———. "Thwarted Democratization in Tajikistan." In *Conflict, Cleavage, and Change in Central Asia and the Caucasus*, edited by Karen Dawisha and Bruce Parrott, 277–311. Cambridge: Cambridge University Press, 1997.

Avdeev, G. "Dom na Vesal-e Shirazi" [The Building on Vesal-e Shirazi]. *Aziya i Afrika segodnya*, no. 2 (2000): 54–57.

Baer, Robert. *See No Evil: The True Story of a Ground Soldier in the CIA's War on Terrorism.* New York: Crown, 2002.

Baker, James A., III. *The Politics of Diplomacy: Revolution, War and Peace 1989–1992.* With Thomas M. DeFrank. New York: G. P. Putnam's Sons, 1995.

Baker, Peter, and Susan Glasser. *Kremlin Rising: Vladimir Putin's Russia and the End of Revolution.* New York: Scribner, 2005.

Bakhash, Shaul. *The Reign of the Ayatollahs: Iran and the Islamic Revolution.* New York: Basic Books, 1984.

Balzer, Harley. "The Putin Thesis and Russian Energy Policy." *Post-Soviet Affairs* 21, no. 3 (July–September 2005): 210–225.

———. "Vladimir Putin's Academic Writings and Russian Natural Resource Policy." *Problems of Post-Communism* 53, no. 1 (January–February 2006): 48–54.

Baram, Amazia. "Iraq: Between East and West." In *The Iran-Iraq War: Impact and Implications*, edited by Efraim Karsh, 78–97. New York: St. Martin's Press, 1989.

Bazhanov, Ye. P., and V. Ye. Dontsov, eds. *Rossiysko-iranskoye sotrudnichestvo (vzglyad iz Rossii): Materialy mezhdunarodnoy konferentsii* [Russian-Iranian cooperation (the view from Russia): Materials from an international conference]. Moscow: Diplomaticheskaya Akademiya MID Rossii, 2000.

Behrooz, Maziar. "Trends in the Foreign Policy of the Islamic Republic." In *Neither East nor West: Iran, the Soviet Union, and the United States*, edited by Nikki R. Keddie and Mark J. Gasiorowski, 13–35. New Haven: Yale University Press, 1990.

Berntsen, Gary, and Ralph Pezzullo. *Jawbreaker: The Attack on Bin Laden and Al Qaeda: A Personal Account by the CIA's Key Field Commander.* New York: Three Rivers Press, 2005.

Bhatty, Robin, and David Hoffman. "Afghanistan: Crisis of Impunity: The Role of Pakistan, Russia, and Iran in Fueling the Civil War." *Human Rights Watch* 13, no. 3(C) (July 2001).

Blank, Stephen. "Russia Realizes Its Cartel." *Central Asia-Caucasus Analyst*, Central Asia-Caucasus Institute, Johns Hopkins University, November 30, 2005. http://www.cacianalyst.org/issues/20051130Analyst.pdf.

Bovin, Aleksandr Yevgenevich. *5 let sredi evreev i midovtsev* [Five years among the Jews and MFA-ers]. Moscow: Zakharov, 2000.

Bowden, Mark. "The Kabul-ki Dance." *Atlantic Monthly* 290, no. 4 (November 2002): 65–87.

Boyer, Peter J. "The New War Machine." *New Yorker*, June 30, 2003, 55–71.

Bremer, L. Paul. *My Year in Iraq: The Struggle to Build a Future of Hope.* With Malcolm McConnell. New York: Simon & Schuster, 2006.

Brutents, Karen Nersesovich. *Tridtsat' let na Staroy Ploshchadi* [Thirty years on Old Square]. Moscow: Mezhdunarodnyye Otnosheniya, 1998.

Chernyayev, Anatoliy Sergeyevich. *Moya zhizn i moye vremya* [My life and times]. Moscow: Mezhdunarodnye Otnosheniya, 1995.

———. *Shest' let s Gorbachevym* [Six years with Gorbachev]. Moscow: Progress-Kul'tura, 1993.

Chubin, Shahram. "Iran and the War: From Stalemate to Ceasefire." In *The Iran-Iraq War: Impact and Implications*, edited by Efraim Karsh, 13–25. New York: St. Martin's Press, 1989.

———. *Iran's National Security Policy.* Washington, DC: Carnegie Endowment, 1994.

———. *Iran's Nuclear Ambitions.* Washington, DC: Carnegie Endowment for International Peace, 2006.

————, and Charles Tripp. *Iran and Iraq at War: A Developing State in a Zone of Great-Power Conflict.* Boulder: Westview Press, 1988.

————, and Sepehr Zabih. *The Foreign Relations of Iran.* Berkeley: University of California Press, 1974.

Clawson, Patrick. "Iran as Part of the Axis of Evil (Part II): U.S. Policy Concerns." Washington Institute for Near East Policy. *PolicyWatch,* no. 601, February 5, 2002. http://www.washingtoninstitute.org/templateC05.php?CID=1479.

Clinton, Bill. *My Life.* New York: Knopf, 2004.

Cold War International History Project. Woodrow Wilson International Center for Scholars, Washington, DC. *Bulletin,* no. 8–9, Winter 1996–1997.

Cold War International History Project. Woodrow Wilson International Center for Scholars, Washington, DC. *Bulletin,* no. 14–15, Winter 2003–Spring 2004.

Coll, Steve. *Ghost Wars: The Secret History of the CIA, Afghanistan, and Bin Laden, From the Soviet Invasion to September 10, 2001.* New York: Penguin Books, 2005.

Cordesman, Anthony, and Nawaf Obaid. "Saudi Militants in Iraq: Assessment and Kingdom's Response." Center for Strategic and International Studies, Washington, DC, September 19, 2005. http://www.csis.org/ press/wf_2005_0919.pdf.

Cordovez, Diego, and Selig S. Harrison. *Out of Afghanistan: The Inside Story of Soviet Withdrawal.* New York: Oxford University Press, 1995.

Cottam, Richard W. "U.S. and Soviet Responses to Islamic Political Militancy." In *Neither East nor West: Iran, the Soviet Union, and the United States,* edited by Nikki R. Keddie and Mark J. Gasiorowski, 265–288. New Haven: Yale University Press, 1990.

Council on Foreign Relations. *Russia's Wrong Direction: What the United States Can and Should Do.* Task Force Report, no. 57. John Edwards and Jack Kemp, chairs, and Stephen Sestanovich, director. March 2006. http://www.cfr.org/content/publications/ attachments/Russia_TaskForce.pdf.

Critchlow, James. "Caravans and Conquests." *The Wilson Quarterly* 16, no. 3 (Summer 1992): 20–32.

Dawisha, Karen, and Bruce Parrott, eds. *Conflict, Cleavage, and Change in Central Asia and the Caucasus.* Cambridge: Cambridge University Press, 1997.

————, eds. *Democratic Changes and Authoritarian Reactions in Russia, Ukraine, Belarus and Moldova.* Cambridge: Cambridge University Press, 1997.

————, eds. *Russia and the New States of Eurasia: The Politics of Upheaval.* Cambridge: Cambridge University Press, 1994.

Degras, Jane, ed. *Soviet Documents on Foreign Policy.* Vol. 3. London: Oxford University Press, 1953.

Djalili, Mohammad Reza, and Frederic Grare. "Regional Ambitions and Interests in Tajikistan: The Role of Afghanistan, Pakistan and Iran." In *Tajikistan: The Trials of Independence,* edited by Mohammad Reza Djalili, Frederic Grare, and Shirin Akiner, 119–131. Richmond, Surrey: Curzon Press, 1998.

Djekshenkulov, Alikbek. *Novye nezavisimye gosudarstva Tsentral'noi Azii v mirovom soobshchestve* [The new independent governments of Central Asia in the world community]. Moscow: Nauchnaya Kniga, 2000.

Duncan, W. Raymond, and Carolyn McGiffert Ekedahl. *Moscow and the Third World Under Gorbachev.* Boulder: Westview Press, 1990.

Eggert, Konstantin. "'Meteor' for the Ayatollahs: Iran Needs Ballistic Missiles in Order to Become a World Power." *Izvestiya,* October 21 and 22, 1998 [FBIS].

Ehteshami, Anoushiravan. *After Khomeini: The Iranian Second Republic.* London: Routledge, 1995.

Eisenstadt, Michael. "Dilemmas for the U.S. and Iran." Washington Institute for Near East Policy, *PolicyWatch*, no. 414 (October 8, 1999). http://www.washingtoninstitute.org/.

———. *Iranian Military Power: Capabilities and Intentions.* Washington, DC: Washington Institute for Near East Policy, 1996.

———. "Russian Arms and Technology Transfers to Iran: Policy Challenges for the United States." *Arms Control Today*, March 2001. http://www.armscontrol.org/act/2001_03/eisenstadt.asp.

Entekhabi-Fard, Camelia. "Afghan Leader's Visit to Iran Hands Political Victory to Reformists in Tehran." *Eurasia Insight*, February 27, 2002. http://www.eurasianet.org.

———. "US National Security Expert Says Internal Rivalries Influence Iranian Foreign Policy." *EurasiaNet Q&A*, March 15, 2002. http://www.eurasianet.org/departments/qanda/articles/eav031502.shtml.

———, and Idi Verani. "Afghan Reconstruction Effort Poses Major Test for Iranian Policy Makers." *Eurasia Insight*, February 27, 2002. http://www.eurasianet.org.

Escudero, Stanley T. "Rat-a-tat-tat in Tajikistan: U.S. Embassy People Have to Get Out." *State*, no. 365 (April 1993): 13–18.

Esfandiari, Golnaz. "Iran: Former Nuclear Negotiator Arrested on Security Charges." RFE/RL, May 3, 2007. http://www.rferl.org/content/article/1076263.html.

Fane, Daria. "Tajikistan: Conflict and Conflict Resolution." Paper presented at annual meeting of the Association for Studies of Nationalities, Columbia University, New York, April 1999.

Felgenhauer, Pavel. "Iran Takes Delivery of Russian TOR-M1 Missiles." Jamestown Foundation, *Eurasia Daily Monitor* 4, no. 12 (January 17, 2007). http://www.jamestown.org/print_friendly.php?volume_id=420&issue_id=3975&article_id...

Feuchtwanger, E. J., and Peter Nailor, eds. *The Soviet Union and the Third World.* New York: St. Martin's Press, 1981.

Foreign Broadcast Information Service [FBIS]. Since November 2005, reorganized as Open Source Center, or OSC (for U.S. government users only). https://www.opensource.gov.

Foreign Broadcast Information Service [FBIS]. FBIS/OSC material also available through World News Connection (for non-U.S. government users). http://wnc.dialog.com.

Foreign Broadcast Information Service. *Daily Report for the Soviet Union* [FBIS-SOV] (Springfield, VA: National Technical Information Service, various years).

Forsythe, Rosemarie. *The Politics of Oil in the Caucasus and Central Asia.* IISS, Adelphi Paper 300. Oxford: Oxford University Press, 1996.

Franklin, Simon, and Jonathan Shepard. *The Emergence of Rus: 750–1200.* London: Longman, 1996.

Frantz, Douglas, and Catherine Collins. *The Nuclear Jihadist: The True Story of the Man Who Sold the World's Most Dangerous Secrets . . . and How We Could Have Stopped Him.* New York: Twelve, 2007.

Freedman, Robert O. *Moscow and the Middle East: Soviet Policy Since the Invasion of Afghanistan.* Cambridge: Cambridge University Press, 1991.

———. *Soviet Policy Toward the Middle East Since 1970.* 3rd ed. New York: Praeger, 1982.

Freidin, Gregory. "The Horror in Tajikistan." *Central Asia Monitor*, no. 5 (1992): 8–10.

Fuhrman, Peter. "Robber Baron." *Forbes* (September 11, 1995): 208–220.

Fuller, Elizabeth. "Azerbaijan at the Crossroads." In *Challenges for the Former Soviet South*, edited by Roy Allison, 131–139. Washington, DC: Brookings Institution Press for the Royal Institute of International Affairs, 1996.

Gaidar, Yegor Timurovich. *Days of Defeat and Victory*. Seattle: University of Washington Press, 1999.

Garthoff, Raymond L. *Détente and Confrontation: American-Soviet Relations From Nixon to Reagan*. Rev. ed. Washington, DC: Brookings Institution, 1994.

Gevorkyan, Nataliya, Natalya Timakova, and Andrei Kolesnikov. *First Person: An Astonishingly Frank Self-Portrait by Russia's President Vladimir Putin*. New York: Public Affairs, 2000.

Girardet, Edward. *Afghanistan: The Soviet War*. New York: St. Martin's Press, 1985.

Gleason, Gregory. *The Central Asian States: Discovering Independence*. Boulder: Westview, 1997.

Golan, Galia. *Soviet Policies in the Middle East: From World War Two to Gorbachev*. Cambridge: Cambridge University Press, 1990.

Goldberg, Jeffrey. "A Reporter at Large: The Unknown." *New Yorker*, February 10, 2003, 40–47.

Goltz, Thomas. *Azerbaijan Diary: A Rogue Reporter's Adventures in an Oil-Rich, War-Torn, Post-Soviet Republic*. Armonk, NY: M. E. Sharpe, 1998.

Gretsky, Sergei. "Civil War in Tajikistan: Causes, Developments, and Prospects for Peace." In *Central Asia: Conflict, Resolution, and Change*, edited by Roald Z. Sagdeev and Susan Eisenhower, 217–247. Chevy Chase, MD: CPSS Press, 1995.

———. "Russia and Tajikistan." In *Regional Power Rivalries in the New Eurasia: Russia, Turkey, and Iran*, edited by Alvin Z. Rubinstein and Oles M. Smolansky, 231–251. Armonk, NY: M. E. Sharpe, 1995.

Gromov, Boris Vsevolodovich. *Ogranichennyi Kontingent* [Limited contingent]. Moscow: Progress-Kul'tura, 1994.

Gromyko, Anatoly Andreyevich. *Andrey Gromyko: V labirintakh Kremlya* [Andrey Gromyko: In the labyrinths of the Kremlin]. Moscow: Avtor, 1997.

Grummon, Stephen R. *The Iran-Iraq War: Islam Embattled*. New York: Praeger, 1982.

Gusher, A., and A. Slavokhotov. "Strategiya natsional'noi bezopasnosti Rossii na yuge" [Russia's strategy of national security in the south]. *Aziya i Afrika segodnya*, no. 1 (1997): 28–35.

Halliday, Fred. "The Iranian Revolution and Great-Power Politics." In *Neither East nor West: Iran, the Soviet Union, and the United States*, edited by Nikki R. Keddie and Mark J. Gasiorowski, 246–264. New Haven: Yale University Press, 1990.

Hanhimäki, Jussi, and Odd Arne Westad. *The Cold War: A History in Documents and Eyewitness Accounts*. New York: Oxford University Press, 2003.

Harris, George S. "The Russian Federation and Turkey," in *Regional Power Rivalries in the New Eurasia: Russia, Turkey, and Iran*, edited by Alvin Z. Rubinstein and Oles M. Smolansky, 3–25. Armonk, NY: M. E. Sharpe, 1995.

Herrmann, Richard. "The Role of Iran in Soviet Perceptions and Policy." In *Neither East nor West: Iran, the Soviet Union, and the United States*, edited by Nikki R. Keddie and Mark J. Gasiorowski, 63–99. New Haven: Yale University Press, 1990.

Hersh, Seymour M. "The Iran Plans: Would President Bush Go to War to Stop Tehran From Getting the Bomb?" *New Yorker*, April 17, 2006, 30–37.

———. "Watching Lebanon." *New Yorker*, August 21, 2006, 28–33.

Herzig, Edmund. *Iran and the Former Soviet South*. London: Royal Institute of International Affairs, 1995.

Herzog, Chaim. "A Military-Strategic Overview." In *The Iran-Iraq War: Impact and Implications*, edited by Efraim Karsh, 255–268. New York: St. Martin's Press, 1989.

Hiro, Dilip. *Iran Under the Ayatollahs*. London: Routledge & K. Paul, 1985.

————. *The Longest War: The Iran-Iraq Military Conflict.* New York: Routledge, 1991.

Hoffman, David E. *The Oligarchs: Wealth and Power in the New Russia.* New York: Public Affairs, 2002.

Hunter, Shireen T. "Greater Azerbaijan: Myth or Reality?" In *Le Caucase Post Sovietique: La Transition Dons le Conflict,* edited by Mohammad-Reza Djalili, 115–142. Brussels: Bruylant, 1995.

Indyk, Martin. "The Clinton Administration's Approach to the Middle East." Washington Institute for Near East Policy, Soref Symposium, 1993. http://www.washingtoninstitute.org/print.php?template=C07&CID=61.

International Crisis Group. "Uzbekistan: The Andijon Uprising." Update Briefing, Asia Briefing, no. 38. Bishkek/Brussels, May 25, 2005. http://merln.ndu.edu/archive/icg/uzbekistanandijonuprising.pdf.

Jack, Andrew. *Inside Putin's Russia.* Oxford: Oxford University Press, 2004.

Janusz, Barbara. *The Caspian Sea: Legal Status and Regime Problems.* Russia and Eurasia Program, Briefing Paper, REP BP 05/02. London: Chatham House, August 2005.

Jawad, Nassim, and Shahrbanou Tadjbakhsh. *Tajikistan: A Forgotten Civil War.* Manchester, UK: Manchester Free Press, 1995.

Kandaurov, Sergey. "VTS Between Russia and Iran: Possibilities and Prospects." *Eksport Vooruszheniy,* November–December 2000, 5–10 [FBIS].

Karsh, Efraim. "From Ideological Zeal to Geopolitical Realism: The Islamic Republic and the Gulf." In *The Iran-Iraq War: Impact and Implications,* edited by Efraim Karsh, 26–41. New York: St. Martin's Press, 1989.

Katz, Mark N. "Losing Balance: Russian Foreign Policy Toward Iraq and Iran." *Current History* 102, no. 666 (October 2003): 341–345.

————. *Russia & Arabia: Soviet Foreign Policy Toward the Arabian Peninsula.* Baltimore: Johns Hopkins University Press, 1986.

Kauzlarich, Richard D. "Time for Change? U.S. Policy in the Transcaucasus." New York: Century Foundation, 2001.

Kazemzadeh, Firuz. "Iranian Relations With Russia and the Soviet Union, to 1921." In *The Cambridge History of Iran,* edited by Peter Avery, Gavin Hambly, and Charles Melville, 7: 314–349. Cambridge: Cambridge University Press, 1991.

————. "Soviet-Iranian Relations: A Quarter-Century of Freeze and Thaw." In *The Soviet Union and the Middle East: The Post-World War II Era,* edited by Ivo J. Lederer and Wayne S. Vucinich, 55–77. Stanford: Hoover Institution Press, 1974.

Kelly, Laurence. *Diplomacy and Murder in Tehran: Alexander Griboyedov and Imperial Russia's Mission to the Shah of Persia.* London: I. B. Tauris, 2002.

Kemp, Geoffrey. "U.S.-Iranian Relations: Competition or Cooperation in the Caspian Sea Basin." In *Energy and Conflict in Central Asia and the Caucasus,* edited by Robert Ebel and Rajan Menon, 145–162. Lanham, MD: Rowman & Littlefield, 2000.

Kenjaev, Safarali. *Perevorot v Tadzhikistane* [Upheaval in Tajikistan]. Vol. 1. Dushanbe: Dushanbinskiy Poligrafkombinat, 1996.

————. *Tabadduloti Tojikiston* [Upheaval in Tajikistan]. 3 vols. Dushanbe: Fondi Kenjaev, 1993–95.

Khaidarov, Gapur, and Maksudjon Inomov. *Tajikistan: Tragedy and Anguish of the Nation.* St. Petersburg: LINKO, 1993.

Khalaji, Mehdi. "Iran: International Pressure and Internal Conflict." Washington Institute for Near East Policy, *PolicyWatch,* no. 1106, May 24, 2006. http://www.washingtoninstitute.org/.

———. "Larijani's Resignation: Implications for Iranian Nuclear Policy and Internal Politics." Washington Institute for Near East Policy, *PolicyWatch*, no. 1296, October 25, 2007. http://www.washingtoninstitute.org/.

Khudonazar [Khudonazarov], Davlat. "The Conflict in Tajikistan: Questions of Regionalism." In *Central Asia: Conflict, Resolution, and Change*, edited by Roald Z. Sagdeev and Susan Eisenhower, 249–263. Chevy Chase, MD: CPSS Press, 1995.

———. Interview by Yevgeniy Tsymbal. "Ya daval slovo, chto budu delat' vsyo, chto smogu. I ya starayus' eto slovo derzhat'" [I gave my word that I will do everything that I can. And I am trying to keep my word]. *Vestnik Instituta Kennana v Rossii* (Moscow), no. 2 (2002): 67–77.

Kimmage, Daniel. "Eurasia: Central Asian Gas Powers Regional Aspirations." RFE/RL, January 25, 2006. http://www.rferl.org/content/article/1065068.html.

———. "Turkmenistan: The Achilles' Heel of European Energy Security." RFE/RL, June 30, 2006. http://www.rferl.org/content/article/1069597.html

Kirillin, Mikhail. Interview by *Yadernyy Kontrol.* "Mikhail Kirillin: Several U.S. Firms Engaged in Developing Missile Equipment Have Links With Iranians." *Yadernyy Kontrol* 38, no. 2 (March–April 1998): 37–43 [FBIS].

Klaits, Alex, and Gulchin Gulmamadova-Klaits. *Love and War in Afghanistan.* New York: Seven Stories Press, 2005.

Korgun, V. G. *Afganistan: politika i politiki* [Afghanistan: Politics and politicians]. Moscow: Institute of Oriental Studies of the Russian Academy of Sciences, 1999.

Korniyenko, Georgiy Markovich. *Kholodnaya Voyna* [Cold War]. Moscow: Mezhdunarodnyye Otnosheniya, 1995.

Kosach, Grigorii G. "Tajikistan: Political Parties in an Inchoate National Space." In *Muslim Eurasia: Conflicting Legacies*, edited by Yaacov Ro'i, 123–142. London: Frank Cass, 1995.

Kupchinsky, Roman. "East: Ukraine, Russia Spar Over Turkmen Gas." RFE/RL, April 18, 2005. http://www.rferl.org/content/Article/1058531.html.

Kuzichkin, Vladimir. *Inside the KGB: My Life in Soviet Espionage.* New York: Pantheon Books, 1990.

Lang, David Marshall. *Lives and Legends of the Georgian Saints.* 2nd rev. ed. Crestwood, NY: St. Vladimir's Seminary Press, 1976.

Latynina, Yuliya. *Okhota na izyubrya* [Stag hunting]. Moscow: Olma-Press and Neva, 1999.

Lenczowski, George. *Russia and the West in Iran, 1918–1948: A Study in Big-Power Rivalry.* Ithaca: Cornell University Press, 1949.

Lewis, Michael. "The Satellite Subversives." *New York Times Magazine*, February 24, 2002, 30–35.

Limbert, John W. *Iran: At War With History.* Boulder: Westview Press, 1987.

Litwak, Robert S. "The Soviet Union and the Iran-Iraq War." In *The Iran-Iraq War: Impact and Implications,* edited by Efraim Karsh, 200–214. New York: St. Martin's Press, 1989.

Lowe, Robert, and Claire Spencer, eds. "Iran, Its Neighbours and the Regional Crises." Royal Institute of International Affairs, Chatham House, Middle East Programme Report, August 23, 2006. http://www.chathamhouse.org.uk.

Mackey, Sandra. *The Iranians: Persia, Islam, and the Soul of a Nation.* New York: Plume Books, 1998.

Maleki, Abbas. "The Legal Status of the Caspian Sea: Discussions of Different Iranian Views." Tehran: International Institute for Caspian Studies, January 2001. http://www.cpf.az/caspsea/109-the-legal-status-of-the-caspian-sea.html.

Maley, William. *The Afghanistan Wars.* Houndmills, Basingstoke, Hampshire: Palgrave Macmillan, 2002.

Matlock, Jack F., Jr. *Autopsy on an Empire: The American Ambassador's Account of the Collapse of the Soviet Union.* New York: Random House, 1995.

McNaugher, Thomas. "Walking Tightropes in the Gulf." In *The Iran-Iraq War: Impact and Implications,* edited by Efraim Karsh, 171–199. New York: St. Martin's Press, 1989.

Menashri, David. "Iran and Central Asia: Radical Regime, Pragmatic Politics." In *Central Asia Meets the Middle East,* edited by David Menashri, 73–97. London: Frank Cass, 1998.

———. *Revolution at a Crossroads: Iran's Domestic Politics and Regional Ambitions.* Policy Paper, no. 43. Washington, DC: Washington Institute for Near East Policy, 1997.

Menon, Rajan. *Soviet Power and the Third World.* New Haven: Yale University Press, 1986.

Mesbahi, Mohiaddin. "Gorbachev's 'New Thinking' and Islamic Iran: From Containment to Reconciliation." In *Reconstruction and Regional Diplomacy in the Persian Gulf,* edited by Hooshang Amirahmadi and Nader Entessar, 261–296. London: Routledge, 1992.

———. "Iran and Tajikistan." In *Regional Power Rivalries in the New Eurasia: Russia, Turkey, and Iran,* edited by Alvin Z. Rubinstein and Oles M. Smolansky, 112–143. Armonk, NY: M. E. Sharpe, 1995.

———. "Tajikistan, Iran, and the International Politics of the 'Islamic Factor.'" *Central Asian Survey* 16, no. 2 (1997): 141–158.

Mikhaylov, Viktor Nikitovich. Interview by I. N. Arutyunyan. "Nuclear Cooperation With Iran: The View From Ordynka." *Priroda,* no. 8 (August 1995): 3–11 [FBIS].

Milani, Mohsen. "Iran's Policy Towards Afghanistan." *The Middle East Journal* 60, no. 2 (Spring 2006): 235–256.

Millar, T. B., with Robin Ward, eds. "Treaty of Friendship Between Persia and the Russian Federal Soviet Republic." In *Current International Treaties,* 408–416. New York: New York University Press, 1984.

Miller, Laurel, and Robert Perito. "Establishing the Rule of Law in Afghanistan." U.S. Institute of Peace, Special Report 117, March 2004. http://www.usip.org/pubs/specialreports/sr117.html.

Milov, Vladimir. "Gazoviy Prezident." *Novaya Gazeta,* no. 97 (December 26, 2005). http://www.NovayaGazeta.Ru/data/2005/97/17.html.

Moaveni, Ardeshir. "Iran Probes for Diplomatic Openings to Avoid Strategic Encirclement." *Eurasia Insight,* August 20, 2002. http://www.eurasianet.org

Naumkin, V. V. "Rossiya i Iran v Tsentralnoy Azii i Zakavkaz'ye v Regional'nom i Global'nom Kontekste" [Russia and Iran in Central Asia and the Caucasus in regional and global context]. In *Doklady Rossiyskikh Uchastnikov 5-oy Konferentsii "Kruglogo Stola" po Rossiysko-Iranskim Otnosheniyam* [Reports by Russian participants in the fifth "round table" conference on Russian-Iranian relations], edited by V. V. Naumkin, 20–30. Moscow: Tsentr Strategicheskikh i Politicheskiykh Issledovaniy, 1999.

Nikitin, A. I., O. N. Khlestov, Yu. E. Fedorov, and A. V. Demurenko. *Mirotvorcheskiye Operatsii v SNG* [Peacemaking operations in the CIS]. Moscow: Moskovskii Obshchestvennii Nauchnii Fond, 1998.

Nikolayev, Andrey Ivanovich. *Na perelome: Zapiski russkogo generala* [At the turning point: Notes of a Russian general]. Moscow: Sovremennyi pisatel, 1999.

Nissman, David B. *The Soviet Union and Iranian Azerbaijan: The Use of Nationalism for Political Penetration.* Boulder: Westview Press, 1987.

Olimova, Saodat Kuziyevna, and Muzaffar Abduvakkosovich Olimov. *Tadzhikistan na poroge peremen* [Tajikistan on the threshold of change]. Moscow: Tsentr strategicheskikh i politicheskikh issledovaniy; Nauchno-analiticheskiy tsentr "Shark," 1999.

Orlov, Vladimir. "Patient in Coma?" *Russia in Global Affairs* 1, no. 3 (July–September 2003). http://www.ceip.org/files/projects/npp/resources/moscow2003/orlovreport.pdf.

Packer, George. "Letter From Basra: Testing Ground." *New Yorker*, February 28, 2005, 36–45.

Parker, John W. *Kremlin in Transition*. Vol. 1, *From Brezhnev to Chernenko, 1978 to 1985*. Boston: Unwin Hyman, 1991.

———. *Kremlin in Transition*. Vol. 2, *Gorbachev, 1985 to 1989*. Boston: Unwin Hyman, 1991.

Parsi, Trita. *Treacherous Alliance: The Secret Dealings of Israel, Iran, and the United States*. New Haven: Yale University Press, 2007.

Perito, Robert M. "The U.S. Experience With Provincial Reconstruction Teams in Afghanistan." U.S. Institute of Peace, Special Report 152, October 2005. http://www.usip.org/pubs/specialreports/sr152.html.

Pickering, Jeffrey. *Britain's Withdrawal From East of Suez: The Politics of Retrenchment*. New York: St. Martin's Press, 1998.

Pollack, Kenneth M. *The Persian Puzzle: The Conflict Between Iran and America*. New York: Random House, 2004.

Poujol, Catherine. "Chronology of the Russian Involvement in the Tajik Conflict, 1992–1993." In *Tajikistan: The Trials of Independence*, edited by Mohammad Reza Djalili, Frederic Grare, and Shirin Akiner, 111–118. Richmond, Surrey: Curzon Press, 1998.

Pribylovskiy, V., and I. Suchkova. *Rukovoditeli Gosudarstv na Territorii Byvshego SSSR* [Leaders of governments on the territory of the former USSR]. Moscow: Panorama, 1999.

Primakov, Yevgeny Maksimovich. *Gody v bol'shoi politike* [Years in big politics]. Moscow: Kollektsiya "Sovershenno Sekretno," 1999.

———. *Minnoye pole politiki* [The minefield of politics]. Moscow: Molodaya Gvardiya, 2007.

———. *Vosem' mesyatsev plyus* . . . [Eight months plus . . . ]. Moscow: Mysl', 2001.

Radio Free Europe/Radio Liberty. *RFE/RL Iran Report*. http://archive.rferl.org/reports/Archive.aspx?report=571&year=2008

Ramazani, Rouhollah K. *Iran's Foreign Policy, 1941–1973*. Charlottesville: University Press of Virginia, 1975.

Rashid, Ahmed. "Jockeying for Influence, Neighbors Undermine Afghan Pact." *Eurasia Insight*, January 15, 2003. http://www.eurasianet.org/.

———. *The Resurgence of Central Asia: Islam or Nationalism?* Atlantic Highlands, NJ: Zed Books, 1994.

———. *Taliban: Militant Islam, Oil and Fundamentalism in Central Asia*. New Haven: Yale University Press, 2000.

Rubin, Barnett R. *The Fragmentation of Afghanistan: State Formation and Collapse in the International System*. 2nd ed. New Haven: Yale University Press, 2002.

———. *The Search for Peace in Afghanistan: From Buffer State to Failed State*. New Haven: Yale University Press, 1995.

Rubin, Michael. *Into the Shadows: Radical Vigilantes in Khatami's Iran*. Washington, DC: Washington Institute for Near East Policy, 2001.

Rubinstein, Alvin Z. "Moscow and Tehran: The Wary Accommodation." In *Regional Power Rivalries in the New Eurasia: Russia, Turkey, and Iran*, edited by Alvin Z. Rubinstein and Oles M. Smolansky, 26–61. Armonk, NY: M. E. Sharpe, 1995.

Rumer, Eugene B. *Dangerous Drift: Russia's Middle East Policy.* Washington, DC: Washington Institute for Near East Policy, 2000.

Safranchuk, Ivan. "Scientific Notes No. 8: The Nuclear and Missile Programs of Iran and Russian Security—The Framework of Russian-Iranian Collaboration." *Nauchnyye Zapiski* 8 (May 5, 1999): 1–36 [FBIS].

Safronchuk, Vasiliy Stepanovich. "Afghanistan in the Amin Period." *International Affairs,* February 1991, 79–96.

———. "Afghanistan in the Taraki Period." *International Affairs,* January 1991: 83–92.

———. "Afganistan pri Babrake Karmale i Nadzhibulle" [Afghanistan under Babrak Karmal and Najibullah]. *Aziya i Afrika segodnya,* no. 6 (1996): 8–15; no. 8 (1996): 25–32; no. 10 (1996): 68–69; no. 1 (1997): 36–41; and no. 5 (1997): 37–41.

Saikal, Amin. "Iranian Foreign Policy, 1921–1979." In *The Cambridge History of Iran,* edited by Peter Avery, Gavin Hambly, and Charles Melville, 7: 426–458. Cambridge: Cambridge University Press, 1991.

———, and William Maley. *Regime Change in Afghanistan: Foreign Intervention and the Politics of Legitimacy.* Boulder: Westview, 1991

Samii, A. William. "Drug Abuse: Iran's 'Thorniest Problem'" *Brown Journal of World Affairs* 9, no. 2 (Winter–Spring 2003): 283–299.

———. "Iran: Distrustful of Russia, Legislators Want Nuclear Diplomacy." Radio Free Europe/Radio Liberty, January 25, 2006. http://www.rferl.org/content/Article/1065078.html.

———. "The Nation and Its Minorities: Ethnicity, Unity State Policy in Iran." *Comparative Studies of South Asia, Africa and the Middle East* 20, nos. 1–2 (2000): 128–142.

Schroen, Gary C. *First In: An Insider's Account of How the CIA Spearheaded the War on Terror in Afghanistan.* New York: Ballantine Books, 2005.

Schuyler, Eugene. *Turkistan: Notes of a Journey in Russian Turkistan, Kokand, Bukhara and Kuldja.* Edited with introduction by Geoffrey Wheeler and abridged by K. E. West. New York: Praeger, 1966.

Sezer, Duygu Bazoğlu. "Turkish-Russian Relations: From Adversity to 'Virtual Rapprochement.'" In *Turkey's New World: Changing Dynamics in Turkish Foreign Policy.* Edited by Alan Makovsky and Sabri Sayari, 92–115. Washington, DC: Washington Institute for Near East Policy, 2000.

Shaffer, Brenda. *Borders and Brethren: Iran and the Challenge of Azerbaijani Identity.* Cambridge: MIT Press, 2002.

———. "The Formation of Azerbaijani Collective Identity in Iran." *Nationalities Papers* 28, no. 3 (September 2000): 449–477.

———. *Partners in Need: The Strategic Relationship of Russia and Iran.* Policy Paper, no. 57. Washington, DC: Washington Institute for Near East Policy, 2001.

Shanahan, Rodger. "The Islamic Da'wa Party: Past Development and Future Prospects." *Middle East Review of International Affairs* 8, no. 2 (June 2004): 16–25.

Shapiro, Leonard, ed. *Soviet Treaty Series.* Vol. 1. Washington, DC: Georgetown University Press, 1950.

Shebarshin, Leonid Vladimirovich. *Ruka Moskvy: Zapiski nachal'nika sovetskoi razvedki* [The hand of Moscow: Notes of the chief of soviet espionage]. Moscow: Tsentr-100, 1992.

Shevtsova, Lilia. *Putin's Russia.* Revised and expanded edition. Washington, DC: Carnegie Endowment for International Peace, 2005.

Sick, Gary. "Slouching Toward Settlement: The Internationalization of the Iran-Iraq War,

1987–1988." In *Neither East nor West: Iran, the Soviet Union, and the United States*, edited by Nikki R. Keddie and Mark J. Gasiorowski, 219–245. New Haven: Yale University Press, 1990.

Simonia, Nodari. "Domestic Developments in Russia." In *Russia and Asia: The Emerging Security Agenda*, edited by Gennady Chufrin, 52–81. Oxford: Oxford University Press, 1999.

Slavin, Barbara. *Bitter Friends, Bosom Enemies: Iran, the U.S., and the Twisted Path to Confrontation.* New York: St. Martin's Press, 2007.

Sluzhba vneshnei razvedki Rossii. Otkrytyi doklad SVR za 1993g. "Novyi vyzov posle 'kholodnoi voiny': rasprostraneniy oruzhiya massovogo unichtozheniya: Iran." http://svr.gov.ru/material/2-1.html and http://svr.gov.ru/material/2-13-9.html.

Sluzhba vneshnei razvedki Rossii. Otkrytyi doklad SVR za 1995g. "Dogovor o nerasprostranenii yadernogo oruzhiya: Problemy prodleniya: Iran." http://svr. gov. ru/material/4-0.html and http://svr.gov.ru/material/4-iran.html.

Smith, R. Grant. "Tajikistan: Implementing the Peace Accords." Paper presented at the UN University for Peace Conference, Dushanbe, Tajikistan, June 2002.

———. "Tajikistan: The Rocky Road to Peace." *Central Asian Survey* 18, no. 2 (1999): 243–251.

Smolansky, Oles M. "Turkish and Iranian Policies in Central Asia." In *Central Asia: Its Strategic Importance and Future Prospects*, edited by Hafeez Malik, 283–310. New York: St. Martin's Press, 1994.

———. *The USSR and Iraq: The Soviet Quest for Influence.* With Bettie Smolansky. Durham: Duke University Press, 1991.

Sonboli, Nabi. "Iran and the Post-9/11 Security Environment of Central Asia." *Central Asia and the Caucasus Review*, no. 37 (Spring 2002): 103–122 [FBIS].

Stewart, Rory. *The Places in Between.* Orlando, FL: Harcourt, 2004.

Suny, Ronald Grigor. *The Making of the Georgian Nation.* Bloomington: Indiana University Press, 1988.

Swietochowski, Tadeusz. *Russia and Azerbaijan: A Borderland in Transition.* New York: Columbia University Press, 1995.

Takeyh, Ray. "Iran: Scared Straight?" Washington Institute for Near East Policy. *PolicyWatch*, no. 622, May 3, 2002. http://www.washingtoninstitute.org/templateC05. php?CID=1500.

Talbott, Strobe. *The Russia Hand: A Memoir of Presidential Diplomacy.* New York: Random House, 2002.

Tarzi, Amin. "Is Herat a Prelude to the End of Afghan Warlordism?" *Eurasia Insight*, September 26, 2004. http://www.eurasianet.org.

Tregubova, Yelena. *Bayki kremlevskogo diggera* [Tales of a Kremlin digger]. Moscow: Ad Marginem, 2003.

Trenin, Dmitri. "Russia Leaves the West." *Foreign Affairs* 85, no. 4 (July–August 2006): 87–96.

Tsereteli, Mamuka. "The Blue Stream Pipeline and Geopolitics of Natural Gas in Eurasia." *Central Asia-Caucasus Analyst*, Central Asia-Caucasus Institute, Johns Hopkins University, November 30, 2005. http://www.cacianalyst.org/issues/ 20051130Analyst.pdf.

Turajonzoda, Akbar. Interview by David Nalle with Sergei Gretsky. "Interview With Qadi Akbar Turajonzoda." *Central Asia Monitor*, no. 2 (1995): 9–11.

———. "Religion: The Pillar of Society." In *Central Asia: Conflict, Resolution, and Change,* edited by Roald Z. Sagdeev and Susan Eisenhower, 265–271. Chevy Chase, MD: CPSS Press, 1995.

Turner, Jefferson E. "What Is Driving India's and Pakistan's Interest in Joining the Shanghai Cooperation Organization?" *Strategic Insights* 4, no. 8 (August 2005). http://www.ccc. nps.navy.mil/si/2005/Aug/turnerAug05.asp.

Urban, Michael, and Vladimir Gel'man. "The Development of Political Parties in Russia." In *Democratic Changes and Authoritarian Reactions in Russia, Ukraine, Belarus and Moldova*, edited by Karen Dawisha and Bruce Parrott, 175–219. Cambridge: Cambridge University Press, 1997.

Uspenskiy, Nikolay. "Export Control Is a Key Element of National Security." *Yadernyy Kontrol*, no. 3 (May–June 1999): 5–8 [FBIS].

Valdez, Jonathan. "The Near Abroad, the West, and National Identity in Russian Foreign Policy." In *The Making of Foreign Policy in Russia and the New States of Eurasia*, edited by Adeed Dawisha and Karen Dawisha, 84–109. Armonk, NY: M. E. Sharpe, 1995.

Vassiliev, Alexei. *Russian Policy in the Middle East: From Messianism to Pragmatism*. Reading: Ithaca Press, 1993.

Verkhovskiy, Aleksandr. *Srednaya Aziya i Kazakhstan: Politicheskiy spektr* [Central Asia and Kazakhstan: Political spectrum] 2nd ed. Moscow: Informatsionno-ekspertnaya gruppa "Panorama," October 1992.

Vishniakov, Viktor. "Russian-Iranian Relations and Regional Stability." *International Affairs* 45, no. 1 (1999): 143–153.

Vorontsov, Valeriy. *V koridorakh bezvlastiya (Premyeri Yeltsina)* [In the corridors of anarchy (Yeltsin's premiers)]. Moscow: Akademicheskiy Proyekt, 2006.

Westad, Odd Arne. *The Global Cold War: Third World Interventions and the Making of Our Times*. New York: Cambridge University Press, 2005.

———. "Prelude to Invasion: The Soviet Union and the Afghan Communists, 1978–1979." *The International History Review* 16, no. 1 (February 1994): 49–69.

Whitlock, Monica. *Land Beyond the River: The Untold Story of Central Asia*. New York: St. Martin's Press, 2002.

Woodward, Bob. *Bush at War*. New York: Simon & Schuster, 2002.

———. *State of Denial*. New York: Simon & Schuster, 2006.

Yakovlev, Aleksandr. *Omut pamyati: Ot Stolypina do Putina* [Whirlpool of memory: From Stolypin to Putin]. 2 vols. Moscow: Vagrius, 2001.

Yapp, Malcolm. "Colossus or Humbug? The Soviet Union and its Southern Neighbours." In *The Soviet Union and the Third World*, edited by E. J. Feuchtwanger and Peter Nailor, 137–163. New York: St. Martin's Press, 1981.

Yegorova, Natalia I. "The 'Iran Crisis' of 1945–1946: A View From the Russian Archives." Woodrow Wilson International Center for Scholars, Cold War International History Project, Working Paper, no. 15, May 1996.

Zviagelskaya, Irina. *The Tajik Conflict*. Moscow: Russian Center for Strategic Research and International Studies, 1997.

———. "The Tajikistan Conflict." In *SIPRI Yearbook 1999: Armaments, Disarmament and International Security*, 63–75. New York: Oxford University Press, 1999.

# Index

# About the Author

**John W. Parker** is chief of the Division for Caucasus and Central Asia, Office for Russian and Eurasian Analysis, Bureau of Intelligence and Research, U.S. Department of State. During the final years of the Soviet Union, 1989–91, he served in the American embassy in Moscow as chief, Political/Internal Section. For the prior decade he was an analyst of Soviet foreign policy in the Office for Soviet and East European Analysis, U.S. Department of State. He has been a scholar at the Woodrow Wilson International Center for Scholars in Washington, D.C. (1999–2000) and at the Brookings Institution in Washington, D.C. (1973–74). He holds a Ph.D. from Yale University. Parker is the author of *Kremlin in Transition*, two volumes (Boston: Unwin Hyman, 1991).